Living
Human Development through the Lifespan

Janice T. Gibson
University of Pittsburgh

Random House New York

Library of Congress Cataloging in Publication Data

Gibson, Janice T.
  Living, human development through the lifespan.

  Bibliography: p.
  Includes index.
  1. Developmental psychology.   I.   Title.
[DNLM: 1. Human development.   BF 713 G449L]
BF713.G53 1983   155   82-8728
ISBN 394-34912-1   AACR2

First Edition

9876543

ISBN 0-394-34912-1

The text of this book was composed on a Linotron 202 in ITC Garamond by the Clarinda Company.

Manufactured in the United States of America

Preface

The book you are about to read deals with an exciting topic: human life from conception to old age. I have used the research literature of developmental psychology to describe and explain the changes that take place during the developmental process in the body and the mental processes involved in thinking and understanding and in developing likes, dislikes, attitudes, values, beliefs, and adjustments to the world.

The task of compiling and interpreting literature was a personally sensitive one that evoked strong emotions. The reason is that the research of my colleagues often describes events with which I am personally familiar from my own life or from the lives of those I know and love. The joys, fears, and development described in the research are personally familiar to me because of my own observations of the growth and development of my children. The adjustments made to marriage and then to divorce are painfully familiar because, just as a high percentage of American women, I have been both married and divorced. Finally, the adjustments of adulthood and aging are known to me through my own life experiences as well as those of my husband and parents. All of us have passed through many of the stages described in the book.

Lifespan development is a highly personal topic of study, not just for me but for anyone who has been close to people or interested in explaining reactions to life events. Understanding the changes expected with development is, after all, understanding the human condition.

Lifespan development is a study not only of similarities among people in their progression from early to late development but also of the differences that make each a unique and interesting creation. The research describes the changes that can be expected for each person, regardless of his or her racial, socioeconomic, or cultural background. It also describes the differences that occur because of learning experiences, nutrition, opportunity to learn, and a host of other factors that can directly enhance or slow the rate of development. It examines a number of cultural factors that affect our life-styles and therefore the progress of development. In the book, I have provided data to explain that some of the problems that tend to exist at certain periods of development do indeed occur, and I have provided some ways of dealing with these problems.

Current research literature is exacting in its descriptions, not only for the early years of life but also for what psychologists remind us is the second half of life. Developmental psychologists have recently examined adulthood and old age with much the same rigor that they previously examined the first half of life. *Living: Human Development through the Lifespan* not only describes what takes place but also provides theoretical underpinnings for each of the stages that occurs.

Chapter 1 provides the reader with both an overview of developmental theory as a preparation for the descriptions of the stages of the lifespan that follow in later chapters and an explanation of the environmental factors that can alter the developmental process. Later chapters deal with the stages of the lifespan, beginning with the prenatal period and birth and ending with the older adult years and finally death, what one psychologist has called "the last stage of life." The emphasis is on those periods of life in which the greatest changes occur, as in prenatal development, infancy, and adolescence. Emphasis is also on the second half of life, including middle age, and older adulthood, and aging. Recent research by stage theorists has contributed a number of interpretations about the adult years, and these are explored in some detail.

How should this book be used? It is designed as an introduction to the study of human development. For this reason, many teaching aids have been placed within the text. These are designed to make the book useful for students with different interests in the lifespan. The Prologue, "Looking Ahead: An Interview with New Parents," and the Epilogue, "Looking Back: An Interview with an Octogenarian," both provide for the reader some human and humane personalities who are in the process of experiencing themselves in the process of development. The "Interview with New Parents" introduces readers to many social issues faced by people responsible for raising a child in our society today. The interview was conducted with two young people who are immensely awed by the responsibility that they see facing them for the next several decades. The "Interview with an Octogenarian" provides a review of many issues critical to the development of all human beings. The eighty-five-year-old who agreed to the interview sees life very differently from the young parents. This octogenarian has no more responsibilities other than to see his own last stage of life. His memories constitute a very personal description of the human life cycle, with all of its complexities, interwoven problems and solutions, delights, tragedies, and successes.

Learning aids are provided throughout the text and also are available in supplementary learning materials. Sections of the text are boxed to highlight certain items of current social interest. Each Highlight is related to theoretical concerns of developmental psychologists and includes Questions for Thought for the students and faculty member. Detailed case histories for class discussion are included at the end of each chapter, with questions designed to provoke thought about important issues discussed in the chapter. In addition, preview questions, detailed summary statements, and annotated bibliographies appear in each chapter.

For students who want help in preparing for examinations, a student study guide reviews key concepts and provides self-administered quizzes and answers. An instructor's manual suggests varieties of classroom exercises that instructors can use with both large and small classes.

Human beings constitute exciting subjects for research, whether they are young or old, whether we find them in psychological research centers or sitting opposite us at our own dinner tables. Many of the case studies come from very personal experiences with students, friends, and close family members. *Living: Human Development through the Lifespan* is filled with personal memories, from the first sight of my own new babies in the hospital to the last sight of my aged grandfather in a nursing home. To all of these people, I owe gratitude for help in providing many of the insights I have described here. These insights are, of course, strengthened by extensive research findings. A sincere debt is owed to my many colleagues whose research is cited in this text.

Certain of my colleagues have provided particular assistance that should be mentioned here. Particularly, I should like to thank the following individuals who read through and offered valuable commentary on the text as it was being prepared: Dene G. Klinzing, University of Delaware; Ann L. Bradford, California State University-Sacramento; Janet Fritz, Colorado State University; Paul Muhs, University of Wisconsin-Green Bay; Joan McNeil, Kansas State University; Sara Lynn, Tennessee Tech University; William Tranchell, Erie Community College South; Thomas Ludwig, Hope College; Malcolm Wetherbee, Suffolk University; Janet Kulberg, University of Rhode Island; John C. Johnson, Weatherford College; Robert Brashear, Western Michigan University. At Addison-Wesley, Kathe Rhoades provided extensive reviewing and editing. Dr. Steven Kanter did the background research, providing a great deal of the data that was incorporated into the text. Without his aid, it would not have been possible to complete the required research in time to allow it to deal with up-to-date current issues related to human development. Finally, Dolores Mokwa typed flawless copy under severe pressure and always on time. To all these people, I owe a sincere debt of gratitude.

Pittsburgh, Pennsylvania   J. T. G.
November 1982

To Marjorie and
Peter Thorne

Contents

PROLOGUE

LOOKING AHEAD: AN INTERVIEW WITH NEW PARENTS

I interviewed Dot and Pete Richards in Dot's hospital room just three days after their baby was born. Dot was sitting up in bed when I came in. She had just finished combing her long blonde hair into one braid that hung down her back and was stirring a spoonful of sugar into a cup of tea. Pete, in an easy chair next to the bed, was studying the Sunday paper. Pete had telephoned me the evening before to let me know they were ready to see me. Dot was anxious to talk about the new baby. Pete was just as excited and as interested in talking about the baby as was his wife.

Peggy is the Richards' first child; if Dot and Pete do not change their minds, she will be their only child. Dot began by describing what she remembered of her twelve-hour labor and delivery. Pete listened, interrupting frequently to describe details that Dot omitted. Pete told me that he had been in the labor room, wiping Dot's brow, squeezing her hands with each contraction. He had attended his wife in the delivery room. After Peggy was born, examined, weighed in, and put to bed, and after a very tired Dot finally fell asleep, only then had Pete gone home to telephone the news to friends and relatives and finally to get some rest himself. He was back at the hospital first thing in the morning.

I asked Pete and Dot to talk to me about their plans for Peggy and their expectations for the future of their family.

Me: Could you talk to me today about your plans for the three of you? It's difficult, I know, to predict exactly what you will be doing. But you might have some ideas, plans, hopes for the future.

Dot: We have had plans, not so much for Peggy's future as for just "beginning Peggy." Pete and I planned for about five years to have a baby. With the economy in the state that it's in, it was difficult to save enough money so that we could comfortably live on Pete's salary alone for awhile. Right now I plan to go back to work in about a year—that is, if there are openings in my field at that time and if we can find a suitable way to take proper care of Peggy. We haven't worked out all of these plans, but are really "muddling through."

Pete: We thought a lot about Peggy's future in a different way. Dot is thirty-seven years old, and we were particularly worried about the increased possibility of her having a child with Down's syndrome. We agreed that the best thing to do was to arrange for Dot to have amniocentesis.

Dot: I don't think I had a relaxed moment from the time I went into the doctor's office until we got the results that she didn't carry the defect. I guess that really was a major step in planning for Peggy's life ahead. After that point, we started to think more and more seriously about the tremendous responsibility we were facing—why, we're the *sole* people truly responsible for the health and welfare of a helpless new human being!

Me: What do you think that the two of you will do specifically to help?

Dot: That's a hard one to answer . . . for starters, we need to provide proper care . . . you know, the best food, medical care, attention we can. I want to do all that myself, at least when she's so tiny and helpless. I can't imagine trusting anyone else.

Pete: That's why we're not really sure when Dot should go back to work. Before Peggy was born, we thought it was going to be an easy decision. Dot has always loved her job, and she does it very well. But now we can see that it is going to be more difficult than we'd thought.

Me: Have you given any thought yet to Peggy's growing up? She won't always be a baby.

P R O L O G U E

Dot: A little. It's hard to think of that tiny creature becoming a grownup. We hope and expect that she will grow up strong and healthy . . .

Pete: Beautiful . . .

Dot: And beautiful, of course. We expect her to be smart and a good student . . . I suppose I expect her to have a career of some kind when she grows up . . . .

Pete: It seems impossible to think so far into the future, particularly with conditions changing in the world as rapidly as they are now. Who knows what the world will be like by the time Peggy grows up?

Dot: The best we can do is to provide Peggy with as much help as possible to be flexible . . . for the best adaptation to whatever the future will bring.

Pete: Immediate plans are easier to talk about. We expect to do our best to provide a happy, healthy childhood. As for the future, that's more complicated. I suppose we could say that we want her to have "the better things of life" when she grows up.

Me: What exactly do you mean by "the better things of life"?

Pete: That's another hard one . . . What's "better" for us may not be better for her, just as what was "better" for our parents is not what many of us think as "better" today. Dot's mother thinks that the "better life" is being a wife, mother, and housekeeper. Dot thinks it involves an exciting life and an interesting career as well as a family. Who knows what Peggy will think twenty years from now?

Dot: I *hope* she'll want to marry and to have a child like her parents did.

Pete: You want her to have a profession and be like you, don't you?

Dot: Yes . . . I suppose I want that, too.

Pete: Who knows? Today most of our friends are breaking their backs trying to save enough money to buy their own homes. Maybe by the time Peggy grows, it will be easier . . . .

Dot: Or, maybe it will be even more difficult than it is now. Who knows? I think that a woman needs to be able to take care of herself in case the future doesn't bring what she expected. It isn't like two generations ago when she expected to be in charge of a household all her life. And, if she is working, let's say eight hours a day or one-third of her adult life, she ought to be doing what she wants to do and enjoys.

Me: You've both really said a lot here. Can you come up with what you think is most important? What you really want for Peggy?

Dot: What do we want for Peggy? Well, for the first, to be happy and healthy . . .

Pete: She'll need us for that . . . In the beginning, love and affection, good nutrition, and so forth . . . .

Dot: A good education . . .

Pete: If things go well, she'll live a long life and do many different things that she wants to. Someday she'll look back and think of all the different experiences of her life. At that point, I hope that she will be glad that we brought her into the world.

The interview was over. The nurse came to the room at that moment to help Dot get ready to nurse her baby. She handed a small bundle wrapped in a light cotton blanket to the new mother. Peggy was whimpering and moving her tiny mouth in search for her mother's breast. Dot cuddled the baby in her arms. She opened the front of her nightgown, and Peggy began to nurse.

Introduction

Part I

Preview Questions

- What are the eight stages of the lifespan and the principal features of each?

- Can you describe five principles that govern all aspects of development?

- How does the idea of sensitive periods of development compare with Havighurst's concept of developmental tasks?

- Can you describe the developmental stage theories of Piaget, Kohlberg, Freud, and Erikson and explain the major focus of each?

- What are four learning-environmental theories and how does each account for development?

- How would you compare the experimental and descriptive methods of research?

- Can you describe both longitudinal and cross-sectional research designs and explain the advantages of each?

- What are three ways in which research data may be collected and some major advantages of each?

- How do codes of ethics attempt to solve the moral problems that arise in developmental research?

I

The Study of Human Development

The development of a human being begins with the development of a one-celled fertilized egg at conception to an infinitely complex organism at birth. The person becomes a schoolchild with interests, attitudes, abilities, and expectations; a college student planning a career; a parent; a citizen involved in local politics; a grandparent; a senior citizen. Development is an amazingly complex process.

To create this scenario in the lifespan of any individual, changes have occurred in many dimensions—biological, social, and psychological. The individual has grown biologically and has changed both in size and in the complexity of bodily systems. Individuals develop gradually changing methods of interacting with others and satisfying their needs. Psychologists refer to all of these orderly and sequential changes as development. Development includes processes that are determined genetically and biologically, such as physical growth. It also includes many processes that take place because of learning or interaction with the environment.

In some respects, the process of development makes each of us increasingly different from others as we grow older. We choose different careers; our personal lives differ; our interests and attitudes differ from one another. Our development in other respects reflects continuity. Many interests and attributes that we develop early in life affect later choices and patterns of living. The fifty-five-year-old physicist who might win a Nobel prize next year was a creative student during her high school years and has demonstrated since her childhood an interest in all subjects related to the functioning world around her. The thirty-five-year-old man who elects to give up his teaching career, raise his family in a rural area, and earn his living by farming probably always had a strong interest in the land.

The emergence of developmental psychology, the study of human development throughout the lifespan, is a relatively new field of interest in the United States. As a new branch of study emerging from the field of psychology, it has been greatly influenced by social and political change in this country. Because of popular acceptance in the 1930s of the notion that childhood is an important part of development and that children should be helped to lead constructive lives, major American universities at that time began to establish child development centers (Aries 1962). With the increase in behavior problems among young people in the 1960s, adolescence became popular as a topic of research interest. As the average age of our population began to increase, developmental psychologists began to gather information on the development of young adults. Today, as the number of older people increases in our population, developmental psychologists are including the study of aging, or geriatrics, in their research. Neugarten (1979, p. 899) suggests that this period of life may well be the most interesting, because "the longer the life, the more twists and turns it has had and the more challenging puzzle it is to unravel."

Developmental psychology today involves many issues studied in other fields of psychology; it includes perception, motivation, intelligence, and neuropsychology. All of these concepts are used to explain the individual's development at each stage of the life cycle. Because human interactions—from the very first stages of development through old age—involve great numbers of people, differing life-styles, and differing social, political, and economic events, the study of human development also includes information from many fields other than psychology.

STAGES OF THE LIFE CYCLE

There is no one "correct" way to divide the human lifespan for study. Researchers agree about specific changes that we can expect of most people at specific ages. For example, we expect children's teeth to erupt at certain ages. We expect growth spurts to occur about the time of puberty. The presence of these changes is affected, however, by changes in the different environments in which children grow and develop. Children who are not provided proper nourishment may not grow teeth at the time they would otherwise, or they might lose them shortly after they appear. Puberty and the growth spurt associated with it can be similarly retarded by under-nutrition. American children approximately between the ages of eleven and eighteen tend to exhibit a variety of behaviors, such as rebellion, which American adults term "adolescent." Some American children go through a rebellious period earlier than others; some go through it later. Children growing up in societies other than America may never exhibit rebellious adolescent behavior. Children in some preliterate societies in sub-Saharan Africa, for example, never exhibit rebellion and instead change their behaviors from "childlike" to "adultlike" during the course of specific prescribed puberty rites. For these individuals, adolescence is not descriptive of a stage of development.

The eight time periods, or stages, of the lifespan cited in this book are typical for Americans during their lifetimes. They were chosen for two reasons. First, we assume that readers are interested in the manner in which individuals grow and develop in cultures similar to that of the United States. When development of individuals growing up in America differs considerably from development for people in other parts of the world, we will point it out. Second, many psychologists have based their own research on these time periods because they coincide with important events in the life cycle.

The first stage, the prenatal stage, begins with conception and continues through birth. This is the only stage for which all researchers agree on a fixed beginning and ending. The second stage, infancy, begins at birth and continues until approximately age two when most children have begun to acquire language and thought. During infancy, individuals need a great deal of care and attention to develop properly. Unlike the prenatal stage, infancy and all stages that follow it are fluid, or subject to some change in beginning or ending. For example, two-year-olds may be ready to enter the next stage of development on the basis of some of their acquired thinking abilities, but they remain physically in the infancy stage on the basis of slowed motor development.

Today many developmental psychologists study not only infancy and childhood but the entire lifespan.

The third stage, childhood, includes the preschool years from roughly age two to ages five, six, or seven, during which time children typically become socially involved with others outside their immediate families. It also includes what we have chosen to call middle childhood, the five to eight years during which children often first attend elementary school, and older childhood, which includes nine to twelve-year-olds.

For most children, the period we term adolescence begins at eleven or twelve years. The specific time period for adolescence is somewhat less well defined than for earlier stages because children vary considerably in the age at which they begin and end the physical and behavioral attributes associated with this stage. In addition, Malina (1979) reports that adolescent physical changes are coming earlier than they were a generation ago.

Youth and young adulthood follow the rebellion of adolescence. Youth, a concept coined to describe behaviors that do not exist for all young people but are increasingly common among Americans and young people from other Western industrial societies, has been used to describe those young people who have given up the rebellion of their adolescent period but who are not yet ready to take on the responsibilities and commitments required of young adults. When they finally are ready, young people at the young adult stage commit themselves to life-styles and careers and often to lifetime mates.

Adulthood, described in this text as the period from roughly twenty-five years to sixty-five years, includes that period in which most Americans are committed to maintaining life-styles, raising families, pursuing careers, and helping their children become young adults who take on their own responsibilities. These are the "working years" for most Americans. The newest stage of development to be studied by developmental psychologists is older adulthood. The stage includes the after-retirement years, for most a period of life in which the individual adjusts to decreasing physical abilities and other psychological stresses.

The last stage of life, described extensively by Kübler-Ross (1975), is death. Death and dying are the end of the life cycle for all people, regardless of their beginnings or cultural backgrounds.

PRINCIPLES GOVERNING DEVELOPMENT

Some developmental psychologists study individuals for the purpose of describing and explaining the principles by which they develop. The purpose of this research is not only to help explain the behavior of any individual at a particular age but also to help make predictions about the behavior of groups of people at any given stage in their development. The principles that follow govern all aspects of development, whether we are talking about physical or behavioral development or about motor, cognitive, or social–emotional development.

1. *Development proceeds qualitatively, from simple to complex.* To explain this principle, we must first distinguish between what we have been calling "growth" and what we have been calling "development." All human beings increase in size as they get older. At the same time, the number of different responses they are able to make increases as well. These are quantitative changes, or what we call **growth.** One example of growth is that children add to the number of words they can produce and respond to, from an average of three words at one year of age to approximately 2500 words at six years (J. Gibson 1978). At the same time, development proceeds qualitatively; it progresses from simple to complex. Not only do humans grow larger, but they also change from single-celled organisms at conception to highly complex creatures of varied structure and function. The process by which this occurs is **development.** Similarly, while the sizes of children's vocabularies increase (quantitative growth), children are simultaneously developing the ability to use their words in more complicated ways and to give them more involved meanings (qualitative development).

2. *Development proceeds from the general to the specific.* Together with the change toward complexity comes an increase in specificity. In the body's physical development, as its cells change in character, specific kinds of tissues with specific functions are developed (skin, bones, blood, etc.). In behavioral development, however, a baby makes general arm movements long before specific responses, such as reaching for objects. Similarly, as older children find more ways to use

words, they develop very specific uses for certain words. Long before adult-hood, specific body mannerisms, facial movements, or hand gestures typical of a given individual are fixed for life.

3. *Development proceeds directionally.* The **cephalo-caudal principle** indicates that development (as well as growth) always proceeds directionally from head to foot. We can see this principle demonstrated in physical growth simply by comparing the changes that take place in the comparative sizes of different parts of the body. At birth, babies' heads are large in comparison to the rest of their bodies. As individuals grow older, the rate of growth increases in the lower extremities of the body. As this occurs, the head gradually begins to look smaller in relation to the rest of the body (see Fig. 1.1). Some approximate comparisons between newborn and adult bodies are (1) an infant's head is one-half the length of an adult head, (2) an infant's trunk is one-third the length of an adult trunk, and (3) an infant's legs are one-fifth the length of adult legs.

   Development also proceeds according to the **proximo-distal principle**—that is, it proceeds from areas closest to the central nervous system outward to the extremities of the body. For this reason, arm muscles develop before finger muscles; babies learn to control arm movements long before they can manipu-late their fingers at will. In fact, they will not develop control of their fingertips sufficiently to make the very fine movements required in writing until some-where near the age of six years. Very fine control, as is necessary in playing musical instruments, often cannot be accomplished until much later.

4. *Development continues throughout life.* Changes that are controlled by the de-velopmental process are orderly and tend to occur in unvarying sequence. This means that a person's body and behaviors continue to change in predictable ways as long as the person lives. Every baby can be expected to sit before standing, to stand before walking. All aging persons can be expected gradually to lose some of the abilities they once had. It is this fact that led Havighurst (1952) and other psychologists to outline the developmental tasks expected for all of the lifespan. It has led Kübler-Ross (1975) to describe death as "the last stage of development."

   Since development is continuous, what happens at one stage influences all ensuing stages. The child who receives little maternal affection in the first year of life can be expected to exhibit predictable social problems in later stages of development. Accordingly, many psychologists today are interested in studying child development in order better to understand the behavior of adults.

5. *The rate of development varies.* Any two individuals born at the same time can be expected to differ somewhat in height, weight, level of motor development, and so on. Another way to say this is that each individual is unique; each tends to be distinctive in both inherited characteristics and in rate of growth and development. Development also is discontinuous. It varies from age to age for

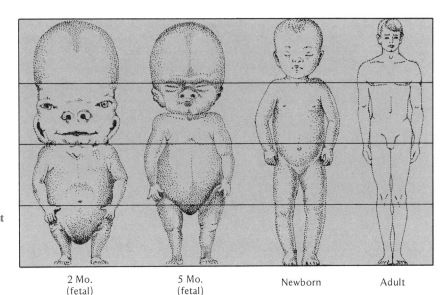

Figure 1.1 Changes that occur in body form and proportion over the lifespan.

| 2 Mo. (fetal) | 5 Mo. (fetal) | Newborn | Adult |

any given person; it is not smooth and gradual. Sudden spurts in development occur from time to time. This is particularly noticeable at certain periods in everyone's life, as with during the first year of life and again at puberty. Developmental rate is asynchronous. It varies for different aspects of development.

Relationships exist among different aspects of development. For example, a marked relationship exists between the rates of physical and mental development. A good example is the relationship between sexual maturation and specific patterns of interest and behavior common to adolescents. Another is the relationship between physical decline in the later years and interests of the elderly.

Maturation, Readiness, and Sensitive Periods of Development

Some aspects of development depend on the process we call **maturation,** a process controlled by biological inheritance. One such aspect is physical development. Biological inheritance controls to a large extent the rate of physical development. It also sets some limits on it, as exemplified by the defect known as "Down's syndrome." Children with Down's syndrome rarely live long lives no matter what experiences they have after birth, and they never can learn to think and solve problems as well as normal people. We say that their maturation process differs from that of normal people.

HIGHLIGHT 1.1   IMPRINTING: MATURATION OR LEARNING?

A research topic of major interest to psychologists concerned with the relationship between maturation and learning is **imprinting.** Dr. Konrad Lorenz, the pioneer researcher in the area of imprinting, noted that some animals are born with a tendency to accept a certain range of "mother figures." Once a mother figure has been accepted by the young animal, it will follow that mother figure everywhere. Imprinting is the term used to refer to the bond that apparently develops between the young animal and the mother figure it adopts. Lorenz's

Konrad Lorenz, the "imprinted mother" to these goslings, leads his charges on a morning stroll.

The ability to walk is a good example of the way maturation affects development. Walking is affected only minimally by learning experience or interaction with the environment. Hopi Indian mothers used to bind their babies to cradle boards that they carried on their backs. Babies remain attached to these boards most of the time during the first three months of their lives and for part of each day after that. Because they were unable to move their legs while attached to the boards, they had almost no experience using the muscles required for walking. Yet, when removed from the cradle boards, they walked at approximately the same age as other children. Apparently, lack of opportunity to practice moving their arms and legs did not hamper development of walking (Mussen 1973).

most famous research involved geese (Lorenz 1952). He discovered that shortly after hatching, young goslings will follow the first moving object that comes into their field of view. They thereafter "imprint" that object. Of course, normally the first moving object present is the mother goose. Lorenz, however, was able to produce artificial situations in which the first moving object the baby goslings saw was Lorenz himself. Imagine this great biologist waddling across a field, waving his arms, followed by his troupe of imprinted goslings!

Lorenz and colleagues found that many animals, including geese, chickens, goats, and sheep, exhibit this imprinting response (Moltz and Stettner 1961). They discovered a number of interesting pheonomena related to this event. Apparently, there is a sensitive period in the life of the young animal for imprinting. In geese, approximately three days after hatching, imprinting no longer takes place. The sensitive period, however, seems to be extended considerably if the animal is kept in an almost structureless environment after hatching.

QUESTIONS FOR THOUGHT

1. Psychologists have long been interested in the relationship between what Lorenz called imprinting and what child psychologists call attachment, the emotional tie that develops early in life between an infant and its care giver. Do you think that what Lorenz was measuring is the same attachment response that develops in human infants? Why or why not?

2. If there is a sensitive period in the development of human infants after which attachment no longer develops, just as there is a sensitive period in the development of goslings after which imprinting does not occur, what do you think might be the effects of depriving a human infant of interactions with its mother at this age?

Maturation brings with it **readiness** for new and more complex behaviors. In some cases, readiness refers to behaviors of which the developing person is capable, but only if certain kinds of learning experiences are provided. We call this readiness to learn. We say that children who have matured sufficiently and developed perceptual skills are ready to learn to read. During what developmental psychologists call **sensitive periods of development** (Oyama 1979), responsiveness is heightened to certain kinds of learning. During these periods, certain interactions with the environment must take place if development is to progress and to result in permanent changes in behavior. Thus the child who never practices perceptual skills may never learn to read properly.

The crucial factor affecting sensitive periods is often timing. If people are not provided certain types of environmental interactions at very specific periods of their lives, development may be slowed or completely stopped. An extreme example is feeding during prenatal development and infancy. A fetus or infant who is not provided adequate protein may suffer in a terrible way: Because the brain is developing more rapidly during this period than any other of life, inadequate nutrition may cause irreversible damage and in severe cases, mental retardation (Coles *et al.* 1967).

Developmental psychologists have determined specific time periods in our lives when certain kinds of stimulation are most useful. Many argue that the preschool years are particularly important for intellectual development, and they advocate systematic early-intervention programs to help children who have received little cognitive stimulation in infancy (Glaser and Resnick 1972).

The concepts of readiness and sensitive periods have been used widely by psychologists concerned with social, emotional, and other forms of development. Bowlby (1965) suggested, for example, that delaying the formation of close attachments much past the age of six months may impair a baby's later ability to form close personal attachments to other people. Psychiatrists worry about effects of social and maternal deprivation, particularly in the first year of life. They attribute many problem behaviors of later life to this type of early deprivation.

Developmental Tasks

At each period of their lives, people are confronted with new and different tasks that society expects them to learn. Havighurst (1952) divided the lifespan into six basic periods. He then described the **developmental tasks** expected of people in our society. According to Havighurst, developmental tasks must be mastered at the proper and accepted developmental stage if the individual is to develop normally. Tasks vary from society to society; what is acceptable in one society may not be acceptable in another. People successful at accomplishing each task at the appropriate age prescribed by their own societies are able to move on to complete new tasks successfully. Failure at any developmental task is likely to hamper development in succeeding stages. For example, learning to read is a critical task for children in our society. The person who does not learn to read until adulthood is likely to suffer greatly in the delay. Functionally illiterate adults in America usually suffer terrible feelings of humiliation.

THEORIES OF DEVELOPMENTAL STAGES

The concept of **developmental stages** grows logically from the principles of development. According to these principles, individuals develop in a systematic and orderly fashion. Although development is continuous throughout life, it is not perfectly correlated with age. Researchers have been able nevertheless to specify fairly distinctive stages characterized by special behaviors.

Explorations of broad aspects of behavior have led psychologists to make generalizations about the sorts of behavior we can expect of individuals at various ages throughout their lives. Some researchers point out that the concept of the developmental stage becomes most useful when it describes not just one behavior, but an interrelated or unifying set of behaviors associated with a given age level (Wohlwill 1973). Inhelder (1953) considers this set of behaviors as a structured whole as opposed to any isolated pieces of behavior. Such sets of behaviors include those associated with infancy, adolescence, or old age.

Developmental stages are used to provide descriptions of the sequences of changes expected as individuals increase in age. The term *adolescence,* for example, means to most of us behaviors associated with developing sexuality, with achieving greater independence from home and parents, with more time spent with peers away from home, and so forth. Descriptions of developmental stages are based on the "average" person's behavior—that is, behavior expected of most people at any given age. They serve as a kind of concise summation of what happens to individuals at a given point in their development.

Developmental stages are more than simply descriptions of age-related behavior. Piaget (1960) argued that developmental stages, by definition, describe certain sequences of behavior, that they describe behaviors that gradually and predictably change in some specific order. Developmental stages describe behaviors that are related one to another in different ways. To describe a developmental stage, psychologists must do more than describe behaviors common to a general age level. They must also be able to describe and explain the "inter-patterning among the changes of responses" (Wohlwill 1973, p. 219).

Developmental stages are the result of a combination of maturation, learning, and behavioral changes due to interaction of the individual with the environment. Characterization of any stage is rarely, if ever, free of the environment in which the individual acts. For this reason, many developmental stages cannot clearly be separated from one another. Transitions from one stage to the next are gradual and occur at slightly different times for individuals with different learning experiences. Occurrences at different developmental stages may explain behavior at later stages. Individuals who are deprived of maternal or other parental affection during infancy, for example, may not develop attachment responses. These individuals may be expected to have superficial relationships with others in adulthood (Bowlby 1965).

Several theories have been formulated to describe many different aspects of developmental stages. A representative few, designed to describe cognitive development, the development of moral thinking, personality development, and social development are discussed here. Later chapters will discuss the stages in greater detail as they relate to specific chronological ages.

HIGHLIGHT 1.2 DEVELOPMENTAL TASKS OF LIFE

Following is the list of developmental tasks from the first years of life through old age, as Havighurst viewed them for people growing up in the United States:*

Birth to Six Years (infancy and early childhood)

Learning to take solid foods
Learning to walk, talk, and control elimination of wastes
Developing trust in one's self and others
Exploring the environment
Learning to identify with one's own sex
Learning to relate socially and emotionally to others
Learning to distinguish right from wrong

Six to Twelve Years (middle childhood)

Expanding knowledge of the physical and social world
Learning appropriate sex role
Developing confidence and self-esteem
Acquiring academic skills, reasoning, and judgment
Learning physical and social skills

Twelve to Eighteen Years (adolescence)

Developing self-assurance and a sense of identity
Adjusting to bodily changes
Acquiring sexual interests and more mature relationships with peers
Achieving emotional independence from parents
Exploring interests and abilities, selecting an occupation

Eighteen to Thirty-Five Years (early adulthood)

Completing formal education and beginning profession
Finding and learning to live with a mate
Developing responsibility to care for family needs
Developing basic philosophy of life

*This list of tasks is compiled from data described in Havighurst (1952).

Thirty-Five to Sixty Years (middle age)

Accepting greater social responsibility

Establishing a pattern and standard of living

Helping one's children become effective adults

Adjusting to one's aging parents

Accepting the physiological changes of middle age

Later Life (aging)

Adjusting to increased physical limitations

Adjusting to reduced income

Affiliating with one's own age group

Accepting retirement

QUESTIONS FOR THOUGHT

1. Havighurst's developmental tasks are related directly to the culture in which people grow and develop. Can you give examples of ways that some of these tasks may differ from culture to culture?

2. What is the major difference between the tasks ascribed to individuals in early and later life?

Piaget's Theory of Cognitive Development

Jean Piaget spent the bulk of a long career observing the ways that children of different ages think and solve problems. Piaget watched infants and children react to problem situations of many kinds. He was interested not in whether they solved these problems correctly, but in the reasons they responded as they did. From his painstaking, detailed observations, Piaget derived a theory to explain the development of **cognition,** or the thinking processes. According to Piaget's theory, thinking processes change in many different ways with age. He proposed a progression of different cognitive stages, each stage permitting children to solve problems using qualitatively different processes.

Piaget's Stages of Cognitive Development. The stages of cognitive development refer to what individuals are capable of learning as they become older. Because of the importance of cognition to development, later chapters will refer to different stages of cognitive development as they describe, in turn, different periods of life. For now, we will provide a brief description of major stages as an aid to understanding Piaget's approach.

A child's first two years are devoted to the development of sensorimotor skills. Piaget called this the **sensorimotor stage** of development. Throughout this period, infants learn to make use of the sensations coming to them from the outside world and to manipulate and control the muscles of their bodies. Young infants use responses that do not require use of symbols or language. Piaget saw many major and predictable changes taking place during the sensorimotor period. He described them in a number of stages. These include a stage in which innate responses become efficient, which means that babies willfully repeat acts over and over again, first for their own sakes, later to watch the results, and finally to obtain particular goals, and that babies learn to think about the effects of responses before they make them.

Children, according to Piaget, enter the stage of **preoperational thought** at the end of the second year. During the early part of this stage, they develop use of language and then use this ability to help them use signs and symbols to solve increasingly complex problems.

Older children, at Piaget's **intuitive stage,** can solve a variety of complex problems involving what Piaget called imaged-based thinking, which uses symbols to represent stimuli in the environment. Children, who enter this stage at about four, still have a great deal of difficulty using logic. At this age, according to Piaget, children's problem solutions are likely to be based on one stimulus dimension only—that is, only one aspect of the problem is used to help find the solution. For this reason, the child will often make mistakes in problem solving. For example, a four-year-old might decide that the taller of two containers always contains more liquid, even though the shorter container is wider and holds a greater volume. Piaget would say, in this case, that the only stimulus dimension the child is considering is height.

The intuitive stage ends with what Piaget called the **concrete operational stage,** at about age seven. It is at this point, according to Piaget, that true reasoning first develops. It begins with reasoning requiring concrete examples. A child will no longer think that two containers of equal volume hold different amounts of liquid if it is possible to test the hypothesis by examining the containers and perhaps test-pouring the liquid from one container to the other. Later, beginning at about twelve to fifteen years, children develop ability to reason using abstractions. Piaget called this stage the **formal operational stage.** At the formal operational stage, children, and later adolescents and adults, gradually develop ability to think about and solve problems of many varied and complex types.

Equilibration. How do all the changes that Piaget described take place? According to Piaget, cognitive development consists essentially of activity directed toward **equilibrium** (Piaget 1967). Equilibrium, in the sense that Piaget used the term, means a well-balanced set of ideas, organized into a coherent mental system that ties together what has been learned with what is being perceived in the environment. Piaget called this system a **cognitive structure** or **schema.** As people become adults, most are able to solve increasingly complex problems. This is due to learning and perceptions that allow cognitive structures of increased complexity.

According to Piaget, individuals progress from one cognitive stage to the next in each type of problem solving. At the same time, they go from periods of **disequilibrium,** in which the environment is not matched by their capabilities to use it, to periods of equilibrium, in which they are maximally capable of using the environment. For example, students first entering college have available to them the same research tools and access to the library that are available to juniors and seniors. They often are not, however, ready to use them to best advantage. We say they are in disequilibrium. By their senior year, these same students may be solving complex problems using all the stimuli in their academic environments. We say they are now in equilibrium. **Equilibration,** the process by which increased ability to respond takes place, requires two separate processes, each following the other. **Assimilation** occurs when individuals use new stimuli in their environments to perform activities they already know how to do. An example of assimilation is finding a source book on theories of ancient writers and using it to explain modern-day problems in political science.

Accommodation, the second process that must occur for equilibration to take place, occurs when individuals add new activities to their repertoires or modify old behavior. Children may stay in their playpens for long periods of time before suddenly realizing that they might use the bars of the playpen to perform new activities. The first time a child comes to a standing position in the playpen is an example of accommodation.

We will discuss other examples of assimilation and accommodation in other chapters as we discuss problem solving at each stage of life in the book. At all ages, as individuals assimilate, they increase their abilities to accommodate. It follows that without new learning experiences both processes necessarily would stop. Children whose parents do not provide visual and auditory stimulation will slow down in the development of their thinking. Adults who stop reading when they leave school slow down in similar fashion.

Suitable input, according to Piaget, consists of stimuli matched in complexity to the individual's cognitive structure. Piaget was skeptical of attempts to teach children advanced and complex concepts at early cognitive stages. He felt that such attempts too often do not provide stimuli properly matched to the cognitive structures of the children and thus are not likely to succeed.

Piaget did not assume that the stages he described were entirely separate. Nor did he specify exact ages at which they occurred. Instead, he described a series of stages that varied somewhat in their timing and that sometimes overlapped one another slightly, depending on the type of problem solving studied. His point was that they always occurred in the same fixed order; more complex or higher stages always following less complex ones.

Piaget explained stages as a mixture of maturation and learning. His detailed descriptions, as well as his theoretical writings, make clear his belief that interaction with the environment is necessary for cognitive change to occur. Piagetian theory predicts that individuals reared in isolation from outside stimulation will have significantly slowed rates of cognitive development.

Psychologists studying learning agree with developmental-stage researchers that behavior changes relate in some ways to chronological age. They disagree, however, as to the cause of that relationship and to the emphasis placed on it. Gagne (1968) suggested that Piaget's stages of cognitive development depend on two factors: (1) what the individual already knows and (2) how much still has to be learned in order to reach the goal. According to Gagne, the reason that the individual progresses from one point to the next in development is that individuals learn an ordered set of capabilities that build on each other in progressive fashion. A person is ready to learn a new skill only when prerequisite skills have been learned. Every higher level of learning requires previous lower-level learning. As individuals grow older, they are more likely to have completed more lower-level learning. Thus older individuals are usually better able to solve problems requiring these lower levels of learning successfully.

Kohlberg's Theory of Moral Development

A refined extension of Piaget's concepts was proposed by Lawrence Kohlberg (1969), who hypothesized stages in moral reasoning that form an unvarying and universal

According to Piaget, in order to get the toy through the bars, this baby first uses familiar grasping behavior (assimilation) and then modifies this skill with new knowledge (accommodation).

sequence (see Table 1.1). Kohlberg gathered his information in the following fashion: He interviewed boys aged ten to sixteen and asked them to respond to problems containing hypothetical moral dilemmas involving conflicts.

Kohlberg's problems are complex; there are no "correct" answers. In each problem, individuals can give answers based on anything ranging from conformity to societal expectations, from adherence to law to certain higher considerations, as the welfare and rights of others. A typical problem raises the issue of stealing a drug to save a dying woman. The inventor of the drug is selling it for ten times what it costs him to make. The woman's husband cannot raise the money, and the seller refuses to lower the price or wait for payment. The question posed by this problem is, "What should the husband do?"

Kohlberg described stages ranging from what he considered the lowest stage of moral development, obedience and punishment orientation, to a sixth and highest level involving conscience or principle orientation (Kohlberg 1969, p. 376). Like Piaget, he found a positive relationship between age and stage of development. He also noted that stages of moral reasoning, like cognitive stages, seem to be the product of an individual's interaction with the environment. Kohlberg stressed that increases in the development of moral reasoning do not occur through direct teaching—that is, they cannot be taught through traditional schooling and lessons. Rather, they develop through complex processes involving, among other factors, interaction with others. Kohlberg notes that most people in our society never reach the highest stage, that of morality based on universal ethical principles. He suggests that perhaps only five to six percent of adults reach this highest level (Sanborn 1971).

Table 1.1
Kohlberg's Stages of Moral Development

Stage	Illustrative Behavior
Level I. Premoral	
Stage 1. Punishment and obedience orientation	Obeys rules in order to avoid punishment
Stage 2. Naïve instrumental hedonism	Conforms to obtain rewards, to have favors returned
Level II. Morality of conventional role conformity	
Stage 3. "Good-boy" morality of maintaining good relations, approval of others	Conforms to avoid disapproval, dislike by others
Stage 4. Authority-maintaining morality	Conforms to avoid censure by legitimate authorities, with resultant guilt
Level III. Morality of self-accepted moral principles	
Stage 5. Morality of contract, of individual rights, and of democratically accepted law	Conforms to maintain the respect of the impartial spectator judging in terms of community welfare
Stage 6. Morality of individual principles of conscience	Conforms to avoid self-condemnation

Source: Kohlberg (1958).

Specific stages described by Kohlberg include

1. *Orientation to punishment and reward and to physical and material power.* In this and the next stage, young children and older delinquents decide on the basis of specific rewards or punishments they might receive. In the case of the preceding problem, this would be determined by the husband's ability to get the medicine and the likelihood of his being caught if he steals it.

2. *Hedonistic orientation with an instrumental view of human relations.* This stage involves beginning notions of reciprocity but with emphasis on exchange of favors. Those at this stage of development think of people other than themselves, but the purpose, in the end, is to get what they want. Such a person might decide to have the husband steal the medicine because a wife is a more important (and useful) figure than a druggist.

3. *Good boy/good girl orientation.* This stage involves seeking to maintain expectations and win approval of one's immediate group. Individuals operating at the good boy/good girl stage define morality by what their peers think. If the peer group thought badly of stealing, a person at this stage of development might decide to let the wife die; if the peer group did not mind, this person might decide to save the wife by stealing the drug.

4. *Orientation to authority and duty and to maintaining a fixed order,* whether social or religious, which is assumed as a primary value. Individuals at this stage of development would decide on the basis of legality, regardless of the consequences.

5. *Social contract orientation,* with emphasis on equality and mutual obligation within a democratically established order (e.g., the morality of the United States Constitution). Here, morality comes seriously into play. The individual who decides to steal the drug might do so because, in a democratic society, all people should have equal access to life-saving drugs.

6. *Conscience or principle orientation.* Morality or individual principles of conscience have logical comprehensiveness and universality. Highest value at this stage is placed on human life, equality, and dignity. Decisions concerning the husband's response are based on the effects of this decision on the persons concerned. Whatever choice is made is consistent with other decisions made in response to other problems.*

Freud's Psychoanalytic Theory of Personality

The first researcher to propose developmental stages as an explanation for personality and social development probably was Sigmund Freud, an Austrian psychiatrist whose major works were written during the early part of this century.

Freudian theory, also called **psychoanalytic theory,** stresses the vital role of experience in interacting with internal instinctual urges. Psychoanalytic theory maintains that unless basic needs for food, love, warmth, and security are met at early stages in life, development of personality will be arrested. Freud called this **fixation.** He felt that fixation at early ages, caused by frustration of basic needs, affects personality at all later stages. In this sense, each stage constitutes a sensitive period in the life of the individual. Without fixation, Freud thought that people would pass through the stages of development in specific sequential order. With fixation, however, a person's basic personality structure would be flawed in whatever area the deprivation occurred.

Freud hypothesized five basic stages of development, each stage characterized by a new socialization problem confronting the individual. The first stage, occurring during infancy, is characterized by passive and dependent behavior on the part of the child. The organized source of gratification at this age is sucking. The child's life

---

*Kohlberg has found almost no subjects who reach this stage of development.

In Freudian theory, the anal stage of development is characterized by gaining control of bladder and bowel functions and, by extension, of the environment.

centers about the mother, the nipple, and the thumb. Freud called this the **oral stage.** According to psychoanalytic theory, children who do not receive sufficient gratification at this stage of development are likely to become fixated. Such individuals, when they are adults, may display a variety of symptoms: thumb sucking, pencil or pipe chewing, and nail biting are a few examples.

The next period of development, according to Freud, is associated with concerns for control of bladder and bowels. Freud called this the **anal stage.** Children at this stage are learning to exercise control over their environments. They are able to give or not give feces. They are acquiring language and communication skills. Fixation at this stage of development causes characteristics different from oral fixation. According to psychoanalytic theory, the individual may either become overly controlled, orderly, and rigid or do the reverse and become extremely messy, disorderly, and irresponsible.

The **phallic stage** occurs when the child becomes aware of genital differences and the pleasures associated with them. Freud thought that this occurred in early childhood. At this time, the child develops increased affection for the parent of the opposite sex. Personality, according to Freud, now begins to take shape. The child begins to explore the world and to internalize a value system.

The phallic stage is followed by what Freud termed the **latency stage** of middle childhood. The individual now begins to divert primary love attentions to those outside the home. Interest in peers and sex-role identification increase. Some authors have referred to this stage as the calm before the storm of puberty (Westlake 1973). Freud's fifth stage, the **genital stage,** is that storm. With adolescence, Freud said, comes an upsurge of instinctual sexual drives, a need to dissolve parental attachments, and a set of conflicts well known in our society.

Erikson's Psychosocial Approach to Personality

Erik Erikson (1963) has expanded and elaborated on Freud's theories. Erikson outlined **psychosocial** stages of development to parallel Freud's stages (see Table 1.2). Erikson claimed these stages describe the individual's orientation to self and to his or her social world. Erikson, unlike Freud, felt that personality is not defined in early childhood but continues to develop throughout life. In this sense, many feel that Erikson has rectified what they consider Freud's one-sided emphasis on childhood as the beginning and the end of personality development (Elkind 1970).

Table 1.2
Erikson's Eight Stages of Psychosocial Development

Stages	Psychosocial Crises	Significant Social Relations	Favorable Outcome
1st year	Trust vs. mistrust	Mother or mother substitute	Trust and optimism
2nd year	Autonomy vs. doubt	Parents	Sense of self-control and adequacy
3rd through 5th years	Initiative vs. guilt	Basic family	Purpose and direction, ability to initiate one's own activities
6th year to puberty	Industry vs. inferiority	Neighborhood, school	Competence in intellectual, social, and physical skills
Adolescence	Identity vs. confusion	Peer groups and out groups, models of leadership	An integrated image of oneself as a unique person
Early adulthood	Intimacy vs. isolation	Partners in friendship; sex, competition, cooperation	Ability to form close and lasting relationships, to make career commitments
Middle adulthood	Generativity vs. self-absorption	Divided labor and shared household	Concern for family, society, and future generations
The aging years	Integrity vs. despair	"Human Kind," "My Kind"	A sense of fulfillment and satisfaction with one's life, willingness to face death

Source: Adapted from Erikson (1963).

Erikson, like Freud, believed in sensitive periods of development. These periods, he felt, are characterized by crises or potential turning points. They are due to radical changes in the child's perspectives. If a problem is not resolved, it will appear again and again at each successive stage. Unlike Freud, however, Erikson was optimistic in his belief that failures at one stage can be corrected by successes at later stages. He felt further that resolution of problems at one stage does not necessarily require resolution of other past problems.

Erikson described eight stages of psychosocial development, each increasing in complexity and developing directly from the preceding stage. The first stage, **trust vs. mistrust,** is characterized by children's learning to trust or mistrust the environment. During the first two years of life, according to Erikson, if children's needs are satisfied by warm, loving parents, they will learn to trust; cold, unsupporting parents will create mistrusting adult personalities.

The second stage of childhood, **autonomy vs. doubt,** from age two to age three, is characterized by the learning of either autonomy or doubt, as children emerge from total dependence on a parent or other caregiver. The child may learn to control the environment successfully during this period if adequate support is given by parents or caregivers. An overprotected child may learn to fear the environment. Too little protection and resulting unpleasant experiences may produce similar fear.

Initiative or guilt is developed in the fourth and fifth years, depending on the responses of surrounding individuals to the child's continued experimentation with the environment. This stage of development, termed **initiative vs. guilt,** corresponds to Freud's genital stage.

The early school years, ages six to eleven, are the years in which the child develops industry or inferiority feelings. It is in these years that the child learns to relate with peers, to play by the rules, and to perform academic tasks. Reward for learning and assistance in learning leads to industry. Inability to deal with this environment may lead to feelings of inferiority throughout life. Erikson called this stage **industry vs. inferiority.**

Erikson probably is known best for descriptions of adolescent development. According to Erikson, adolescence, the period from twelve to eighteen years, is a period during which developing youngsters may learn either identity or role confusion, depending on what happens in their interactions with the world. The stage is therefore termed **identity vs. role confusion.**

Erikson's sixth stage concerns young adulthood and deals with development of either intimacy or isolation, depending on whether the young person is able to develop satisfactory interpersonal attachments at the time of life when such relationships usually develop. Erikson called this stage **intimacy vs. isolation.** Isolation, according to Erikson, will keep young people from satisfactions that might occur in middle age and beyond. In particular, it will make it more difficult for adults to develop what Erikson refers to as generativity during the childrearing and middle years. Generativity is the ability to deal with the concerns of others, including children, other members of the household, and persons with whom one interacts on a day-to-day basis. The nongenerative person is considered to be the opposite, or self-absorbed. The stage is therefore called **generativity vs. self-absorption.** Finally, the crisis of old age involves the development of ego, or **integrity vs. despair.** The integrated person knows that he or she has been the generator for others and the generator of things or ideas; the despairing individual gives up. This stage is affected strongly by all the preceding stages.

LEARNING—ENVIRONMENTAL THEORIES

Learning, a relatively permanent change in behavior due to experience, is a strong determinant of development. Learning can be used to explain much of what happens as we grow and develop.

Many learning psychologists identify principles common to learning in all people. One approach restricts study of learning to only what can be observed—behavior itself. Another approach explains behavior as what goes on inside people—their thinking processes and their needs, drives, and motives. We will consider each of these approaches.

Classical Conditioning

Psychologist John Watson showed in laboratory experiments that learning occurs through a process of association. In a now-famous study, Watson and Raynor (1920) demonstrated that an eleven-month-old baby could be taught to exhibit fear responses to a white rat. To accomplish this, they first showed that their subject, Baby Albert, responded without fear (smiling and cooing) when a white rat was presented to him. At the same time, he exhibited fearful responses (crying) when subjected to a loud noise. After Watson and Raynor presented the rat many times together with the loud noise, Baby Albert began to show fear when the rat was presented alone. Later, Watson and Raynor noted that Baby Albert generalized this fear to all white furry animals.

Watson and Raynor did their studies of Baby Albert more than sixty years ago. In the most recent several decades, psychologists have become more concerned about the welfare of the subjects of their research. Today, studies that involve frightening or endangering children are no longer allowed. Ethics committees composed of psychologists monitor research involving human subjects to ensure that they are treated humanely.

Baby Albert's learning is called **classical conditioning.** Classical conditioning occurs when an initially neutral or **conditioned stimulus** (CS) (in this case, the

28 THE STUDY OF HUMAN DEVELOPMENT

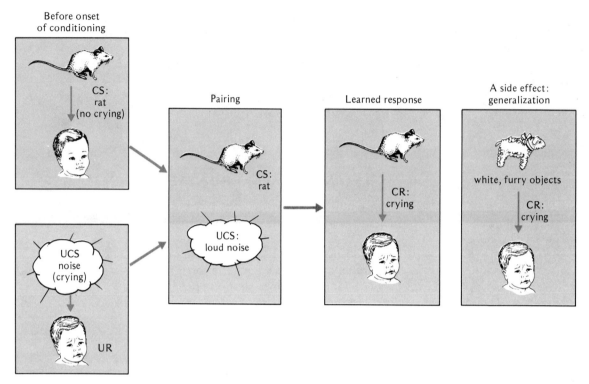

Figure 1.2 The classical conditioning of Baby Albert. During the conditioning process, the white rat (CS) was presented before the loud noise (UCS). Together CS and UCS evoked crying (UR). After conditioning, it was no longer necessary to present the loud noise to make Baby Albert cry. The CS has become a substitute for the UCS. It now evokes the response labeled the conditioned response of crying (CR).

white rat) is associated with an **unconditioned stimulus** (UCS) (the loud noise). Albert's learned fear response to the conditioned stimulus is called a **conditioned response** (CR). His initial unlearned fear response to the unconditioned stimulus is called an **unconditioned response** (UCR). In Watson and Raynor's study, Albert's conditioned fear response was generalized to other stimuli similar to the conditioned stimulus. He thus became fearful of all white furry animals. Figure 1.2 describes the steps that took place in Baby Albert's conditioning.

Classical conditioning occurs frequently in everyone's life. This morning, for example, when the alarm clock rang, most of us turned it off, sat up, rubbed our eyes, and got out of bed. The ringing of the alarm clock is associated with getting up.

Operant Conditioning

Classical conditioning is learning caused by stimuli that precede the learned response. In another type of learning, the learned response is followed by certain kinds of stimuli. This second type of learning is called **operant conditioning.**

A great deal of behavior is affected by what follows it. For example, if you study this chapter carefully tonight and receive an A on a quiz in class tomorrow, you will be more likely to use this same careful method of studying for future quizzes than you would if you had received a lower grade. Careful study behavior, in this example, is called an **operant response:** You are operating on what for you is a desired result. Operant conditioning sometimes is referred to as **instrumental conditioning** because the response made is instrumental in producing a given result.

Operant conditioning occurs when behavior is followed by a reward or reinforcement. A **reinforcement,** according to the operant theorist, is any stimulus that has the effect of increasing the immediately preceding response. Feedback on a test is a reinforcement. The value of any particular stimulus as a reinforcer depends on the person being reinforced. To most college students who want to achieve in school, high grades serve as potent reinforcers. To a teenage gang leader, on the other hand, social approval from peers is likely to be a much more powerful reinforcer than any feedback a teacher is able to give.

Some stimuli, called **primary reinforcers,** are necessary for physical survival. Among primary reinforcers are food for a hungry person or shelter for an individual lost in the wilderness. Other stimuli, such as grades and social approval, are unnecessary for physical survival, but they still strongly affect behavior. These are called **secondary reinforcers.** A secondary reinforcer initially is not reinforcing but comes to be so through repeated association with one that is. A newborn infant certainly will not change behavior because of a high grade. Nor are infants at very early ages affected by parental approval. It is only later, when approval has come to be associated with satisfaction of primary needs and grades have come to be associated with approval, that these become secondary reinforcers. Money is a powerful secondary reinforcer for many adults in our society because it is closely associated with the primary reinforcers it can purchase.

Reinforcement may occur immediately after a response is made, or it may occur sometime later. Psychologists have discovered that the longer the delay of reinforcement, the less its effect on the response. Thus, your good grade in child psychology will have a stronger effect on your future study habits if your instructor grades your quiz immediately instead of waiting two weeks to tell you how you did. The ability to learn with delayed reinforcement develops only gradually. Promises that studying will lead to great success in adult life will have very little effect on the behavior of a first grader. The same is true of promises of good health in later life as the child observes the doctor preparing the vaccination with that big, long needle! A much more effective reinforcer might be strong social approval exhibited openly by everyone—parents, doctor, and nurses—for receiving the shot without commotion.

Scheduling of Reinforcement. In any learning situation, reinforcements can be provided after each desired response is made. They also can be provided after a few desired responses occur. The pattern by which reinforcements are provided is called a **reinforcement schedule.** Researchers have conducted extensive study on the effects of different types of schedules on behavior. A **continuous** (or 100-percent) **reinforcement schedule** provides reinforcement after every single desired response is made. Researchers have found that continuous schedules of reinforcement lead most rapidly to regular patterns of responding. A production worker who always receives a reward from the boss when achieving a certain production rate on the assembly line can probably be expected to maintain that rate.

It is not always possible or even profitable, however, to reinforce on a continuous schedule of reinforcement. The boss on the production line, for example, may decide to wait until the workers are producing double what they did before and give out rewards when this goal has been met. For this method to work effectively, workload requirements must be increased gradually. We call this **shaping** behavior. Behavior can be shaped by reinforcing gradually increased methods. It can also be shaped by gradually increased reinforcing of more and more complex responses.

Reinforcements may be distributed on a number of different schedules. Workers who are provided pay incentives based on the number of items produced are being reinforced on what is called a **ratio schedule. Interval schedules** are frequently used in formal education. An example is a planned schedule in which an instructor provides weekly quizzes. Students know, after taking a quiz, that there will not be another quiz for a week. We call this particular schedule a **fixed schedule of reinforcement** because students know the fixed period of time that will elapse before the next quiz. If an instructor gave pop quizzes, we would say that the students were on a **variable schedule of reinforcement.** In this case, they would know that an interval must pass before the next quiz takes place, but they would not be able to determine the length of that interval.

On any schedule, once reinforcement is stopped, the learned response will gradually drop off. We call this **extinction.** Some human behavior seems to be virtually inextinguishable, even though no one seems to be rewarding it in any way. Behaviorists point out, however, that if we look closely, there is virtually no situation where behavior continues and some form of reinforcement is not being given. Small children frequently continue to talk to themselves, often for long periods of time, when there is no one around to listen or respond. Talking seems inextinguishable. The reason is that this verbal behavior by itself is very rewarding. Lovaas *et al.* (1977) suggest that it forms its own source of sensory reinforcement.

Positive and Negative Reinforcers. All the reinforcements we have been talking about so far have led to increases in the immediately preceding responses. These reinforcements are pleasant; people want them to occur. We call these **positive reinforcers.** Many stimuli are unpleasant. **Negative reinforcers** are stimuli that we try to avoid. These stimuli strengthen escape responses—that is, whatever we do to allow ourselves to escape the negative reinforcer will be more likely to occur in the future (Hilgard and Bower 1975). Most of us have at one time or another received parking tickets. The parking ticket is designed as a negative reinforcer: It is supposed to teach us either to park in a different spot or to put money in the parking meter if we are in a proper spot. In order for socially desirable responses like parking in the proper spot to develop through use of a negative reinforcement, we must be able to behave properly in the first place (Holz, Azrin, and Ayllon 1963; Solomon 1964). In this example, a parking space in which one would not get a ticket must be available.

Cognitive Learning Theories

Many learning psychologists believe that the behavioral description of learning is too simple. They feel that learning is more than the result of connections between stimuli and responses. It is instead a result of the combination of these factors as they are affected by the methods that we use to organize and process information. In explaining the learning process, cognitive learning psychologists describe the

---

USING OPERANT CONDITIONING   HIGHLIGHT 1.3

Rodney was an extremely active ten-year-old in the fourth grade. Ms. Murphy, his teacher, reported to the school psychologist that Rodney continually jumped out of his seat and disrupted the class. It had gotten to the point that the teacher had to stop what she was doing every few minutes to ask Rodney to sit down.

Dr. Hughes, the school psychologist, stayed in Ms. Murphy's classroom one morning to observe. Later the psychologist gave Ms. Murphy a sheet of paper and asked her to note the time whenever Rodney jumped out of his seat. She also told her to write down exactly what occurred immediately after this happened. When Dr. Hughes and Ms. Murphy sat down together a day later to look at the paper, Ms. Murphy said, "Each time he jumped up, the same thing happened: I stopped, told him to sit down, and went back to my work."

The psychologist explained to Ms. Murphy that any stimulus in the environment can be a reinforcer to some children. Often the only way we can identify the reinforcer is to find out what always follows the unwanted behavior. "In this case," Dr. Hughes said, "probably the attention given to Rodney when he jumps up is the reinforcer. We should test it by ignoring the jumping re-   Continued sponse." Dr. Hughes recommended that Ms. Murphy continue recording the times that Rodney jumped up and showed her how to plot the responses on a graph.

A week later, Dr. Hughes and Ms. Murphy studied the graph Ms. Murphy had drawn. It looked like this:

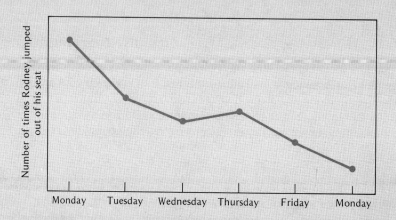

The first day, Rodney jumped out of his seat almost every two minutes. Ms. Murphy had trouble simply counting Rodney's jumping responses because they occurred so frequently. The second day, he jumped up half the number of times and spent most of the remaining time sulking. By the third day, Rodney began to spend his time looking at his schoolwork. It was clear by now that Ms. Murphy's attention was the reinforcer. On the fourth day, Rodney first tried to get attention by raising his hand. He was greatly surprised and delighted when Ms. Murphy smiled at him. It was a very pleasant and novel (for him) type of attention. By the time Dr. Hughes came back to the class, Rodney was jumping up from his seat only a few times per day. The unwanted behavior was almost completely extinguished.

QUESTIONS FOR THOUGHT

1. Did Ms. Murphy use positive or negative reinforcement to stop Rodney's behavior? How do you know?

2. What do you think might have happened to Rodney's behavior if Dr. Hughes had responded to his jumping up and down by severely punishing him?

ways we perceive the world around us. Individuals with histories of failure in school, they point out, are likely to perceive a college course as much more threatening than individuals who have always done well academically. Adults entering a second marriage usually perceive the rewards and potential dangers with much more sensitivity than they did when they were several years younger and contemplating their first marriage.

Individuals also differ in the methods they use to think and to solve problems. **Cognitive styles** include individual preferences in methods of perceiving, thinking, remembering, and solving problems. In addition, some psychologists believe that cognitive styles are reflections of individual differences in personality and motivation (Ausubel, Novak, and Hanesian 1978).

Motivational Theories

Psychologists who study motivation point out that to explain behavior fully we need to know more than what goes on in the environment and what method of thinking

The student's need to achieve is extremely important to later adjustment.

a person uses. **Motivational theory** suggests that without describing the needs, drives, and motives of people we can never fully explain why they behave as they do.

A **need** is a lack of some kind that must be reduced for satisfactory adjustment to the environment. Babies have very simple or primary needs for food and for love. Later, when they get older, they develop other learned needs that are not so important for physical survival but are necessary for optimal adjustment to the environment. A student's need to achieve is learned and extremely important to later adjustment. Many adults' needs for relationships are also learned and equally important to adult adjustment.

Psychologist Abraham Maslow (1943; 1954) has described what he considers to be the basic needs of human beings in terms of a hierarchy arranged from the simplest to the most complex in which each need becomes dominant when needs lower on the hierarchy are reduced. According to Maslow, physiological needs, the foundation of motivational theory, are dominant unless they are satisfied. Children who are hungry will not be concerned, for example, with meeting needs for social approval; the usual social reinforcers will have little effect on their behavior. Safety needs, the needs for a safe, stable environment, follow. These needs dominate the lives of some unfortunate children whose unstable environments mean that their lives are in turmoil. Needs for love and belonging come next. Youngsters who feel unwanted or who feel no rapport with peers in school often become major behavior problems. Needs for esteem are met through achievement; teachers and parents can help by rewarding success and by providing opportunities for success. According to Maslow, however, even if these needs are satisfied, the child will feel discontented and restless without doing what he wishes and what he is capable of doing. This is what Maslow calls the need for self-actualization. It is only by meeting this need that a child can begin to satisfy the need to know and to understand.

Maslow's hierarchy makes a great deal of sense when we attempt to explain why many peoples in underdeveloped countries have accepted American financial aid and have then backed nondemocratic governments. Until hunger drive is reduced, we cannot expect people to consider needs for self-actualization, according to Maslow. Figure 1.3 is a graphic portrayal of Maslow's hierarchy of needs.

Needs give rise to what psychologists who study motivation call **drives,** internal states compelling individuals to act. When babies have primary needs for food, they become active, squirm about, and cry. When college students have high needs to do well on examinations, they sometimes act in ways associated with anxiety. A student with a high need to achieve often enters the examination room with perspiring palms and increased pulse and heart rates. At first, drive states are undirected; newborn babies cry because of hunger even when they have not yet learned that they "want" a bottle. The highly anxious university student may not have prepared for the examination at all; sometimes, in fact, anxiety reduces the ability of the student to study. Once people learn to direct their drive states in order to get what they want and reduce their needs, we can expect them to behave in similar ways in the

Desires to know
and to understand

Self-actualization needs

Esteem needs

Love and belonging needs

Safety needs

Physiological needs

Figure 1.3   Maslow's hierarchy of needs.

future. Now, when their behavior is goal directed, we say that they act with **motivation** or are motivated.

Developmental psychologists tell us that different types of motives predominate at different ages. According to Kagan (1971, p. 64), "the motives that are preoccupying are usually those linked to goals that one is uncertain of attaining. These foci of doubt change as the child matures." Kagan suggests that, in the beginning months of life, the infant is guided only by goals associated with satisfaction of physiological needs.

The early school years are characterized by growing needs for competence, according to Kagan. During this period, desire both for competence and for acceptance from peers is strong. First graders have great needs for evidence that they are valued. Praise is as effective as a hug; they often will work hard at school tasks just to receive praise from the teacher. First graders who have difficulty learning to read not only feel unworthy because of lack of achievement, but they also are keenly aware that peers can see their failures.

Adolescence brings strong sexual motives to the forefront. The adolescent needs evidence of sexual attractiveness in order to feel desirable. Sex-typed behavior, learned gradually through childhood, now becomes extremely important. The high school girl who seeks strongly to gain her father's or boyfriend's praise at this age may do so in a variety of ways, including spending hours combing her hair and experimenting with makeup. An adolescent boy who thinks that his father will be proud of him for his athletic ability may work out long hours in the gym. Of course, changes in cultural stereotypes affect sex-typed behaviors, but the need for acceptance exists, no matter what behavior is chosen as culturally correct.

Adulthood and aging bring with them needs to adjust to new forms of stress. Adults need to learn to cope with the world of work and to develop satisfactory interpersonal relationships. People who reach this goal are more often satisfied with their lives than those who have not, and they more often adjust in satisfactory fashion to the phases that are to come.

CONDUCTING RESEARCH ABOUT HUMAN DEVELOPMENT

Whatever the theory of human development, research may take a variety of directions. Some researchers gather their information through laboratory studies in order to control all variables (factors in the environment that vary in some way) that may affect their results. Others use real-life settings to study human beings. Some researchers use the information they gather to develop theoretical models and to predict future behavior. Others study the effects of certain kinds of day-to-day experiences on human behavior. Some others are primarily concerned with the applications of research, such as treatment of problem behavior, and work with families, in schools, directly in the community, and in guidance clinics.

Contemporary developmental psychology centers frequently on problems of interest to society. With increasing evidence of the great importance of the prenatal and early-infancy environments, attention is being given to such questions as "How do we provide the best prenatal environment possible for the developing infant?" "What specific effects do early child care and infant learning have on later development?" The high divorce rate in the United States has prompted researchers to pay attention to the effects of divorce on people's lives. Because the number of older adults in our society is steadily increasing, investigators are attempting to determine what living styles might best be suited to the needs of the elderly.

Research Methods

Developmental psychologists are interested both in describing what takes place in the course of human development and in describing why development occurs the way it does. The **descriptive method** of research, also called **naturalistic observation,** is used to study people in natural settings. Descriptive research describes what takes place; researchers make no attempt to alter environmental conditions. The **experimental method** of research is used to study people in carefully controlled situations. Experimental researchers manipulate and control environmental conditions and then measure the consequences in order to provide some evidence of the reasons people behave as they do.

The Descriptive Method. Descriptive research has been used for a long time. Some famous early descriptive studies include use of baby biographies, in which observers studied and kept careful records of day-to-day changes in a baby's behavior. *Emile,* written by the famous philosopher Rousseau (1762), is an example.

Many researchers in Rousseau's time used the baby biography to study the development of babies and young children. Pestalozzi, the 18th century educator, prepared a diary describing the behavior of his son during the first forty-two months of life (DeGuimps 1906). Pestalozzi used the diary as the basis for his description of child development. Later, the diary was used as a rationale for procedures used in his famous experimental schools. Another famous baby biography published a cen-

Psychologist Arnold Gesell developed one of the first child development centers at Yale University in the 1930s. Gesell used the descriptive method to study the changes that occur during the first five years of life.

tury later was Charles Darwin's (1887) biography of his son. Darwin used this descriptive diary of his child's early development to produce evidence for his theory of evolution.

The biographical method still appears today in various forms. One variation is the **anecdotal record** kept by many public school systems to describe observations of student behaviors. Teachers prepare these records by describing, on a day-to-day basis, behaviors they consider sufficiently important to be remembered and passed on to future teachers.

In addition to keeping biographical records, other ways to conduct descriptive research are available. One frequently used method is called **time sampling.** If we wish to study the interactions between parents and their children in day-to-day situations, we can do so by using some method of observation. It is impossible, however, to measure any family situation continually. Researchers therefore record samples of behavior at particular intervals of time—perhaps videotaping a family at the dinner table three days per week, one hour per session, for a period of fifteen weeks. Researchers using time-sampling techniques have been able to provide interesting and provocative information concerning the interactions that go on in family settings. Rebelsky (1973) reported, for example, that American mothers at home spend an average of fifteen minutes per day in face-to-face contact with their preschool children. Robinson *et al.* (1973) found that fathers spend as little as twenty to thirty-eight seconds per day in direct interaction!

Event sampling is used when certain events in the life of an individual are to be described, as with interactions among siblings in free-play situations. It is not possible to sample interactions every time siblings interact with one another. Researchers therefore select certain of the events for investigation.

The Experimental Method. To explain the experimental method, let us use one famous experimental study as an example. Hilgard (1933) devised this study to determine whether development of certain basic skills is due to training or to normal maturing processes. Hilgard's subjects were sets of young identical twins. He knew that because they were identical twins, their heredity component was identical. Any differences in behavior had to be due to learning rather than to normal maturing processes controlled by heredity.

The basic procedure used with each set of identical twins was as follows: First, one young twin was given training at some skill, while the other was not. Sometime later, the skill was measured in both twins. If Hilgard found that training one child increased that child's skill competence above that of the other, he concluded that the skill was developed through training. If both twins performed equally well, even though only one was given special training, then Hilgard concluded that the increase in skill was due to identical maturation processes. Hilgard's experiments involved a variety of relatively simple motor skills, such as tossing a ring over a peg and walking along a narrow board. Since most sets of twins performed equally well at the skills

Identical twins are ideal subjects for experimental study because of their identical genetic makeup and similar environments.

when they were measured, Hilgard concluded that ability in these skills increases normally with age and cannot be enhanced through early training.

In Hilgard's study, as in all experimental studies, one feature of the environment was manipulated by the researcher. This manipulated feature is known as the **independent variable.** In the case of Hilgard's co-twin control study, the feature manipulated, the independent variable, was the training experience. The variable that might be affected by this independent variable is known as the **dependent variable.** In Hilgard's study, the dependent variable measured was skill at performing the required tasks.

Two types of subjects, experimental and control, are used in an experimental study. The experimenter must ensure that they are as alike as possible in all respects but one: The **experimental subject** has access to the independent variable, but the **control subject** does not. In the Hilgard study, the twins receiving training were experimental subjects. The twins receiving no training were control subjects. Identical twins, of course, are perfect control subjects, for they are as identical as any two human beings possibly can be, both in genetic makeup and in most family experiences.

Animals for Experimental Study. Human beings are very complicated creatures. In experimental research with humans, it is impossible for the experimenter always to control outside conditions affecting behavior. Invariably, some variables that might affect the behavior of the subjects cannot be controlled by the experimenter. In studying child behavior, the experimenter often is limited in ability to evaluate accurately the individual's present environment, history of interaction with the past environment, and, in most people, exact genetic endowment. In the case of Hilgard's co-twin study, Hilgard could tell that, because the subjects were identical twins, they were identical in genetic characteristics. He could not, however, control all of the personal experiences that each of the twins might have had during the courses of their lives outside the experimental situation. And, even if it were theoretically possible to control all of these outside experiences, Hilgard would have been prohibited from doing so by ethical considerations.

For these reasons, many researchers concerned with questions related to the nature of development have relied on nonhuman subjects for their experimental data. Initially, it may seem meaningless to study the effects of changing environments on the development of chimpanzees, puppies, or rats if one is interested in child development. On the other hand, particularly when researchers are interested in studying the effects of independent variables that might produce long-term harmful effects on the subjects being studied, as with sensory deprivation, for example, it is advantageous to study nonhuman species first.

Types of Research Design

A basic concern of developmental psychologists, regardless of the method of research they use, is to provide some information about people of different ages. One way to do this is to study the same people over time. We call this a **longitudinal design.** The second way is to study many people of different ages at the same time. We call this a **cross-sectional design.**

Longitudinal Design. One very famous study of the behavior of gifted people was conducted over a thirty-five-year period (Terman 1925–1959). Terman's study was descriptive. He made no attempt to change the environments of any of the people he studied. Instead, he subjected them to a repeated battery of tests over the years to compare their responses to those of less-gifted individuals. If Terman had included two groups of people in his study and had provided one of the groups with a special educational program for gifted individuals to determine whether such a program changes the "normal" course of development, then his study would have been an experimental longitudinal study.

It took Terman more than three decades and a great deal of time, money, and effort to gather his information. Longitudinal studies are difficult to conduct because of the long time period involved. It takes a very long time, as long as a human lifetime, to describe lifespan development. An additional problem is the result of the high mobility rate of Americans today. It is extremely difficult to keep close track of one individual's activities over an extended period of time.

Cross-sectional Design. This design helps solve some of the problems of the longitudinal design by studying people of different ages over a brief period. Piaget used a cross-sectional design to observe the behavior of children while they solved problems requiring the ability to think and to understand. Piaget systematically observed and described both verbal and nonverbal behavior in his studies. He attributed differences found to differences in age.

Methods of Data Collection

Many research tools have been developed to aid psychologists at their tasks of collecting data that will enable them to describe and explain the process of development. The **questionnaire,** first developed by G. Stanley Hall and his students to explore "the content of the mind" (Hall 1891), is still used frequently, especially when large numbers of people are being studied. Persons may be asked to write their answers or, in some cases, to respond orally. The questionnaire is useful only when it is complete and objective. Persons writing questionnaires must prepare each question with extreme care to make certain the wording does not bias the person answering. The **interview,** in which questions are administered orally, is a second means of gathering information.

Varieties of **standardized tests,** on which typical scores have been obtained for sample populations (groups of people), are also used. Researchers using these tests compare the scores of the people they are studying to typical scores of the sample population in order to note similarities and differences. Tests can be used to measure many characteristics of people. Today we have tests of intelligence, achievement, psychomotor ability, personality, and so on. Many of these tests, as well as a variety of other tools used to study development, will be described in later chapters.

Ethical Problems in Human Developmental Research

Many studies of human development are carried out to find information that will be useful to society. In some cases, researchers note that their studies involve some risk to the human beings being studied but feel that this risk is warranted by the benefits of the results. In some cases, however, although researchers feel that the study will provide an important contribution to society, others do not agree. Ethical dilemmas often are the result. Dr. Patrick Steptoe, the developer of *in vitro* fertilization (popularly known as test tube fertilization), for example, points to the birth of

Louise Brown as evidence of a method that allows women who otherwise cannot bear children to become mothers. Many agree. Some, however, point to ethical questions that the procedure raises: Might the method produce more harm than good? Some physicians believe that the baby conceived through *in vitro* fertilization is born at higher risk and with a greater possibility for physical or mental damage than babies conceived through normal methods.

Today, in America as in many other countries, research involving human beings is the subject of great controversy. What is safe for the subject? What is safe for society? What is ethical? Disclosures at the famous Nuremburg trials of Nazi war criminals demonstrated how damaging uncontrolled research on human beings can be. Reports of those trials disclosed research on the effects of various aversive drugs on prisoners, studies of the length of time prisoners could remain alive immersed in cold water, and far worse. To ensure that such atrocities could never again be permitted under the guise of scientific research, the international Nuremburg and Helsinki Codes of Ethical Research (reprinted in Ladimir 1969–1970) were formulated and later became the foundation of law in many nations. The codes established the right of any human subject participating in clinical research to informed consent. Informed consent, according to the codes, means that the subject clearly and fully understands what the research entails before agreeing to participate.

The question of informed consent is a complicated one. When researchers are studying the behavior of individuals with restricted abilities to understand what the research is all about—as with small children, the mentally incompetent, or even simply uneducated adults—or when they are studying the behavior of individuals who do not have the freedom to give or withhold consent—as with prisoners—this question becomes difficult indeed.

Many questions regarding informed consent are being asked today, both by researchers and by the public. For example, when does volunteering for an experiment change from a free decision to coercion? When the researcher is a teacher "requesting" students in the class to volunteer for a study in learning, how many students feel they "must" volunteer? If an experimenter is paying impoverished subjects to volunteer for a study and the subjects are clearly in need of money, is this really freedom of consent, or is it coercion? And if a researcher requires consent of parents to study the behavior of small children, how much information about the study must be given these parents before the requirements of informed consent are met?

Ethics Codes. Complicated questions like these led the United States government in the 1960s to enact the first federal law and agency regulation on medical experimentation of humans (Durran, Smhyg, and Beecher 1969). The American Psychological Association, after considerable debate about the advantages and disadvantages of controlling human behavioral research, also developed a code of ethical standards for research with human subjects. Because of the special implications of conducting behavioral research with children, the Division on Developmental Psychology of the American Psychological Association established its own position on ethical standards (American Psychological Association 1968).

Federal guidelines governing the use of humans are still being established; state guidelines supplement federal guidelines. Universities have developed their own explicit procedures for conducting research with all humans. To protect the rights of children, for example, all of these ethical codes make the same several requirements. They require that parents be notified, be given all details and facets of the proposed research important to the child, and be told how the information obtained from the child will be used.

Psychologists today agree that research with children and adults should not involve invasion of privacy. They agree also that research involving humans should involve procedures guaranteed safe for the subjects being studied. Studies involving the effects of frustration, for example, have been criticized by many authorities because of the possibilities of the subjects' suffering long-term detrimental effects. The code of the American Psychological Association states that researchers must avoid at all costs the possibility of exploiting subjects in the name of science.

THE CASE OF ALEX BARNES—A QUESTION OF INFORMED CONSENT: A CASE STUDY FOR CLASS DISCUSSION

I. Identification and Sources of Information

Name: Alex Barnes
Address: 15 Philips Street, New City, Cal.
Race: White
Sex: Male
Age: Forty-seven years
Sources of information:

1. Interview with Mr. Barnes
2. Interview with John Delaney, prison psychiatrist
3. Interview with Mr. Barnes's psychiatrist
4. Interview with Dr. Ellsworth, psychological researcher.

II. Family History

Alex Barnes is forty-seven years old. He has been married for twelve years and has two children, Alex Jr. and Stephanie. Alex has lived in New City all of his life and is a graduate of New City High School. He has worked as a carpenter for the past twenty years. Two years ago, he was arrested on a burglary charge. It was his first arrest. He was sent to prison and was released six months ago. While Alex was in prison, his older brother Bill died in New City of a heart attack.

III. Case History

Reports of Alex Barnes's trial showed him to be penitent. He admitted guilt and blamed his behavior on serious financial problems. He was a model prisoner and spent a great deal of time seeking counseling while in prison, so as to ease his way back to society. When his brother died, Alex requested an early parole. Parole was denied. Later, when Dr. Ellsworth came to the prison to solicit volunteers for a study in social psychology, Alex decided to volunteer. He reported to the prison psychiatrist that he did so "in

Continued

THE CASE OF ALEX BARNES *(Cont.)*

order to make my record look better for parole." The psychiatrist pointed out that it had nothing to do with parole. But Alex answered, "It couldn't hurt." In fact, he was paroled just three months later.

Dr. Ellsworth reported that his research involved studies of moral decision making. He presented prisoners a series of problems in which they had to choose between their own welfare and that of others. He then compared their responses to those of individuals who had never committed crimes. Dr. Ellsworth had his research proposal approved by a group of his peers, and he had required all subjects to sign papers stating that they understood the nature of the experiment and volunteered willingly.

Alex Barnes began to have bouts of depression several weeks after participating in the study. At the time, he related the depression to guilt at being in prison while his brother died and while other family members were coping with their difficulties alone. He discussed the matter several times with the prison psychiatrist, who felt that Alex would improve when he got out.

The depression grew worse, not better, after Alex's release from prison. A series of sessions with a psychiatrist revealed deep guilt that he had answered some of Dr. Ellsworth's questions in ways that demonstrated that he cared for no one but himself. Dr. Ellsworth had explained the purpose of each research question in a debriefing after the study and had given examples of answers that Alex thought resembled his own.

Alex began to blame himself for Bill's death. Later he blamed himself for all of his children's problems as well. It became impossible for him to work as he withdrew more and more from reality. Although his wife attempted to reassure him that he was not responsible for his brother's death, Alex was inconsolable. He also continued to feel guilty about having been in prison and the difficulties this had caused his family.

IV. Present Status, Diagnosis, and Recommendation

Alex's psychiatrist reports that Alex was, at the time of the psychological study, particularly vulnerable to feelings of guilt, and suggests that the psychological research probably served as a catalyst for Alex's present difficulties. He suggests further psychotherapy.

The Barnes's family attorney has announced that he plans to file legal suit against Dr. Ellsworth and the prison system for allowing the research. He states that his client did not understand the implications of the study, or he would not have volunteered. In effect, he suggests that Alex Barnes was coerced into volunteering. Regardless of whether or not a group of researchers say it is a safe study, the attorney asserts, the psychiatric evidence shows that problems did develop. Alex Barnes probably would not have participated had he expected them. Moreover, he probably would not have participated if he had not thought that participation might lead to an early parole.

Questions for Class Discussion

1. The issue of informed consent is a complicated one. Do you think that Alex Barnes was coerced into volunteering? Can a prisoner who thinks he might be paroled earlier if he is a "good" prisoner ever provide true informed consent?

2. Dr. Ellsworth's study was an observational one. He did not manipulate the environment for any of his subjects in any way at all. All he did was to ask them a series of questions. Even so, problems developed. What could he had done to protect his subjects more effectively than he did? How can we ethically study prisoners? How can we ethically study other people who have little education and who might not understand the implications of what is taking place?

SUMMARY

Psychologists refer to the biological, social, and psychological changes that occur in an individual's lifespan as development. Development includes processes that are determined genetically and biologically as well as those that take place because of learning or interaction with the environment.

The human lifespan can be divided into eight stages: prenatal, infancy, childhood, adolescence, youth and young adulthood, adulthood, older adulthood, and death.

Certain principles govern all aspects of development: (1) it proceeds qualitatively, from simple to complex; (2) it proceeds from the general to the specific; (3) it proceeds directionally from head to foot and from areas closest to the central nervous system outward to the extremities of the body; (4) it continues throughout life; (5) the rate of development varies among individuals, from age to age for any given person, and for different aspects of development.

Psychologists have identified so-called sensitive periods of development in the maturation process, during which individuals exhibit heightened responsiveness to learning. During these periods, certain interactions with the environment must take place if development is to progress.

Psychologists use developmental stages to describe the sequences of changes expected as individuals age. The stages are the result of a combination of maturation and learning, and occurrences at different developmental stages may explain behavior at later stages.

Jean Piaget's approach to cognitive development outlines major and predictable stages during which children solve problems using qualitatively different processes. Lawrence Kohlberg, with an approach similar to Piaget's, outlines the ways that individuals solve problems involving moral dilemmas.

Sigmund Freud stressed the vital role of experience interacting with internal instinctual urges. Freud hypothesized five stages of personality development, each characterized by a new socialization problem confronting the individual. His theory held that individuals who do not receive gratification at each successive stage of development may become fixated at that stage. Erik Erikson, expanding on Freud's views, suggested that personality is not defined in early childhood but instead continues to develop throughout life. Unlike Freud, he was optimistic in his belief that failures at one stage can be corrected by successes at later stages.

Learning is a relatively permanent change in behavior caused by experience. Classical conditioning is learning caused by stimuli that precede the learned response. Operant conditioning occurs when behavior is followed by a reward or reinforcement. The type of reward or reinforcement and the initial schedule under which learning has taken place strongly affect the strength of the learned behavior.

Many learning psychologists believe that behavioral descriptions of learning are too simple; cognitive learning psychologists, for example, explain how the many different ways we perceive the world affect our development. Motivational psychologists point out that to fully understand behavior at any point in the lifespan, we need to understand the needs, drive, and motives of the people involved. Abraham Maslow has described a hierarchy of human needs in which each need becomes dominant when needs lower on the hierarchy are reduced.

Researchers use a variety of ways to study the developmental process. Descriptive researchers study individuals in natural settings, using such methods as biographical records, time sampling, and event sampling to collect data. Experimental researchers study the effects of independent variables on dependent variables, using an experimental group that has been manipulated in some way and a control group that has not. They frequently use nonhuman species for the experiments. Both descriptive and experimental researchers may gather their data using either longitudinal or cross-sectional research designs. Both research methods may use any of a variety of research tools.

FOR FURTHER READING

Bronfenbrenner, Urie (ed.). *Influences on Human Development.* Hinsdale, Illinois: Dryden, 1972. This collection of readings covers a number of topics in child development, including early deprivation, the effects of television violence on children, experiments in group upbringing, and the socialization of student activists.

Gelfand, D. (ed.). *Social Learning in Childhood.* Monterey, California: Brooks/Cole, 1975. Gelfand has collected in this volume a large number of theoretical and research studies dealing with social learning, imitation, and identification in children. The text provides an excellent survey of the literature in the field.

Gruber, H., and J. Voneche (eds.). *The Essential Piaget.* New York: Basic Books, 1978. *The Essential Piaget* is a source book that presents the whole panorama of Piaget's work by means of carefully chosen excerpts from his own articles and books. Sections are arranged chronologically, according to the interests and researches of Piaget at different stages of his own life. They include his early naturalistic work, excerpts from his early work on egocentric thought when he was influenced by Freud, his classic studies of his own three children when they were infants, material on the logical–mathematical thinking of school-age children, and selections that reveal his more abiding concerns: education, philosophy, and the relationship between biology and the process of knowing. The editors have added introductory notes and footnotes, which are useful to the student of Piagetian theory in fitting each piece into the general context of Piaget's voluminous works.

The Prenatal Period
and Infancy

Part II

Preview Questions

- Why is it important to study the prenatal period of development?

- Can you explain how heredity and environment interact to produce human development and how its genetic basis is established?

- What are the three stages in prenatal development and the significant events featured in each?

- Can you list six critical prenatal influences on the child and explain what precautions are indicated by each?

- What are three recent advances that have revolutionized conception and prenatal screening?

- Can you describe the three stages of the birth process and list some complications that may arise during that time?

- What is a caesarean section and what are some conditions that make it necessary?

- Can you explain why people advocate each of the following: prepared childbirth, family-centered childbirth, home births, birth without violence?

- What are some advantages and disadvantages of allowing nurse-midwives to deliver babies?

2

The Beginnings of Life

THE PRENATAL PERIOD AND BIRTH

Most of us are accustomed to thinking of our birthdays as the beginnings of our lives. Yet in fact, human life and human development begin long before birth. At the instant of conception, our hereditary characteristics are set for all time. From that instant and for the next nine months, as we develop *in utero,* we also change in extraordinary ways. Birth is the result of a highly complex prenatal period of development.

THE INFLUENCES OF HEREDITY AND ENVIRONMENT

Our heredity affects us in many ways that we usually take for granted. For example, our physical resemblance to our parents is something we all expect. Neighbors look at the new baby and remark, "He has his daddy's smile" or "Those are her mother's eyes." Heredity controls many obvious factors, such as the color of eyes, hair, and skin. It obviously affects our heights as adults. Many other physical characteristics are also passed from one generation to the next.

People's abilities, like their physical characteristics, are affected by heredity. The link, however, is not always direct. Inherited abilities are influenced and shaped in various ways by the environment. As a result, each individual exhibits unique capabilities and behaviors. Psychologists do not understand all the mechanisms by which this takes place.

The Heredity vs. Environment Controversy

Which is more important, heredity or environment? Just a few years ago, social scientists engaged in a debate of this question that mushroomed into public furor. Using the average difference that occurs in the IQ scores of black and white populations in the United States as evidence, Arthur Jensen (1969; 1972; 1980) proposed that heredity far outweighs other factors in explaining differences in mental ability. Jensen proposed further that differences in innate ability are the reason that compensatory education programs in this country often have failed to produce IQ or achievement gains.

Jensen's argument is backed by some biochemists who report that biochemical processes play clear-cut roles in the development of brain structures necessary for intelligence (Ungar 1976). Critics point out, however, that the jump from research in biochemical processes to educational differences between ethnic or racial groups is a gigantic one. Critics also charge that Jensen and others supporting him fail to take into account such environmental factors as educational differences known to affect IQ scores. They point out the cultural bias of the tests used. Learning environmentalists as well as geneticists also criticize the statistical bases of Jensen's arguments. Public criticism charges that Jensen's position serves to retard hard-won social improvements in our country rather than adding to our information base. (For a review of the controversy, see critics Crow 1969; Hunt 1969; Bodmer and Cavalli-Sforza 1970; Bronfenbrenner 1970; Hebb 1970. See also Jensen advocates Eysenck 1971; Herrnstein 1971.)

In considering the controversy and its importance to society, it is important to note that, over two decades ago, social scientists had reviewed this same literature. They concluded then that the "nature vs. nurture" question simply is not answerable and that those who accept either absolute hereditary or environmental choices were not providing a complete picture. In a classic article, psychologist Anne Anastasi (1958, p. 197) proposed that "the reacting organism is a product of its genes and its past environment, while the present environment provides the immediate stimulus for current behavior." Anastasi was concerned with the complexities of the interactions between heredity and environment. She stated that it is this interaction that is most important to the developing individual.

Hereditary Influences. Anastasi distinguished between hereditary influences that are directly responsible for specific traits and influences that are indirectly responsible. We have mentioned already examples of direct hereditary influence. Eye color, for example, is due to the **genotype** or genetic makeup of the individual and is irreversible.

Indirect hereditary influences, like direct influences, are determined at conception. The direction that they take, however, is affected by environmental interaction. A **phenotype** is the detectable expression of the interaction between the genotype and the environment. Many visible characteristics of children are phenotypic. For example, artistic talent, social ability, and ability to perform on tests of intelligence are caused by the interaction of a large number of genetic and environmental factors. Persons with inherited susceptibility to certain physical diseases must actually encounter the specific disease organisms before they are visibly affected. In other words, an individual with an inherited susceptibility (genotype) might become diseased (phenotype) or might live life fortunate enough never to encounter the organism. In this case, the person's phenotype would not reflect the genotype, and we probably would never discover the susceptibility.

Some psychologists have suggested that schizophrenia may be a phenotypic trait. They suggest that susceptibility to this mental illness may be inherited but that certain environmental conditions are necessary for the susceptibility to manifest itself (Eisenberg 1968; Villet 1978). Many researchers point to differences in normal everyday behavior, which they think are due in large part to heredity. For example, researchers studying newborn behavior in different countries report noticeable differences in temperament (Thomas, Chess, and Birch 1970). Freedman (1979) reported striking differences in temperament and behavior in babies only a few days old that characterize different ethnic groups. Other studies (Chess, Thomas, and Birch 1968) point to the stability of these temperamental differences from birth to twelve years of age. Researchers suggest that although some differences might be explained away by differences in environment, many cannot be. They conclude that whatever else we say, it is not true that we are born alike regardless of our hereditary backgrounds.

Environmental Influences. Environmental influences, like hereditary influences, may be direct or indirect. One example of a direct environmental influence is severe protein deficiency at certain stages of development, which is known to cause brain damage (Dobbing and Smart 1974). Infant hospitalization is an example of an indirect environmental influence. Although the illness causing the hospitalization by itself may have no direct aftereffect, maternal absence associated with hospitalization might permanently affect the developing personality.

Both hereditary characteristics and environment clearly affect all of an individual's experiences with the world. What Jensen and his followers neglected to consider is that it is impossible to separate the two effects. Take, for example, a hereditarily malformed infant born with dwarfed limbs. The life experiences of this child will differ so drastically from those of a more normal child that it will always be impossible to determine precisely the effects caused by heredity and those caused by experience. Consider the more subtle (and common) experience of a child born with skin color different from most other children in the immediate environment. This child also will be affected by the environment in many subtle ways. The issue is complex and important; neither heredity nor environment alone governs the developing child, as the purists would have us believe. Rather, it is a complicated interaction between the two variables that is critical to the development. As Freedman (1979) suggested, we are, in fact, biosocial animals. In order fully to understand our behavior, we must examine both our heredity and the environmental influences that affect it.

The Genetic Basis of Development

What about that part of development that is controlled by heredity? Biological inheritance of traits begins when two **gametes,** a male sperm and a female ovum (egg cell), unite to produce a fertilized egg or **zygote.** If we were to examine these gametes under a microscope and the cells were stained with dye so as to make their separate parts visible, we would see twenty-three rod-shaped bodies in each. These are the **chromosomes.** Each chromosome is composed of thousands of smaller genetic units called **genes.** Genes carry the genetic information from parent to child.

The real key to understanding the way genes carry hereditary characteristics is a complex chemical called **deoxyribonucleic acid (DNA),** which provides the basis of all life, from amoebas to human beings. Biologists Francis Crick and James Watson discovered that genes are formed by two tightly intertwined strands, "the

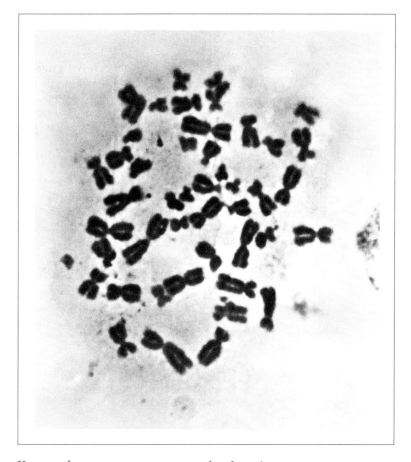

Human chromosomes as seen under the microscope.

double helix," each made of four chemicals composed of nitrogen bases (Gwynne, Begley, and Hager 1979). The way that these nitrogen bases are arranged within each gene provides the specific genetic information that results in what we have called the genotypic pattern. In some cases, the DNA within a single gene may determine one or even several inherited traits. Eye color is an example of a trait determined by just one gene. More often, however, a combination of genes forming larger DNA chains establish what are known as complex or **polygenic traits.** Skin color is a polygenic trait caused by a combination of many genes. A single gene may simultaneously affect a number of traits, leading to an amazing complex of interactions. In some cases, a gene derived from one parent may interact with a gene from the other to produce a trait that does not appear in either parent. It is therefore possible for children to bear little resemblance to either of their parents.

To complicate this issue still further, there are two basically different types of genes: **dominant genes** and **recessive genes.** If a dominant gene appears in the fertilized egg, the trait or traits determined by that gene will appear in the child. We know, for example, that the gene responsible for brown eye color is dominant; the gene responsible for blue eye color is recessive. A child who receives one brown eye-color gene and one blue eye-color gene will have brown eyes. This is true because brown eye color is dominant over blue. Only children who receive two genes responsible for blue eye color will have blue eyes. It is clear from this example that all brown-eyed children do not carry the same genetic pattern for eye color; some carry recessive blue-eyed genes. Two adults with brown eyes are able to produce a blue-eyed baby. It is not possible, however, for two blue-eyed parents to produce a brown-eyed child. The same rule applies to other traits controlled by dominant and recessive genes.

A defect in a single gene may interrupt normal development of both simple and polygenic traits. The gene that causes lack of iodine in the body essential to the development of thyroid hormones is an example of such a defective gene. This gene results in the genetic defect known as cretinism. Infantile amaurotic family idiocy results from an hereditary defect in the nerve cells of the brain and spinal cord. The disorder appears to be caused by the inheritance of specific recessive genes from both mother and father. Another type of hereditary defect occurs in abnormalities of chromosomal structure. An example of this is **Down's syndrome,** a genetic defect caused by forty-seven rather than forty-six chromosomes. Children with Down's syndrome are mentally retarded.

All of us carry some defective genes. Luckily for most of us, these defective genes represent only a tiny proportion of our genes. Furthermore, most of these are recessive and therefore are less likely to affect our children. The average number of seriously defective recessive genes for each of us is thought to be between four and twelve. The existence of so many different defective genes together with continual mutations (changing of genes) causing possible additional genetic defects has been of great concern to geneticists.

With the forming of the zygote, the genotypic pattern is set. Each of the forty-six chromosomes now duplicates itself in a process called **mitosis.** When the newly formed cell divides, each of the two new cells receives forty-six chromosomes matching the originals. Eventually, with repeated cell division, a totally new child develops, carrying in each body cell identical chromosomes, genes, and DNA.

No two individuals developing from different zygotes have exactly the same combination of chromosomes or genes. With each chromosome containing approximately 20,000 genes, it is no wonder that each of us develops in unique ways. The only children born with identical hereditary characteristics are identical twins, who

Down's syndrome is a hereditary disorder caused by chromosomal abnormality. Children with this disorder exhibit certain physical characteristics and are mentally retarded.

develop from the same zygote. Brothers and sisters and even fraternal twins developing at the same time in the same uterus from different eggs have different heredities. They may have some genes in common, but they are never completely identical.

Each body cell has forty-six chromosomes. Exceptions are the cells of a person with Down's syndrome and reproductive cells. Sperm and egg cells are produced by a process called **gametogenesis.** During gametogenesis, a cell division called **meiosis** takes place in which four cells rather than two are produced. Each of these four reproductive cells has twenty-three chromosomes. The sex of the developing individual is determined at conception by one special pair of these chromosomes. The female egg cell carries only what are known as X chromosomes; the sperm cell carries either X or Y chromosomes. If the resulting zygote carries an XX combina-

HIGHLIGHT 2.1 EUGENICS: THE DANGERS OF INAPPROPRIATE USE

The term **positive eugenics** refers to the increasing of desirable characteristics in the human population through specific types of selective breeding. **Negative eugenics** refers to the improvement of the human species through elimination of undesirable characteristics. Both positive and negative eugenics have been advocated from time to time throughout recent history by politicians or philosophers. Sir Francis Galton, the nineteenth-century director of the British Laboratory for National Genetics, for example, proposed that physically and mentally "unfit" individuals should not reproduce. In that way, he claimed, they would not pass on their negative characteristics to future generations.

Negative eugenics is practiced to some extent in all societies today. For example, no contemporary society allows marriage between siblings or other close relatives. Incestuous inbreeding is considered a serious crime, for although inbreeding may increase desired traits, it also greatly increases the probability of harmful recessive genes appearing. (Notably, in the few exceptions to the rule against incestuous mating—as, for example, in royal families—trends toward genetic defects exist. Hemophilia among royal families today is an example of such a defect. Among the ancient royal families of Egypt and Hawaii, in which incestuous mating commonly was practiced, infanticide to remove defective offspring was condoned. Only those babies carrying desired characteristics were allowed to survive.)

In the wrong hands, eugenics can be used to the detriment of all people. The negative eugenics programs of the Nazis before and during World War II are now infamous. The Nazi party, when first gaining power in Germany, pronounced as unfit for procreation all individuals carrying "hereditary diseases." On January 1, 1934, legislation implementing both voluntary and compulsory sterilization of unfit persons was enacted. In the following years, large numbers of individuals were sterilized under the provisions of this act. Later, the

tion, the resulting child will be a girl. If the sperm cell has contributed a Y chromosome, the developing child will be a boy. In one special sense, boys inherit more from their mothers than from their fathers. The Y chromosome coming from the father and responsible for producing males carries fewer genes than does its X counterpart. Thus, some of the genes of the X chromosome are unmatched by genes in the Y chromosome. Some sex-linked characteristics are passed on through the unmatched genes and therefore only through the mother. Two examples are hemophilia and color blindness, two sex-linked disorders inheritable only from mother to son.

Nazi negative eugenics program was extended to include the extermination of all people whose characteristics, according to Adolph Hitler, made them "unfit."

The Nazis' positive eugenics programs matched in horror their negative programs. Lebensborn was a positive eugenics program begun in 1933 by the Nazi government. *Lebensborn* (meaning "life source") was designed as a major part of Hitler's larger program to produce a superrace. It began with careful selection of German women carrying what were considered "Aryan genetic characteristics" to bear children fathered by equally carefully selected men. Later, to increase the number of "pure-blooded" children more rapidly, the program accepted from the occupied countries "Aryan-type" women whose physical characteristics matched Hitler's requirements. Approximately 50,000 to 100,000 children were born in these especially established homes and were turned over to the Nazi government to be raised.

What genetic characteristics actually were bred by the program? In a Public Broadcasting Service documentary film, *In Pure Blood,* a nurse who worked in one Lebensborn home and remained there after the war stated for interviewers, "Superrace? Well, not really . . . . There were intelligent and ordinary children there. Also mentally defective children. But they were all withdrawn" (Henry and Hiller 1975). This is not surprising when we consider the importance of environment relative to heredity.

QUESTIONS FOR THOUGHT

1. Under what conditions is a negative eugenics program useful and meaningful to society? Who should make this determination?

2. How can we ensure that such programs as Hitler's Lebensborn do not occur again?

STAGES OF PRENATAL DEVELOPMENT

From the time of conception, the developing individual changes in extraordinary ways. The one-celled organism, or zygote as it is called, grows in the forty-week prenatal period into a complex human being with approximately 200 billion cells at birth. During the period in which this intricate process takes place, the organism lives in the protective and nourishing environment of the mother's uterus. In recent years, the growing realization has been that the period between conception and birth is crucial for the developing individual.

The prenatal period can be divided into three basic periods, or stages of development, each characterized by certain phenomena. The **period of the ovum** begins with conception and lasts for two weeks until the developing cluster of cells attaches itself securely to the lining of the uterus. The **embryonic period** follows and continues for the next six weeks. During the embryonic period, essential body systems develop. The cluster of cells becomes recognizable as a partially functioning human being. During the **fetal period,** from eight weeks after conception until the time of birth, the body organs, muscles, and nervous system mature, and the organism increases in size and takes on clearly human characteristics.

The Period of the Ovum

Within twenty-four hours after conception, the process of cell division called mitosis occurs; at twenty-four hours of age, the zygote already has doubled itself by forming two identical cells. During the two-week period of the ovum, the zygote lives off its own yolk, dividing over and over again until it forms a cluster of cells the size of a pinhead. This cluster gradually moves down a fallopian tube. In the process, it forms a ball of cells in which a cavity called a **blastocele** appears. At this stage of development, the zygote is known as a **blastocyst.** The outer layer of cells of the blastocyst will later develop into nutritive and protective structures. An inner cell mass will develop into the embryo.

While the blastocyst is developing, hormonal changes cause the uterine wall to thicken and increase its blood supply so as to prepare for reception of the new organism. (If the ovum had not been fertilized within the previous month, this supply of blood would have sloughed off, resulting in female menstrual flow.) On about the fourth day, the blastocyst reaches the uterus, where it drifts about for several days. A short time later, tendrils developed by the organism attach themselves to the uterine wall and finally penetrate the blood vessels within. From this instant, the developing organism is able to receive nourishment from the mother. The blastocyst is now ready to develop into an embryo. By the beginning of the third week, the organism is referred to as an **embryo.**

The Embryonic Period

During the third week, or early embryonic period, two cavities begin to develop in the inner mass of the cell cluster, now called the **trophoblast.** One cavity later will become the **amniotic sac** and will be filled with fluid. This will be a protective cushion, will equalize pressure, and will prevent adherence of the embryo to the wall of the uterus (Iorio 1967; 1975). The other, the **yolk sac,** will feed the embryo until the umbilical cord has developed. Between these two cavities is the embryonic area from which the embryo now begins to develop. Figure 2.1 shows the develop-

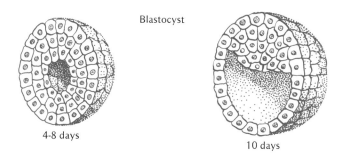

Blastocyst

4-8 days

10 days

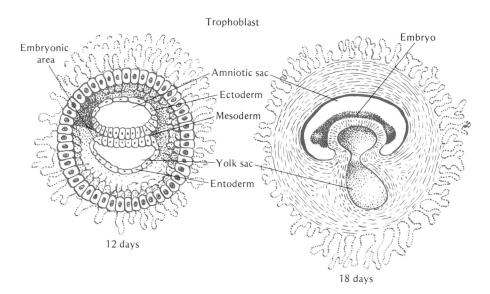

Trophoblast

Embryonic area

Embryo

Amniotic sac

Ectoderm

Mesoderm

Yolk sac

Entoderm

12 days

18 days

Figure 2.1   The development of the fertilized ovum through the stages of the blastocyst and trophoblast.

ment of the fertilized ovum through the stages of both the blastocyst and the tro-phoblast.

As Fig. 2.1 indicates, cells within the embryonic area gradually form three layers: **ectoderm, mesoderm,** and **endoderm.** Later in development, the ectoderm will give rise to skin, certain mucous membranes, and the central nervous system. Blood, muscles, bones, and some internal organs will develop from the mesoderm. The endoderm will turn into lungs, bladder, alimentary mucosa, pancreas, and liver (Keay and Morgan 1974).

The **umbilical cord,** formed by the sixth week of development, is designed to carry food from the mother's blood to the embryo and waste substances from the embryo to the mother. It passes both nutritive substances and waste through an area of the uterine wall called the **placenta.** As the circulatory system of the organism develops, blood is pumped by the fetal heart to the placenta. There the fetus exchanges carbon dioxide for oxygen, which is carried to the fetus by the mother's bloodstream.

It is very important to note that maternal blood and fetal blood never mix in the process of exchanging food and waste materials. Instead, the exchange occurs through the porous walls of closed blood vessels. The placenta, a semipermeable cellular membrane, serves as a protective barrier, selecting and absorbing those substances necessary for nourishment of the fetus and passing them to the fetus from the mother's blood. Similarly, the placenta passes waste materials from fetus to mother. The placenta will tend to reject many potentially dangerous substances in the mother's blood. Some drugs and other potentially harmful substances, however, are sometimes able to pass through the placenta to affect the developing organism.

Growth and development during the embryonic period are rapid. By the end of the third week after conception, the organism is composed of a cluster of cells

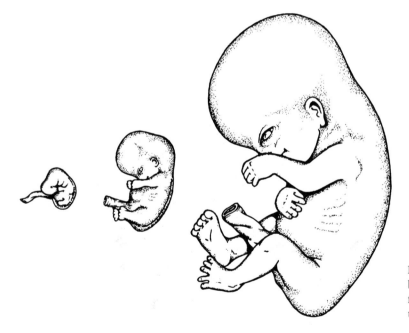

Figure 2.2 Actual size of embryo and fetus at approximately four weeks, eight weeks, and twelve weeks.

totaling only about one-quarter inch from head to the tip of what looks like a tail-like protrusion on the embryo. Even at this stage, the organism is highly complex: A rudimentary heart is just beginning to pulsate; an embryonic brain with two lobes appears.

By the fourth week, the embryonic backbone is apparent. At this point, however, it is so bent that the head almost touches the "tail." The head, at this stage of development, is almost one-third the total length of the embryo. The head develops in size and complexity long before other parts of the body. By this time, the nervous system already has developed extensively and cartilage and muscle development has begun. Neuromotor activity (activation of muscles by nerve impulse), however, has not yet appeared. Rudiments of eyes, ears, and nose as well as stubby arms and legs are noticeable. Even the beginnings of respiratory organs, digestive tract, and stomach are apparent.

By the eighth week after conception, the embryo has a noticeably human appearance. It still is extremely tiny, small enough to fit in a walnut shell and about the same weight as a book of matches. It still is a long way from being able to live without an intimate lifeline to the mother. But it has a well-formed body with a very large head and unmistakably human face, arms, and legs. Fingers have developed on hands. The slower-growing legs have recognizable knees and ankles. The heart has been beating for several weeks, and a brain and nervous system send impulses. The reproductive system has begun to develop. The embryo at this age is growing at the rate of one millimeter per day. At eight weeks, it is approximately one inch in length from head to buttocks and weighs approximately one-thirtieth of an ounce. From this time until birth, the developing organism is called a **fetus.** Figure 2.2 shows the actual size of an embryo and fetus at approximately four weeks, eight weeks, and twelve weeks.

The Fetal Period

During the fetal period, from eight weeks after conception to birth at forty weeks, the skeletal system becomes mature. Embryologists have chosen the appearance of bone cells as the criterion for defining the end of the embryonic period, because bone formation coincides with essential completion of the body.

Bodily systems also mature during the fetal period. Although no new features appear, growth and development progress in a steady and sequential pattern apparent not only by the gradually increasing size and complexity of the body components of the fetus but also by its developing abilities to function.

Extremities of the body develop; fingers and toes are differentiated during this period. Fingernails and toenails now appear. The umbilical cord often is sometimes twisted around the fetus at this stage, evidence of the fetus's ability to move. The first movements are general or mass movements, beginning with head movements.

By the end of twelve weeks *in utero,* the fetus has become sexually differentiated. A swelling appears that will eventually become a penis, if hormones are manufactured by a male testes, or a clitoris if male hormones are not developed. The anatomy of the female reproductive system seems to be basic to human development: Female sex organs will develop if either testes or ovaries are removed or do not function.

The fetus gradually develops the capability of responding to touch. This capability is exhibited by a gradual flexion movement of the head. The fetus also can move its thumb in opposition to fingers and is beginning to be able to make swallowing movements. Not until later will the fetus be able to make specific movements or move a particular limb in response to a touch.

It is interesting that the fetus already shows distinct individuality in behavior. This individuality is due, in part, to the muscle structure, which varies from fetus to fetus. Variations in the uterine environment, however, also lead to differences in fetal behavior. The fetus is now approximately three inches long and weighs about three-quarters of an ounce.

By twenty weeks after conception, heart, stomach, and internal organs near the nervous system have developed. At this stage of development, obstetricians can hear the heartbeat of a fetus in the mother's womb by using an ordinary stethoscope (Babson and Benson 1971). If there are twins, the physician may be able to pick up the sounds of two different hearts at this stage. The lungs, although developing, are not yet sufficiently mature to allow the fetus to survive outside the protective environment of the uterus. At this stage, mothers in first pregnancies report that they feel movement in the womb. This feeling of movement, caused by arms and legs moving independently, is called the "quickening." In subsequent pregnancies, the fetal movements can often be felt earlier. Some mothers learn to recognize the different parts of the fetus's body and learn to distinguish head or buttocks from arms or legs. Some mothers report feeling "knocking" like a series of rhythmic jolts. This is due to hiccuping. The fetus may have hiccups that last as long as a half hour. Basic reflexes involving body extremities are now developed. By the end of twenty weeks, the fetus is approximately ten inches long and weighs about eight ounces. Figure 2.3 shows the actual size of a fetus at this time.

By twenty-four weeks the fetus begins externally to look like a miniature baby. Eyes are completely formed, and the fetus can open and close them. Hair has begun to grow on the head. Eyebrows and lashes now appear. Deposits of subcutaneous fat are beginning to give the fetus a babylike appearance. Quiet and active episodes are experienced by the mother as the fetus alternately sleeps and wakes. The fetus at this stage can be awakened from sleep by loud noises. It is now approximately twelve inches long and weighs about twenty-four ounces.

From the twenty-eighth to the fortieth week after conception, the fetus will mature in all respects, and various body systems will be able to survive outside the

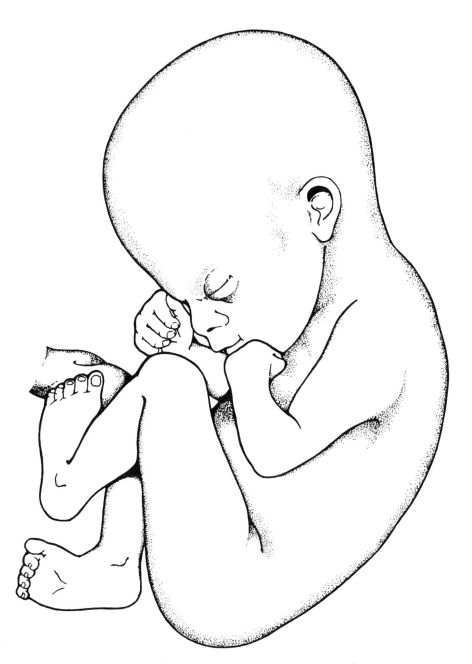

Figure 2.3 Actual size of fetus at approximately twenty weeks.

Table 2.1
Prenatal Development

Time from Conception	Characteristics
1 month (4 weeks)	¼ to ½ inch long. Head is one-third of embryo. Brain has lobes and rudimentary nervous system, appears as hollow tube. Heart begins to beat. Blood vessels form, and blood flows through them. Simple kidneys, liver, and digestive tract appear. Rudiments of eyes, ears, and nose appear.
2 months (8 weeks)	2 inches long. $\frac{1}{30}$ ounce in weight. Human face with eyes, ears, nose, lips, tongue. Hands develop. Almost all internal organs begin to develop. Brain coordinates functioning of other organs. Heart beats steadily, and blood circulates. Complete cartilage skeleton beginning to be replaced by bone. Sex organs begin to be differentiated. Now called a fetus.
3 months (12 weeks)	3 inches long. 1 ounce in weight. Begins to be active. Number of nerve-muscle connections almost triples. Sucking reflex begins to appear. Can swallow and may even breathe. Eyelids are fused shut but eyes are sensitive to light. Internal organs begin to function.
4 months (16 weeks)	6 to 7 inches long. 4 ounces in weight. Body now growing faster than head. Skin on hands and feet forms individual patterns. Eyebrows and head hair begin to show. Fine, downylike hair covers body. Movements may now be felt by mother.
5 months (20 weeks)	10 to 12 inches long. 8 to 16 ounces in weight. Skeleton hardens. Nails form on fingers and toes. Skin covered with cheesy wax. Heartbeat now loud enough to be heard with a stethoscope.

Table 2.1
(Continued)

Time from Conception	Characteristics
	Muscles are stronger.
	Definite strong kicking and turning.
	Can be startled by noises.
6 months (24 weeks)	12 to 14 inches long.
	1½ pounds in weight.
	Can open and close eyelids.
	Grows eyelashes.
	Much more active, exercising muscles.
	May suck thumb.
	May be able to breathe if born prematurely.
7 months (28 weeks)	15 inches long.
	2½ pounds in weight.
	Beginning to develop fatty tissue.
	Internal organs (especially respiratory and digestive) still developing.
	Baby born has fair chance of survival.
8 months (32 weeks)	16½ inches long.
	4 pounds in weight.
	Fatty layer complete.
9 months (38 to 40 weeks)	Birth.
	19 to 20 inches long.
	7 to 7½ pounds in weight (average).
	95 percent of full-term babies born alive in the United States will survive.

protective environment of the uterus. By the twenty-eighth week, the nervous and circulatory systems and other organs are developed sufficiently that the fetus, if born prematurely, will, with special care, have a chance to survive.

In the last twelve weeks before birth, behavioral development proceeds at a rapid rate. Movements become active and sustained. In the ninth month, when the fetus moves, the contours of arms and legs make moving bulges on the mother's abdomen. A kick by the fetus at this age has been known almost to knock a book from the mother's lap (Flanagan 1962). Hands develop the ability to grasp strongly. Finally, before birth, a strong sucking reflex develops. Size changes in these last weeks are dramatic. The fetus grows from an average length of twelve inches and average weight of twenty-four ounces at twenty-eight weeks of age to an average length of twenty inches and average weight of seven and one-quarter pounds at birth. In the last month *in utero,* the fetus gains an average of one-half pound per week! Table 2.1 summarizes the process of prenatal development.

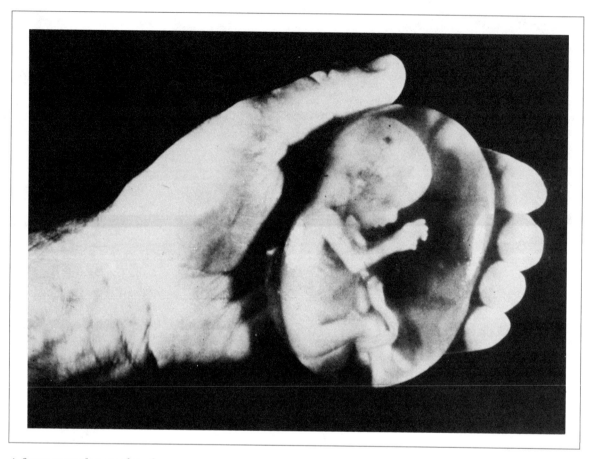

A fetus at twelve weeks of age.

 ## INFLUENCES ON PRENATAL DEVELOPMENT

At one time, a widespread belief held that the unborn child could be affected by the mother's thoughts and experiences. One manifestation of this belief is the idea that going to art museums or attending symphony concerts during pregnancy will help produce artistic or musically talented children. There is no evidence to support such tales. On the other hand, substantial evidence suggests a newer concept of prenatal influence on the unborn child: The child's health and development can be affected profoundly by uterine conditions and by the state of health of the mother.

Nutrition

During prenatal development, the mother's placenta serves as a barrier, absorbing those substances from the mother's blood necessary for fetal nourishment and passing waste materials from fetus to mother. The placenta tends to reject potentially dangerous substances in the mother's blood. Inadequate placental absorption of necessary nutrients as well as absorption of dangerous substances, such as some drugs, can, however, adversely affect fetal development.

It once was believed that reserves accumulated in the mother's body would "spare" the fetus from possible nutritional deficiencies, even if the mother did not eat well during pregnancy. We know now that this is not the case. Good nutrition during pregnancy, as well as before pregnancy, actually can be a matter of life and death for the fetus. At the least, serious malnutrition of the mother affects the growth and health of her child. In periods of famine, babies tend to be abnormally small in size. For example, babies born during the long and severe famine that occurred during the siege of Leningrad in World War II had birth weights 400 to 500 grams lower than normal. A less severe famine at the same time in Holland led to a reduction by 240 grams in the average birth weight of Dutch children (Sterman, McGinty, and Adinolf 1971). Vitamin deficiency in the diets of expectant mothers is known to produce rickets as well as general physical weakness and mental deficiency in newborn infants (Goldenson 1970). Poor maternal diet during pregnancy is known to produce anemia, toxemia, miscarriage, prematurity, and stillbirth. The infants of undernourished mothers are also more vulnerable to serious disease.

Protein deficiency during the period of most rapid brain growth can damage irreparably the developing brain. Animal researchers have shown that cerebellums deprived of adequate amounts of protein during the fetal period actually have been found to weigh less and to have less than the normal complement of nerve cells (Altman 1971; Stone, Smith, and Murphy 1973). Researchers have also found a relationship between prenatal malnutrition and lowered scores of cognitive ability in infancy (Zeskind and Ramey 1978). One group of infants often affected by prenatal malnutrition are infants of impoverished families. (See, for example, Butler and Alberman 1969; Novy 1973; Perkins 1977.) Women with low incomes not only lack the money for adequate diets, but they also often lack knowledge required to maintain balanced diets.

Specific effects of a malnourished prenatal environment, as with any aspect of that environment, is dependent on timing. At some stages of fetal development, gross changes in the environment may produce little or no effect on the fetus. In others, even minor alterations can produce severe complications. Adequate nourishment is most critical during periods of rapid growth. Any interruption of development during these periods may result in complete disruption of the organism. Because different bodily organs and parts develop at different rates, the effect caused by malnutrition at one period may be very different from the effect at another period.

In the case of brain development, the brain grows most rapidly between twenty weeks after conception and two years after birth. During this period, called the sensitive period for brain development, inadequate nutrition inflicts the greatest damage. Damage to the cerebellum caused by malnutrition during its critical growth period has been used to explain clumsiness and greatly reduced motor ability (Cragg 1974; Dobbing and Smart 1974).

In the past, doctors recommended that pregnant women strictly limit their weight gain. Today, however, they believe that gaining too little weight can harm the fetus. Doctors now recommend that mothers gain from twenty to twenty-five pounds in order to maintain proper health both for themselves and their babies.

It is not only the diet of the pregnant woman that determines whether or not the fetus is nourished properly; the maternal metabolic system responsible for changing food into body nourishment and wastes also has a major effect on the nourishment of the child. Metabolic problems in the mother, as with those caused by diabetes, can result in a prenatal environment that is incapable of supplying everything the fetus needs. From the first hours of pregnancy, the maternal metabolic system begins a vast readjustment to provide nutrients to support fetal growth. Unhealthy or undernourished women with metabolic problems apparently are less able to produce good prenatal environments for fetal growth.

Maternal Age and Spacing of Births

Maternal age can also be an important factor in prenatal development. It has long been known that very young women and older women run a greater risk of having a defective child. Down's syndrome, which causes mental retardation, is one hereditary defect that occurs with increasing frequency in women over the age of thirty-five. The probability that this defect will occur increases dramatically in infants born to mothers forty years and older. Very young mothers (under sixteen years of age), however, also have a high risk of bearing children with defects. One possible explanation is that very young mothers are unable to provide a proper prenatal environment to nourish their children. Young mothers, still growing themselves, have high nutritional requirements. It is difficult to meet the requirements of both a growing mother and a growing fetus. Babies of very young mothers are known to have lower birth weights and are more likely to be stillborn or to have birth defects than are babies of mothers in their twenties. This is a particularly serious problem today in America. Each year, more than a million young girls between fifteen and nineteen— plus another 30,000 under fifteen and many as young as eleven or twelve—are expected to become pregnant, and three-fifths of these women carry their babies to full term (Kapp *et al.* 1980). The number is on the increase.

Timing of births also may affect fetal development. Close spacing of children (less than two and one-half years between births) has been related to decreased levels of cognitive ability later in life (Zajonc 1976). It is unclear, of course, whether such decreased levels are due to experiences after birth. Some researchers, however, have hypothesized that close spacing of children, just as early age of mother, may result in an inadequate prenatal environment (Holley, Rosenbaum, and Churchill 1969).

Disease

Maternal infection from bacteria, protozoa, and viruses also may have adverse effects on prenatal development. As with inadequate nutrition, timing is crucial. If the mother does not take in a sufficient amount of oxygen, because of acute respiratory infection or chronic anemia during the first three months of pregnancy, the child could be born with a cleft palate or a harelip.

Diabetes, a metabolic disease in which glucose cannot be used as an energy source, always has caused high mortality rates in both mothers and children. Only in the past forty years have medical advances, including judicious use of insulin, made it possible for diabetic mothers to expect to bear healthy children. Even today, infants of diabetic mothers whose disease is not well controlled are more likely than other infants to have congenital abnormalities and are more subject to infant infections. Researchers hypothesize that these, like many other complications, are due to insufficient nutrients provided to the fetus. Diabetic mothers must metabolize fats and amino acids to meet their energy requirements, and thus a diabetic mother might restrict the supply of amino acids to the fetus (Fletcher 1975).

Maternal disease can affect the fetus in direct as well as indirect ways. For example, rubella (German measles) occurring in mothers during the first three months of pregnancy can invade placenta and fetus, infecting the fetus and causing defective or undersize infants. Fetal infection with gonorrhea or syphilis from an infected mother, unfortunately, is not at all uncommon today and is increasing in frequency throughout the world. Gonorrhea, which is passed to the fetus at birth, used to be the major cause of congenital blindness. The incidence has been greatly reduced through the use of silver nitrate eyewash administered shortly after birth. Fetal syphilis can lead to abortion, fetal death, prematurity, and deformity. Because the fetus under eighteen weeks of age is not susceptible, treatment of the mother during early pregnancy can save the life of the newborn child.

Cigarettes, Drugs, and Alcohol

Smoking has been found to be related to premature birth, stillbirth, and decreased birth weight. Researchers hypothesize that carbon monoxide replaces oxygen in the mother's blood and placenta to cause these damages (Ounstead 1969; Babson and Benson 1971). In addition, studies show that pregnant women who smoke more than a half a pack of cigarettes per day significantly increase their chances of having babies with severe brain damage (Naeye 1978). Children of smoking mothers have blood vessels that show signs of lesions (tissue damage) and clogging—the heavier the smoking, the more the damage (Asmussen 1978).

Prescription and over-the-counter drugs are known seriously to affect the fetus, both directly and indirectly. Directly, many products can, by crossing the placenta, affect the fetus in ways similar to those in which they affect the mother. Indirectly, such drugs alter the maternal physiology and thereby change the uterine environment. A famous example is thalidomide, now known to produce severe abnormalities. Thalidomide was prescribed in England during the early 1960s for women who had had histories of miscarriages. The drug was removed from the market after a series of widely publicized tragedies, in which women who had taken the drug gave birth to severely deformed infants.

More commonly used drugs pose risks as well. In a study of pregnant women, eighty-two percent reported that they received prescribed medication. Almost as many took self-prescribed medication. The major drug categories used included iron, analgesics, vitamins, barbiturates, diuretics, antibiotics, cough medicines, antihistamines, and tranquilizers (Marx 1973). Physicians now consider it possible that large doses of antihistamines, some antiinfectant drugs, and even vitamin D during pregnancy can produce serious defects in babies. The use of some commonly used sedatives by pregnant women has been related to neonatal bleeding and to retardation in infants (Babson and Benson 1971; Vulliamy 1972; Driscoll 1973). Some doctors warn of the possibility of danger to the unborn infant from caffeine, which is present in coffee, tea, and many soft drinks. Even aspirin may cause fetal abnormalities.

The use of hallucinogens, such as LSD or mescalin, has been associated with chromosomal damage capable of injuring the fetus even before conception (Dishotsky *et al.* 1971). The number of newborns affected by narcotics, such as heroin, cocaine, morphine, and alcohol, also is increasing. Reports by the National Institute on Drug Abuse (1976) indicate that the high rate of illegal drug use that characterized the 1960s did not abate in the 1970s, and for several drugs, like cocaine, usage is on the increase. Alcohol continues to be the national drug of choice. Drug or alcohol dependence occurs in fifty percent of infants born to dependent mothers. Offspring of alcoholic mothers who drink heavily during pregnancy are at higher risk of physical and mental deficiencies. Even moderate drinking during pregnancy may have detrimental effects on the birth weights and behavior of infants (Streissguth 1977).

Prenatal drug dependence can lead to prematurity, infant mortality, and withdrawal symptoms after birth. A now well-recognized syndrome frequently occurs in babies born to narcotic-dependent mothers. It is fundamentally a withdrawal syndrome, manifested by hyperirritability, trembling, shrill crying, rapid respiration, and vomiting.

The adverse effects of drugs and alcohol on infants may not be caused by maternal influences alone. Doctors suspect that some drugs affect sperm adversely during or after their development, change the nature of the seminal fluid in which sperm are transported, or allow altering of mating habits such that harmful hormonal effects are caused in the female. One physician (Bartoshevsky 1979) reported on the case of a baby born with signs of **fetal alcohol syndrome.** Only the father was a heavy drinker!

Radiation

The fetus can also be affected adversely by modern technology. For example, radiation is known to be a hazard to the newborn. X-ray treatments, commonly used to treat a variety of illnesses in the United States, can cause damage to unborn infants. It is well known that X-ray treatment in the pelvic region—for example, in therapeutic treatments for tumors or cancer—is extremely dangerous. Radiation from X-ray treatment in other body areas also can be harmful. Pregnant women therefore are advised to avoid even routine X-rays.

Rh Factor

Rh factor is the name given to genetically determined differences between blood types that make fetus and mother incompatible. Medical researchers have explained the difficulties the Rh factor can cause the fetus as follows: The Rh-positive fetus produces antigens that enter the mother's bloodstream through the placenta. The mother's blood in turn produces antibodies with the capability of destroying red blood cells. Miscarriages, stillbirths, defects, and early deaths all have been attributed to the Rh factor. In recent years, medical research has developed ways to deal with the problem. Transfusions given to the infant after birth is one method commonly used. An afflicted infant now has a much greater possibility of living a normal life than did an infant just a few years ago. Expert attention and parental education are, of course, required.

Emotional Stress

Can a mother's emotional stress affect fetal development? While there is no guarantee that a happy mother will have a happy and healthy child, increasing evidence shows that mothers under emotional stress may have offspring with negative effects. Psychosocial stress has been related in a number of studies to risk in pregnancy, tensions or vomiting in babies, respiration difficulties at birth, and excessive childhood illnesses (Stott 1977; Digges, 1978).

It is known that fetuses move more actively within the uterus while the mother is in a state of stress than when she is calm and further that maternal stress is related to **colic,** a general term for excessive crying and general irritability in the infant. Researchers suggest that tension during pregnancy alters hormonal balance and af-

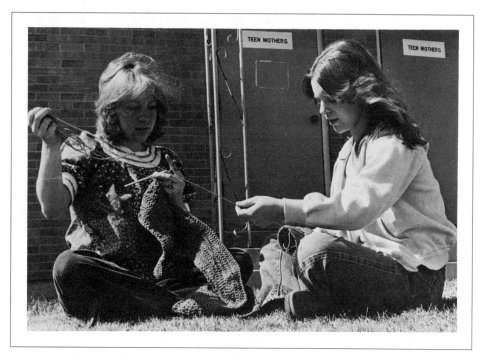

Very young mothers are at higher risk of bearing children with defects.

fects the delicate maternal–placental–fetal relationship. Tension also affects the fetus by liberating chemicals in the bloodstream and modifying cell metabolism. While anxiety before pregnancy is unrelated to prenatal complications, anxiety during pregnancy has a clear relationship to later-found abnormalities (Gorsuch and Key 1974).

Maternal tension affects fetal development in other more indirect ways as well. Tense mothers are more likely to smoke and to use tranquilizers, for example, and, as we have seen, both smoking and drug use are related to complications. Whether tension produces problems directly or indirectly, however, it appears that tense women are more likely to suffer complications in their pregnancies.

Stress, of course, cannot always be eliminated. Stress related to fears regarding pregnancy, however, can be reduced by good prenatal care and education. A good physician–patient relationship and adequate prenatal counseling can help significantly in alleviating stress.

ADVANCES IN PRENATAL SCREENING AND FERTILITY

The past twenty years have brought major increases in scientific knowledge of genetics and biomedicine. Reliable screening of infants for genetic diseases has increased dramatically, and treatment of genetic diseases has improved. In addition, methods have been developed to help childless couples bear their own children. Most dramatic is the recent development of a procedure known as amniocentesis. In addition, methods to increase fertility have been developed and are being used with increasing success.

Amniocentesis

In 1955, researchers first reported the discovery of chromosomes of fetal cells in fluid surrounding the fetus. Later, a technique known as **karotyping** was developed to make it possible to study the number, form, and size of the chromosomes in these cells. **Amniocentesis,** the procedure for removing the fluid, is performed in the obstetrician's office and requires only a local anesthetic. A long, thin needle is attached to a syringe and inserted through the lower abdominal wall when the fetus is between fourteen and sixteen weeks old. A small amount of amniotic fluid surrounding the fetus is withdrawn into the syringe. The fetal cells in the fluid are then grown in a laboratory by tissue-culture techniques and tested for abnormalities.

Amniocentesis can detect a variety of hereditary defects prior to birth. It is the first technique that, if used properly, can determine with complete accuracy that some genetic diseases do or do not exist in the fetus. In the cases of Down's syndrome or Tay-Sachs Disease, amniocentesis is the only technique that can detect the additional defective chromosome that causes the damage. An estimated forty percent of all childhood deaths and eighty percent of births of the three million mentally retarded people in the United States could have been prevented if parents had chosen to use this procedure together with abortions of defective fetuses. The procedure is of particular importance in the case of Down's syndrome. The incidence of this defect rises dramatically from one in fifteen hundred for infants born to mothers in their twenties to one in forty for infants born to mothers forty years or older. In the 1980s, when an increasing number of middle-class urban women are marrying later, remaining in the work force, and delaying childbirth often until their later thirties, amniocentesis can provide parents who choose to use it together with abortion an alternative to delivering infants with this inherited defect.

In addition to the moral concerns of individuals who do not believe in aborting defective infants, amniocentesis carries some dangers, including slightly increased chances of spontaneous abortions. In one study (Milunsky and Atkins 1975), approximately three and one-third percent of women who underwent amniocentesis were reported to have major birth complications. Parents who have received reports of birth defects discovered through amniocentesis may require psychological counseling to deal with the moral issues provided by the option to abort. Medical doctors often are unprepared to provide this help. Finally, since amniocentesis cannot be done until the second trimester of pregnancy, abortion, if it is decided upon, cannot be performed until this time, making the procedure more dangerous than if it were done earlier in the pregnancy. Physicians' groups have established guidelines to help doctors and clinics deal with the problems involved in psychological counseling in these situations. They point out, among other issues, that doctors must be extremely careful to avoid coercing their patients into decisions and to respect family views on abortion, whether or not these views coincide with their own (Genetics Research Group of the Hastings Center 1979). Still, dealing with these issues falls into a murky ethical area for many doctors.

Artificial Insemination

Artificial insemination reportedly was used at the end of the eighteenth century. Today, it is a common way to help infertile couples have children. Artificial insemination is a simple procedure that can be performed in a doctor's office. During a woman's peak fertility period, a syringe containing semen is inserted at the opening of the uterus, and the semen is deposited. Biologically, it is largely irrelevant whether the semen is provided by the husband or a donor. A donor's semen usually is used when the husband is infertile.

Despite the popularity of artificial insemination, complex ethical issues are involved. Not all states have laws protecting the rights of children conceived through artificial insemination, and some states have actually held these children to be illegitimate, with few rights of inheritance. Some women have been volunteering in recent years to serve as surrogate mothers and produce babies for infertile couples. When the woman inseminated is a surrogate, the legal and ethical issues can be perplexing. What if the surrogate mother refuses to give up the baby? What happens if the child is defective, and the adoptive couple decide they do not want to take the responsibility? Is it ethical to pay surrogate mothers for carrying babies? These questions already are being considered, but it is likely to be many years before all the issues are resolved.

In Vitro Fertilization

In 1978, banner headlines in British newspapers proclaimed "Our Miracle" and "Baby of the Century." Louise Brown, the first human being every conceived outside the body of her mother, was born in Oldham, England, on July 25, 1978. In a technique developed by British doctors Patrick Steptoe and Robert Edwards, an egg was surgically removed from Mrs. Brown and fertilized by Mr. Brown's sperm in a laboratory dish. Then the fertilized ovum was incubated as it began to divide. Finally, it

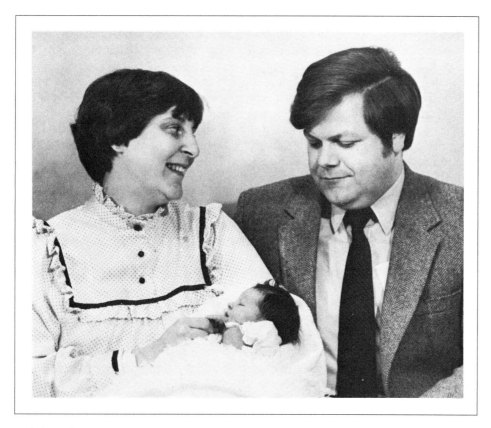

Judith and Roger Carr display their newborn daughter Elizabeth, the first baby in the United States to be conceived by *in vitro* fertilization.

was implanted in Mrs. Brown's uterus, where it developed normally and was born at full term.

By 1981, several babies had been born through the method of *in vitro* fertilization, and the first United States clinic for the conception of human embryos outside the mother's body had been opened in Norfolk, Virginia. Couples who were infertile because of physical damage to the prospective mother's fallopian tubes or because of other damages that prohibited the mother's eggs to enter her fallopian tubes were delighted at the new prospect of producing offspring in this manner. The clinic's opening was not, however, without opponents. Payl Ramsey, Professor of Christian Ethics at Princeton University, had already summed up the views of the opposition and outlined a series of new problems with which humankind now will have to deal. First, he pointed out, physicians and parents engaged in the practice of human *in vitro* fertilization must be willing to discard mishaps at any point in the prenatal period "which do not come up to the standards of an acceptable human being" (Ramsey 1976, p. 44). Amniocentesis obviously provides a solution to the problem of detecting defective fetuses, but what about defects found late in the prenatal period, after that time deemed safe for the mother to abort, or after birth? Other writers contend that other equally perplexing issues might develop. The Norfolk, Virginia, clinic planned, when it opened, to perform *in vitro* fertilizations only for childless married couples. But what if one woman should decide to provide the uterus for an egg donated by the other? Who would be the legal mother? Sociologists project some advantages for modern working mothers—a future "wombs for hire" industry in which women who are unwilling to complete their own pregnancies may pay someone else to do it for them.

These issues do not appear to dissuade large numbers of infertile couples: In December 1979, before the opening of the Norfolk clinic, the *New York Times Magazine* reported that more than 2500 women had already signed up for the proposed program and that thousands more had made inquiries (Kleiman 1979).

THE BIRTH PROCESS

The end of prenatal development comes with birth itself, usually forty weeks after conception. Today, while fathers or other family members sometimes assist in home deliveries, childbirth in America usually takes place in hospitals under conditions far more antiseptic than those in either medieval times or even a few generations ago. Childbirth in America today differs considerably from present-day childbirth in many other societies as well. The Jarara of South America, for example, give birth to their infants publicly, in view of everyone in the village. The San Blas Indians of Panama, by contrast, deliver their babies away from the village in the forest. Women preparing to deliver leave in sufficient time that children in the village do not have the opportunity to witness the preparation for childbirth (Jelliffe et al. 1961). Today in the Soviet Union, babies usually are delivered in hospitals, but unlike in America, fathers and other relatives are not permitted to participate in any way. They are not even permitted to see the mother or infant until they are ready to come home from the hospital (Gibson and Vinogradoff 1981).

Stages of the Birth Process

Birth occurs in three stages. The first stage of **labor,** as the process is known, is the longest of the stages, lasting from approximately six to twenty hours for most women. First-stage labor begins with uterine contractions, which may be mild or intense and spaced as close together as four or five minutes, as far apart as twenty to thirty minutes, or longer. As labor progresses, the contractions increase in frequency and intensity until the cervix finally is dilated sufficiently to enable the baby's head to pass through the vaginal canal. A woman's first labor usually takes longer than her labors in succeeding births. When we hear of mothers delivering their babies moments before arriving at the hospital, it is usually mothers who are delivering their second or third child. Even so, there are many exceptions in length of delivery.

The second stage of labor, the actual birth of the baby, generally lasts from thirty minutes to two hours. The baby is expelled from the vaginal canal with the help of continuing uterine contractions and eventually emerges from the mother's body. The first part of the baby to emerge in a normal delivery is the head. First, it crowns or becomes visible, a stage known as **crowning.** More and more of the head emerges with each contraction until the person assisting with the delivery can support it, gently turn the baby when the shoulders emerge, and ease the baby from the mother's body. In most births, the baby is born head first and face upward. Some babies, however, are born in a **breech presentation,** with the bottom entering the vaginal canal before the head, or in a **posterior presentation,** with the back rather than the face facing upward. With breech and posterior births, special care may have to be provided to prevent injury to both mother and infant.

The final stage of the birth process occurs after the baby has completely emerged. From two to twenty minutes after delivery, the mother expels the **afterbirth,** or placenta, consisting of the remaining amniotic sac, and whatever is left of the umbilical cord.

The birth cry that marks the infant's first breath symbolizes for most the beginning of the infant's life. The doctor or midwife assisting in the delivery watches the first breath of air closely, because it marks the first use of the infant's lungs. One minute and then five minutes after delivery, the infant is given a rating on the **Apgar scale,** which measures such vital signs as pulse rate, muscle tone, skin color, reflexes, and responsiveness to the environment (Apgar 1953; Apgar and James, 1962; Brazelton 1973). Table 2.2 shows the scoring system of the Apgar scale.

Complications of the Birth Process

Birth is usually a normal event in the life of parents and child. Nevertheless, complications that require intervention or special care may sometimes occur in the birth process.

Problems Related to Anesthesia. Anoxia is inadequate oxygenation of the blood. All infants are subjected to varying degrees of oxygen deprivation during labor. In most births, this is tolerated without difficulty. In some situations, however, inadequate uterine environments pose additional risks, so that normal changes of labor are more than the infant can tolerate successfully. If supplies of oxygen to the nerve cells of the brain are reduced sufficiently, serious brain damage or death can result.

Table 2.2
Apgar Scoring System for Infants

Vital Signs*	Scores		
	0	1	2
Pulse	Absent	Less than 100	More than 100
Breathing	Absent	Slow, irregular	Strong cry
Muscle tone	Limp	Some flexion of extremities	Active motion
Reflex response	No response	Grimace	Vigorous cry
Color (For nonwhites, alternative tests of mucous membranes, palms, and soles are used.)	Blue, pale	Body pink, extremities blue	Completely pink

Source: Apgar 1953 Reprinted by permission of the International Anesthesia Research Society.
*Each sign is rated for its absence or presence from 0 to 2. The highest overall score is 10. Ninety percent of infants score 7 or higher; a score of 4 or less means the infant is in danger and requires immediate treatment.

Milder anoxia has proportional effects. Anoxia can produce irritable infants, muscular tension, rigidity, and motor defects (Graham, Matarazzo, and Caldwell 1956; Lewis *et al.* 1967).

One factor that has been isolated as a primary cause of anoxia is anesthesia given to the laboring mother. Excessive medication may reduce oxygen intake of the mother and can dangerously deplete oxygen supply to an infant already experiencing stress. Today, most infants born in private hospitals in the United States are delivered with the mother receiving some form of inhaled anesthesia or analgesia.

What effect does medication to relieve maternal pain have on the newborn infant? When a drug is given to the mother in labor, the extent of its effect on the baby depends on a number of factors. Let us begin with the mother's health. The blood level of the drug in the mother will remain high if her liver or renal functioning is impaired, and therefore the drug will pass more readily to the fetus. Similarly, if maternal serum protein is low, any protein-bound drug will reach the fetus in greater quantity.

The dangers of anoxia and resulting brain damage during long labors are high. In shorter labors, where less medication is likely, effects may not be so severe. Onset of respiration, however, still may be less prompt and less vigorous when sedative drugs are given than when they are withheld.

Effects on the infant also depend on choice of medication. All of the inhaled anesthetics commonly used today are known to cross the placenta easily and enter fetal circulation (Giacoia and Yaffee 1975). Barbiturates, if short acting and given

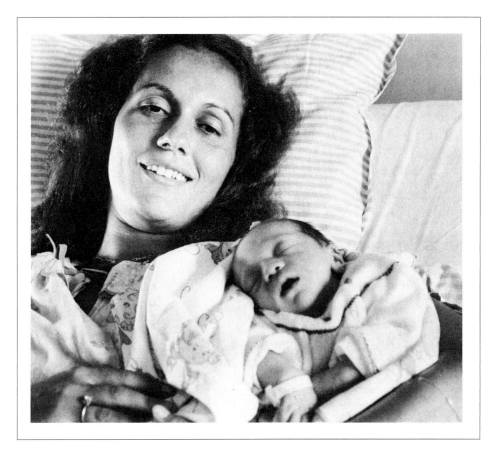

More women today than in the past are choosing nonmedicated childbirth.

well before delivery, may not have a measurable effect on the infant, but some commonly used drugs, such as reserpine, may result in infant lethargy for twenty-four hours after birth. Morphine, although safe two hours before delivery, may cause breathing problems and anoxia at birth if used later in the labor process. Regional anesthetics such as the spinal block, while having no direct effect on the fetus, have been known to produce extreme hypotension or low blood pressure in the mother. Thus these also are not free of risk (Bowes 1970; Vulliamy 1972).

Physicians long have known that a drug's effect is related directly to the size of the patient. Thus even the larger newborn is affected by a given drug dosage much more than the mother. Since the fetus and newborn do not have well-developed mechanisms for elimination, drugs can be stored in infant tissues for many days (Kron, Stein, and Goddard 1966). Examples of retarded development of drug-

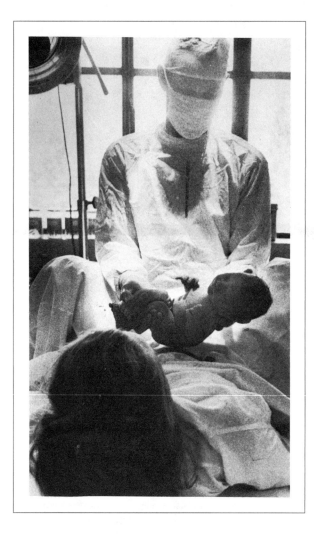

The timing and type of
medication given during
labor may influence the
effects on the infant.

affected infants have been reported up to four weeks after delivery. Daily increases
in sucking behavior in infants after medicated deliveries have been attributed to
recovery from drug effects. Brazelton (1961) reported that mothers who used anesthetics during delivery needed to stimulate their infants far more to maintain sucking
than did mothers who delivered without anesthetics. Some psychologists feel that
these effects, even though they are temporary, may well affect feeding patterns and
personal interrelationships in later life. Some researchers have suggested that "some
of the psychological effects may be pervasive if not permanent" (Stone, Smith, and
Murphy 1973, p. 112).

More recent research involving a seven-year study of some 3500 babies confirms the possibility of long-term behavioral damage to children as a result of certain anesthetics and pain killers prescribed during delivery. Some researchers (Brackbill 1979; Research News 1978; Brackbill and Broman 1979) found strong relationships between some commonly used drugs and developmental lags in children during the first year. They report that many of the children sat up, walked, and talked late. In some cases, preliminary findings show that additional lags in language and learning skills persisted until age seven. Brackbill and Broman suggest that scientists may someday be able to establish relationships between drugs administered during pregnancy and childbirth and behavioral measures as different as IQ and personality.

The Brackbill and Broman study also suggests that the amounts and kinds of medications ordered at delivery might serve the needs of the physicians rather than the patients. The study suggests that it might often be easier for the physician to accommodate a patient requesting relief from pain than to explain why she should not have further medication and to provide additional assistance necessary for her to deal with the pain without further anesthesia. In some American hospitals, over ninety-five percent of normal deliveries to healthy women still use some form of anesthesia. While drug use at delivery still is increasing, critics complain that little information on anesthetics and their complications is being provided to patients (Restak 1979a).

Internal Hemorrhaging. In births in which the mother has been given pain-relieving drugs, obstetricians may sometimes use a **forceps delivery.** Forceps are tongs that fit around the baby's head to help ease the child from the mother's body. This technique is sometimes regarded as necessary when the anesthesia deprives the mother of the spontaneous urge to bear down and push the baby out of the birth canal. One possible danger of forceps comes from excessive pressure that can be applied accidentally. Excessive pressure can cause internal hemorrhaging (bleeding) and destroy brain cells. Critics of modern hospital obstetrics in this country report that use of forceps is increasing and, in more cases than necessary, results in brain damage (Arms 1975).

Prematurity. A newborn infant is considered premature if born less than thirty-seven weeks after conception or, more commonly, if the birth weight is less than five and one-half pounds. By this definition, 7.6 percent of hospital births in the United States are premature. Approximately twice as many American as Swedish infants fall into this category; twice as many of these are nonwhite as are white babies (Behrman 1973). Prematurity has been related to a number of prenatal influences, including poor maternal diet, illness and infant malnutrition, excessive smoking and drinking of the mother, and drug abuse during pregnancy.

Prematurity is predictive in many respects of later development. Although recent medical advances have greatly increased their chances, premature infants still

---

HELPING PARENTS OF EXTREMELY PREMATURE INFANTS

Until very recently, extremely premature infants (born before thirty weeks after conception) usually died. Today with modern technology, more survive, but many still face severe problems. Being the parents of an extremely premature infant can be the most emotionally draining experience of a lifetime. First, the infant is taken away immediately after birth and placed in an incubator. The first meeting of parents and child is a frightening one: The infant, tiny and strangely colored, rests among a mass of tubes and wires. Parents immediately are faced with very realistic fears that the infant may not survive or may be abnormal. The physician can give no assurance. Parental feelings often include guilt as well as anxiety. Parents feel that somehow they are at fault. Often for weeks after birth, sudden ups and downs in the infant's responding keep this fear alive.

What can be done to relieve parental anxiety and to help parents gain rapport with their newborn infant? Physicians suggest first that the baby be shown to the parents immediately in the delivery room, even before being placed in the incubator. From then on, parents should be encouraged to visit the nursery often. They should be counseled as to what modern medical care now can do. All good news should be reported immediately.

Parents also should be counseled as to what to expect of their infant when they are able to take the baby home. Many parental fears relate to the doctor's careful precautions in the hospital. Parents, already anxious, fear they might not be capable of caring for the infant properly away from the hospital. Many premature infants later become excessively timid children and exhibit behavior disorders related to overprotection—for example, nail biting, thumb sucking, and temper tantrums. When lasting effects of a psychological nature are found in "preemies," they are likely to be due to parental attitudes related to parental fear rather than to the prematurity itself. Physical development of the premature infant can be expected to be retarded in the first few months of life. Parents should be fully informed as to what to expect: Extremely premature infants sit, stand, and walk considerably later than do full-term babies. Speech development is apt to be delayed; baby talk persists longer; and stuttering is more frequent than among full-term infants, although by the time they are ready for preschool, most of these children catch up.

QUESTIONS FOR THOUGHT

1. What are the advantages of parents having immediate contact with premature babies, even in the delivery room?

2. Why is guilt a common reaction among parents of premature infants?

have less chance to survive than babies born at full term or at average birth weights. Today, prematurity accounts for one-third of infant deaths in the first year. Mortality in the first two years for infants who survive to be discharged from the hospital is three times that of full-term infants.

Incidence of **sudden infant death syndrome,** also called SIDS or crib death, is increased among premature infants. Crib deaths occur in apparently healthy babies who are put to sleep for the night or for a nap and are later found dead with no apparent cause of death. Autopsies of infants who have died from SIDS, however, consistently show excessive red blood cell production and thickened arterial walls. The results of these autopsies are consistent with theories that suggest the infants suffer from lack of oxygen. Premature babies more frequently die from crib death than do full-term babies, suggesting that immature breathing mechanisms and weak defensive reflexes at birth partly account for the respiratory failure (Lipsitt 1978).

One new technique that some doctors are using to help with infants diagnosed as having weak defensive reflexes, which in turn makes them likely candidates for SIDS, is a monitor with a beeper attached to the infant's abdomen. If an infant wearing this beeper stops breathing, the beeper sounds and alerts the parents to begin assisting the infant. Usually the sound of the beeper is sufficient to cause the child to begin breathing again.

Caesarian Section

Most births, with or without medication, occur vaginally. In five to ten percent of births in American hospitals in recent years, however, physicians elected to perform what is known as a **caesarian section.** This procedure involves the surgical removal of the infant and placenta from the uterus through an incision made in the mother's abdominal wall. Some reasons that obstetricians give for delivery by caesarian section include excessively large fetuses that might have difficulty passing through the mother's pelvis, such fetal distress as weakened heart beat or breech or posterior presentation, such metabolic disturbances of the mother as **toxemia** (poisoning of the body) or diabetes, weak contractions, and pelvic disorders.

In the past, once a woman delivered a baby by caesarian section, it was more difficult for her to deliver future babies vaginally. The reason for this was that the surgery involved a large incision through the wall of the uterus, which was then no longer as strong as before the surgery. Recent medical advances, such as smaller incisions to strengthen the uterine wall, now make it possible for more women to deliver vaginally after once having caesarian sections.

Critics of caesarian section believe that many babies are delivered by this method unnecessarily when vaginal childbirth might be perfectly safe. Unnecessary surgery, these critics point out, carries high risks. Critics also point out that it is extremely difficult to predict accurately when babies are ready to be born. As a result, some caesarian sections are performed unnecessarily.

CHILDBIRTH METHODS AND SETTINGS

Although most Americans give birth in hospitals and with the attendance of nurses and obstetricians, this was not always the case. Medieval historians describe more natural childbirth of peasant women who reportedly often gave birth simply by stopping their work and squatting in the fields, often with no other person in attendance. Vinogradoff (1978) reports a description of childbirth in the home of a wealthy, educated family in Europe at the turn of this century. In this case, a physician was called to the home of the parents to assist in the delivery. Everyone in the family assisted, including the father and the servants. Candles were lit so that the doctor could see what she had to do. At that time, Vinogradoff reports, only babies born to urban poor families were born in hospitals. Those who had the money to have the assistance of a doctor or midwife delivered their babies at home.

In recent years, many parents have come to feel that modern hospital obstetrical procedures pose a number of difficulties. There is evidence that a variety of routinely used procedures may be detrimental to mother and child alike. Excessive use of medication and forceps, artificial induction of labor, and impersonal care of mothers and infants are some of the procedures causing growing concern. As a result many parents are investigating alternative birthing methods that give them more control over this most personal experience.

Prepared Childbirth

One outgrowth of the criticism of modern hospital delivery in America is an increasing trend toward more "natural" methods of childbirth, similar in some ways to the manner in which babies were delivered before sophisticated technology was developed. **Prepared childbirth** involves a labor and delivery process with little or no use of anesthetics. It involves special preparation through exercises during pregnancy that will develop muscles that will aid the body in labor and delivery.

Prepared childbirth was first made popular by obstetricians Grantly Dick-Read and Fernand Lamaze. Dick-Read's method uses as its key the preparation of the mother. Dick-Read (1953) argued that pain normally associated with childbirth comes primarily not from physiological causes but from exaggerated fear and the tension that accompanies it. Dick-Read pointed out that if mothers learned precisely what the birth process is about and what to expect, they would be less frightened and more relaxed. He hypothesized further that this process would lead to reduction of pain and less need for anesthetics or other forms of medication during delivery.

Lamaze (1970) describes his approach as involving preparation, limited medication, and participation. The Lamaze technique is strikingly similar to that used by obstetricians in the Soviet Union, who call their method "psychological delivery." The Soviet process includes a preparatory set of talks by physicians to improve maternal understanding and special exercises to strengthen the muscles of the abdomen, pelvis, and diaphragm. The final step is the delivery exercises. Unlike the Lamaze technique, however, the Soviets do not use limited medication during delivery. Except in very unusual and difficult cases they use no medication at all because of its danger to the unborn infant (Gibson and Vinogradoff, 1981).

Western as well as Soviet proponents of prepared childbirth today agree that if the mother is prepared psychologically and physically for labor, pain will be minimized. Many American doctors now agree to prepared childbirth, but many also point out that it is important to recognize that this need not be an "all-or-none" method. Unlike Soviet childbirth procedures, the amount of anesthetic used in American hospitals when childbirth is prepared will, in the end, normally depend on the mother's final desires as well as on the doctor's assessment of her physical state and that of the baby.

Family-Centered Childbirth

Along with the trend toward prepared childbirth have come demands for increased participation of the father in the birth process. Proponents of father-present deliveries in the hospital suggest that the father can provide much needed psychological support. Associations such as the International Childbirth Education Association, the American Society for Psychoprophylaxis in Obstetrics, and the LaLeche League International have long supported the father's presence in the delivery room as part of the procedure for making childbirth more humane. Some hospitals in the United States today allow fathers to be present during the births of their children. Some doctors, opposed to the father's presence, point out the dangers of increased possibility of infection and stress that the delivery room is no place for sentimentality. Parents also seem to be divided as to the desirability of the father's presence during childbirth. In 1968, when St. Mary's Hospital in Grand Rapids, Michigan, first allowed fathers in the delivery room, only nine percent of fathers chose to be present (Shu 1973). In recent years, however, this percentage has increased considerably (Furstenberg 1976).

Home Birth. Some mothers today who choose family-centered childbirth choose to deliver their babies not only in the presence of the fathers but sometimes in the presence of other family members. Even children, in some cases, may watch the birth of a sibling. With this type of family-centered childbirth, delivery usually takes place in the home. Statistics on home delivery are scarce, although it appears that an increasing number of parents are opting for this alternative. In this case, a midwife or doctor usually assists at the delivery, with family members assisting the professional staff. Parents delivering their babies at home report it to be, at once, the most intimate of experiences and the most public of events to be shared with loved ones.

Many obstetricians, however, do not favor home birth. They suggest that the trend to home delivery deprives the patient of advances in obstetrical care. Many hospitals, they point out, routinely measure the fetus's heart rate to detect fetal distress during labor by means of a fetal monitor. Two types of fetal monitors are used routinely, an external type that records the heartbeat by means of two belts placed around the mother's abdomen and an internal type that uses a plastic tube containing electrodes inserted into the vagina and attached to the baby's head. It has been estimated that doctors using fetal monitors can be ninety-percent more effective in detecting problems than they can be without this equipment (Boston Women's Health Book Collective 1976). Lack of this sort of modern technology to provide advance warning of complication is the difference that many obstetricians feel make home delivery more dangerous than hospital delivery. Even when fetal monitoring is done in home delivery, they point out, there might not be sufficient time to get the mother to the hospital in event of serious complications.

Proponents of home delivery argue that dangers are inherent in overdependence on equipment like the fetal monitor. If the fetal monitor errs in its measurement, these proponents point out, it is possible that a doctor relying too heavily on it may perform an unnecessary caesarian delivery. Proponents of home delivery point out further that most couples who choose home delivery today are screened carefully by physicians, attend classes in order to prepare adequately, and make provision in advance for back-up care if it is needed. Finally, they believe that the issue of home delivery vs. hospital delivery today is a political issue for some physicians who are uncomfortable with the use of midwives in delivery, whether the delivery takes place at home or in a hospital.

Hospital Birthing Rooms. In response to the desires of parents who want family-centered childbirth, more and more hospitals are offering alternative facilities that provide homelike qualities and, at the same time, allow for technology, such as fetal monitoring and other back-up services, nearby. The so-called **birthing rooms** are made to look as homelike as possible, sometimes even with rocking chairs, hanging plants, and stereo sets. Fathers are invited to be present and to assist. Instead of the mother's going to a recovery room after delivery, father, mother, and baby are allowed to remain together.

In some birthing room facilities, there are no restrictions on visits by other children in the family. Some doctors feel that, as long as the brothers and sisters are educated in advance as to what will take place, letting them join in the experience, at home or in the birthing room, reduces their fears about their mother's well-being and makes them feel a part of the family experience. The contact between the baby and parents in the first minutes and hours of life, many feel further, causes stronger infant–mother attachment, what psychologists call **bonding.**

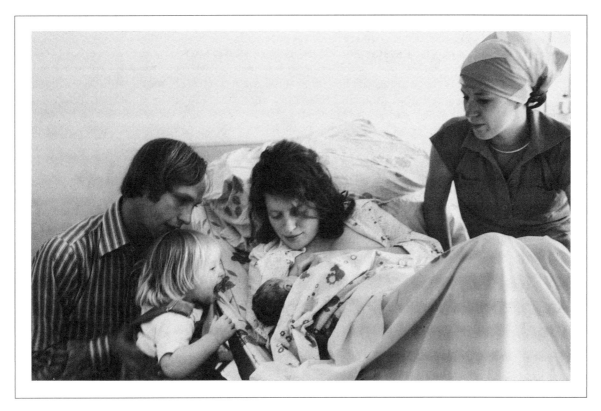

In homelike hospital birthing rooms, fathers may assist during labor, and children are often allowed to be present.

"Birth without Violence"

A recent alternative in childbirth procedures was developed by Dr. Frederick Leboyer, a French obstetrician whose book, *Birth without Violence* (1975), became a best seller in the United States. Leboyer is concerned with the emotional impact of childbirth on the neonate, and questions the "harshness" of traditional childbirth practices. The **Leboyer method** includes dimming delivery room lights so that the baby will not be startled unduly by bright lights. Immediately after birth, the newborn infant is placed on the mother's abdomen and allowed to retain as long as possible the prenatal curved spinal position. The umbilical cord is not cut until the baby's respiration is well established. The baby continues, for up until six minutes after birth in some cases, to receive oxygen through its prenatal respiratory system. After the cord is cut, the baby receives a warm, comfortable bath, often to soft music.

HIGHLIGHT 2.3 **THE TJARKOVSKY METHOD:
TAKING LEBOYER ONE STEP FURTHER**

Physicians in the Soviet Union have expanded on the Leboyer approach with an even more radical experimental technique. Dr. Igor Borisovich Tjarkovsky has developed an extraordinary, controversial method of delivery in his laboratory hospital in Moscow, in which birth reportedly takes place in a large tank of liquid. The baby is delivered into liquid of the same temperature and viscosity as that in the mother's womb and remains there for a period of time with the umbilical cord still attached so as gradually to adjust to its new state. The purpose of the Tjarkovsky method, like the Leboyer method, is to decrease as much as possible the shock of childbirth. Only when the infant has had some time to adjust to its new expanded environment in the tank is the baby removed from the liquid and brought into the air. The umbilical cord is then cut, and the baby begins breathing air (Magalhaes 1979).

The Tjarkovsky method is not used regularly in the Soviet Union, and it is still being studied. Through studies, Soviet researchers hope in the next few years to be able to document positive effects on the development of infants born through this technique.

QUESTIONS FOR THOUGHT
1. What are the advantages of this radical method to the baby? To the mother?
2. What might be the major disadvantages?

Critics of the Leboyer method point out that these procedures might in some cases be dangerous. Bright light is necessary to see signs of distress and fetal color. The cord should be cut as quickly as possible after it stops pulsating so as not to risk infection. The doctor needs to hear the cry of the baby to be sure of normal breathing.

Advocates of "birth without violence" point out that precautionary measures can be used although they are seldom necessary. For example, hospital lights can be turned up if a problem develops. Leboyer's supporters contend that follow-up studies of French babies born by the Leboyer method seem to show that these children are healthier and noticeably more active, exhibiting avid interest in the world about them (Englund 1974).

Nurse-Midwifery

Another major change in recent years in obstetrical procedures in the United States has to do with determining who actually assists in delivery of the baby. Because of increased requests for more attention and, at the same time, for lower costs, a new trend toward assistance by midwives is occurring. Today, nurse–midwives are reg-

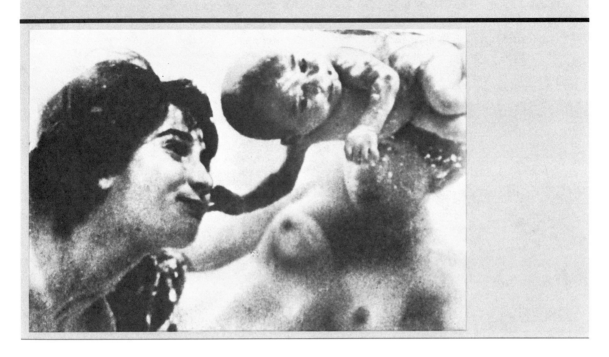

istered nurses with special training in delivering babies. Midwifery has always been practiced in other countries and, in fact, is the most common assistance available in the world for childbirth. In the United States, with its interest in technology and doctoring, the trend to delivery assistance by midwives is only now beginning to come into vogue. Today there are some twenty-four schools that train nurse–midwives at the rate of about 200 graduates per year. In 1980, there were approximately 2200 midwives in the United States.

Most midwives are capable of handling routine births as well as prenatal and postnatal care without a doctor's assistance. While nurse–midwives today assist in home deliveries, the largest number assist in short-stay hospital delivery units or birthing rooms. In hospital settings, midwives may deliver babies, but physicians and medical back-up are available in the event that birth complications develop. In normal deliveries, mother and infant often leave for home in less than twelve hours. The facilities, together with the nurse–midwife, reduce expenses for many parents and allow them to assume more immediate responsibilities for the baby (Rawlings 1973). Mothers who deliver their babies in birthing rooms may elect to stay longer, while still enjoying the advantages of the less expensive nurse–midwives and the opportunity to share responsibilities in caring for the newborn infant.

THE CASE OF THE DUGAN FAMILY—AN EXAMPLE OF FAMILY-CENTERED CHILDBIRTH: A CASE STUDY FOR CLASS DISCUSSION

I. Identification and Sources of Information

Names: Bill and Yvonne Dugan, parents, ages twenty-seven and twenty-six years, respectively
Bill Dugan, Jr., age five years
Sally Dugan, born during observation period

Address: 1313 W. Street, Pittsburgh, Pennsylvania

Race: White

Professions (of parents): Schoolteachers

Sources of information:

1. Interview with Bill and Yvonne Dugan

2. Interview with Billy Dugan

3. Personal observation

II. Family History

Bill and Yvonne Dugan have been married for seven years. They met while attending the state college and married immediately after Yvonne had received her bachelor of education degree. Bill had received his college degree the year before and was already working at Wadsworth Elementary School at the time. After their marriage, Yvonne began teaching kindergarten at Wadsworth and remained there until Bill Jr. was born. She left Billy each day with her mother, who lives a block away, when she returned to work a year later. Yvonne had read about the Lamaze method before Billy's birth but had not had the time to prepare the exercises. She opted for traditional delivery. Billy's birth was normal. Bill remembers taking Yvonne to the hospital when the pains were about five minutes apart. "When we got there," he said, "I could hardly believe it. They whisked Yvonne away, and I waited for fifteen hours in the bull pen— you know—with the other fathers." Bill remembers smoking about three packs of cigarettes, walking back and forth, jumping (just like all the other fathers) whenever someone came out of the labor or delivery rooms with news. "We tried to talk with each other, but we were all too nervous. Every hour or so, one of us would get called with news. Then back to the waiting." When Billy was finally born, Bill was allowed to see him for a moment through the nursery window. He waited until Yvonne left the recovery room, kissed her congratulations, and then went home to call the grandparents and get some sleep. Yvonne remembers a little more about Billy's delivery than does Bill, but, she complained, "not much more. Billy was a breech birth and came out bottom first. The doctor decided that the best thing was to put me out. I tried to 'will' myself to stay awake, but after they put the mask over my face, I felt a terrible pain. Then I didn't remember anything until the recovery room. The doctor told me that I had looked at Billy and said I was glad he was a boy, but I don't remember even that."

Bill and Yvonne, although satisfied with their doctor and the outcome of Billy's delivery, decided that they wanted to play larger roles in the birth of their next child. When Yvonne became pregnant with Sally, they were prepared. Yvonne and Bill joined a family-centered childbirth class at the local "Y." They decided not simply to have a family-centered childbirth in which Yvonne could give her full participation without the dangers posed by anesthetics ("Billy wasn't damaged, but when we read what could have happened, it really frightened us," recalls Yvonne), and Bill could assist her during the entire process. They decided to have the baby at home. "We wanted Billy Jr. to see his new brother or sister just as soon as the baby was born and to be part of our family process," explained Bill. The Dugans found a nurse–midwife willing to come to their home to assist. Bill and Yvonne spent a great deal of time preparing Billy as to what to expect.

THE CASE OF THE DUGAN FAMILY

III. The Delivery

Yvonne went into labor two days before she was scheduled to do so, but the Dugans were prepared. Bill had just come home from work, and the couple started timing contractions together. During the early stages of labor, Yvonne prepared Billy's supper, and his father put him to bed for the night after reading him his favorite bedtime story. Billy asked to be awakened when the baby came; his parents promised they would call him. When the contractions began to come close together, Bill called Mrs. Oliver, the midwife, who came right over. She gave Bill directions on how to support Yvonne during the contractions. She stood by Yvonne's side and assisted Yvonne with her breathing control. The breathing exercises that Yvonne had practiced before delivery helped, but it apparently was necessary for Mrs. Oliver to remind her at the end just what to do.

About an hour before Sally was born, Yvonne's mother arrived, together with Yvonne's sister, to provide additional support. Yvonne's mother had just gone to the kitchen to make some coffee for everyone when Mrs. Oliver called her back. "Not now! It will be here soon," she said quietly.

"Oh, my God, it's coming!" Yvonne screamed. The infant's head suddenly crowned. Then more and more of it appeared. Bill and his mother-in-law yelled, "Push! Push!" The midwife put her hands around the baby's face and turned it gently. The shoulders appeared. Mrs. Oliver took hold of the baby and completed the task.

Sally did not cry right away. Mrs. Oliver quickly held her up and cleared some of the mucus from her throat. After ten seconds, she started to cry. As soon as she did, everyone in the room began to laugh and cry at the same time. Mrs. Oliver held the baby up for a moment for Yvonne to see and then placed her in her mother's arms. After the umbilical cord stopped pulsating, Bill cut the cord. Bill went to the other room then to get Billy Jr. from his bed. Billy got into the bed next to his mother and snuggled against her, peering at the tiny infant on her other side. His father let him stay for a few minutes before the placenta was delivered.

IV. Present Status, Diagnosis, and Prognosis

Two weeks after the delivery, the Dugan family is doing very well. Billy Jr. reports that his sister "weighed seven pounds, one ounce the night she was borned." Yvonne's breast-feeding is going well. Bill bought Billy a baby doll to play with when Yvonne takes care of Sally. "Billy tries to breast-feed the doll," Yvonne laughs. "But his interest in that seems to be wearing off." Bill described the only aspect of the delivery that disappointed him. "I had planned to take moving pictures so that someday we could show Sally her first moments of life in the Dugan family. I had already gotten the camera out with new film in it, and it was sitting on the dresser during the entire delivery! But I never even once thought about it during the entire ten hours. I was so excited about what was going on! Billy remembered though and reminded us. We did get some scenes of him in bed with Yvonne and Sally. He wasn't nearly as excited as the rest of us . . . just interested in cuddling with his mother before going back to sleep."

Questions for Class Discussion

1. In what ways was the birth of Sally Dugan a more pleasurable experience for the Dugan family than was the birth of Billy Jr.? What were the extra hazards posed by Billy's birth? By Sally's birth? How could each of these have been reduced?

2. What sorts of experiences did Billy and Sally share that children whose parents select traditional obstetrics methods in the United States do not have? What effect might these experiences have in the future on each member of the family?

SUMMARY

Researchers have long been debating the relative importance of heredity and environment to the developing human being. Neither absolute hereditary nor environmental choices, however, provide a complete picture; it is the complicated interaction between heredity and environment that is most important to the developing individual. Hereditary influences are caused by chromosomes and the thousands of smaller genetic units, called genes, of which they are composed. The genes, which are either dominant or recessive, carry hereditary characteristics through DNA, which is the basis of all life. The genotype is set with the forming of the fertilized egg, or zygote.

The prenatal period can be divided into three basic developmental stages. The period of the ovum begins with conception and lasts for two weeks until the developing cluster of cells attaches itself securely to the lining of the uterus. During the embryonic period, lasting for the next six weeks, essential body systems develop, and the cluster of cells becomes recognizable as a partially functioning human being. During the fetal period, from eight weeks after conception until the time of birth, the body organs, muscles, and nervous system mature, and the organism increases in size and takes on clearly human characteristics.

Although heredity is determined at conception, a child's health and development can be affected profoundly by uterine conditions. Adequate nutrition of the mother during and even before pregnancy is critical to normal fetal development, and protein malnourishment, in particular, can have devastating effects on the fetus.

Maternal age can also be a factor in prenatal development. Very young women and older women run a greater risk of having defective children. Maternal infection and disease can affect the fetus in direct as well as indirect ways, as can the use of cigarettes, drugs, and alcohol. Radiation, as from X-ray treatments, is a hazard to both the fetus and the newborn. Emotional stress of mothers has also been related to risk in pregnancy, tension and vomiting in infants, respiration difficulties at birth, and excessive childhood illness.

In the past twenty years, reliable screening of infants for genetic diseases has increased dramatically, and treatment of genetic diseases has improved. Most dramatic is the development of a procedure known as amniocentesis, in which fluid is removed from the amniotic sac and tested for genetic characteristics.

In addition, methods to increase fertility have also been developed and are being used with increasing success. Artificial insemination is a simple procedure that can be performed in a doctor's office. *In vitro* fertilization, fertilization of an egg in a laboratory dish, followed by implantation of the fertilized egg into the womb of the mother, has enabled couples who were infertile either because of damage to the prospective mother's fallopian tubes or because of other damages prohibiting the mother's eggs from entering her fallopian tubes, to have babies.

Birth occurs in three stages. The first stage, labor, begins with mild contractions, initially spaced far apart, that increase in intensity and duration until the second stage, birth. Birth occurs when the mother's uterine contractions finally push the baby through the vagina. Afterbirth occurs after the baby has emerged into the world outside, when the mother expels the placenta, remaining amniotic sac, and whatever is left of the umbilical cord.

Modern obstetrics, even with the advent of such technology as the fetal monitor that can detect problems early in delivery, still pose a number of potential hazards during the birth process. These include anoxia, or inadequate oxygenation of the blood, the possibility of internal hemorrhaging, adverse effects on the developing infant of the anesthetic used to help the mother, and prematurity. Some critics of modern obstetrics complain that caesarian sections are performed too often.

Critics of modern hospital obstetrics have proposed a number of alternative methods of childbirth that allow parents more control over the birth experience. These include prepared childbirth, family-centered childbirth, home delivery, the use of hospital birthing rooms, and the practice of such procedures as the "birth without violence" proposed by Leboyer. Also, more and more midwives are assisting in delivering babies in the United States.

FOR FURTHER READING

Hathaway, M., and J. Hathaway. *Children at Birth.* Chicago, Illinois: Cinema Medica, 1980. *Children at Birth* presents a controversial and provocative argument that children should be present at siblings' births. The Hathaways discuss pros and cons and use professional interviews and children's own reports of the effects of watching childbirth.

Stewart, D., and L. Stewart (eds.). *Safe Alternatives in Childbirth.* Chicago, Illinois: Cinema Medica, 1980. Care is given in this book to present a forum providing a variety of philosophies and scientific studies on the safety of various alternatives in maternity care and childbirth. The book advocates, among other things, safe births outside the hospital.

Preview Questions

- Can you describe how the neonate looks and acts?
- What are three major advances in physical development that are made during infancy?
- How does a child's general sensorimotor behavior change during infancy?
- Can you describe some infant behaviors that signal the beginnings of language?
- What are the six stages Piaget identifies during the sensorimotor period and what behaviors characterize each?
- How do conditioning and motivation bring about changes in an infant's behavior?
- Can you explain what is meant by social learning and describe five changes in infant behavior that result from this process?
- What are some developmental tests of infant learning and how can their results be used?
- How does improper nutrition affect the development of the infant and what are the causes of high-risk births and the failure-to-thrive syndrome?
- Can you describe some biological and environmental factors that are key influences in producing individual differences among infants?

3

Infancy
and Toddlerhood

THE NEONATE

For the first two weeks of life, the infant is called a **neonate.** The tiny newborn, although vulnerable to many hazards in the environment, has all body structures present, if not yet matured. The behavior of neonates demonstrates that they are well adapted for life in their new environment.

Physical Characteristics

Neonates are red, wrinkled, and, at birth, wet with amniotic fluid. The skin is coated with a protective cheeselike substance. The bones of the skull protecting the neonate's brain are soft and connected by fibrous tissue. The skull contains six soft spots or openings called **fontanels,** where the bones have not yet grown together. The largest fontanel is on the top of the head and will not close until the baby is more than a year old.

Neonatal Behavior

Neonates spend most of the time sleeping. When they are awake, they may cry spasmodically without tears. Crying usually means the infant is hungry, thirsty, or uncomfortable. It is unusual for an adequately fed baby who is given sufficient attention to cry for more than a total of two hours in a twenty-four-hour period.

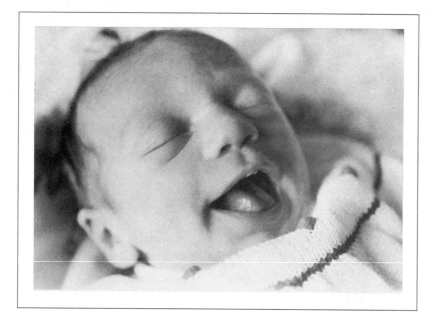

For the first two weeks of life, the infant is called a neonate.

NEONATAL STATES OF ACTIVITY　　　　　　　　　HIGHLIGHT 3.1

Psychologists have described neonatal states of activity in various ways. The following categories were used by Wolff (1966) in describing sleeping infants:

Regular sleep: Closed eyes, slow even breathing, relaxed facial features

Irregular sleep: Closed eyes, quick uneven breathing, variable body movements

Drowsiness: Eyes open and shut intermittently, regular breathing, relatively slow body movements

Alert inactivity: Open eyes, relatively inactive body movement, relaxed facial features

Waking activity: Open eyes, diffuse motor activity involving whole body, irregular respiration

Crying: Vocalization associated with vigorous motor activity.

QUESTIONS FOR THOUGHT

1. Newborns, when left alone and unstimulated, spend most of their time sleeping. Why do some parents feel that their infants seem to cry all night and then sleep all afternoon, just when friends and relatives want to see them?

2. Are these babies really crying all night? What do you think makes their parents think they do?

States of Activity. Neonatal behavior often is described by the infant's state of activity. Together, these states form a continuum of consciousness or alertness, ranging from vigorous activity to regular sleep. Parents' inability to regulate their babies' sleep–wake cycles by keeping them up longer in the daytime demonstrates that the regulatory mechanism cannot be controlled by external manipulation.

Reflexive Responses. The neonate at birth is capable of making specific reflexive or involuntary motor responses with some regularity to certain stimuli. For example, the **rooting response,** well known to mothers of newborn infants, occurs when the baby's mouth is stimulated. The baby responds by turning mouth and head toward the source of stimulation. If the stimulus is a milk-producing nipple, rooting behavior automatically will be followed by sucking. Finger and toe flexion can be elicited by pressure on the palms or the soles of the feet at the base of the toes.

The neonate will grab a person's finger when it is placed in the infant's hand and touches the palm, a response known as the **Palmar grasp.** If the middle of the baby's sole is stroked where the arch will be, the opposite of flexion, called the **Babinski response,** occurs, and the neonate's toes fan up and outward. This reflex occurs only at this early stage of development. The **Moro (startle) response** is elicited by withdrawal of support or by a loud noise. It consists of a rapid flinging out and upward of the neonate's arms. The neonate also produces what is known as a reflexive smile. These reflexive responses disappear after a few months as the

Table 3.1
Neonatal Reflexes

Reflex	Description
Rooting	When an infant's cheek is touched, the head turns toward the stimulus, and the mouth opens as if to find a nipple. This reflex disappears after about 3 months.
Sucking	When a finger is put in an infant's mouth, the infant responds by sucking and making rhythmic movements with mouth and tongue.
Flexion (Palmar)	When a finger is placed in an infant's palm, the infant grasps it tightly and strengthens the grasp as the object is pulled away. This reflex disappears after about 5 months.
Plantar	When an object or a finger is placed on the soles of an infant's foot near the toes, the infant responds by trying to flex the foot. This reflex disappears after about 9 months.
Babinski	When the sole of an infant's foot is stroked from heel to toes, the infant will spread the small toes and raise the large one. This reflex disappears after about 6 months.
Startle (Moro)	When an infant is startled by a loud sound or by being suddenly dropped, the arms spread, and the fingers stretch out. Arms are then brought back to the body, and fingers are clenched. This reflex disappears after about 4 months.
Babkin	When objects are placed against both palms, an infant reacts by opening the mouth, closing the eyes, and turning the head to one side. This reflex disappears after about 4 months.
Tonic neck	When an infant's head is turned to one side, the arm and leg on that side are extended, and the arm and leg on the opposite side are flexed as in a fencing position. This reflex disappears after about 4 months.
Stepping (walking)	When an infant is held upright with feet against a flat surface and is moved forward, the infant appears to walk in a coordinated way. This reflex disappears after about 2 to 3 months.
Placing	When an infant's feet are put against a table edge, the infant attempts to step up onto it. This reflex disappears after about 2 months.
Swimming	When an infant is placed in water in a prone position, the infant will attempt to swim in a coordinated way. This reflex disappears after about 6 months.

nervous system matures. Psychologists believe that the appearance of reflexive behavior very early in life serves particular adaptive purposes. Table 3.1 lists some of these reflexes and the ages at which they tend to disappear.

Sensory and Perceptual Responses. Infant **sensation** is awareness that results from stimulation of one of the infant perceptor organs—for example, the skin or the ears. **Perception** involves the infant's abstracting information from sensory experiences. The newborn infant senses touch and sound and perceives a mother's presence by learning to associate certain touch and voice sensations with the mother being there.

Behavioral scientists used to believe that neonates had very limited sensory and perceptual abilities. Researchers today, however, believe that neonates have greater sensory and perceptual abilities than was previously believed. Indeed, neonates are now known to possess many perceptual abilities even in the first hours of life.

What is the neonate capable of perceiving? Neonates at birth can feel and respond to touch. They can remove irritants from their noses with their hands and from their opposite feet (Bower 1977b). They turn away from unpleasant odors, prefer sweet-tasting food, and demonstrate some ability to localize sound by turning their eyes. This last ability is present just a few minutes after birth.

Infants at birth seem to be capable of depth perception; they make defensive movements to approaching objects by retracting their heads or moving their arms. Neonates have been shown to imitate. Bower (1977b) reported cases of newborns who, after watching their mothers stick out their tongues, open their mouths, or flutter their eyelids, followed by performing the same activity. By only two weeks, these infants expressed more interest in their mothers' faces and voices than in those of strangers.

THE INFANT

Development during infancy proceeds at an amazingly rapid pace. In fact, humans grow more quickly during the first year of life than at any other phase of their development after birth. Babies born in the 1980s probably will grow even more quickly than babies born in past decades. The reason for this is that as a nation, we have better nutrition and living conditions, and we have learned how to cure many illnesses that previously retarded infant growth. Our community health services are also much improved over the past.

Physical Development

The average infant at delivery measures approximately twenty inches in length and weighs an average of seven pounds. Gains in length and weight from this moment on are impressive. After four months, the average infant has doubled in weight, weighs between twelve and fifteen pounds, and has grown four or more inches. Important changes also take place in body proportion and composition. Growth and development proceeds in a cephalo-caudal (head-to-toe) direction during the first year just as it did during the prenatal period. At delivery, infants' heads measure almost one-third of their body length. During the first year of life, the head continues to grow, both in size and brain complexity, at a more rapid rate than the rest of the body. Brain weight alone increases thirty-five percent by the time the baby is two years old! After that, growth becomes more rapid in parts of the body farther from the head. We can judge fairly accurately the age of children on the basis of the relative sizes of their heads as compared to the rest of their bodies: The head of a six-year-old child is much smaller in comparison to body length than that of a six-month-old. Adults' heads, as we learned in Chapter 1, are always considerably smaller in proportion to the rest of their bodies than they were in infancy.

Other very noticeable changes take place in the first year as well. Neonates enter the world toothless, although their teeth already have developed below the gum line prior to birth. The first tooth usually erupts at four or five months. By the time most children are two years old, they have the twenty baby teeth, including primary teeth, first and second molars, and cuspids. Teething often is memorable for parents because it signals a more grown-up facial appearance and the ability to eat more solid foods. In addition, parents remember the discomfort that sometimes accompanies the tooth eruption.

Infants very gradually develop muscles; their muscular strength increases, and their dexterity improves. Skeletal structure passes through successive stages from basic connective tissue to cartilage to osseus tissue (hard bone). The central nervous systems grow and mature more rapidly during infancy than during any other period of life. We learned that, as the nervous system becomes more complex, some of the neonatal reflexes disappear. New reflexes develop that were not present at birth. At thirty days, for example, the **labyrinthine reflex,** or righting reflex, appears. This reflex allows infants to attempt to right themselves when they are held downward.

Perception

Infants' sensory and perceptual abilities increase rapidly in the first twenty-four months.

Vision. A good deal of research has been done on the visual perception of infants. It has been demonstrated, for example, that infants prefer moderate lighting, particularly in the early weeks of life and that they are unhappy in brightly lit rooms. They can discriminate among colors and seem to prefer (by paying more attention to) clear reds and blues. They watch moving objects and usually are able to track a toy moving across the visual field by the time they are three months old. It is at this age

---

THE PREDICTION OF ADULT SIZE

Often, when we see a big, strapping baby, we say, "My, he's going to be a football player" or "Don't we have a prospective weight lifter" or "He'll make a basketball star." The assumption usually is that we can predict adult height, weight, and physical capability from size in infancy. Is this possible? One researcher (Krogman 1972) suggests that it is possible to some extent and provides us with a rule of thumb:

Boys: 2 × height at age 2 = adult height;
5 × weight at age 2 = adult weight.
Girls: 2 × height at 1$^1/_2$ years = adult height;
5 × weight at 1$^1/_2$ years = adult weight.

Krogman cautions, however, that this rule works only with infants who fall within an average range of height or weight. Furthermore, an early-maturing child will probably be shorter as an adult than predicted by this formula, and a late maturer might well be taller. Infant weight and adult weight, just as infant length and adult length, are apparently related, but so many factors affect a child's growth that really accurate predictions cannot be made.

QUESTIONS FOR THOUGHT

1. If your baby falls within an average range of height or weight so that you could use Krogman's rule of thumb with at least some accuracy, how might this information be useful to you in predicting anything about the child's future?
2. What other factors, besides early or late maturing, might affect adult size?

---

that a mobile hanging over the crib becomes an exciting toy. The visual system approximates adult capability by the time the infant is about four months old.

Vision is extremely important to development. In the first month of life, infants spend approximately ten percent of the time scanning their surroundings with rapid eye movements and frequent changes of direction. Vision provides the bases for both sensorimotor and cognitive functioning. Complex patterns of responding, as with crawling toward and picking up objects, are achieved through coordination of vision with developing motor ability.

Research has demonstrated that infants can perceive depth quite early in life. Gibson and Walk (1960) developed what they called the "visual cliff" to test infant depth perception (see Fig. 3.1). Infants were placed on a surface that appeared to end in a cliff with a large drop to the floor; actually, the "drop-off" was covered with transparent glass that allowed them to see the floor below. Six-month-old infants

Figure 3.1 The "visual cliff" apparatus used by Gibson and Walk in their studies of depth perception in infants. (From E. J. Gibson and R. D. Walk, The "visual cliff," in *Scientific American*, 1960, Vol 202(4), 80–92. Photograph by William Vandivert.)

could not be coaxed to crawl across the glass surface. Apparently, human infants perceive depth and avoid such a visual cliff as soon as they are able to crawl. Gibson (1970) has hypothesized that these avoidance responses might occur at earlier ages, as they do with animals lower on the phylogenetic scale, if motor development allowed human babies to make the necessary movements.

Infants show particular interest in the human face. Three- to five-week-old infants pay much more attention to human faces than to other stimuli they see. By two months of age they pay the greatest attention to the faces of their mothers (or other caregivers). At this age, babies stare continuously at the faces around them. By four months, interest in faces intensifies still further. Babies now prefer to watch all stimuli resembling faces, even line drawings of faces. Apparently, drawings of other objects are not nearly so fascinating, for attention to these objects is much shorter. Figure 3.2 shows the stimuli that interest babies from two to three months of age and the stimuli that interest those older than three months, according to research by Fantz (1961).

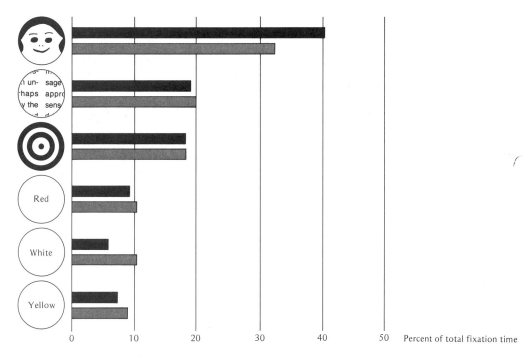

Figure 3.2 Stimuli that interest babies of different ages. Importance of pattern rather than color or brightness is illustrated by infants' responses to a face, newsprint, a bull's-eye, and plain red, white, and yellow disks. Black bars show the results for infants two to three months old. (From Robert L. Fantz, The origin of form perception, in *Scientific American*, 1961, vol. 204. Copyright © 1961 by Scientific American, Inc. All rights reserved.)

The Nonvisual Senses. The other sensory systems critical to early development also mature during infancy. Much less, however, is known about the nonvisual senses than about sight. The **tactile sense** (touch), used throughout life as a major source of information about the outside world, clearly begins to function during this stage. Infants constantly explore the environment by putting things in their mouths or touching them with their hands or feet. They also are extremely responsive to being touched by others. A parent's touch, for example, is capable of changing the neonatal state from sleep to wakeful activity. Touch is also important to the development of both social and cognitive functioning, as we shall see in Chapter 4.

   Audition, the ability to hear sounds and to discriminate among them, increases rapidly with chronological age. Infants as young as five or six weeks discriminate among different specific sounds (Appleton, Clifton, and Goldberg 1975). By four or five months they look in the correct direction for a rattle when a parent shakes it and then hides it from sight. The **olfactory sense** (smell) also is present at birth and develops with age. Infants a few months old are likely to exhibit strenuous

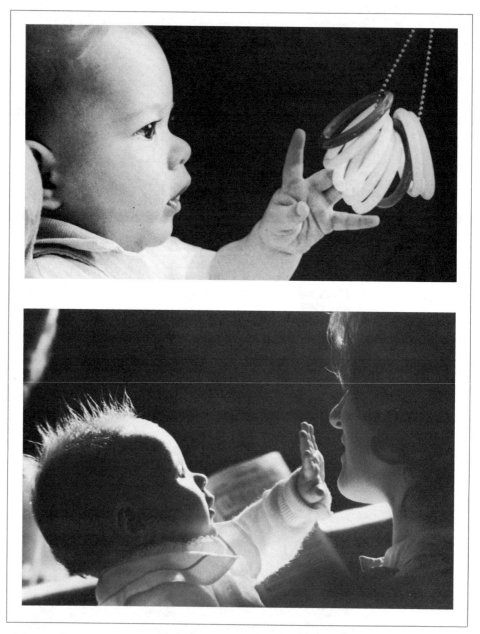

Vision and touch are important means by which the infant explores the environment.

avoidance responses, such as squirming or crying when they come in contact with extremely unpleasant smells.

The various sensory systems develop in relationship to one another and to the learned perceptual ability in the developing infant. For example, the **vestibular sense,** concerned with perception of body position and movement, is mediated through the inner ear and stimulated by the starting and stopping of head movements. This complex sense provides a good example of sensory interrelationship. The development of both vestibular and tactile orientation to the outside world is related in many ways to visual perceptual ability. When parents touch their babies and hold them in vertical positions, the infants are noticeably more visually alert (Korner and Thoman 1970). Newborn infants are relatively insensitive to pain; parents can lightly pinch them without getting much of a response. But sensitivity to pain increases rapidly with age.

Researchers have been increasingly interested in discovering whether the senses of infants are integrated and coordinated. Bower (1977*b*) believes that the senses are coordinated and that this coordination is innate. He uses as his evidence that infants look toward the sources of sounds and that they try to grasp objects they see. Bower, Broughton, and Moore (1970) showed that infants as young as seven days to six months had sight and grasping coordinated. They gave infants specially designed goggles and showed them objects projected by a shadow caster. The infants responded to the sight of the images by crying. Bower and his colleagues assumed that the crying was evidence of frustration caused by their not being able to reach the objects. They used this study as evidence that grasping and vision are coordinated.

Other researchers, while agreeing that vision, audition, and touch are coordinated at an early age, disagree with Bower and his colleagues that this coordination is innate and present at birth. Some researchers have been unable to cause distress in infants under five months when he presented them with objects that they could see but not touch. Clearly, coordination of the senses occurs at early ages. Whether or not this coordination is present at birth, however, is still unclear.

Sensorimotor Behavior

As mentioned in Chapter 1, Piaget (1952*b*) described the first two years of life as the sensorimotor period. It is during this period that the abilities to sense and to perceive the outside world and the motor behaviors appropriate to these perceptions are developed. During the first two years, according to Piaget, sensorimotor development causes the beginning of truly intelligent behavior. Increased ability to respond occurs largely through coordination of sensory and motor functioning. Large muscle activities (usually referred to as gross motor behavior) related to posture and locomotion develop. Small muscle activities (referred to often as fine motor-adaptive activities) coordinate sensory input with muscle movement. A good example of the way fine motor-adaptive behavior increases the ability to manipulate this environment is the baby's increasing ability to manipulate objects. The infant first learns to shake a rattle to make noise and later learns to find blocks hidden under a blanket. When older, the baby will learn to use a knife, fork, and spoon. By learning to control his or her body and the objects in the world around, the infant evolves from an individual with limited mobility to a highly mobile person.

Neonates are born with what Pavlov (1927) called **orienting responses.** They are capable of turning their sensory receptors toward particular stimuli. They also are born with ability to produce change in the environment. For example, newborns can turn their heads, changing the visual and kinesthetic stimuli surrounding them. They can cry, creating new sounds. They seem at this early age to be looking at the world almost as if it were a continuous panorama of fleeting images. Young infants are unable to control arm and hand muscles and thus are prohibited from reaching out and stopping the objects passing before them. Their grasping reflexes, however, do develop rapidly into reaching responses. Soon they will be able to reach out, grasp, and stop these objects.

Prehension: Reaching and Grasping. The first step toward the development of **prehension** (ability to reach for and grasp objects) occurs with control of arm movements. Such control develops gradually through a series of steps. Arm movements eventually become coordinated with already-present responses to produce successful grasping behavior. Between five and eight months, infants approach and grasp toys presented to them. After six months, they can let go of the toys voluntarily once they have grasped them. Before that time, they often hold on until the object is pried loose. They can use their thumbs and index fingers to pluck small objects (such as raisins) from flat surfaces (Cratty 1979). By a year of age, they have even more motor control and try to build towers of two (and sometimes even more) blocks. By eighteen months, most infants can build four-block towers; they also are able to hold toys a way that enables another person to take them. By two years, six- or seven-block towers are likely.

Most two-year-olds also can turn the pages of a book at will; moreover, they can turn them one at a time, an extremely complex task! They have already learned to scribble with crayons and can make a variety of patterns with multiple- and single-line crossings (Cratty 1979). Voluntary control of the body to obtain what is wanted has been termed **volition** (Bruner 1968). Children now are purposeful in their grasping and reaching behavior. They enjoy picking up objects and placing them one after another in a container or throwing them out of the container onto the floor. They like to reach out and touch other people. They are capable of eye-to-eye contact.

This Russian baby displays fine motor coordination for his age (twelve months) when he places spools on a peg.

Locomotion. Figure 3.3 illustrates the sequence of motor development. Sensori-motor development proceeds in a cephalo-caudal (head-to-foot) direction. Development of the upper part of the body (including arms and hands) proceeds earlier and at a more rapid rate than development of lower parts of the body. Cross-cultural research has shown that infants reared in traditional preindustrial communities in Africa, Asia, Australia, and Central America tend to show a distinct acceleration in development of their neck and back muscles when compared to American babies during the first six months of life (Werner 1979).

Although there is a great deal of variation, both from culture to culture and from individual to individual, in the ages that babies develop ability to make certain responses, researchers have noted some ages that most American babies develop specific abilities. In the third month, for example, many infants can turn from their backs to their stomachs by themselves. At three or four months of age, they usually

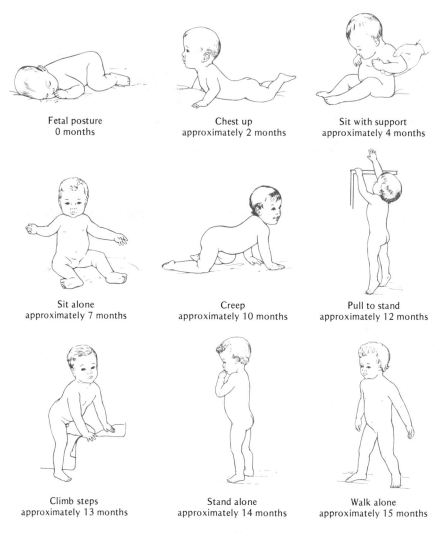

Fetal posture
0 months

Chest up
approximately 2 months

Sit with support
approximately 4 months

Sit alone
approximately 7 months

Creep
approximately 10 months

Pull to stand
approximately 12 months

Climb steps
approximately 13 months

Stand alone
approximately 14 months

Walk alone
approximately 15 months

Figure 3.3   The sequence of motor development (Adapted from Shirley 1933).

can sit for several minutes with support. At about seven or eight months, they are usually able to sit for several minutes without support, a major step toward ability to move about in the environment. By about nine months, most infants are able to sit unsupported for longer periods of time, usually for about ten minutes.

Most infants begin to creep (get around on all fours) at about six or seven months and can move about quite skillfully this way by eight and one-half months. All babies progress from sitting to creeping to walking stages in the same order, although some babies skip one or more of the intermediate steps. Before the end of the first year, many babies begin pulling themselves to a standing position. The average age for walking without support is about fifteen months for babies in the United States, although many babies can walk unaided by twelve months or earlier. Walking adds a new dimension to the infant's control of the physical and social environment. Psychologists have reported that during this period, children demonstrate new feelings of competence, accompanied by attempts to assert themselves. Assertion is exhibited in a number of ways. A one-year-old's behavior is characterized by a large number of negative responses; although parents rarely mention it, the first word of a twelve to fifteen-month-old baby is often, "No!"

THE BEGINNINGS OF LANGUAGE

Within a few weeks after birth the infant begins to create new sounds. Noncrying vocalization has been reported in infants as young as three weeks old. Three-week-old babies make fussing sounds. By four months, nearly all babies smile, laugh, and coo selectively. The number of vowel sounds gradually increases in the infant's response repertoire, from 4.5 sounds at two months to 11.4 sounds at thirty months. The number of consonants increases from 2.7 sounds at two months to 15.8 sounds at thirty months (Chen and Irwin 1946).

Babbling consists of repeating vowel and consonant sounds. From three to six months, the baby babbles when excited. The amount of babbling has been found to be associated with the amount of attention given the infant. Three-month-olds babble more when their parents respond to this behavior with smiles and touching (Rheingold, Gewirtz, and Ross 1959). At six months, babies babble socially and use their growing repertoire of sounds to attract and respond to adult vocalizations.

Infant understanding precedes speech. Understanding of simple adult speech has been reported in infants eight and nine months old (Church 1966). But although eight- or nine-month-old babies often understand what their parents mean when they say "no!," they will not begin to say "no!" themselves until three to six months later.

At between ten months and one year, the first linguistic utterances occur. Earliest speech is made up of reduplicated syllables formed from sounds the baby hears and imitates. Typical baby words are "bye-bye," "Mama," "Dada," and "no." This early speech, referred to as **holophrastic speech,** includes single-word utterances used to express whole ideas (Dale 1972). When year-old children say "milk," they might mean that they want milk, or they might mean that they want the listener to look at the glass of milk on the table. Both context and intonation can help the listener understand what a child's holophrastic speech means.

During the first half of the second year, the young child builds a vocabulary from about three words to fifty words. By two years, holophrastic speech decreases. Two-word phrases and short sentences are common in two-year-old speech.

HIGHLIGHT 3.3   FROM HOLOPHRASTIC SPEECH TO SENTENCES

The following conversation is between a 19-month-old girl and her mother, who has just come home from work. The child is in the process of changing from holophrastic speech to more complex phrasing and sentences.

Child: "Mommy."

Mother: "Hi, Sally. Where did you get that truck?"

Child: "Truck."

Mother: "Can you make it go?"

Child: "Go fast. See. Truck."

Mother: "Yes, the truck is red."

Child: "Dress off."

Mother: "Yes, I'm taking off my dress."

Child: "Dress chair."

Mother: "Where's Daddy?"

Child: "Daddy there."

Mother: "Let's go see Daddy."

Child: "Daddy."

Mother: "Why don't you stay with Daddy, and I'll see what's happening in the kitchen."

Child: "Daddy."

Mother: "I'll get dinner on the table soon."

Child: "Sally hungry."

Mother: "Would you like chicken soup?"

Child: "Chicken." "Pick napkin."

Mother: "Thank you for picking up the napkin. Put it on the table, please."

Child: "Napkin table."

Mother: "Now let's wash you before dinner."

Child: "Wash off."

Mother: "Where's the washcloth?"

Child: "Washcloth. Here. Dirty all gone."

QUESTIONS FOR THOUGHT

1. Which of the child's utterances demonstrate the holophrastic speech?

2. Which speech involves more complex phrasing?

Language development is related directly to the child's growing motor ability. Indeed, language development is even more directly correlated with motor development than it is with chronological age. Children who have little or no opportunity to hear spoken language will, however, develop language deficits, regardless of their motor development.

COGNITIVE DEVELOPMENT: THE SENSORIMOTOR PERIOD

According to Piaget, early sensorimotor development accounts for future cognitive functioning. Piaget described the changes that characterize the developing child during the first two years (the sensorimotor stage) as a series of discrete and qualitatively different substages. These stages enable the child progressively to respond to the environment in increasingly complex ways and eventually to think and solve problems in mature ways.

Intellectual development occurs as the young child begins to organize sets of ideas into a coherent mental system that can be used to solve problems. As noted in Chapter 1, Piaget calls this the child's cognitive structure or schema. According to Piaget, in the first two years, the cognitive structure develops through increasing sensorimotor abilities. Infants respond to the world around them through their senses. Their growing abilities to respond to perceived stimuli allow them to progress from simpler to more advanced stages of development. As they progress from one stage to the next, they go from periods in which they are in the process of learning to make use of objects (disequilibrium) to later periods in which they become capable of using these objects in useful ways (equilibrium).

This equilibrium is not permanent. It allows infants to extend their environments and to create a new disequilibrium. The six-month-old baby in the playpen has not developed sufficient muscular strength to use the playpen bars as a way to pull to a standing position. As the baby works on this task, we say the child is again in a state of disequilibrium. For a time after mastering the task of standing, the child will be in equilibrium but quickly will begin to use the bars in new ways and to learn to make new types of responses. Babies have access to a great many new objects, most of which they have to learn to use. As a baby works on each new task, we say that the child is in a state of disequilibrium.

Equilibration, Piaget's name for this continuous process, assumes the interplay of two processes discussed in Chapter 1, assimilation and accommodation. Assimilation occurs when infants use new objects to perform activities they already know how to do. A good example of assimilation by young babies is adjusting to sucking bottle nipples after having been exclusively breast-fed. Accommodation occurs when new activities are added to the infant's repertoire of responses. As infants increase the number of stimuli to which they respond (assimilate), they simultaneously increase the number of new responses they are able to make (accommodate).

Compared to Western babies, African infants tend to develop sensorimotor abilities far more quickly. Konner (1977) studied nomadic and rural African and Asian infants and suggested that their accelerated sensorimotor development seems to be related to a greater amount of stimulation, particularly touch provided by their care givers, as compared to that provided Western babies.

The following order of stages occurs for all infants. The specific age at which each state is predicted, however, applies directly only to infants brought up in our own Western culture. Cross-cultural studies of children from five continents have verified the sequence and structural properties of these stages (Werner 1979). The quantitative aspects of the theory (the rate of development through the stages) are, however, subject to considerable variation.

Reflexive Stage

During the first month of life, the infant proceeds through what Piaget calls the **reflexive stage** of development. During this time, innate reflexive responses, such as sucking and grasping, become more efficient and more generalized. For example, infants' reaching abilities improve, and they learn to reach out not only for their mothers' nipples but also for rattles placed in the line of vision. These accommodative responses allow the infant, in turn, to assimilate the objects grasped into the cognitive structure.

Primary Circular Reactions

After one month and through the fourth month, infants begin to perform more and more complex behaviors. They do this through what Piaget described as a series of circular (repetitive) reactions to the environment; these are active behaviors that gradually accommodate infants to the experiences around them. At first, they willfully repeat new actions over and over again, apparently for the sake of performing them. For example, infants wave their hands over their heads over and over again or kick the side of the crib repeatedly with the same motion. Piaget is careful to point out that at this stage, babies lack apparent intention—that is, "even when the child grasps a new object to suck or look at it, one cannot infer that there is a conscious purpose" (Piaget 1952b, p. 143). Piaget called this the **primary circular reaction stage.**

For the first two months, infants prefer familiar stimuli. Even at this early age, memory of some sort exists. One evidence of infant memory is that before ten weeks of age, infants show **habituation**—that is, they become accustomed to familiar stimuli and pay less attention to them. For example, they will stop responding to household sounds they are accustomed to hearing.

At three months, the infant has no sense of the permanence of objects. "Out of sight, out of mind" is an apt description at this stage. If the parents of a three-month-old lean over the crib to play and then leave, the baby will not look around for them. At this age, infants show no fear of strangers. Parents usually can take their baby with them when they go to a friend's for an evening. Fear of strange people and places will not be a concern until much later.

Secondary Circular Reactions

This stage, **the secondary circular reaction stage,** begins during the fourth month and lasts until the eighth month. At this point in cognitive development, infant behaviors give the appearance of being "almost intentional." The baby might reach for a string of rattles hanging over the crib, shake them, and exhibit surprise at the result. The infant will now begin to repeat the action in order to observe the results.

At about six months, babies begin to demonstrate some understanding of the notion of object permanence. Gradually, they begin to search for hidden objects. When a parent displays a rattle and then hides it from sight, the six-month-old will look around for it. At first, the infant does not remember easily where the rattle last appeared and the baby searches in the wrong places.

Coordination of Secondary Reactions and Schemata

During the period of development from eight or nine months of age through the first year, babies begin to apply what they have already learned to new situations. They still repeat behaviors again and again to draw attention to themselves. They exhibit a definite sense of intention and goal direction in engaging in an activity. They are gaining more sense of object permanence. By twelve months, the baby will look for an object that has been seen and then hidden.

Tertiary Circular Reactions

The period from twelve to eighteen months marks what Piaget termed the **tertiary circular reaction stage.** Major achievements of this period are the infant's understanding of the notion of causality (cause and effect) and the concept of **object permanence,** the realization that objects continue to exist when they are out of sight, touch, or some other perceptual contact. The infant is now getting ready to begin naming objects, the first step toward putting them into categories, what Piaget called **classification.**

By eighteen months of age, children have learned that objects still exist and that they can move about to find them, even though the objects might not be seen. Now when a parent removes a Teddy bear from the crib to be cleaned in the washing machine, the baby will hunt for it. This period of development is a period of exploring the environment and learning by trial and error.

Object permanence develops gradually. This infant pays attention to the toy when it is directly in view (a), but when it is blocked, she does not seem to realize that it is still there (b). An older infant would look for the toy behind the paper.

Mental Combinations

The period from eighteen to twenty-four months marks what Piaget termed the **mental combination stage.** The cognitive structure now enables children to think before they act. They spend less time in searching for items they cannot find and use their memories to help locate what they want. Piaget described a situation in which his daughter Jacqueline was playing with a number of toys—a fish, a swan, and a frog. Later, while putting all of the toys in a box, Jacqueline noticed that the frog was missing. She then carefully took the toys out, put them together in a group, and only then began systematically to hunt for the frog. Careful planning was used in her search (Piaget 1952*a*).

INFANT LEARNING

In the first two years, infants are capable of many different types of learning. Here we will consider the major theories explaining the way infant learning takes place.

Conditioning

According to learning theorists, learning in infancy occurs through both classical and operant conditioning. Neonates, for example, can be classically conditioned to make sucking responses when such signals as sounds or lights are paired with presentation of milk (Lippsitt and Kaye 1964; Brackbill and Koltsova 1967). Ten-day-old infants also have been classically conditioned to blink when a tone signals a puff of air to the eye (Little 1971). Sucking responses of newborns have been conditioned by operant procedures as well (Siqueland and Lipsitt 1966; Stone, Smith, and Murphy 1973).

Research has shown that the infant also is capable of learning simple intellectual skills and cognitive strategies through operant conditioning. Operant-conditioning studies using five-month-old babies have shown that infants at this age can learn, under experimental conditions, to make certain responses, such as sucking hard on a nipple attached to devices that measure strength of sucking. By doing so, the infant obtains reinforcements, such as pleasurable sounds (Papousek 1967). Once babies have learned to make specific responses in specific situations, however, it is very difficult for them to change their behavior. This is true even when the behaviors are no longer useful to them (Appleton, Clifton, and Goldberg 1975).

Motivation

Infant learning has also been explained by motivational theory. One response studied frequently by motivational theorists is the infant's sucking response. Newborn infants rather quickly develop strong needs for food. We cannot assume that they know that feeding will reduce their need for food; they have not yet been fed through their mouths. According to motivational theorists, babies' hunger drives compel them to activity, accounting for much of an infant's early crying behavior. The longer babies go hungry, the longer they can be expected to cry. When they are fed, motivational theorists assume, drive reduction takes place, and crying behavior therefore ceases. As babies get older, they experience drive reduction through their mothers' breasts many times and come to learn that breast-feeding reduces hunger drive. Now, according to the motivation theorist, motivated behavior occurs: The babies have learned to direct their activities toward obtaining a very particular goal, the breast. At this point, many mothers report that their babies have learned also to communicate their needs. The mother now can tell whether a baby is hungry or wet or sick by the particular sound of the baby's cries.

Another drive often discussed by motivational theorists is the **exploratory drive.** According to some psychologists, infants have a need to explore their environments. This need is manifested through a variety of exploratory activities—throwing toys, putting objects in their mouths, touching them with their hands. Exploratory play is thought by many psychologists to be a necessary part of learning.

Social Learning

Much of a baby's first learning of social behavior occurs through imitation of adult behavior. Psychologists studying social learning of babies report that early imitative responses involve immediate repetition of what the baby sees and hears. Familiar gestures and sounds, such as those the parents make to the infant, are copied (Bohannon and Marquis 1977; DePaulo and Bonvillian 1978). For example, when mother or father smiles at baby, baby smiles back. Similarly, the baby will babble in imitation of the parents' vocalizations. At first, babies are not able to reproduce what they see and hear with much accuracy. They have very short memory spans and so are able to imitate only what has occurred most recently. As they get older, however, imitative responses become more and more accurate. Eye contact between parents and their infants is very important in this phase of development (Riess 1978). Toward the end of the second year, children imitate sounds with great accuracy and may deliberately imitate behavior they have seen or heard hours or even days earlier, such as what directions their mother or father gave them about getting ready for dinner (Piaget 1951). Parents can learn a lot about developing verbal behavior of their offspring by listening to the baby alone in the crib.

Social-emotional Responding. Emotional behavior—that is, behavior expressive of the infant's feelings—does not seem to be present at birth. Even though the baby cries, this crying seems to be a reflexive response rather than an emotional one. Many years ago Watson (1919) first described what he called "response systems" present in the neonate at birth. He identified three major emotional responses: (1) love, characterized by a calm demeanor elicited in the neonate when stroked gently; (2) fear, an outgrowth of the startle response elicited by sudden movements, loss of support, or sudden loud noises; and (3) rage, crying, excited movement, and a flushing of the face, caused primarily by preventing movement of the infant's arms and legs.

Bridges (1932) gave another picture of developing emotional behavior in the infant. She suggested that neonatal behavior is expressive of one emotion only, excitement. According to Bridges, other emotions develop gradually and are characterized by an increasing number of responses as the infant gets older. For example, noticeable fear responses first became apparent at about one month, noticeable delight at two months. Later, anger, fear, disgust, jealousy, and other emotions gradually make their appearance.

Why do different emotional behaviors appear at different ages? The answer is not clear. Some psychologists, Bridges among them, assume simply that emotional behavior matures. Others theorize that interaction with the environment significantly affects the developing emotional response. Still others stress that it is difficult to differentiate specific emotions in infants. It is clear that the extent to which objects in the environment do affect emotional responding increases with the age of the child. In addition, the range of objects that can produce excitation and later distress is greater than the range of those that elicit calm behavior (Reese and Lipsitt 1970).

Fear Responses. Watson, Bridges, and other researchers who have studied the development of emotional behavior have noted that such responses as crying, responses that we associate with fear, appear very early in life. Loud noises, sharp movements, lack of support and pain all can produce crying in one-month-old babies.

Many other acquired fears appear after about nine months of age. The famous case of Baby Albert (described in Chapter 1) who was classically conditioned to fear white rats and other soft furry animals is an example of one way that fears can be learned through conditioning. Fear responses are also learned through modeling. Parents who fear insects are likely to have children who also are afraid of them.

Attachment and Stranger Anxiety. Mothers of very young infants generally can soothe their babies with soft, gentle movements and gentle contact. Mothers of young infants often hold their babies when they want them to sleep, cooing softly and rocking them. Later, when babies reach seven or eight months, they develop feelings of **attachment** or affection toward their mothers or other primary caregivers. In Chapter 4, we will discuss ways that caregivers increase this attachment.

Stranger anxiety, fear of strange people, also appears in babies at about seven months and reaches a peak at about eight months. The typical responses of the fearful baby to a new person are whimpering and clinging to the mother. Ainsworth (1967) noted that the infant's anxiety develops at the same time as the growing understanding that the presence of her mother or primary caregiver coincides with safety and security. Ainsworth hypothesized that an unfamiliar person represents to the infant a discrepancy between what is known, familiar, and therefore safe and what is unknown and therefore potentially threatening. Her hypothesis, known as the **discrepancy hypothesis,** suggests that stranger anxiety develops from a fear of this discrepancy, which in turn develops from an increasingly complex and sophisticated set of expectations. The child assumes that it is far safer to remain in an environment where one knows that one is safe than to remain where there are strange and therefore unpredictable people.

Schaffer (1974) theorized that stranger anxiety develops in a series of stages. He proposed that stranger anxiety, as it appears in young, seven-month-old infants, is due to these infants' becoming aware that a stranger does not match any images of people they already know and that they have stored in their memories. Stranger anxiety as it appears in older infants (eight months and beyond) may occur for more complex reasons. The older infant may perceive the stranger not only as discrepant in many respects with images of known people stored in the memory, but also as similar in many respects. Older infants are confused by the knowledge that the appearance of a new stranger matches their own mother's in many ways, yet at the same time, the stranger is not a parent. The resulting confusion causes an infant to withdraw from a stranger.

Trust and Autonomy. Erikson (1963) pointed out that the development of trust or mistrust begins in the first year of life as the infant learns from early caregiving just how safe the environment is. Infants who receive sufficient attention and affection as well as consistent handling from their caregivers gradually learn that the world is a safe and secure place in which to live. Infants who receive painful or inconsistent treatment from their caregivers learn that the world is untrustworthy and unpredictable.

Toddlers, as they continue to discover their own bodies and to explore feeding, dressing, and toileting, develop responses that Erikson termed autonomy or doubt. Toddlers who are successful in their attempts to do things for themselves and are rewarded for these attempts develop feelings of autonomy. Toddlers who fail in their attempts or who are punished by their caregivers develop senses of self that include feelings of self-doubt.

Social Smiling and Parallel Play. Smiling is another social response that has received attention from child psychologists. Reflexive smiling occurs at birth. It appears in bursts and occurs more frequently in premature babies than in full-term infants. After two and one-half to three months, a baby smiles in response to many stimuli in the environment.

By far, the stimulus that produces the greatest amount of smiling is the human face. At four months, infants will smile at faces that smile back. They even will smile at a photograph of a human face. By seven months, babies learn not only to smile

One-year-old infants engage in egocentric play. Although other infants are nearby, each seems uninterested in what the others are doing.

at faces but also to respond differently to different facial expressions. Wolff (1963) charted the course of babies' smiles in response to human faces and found that the behavior of smiling at human faces peaked somewhere between sixteen and twenty weeks. After this age, babies apparently begin to discriminate between faces they will respond to by smiling and those to which they will not respond to at all.

Infants also gradually begin to interact in other social ways. One-year-olds engage in **egocentric play**—that is, they are absorbed in their own play and seem uninterested in what other children playing near them are doing. At age two, **parallel play** develops. At this point, the child does not truly interact with peers but imitates their play behavior step by step. Social stimuli are very exciting to the two-year-old, who is likely to want the blocks or balls with which other toddlers are playing.

Developmental Tests of Infant Learning *notes.*

A number of tests have been designed to measure various aspects of infant development. The purpose is to make it possible to compare any one infant with other infants of the same age. Because children under two years of age cannot solve complex cognitive problems, most scales make use of sensorimotor perceptual tasks for this age level. Gross motor behaviors, vocalizations and language behaviors, fine motor behaviors, and social behaviors have been studied in relation to sensorimotor abilities.

One example of a typical and popular developmental test measuring these abilities is the Denver Developmental Screening Test (Frankenburg and Dodds 1969). A scoring sheet from this test as well as a set of directions for the tester are shown in Fig 3.4. Children taking the test are measured on such factors as ability to kick a ball forward, throw a ball overhand, point to various parts of the body, build towers of blocks, care for oneself (feeding, dressing, toileting), and help at specific household tasks.

Psychologists generally agree that the developmental state of an infant in the first year, as measured by these tests, is a poor predictor of later development. The data seem to suggest, however, that cognitive and perceptual–motor development are related. For example, items on the California First Year Mental Scale that measure perceptual–motor ability have the greatest predictive value for estimating later cognitive ability. Such items include problems requiring eye–hand coordination, attention, and ability to continue searching for an object after it is hidden.

Studies using the Bayley Scale, another popular scale of development, show that before fifteen months, no differences in developmental scores can be determined for babies of different races, sexes, birth orders, geographical locations, or parent educations (Bayley 1965). This seems to suggest that many of the differences in ability that we observe in older children are related to their experiences.

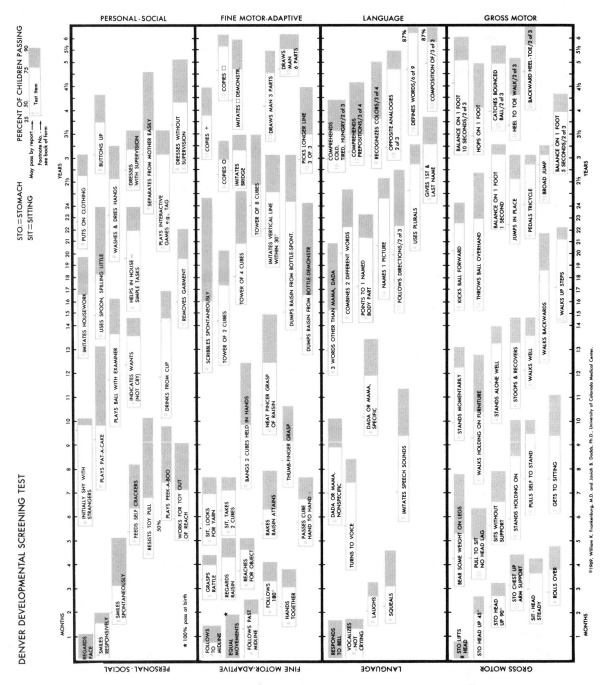

Figure 3.4 Denver Developmental Screening Test. (left) A scoring sheet showing ages at which children are expected to perform gross motor, language, fine motor–adaptive, and personal–social tasks. (right) Directions for administering the test. (Reprinted by permission of William K. Frankenburg, M.D. and Josiah B. Dodds, Ph.D. University of Colorado Medical Center.)

1. Try to get child to smile by smiling, talking or waving to him. Do not touch him.
2. When child is playing with toy, pull it away from him. Pass if he resists.
3. Child does not have to be able to tie shoes or button in the back.
4. Move yarn slowly in an arc from one side to the other, about 6" above child's face.
   Pass if eyes follow 90° to midline. (Past midline; 180°)
5. Pass if child grasps rattle when it is touched to the backs or tips of fingers.
6. Pass if child continues to look where yarn disappeared or tries to see where it went. Yarn
   should be dropped quickly from sight from tester's hand without arm movement.
7. Pass if child picks up raisin with any part of thumb and a finger.
8. Pass if child picks up raisin with the ends of thumb and index finger using an over hand
   approach.

  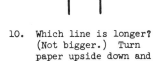

9. Pass any en-   10. Which line is longer?   11. Pass any   12. Have child copy
   closed form.   (Not bigger.) Turn   crossing   first. If failed,
   Fail continuous   paper upside down and   lines.   demonstrate
   round motions.   repeat. (3/3 or 5/6)

When giving items 9, 11 and 12, do not name the forms. Do not demonstrate 9 and 11.

13. When scoring, each pair (2 arms, 2 legs, etc.) counts as one part.
14. Point to picture and have child name it. (No credit is given for sounds only.)

15. Tell child to: Give block to Mommie; put block on table; put block on floor. Pass 2 of 3.
    (Do not help child by pointing, moving head or eyes.)
16. Ask child: What do you do when you are cold? ..hungry? ..tired? Pass 2 of 3.
17. Tell child to: Put block on table; under table; in front of chair, behind chair.
    Pass 3 of 4. (Do not help child by pointing, moving head or eyes.)
18. Ask child: If fire is hot, ice is ?; Mother is a woman, Dad is a ?; a horse is big, a
    mouse is ?. Pass 2 of 3.
19. Ask child: What is a ball? ..lake? ..desk? ..house? ..banana? ..curtain? ..ceiling?
    ..hedge? ..pavement? Pass if defined in terms of use, shape, what it is made of or general
    category (such as banana is fruit, not just yellow). Pass 6 of 9.
20. Ask child: What is a spoon made of? ..a shoe made of? ..a door made of? (No other objects
    may be substituted.) Pass 3 of 3.
21. When placed on stomach, child lifts chest off table with support of forearms and/or hands.
22. When child is on back, grasp his hands and pull him to sitting. Pass if head does not hang back.
23. Child may use wall or rail only, not person. May not crawl.
24. Child must throw ball overhand 3 feet to within arm's reach of tester.
25. Child must perform standing broad jump over width of test sheet. (8-1/2 inches)
26. Tell child to walk forward, ⤳ heel within 1 inch of toe.
    Tester may demonstrate. Child must walk 4 consecutive steps, 2 out of 3 trials.
27. Bounce ball to child who should stand 3 feet away from tester. Child must catch ball with
    hands, not arms, 2 out of 3 trials.
28. Tell child to walk backward, ⤺ toe within 1 inch of heel.
    Tester may demonstrate. Child must walk 4 consecutive steps, 2 out of 3 trials.

DATE AND BEHAVIORAL OBSERVATIONS (how child feels at time of test, relation to tester, attention
span, verbal behavior, self-confidence, etc,):

DEVELOPMENTAL HAZARDS IN INFANCY

The first two years of life are critically important in human development. They are exciting to parents and caregivers who regard each change as a signpost that new stages are being reached and new abilities are being accomplished. Unfortunately, some infants encounter difficulties during their development that may threaten their mental or physical growth. We know, for example, that babies deprived of adequate sensory stimulation or nutrition during infancy may well be retarded in later life in many aspects of their development. It is no accident that American pediatricians are more and more frequently advising breast-feeding if American mothers can manage it. The 1978 report of the Committee on Nutrition of the American Academy of Pediatrics devoted considerable space to advocating breast-feeding, not only because of the nutritional and biochemical advantages but also because of the greater intimacy and tactile stimulation it provides the infant.

Crises in infancy may occur for a variety of reasons. One developmental hazard that is increasingly prevalent is lack of adequate nutrition.

Inadequate Nutrition

Poor nutrition produces detrimental and often irreversible effects on the development of the skeletal system, bodily organs, brain, and other parts of the central nervous system. In the prenatal period, as we have already noted, the brain develops faster than other parts of the body and is particularly vulnerable to damage.

Inadequate nutrition caused by insufficient calories, protein, or both can retard ability to learn and can impair memory. Nutritional problems are the cause of fundamental deficits in attention. Because of low energy levels, one-year-olds who are malnourished often have difficulty making appropriate orienting responses to and learning from new stimuli. Protein deficiency is related to apathy in infants and to abnormalities in their encephalographic records (recordings of brain waves). (See, for example, Citizens' Board of Inquiry into Hunger and Malnutrition in the United States 1968; Eichenwald and Fry 1969; Lester 1975; 1976.) Long-term effects, such as abnormally slow gains in height and weight, anemia, and problems of social adjustment, continue to affect these unfortunate children, although in some cases, if nutritional problems are totally corrected after the first two years, many of the worst results might be decreased (Winick, Meyer, and Harris 1975). Figure 3.5 shows graphically the effect of different animal protein intake on scores of preschool children on tests of mental capability.

Undernutrition is related to social behavior of young children and their caregivers and to psychological and physical problems of young children. Guthrie, Masangkay, and Guthrie (1976) reported examples of infants from impoverished backgrounds with histories of undernourishment. By the time these infants were eighteen months old, even when food was available, they tended to resist parental urging

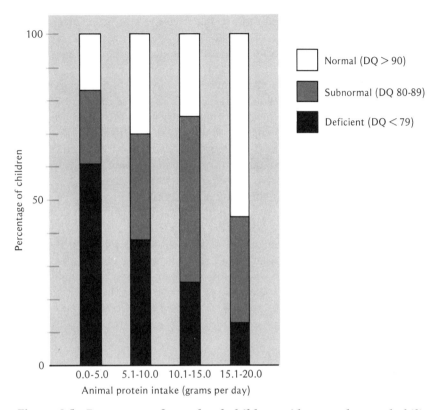

Figure 3.5 Percentage of preschool children with normal mental abilities and mental deficiencies (as measured by the Gesell test of ability) and with differing amounts of animal protein intake (Moenckenberg 1973).

to get them to eat or to behave actively. They tended to avoid responding in any way whenever possible; often they refused to eat when food was presented, avoided eye contact, and even refused to answer. The result was a vicious cycle: Infants who were undernourished developed social behaviors that continued the pattern of undernourishment.

Nutritional deficiency has been related indirectly to mental capability. One researcher (Cravioto 1969) pointed out three ways in which this can happen: (1) Children who are undernourished become ill more often than properly nourished children and thus miss out on many opportunities to learn; (2) hungry, undernourished children frequently have low levels of concentration and low motivation in school; and (3) malnutrition is linked to poverty. Undernourished children often are deprived of the social learning situations associated with mealtime in middle-class families when they do not have the opportunity to participate in dinner table conversation.

Unfortunately, the last decade has brought increased undernutrition in many parts of the world. Today, more than half the children of the world may suffer the effects of early undernutrition. Alarming dietary deficiencies exist among the poor in our own country as well as in less developed countries, such as India, Cambodia (Kampuchea), and many African countries where famine is common.

It is important to realize that these detrimental effects are not, however, restricted to poor people. They can and do occur with any population, poor or financially sound. High income alone does not ensure good diet or good health. Today, middle-class and affluent Americans often give their children such nonnutritive foods as potato chips and soft drinks.

Overfeeding and excessive nutrition can cause problems just as well as undernutrition. Researchers know now that the fat cells that are formed in the first year of life remain in the body through adulthood. The baby who becomes obese during the first year of life stands a greater chance of becoming an obese adult than does the baby who gains a proper amount of weight (Wyden 1971). A problem in our affluent society today, ironically, is obesity of infants as well as adults.

This Guatemalan infant shows the effects of malnutrition during both the prenatal and postnatal periods.

High-risk Babies. Infants categorized at birth as high-risk babies may have a variety of problems. Some high-risk babies are so labeled because of low birth weights. Others may be so labeled because of other problems, such as respiratory distress (breathing problems). We discussed in Chapter 2 the sudden infant death syndrome (SIDS), which each year causes some 10,000 infants in the United States to die suddenly and unexpectedly, apparently because of respiratory disorders.

Failure-to-Thrive Syndrome. Another developmental hazard that affects as many as three percent of infants is the **failure-to-thrive syndrome** (FTTS). FTTS babies fail to achieve normal physical growth even though physicians cannot detect any physiological disorder. Before four months, FTTS babies show a number of behavioral symptoms: They tend to be more watchful than other babies, smile far less frequently, and make fewer sounds. In the next six months, they are noticeable for their lack of stranger anxiety, lack of attachment to their primary caregivers, general passivity, retarded motor development, and abnormally quiet behavior.

One cause of many of these behavioral symptoms is undernutrition. Researchers have noted that FTTS babies frequently exhibit a feeding disturbance in which they refuse food or accept only very small quantities (Leonard, Rhymes, and Solnit 1966). Thus they often deprive themselves of proper nutrition even when adequate nourishment is available to them.

What causes such apparently self-destructive behavior? Ramey, Hieger, and Klisz (1972) suggested that a primary problem is learning insufficiency caused by inadequate caregiving. Mothers of FTTS infants tend to ignore their babies far more than do mothers of normal infants. When they do respond to their infants, it is often in negative ways. These mothers, for the most part, seem to be unaware of their infants' needs and unaware that they are not providing enough attention (Pollitt, Eichler, and Chan 1975; Pollitt and Eichler 1976).

Although the specific mechanisms that appear to cause FTTS are not completely clear at this time, Lipsitt (1979) suggests that it is possible that these babies have not learned or been taught to produce adequate responses necessary for proper development. In many cases where mothers are taught how to respond to their infants, FTTS babies gradually develop normal responding. In other cases, parental education is not sufficient to counteract the apparently self-destructive behavior. Weakened by undernourishment, some FTTS infants succumb to other disorders. Lipsitt (1979, p. 972) points out that these infants "may be the victims of learning disabilities that we are only beginning to understand."

INDIVIDUAL DIFFERENCES IN INFANT DEVELOPMENT

No two babies develop in exactly the same way in exactly the same time span, even when they encounter no developmental crises. Some babies are more active or more vocal than others; some develop their motor abilities more rapidly than others, some have far higher levels of stranger anxiety than do others, even when there are no noticeable differences in the caregiving they have received. Evidence to explain individual differences comes from two sources, research concerned with biological causes and research concerned with general environmental causes.

Biological Factors

Freedman (1979) pointed out striking differences in both temperament and behavior of babies from different ethnic groups. These differences, Freedman reported, were noticeable as early as the first few days of life and continue in childhood. Freedman suggests that Navajo Indian babies, for example, may remain calmly wrapped on their swaddling boards until they are about six months old, whereas non-Indian babies whose mothers have tried to use similar cradle boards found that their infants simply would not tolerate the confinement. Similarly, children in mainland Chinese preschools who have been observed by American psychologists were reported to be "far less restless, less intense in their motor actions," and displayed "less crying and whining than American children in similar situations" (Freedman 1979, p. 42).

Individual differences in physical makeup may affect development in a variety of ways. Physical handicaps or deformities noticeable at birth, for example, can affect later developmental progress. A good example is the infant who requires surgery in the first month or year of life, and who suffers maternal deprivation because of remaining in the hospital for long periods of time. Infants whose handicaps cannot be treated may be retarded in their motor, speech, or mental ability as they get older. These infants and their development will be discussed in Chapters 5, 6, and 7.

While some developmental differences may be more influenced by biological factors and others by environmental factors, it is extremely difficult to separate the two. Connell (1976) hypothesized that babies who tend to develop highly anxious attachments to their parents (see Chapter 4) might well be constitutionally different from other babies. At the same time, these babies may also be more affected by parental unresponsiveness than other babies. Freedman believes that biological makeup and environmental conditions are as inseparable as objects and their shadows. He suggests that many characteristics may develop before birth and later interact with environmental influences to produce different characteristics in different individuals.

Environmental Factors

The most important environmental cause of individual differences among babies in their first twenty-four months clearly is the caregiver. The importance of caregivers in providing stimulation and love cannot be underestimated. Those who provide adequate nourishment and stimulation tend to have babies who develop at more rapid rates than those who do not. Very young children whose parents tend to spend a great deal of time talking to them learn to speak early and are able to speak clearly and in a fashion similar to that of their parents (Ringler *et al.* 1978). Children who receive little verbal stimulation tend to develop speech much more slowly.

Lack of attention and stimulation by caregivers, whether they love their infants but are too busy to provide them with a great deal of attention or are simply uninterested in their youngsters, tends to produce retarded development. We will discuss caregiver–infant interaction in some detail in Chapter 4.

Birth order has been shown to be related to intellectual development in the early years. Zajonc (1976) developed a **confluence model,** which proposes a direct relationship between birth order and intellectual development when there is close spacing between children. Zajonc suggested that the reason for decreasing performance is that parents simply have less and less time to spend with each new infant born into the family. Thus successive infants receive less stimulation. He proposed therefore that parents allow more than two years between the births of successive children to give the older children the benefits of being in a smaller family for a longer period of time (Zajonc 1976, p. 230). Zajonc's theory has been supported by other researchers who also showed that IQ and birth order are related in the early years (Marjoriebanks 1978).

THE CASE OF SUSIE QUILLAN—A NORMALLY DEVELOPING, TWO-YEAR-OLD AMERICAN: A CASE STUDY FOR CLASS DISCUSSION

I. Identification and Sources of Information

Name: Susie Quillan

Address: 50 Oak Lane, Greenville, Oklahoma

Race: White

Age: Two years

Sources of information:

1. Personal observation
2. Interview with Susie's parents
3. Interview with Susie's pediatrician

II. Family History

Susie is the first child to be born to Mr. and Mrs. Quillan. Mr. and Mrs. Quillan, both 26 years old, live together with Mr. Quillan's parents on their farm. Mr. Quillan works daily with his father and expects to take the farm over when his dad retires in a few years.

Both the Quillans completed high school together in Greenville; Mr. Quillan continued his education for two years at a local agricultural college. The Quillans married when he returned and have made their home at the farm since. Mrs. Quillan worked as a dental hygienist in town until Susie was born. She has remained on the farm since that time, helping out with farm chores and sharing the raising of Susie with her mother-in-law.

III. Case History

Susie was born without complications at Greenville General Hospital. Her mother had practiced exercises for prepared childbirth and chose not to have any anesthetic administered during labor or delivery. The labor took seven hours. Susie was twenty-one inches long and weighed six pounds and eleven ounces. At two years old, she weighs twenty-seven

Continued

THE CASE OF SUSIE QUILLAN *(Cont.)*

pounds and is thirty-five inches tall. Susie has cut all of her baby teeth and, since she was twenty months old, has been eating regular foods at the table with the family. Susie's grandmother reports that Susie ate solid foods at an earlier age than she remembers giving it to her own babies. But the pediatrician advised it, and it seems to be working well.

Susie likes to play with toys, particularly a large rubber doll that her grandfather bought her as a Christmas present. When she was asked to do so, she named all the parts of the doll's body, including its fingers and fingernails. Another favorite toy is a book made from starched cloth that her mother sewed for her. Each page has pictures of different household items—forks, knives, plates, furniture of various sorts—and people. Susie can turn the pages of the book, and the family currently is working on teaching her the names of the people and objects in the pictures. When we asked Susie to tell us what some of the pictures were, however, she was not interested and sucked the book instead. When we moved the book away, however, she began to look for it. Not finding it among her other toys, she whimpered until we brought it back.

Susie has walked without support since she was fourteen months old, her mother told us proudly. The pediatrician told us that unlike most babies, Susie never creeped. She dragged herself around the floor on her arms. Then one day, she suddenly pulled herself to a standing position. The pediatrician chuckled, "The whole family was worried that something was wrong, even though I told them that many babies do this. They didn't stop worrying until she decided to stand and then walk—just like that."

Susie's speech has developed in similar fashion to most other babies. She has learned names for four critical people in the family, her parents and grandparents. She calls her mother and grandmother by the same name, "Mamama." The family has tried to teach her to call her grandmother "Grandma." Even though she repeats the word on request, however, whenever she wants either woman, she uses the basic "Mamama." Either woman seems to satisfy her and keeps her from being frightened in new situations. She is content as long as one of the women is within eyesight. Susie's mother was not able to breast-feed Susie because of an infection that caused her to be hospitalized for a brief time shortly after Susie's birth. Susie's grandmother took care of Susie while her mother was recuperating. Mrs. Quillan wonders whether Susie might have developed stronger feelings for her—"enough at least to distinguish me from my mother-in-law," she said somewhat plaintively—had she been able to breast-feed the child. But bottle-feeding had not seemed to hurt the baby.

Susie calls her father "Papapa." She sees her father at mealtimes and in the evenings, and she enjoys being put to bed and tucked in by him. Susie enjoys having her father take care of her at times when her mother and grandmother are busy with other things.

Susie's one single fear that the Quillan family worries about is the "spot on the wall." Susie does not like her parents to turn off the light in her room at night, and she cries when it is time to go to sleep. "The 'pot is there! The 'pot is there!" is the usual complaint. Once her parents understood what she was worried about (the "spot") they realized that what troubled her was a small shadow that came from the moonlight streaming across the tree outside her window. Susie does not like the window shade pulled, and today she still whimpers about the " 'pot," even though it is winter and all the leaves have fallen from the tree so that there is no sign of a shadow spot on the wall. Mrs. Quillan usually takes her hand and wipes off the wall just after turning off the light; " 'pot all gone," Susie says, and snuggles down in her crib.

IV. Present Status, Diagnosis, and Prognosis

According to information gathered both from observations and interviews, Susie Quillan is a normally developing two-year-old. Slightly long at birth, she

THE CASE OF SUSIE QUILLAN

remains slightly taller and heavier than the average two-year-old. Her physical and motor development, as measured by the Denver Developmental Screening Test, show her to be responding at such tasks as ball throwing, block building, and the like at just the norms expected for her age. Her vocabulary development is somewhat more rapid than that for most children of two. She has progressed to using short sentences on a regular basis. Susie's speech development is enhanced, no doubt, by her being an "only child" in a household of four adults. Her parents and grandparents are devoted to teaching her and spend a great deal of time paying attention to all phases of her growth and development.

Susie's fear of the spot on her wall is probably an acquired fear, reinforced by parental attention. Her mother was very frightened in the early stages of the development of this fear; she thought that something was wrong for Susie to be so concerned. She spent hours rocking Susie, only to put her back in the crib and have her cry again, " 'pot! 'pot!" Wiping off the imaginary spot from the wall now solves the problem temporarily; it provides a small amount of attention that has gradually built itself into a bedtime ritual. Susie probably will outgrow it eventually. Even if it takes some time, it does not seem at this point to pose a hazard to normal personal–social development.

Questions for Class Discussion

1. How can you tell that Susie's development is normal for her age?

2. How has the caregiving in the Quillan family affected Susie's development of attachment? What do you think are the advantages and disadvantages to Susie's future development of having more than one primary caregiver? Why?

3. Susie, like a relatively small number of normal babies, skipped the creeping stage of development. Do you think that Susie's parents could have changed Susie's developmental process by giving her crawling lessons? What do you think would have been the result of those lessons? Why?

SUMMARY

The neonate, or newborn, has all body structures present. At birth, neonates are capable of making a number of specific reflexive responses, which psychologists believe serve particular adaptive purposes. They also possess many sensory and perceptual abilities even in the first hours of life.

Humans grow more quickly during the first year of life than at any other phase of their development after birth. The head continues to grow at a more rapid rate than the rest of the body.

Infants' sensory and perceptual abilities increase rapidly in the first twenty-four months. Vision provides the basis for both sensorimotor and cognitive functioning. The other sensory systems critical to early development—tactile, auditory, olfactory, and vestibular—also mature and are coordinated during infancy.

Piaget described the first two years of life as the sensorimotor period, during which the beginnings of truly intelligent behavior emerge. The increase in a baby's ability to respond occurs largely through coordination of sensory and motor functioning.

The infant begins to create new sounds within a few weeks after birth. At between ten months to one year, the first linguistic utterances occur. Early speech, which is holophrastic, includes single-word utterances used to express whole ideas. Language development is related directly to the child's growing motor ability.

According to Piaget, early sensorimotor development accounts for future cognitive functioning. During the sensorimotor period, the developing child passes through a series of stages that lead to the development of a cognitive structure. As children progress from one stage to the next, they go from periods of disequilibrium to equilibrium, a process called equilibration.

During the first of Piaget's stages of development, innate reflexive responses, such as sucking and grasping, become more efficient and more generalized. A series of circular reaction stages follow in which babies perform more and more complex behaviors in a series of repetitive (circular) reactions that gradually accommodate to the environment. During the first half of the second year, the tertiary circular reaction stage, infants learn the concepts of causality and object permanence as well as the beginnings of classification. In the second half of this year, the mental combinations stage, their cognitive structure enables them to think before they act.

In the first two years, infants are capable of many different types of learning. According to learning theorists, learning in infancy occurs through both classical and operant conditioning. Motivational theorists see unfulfilled needs, such as hunger, compelling infants to such activities as crying. Much of babies' social learning occurs through imitation of adult behavior; imitative responses grow more and more accurate as the baby grows.

Attachment to the primary caregiver shows itself usually by seven or eight months, as does stranger anxiety. The importance of the primary caregiver is also reflected in the development of trust or mistrust in the first years of life and the development of autonomy or self-doubt in toddlers.

A number of tests have been designed to measure infant development. Psychologists agree, however, that the developmental state of an infant in the first year, as measured by these tests, is a poor predictor of later development.

Many potential hazards exist for babies' normal development. Early undernutrition especially produces detrimental and often irreversible effects on the development of the skeletal system, bodily organs, brain, and other parts of the central nervous system.

No two babies develop in exactly the same way in the same time span, even when they encounter no developmental problems en route. Some researchers offer evidence that some babies are constitutionally different from others and that biological makeup and environmental conditions are inseparable. Researchers stress the major importance of early stimulation and point out that differing amounts of stimulation provided by the same caregivers to different children produce different behaviors.

FOR FURTHER READING

Appleton, T., R. Clifton, and S. Goldberg. The development of behavioral competence in infancy. In F. Horowitz (ed.), *Review of Child Development Research.* Chicago: University of Chicago Press, 1974. This chapter is devoted to careful descriptions of the behavior expected of infants at each stage of development. The charts describing particular aspects of behavioral development month by month are particularly useful to students seeking a detailed account of what to expect of infant behavior.

Cratty, B. *Perceptual and Motor Development in Infants and Children.* Englewood Cliffs, New Jersey: Prentice-Hall, 1979. This comprehensive text not only describes the changes that take place in children as their chronological ages increase, but it also provides provocative and useful questions for discussion as well as projects, observations, and learning experiences for those with extensive interest in early development.

Lehane, S. *Help Your Baby Learn: 100 Piaget-Based Activities for the First Two Years of Life.* Englewood Cliffs, New Jersey: Prentice-Hall, 1976. In *Help Your Baby Learn,* Dr. Lehane shows how to recognize subtle developmental changes and explains Piaget-based activities parents can use to facilitate infant development as their babies become ready to learn.

Preview Questions

- What are the characteristics of caregivers who promote healthy child development?

- What are some infant characteristics that influence the sort of care they receive from others?

- How do the caregiving roles of mothers and fathers usually differ?

- Does caregiving in one-parent families differ from that in two-parent families?

- What are some effects of different levels of sensory stimulation?

- What are three types of attachment, and which should a caregiver strive for?

- Can you describe the process of identification and explain how it may influence a child's dependency and sex-role learning?

- What are the effects of hospitalization and longer term institutionalization on child development?

- Are there any differences in the effects of maternal and paternal deprivation?

- Can you describe several different systems of caregiving and compare them with the nuclear and extended family systems?

- How would you compare the communal care programs of the U.S.S.R., People's Republic of China, Israel, and Sweden with those in the United States?

4

Infant-Caregiver Relationships

From birth, infants process information and respond to sensory input. They play active roles in their relationships with the environment. Their caregivers respond to this activity by smiling, cuddling, meeting their needs for nourishment, keeping them dry, and so forth. Since infant survival itself is dependent on the attention provided by caregivers, it is not at all surprising that the infant's earliest adaptive responses are made toward their caregivers. Many researchers suggest that the effects of the infant–caregiver relationship last for long periods in the development of the individual, perhaps for a lifetime.

INFANT–CAREGIVER RELATIONSHIPS: A CIRCULAR PROCESS

The relationship between infants and their caregivers is by no means a one-way street: Just as the child's behavior is influenced by the caregiver's responses, the caregiver, in turn, is affected by his or her charge. Babies whose physical and emotional needs are met tend to have proud, contented parents. The impact of the baby's response on the parents can also be powerful. Bell (1979) points out the discrepancy between the baby's small size and large power: Eye-to-eye gazing, smiling, crying, appearing helpless, or thrashing about can have dramatic effects on a parent.

Even the behavior of a newborn can exert a powerful influence, shaping the reaction of the nursing mother even before she brings her baby home from the hospital. For example, the mother of an infant who cries a great deal is likely to develop anxieties related to her ability (or inability) to care for her child. Unfortunately, the interaction is circular: The anxious mother, because of her anxiety, is more likely to have a baby who cries frequently. It is not surprising that researchers investigating the relationships between maternal needs and infant behavior report striking personality similarities between mothers and their infants (Murphy 1971; Caldwell *et al.* 1973). It is important to remember, however, that these relationships, by themselves, do not prove causality.

The infant–caregiver relationship is not only complex, but it is also extremely important. Both caregiver and infant affect one another in more and more complicated ways as the relationship develops. During infancy, children first learn to trust or mistrust their environments. Caregivers who provide safe, warm, loving environments are likely to have trusting, contented children. Caregivers who somehow teach their infants that the world is not a safe place in which to live and that they cannot always expect to have their needs met easily are likely to have frightened, mistrustful children (Erickson 1963; 1968).

Caregiver Characteristics and Infant Development

Landreth (1967, p. 98) listed the following attributes of caregivers as critical to optimal infant development: "amount of physical contact, speed of response, soothing, physical closeness, achievement stimulation, social stimulation, communication stim-

Caregivers who provide a warm, loving environment encourage the child's feelings of trust in the world.

ulation, stimulus adaptation, positive–affective expression, consistency, emotional involvement, acceptance–rejection, and individualization of care." Also cited were "time spent looking at baby, looking at baby's face, talking, talking to infant, patting, showing affection, playing, holding, diapering, bathing, feeding, dressing, adjusting position, and rocking."

Research shows that the most important factor in personality development is not simply the presence of the caregiver but also his or her reaction to the child. In some nuclear families (consisting of mother, father, and children) the mother provides a constant physical presence, yet she may rarely interact with her children in a playful, affectionate, and stimulating manner. Studies have shown that American mothers tend to interact less frequently with their children in day-to-day situations than mothers in many other cultures do (Wurst 1978; Gibson, Wurst, and Cannonito 1982).

According to most psychologists, the ideal caregiver is one who is warm, loving, consistent, and nonrejecting (see, for example, Coopersmith 1967; Erikson 1968; Margolin 1974). This type of caregiver is sensitive to the child's needs and distress signals and responds promptly and appropriately. He or she spends time interacting with the infants, looking at them, stimulating them, and playing with them. The caregiver has a healthy outlook on life and thus is able to attend to the children's needs. Most interactions with the infant are mutually pleasurable.

Psychologists have shown that happy, loving mothers with positive, accepting attitudes tend to provide warm physical handling. These same mothers tend to have affectionate, smiling babies, regardless of the specific child-rearing methods used. Mothers who provide a great deal of verbal stimulation tend to have babies with high levels of cognitive development (Clarke-Stewart 1973); those who feel they are unable to solve the day-to-day problems in caring for an infant tend to have infants who do not thrive. In one study of infants who were retarded both behaviorally and physically, even though they had no known organic dysfunction, researchers found that the mothers reported themselves to be "inadequate" (Leonard, Rhymes, and Solnit 1966). Similarly, Carey (1968) found that mothers of colicky infants tended to be uncertain in their descriptions of their roles as mothers. These mothers gave attention to their infants, but they often were inconsistent in their manners of responding to their offspring.

The ideal caregiver is more than just available. He or she interacts in specific and direct ways and is generally competent in many areas of life. Finally, the ideal caregiver is prepared to help increase a child's sensory–motor skills through touch, contact, and interaction. It is important to remember, of course, that no caregiver is all of these things all of the time; the ideal caregiver, however, provides a great deal most of the time.

Infant Characteristics Affecting Caregiving

Just as the caregiver affects the development of the baby, the baby, in turn, affects the caregiver's attitudes as well as the specific type of infant–caregiver interaction. One example of this relationship is that babies who are born at what is called high risk—who are premature, underweight, or have serious defects and require intensive care during their early lives—tend to have mothers who display negative attitudes toward them. Cross (1978) interviewed mothers of babies in intensive care at three weeks and then again at ten weeks and found that the mothers gave consistently more negative descriptions of their infants than did mothers of normal babies.

The sex of infants might affect the attitudes and behaviors of caregivers as well. Schwartz (1979) points out that males have a four-to-eight times greater incidence

---

NURSERIES IN THE JAILHOUSE: A CASE OF BENEFICIAL MUTUAL INTERACTION

The German government demonstrated its belief that babies should all be provided ample opportunity to interact with those individuals who will give them the greatest attention. In West Germany mothers jailed for serious crimes are being given the chance to provide their children with love and support. The theory is that if preschool children are allowed to remain with these mothers, the children, the mothers, and ultimately, society will benefit.

In the West German town of Preungesheimin, in a high-walled century-old prison, is the prison Kinderheim or "children's home." Completed in the spring of 1975 at a cost of $800,000, the Kinderheim is capable of housing twenty women prisoners and up to twenty-five of their children. The prisoners have been convicted of many crimes, including shoplifting, burglary, drug addiction, and prostitution.

What attention do the children in the Kinderheim receive? Their mothers live with them in a special section of the prison. Their cells are brightly painted and contain windows and modern furniture. Except for the forty hours per week that each mother is required to work in the prison, mothers are free to spend all of their time playing with their children, engaging in activities in the Kinderheim, or watching TV with them. Children in the Kinderheim have far more attention from their caregivers than most would have received otherwise in foundling homes or the like.

Every three months, mothers are allowed to leave the prison to shop. With good behavior, each mother is allowed a brief vacation home with her child after six months.

Critics of the Kinderheim program make many of the same points that critics of prison reform in the United States have made. They suggest that the Kinderheim "coddles" its inmates so much that their return to the outside world may provide a rude shock. But of the fifty prison inmates who have thus far lived in Kinderheim and returned to the outside world, only one has been returned to prison. Most of their children have the opportunity to grow up in homes much like those of children whose mothers never went to prison. It appears that the mutual interaction of preschoolers and loving caregivers, even in the confines of a prison, can be a highly beneficial one (Sheils and Agrest 1976).

QUESTIONS FOR THOUGHT

1. What, specifically, do you think is the major benefit to mothers and their children of this program?

2. Do you think that the prison system in the United States ought to consider a policy similar to the Kinderheim policy for female criminals and their young children? Why?

of infantile autism as well as some other psychological disorders during the early years. He suggests that these disorders might be related to innate predispositional differences between the sexes that are somehow reinforced by sex-stereotyped specialization. Male infants, according to this hypothesis, may well be treated differently by their caregivers when still in the cradle; the differences may be subtle, so that the caregivers might not even notice.

Other psychosocial disturbances that appear in infancy are due to complex interactions of infants and their caregivers. A good example, described in Chapter 3, is the failure-to-thrive syndrome (FTTS). This syndrome is characterized by a number of symptoms: Not only do the infants fail to thrive without any recognizable physical difficulty as the cause, but they also fail to eat and sleep properly and are generally unresponsive to their external environments. Ramey *et al.* (1972) contend that a primary cause of FTTS is inadequate caregiving. Children exhibiting FTTS symptoms tend to come from homes in which parents are intensely hostile or rejecting toward their children. Current theory suggests that, for some infants at least, emotional stress generated by tense family relations somehow triggers a reaction of the pituitary gland, the master regulator within the brain responsible for orchestrating the body's normal hormonal secretions. Yet not all rejected children or children whose primary caregivers are hostile toward them develop FTTS. What then makes the difference? From early infancy, FTTS children are often described as difficult and unresponsive, crying excessively, and rejecting interaction. Most probably, the behavior of these infants helps trigger rejecting behavior in their caregivers. This is one more example of the powerful effect of a combination of the infant's early behavior and the parent's reaction to it. Kagan (1968) referred to it as something similar to a ballet in which each partner dances to the steps of the other.

Maternal and Paternal Roles in Caregiving

In the United States, mothers traditionally have had primary responsibility for child-rearing, at least during the first two years. For this reason, maternal interactions with and attitudes toward offspring have been studied extensively.

How much actual time is spent by most mothers interacting with their infants? In a study of American families, Clarke-Stewart (1973) showed that, even though mothers of extremely young infants usually remain in close physical proximity to their offspring, a relatively short amount of time is actually spent interacting with infants. The study made repeated observations in the homes of thirty-six American mothers and their first-born infants, from the time the infants were nine months old until they were eighteen months old. Only thirty-six percent of these infants' waking hours was spent in infant–mother interaction. The remainder of the time was spent in observing and interacting with other objects in the environment, such as toys, household objects, and, in some cases, other people. Between nine and eighteen months, the mothers studied tended gradually to decrease both attention given and interactions with their offspring. At the same time, the infants developed reciprocal responses: They gradually spent less and less time showing interest in their mothers or responding directly to them, and they spent more and more time interacting with and displaying increasing interest in the outside world.

In most societies today, fathers spend less time interacting with their infants than do mothers. This is caused by the roles of fathers in most societies, which do not assign them primary responsibility for childrearing. In Western industrial societies, fathers usually spend large portions of their time on the job and away from the home during their infants' waking hours.

The roles of fathers in relation to infants and young children are similar across most cultures. Because most societies relegate major responsibility of infant care to mothers, fathers usually are assigned assisting roles. While mothers take day-to-day responsibility for most aspects of infant care, fathers take on caregiving chores when mothers are off at other activities. When babies are bottle-fed, fathers can participate in the major task of feeding. This may be a factor in the decision of some parents today to bottle-feed rather than to breast-feed their infants.

In situations in which mothers are not present, of course, fathers may play the role of primary caregiver. In Sweden, the federal government has attempted legally to provide fathers the opportunity to participate equally with their wives in the rearing of their infants. The expression "male emancipation" has been coined to denote the rights of husbands in Sweden to remain at home while their children are extremely young.

Clearly, many fathers want to play important roles in the development of their children. But how important are fathers to their children's day-to-day development? The answer to this question varies from father to father. Studies have shown that fathers can be as competent and responsive as mothers in providing everyday care (Parke 1979). Researchers comparing the different ways that mothers and fathers interact with toddlers in social situations—vocalizing, gesturing, making body contacts, and playing games of various sorts—find that although a typical father's type of play is more physical (as, for example, tossing the child) than is a typical mother's style, there are no important differences either in the ways fathers interact with their toddlers or, equally important, in the ways the toddlers respond in return (Collins 1979; Vandell 1979).

Caregiving in Single-parent Families

Together with the increasing number of women in the work force and the increasing number of divorces in our country, more and more single parents are raising children. Today, thousands of single men and women raise their children without the help of another parent, and they play the roles that both mother and father have traditionally played in the rearing of their children. The single parent faces a number of obstacles in caring for the young child that the two-parent family does not face. It simply is more difficult for one person easily to supply the same individual attention and affection that two parents can provide. In spite of the financial and personal

HIGHLIGHT 4.2 "MOTHERING:" A VASTLY UNDERRATED OCCUPATION

"Mothering" is the word usually used in this country to describe childrearing as well as the relationship that exists between the mother and her child. The reason for the term is clear: until recently, at least in the United States, most infant care was done by mothers in their own homes.

Today, the increase in our country of women working outside the home, single-parent families, and communal childrearing practices leads to many instances in which people other than the natural mothers are doing the actual caregiving. For this reason, many psychologists feel that the term *mothering* should be changed to the term *caregiving*.

The following statement made by a child psychologist amplifies the role of mothering, or caregiving:

> . . . the mother's direct and indirect actions with regard to her one- to three-year-old child are . . . the most powerful formative factors in the development of a preschool child. Further, I would guess that if a mother does a fine job in the preschool years, subsequent educators such as teachers will find their chances for effectiveness maximized. Finally, I would expect that much of the basic quality of the entire life of an individual is determined by the mother's actions during these two years. Obviously, I could be very wrong about these declarative statements. I make them as very strong hunches that I have become committed to, as a kind of net result of all our inquiries into early development. Let me quickly add that I believe most women are capable of doing a fine job with their one- to three-year-old children. Our study has convinced us that a mother need not necessarily have even a high school diploma, let alone a college education. Nor does she need to have very substantial economic assets. In addition, it is clear that a good job can be accomplished without a father in the home. In all of these statements I see considerable hope for future generations.*

QUESTIONS FOR THOUGHT

1. The author of this statement is optimistic about the future of caregiving in our society. Do you agree with him?

2. The author talks about the mother's "direct and indirect actions" with regard to her child. What, specifically, are the important interactions between a mother or caregiver and child that he is referring to?

---

*First published by the Ontario Institute for Studies in Education in *Interchange*, Vol. 2, No. 2, 1971.

Tactile stimulation, as well as warm, affectionate attention in the course of play, helps to promote normal sensorimotor development.

setbacks that have resulted from the loss of mate through divorce or death, however, many single parents report that they have made good adjustments, are successfully coping with many of the problems of being one-parent families, and are able to provide consistent and warm interactions with their children.

The Importance of Sensory Stimulation

No matter how much love and attention caregivers provide, it is essential to normal development that they also provide comfort through physical contact. Research with both human children and primates confirms this. Harlow (1958), for example, compared the effects on the behavior of baby monkeys of receiving and not receiving contact stimulation from monkey caregivers (see Fig. 4.1). Specifically, he compared

Figure 4.1 Harlow's baby monkeys spent much time clinging to their soft, padded mother substitutes. (From H. Harlow, The nature of love, *American Psychologist* 13, 1958:675. Copyright © 1958 by the American Psychological Association. Reprinted by permission.)

the behavior of monkeys reared with their own mothers, who touched them constantly, with that of baby monkeys kept with monkey-mother surrogates. Harlow's experimental group was kept in cages isolated from other monkeys. Instead of their live mothers, each monkey was given two substitute mothers, one made of hard wire and one made of soft terry cloth. A control group of monkeys was raised in cages together with their own natural mothers. These monkeys spent a large proportion of their days clinging to their mothers, both during feeding and at other times. In the experimental group, the "wire mother" was the sole source of food. Nursing bottles were built into the center of the wire mothers' chests with the nipples protruding. To nurse, the baby monkeys had to climb onto the fronts of the "wire mothers" and hang on with all four limbs. When not eating, they spent much of their time clinging with all four legs to the comfortable, soft padded mother substitute. Other than when nursing, not much time was spent in close contact with the "wire mother."

Harlow's study made clear that his independent variable, type of mother or mother substitute, strongly affected the baby monkeys' behavior. It showed something else as well. In the experimental group of monkeys, even when food did not come from the soft cloth mother, the latter provided an apparently necessary contact and was uniformly preferred by her monkey "children." Harlow showed that when baby monkeys are offered both hard and soft substitute mothers, even though the hard substitute "feeds" the baby, the baby still prefers touch contact with the soft, padded "mama." Harlow's study thus demonstrated that contact comfort is more important to the development of a strong affectional response in baby monkeys than is satisfaction of the hunger drive.

In a later report, Harlow (1962) noted that early deprivation suffered by the experimental monkeys in his study led to long-lived retardation in development in aspects other than affectional responding alone. All baby monkeys who were raised initially with live monkey mothers eventually developed normal adult heterosexual and maternal responses. None of the babies raised with wire or cloth mother surrogates, however, developed either mature adult heterosexual behavior or, in females, maternal responses toward their young.

Human studies provide detrimental results in some ways similar to that found by Harlow. As we shall see in discussing children who have been institutionalized and deprived of contact stimulation, lack of sensory stimulation leads to retarded infant development. Other studies of children receiving less than an adequate amount of contact stimulation show similar results. Brossard and DeCarie (1971) demonstrated that such children often are retarded physically, emotionally, and cognitively.

Whereas insufficient physical contact interferes with normal development, research has shown that substantial amounts of physical contact can produce accelerated motor development. Advanced motor development of infants in Uganda and other African countries has been frequently reported (Ainsworth 1967). Babies in these countries usually are carried upright on their mothers' backs. They are in constant skin contact with their mothers and also are handled frequently. Many Ugandan infants can hold up their heads and straighten their backs when pulled to a sitting position in the first days of life. They can also follow moving objects with their eyes. This advanced rate continues, apparently for many months. In one study (Geber 1958), some babies were reported to sit unsupported for a few seconds at three months. By five months, all babies studied could sit unsupported for thirty minutes. It may be that rapid motor development is related to the particular style of handling. When Ugandan infants are reared in the European tradition of a horizontal crib position and more rigid feeding schedule, they do not exhibit this advanced development. Similarly, Soviet psychologists have shown that babies who are handled continuously increase their rates of motor development dramatically.

Stimulation by the caregiver or caregivers is of major importance in affecting far more than motor development. The quality and amount of caregiver stimulation determine the infant's ability to explore and play with objects in the day-care environment. Children in the first twenty-four months of life are at what Piaget termed the sensorimotor stage of development. It is at this stage that children learn to co-ordinate movements in order to make definite actions. By eighteen months, they are ready to think before they act, provided that they have received stimulation to do so. This stimulation is considered so critical today that both caregivers in day-care programs and parents at home are being taught to provide optimal amounts of stimulation. In the winter of 1979, Blue Cross and Blue Shield first sponsored a pilot program for infants and their parents called "Fitness in Diapers." The purpose was to teach parents exercises to perform with their babies to increase spatial awareness and balance and to stimulate the brain and nervous system (Gregory 1979). It is interesting that the Fitness in Diapers program matches in many basic ways the exercises and forms of stimulation planned for years by preschool educa-tors for Soviet children in the state-controlled nurseries (Gibson and Vinogradoff 1981).

Many theorists, including Piaget, have argued that infant exploration of the ob-jects in the immediate environment is the single most important learning experience of the child. Infant behavior during what Piaget called the primary circular reaction stage, in which babies repetitively hit their rattles or throw toys out of their playpens, is crucial in learning the ways the world works. The caregiver who picks up toys repetitively when they are tossed out and returns them to the infant teaches that infant actions affect caregiver reactions. Infants whose caregivers encourage their exploration by providing new stimulation through all of the senses learn to operate in the world in increasingly novel and creative ways.

 ## DEVELOPING ATTACHMENT

Attachment, as we discussed in Chapter 3, is an ongoing, durable affectional tie between caregiver and infant. It describes what most people think of as "love." In infancy, attachment is manifested through clinging, following, smiling, and watching the caregiver, as well as crying and protesting at separation.

Early studies of attachment (Bowlby 1951; 1958; 1969) suggested that it occurs as the natural result of infants' associating their mothers with drive reduction (satis-faction of needs). Harlow's research (1958), as discussed, demonstrated that the need for touch contact plays a major role not only in the development of adult behavior but also in the development of attachment. In his studies, infant monkeys with access to terry cloth "mothers" developed attachment to these surrogates and spent most of their time clinging to them.

Many researchers describe attachment as responses directed to only one per-son, usually the mother (Bowlby 1969). Others, however, showed that infants may become attached to more than one caregiver, although they are highly selective regarding who that caregiver is (Schaffer and Emerson 1964; Ainsworth 1967). The fact that babies may have several attachment figures does not mean that all caregivers are equally important. Bowlby (1969) proposed one principal attachment figure, usually the primary caregiver, and one or more secondary figures. The question is whether babies of mothers working outside the home develop strong attachment to their baby sitters or day-care caregivers as secondary attachment figures. The question is an important one and will need to be answered as more and more mothers of infants join the work force.

Who is the principal attachment figure likely to be? Fathers as well as mothers are objects of attachment in traditional family settings. Cohen and Campos (1974) reported that infants as young as ten months often relate strongly to their fathers as attachment figures, although these fathers rated second to the babies' mothers. This latter fact is not surprising because babies typically spend far more time interacting with their mothers. The anecdotal evidence available shows that babies who spend a great deal of time with baby sitters also become attached to these caregivers.

Why is attachment important? Bowlby (1969) reported that attachment forms the basis of learning experiences that, in turn, lead to socially desirable responding.

In infancy attachment is often expressed through smiling, clinging, watching and other expressions of pleasure in the presence of the caregiver and protesting at separation from the caregiver.

Young babies first learn through interactions with their principal attachment figures the responses that are appropriate for that caregiver to satisfy their needs. At first, they do not know whether these same responses will be equally effective in their interactions with other people. Later, through continued interactions with the primary caregiver, they develop self-assurance in their decisions about responding in each new situation.

Type of Attachment

Ainsworth (1979) suggested that three basic types of attachment develop and that each type is related to a certain style of parent–infant interaction. These can be described as **secure attachment, anxious attachment,** and **anxious-avoidance attachment.**

Securely attached infants tend to use their caregivers as secure bases from which to explore and learn from the world around them. When their attachment figure goes away, some of this security vanishes. They are often upset by the separation and are glad to see their caregivers return. The infants tend to stop their exploration and often may cry. Mothers of securely attached infants tend to be more sensitively attuned to infant behavioral signals than are the mothers of the other two groups of infants (Ainsworth *et al.* 1978).

A second group, the anxiously attached, tends to show a great deal more anxiety than the first, even when their attachment figures are still present. They are much more upset by separation. But when their mothers return, they are ambivalent: They seek close contact and at the same time resist interaction. Much time is spent in indecision rather than in exploration of the environment. Connell (1976) hypothesized that these babies may, as newborns, be "constitutionally different" from other babies. Particularly if their mother's personalities or general behavior patterns make it hard for them to be responsive to their babies' cues, such babies seem likely to develop this anxious type of attachment.

A last group develops what we have called an anxious-avoidance attachment. These babies, unlike those in the other two groups, rarely cry in the separation episodes. In the reunion episodes, they avoid or ignore the mother altogether. They tend to be quiet, apathetic, and show little interest in exploring their environments. Mothers of such babies tend to have problems of their own, often expressed by deep-seated aversion to close bodily contact. In addition, these mothers are more rejecting, more often angry, and more restricted in their expressions of affection than are mothers of other babies. Ainsworth concludes that maternal sensitivity to infant behavioral cues is essential for healthy attachment to occur and, of course, to all the infant learning developing from successful attachment. Secure attachment is the kind that mothers need to foster if they want their infants to learn easily to interact successfully with others.

Identification

Identification is the process by which individuals gradually adopt for themselves the behavior and standards of another individual who serves as a model by which they can judge their own behaviors. Early **anaclitic identification** first begins in infancy and is a plausible explanation for attachment to the caregiver.

According to motivational theorists, anaclitic identification begins when the infant is physically and emotionally dependent on the caregiver. In societies in which mothers usually are the first caregivers, identification usually is with them. At this stage, infants seek out their mothers to satisfy their own basic needs. Later, infants come to derive pleasure from mothers' presence alone. After babies are nine months of age or older, mothers gradually tend to spend less and less time interacting with them. Thus as babies get older, they gradually are deprived of the pleasure of their mothers' presence. At this point, by some mechanism that has never satisfactorily been described, they begin to imitate their caregivers (Sears, Rav, and Alpert 1965). Sounds and smiles are among the first imitated responses. Some psychologists hypothesize that babies use this early imitation as a substitute for the pleasure of their mothers' presence. Babies who learn quickly to imitate become less dependent on their mothers. They learn more easily to interact with other objects and people in the world around them. Later, children learn not only to copy maternal behaviors but also to internalize them. The mothers' attributes gradually become part of the infants' "psychological organization," so that they begin to react to events as their mothers would react (Kagan 1958).

Anaclitic identification first involves imitation of the caregiver, and then identification of the perceived attributes. **Defensive identification,** in which children internalize the prohibitions of the caregiver model, involves a similar process of imitation followed by identification. For example, the baby's first word is often the prohibition *no!* As children get older, they enjoy using this prohibition in situations in which they have heard their parents use it.

According to motivation theorists, identification enables babies gradually to decrease their attachment to their caregivers. At the same time, it provides a primary vehicle through which acceptable and necessary responses for socialization are learned. Thus factors necessary for identification are necessary also for the learning of social responses. Sears, Rav, and Alpert (1965) listed these necessary factors as (1) high early dependency, (2) high adult nurturance, (3) high use of love-oriented discipline, and (4) clear presentation of models—that is, babies (1) who at early ages are highly dependent on their caregivers, (2) who receive a large amount of loving and affection rather than punitive discipline, and (3) whose parents provide good models to imitate learn social responses more easily than do other babies. For babies to have what they need to learn social responses, they need caregivers who interact frequently, consistently, and with warmth and affection.

HIGHLIGHT 4.3 DO PARENTS SEX STEREOTYPE THEIR BABIES?

Research has shown that, despite efforts of many people to reduce the effects of sex stereotyping, parents still think of their infants in different ways, depending on whether they are male or female.

Several studies seem to indicate this stereotyping begins in earliest infancy. Adjectives that parents use to describe their babies are related more to the sex of the babies than to their actual characteristics. In one study, parents of newborn infants were asked within twenty-four hours after delivery whether their babies were boys or girls and what their babies were like. Daughters were rated as significantly softer, finer featured, smaller, and more inattentive, even though there was no difference in actual size or weight of male and female babies. Fathers tended to engage in more of the sex typing than did mothers.

The expectations of these parents are in no way unusual. Expectations of sex-typed attributes and behaviors occur regularly in our society. A second study required college students to examine pictures of a week-old infant named Sandy and then to describe the baby. The subjects in this study exhibited sex typing similar to that in the first study. Students who were told that Sandy was female proceeded to describe the baby as smaller, weaker, and more cuddly than did students who were told Sandy was male.

QUESTIONS FOR THOUGHT

1. With increasing numbers of adult women holding jobs in fields previously dominated by men, should we expect our perceptions of male and female attributes gradually to change?

2. With "true" equality of sexes, should we expect parental perceptions of male and female babies to differ, as these studies have shown?

Sex-role Identification. Sex-role identification is the process whereby young children gradually internalize the roles considered appropriate to their sex and the reactions characteristic of that role. It begins in infancy with caregiver identification. Historically, in American society where principal caregivers have been women, both male and female babies' first identification has been with women.

The learning of **sex typing,** selection of acceptable behaviors and attributes on the basis of sex, begins in infancy. Kagan (1971), for example, noted that American mothers tend to respond more physically to their male six-month-old infants and more verbally to their female infants at the same age. In America, we are all familiar with the tradition that newborn baby boys come home from the hospital to nurseries decorated in blue and filled with Teddy bears, and newborn baby girls come home to pink nurseries with baby dolls in them. Sex-typed toys and room decorations, of course, are merely symptomatic of different attitudes toward males and females. They are not nearly so important to the development of sex-role identification as the hundreds of little things that parents do all day long in the course of caring for their infants. Sex-role identification is learned in subtle ways through the manner in which parents hold their babies, pick them up, and talk to them.

Most societies seem to teach sex typing at early ages. Sex differences in the care of infant boys and girls have been noted by Super (1977) in a comparison of thirteen societies in Africa, Latin America, Europe, and the United States. In the majority of samples studied, Super found that infant sons were more likely to be touched (or held) by their mothers than were infant daughters. Graves (1976) reported further that in at least one Asian society studied, mothers of seven- to eighteen-month-old infants interacted with their sons across a distance and initiated interaction significantly more than they did toward their infant daughters.

MATERNAL AND PATERNAL DEPRIVATION

Care given infants is crucial to their development. What happens when the primary source of this care is removed abruptly? The research has demonstrated that even brief separations, such as those caused by hospitalization, can produce disruptions in infant development.

Hospitalization

Research has shown that infants who are suddenly hospitalized for serious illness may display decreased exploratory behavior and even retarded physical and psychological development (Collard 1971). To compensate for some of the isolation imposed by hospitals, many pediatric units in hospitals today provide for mother rooming in and train parents so that they can be involved in the care of their child (Jay 1977; 1978). Also, some hospitals have child life specialists trained in child development. After assessment with a nurse and/or physician of the child's needs, the child life specialist plans appropriate activities. Exploration and involvement with parents is often part of the play therapy used.

Disruption seems to be greater after the age of six months than before (Landreth 1967). Of course, many other potentially pertinent factors often accompany developmental disruptions—pain, illness, and strange people and procedures, to name just a few. Whatever the circumstances, absence of the primary caregiver itself seems to be the key factor in delayed development. Infants even tend to tolerate surgery well as long as primary caregivers stay with them in the hospital.

Longer-term instutionalization

A great deal of research has been done on the effects on infants of long-term institutionalization. Infants reared in extremely barren, understaffed facilities have consistently displayed retarded development and symptoms of apathy. They have displayed disrupted behavior ranging from listlessness and loss of appetite to a condition known as **marasmus,** which involves a general wasting away that continues sometimes even to the point of death.

Much early research was conducted on effects of institutionalization on babies separated from their parents during World War II (Freud and Burlingame 1943; 1944). Spitz (1945; 1946) reported in a study of homeless children who were orphaned or separated from their parents that one of the major orphanages in Germany during the war had a mortality rate of over seventy percent for children during the first year of life. Spitz's studies related this developmental impairment to a lack of single mothering or caregiving figure. Psychologists, however, are by no means agreed as to the primary cause of the developmental damage. Institutionalized infants studied by all were deprived of more than primary caregivers; they were deprived of environmental stimulation of all sorts. Many researchers have suggested that this lack of environmental stimulation was a much more important cause of retardation than lack of close association with any single caregiver (Rheingold and Bayley 1959; Casler 1961; Gardner, Hawkes, and Burchinal 1961).

Other studies of institutionalization report similar developmental disruption. In a study of one hundred Lebanese orphan babies institutionalized in a Beirut orphanage, Dennis and Najarian (1957) reported that these babies exhibited continual listlessness. Toward the end of their first year, they showed significantly decreased abilities to perform both intellectually and on motor tasks, as measured by developmental scales, when compared with Lebanese infants of comparable backgrounds who were reared with their own families.

The caregivers in the Beirut orphanage in which Dennis and Najarian conducted their investigation provided for the physical needs of the babies in indifferent and apathetic ways. In addition, they appeared to be unresponsive to signs of interest or affection from the infants. Because of a large infant–caregiver ratio of ten to one, bottles often were propped by pillows during feeding, and contact during feeding was quite limited. Individual caregivers were not assigned to individual children, so that attachments to particular caregivers were not developed. Few toys were provided. Infants spent most of their time in cribs, later in playpens. Cribs were equipped with canvas sides so that infants could not see out of them.

In what ways did the few apathetic caregivers affect the development of the institutionalized infants studied by Dennis and Najarian? Clearly, they affected the infants both by their lack of presence and by their inability to interact directly with them. Even the presence of a caregiver's face is known to affect infant development. Young babies show more interest even in line drawings of human faces than in other pattern types (Fantz 1961a). But this interest is restricted to babies who see faces regularly. Fantz and Nevis (1967) showed that socially isolated infants show no more interest in human faces than in any other patterns presented them. Institutionalized Israeli infants were observed to smile less frequently at the presentation of a human face than either family- or kibbutz-reared infants (Wolff 1963). It is not surprising, therefore, that institutionalized babies who rarely have the opportunity even to see a human face are disrupted in their development.

Rheingold and Bayley (1959) studied sixteen babies living in a state institution for the first nine months of their lives. Half of the babies in the study were provided extra attention by one caregiver from the sixth to the eighth month. Tested after a year, these babies were more socially responsive than the babies who had not received this special attention, but they did no better on tests of developmental progress than did babies who had received much less attention. The authors suggested that this was an example of too little attention provided too late. Their hypothesis was confirmed by another study conducted ten years later on children reared in their own homes by low-income mothers (Gordon 1969). In this two-year study, low-income mothers were specially trained in ways to stimulate their infants. At the end of the first twelve months, the stimulated infants did far better on developmental tests than did their nonstimulated counterparts. After the experiment had been discontinued for twelve months, however, differences in development between the two groups of babies disappeared. Adequate stimulation, to be effective, must begin early and must continue to be provided.

Skeels (1966) reported a twenty-year study of subjects who, as infants, had resided in an orphanage. At the outset of the study, all were classified as mentally retarded. Skeels arranged for thirteen of these babies, all under two years of age, to be transferred from the orphanage to a resident institution for the mentally retarded. This institution, paradoxically, was able to provide more caregiving and stimulation for the babies than the orphanage. Babies received individual attention from older retarded inmates who enjoyed serving as mother figures. The babies played often with others and joined in group activities. Unlike the IQs of control subjects left in the original orphanage, the IQs of all thirteen of these babies increased sufficiently to permit later adoption. Skeels's twenty-year follow-up study reported finally that all thirteen subjects, when adults, were self-supporting, had gained economic independence, and exhibited no antisocial behavior. Control subjects, left in the unstimulating orphanage, had completed lower levels of education and were employed in considerably lower-level occupations. Only seven were employed at all, and four remained institutionalized in adulthood.

One major cause of the problems that the institutionalized children in all of these studies faced is lack of stimulation of all kinds—tactile, visual, and auditory, as well as emotional. The importance of physical contact has been demonstrated by much research, including studies by Soviet psychologists who have reported that babies who are not picked up frequently receive less vestibular and kinesthetic feedback. The physical development of these babies often is retarded (Kistiakovskaia 1960). The Soviet belief in the importance of handling babies has resulted in large numbers of caregivers provided in the state nurseries.

SYSTEMS OF CAREGIVING

Only slightly more than a quarter of households in societies across the world have what we have far more frequently in America, that is, monogamous nuclear households containing mother, father, and children. Most households in the world have more adults living in them than do typical American households. Much recent research has compared the effects on childrearing of different types of households. Data gathered so far suggest that the amount of warmth, affection, and attention shown to the child varies directly with the number of adults in the home: the larger

In the United States today, as more mothers work outside the home, it is becoming common for children to spend some portion of the day with other caregivers.

the number of adults in the household, the greater the warmth, affection, and attention given to the children. Thus the greater tendency is to treat the young in a tolerant and kindly manner, what psychologists refer to as indulgence, in extended families, where children are raised simultaneously by many adults, rather than in households with only one or two parental figures (Whiting 1961; Werner 1979). Observations of children raised communally with many caregivers, as with those raised on kibbutzim in Israel or in day-care centers in the Soviet Union, have generally supported the view that carefully planned multiple caregiving systems do not have harmful effects on the child (see, for example, Bronfenbrenner 1969; 1977). In fact, these systems can serve certain useful functions.

Both the extended family and the collective society have a unique advantage absent in the typical nuclear household: They offer children the availability of several caregivers who can take turns responding to their needs. In such arrangements—when the child's mother is pregnant, for example, or busy taking care of a new baby—the older children can still receive the same amount of attention. Lusk and Lewis (1972) found, in studies of Senegalese extended families, that attention provided infants was similar, whether the primary caregiver was seven or seventy years old, the natural mother, the grandmother, the infant's sister, or a distant cousin. Whiting and Whiting (1975) reported similar results in an extensive study of six cultures in which children were raised in extended families.

The Lusk and Lewis study and the Whitings' study both suggest some disadvantages inherent in nuclear family living. Margolin (1974) agrees that in the nuclear family, a parent with several children simply may not have enough time or energy to care adequately for all of them. Ainsworth (1967) adds, furthermore, that losing a parent might be less traumatic for a child accustomed to other caregivers than for a child who has depended on one parent exclusively.

Substitute Caregiving

Although increasing numbers of American women, including mothers of small children, are working outside their homes today, most of them out of economic necessity, the United States is one of the few industrial nations that does not have a national system of child care. Today, 53.1 percent of divorced American mothers of preschoolers and 40.9 percent of married mothers of preschoolers work outside the home. Employment rates are highest for parents in single-parent families and are expected to increase during the 1980s (U.S. Dept. of Labor 1980).

How do American working parents cope with the problem of child care? What are the effects on the developing child of having two working parents? Studies of short-term parental separation show very different results from those of institutionalization in barren environments. It is clear that care given infants during their separation periods from their parents is critical; yet no evidence today shows that toddlers whose primary caregiver works away from home need suffer adverse effects.

Hoffman (1979) reported no evidence that the best caregiver has to be the mother or that this role is better filled by a male or a female. Further, she points out, working women in the United States today often do not put their babies in any kind of substitute care. Today, most preschool children of mothers who work away from home are cared for in their own homes.

Substitute caregiving for toddlers of working parents has been a subject of great controversy in this country in recent years. Many studies published in the early 1970s criticized the quality of American day care, pointing to large numbers of day-care facilities in the United States that were understaffed and had inadequate facilities. Many suggestions were made for drastic improvements (see, for example, Keyserling 1972; Robinson *et al.* 1973). Recent reports, however, have suggested considerable diversity in the quality and types of American day care provided and report that, in many cases, substitute care programs are excellent. Belsky and Sternberg (1978) and Rubenstein and Howes (1979), for example, have reported high-quality care in day-care centers they investigated. Clearly, parents of toddlers need to look carefully at the situations in which they place their infants who cannot tell them in words what happens to them each day.

One concern of many Americans regarding substitute infant care, regardless of the quality of the caregiver or setting, is the quality of parent–child interactions, particularly during the first year. Do working parents spend less time or interact less with their infants when they are at home? If so, does this result in differences in the quality of attachment? In this respect, Cohen (1978) found no difference between the behavior of one-year-old infants of middle-class mothers working outside the home and those of mothers at home. She did, however, note differences in two-year-olds. Children of mothers at home interacted more with their parents, talked more, and performed better on developmental tests, presumably because of greater amounts of attention given them. The question, however, is not a simple one. Studies of low-income parents and their young children show that there may be many advantages of working both to these parents and their toddlers. With higher per-capita incomes, parents are able to supply better nutrition, better living conditions, and better health. Among the poor, Cherry and Eaton (1977) found that the children of mothers employed outside their homes were ultimately more advanced in their physical and cognitive development.

Day-care Facilities

The term day care as we have been using it covers a range of child care. It includes care in an organized day-care center, and family day care in a private home where a caregiver provides for children of working parents. Care by fathers, older siblings, other relatives in the infant's own home, or a combination of such arrangements are also methods of providing child care. The Administration on Children, Youth and

Families estimated in 1976 that one-third of preschoolers were cared for in family day-care homes, with the other two-thirds cared for in special centers with staffs hired as caregivers.

Kamerman and Kahn (1979; 1981) noted that by 1978 the figures had reversed. Of the 6.9 million American children of mothers working outside the home in 1978, sixty percent were cared for by relatives, including older siblings; thirty percent were cared for by day-care providers outside the home or by in-home baby sitters; and ten percent were cared for in formal day-care centers.

In general, parents prefer child-care facilities near their homes rather than near their work so that their children will have less distance to travel. Many parents prefer having their relatives care for their children rather than sending them to day-care centers. Today, most parents of preschoolers patch together several types of care in a single day. For example, a father may leave his child with a neighbor for several hours; then someone else may take the child to a part-day program until the close of the working day.

Today, with increasing cost of organized day-care centers and with decreasing funding available from the federal government to assist low-income families, the use of both formal day-care centers and licensed day-care homes by low-income families has decreased. At the same time, companies have begun to take over for America's middle class what our federal government previously had helped provide for our poor. An increasing number of day-care programs were incorporated in the late 1970s to cater to young children, including infants in diapers, from 7 A.M. to 6 P.M. These programs offer hot breakfasts and lunches, such activities as swimming, and kindergarten-style teaching. Many programs offer, in addition, afternoon day care for elementary school children. Because of recently declining school enrollments, many day-care centers are staffed by elementary school teachers who have lost jobs in the school systems.

The effects of these new programs on middle-class children seem to depend on the quality of the caregiving and the program offered. Well-designed and well-staffed programs generally produce beneficial effects on the toddlers; poor programs produce less beneficial effects. For example, research indicates that toddlers in high-quality programs can increase in their cognitive and social development (Rubenstein and Howes 1979). Some researchers caution, however, that our knowledge of the effects of day care on child development is still very limited, and that some of it is contradictory. Portnoy and Simmons (1978) tell us that young children develop normal attachments to their parents even when they spend large portions of their time in day-care centers. Children studied by Portnoy and Simmons showed attachment responses to their parents similar to those of children who had never attended day-care centers and who spent all of their time in nuclear households. Others, however, point out that this fact does not address an equally compelling issue. Belsky and Sternberg (1978), for example, question the long-term impact of day care on the families and family relations. They point out that we really do not know the effect of day care on the parents and on the relationships between them and their children.

Today, the use of American day-care facilities, with multiple substitute caregivers providing for infant needs while parents work outside the home, is similar in many ways to the use of multiple caregivers in societies outside the United States. Kagan (1979, p. 888) reminds us that "Mothers in most societies in the world share caretaking responsibilities with older daughters and have done so for centuries. If this practice (of multiple caregiving) produced insecure infants and adults with fragile defenses, one would expect these societies to have abandoned those practices."

Alternative Methods of Infant Care

In the last twenty-five years, the condition of the world's children has become an issue of broad concern. In 1979, the "International Year of the Child" represented an international effort toward making the world aware of the special nutritional and emotional needs of children. Today, even at a time when economic pressures in many Western societies are causing funding for improving the care of young children to decrease, there is still growing recognition that strong governmental commitment to improved child care and child development is crucial to the improvement of society. Many developed countries are focusing on the changes in traditional sex roles and family relationships and on the effects of these changes on children. Many developed nations are also attempting to find ways whereby men can be encouraged to work and also assume more household and child-raising responsibilities. Many behavioral scientists are also examining alternative methods of childrearing, with closer looks at the advantages and the disadvantages both to young children and their families (see, for example, David and Baldwin 1979).

Communal Childrearing in Preliterate Societies

Margaret Mead and other anthropologists have studied a variety of preliterate societies to determine, among other things, the effects of infant and childrearing on development. Mead (1928; 1935; 1959) noted in a number of now-famous studies that in societies in which infants and children are reared in groups by a number of caregivers, children develop attachment responses to more than one person. Moreover, these children do not develop separation anxiety and fear of strangers. These differences in their development, she asserted, are important assets in a society where change of companions is frequent. Mead concluded that attachment to a single caregiver is not necessary for all healthy, interpersonal relationships. There may be many advantages to American children of working parents today to develop attachment responses to more than one person, particularly because their lives will be filled with many interpersonal relationships. Consider for a moment the children who develop multiple attachments to multiple caregivers in day-care centers. If Mead's assertion is correct, these children will be less fearful and less likely to "hang on to their mothers' skirts" when they are ready to enter kindergarten.

Communal Infant and Childrearing in Industrial Societies

Democratic and socialistic governments have, in recent years, established programs designed to provide infant and early child care to children of mothers who work outside their homes.

Nursery Programs in the Soviet Union. Communal childrearing in the Soviet Union begins usually at three months of age. Mothers in the Soviet Union are given three months' leave from their jobs with full pay after the birth of each child. After three months, large numbers of Soviet women bring their children to the state-run

Soviet children playing basketball in a kindergarten. Millions of children in the Soviet Union attend nurseries and kindergartens during their parents' working day.

**HIGHLIGHT 4.4 THE GROUP PLAYPEN:
A SOURCE OF SOCIAL STIMULATION**

Maria Vincze (1971), a researcher for the National Methodological Institute for Infant Care in Budapest, Hungary, studied infants from three months to thirty months of age who were placed in a day-care program while their mothers were working. The object of her study was to determine whether large playpens that hold several babies simultaneously during most of their waking hours aid in providing social stimulation important to infant development.

Soviet toddlers in a group playpen similar to that advocated by Vincze.

day-care program for childrearing. Day-care centers are open during working hours and provide facilities for nutritional, medical, physical, and social care of infants and small children at nominal fees.

The Soviets have long known the importance of attention in the development of infants. As noted earlier, they have gone to great lengths to ensure that infant–caregiver ratios are kept low, particularly for the youngest infants. The caregiver-to-infant ratio in Soviet infant programs is reported to be one to four. Attention is provided through continual visual and auditory stimulation, exercise, and constant physical contact. Brightly colored objects are available at all times for play and ex-

Vincze studied the following social interrelations among the babies: contacts made among them by looks, smiles, vocalizations; contacts made through gestures or locomotion; touching; pulling at objects held by other babies; giving objects to other babies; imitation; verbal communication; common activities performed together; and imitation of adult caregivers in interactions among them.

Vincze found that babies who spend their play hours in these communal settings, where they have the opportunity to interact with one another, develop far more social behavior than babies kept in separate playpens without such opportunity. Social contact, Vincze reports, occurs even as young as two to three months. Even though the babies cannot move toward one another yet, they do make eye contact. By seven months, they tend whenever possible to crawl or scramble over one another. As their motor development progresses, the forms of social contact become more varied. The pens used in many day-care programs across the world today provide a new source of stimulation particularly important when there is no one-to-one infant-to-caregiver ratio. Other babies, in addition to caregivers, serve as sources of stimulation. Vincze's findings suggest then that the group playpen may be the solution to one of the major problems of day care for infants.

QUESTIONS FOR THOUGHT

1. From Vincze's research, what can we conclude about the age at which infants are ready to learn social responding?

2. Why do you think we tend in this country to keep infants separated from others in the household by placing them in playpens? What do you think is the result of this tendency?

ploration. When babies are placed in playpens in Soviet preschools, they are almost never alone. Soviet playpens hold several babies at the same time.

Nursery Programs in the People's Republic of China. Children in the People's Republic of China also are reared in programs similar in many respects to those of the Soviet Union. Infants in China begin their nursery training at fifty-six days of age. Like Soviet infants, they are reared in communal settings. When they are not being held or played with by their caregivers, they are placed in communal playpens. Like the Soviets, the Chinese are well aware of the importance of physical contact. The caregiver–infant ratio in Chinese preschools is one to four. Visitors to China who have observed infants report that they tend to be happy, healthy, alert youngsters (Alston 1976).

Infants' Homes on Israeli Kibbutzim. Kibbutzim, or collectives, are characterized by cooperative partnership and shared responsibility; each member contributes to the vitality and productivity of the kibbutz as a whole. Kibbutz infant and child-rearing is designed to develop children well adapted to communal living. The methods used to accomplish this are in some ways similar to those used in the Soviet Union and the People's Republic of China. There are, however, striking differences

Children playing at an Israeli kibbutz.

between the kibbutzim educational programs and nurseries in either the Soviet Union or China. Perhaps most important is the lack of a single national plan for kibbutz education, as in each of these other countries. The kibbutz programs differ in philosophy and methods of infant and childrearing, as well as in family patterning. What is true of one kibbutz's infant home may not be true of another.

In most kibbutzim, infants enter infant homes to be reared communally at very young ages, usually when they are four to seven days old. On some kibbutzim, infants remain overnight; on others, they return to their parents' rooms at the end of each day. At this early stage, mothers remain for most of the day to feed, wash, and care for their infants. Only gradually do mothers turn these activities over to the nurses, or metapelot. Most kibbutzim have arranged for small metapelet–infant ratios. One researcher (Marcus 1971) estimated this ratio to be one metapelet for every three to five infants.

The metapelet, according to kibbutz educators, provides a constant caretaker figure who, together with the infant peers, helps to provide constancy in the life of the infant. Kibbutz residents attempt whenever possible to keep the same metapelet or at least, to allow the caregiver to spend transition time with babies when they move to the next nursery, called the toddler home. Life in both the infant home and the toddler home is characterized by much contact both with the parents who visit frequently and the metapelet who provides constant stimulation in their absence (Rabkin 1976).

Observations of kibbutz children have shown that they have warm, close relationships with their peers. What about their relationships with their parents? Most experts agree that kibbutz children develop the same affectional ties as those not raised on kibbutzim (Bronfenbrenner 1969). One study (Rheingold 1956) showed that kibbutz children display the same separation anxiety when their mothers leave them in a room alone with a stranger as do American children reared in nuclear families. Quite possibly, communal child rearing, when warm, loving, attentive caretakers are used, has much less effect on the development of attachment than many people believe.

Full-day Centers in Sweden. Since World War II, Sweden, like other European countries, has been experiencing a declining birth rate and labor shortages. As a result, Sweden has instituted policies aimed at encouraging women to have babies and, at the same time, to join the work force. In Sweden, a total national commitment to the well-being of young children has led to the establishment of full-day centers that provide programs at nominal fees for infants and young children beginning as young as six months. The hours of full-day centers are from 7:30 A.M. to 7:00 P.M. on weekdays and during mornings on Saturdays in order to accommodate children of working parents. Swedish educators and psychologists are aware of the potential hazards of unstimulating institutional care for children between the ages of six months and three years. Therefore the programs provide ample caregiver attention and contact and a stimulating environment for the children to explore. In general, the Swedish programs attempt to nurture and develop attitudes of open expression and individuality. They avoid excessive prohibition and supervision, so as to avoid thwarting emotional development and natural curiosity (Passantino 1971).

American Communal Experiments. During the 1960s and 1970s, some young, usually middle-class Americans made the decision to try communal living. Kanter (1970) estimated the number of communal experiments in the 1960s to measure in the hundreds. Communes appeared in all states of the United States, many growing out of the youth counterculture that rejected what many regarded as the materialism of modern society. Present-day communes are found in both urban and rural areas, although urban communes are becoming more prevalent. They vary widely in both structure and interest, ranging from anarchistic (with no real organization or leadership) to highly organized groups with explicit philosophical systems. In general, the physical and social boundaries of urban communes are less clearly defined than those of a group that seeks rural areas to establish a new life-style. Urban communards are more limited, for example, in the extent to which they can reject the surrounding culture. For instance, the nudity found in many anarchistic rural communes would not be tolerated by city neighbors. Membership is more fluid in the urban than the rural communes, because all that is necessary is a rented house and a group of willing people.

Concerning infant–family relationships, communes range from those that maintain nuclear parental units within the communal families to those that regard children as "belonging" to the commune. In some communes, families live together in large households to share the increasing costs of living but still maintain separate living styles within the household. In others, individuals group together to share a particular style of living. In some communes, individuals group together to share family interests in urban areas where increasingly often, it is feared, family interests are being lost. In some communes, all commune members, including the children, may be present at the birth of the baby. The father may be encouraged to assist in delivery, on the assumption that this will encourage a deep attachment relationship. Breast-feeding is commonly practiced. Babies frequently are carried on their mothers' backs and accompany them most of the time, so there is almost constant physical proximity between mother and child. Intense mother–child relationships between birth and two years are common. In addition, commune members often attempt to develop in the infant generalized feelings of trust. This has been accomplished in some communes by providing multiple caregivers (Eiduson, Cohen, and Alexander 1973). Many communes make no clear distinction between the roles of the parents and those of other commune members. The dominant childrearing ideology often is to allow maximum free expression and creativity.

THE CASE OF BOBBY—A NEGLECTED INFANT: A CASE STUDY FOR CLASS DISCUSSION

I. Identification and Sources of Information

Name: Robert (Bobby) Samuels

Address: Hudson Foundling Home, York City, New York

Race: White

Age: Two years

Sources of information

1. Personal observation
2. Interview with Bobby's mother
3. Interview with staff workers at Hudson Foundling Home

II. Family History

Bobby is the fourth child of Maria Samuels, a thirty-six-year-old unmarried woman who lives with her fifteen-year-old son Philip. Maria quit school at age sixteen after completing ninth grade. Her daughters, Ollie and Sondra, are nineteen and twenty years old and live away from the house. Maria Samuels was divorced shortly after the birth of Philip. She has not seen her ex-husband in more than fourteen years and told us that she does not want to talk about Bobby's father. "He ain't a bad guy—just has his own problems . . . you know, the usual—a wife and a couple kids. He wanted to help with an abortion. But I didn't even know I was having the kid until it was too late. My periods never was regular—and by the time I was sure I was having it, the doc at the hospital told me I couldn't get rid of it. First, I thought I'd put it in a home. Then, after Bobby was born, I decided I wanted him. And I done my best taking care of him—it wasn't too awful hard, even though he cried a lot. It really burned me when the social worker came and took him away."

Maria Samuels was reported to officials by neighbors for leaving Bobby alone—sometimes for most of the day. When Bobby was eighteen months old, officials placed him at the Hudson Foundling Home, where he is being kept pending a legal decision as to his placement. Maria has requested the aid of a public defender to try to get her child back. At the time that officials took the baby, she was employed as a maintenance worker in a packing plant in York City. She worked nights and has told the public defender that she took care of the baby days "and Philip tended him nights." Maria denies neglecting Bobby and says her neighbors were lying when they said she left him unattended. "Sure, they heard him cry a lot. It didn't mean I wasn't there—he just cries more than most kids. The night the police came, I admit he was alone. Philip had gone down to the pool hall—but just for a little while. You know how kids are. He won't do it again."

III. Case History

When the police picked up Bobby, neighbors had reported he had been crying on and off for about twenty-four hours. "Not much noise—kind of a whimpering sound," the woman in the next apartment said. The baby weighed thirteen pounds, seven more than he had at birth. He sat when the policeman who found him picked him up, but he slipped into a prone position quickly when released. Bobby was dressed in a soiled diaper and was lying on a mattress on the floor that he shared with his older brother when the teenager was home. A half-empty bottle of soured milk lay nearby. Police waited an hour to see whether either Philip or Maria would return to the two-room, walk-up apartment. When neither appeared, they took the baby to the foundling home.

Doctors reported that Bobby was undernourished. He refused food for the first twenty-four hours after arrival in the home and appeared listless and uninterested in his surroundings. When Maria Samuels arrived with her son Philip to claim the baby, Bobby showed no interest either in the arrival of his mother and brother or their departure some minutes later. Philip reported that his younger brother "seemed

Continued

THE CASE OF BOBBY (Cont.)

sick." "I don't remember him being so quiet—usually he whined and kept me from hearin' the TV," Philip said. "He was sleepin' when I went out that night, but he still had a bottle he didn't finish that morning, so I wasn't worried or nothin'."

Bobby only gradually began to accept food after a great deal of coaxing from the institution staff. During the first week at Hudson, he took only milk mixed with sugar and water. By the end of the second week, he began to accept small amounts of solid food. He could not chew because he had very few teeth, but he did seem to enjoy puddings. One nurse said that she thought she had seen Bobby give what looked almost like a smile when she came to feed him. But the response was short and did not reoccur.

Bobby's lack of interest in his surroundings continued. By the end of one month in the institution, he had gained two pounds. The staff psychologist administered the Denver Developmental Screening Test. The test indicated that Bobby was retarded. The psychologist reported that the results were inconclusive; Bobby had not adjusted to his environment, and it was unclear as to whether he simply did not want to or could not respond. At the time of the testing, Bobby seemed to understand some simple words and directions. He made some brief eye contact with the examiner. Otherwise, he remained listless and mute. The nurses reported that when alone, he made a repetitive rocking movement and whimpered softly to himself.

Maria and her three children made four visits to the institution during the first month Bobby was there. At no time did he seem to notice them. Maria sat and held and rocked him; Bobby gazed vacantly out the window, his arms by his side.

IV. Present Status, Diagnosis, and Prognosis

Bobby has been at the Hudson Foundling Home for six months. He has gained ten pounds and now is within normal weight range for his age. He eats solid foods and is developing the baby teeth that normally appear in the second year of life.

Bobby sits now without support and can remain standing if he has something to hold. He speaks a few words but usually ignores people who come in to talk with him. He lies for hours at a time in his crib, looking out into the room. He rarely makes eye contact with the nurses or with his family when they come to visit. He still tests as a retarded child on the Denver Developmental Screening Test.

Doctors report that physically Bobby is getting stronger. Socially, however, he has made few advances. He is disinterested both in his caregivers and in the other children in the foundling home. The home hopes to place him in a foster home once a legal decision is made concerning his custody. It is hoped that a one-to-one child-to-caregiver ratio will provide opportunity for him to receive a lot of individual attention and to develop psychosocially.

Maria Samuels will have her court hearing in one month. Her lawyer plans to plead that it is wrong to remove a baby from the natural mother and that whatever mistakes Maria Samuels has made in the past, she is the best person to raise her child. Maria is accused of child neglect, not child abuse. Bobby was not beaten, but he was ignored. Maria plans to engage the assistance of her daughters in caring for her son if she can get him back. She has lost her job and applied for public assistance. Philip has run away from home and has been gone for the past month, so Maria is alone in the apartment.

The court prosecutor hopes to prove that Maria's background and past life make her an unfit mother for Bobby and that Maria wants to keep Bobby home solely for the purpose of adding to her public assistance. The prosecutor plans to use the psychologist as evidence to show the extent of damage caused by neglect and has called several specialists to testify that the natural mother is not necessarily the best caregiver and that, in cases like Bobby's, caregivers

THE CASE OF BOBBY

who provide stimulation can make major changes in children's development.

The prognosis is uncertain. Neither the physician nor the psychologist can predict with certainty the progress of Bobby's development. Both prescribe a great deal of attention and stimulation if there is to be any hope at all for Bobby.

Questions for Class Discussion

1. Compare the development of Bobby as described in this case history with that of Susie Quillan described in the case history in Chapter 3. What are the most important development differences between these two children? Why did you pick these?

2. Bobby was described by the police as a "neglected" baby. What are the most important ways that he was neglected? Is there any evidence that this neglect has affected his development of an attachment response? Explain the reason for your answer. How is this likely to affect future development?

3. There are many arguments, pro and con, to institutionalizing Bobby. Do you think that he should be kept in Hudson Foundling Home permanently, placed in a foster home, or be allowed to return to his natural mother? What do you think is the prognosis for Bobby's development in each situation? Why? Whatever decision is made by the court, what safeguards should be used to protect Bobby?

SUMMARY

The importance to the infant of early caregivers must not be underestimated. It is not only the presence of the caregiver that affects personality development but this person's reaction to the child. The ideal caregiver is warm, loving, consistent, and nonrejecting. Caregivers who are unable to solve their day-to-day infant-care problems satisfactorily tend to have infants who do not thrive. The interactions between infants and their caregivers are complex and affected by such factors as infant health and behavior at birth and the sex of the infant.

Both fathers and mothers can provide adequate caregiving. Studies comparing the ways that fathers and mothers interact with their toddlers show very few differences between the sexes. Although the increasing number of single parents face obstacles that the two-parent family does not face, many report that they have made good adjustments and are successfully coping with these problems.

Research with both human children and primates confirms that physical contact is essential to normal development. Whereas lack of sensory stimulation leads to retarded development, substantial amounts of physical contact can produce accelerated motor development. Stimulation by the caregiver is crucial during the sensorimotor stage.

Attachment between caregiver and infant is important to social learning. Some researchers suggest that babies have one primary caregiver to whom they develop attachment; others suggest there can be more than one. Securely attached infants tend to use their caregivers as secure bases from which to explore and learn from the world around them.

Identification, the process by which individuals gradually adopt for themselves the behavior and standards of another individual, enables babies gradually to decrease their attachment to their caregivers and provides a primary vehicle through which acceptable and necessary responses are learned.

Maternal or paternal deprivation can have adverse effects on infants and young children. It can occur for a variety of reasons. Infants hospitalized because of illness, for example, may suffer retarded physical or psychological development. Long-term institutionalization creates different types of problems; developmental retardation or apathy may be severe if infants are institutionalized in barren environments with little stimulation.

In today's nuclear family, a third type of infant–parent separation takes place when both parents work. Although we do not yet know the long-term impact of day care and substitute caregiving on parents and their relationships with their children, the effects seem to depend on the quality of the caregiving and the program offered. Anthropologists have studied childrearing in a variety of preliterate societies. Margaret Mead noted that in societies where infants and children are reared in groups by a number of caregivers, children develop attachment responses to more than one person.

Democratic and socialistic governments have, in recent years, established childcare programs for children of mothers working outside the home. The Soviet Union, the People's Republic of China, and Sweden all provide quality day-care programs beginning in infancy. Similar to these are the kibbutzim in Israel, which are characterized by much contact both with the mother, who visits frequently, and the metapelet, or nurse, who provides constant stimulation in the mother's absence. In the United States, beginning in the 1960s, a significant number of young, middle-class Americans experimented with communal living and communal childrearing; living patterns for these people vary from commune to commune.

 ## FOR FURTHER READING

Cohen, M. *Understanding and Nurturing Infant Development.* New York: Association for Childhood Education International, 1976. This publication contains papers presented at the 1975 Texas Conference on Infancy. It includes discussions of intervention studies and programs for infants and families, interaction between infants and their caregivers, mutual adaptation of mother and child, discontinuous mothering, and the emergence of self-concept.

Robins, P., and S. Weiner (eds). *Child Care and Public Policy.* Lexington, Massachusetts: D.C. Heath, 1978. This book provides an excellent social perspective of child care in the United States. Chapter 2, in particular, provides a brief and revealing history of the evolving of day care in the United States, the relationship of day care to governmental policy, and the relationship of both to social and historical events.

U. S. Dept. of Health and Human Services. *Parents' Guide to Day Care.* Publication No. (OHDS) 80-30254, LSDS, Department 76, Washington, D.C. 20401, August 1980. This free pamphlet published by the U.S. Dept. of Health and Human Services provides useful information concerning ways of determining what is good day care, whether the family is considering in-home care, family day care or center-based care. A checklist for parents concerning selecting good caregivers for infants, toddlers, preschoolers, and school-aged children is included, along with information regarding state licensure of day-care programs.

Childhood

Part III

Preview Questions

- What are some behaviors of preschool children that illustrate their progress in gross and fine motor skills?

- What are Piaget's two stages of preconceptual thought and some major characteristics of each?

- Which of the following seems to offer the best explanation of the language development of preschool children: learning theory, Chomsky's approach, or Vygotsky's reasoning?

- Can you explain the two major positions in the argument over the relationships between language and thinking?

- How do the experiences of boys and girls bring about differences in their social–emotional development?

- What are some major influences on the development of fear and aggression in preschool children?

- Can you compare the validity of Erikson's and Freud's explanations of the personality dynamics of this stage?

- What are six major influences on the socialization of preschool children and some positive and negative potentials of each?

- What are the major characteristics of the moral development of preschool children as described by Piaget and Kohlberg?

- How do socioeconomic status, birth order, and handicaps produce individual differences in the development of preschool children?

5

The Preschool
Years

Children from ages three to five years have more opportunity than younger children to explore their environments with great amounts of freedom. From three to five years, people outside the immediate family—at home, in church, or in day-care settings—play increasingly important roles in teaching socialization. These important others include not only adults in the child's environment but also, increasingly frequently, playmates and siblings. By the time they are six, most children in the United States enter school, where formal instruction is designed to help socialize them to meet the standards set by society. This chapter deals with preschool development before formal instruction occurs.

SENSORIMOTOR DEVELOPMENT

By the third year of life, most children have made significant progress in their motor skills. They can run with agility and without falling down. Many toddlers climb stairs somewhat clumsily, placing each foot next to the other on the same step and proceeding torturously on the climb up. By three years, however, most children have developed sufficient balance and coordination to manage stairs with very few falls. They gradually develop the ability to use alternate feet going downstairs as well as upstairs, and they will usually accomplish this task satisfactorily by their fourth year. Three-year-olds are able to ride tricycles; by the time they are three and a half, they usually can use the pedals by pressing down with alternate feet. By their fifth year, they will be able to skip, walk across a balance beam without falling, and throw a ball overhand. They can broad-jump from two to three feet, hop fifty feet in about eleven seconds, and if asked, stand on one foot for at least four to six seconds without having to put the other foot on the ground.

At the same time that youngsters develop gross motor skills, they are also improving their fine motor coordination. One area of fine motor skills that has been investigated extensively is drawing (Cratty 1979). Two-year-olds scribble when drawing; most five-year-olds can use crayons or pencils to copy triangles or to draw recognizable human figures. Some preschool children are able to print their first names, albeit sloppily and often in an irregular manner. Right-handed preschool children tend to use a characteristic counterclockwise movement to produce their drawings of circles, squares, or rectangles. They are often unsuccessful at completing these figures, leaving them open at the top, and they cannot draw two-dimensional figures yet (Watson and Lowrey 1967; Cratty 1979).

Children's drawing ability is related directly to what they see around them and to the opportunity they have to practice their newly developing skills. Improved manual dexterity accompanies improved visual and perceptual skills; one set of skills builds on the other. There is considerable variation in the ages at which skills are mastered for individual children. Still, most two-year-olds are still scribbling on their papers. Most of these children have just learned to distinguish between horizontal and vertical lines on drawings shown to them. By five years, when they are already drawing complex figures, most still have some difficulty distinguishing between different lines in a drawing pointing in the same direction. And many five-year-olds become completely confused when presented with letters of the alphabet that have similar basic structure, such as b, p, d, and q. Mistakes in these letters frequently appear in a five-year-old's printing of names.

Children's drawings reflect and follow their understanding of their body images. Two-year-olds who are just beginning to be able to identify the major parts of the body ("tummy," legs, feet, arms, and face parts) usually do not reproduce this new learning in their scribblings. By the time that they are four, however, when they can identify in finer detail more parts of the body (thighs, elbows, shoulders, first and little fingers, and thumb), they often begin crudely drawn human figures. By five, they can draw human figures with all of these parts labeled clearly. Table 5.1 illustrates the emergence of drawing skills by year.

Physical coordination develops rapidly during the preschool years.

Table 5.1
The Emergence of Drawing Skills

Age	Skill
2 years	Scribbling, various positions on paper
	Single- and multiple-line drawings
	Varieties of scribbling patterns
3 years	Space on paper often enclosed
	Simple crossed lines
	"Suns" with lines emanating from them
	Beginning of crudely drawn human figures
4 years	Circles and squares
	Crude houses and cars
	Trees and animals
5 years	More complex drawings of people, buildings, trees, and animals

Source: Age-related skills adapted from Kellogg and O'Dell (1969) and Cratty (1979).

Age 3

Age 5

Age 4

COGNITIVE DEVELOPMENT: STAGES OF PRECONCEPTUAL THOUGHT

Piaget suggested that preschool children improve their abilities to think and to understand by characterizing all new experiences according to past experience. For example, young Susie might pick up a new ball and bounce it on the floor because she knows her old ball bounced when she threw it. Young children assimilate new objects into their cognitive structures when these new objects are similar to others they have encountered previously. They have less ability to generalize from past experience than do older children.

According to Piaget, preschool children tend to concentrate on one aspect of an event to the exclusion of all others. When asked which of two containers holds the larger amount of water, the preschooler is apt to point to the taller of the two containers, regardless of their relative widths. This tendency to concentrate on a single aspect of the event during problem solving sometimes extends through the early school years. This cognitive process is called **centration.**

Another characteristic of preschool thinking is that it is vision–action oriented. Preschoolers solve problems by actively and physically manipulating the environment. When they want to find out what they can do with a toy, they do not think about it. They pick up the toy, pull at it, throw it about, or squeeze it. Bruner, the cognitive psychologist (1964; 1966), called this an **enactive mode of responding.** Children using the enactive mode characteristically use only one habitual active response, such as a motor response, to interact with objects in their worlds.

Cognition of preschool children is characterized by trial-and-error learning. They usually do not stop to decide on a candy from the array presented in a box. Instead they pick one and taste it, and if they do not like it, they pick another. As they grow older, children gradually replace this early responding with directed traits. By the time they are three, children can search for lost objects without having to look in places where they already know the object will not be found.

Piaget described specific stages in the development of the thinking processes of preschool children.

Stage of Symbolic Representation

The preschool years are marked by an increasing interest in and ability to use signs and symbols to represent objects in the outside world. During these years, for example, the young child first learns to treat a doll as a baby and plays at feeding and dressing it. Piaget called this **symbolic representation** or **image-based thinking** and referred to this period of development as the early stage of preoperational thought. Because children at this stage are not yet prepared to deal with conceptual problems, the period is also referred to as the stage of preconceptual thought.

Bruner (1966) referred to the problem solving of children at the preoperational stage of development as the **iconic mode of responding (image representation).** Children using the iconic mode of responding, according to Bruner, actually are describing the outside world to themselves by using images related to the real world by particular sensory correspondences, such as smell or taste. They associate dinner time, for example, with specific smells coming from the kitchen. They associate favorite stuffed animals with their softness. Objects now develop meaning without the necessity of active and physical manipulation by the child, a step up from the enactive mode of responding.

Children using the iconic mode of responding do not define concepts fully and make many errors in learning new concepts. They can, however, understand concretely the ways their responses affect their own worlds. For example, a preschool child understands that hitting mother will make her angry. At this point, however, the child does not understand the concepts of right and wrong. Thus a child will usually choose not to hit because the child wants to please or does not want to be punished but not because of understanding the concepts of right or wrong.

Piaget's theory of cognitive development stresses the importance of matching the complexity of objects presented to the child with the child's cognitive structure. A brightly colored toy presented to a preschooler will be far more effective in increasing exploratory touching and feeling than will a textbook, although the textbook may be very effective in increasing thinking of older children. Bruner's modes of responding also stress matching, both in order to evoke interest on the part of the child and to facilitate developmental progress (Hunt 1973).

Stages of Intuitive Responding

Young children learn gradually to use signs and symbols representing objects in the outside world to test new methods of dealing with these objects. At the same time, they learn to think and solve problems in increasingly complex fashion and to communicate to others about what they see around them. Children, by the time they are four years old, reach what Piaget calls the intuitive stage of preconceptual responding. At this age, although they begin to be able to solve more complex problems, they still have trouble, in many instances, arriving at solutions based on logic. If they want more cookies, they might be satisfied if a parent simply breaks a cookie in half instead of giving them an additional one. Logic does not develop until a later stage of conceptual thinking.

By the time children are four, they use symbols to represent objects in their world. They use dolls to represent babies and stuffed animals to represent live pets. If they want to play with a drum and none is available, for example, they may use the table top for a drum and beat on it with their hands.

As children begin to use symbols to represent objects, they learn also that they can use symbols to imitate what they see happening around them. For example, a child who has watched someone in the house cooking might make mud pies on a make-believe stove. Piaget and Inhelder (1969) called this **symbolic play.**

Sometimes symbolic play takes the form of **fantasy play,** in which children's imaginations allow them to go beyond the limits of immediately perceived events and objects. Children might, for example, "play house" and decide what the mother or father of the house would do if the child refuses to obey. In this sense, they are "taking apart reality" and scrutinizing the parts closely. They may have never decided to disobey in the way they do in the fantasy play. They learn from this experimentation without fear of punishment.

Symbolic and fantasy play clearly are important to more complex thinking. Such play permits the child to practice responses that will be useful in later problem solving. In Piagetian terms, a symbolic play increases the child's ability to assimilate objects in the environment when these objects are not readily obtainable and to find increasingly complex ways to accommodate to these new objects. Researchers have found that fantasy play helps children learn language skills, achieve integration of their experiences, and develop creative thought (Freyberg 1975).

LANGUAGE DEVELOPMENT

A number of generalizations can be made about the ways that preschoolers speak. For one thing, the number of linguistic utterances (the number of different sounds made in a given verbal communication) increases with age (Reese and Lipsitt 1970). When children first begin to speak, they use nouns and content words consisting of verbs and adjectives. Later, **function words** appear regularly in their vocabularies. Now children begin to talk about the ways action is carried out.

At first, children tend to **overgeneralize** when they use words. Two-year-olds, for example often refer to all animals as "doggy." Later, they learn **discrimination** among different categories of words. Four-year-olds are able to discriminate among the different animals and will probably refer to each by its proper name. They also, for the first time, fully understand the meaning of the verbs *to think* and *to know* (Johnson and Moratsos 1977).

Before age three, children appear to use language primarily for the purpose of satisfying their own needs. Typical early sentences might be "want cookie!" or "want ball!" or "want mommy!" Children at this age seem to want constantly! When they are not wanting, they are reporting on events that affect them personally. They might say, for example, "Tommy hit [me]" or "Daddy come" (Schachter *et al.* 1974). Piaget and Erikson both refer to children's thinking during the stage of preconceptual thought and to the speech of that stage as **egocentric speech,** reflecting an inability to separate the self from actions and from the rest of the world (Erikson 1963; Piaget and Inhelder 1969). More recent research, however, seems to indicate that preschoolers frequently adjust their speech to the perceptions and ability levels of their listeners and that it is this accommodation to the needs of the listener that makes preschool speech seem so inner directed. Adult-directed speech often appears more egocentric than peer-directed speech (Gelman 1979).

A second explanation of what Piaget described as egocentric speech was given by the Soviet psychologist Vygotsky (1962). According to Vygotsky, egocentric speech is actually speech used by young children as a method of guiding behavior: They tell out loud what is happening or what should happen. Later, this **overt speech** disappears and is replaced by what Vygotsky called nonverbalized or **inner speech.** Four-year-old children need not tell themselves out loud what they are doing or how they should behave; their inner speech communicates these messages without being apparent to others.

Somewhere about three years of age, children first begin to understand them-selves as entities separate from the rest of the world. Erikson called this period the stage of **ego (self–other) differentiation.** Three-year-olds develop what is called **socialized speech,** or speech that communicates to others what the child is doing as well as what other people are doing.

Theories of Language Development

So far we have described changes that can be expected to occur in the language of children as they grow older. How does the process of language development occur?

Learning Theory. One explanation for the development of language is based on learning theory. According to this view, language, like other behaviors, is learned through operant conditioning. According to learning theorists, particularly B. F. Skin-ner, infant vocalizations that sound like adult words first are reinforced selectively by parental attention. For example, a random vocalization that sounds like "mama" is likely to cause mother to react with pleasure and encouragement. Later, Skinner theorizes, the process becomes more complex. Not only do parents continue to reinforce more complex speech responses, but reinforcement comes also from the child's own increasing ability to obtain desired objects through verbal communica-tion.

Some learning theorists agree with Skinner that caregivers who want their charges to learn to speak need to praise and give attention to their children's verbalizations. Others feel, however, that reinforcement by itself is not sufficient. Bandura, for ex-ample, places major emphasis in language learning on the ability of young children to imitate their caregivers' speech (Bandura and Harris 1966). Thus caregivers who want their charges to learn to speak should spend a great deal of time talking to them. Children do tend to imitate the verbal behavior of their caregivers; this is true even when their imitations are not overtly or noticeably reinforced (see, for exam-ple, Gruendel 1977; DePaulo and Bonvillian 1978).

Some learning theorists believe that imitation explains why function words appear later in the language repertoires of children than do nouns or content words. These theorists offer an interesting explanation for baby talk. They note that parents who use baby talk with their children tend to have children whose first words also are baby talk. They therefore suggest that parental models probably stress nouns and content words rather than function words in their verbal interactions with their children. The children respond primarily with noun and content words. The result is what we call baby talk.

Another learning theorist, Jerome Bruner, suggests that we consider language in the context of the everyday needs and activities of children. Bruner believes that language development is primarily culturally determined. Day-to-day cultural activities, such as games, can be used to teach children to "signal and recognize certain expectancies . . ." In this way, "they learn to manipulate features of language that they must later put together in complex ways" (Bruner 1975, p. 83).

Language development in preschool children is influenced by their peers as well as by their caregivers.

Luria, a Soviet researcher, took Bruner's argument one step further. According to Luria (1974), social conditions play a tremendously important role in speech development. For this reason, he believed that a structured pedagogical approach emphasizing social learning, as used in Soviet education programs, is the most effecitve way to teach language.

The way preschoolers talk has been shown to be affected by all listeners, not just by their parents or other caregivers. Spilton and Lee (1977) studied four-year-olds in free play and recorded their speech. After analyzing the content, these researchers concluded that the children adopted the form of their verbal responses to that of their listeners, and their responses changed with new listeners.

Just as listeners and caregivers reinforce children's speech, children, in turn, reinforce the speaking pattern of those who listen to them. Bohannon and Marquis (1977) tape recorded adults telling the same stories to other adults and to children. These researchers found that the adults used different grammatical structures, sentence lengths, and nouns in the different situations. For example, they referred to parents in the story as "parents" when talking with other adults. When talking to children, they referred to them as "mommies" and "daddies." In the life of the adult caregiver, the child continues to exert control. What is it about preschoolers that makes caregivers speak in what Bohannon and Marquis called "motherese"—that is, why do caregivers call dogs "doggies" when talking to small children? Why don't they call them "dogs" as they do when talking to other adults? The authors assume that when adults use "motherese," the children respond by demonstrating clear comprehension of the story. This reaction is a potent reinforcer for caregivers.

Chomsky's Approach. Noam Chomsky, the linguist, disagrees with the learning explanation of language development. He contends that the learning approach is an oversimplification of a much more complex developmental process. Chomsky (1959) suggested that reinforcement and imitation alone cannot adequately explain the young child's extremely rapid development of complex language and mastery of grammatical rules. Moreover, reinforcement and imitation cannot account for the way children can make up sentences they have not heard before, although this is something that all children do.

Chomsky agrees that imitation and reinforcement are necessary to language learning and that caregivers should provide opportunity for both. In order to explain the infinitely large number of novel sentences that even young children are able to construct, Chomsky suggests that the human nervous system contains innate mechanisms that enable children to process language, construct language rules, and understand complex speech.

Chomsky theorizes that language learning involves early acquisition of what he called **kernel grammar** or **elementary grammar.** This grammar contains the main parts of speech and rules for creating simple sentences (Chomsky 1957; 1965; 1972). From infancy, he believes, children are innately equipped to understand this grammar. According to Chomsky, children's innate mechanisms enable them to grasp more advanced grammatical rules. Using these rules, they are able to create an infinite number of original sentences.

Considerable evidence supports Chomsky's approach. It has been demonstrated, for example, that children all over the world produce new language sounds and develop syntax (the arrangement of word forms to show their meanings in sentences) in essentially the same way. The order of development, from simple to complex forms of speech, also is constant across cultures. Although the number of words spoken at a given age varies from child to child, the order in which each type of word appears is constant.

In addition, similarities occur in the kinds of meanings expressed in children's language, regardless of the individual language learned (Slobin 1972). These similarities occur even though the usual rewards effective in other learning situations have little effect on the teaching of grammar to young children (Brown, Cazden, and Belugi-Klima 1969). Lenneberg (1967) suggested that the best explanation of language development is that it is unrelated to the learning of any single, specific articulatory skill; rather, it is related to the cognitive maturity of the child.

The Relationship Between Language and Thinking

Because language is the basic medium of communication for humans, it is impossible to talk about thinking and problem solving without discussing verbal ability. Theorists have argued for years, however, as to the specific manner in which language and congnition are related.

Piaget believed that the early sounds made by infants and young children are linked to the ways they think and solve problems. He stressed, however, that these utterances are reflections rather than causes of children's thinking. He therefore interpreted these early words as an indication of the stage of development at which a child was operating.

Many psycholinguists (researchers concerned with psychological aspects of language) have disagreed with Piaget's interpretation. They suggest that the words children use actually affect the thinking process and the ways they interpret the world around them (Carroll and Carroll 1956). According to these theorists, retarded speech development will cause children to have difficulty solving certain kinds of problems. Evidence supporting this position was provided by Bernstein (1958), who showed that children whose parents did not teach them complex language had difficulty dealing with problems requiring abstract thought.

Whatever the relationship between language and thinking, it is clear that young children can use their language abilities not only to communicate but also to manipulate their environments in complex fashion (Endsley and Clarey 1975). Preschool children who call their parents and ask whether it is time to come in for dinner may really want to know whether it is dinner time. They might also be asking the question to get a parent to stop and pay attention to them.

**COMMUNICATION IN PRIMATES:
A CONTRADICTION TO CHOMSKY'S THEORY?**

Research brought new studies of language development that have excited psychologists, linguists, and laypeople alike. Scholarly journals, daily newspapers, and magazines began to report a series of studies that purported to show that apes, like humans, are capable of some forms of symbolic communication. Scholarly studies demonstrated that apes can learn simple symbolic communication using sign language and, in some studies, computer language (see, for one example, the work of Fouts 1972).

Using sign language for the deaf, one gorilla, Koko, was able to perform on an intelligence test for nonverbal children with sufficient correct answers that she received an IQ score of between eighty and ninety, the equivalent of a five-year-old child (DeMott 1977). Researchers who asked the question "Does this mean that Koko is as intelligent as a five-year-old child?" were answered "no" (Limber 1977). Limber pointed out, for one thing, that studies of Koko, like those of other apes who have learned to communicate, primarily involve naming rather than reasoning. Koko, for example, could look at her image in a mirror and respond with the sign for "Koko." She could not, however, solve complex problems that involved more than memorizing.

Naming, although it plays an important part in the development of language, is not the only requirement of true language. The syntax that interested Chomsky so much in his interpretation of human language development does not appear in the communications of apes. Limber reports (p. 284) that "any normal three-year-old (human) has far surpassed even the most precocious ape in language structure. Whereas virtually all children use hierarchically structured complex sentences by the beginning of their fourth year at the latest, there is little evidence that any ape ever did." If this is true, Chomksy's notion of the innate mechanisms in humans that enable children to process language, construct language rules, and understand complex speech remains intact. If a chimp or gorilla can master a simple method of communication, all it would mean is that its intellectual capacity and brain structure are more similar to ours than we thought. So-called chimp language is no contradiction to Chomsky's theory.

QUESTIONS FOR THOUGHT

1. The tests used to measure Koko's ability gave her an IQ score of between eighty and ninety, comparable to what a five-year-old might obtain. If Koko could not solve learning problems that require abstract reasoning, do you think this test is a useful one to measure ability to learn in school?
2. Why is it true that Koko's language does not contradict Chomsky's theory?

PERSONALITY AND EMOTIONAL DEVELOPMENT

During the preschool years, children learn to relate socially and emotionally to those around them. Much of preschool personality development takes place through imitation of and identification with model figures. This process, we learned, begins in infancy.

Imitation involves copying the act, not the person. At first the child does not internalize the standards of the person being modeled. Thus a caregiver may wish to instill a desirable behavior but by his or her actions, actually encourages an undesirable behavior. A classic example of imitation producing unwanted behavior is that of the parent who severely punishes the child for aggressive behavior, perhaps by slapping. As a result, the child learns to be aggressive.

Imitation is followed by identification, in which children adopt for themselves not just the behavior but the standards of the model by which to judge their own behavior. Individuals tend to identify not only with models who are similar to them but also with models who provide warmth and loving attention. For the preschooler, this is usually the mother, although it may be the father or other principal caregiver.

Sex-Role Learning

Anaclitic and sex-type identification, described in Chapter 4, usually develop with the mother as the first model. American mothers tend to teach their very young sons sex-typed behaviors by punishing them for behaviors considered feminine. Such behaviors occur because both male and female children usually first imitate their mother's female behaviors. Later, girl children are rewarded for these same behaviors. Boys must unlearn these imitated behaviors in order to learn male sex-typed behavior. These boys often learn sex roles through punishment, while girls learn through reward.

In general, fathers and mothers are more indulgent and protective toward girls than toward boys. When four-year-old Mary falls down and scrapes her knee, her mother or father is likely to pick her up and kiss her. When Johnny hurts himself, his mother or father is more likely to tell him to "be a big boy" or to be more careful. This is largely because our society traditionally has encouraged toughness in boys and dependence in girls. Parents also expect greater aggression from boys in most interactions, in play with peers, with parents, and even with playthings.

Boys often are rewarded for behaving in ways that are "male" and for playing with objects that are considered male. Thompson and McCandless (1970) pointed out that sex-role preference (for example, preferring "male" toys or "male" games) precedes sex-role adoption (as with identification with the male sex in all situations). Girls are usually rewarded for different activities and different play objects. It therefore is not surprising that boys and girls often behave differently in play situations.

Not only do parents behave differently toward boys and girls, they provide them with entirely different environments. Rheingold and Cook (1975) studied the bedrooms of boys and girls under age six. They found striking differences both in the furnishings and the toys selected by parents. Boys' rooms tended to be decorated in "masculine" colors and furnished with educational materials, sports equipment, machines, and military toys. Girls were provided with more dolls, doll houses, and domestic toys.

Today, however, sex-typed clothing and toys are gradually becoming less prevalent. For example, it is harder to guess, simply from watching a group of preschool-age children on a playground, which are boys and which are girls. Both are likely to be clad in blue jeans. It is more usual now to see girls playing with trucks or boys with dolls.

Preschool children learn sex-typed behaviors from peers and other models as well as from their parents. Early in life, children tend to model and identify more with adults than with peers. By the preschool years, however, peers play an increasingly important role in sex typing. One vehicle through which this takes place is through social play. Preschool boys watching other boys exhibit male sex-typed behavior, such as roughness or rowdiness at play, imitate this behavior and are reinforced by the approval of the peers and often by their caregivers. Preschool girls playing with other girls in the playground often learn that when they imitate more common feminine behaviors, such as walking daintily, they also will be reinforced by peers and caregivers alike.

By age four or five, children understand the difference in body structure and capacity of males and females. By age five, they understand the concept of permanent sexual identity as well (Kagan, Hosken, and Watson 1961).

Sex Differences in Social–Emotional Development

Preschool boys tend to be more aggressive than girls. This difference in behavior between boys and girls has been measured as early as eighteen months and in varieties of situations (Maccoby 1974).

Children of both sexes tend to associate sexuality with degree of strength and power. It is interesting that sex-role preference of girls is more variable than that of boys until the age of nine or ten. This had led some psychologists to question whether our society's emphasis on the strength and power of "maleness" has led small girls to be more ambivalent in their desires to play female roles.

By age three, boys in our culture tend to exhibit significantly more aggressive behavior at play than do girls. They also engage in play activities involving the large muscles more often than do girls. Boys spend much of their play time involved in sports, such as ball playing, while young girls tend more often to play games involving observed household activities or work roles. When raised at home, they also respond in ways that reflect significantly more dependence on their mothers than do boys (Cornelius and Denny 1975).

The different socialization of boys and girls begins early. Girls are encouraged to pursue passive, nurturant activities, whereas boys are encouraged to be more active and assertive.

By the time they are three years old, boys are learning to be aware of sex-typed behaviors and objects. By the time they reach six, they are fully aware of sex-role stereotypes (Barry and Barry 1976; Horance 1977).

Aggression

Aggression refers to behavior intended to harm another individual. Preschool children in the United States exhibit a variety of aggressive behaviors that are incompatible with socially acceptable peer interactions. In interactions with peers, preschool aggression can include such antisocial behavior as punching, kicking, biting, verbal abuse, taking away toys, breaking toys, and destroying property. Older preschool children tend more often to be verbally rather than physically aggressive when dealing with younger children. Younger children, on the other hand, are more prone to physically aggressive acts, such as taking away toys, especially when they are dealing with age mates or younger children.

The degree and type of aggression displayed in peer interaction are related only very tenuously to aggression displayed by children in home situations. Aggression in young children, however, can be fostered by harsh or restrictive parents who provide aggressive model figures with whom children identify. In studies of aggression exhibited by preschool children in doll play, severe punishment by parents appeared to correspond directly to preschool children's aggression toward the dolls (Lewin and Sears 1956). Children who are afraid to be aggressive against their parents may well be aggressive toward their own age mates.

Psychologists have distinguished between two basic types of aggressive behavior in preschool children (Bandura and Walters 1963; Feshbach 1970). The first, called angry or **hostile aggression,** seems to occur for its own sake and is its own goal. The preschool bully who calls a smaller child "sissy" in order to make that child cry is exhibiting hostile aggression. The same bully might grab away a toy or break it to achieve the same end. In both these examples, the crying or unhappiness of the smaller child serves to reinforce the bullying child. Reinforcement of hostile aggression may also come from the social approval of other children or through vicarious means, such as identifying with a bullying model parent.

A second type of preschool aggression identified by psychologists is **instrumental aggression.** In this case, the child's behavior is directed toward the achievement of what actually is a nonaggressive goal. For example, a preschool child who wants a toy held by a playmate may first try a variety of nonaggressive responses to get that toy. The child may ask for the toy, offer to trade another toy for it, or cry. If all of these fail, the child may finally resort to the aggressive behavior of grabbing the toy. Frequently, such antisocial behaviors as grabbing, punching, or verbal abuse are designed to obtain a goal unobtainable by other methods. Reinforcement (in this case, obtaining the desired toy) increases the behavior.

Instrumental aggression, whereby the child's aggressive behavior is actually directed at a nonaggressive goal (such as playing with a toy), is common in preschool children.

Instrumental aggression can be learned through identification with parents who daily exhibit instrumental aggression in their interactions with their children. The parent who grabs a teacup roughly and angrily away from the child to keep it from getting broken is likely to have a child who grabs other objects away from other children in a similar rough manner.

Dependence–Independence

Behavior, such as attachment behavior, that is designed to obtain or maintain the attention of the adult caregiver is called dependent behavior. Reinforcement is provided young children through imitating and identifying with caregivers. This behavior helps them later to interact more easily with other people and also to be less dependent on their own parents for reinforcement. With preschool children, dependence on the adult caregiver is related also to the type of child rearing and child-care given. Restrictive discipline in which children are not permitted to try new behaviors on their own, for example, is related to dependence in preschool children; more permissive caregiver behavior seems to lead to greater independence.

Two basic types of dependent behaviors have been studied in preschool children (Goggin 1974). **Instrumental dependency** includes behaviors initiated by children that directly reflect their desire for attention. The instrumentally dependent child asks directly for help or approval. For example, the three-year-old who stops the nursery school teacher every few minutes to ask, "Am I making my drawing right?" or "Is this the right way to put the blocks?" probably is seeking feedback.

Emotional dependency includes behaviors that do not directly appeal for help. These behaviors are designed to obtain attention directly by asking for social approval. Emotionally dependent children will be less likely to ask whether their drawings or block piles are what the teacher wanted. Instead, they might ask whether they are loved, or they might demand that the teacher demonstrate this love by asking, "Let me sit on your lap." Negative attention getting also is a reflection of emotional dependency. Even a spanking, because it requires attention of the caregiver, can provide reinforcement for the emotionally dependent negative attention getter.

Children with high dependency needs exhibit many behaviors evidencing these needs. Situations that do not present opportunities for reinforcement will be perceived by these children as highly stressful. Preschoolers continue to decrease their dependence as they increase their interactions with other people. Psychologists studying preschoolers have found a marked decrease in instrumental dependency on adult caregivers, as well as a corresponding decrease in interest in the nonliving objects around them (Scholtz and Ellis 1975). At the same time, other sorts of contacts with adults increase—for example, helpful contacts in which children give assistance, presents, or information to adults, instead of seeking aid. The five-year-old child who brings home a Valentine's Day present for mommy and daddy is making a helpful contact.

Children, as they grow from three to five years of age, learn more ways to provide helpful contacts both to adult caregivers and to peers. At the same time, they learn new ways to seek and receive help from other people. Similarly, as they develop new skills, young children gradually learn new ways to help themselves and to manipulate the environment to meet their personal needs. They gradually come to require less intimate and less frequent expressions of affection from their caregivers. They play for longer periods of time on their own and enjoy their own accomplishments without having to turn to others for approval. Increasing independence also is demonstrated through adopting more assertive roles in peer interaction.

Fear

Preschool children develop many fears through conditioning. Sometimes even one frightening experience, such as a large dog knocking down a small child, is sufficient to establish long-term fear. Other times, parents unknowingly teach fear to young children through imitation. The father who trembles during a thunderstorm is likely to have a child who also fears thunderstorms.

Jersild and Holmes (1935) found that children's fear of certain tangible and immediate situations decreases between three and six years. For example, they gradually become less afraid of strangers, strange objects, and strange noises. They become more afraid of imaginary creatures. Children do not fear things they have not heard much about, such as nuclear power or disease. They do fear being alone, seeing strange things, or hearing strange sounds. They also fear animals they have heard discussed, even if they have never actually seen the animals (Maurer 1965). Flaste (1977) reported that although what makes any child afraid varies considerably from child to child, still one in ten preschool children name their fathers as the person they are most afraid of.

The majority of children's fears are learned and are common to their culture. Table 5.2 lists some of the most common fears shown by American children in several experimental situations.

Erikson's Initiative vs. Guilt

The preschool years constitute the period in which children learn either initiative or guilt, according to Erikson (1963). During this period, the number of motor and cognitive tasks that children are able to perform increases greatly. If caregivers give

Table 5.2
Fears Shown by Children Age Two to Six in Several Experimental Situations

Situation	Percentage of Children Showing Fear			
	24–35 Months	36–47 Months	48–59 Months	60–71 Months
Being left alone	12.1	15.6	7.0	0
Falling boards	24.2	8.9	0	0
Dark room	46.9	51.1	35.7	0
Strange person	31.3	22.2	7.1	0
High boards	35.5	35.6	7.1	0
Loud sound	22.6	20.0	14.3	0
Snake	34.8	55.6	42.9	30.8
Large dog	61.9	42.9	42.9	0
Total	32.0	30.2	18.1	4.5

Source: Reprinted by permission of the publisher from Arthur T. Jersild and Frances G. Holmes, *Children's Fears* (New York: Teachers College Press, copyright 1935 by Teachers College, Columbia University), Table 14, p. 237.

their charges freedom to run, climb, ride bicycles, or experiment on the playground, they will increase the sense of initiative. If, on the other hand, caregivers are restrictive, children will develop feelings that they do not belong in the adult world, that they are nuisances, and that their role should be to accept passively what is presented to them.

The Phallic Stage

During the preschool years, children become aware gradually of their genitalia. According to Freud (1905), for most children between the ages of three and approximately seven, masturbation becomes the most pleasurable body activity. Freud cautioned that there are conflicts associated with the period. For boys, the major source of conflict is the **Oedipal complex** in which they become aware that they feel sexual love for their mothers and hostile rivalry for their fathers. According to Freud, this leads many young boys to fear a punishment by castration from their fathers. For girls, it is what Freud called the **Electra complex,** in which girls feel sexual love for their fathers and hostile rivalry toward their mothers. Freud concluded that girls feel that they have already been castrated because they have no penises and that they develop what he termed "penis envy." Mishandling of these sexual feelings and behavior, according to Freud, at this stage of development can lead to later sexual problems or inability to handle competitive relationships.

Many psychologists today are concerned that Freudian theory is based on data that Freud's emotionally disturbed patients presented to him and that many of these sources of conflict are not important to well-adjusted young American children (see Thompson and Grusec 1970, for example). In addition, proponents of the women's movement find unacceptable the notion of penis envy and propose that this aspect of Freudian theory is a sexist interpretation. Still, psychologists agree that well-adjusted caregivers can help their preschool charges to adjust satisfactorily and form well-adjusted personalities by being cautious not to punish them either for their feelings or for masturbating. Table 5.3 illustrates the level of development of preschool children in cognitive, psychosocial, psychosexual, and language skills.

Table 5.3
Preschool Development of Cognition, Psychosocial and Psychosexual
Responding and Language

Developmental stage	Level
Cognition (Piaget)	Preoperational (intuitive) symbolic representation
Psychosocial (Erikson)	Initiative vs. guilt
Psychosexual (Freud)	Phallic
Language (Erikson, Vygotsky)	Socialized, inner speech

SOCIALIZATION

An important part of development involves socialization, the process through which children learn to behave in ways acceptable to and desired by society. Socialization skills are learned, in part by imitation and identification and in part by other types of learning. Since most of the preschooler's time is spent either with the family or with a caregiver chosen by the family, an examination of family patterns of child rearing is helpful in understanding the way preschoolers learn socialization skills.

Patterns of Child Rearing

The classic descriptive study of childrearing in the United States was conducted two decades ago at the Harvard University Laboratory of Human Development. Although there have been major changes in family patterning since that time, the study is still pertinent because it describes many practices widely accepted and suggests some important trends in childrearing in this country.

Sears, Maccoby, and Lewin (1957) interviewed American mothers and asked them to describe their day-to-day interactions with their children. They asked the mothers how they took care of their young children, what sorts of play activities they engaged in, what they considered good and bad behavior, how they disciplined their children, and generally how they enjoyed their roles as mothers. From the mothers' answers, the authors developed a list of dimensions of maternal behavior that they considered important to child rearing and to socialization. They then rated the mothers on the bases of these dimensions. The study included only second-generation middle- or upper-working-class mothers who lived with their husbands and were not employed outside the home. Poor families, single-parent families, and families in which both spouses were employed were not included in the study.

Sears, Maccoby, and Lewin determined first that maternal behavior could be measured along the following five dimensions:

1. Maternal permissiveness vs. strictness in dealing with behaviors related to sex play, modesty, table manners, noise, toilet training, orderliness, and neatness

2. Maternal self-esteem and the mother's happiness with her status in the family

3. Warmth of the mother–child relationship as measured by such demonstrable affectional responses as hugging, patting, and smiling

4. Maternal tolerance for child aggression in play and day-to-day activities both with peers and with the mother

5. Types of rewards and punishments used in disciplining the child.

When the researchers rated American mothers along these dimensions, they found them to be generally strict, punitive caregivers. The mothers in the Sears study required their children to observe specific, socially prescribed behaviors at early ages.

For example, children in the Sears study were toilet trained as early as physically possible. Inappropriate behavior was frequently punished. In teaching manners, methods of playing with other children, or ways to interact with adults, American mothers tended to be strict, punitive, and often rigid models for their children. At the same time, they reported personal dissatisfaction and unhappiness with their own statuses in their own families (Harrington and Whiting 1972; Gibson 1981).

One explanation for what appear to be harsh childrearing practices, as described by Sears, Maccoby, and Lewin, is the small unit responsible for caregivers. Mothers in the Sears study all were unemployed outside the home and lived with husbands who were employed. In this population, only a few families included adults other than the mother and father. Mothers served as single, full-time caregivers for their children. In comparing childrearing methods of these American mothers of the 1950s with mothers in many other cultures, including many modern societies and many primitive tribes, the American mothers studied were far more strict, more punitive, and more rigid (Werner 1979; Gibson and Vinogradoff 1981).

The less strict mothers generally come from societies that rear their children communally, with many full-time caregivers sharing the responsibility. (In some societies, the major childrearers are adult women; in others, they are older children.) It can be assumed that mothers in the Sears study had more child-care responsibility for longer periods of time than less strict or punitive mothers. They were more concerned than tribal mothers that their children be toilet trained early and not soil their clothing, clean up after themselves, and generally not cause a fuss around the home. It might be assumed that the American mothers described by Sears were more burdened by their chores and therefore used childrearing methods designed to ease these burdens more often than did tribal mothers.

There has not been as comprehensive an examination of American mothers since the classic Sears study was conducted. Since the Sears study, however, there has been more than a thirty-percent increase in single-parent families in this country. In single-parent families, usually only one adult is responsible for childrearing and all other activities associated with maintaining a home. In addition, a large number of families now have two working parents. For caregivers in these families, the individual attention necessary for teaching socialization is even more difficult to arrange than it was for mothers in the Sears study.

The results of a rapidly changing social system and a decreasing family size in the United States have included not only harsh childrearing methods in the past several decades but greater permissiveness coupled with decreased attention to child rearing (Rebelsky 1973; Garbarino and Crouter 1978).

Styles of Discipline

Discipline, as we use the term here, is not necessarily punitive. *To discipline* means to teach. Parents discipline their children to behave in ways that are socially desirable and will allow the children to adapt satisfactorily to the world in which they will live. Research has shown that the degree to which mothers and fathers are supportive, controlling, hostile, or reasoning in their daily parent–child interactions has a significant impact on their children's overall development. Research has also shown that American mothers often are strict and punitive in the disciplining of their children (Garbarino and Crouter 1978). Is this important to the development of American children?

Sears, Maccoby, and Lewin distinguished in their study between two types of discipline. **Love-oriented discipline** refers to the effort to obtain desired behaviors by giving or withdrawing affection. It involves personal interaction. **Object-oriented discipline** involves obtaining desired behaviors by less personal means. Giving candy when the child behaves or sending the child to his or her room after misbehaving are examples. Love-oriented discipline leads to more and stronger emotional responding than object-oriented discipline. Children whose parents with-

Unhappiness caused by disciplining is quickly compensated by the warmth of the caregiver.

draw affection or who point out to their children that they are making them feel bad are likely to feel guilt along with other emotional responses too.

Becker (1964) suggests two dimensions of discipline that he considers critical to the development of a child's personality. According to Becker, both these dimensions relate not so much to specific parental behaviors as to parental attitudes toward childrearing. Becker's first dimension is love-oriented vs. power-assertive discipline. According to Becker, love-oriented discipline includes praise and reasoning and tends to be used by warm, supportive parents who provide the child with models of appropriate behavior. **Power-assertive discipline** involves the use of parental power and authority to control. Becker found this type of discipline tends to be used by cold, hostile parents and promotes child aggression.

The second dimension suggested by Becker is **restrictive discipline** vs. **permissive** discipline. Parents using **restrictive discipline** tend to dominate their children's behaviors, plan excessively for their needs, and control through frequent criticism. Becker found that children of restrictive parents tend to be more obedient than those of parents using more permissive methods. They do, however, exhibit inhibited behavior, something that does not usually lead to happy, healthy adjustment. As they grow older, they tend also to be more courteous, neat, and polite. **Permissive discipline,** in which more freedom is afforded the young child, tends to lead to uninhibited, less orderly, and more expressive behavior. Table 5.4 shows the consequences of Becker's two dimensions of discipline.

Table 5.4
Consequences of Different Kinds of Parental Discipline*

	Restrictiveness	Permissiveness

Warmth	Submissive, dependent, obedient
	Minimal aggression
	
	Maximum rule enforcement
	  (boys)
	Dependent, not friendly, not
	  creative
	Maximal compliance
		Active, socially outgoing, creative
		Minimal rule enforcement (boys)
		Minimal self-aggression (boys)
		
		Independent, friendly, creative,
		  low projective hostility

Hostility	"Neurotic" problems More quarreling and shyness with peers Socially withdrawn Maximal self-aggression (boys)	Noncompliance Maximum aggression

Source: From Consequences of parental discipline by Wesley C. Becker in *Review of Child Development Research,* edited by Martin L. Hoffman and Lois Wladis Hoffman. © 1964 by Russell Sage Foundation. By permission of Russell Sage Foundation.
*Wherever boys are listed in the table, this response was characteristic of male subjects but not of female subjects.

Gender differences in methods of discipline have been noted. For example, in the American middle-class family, the mother is more likely to discipline the young child verbally, while the father is more likely to discipline physically (Gecas and Nye 1974).

Punitive discipline, whether verbal or physical, often has an effect quite different from what one might expect. Punitive disciplinary techniques used by hostile parents frequently lead to an increase in other unexpected and often unwanted behaviors. Studies of two-and-a-half-year-old children whose parents are punitive have shown that these children are much less likely to exhibit the behaviors desired by their parents than are children of nonpunitive parents (Lytton and Zwirner 1975).

The consistency shown by parents in carrying out their discipline also influences the child's socialization. Parents who are inconsistent in following through with discipline are more likely to have children who learn socialized behaviors more slowly. There is no single link, of course, between specific behaviors in children and method of discipline. Other factors must be taken into consideration. Becker, for example, noted that the effects of discipline can be changed by the overall warmth of the parent. Punishment by a warm, loving parent has a very different effect from punishment by a cold, unaffectionate parent. The former often leads to compliance and obedience, and the latter can lead to high-level aggression.

According to Fritz Redl, the psychoanalytic theorist, the effects of punishment on the young developing child are extremely complex (Redl 1959). Among the many possible outcomes are upsurges of anger, often directed by the child toward himself or herself. The effects of punishment may be severe, particularly if the child being disciplined has any sort of emotional problem.

The Problem of Child Abuse

Researchers have related child maltreatment to the overall balance of stresses and supports in the family (Garbarino and Crouter 1978).

Child abuse—the physical or psychological abuse of children by their primary caregivers—is as old as human society, but because such abuse is rarely reported and easily covered up, it has been difficult to assess its frequency until recently. Now, with attention drawn to the problem by the women's movement, together with the advent of medical technology that allows physicians to measure the extent of old healed fractures and other wounds, it has become increasingly apparent that physical abuse of children is far more prevalent in our society than most of us had imagined.

It is estimated that, in the United States, 1.6 million children per year are victims of child abuse or serious neglect. More than half of these are children under the age of six (Cohen and Sussman 1975). According to statistics gathered for the United States Department of Health, Education and Welfare, at the very least 2000 children die annually from abuse, including beatings, burnings, sexual molestings, and inadequate feeding and care (American Psychological Association 1976). Other research indicates that in America, fourteen of every one hundred children are reported to suffer physical abuse by biting, kicking, punching, hitting with an object, or heavy beating (Farmer 1980).

Abusive parents come from all socioeconomic and cultural backgrounds, although some studies have found a relationship between child abuse and socioeconomic status (Garbarino and Crouter 1978). One reason may be that poor families have greater numbers of stresses and fewer supports. Parental characteristics common to all three types of abuse include a variety of psychological diagnoses, such as low self-esteem, personal–social isolation within the family and community, fear of rejection, and low frustration tolerance. Abused children often have some character istic (for example, a physical deformity) that sets them off from their siblings and causes them to be selected for abuse. Abusing parents often were abused children.

Effects of Changing Family Structures

Divorce and Preschool Children. The United States today has the highest divorce rate among Western nations. By the end of the 1970s, one in every two marriages was ending in divorce, and many divorces were being followed with remarriage. Sudden changes in family structures produce many different effects on small children. Wallerstein and Kelly (1980), in a five-year longitudinal study of children of divorced parents, noted three different results. About twenty-five percent of the children had adjusted successfully five years after the divorce. Fifty percent seemed to be able generally to muddle through, and about twenty-five percent had failed to recover from the divorce or were looking back to the predivorce family with intense longing. Wallerstein and Kelly suggested that what made the biggest difference for the children was not the specific change in the family itself but the same factors that make good adjustment and satisfaction in two-parent families: psychologically healthy parents and children involved with one another in appropriate ways.

It is necessary to know the particular situation before the effects of divorce or separation on children can be assessed. There is no doubt, however, that a divorce creates stress for all family members. Such stress can cause socialization problems, for children often blame themselves for the difficulties they see around them.

Some children believe in the domino theory: "If Daddy goes, why not Mommy?" Many children become overly dependent on the remaining parent. They are likely to resist losing sight of that parent, even by going into another room, for fear the parent might be gone when they come back. They might regress in their toilet training or become possessive of things.

Ages of children at the time of divorce seem to be correlated to ease of adjustment. Family tensions apparently have more detrimental effects on older children than on younger ones. Preschool children whose parents divorce are generally less aware of family conflicts, tend to feel more secure, and exhibit fewer feelings of inadequacy than do older children whose parents divorce. Still, researchers have found angry, sad, and forlorn responses in the great majority of preschoolers whose parents were being divorced. Among the more vulnerable children, these responses have been found to last more than a year, with the children exhibiting such symptoms as excessive need for physical contact, inability to play well with others, and diminished self-esteem (Wallerstein and Kelly 1979). Many children experiencing parental divorce seem to have far greater difficulty following rules and exhibiting "acting out" behavior (that is, aggressive or antisocial behavior) than children who have lost a parent through death (Felner 1977).

In cases where children are particularly vulnerable, crisis intervention from family groups, friends, or psychologists can be helpful. Whatever the therapeutic approach used during crisis intervention, it is important to remember that adjustment comes through reduction of family stress.

The Father-Absent Home. Although an increasing number of fathers are seeking and obtaining custody of their children after divorce, the vast majority of children whose parents divorce live with their mothers. Today, more than thirteen percent of all families with children have no father present in the home. What is the effect of this situation on preschoolers?

The effects of the father's absence have been found to be different for young boys and girls. The father's absence apparently has mixed implications for preschool girls. Some psychologists suggest that lack of male reinforcement for female sex-typed behaviors slightly weakens sex-role identification for young girls (Hunt and Hunt 1977). This result may be somewhat ameliorated, however, by the attitude and behavior of the mother. The mother who serves as a female ideal model, exhibiting strong female sex-typed behaviors and rewarding her daughter for these behaviors, will probably have a daughter with a strong female sex-typed identification. The preschool boy may face a more serious problem. By the age of two, in our society, young boys learn to imitate their father's rather than their mother's behavior. The father's total absence removes a major source of reinforcement for masculine behavior because it removes the male model (Lamb 1975).

Such effects depend on the adjustment of both mother and father to the divorce as well as the child's perception of the predivorce family. Divorce and the father's absence tend to be more traumatic for preschoolers who view their predivorce homes as happy rather than unhappy. The mother's attitude toward the absent father and her feelings toward men in general also play an important role in young children's perceptions of their fathers. This is particularly true for children who no longer have daily opportunities to experience relationships with their fathers, which would have helped to correct distortions provided by the mother. Grossberg and Crandall (1978) found that some children whose fathers were described by their mothers with such terms as "no good," "oversexed," or "promiscuous" seemed to exhibit the most sexual acting out.

Of course, many single parents are capable of providing home environments in which their young children are provided with adequate love and attention as well as appropriate models with whom to identify. One early study (Wright 1965) followed eighty unmarried mothers who decided to keep their babies after first going to adoption agencies for help. Children were judged to be receiving adequate attention in the majority of cases, and most were judged as developing normally without any socialization problems.

Mothers Working Outside the Home and Day Care. Today in American families with preschool children, at least one mother in three holds an outside job. The vast majority of mothers are employed for economic reasons, many because they must help support their families. More and more women, however, are pursuing careers to achieve personal fulfillment or for other noneconomic objectives. Whatever their reasons for working outside the home, many mothers report feeling guilty about the time spent away from their young children.

One factor that clearly affects child socialization when the primary caregiver works outside the home is the quality of the substitute care provided. Cohen (1978) pointed out that not only must the care be adequate but also that primary caregivers must be comfortable with the care and be able, in addition, to interact with their young children adequately themselves.

As noted in Chapter 4, in the United States today, the difference in quality among day-care programs is considerable. Preschool children raised in unstable care programs often give evidence of being insecure. Studies, however, have shown no increase in unwanted behaviors (for example, poor eating, bed wetting, aggression) when children are placed in high-quality, stable day-care programs. The strength of attachment to the mother has been found to be related to the amount of stimulation provided in the day-care center, rather than to whether or not the mothers worked (Etaugh 1974).

Another factor affecting children of mothers working outside the home is the mother's attitude toward working. Early studies of mothers who did not want to work outside their homes or who were ashamed about their economic statuses revealed that children of such mothers generally felt neglected. Mothers with strong guilt about their jobs often pass their anxieties on to their young children. On the other hand, women who enjoy their work and are proud of their accomplishments communicate this pride to their children. Children of these mothers tend to have self-role concepts that demonstrate belief in themselves and high self-esteem (Gold and Andres 1978).

Effects of Television

Preschoolers spend an enormous amount of time watching TV. Kenneth Keniston (1975), Chairman of the Carnegie Council on Children, described television as "a flickering blue parent occupying more of the waking hours of American children than any other single influence—including both parents and schools" (p. 55).

Television and Socialization. Television has alternately been castigated and praised for its role in child socialization. One group of researchers found that for preschoolers the amount of TV watching was inversely related to academic achievement and social ability with peers in the first grade. The children who watched TV the most during their preschool years tended to get lower grades and to get along less well with peers (Burton, Calonico, and McSeveney 1978). Some psychologists have suggested that watching violent programs can promote aggression in children or can promote excessive passivity. They contend that TV watching contributes to a distorted sense of reality and interferes with creativity (see, for example, Friedrich and Stein 1973; Gotz 1975). Others report the dangers of the advertising on TV because advertising so often distorts reality. On the positive side, evidence shows that if used appropriately, TV can provide positive potentials to the socialization of young Amer-

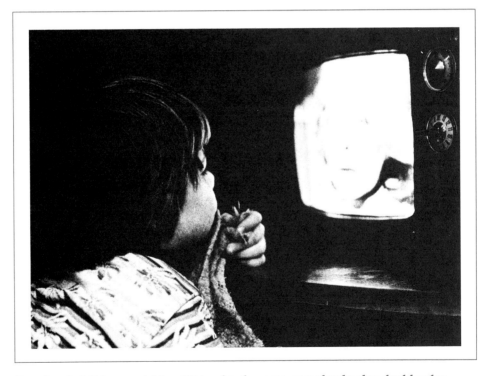

Preschool children watching TV tend to become completely absorbed by the images coming to them from the screen. For many children, the television set is a part-time babysitter.

ican children and to the development of their cognitive skills (Segal and Cooper 1979). For example, children have learned to get along with others on such prosocial programs as "Mister Rogers' Neighborhood" and have learned to identify the letters of the alphabet and count on such programs as "Sesame Street."

Television Watching and Aggression. Ever since Bandura and Walters (1963) reported that filmed violence increases the probability that viewers will exhibit aggressive behavior in stressful situations, Americans have been concerned about the effects of TV watching on children's behaviors. The concern is a real one: Surveys taken in the 1950s indicated that American preschool children then were watching TV an average of one to two hours daily. Systematic content analysis of prime-time TV in the late 1970s, when children were often watching for six hours or more daily, indicated that violent episodes appeared in eighty percent of the programs. During children's cartoons, violent episodes average 25.1 appearances per hour (Friedrich and Stein 1973).

Friedrich and Stein (1973) studied a group of ninety-three children who watched TV daily for four consecutive weeks as part of a nursery school program. Each child was exposed to one of three different types of programs: aggressive programs in which cartoon characters (as in "Batman" and "Superman") committed violent acts regularly, prosocial programs in which the models purposefully taught acceptable social responses (as in "Mister Rogers' Neighborhood"), and neutral programs in which neither aggression nor socially desirable behavior specifically was taught. The results of the study were striking. Preschool children who initially tended to be more aggressive toward their peers than the average of their group exhibited significantly more aggression after the four-week period than before. TV aggression, however, had no such effect on initially nonaggressive children. Similarly, the prosocial program had significant effects on its viewers: Children watching "Mister Rogers' Neighborhood" increased their prosocial behaviors. (It is interesting that "Mister Rogers' Neighborhood" had greater positive effects on higher-IQ children than on lower-IQ children.) The study seems clearly to indicate that TV can produce significant modeling effects, even on preschool-age children. At a time when TV is used more and more frequently as a baby sitter for young children, it is vital that acceptable model figures be provided in the programming.

PEERS AND PLAY

A major developmental task for preschool children in our country is to learn to relate socially and emotionally to peers as well as to adults if they are to get along satisfactorily in day-to-day situations. Successful peer interaction requires learning to cooperate and share in play situations, learning to be generous, and learning the rules that govern behavior in each situation. It also involves learning to handle jealousy and aggression and to become more independent, all difficult tasks for many preschoolers.

In what ways do peers and play aid children in their social development? For one thing, peer contact can compensate for lack of contact with an adult caregiver. This is extremely important in situations in which a caregiver does not provide optimal stimulation or social contact for his or her charges. For example, a primary caregiver may be ill and unable to spend a great deal of time interacting with his or her charge. Peer friendships and play give preschoolers opportunity to learn from one another through imitation and role play.

The Functions of Play

By the age of two or three, children involve themselves more and more frequently in different types of play. **Play,** a behavior engaged in for the child's amusement, can assume many different forms, including games, behavior imitative of adult models, dramatic play in which animals or objects are imitated, and make-believe acting out of socially unacceptable behavior.

Play recently has become a source of major interest to researchers who view it both as a mechanism of socialization and as an activity related to later creative output. For preschool children, play provides an opportunity to imitate and identify with adult models. Peer models also serve as important sources for social learning. Play using peers as models allows children to practice what they have learned and develop skills necessary for later life. Children often use this form of play as an outlet for expression of socially unacceptable behaviors and for working out social problems, as with conflicts with peers (Hartup 1977).

Group norms also can be expressed through role-playing activities. In societies where group roles are reinforced, understanding of group norms can develop as early as two years of age. Studies of kibbutz children have shown that two-year-olds already have a clear understanding of the difference between *we* and *they* (Faigin 1958).

Play often involves fantasy in which children make believe. This fantasy is firmly grounded in social reality and in what has already been learned. For example, children who pretend that they are parents when they play house probably will perform many activities they have seen their own parents perform, such as preparing meals, doing the laundry, coming home after a day at work, and the like.

Fantasy is used often as a socially acceptable outlet for socially unacceptable behaviors. Children who are jealous of the arrival of a new baby brother or sister would be punished if they were physically to harm the new baby. No such punishment, however, will be meted out if the jealous child hits a doll as a substitute for the unwanted sibling.

The Steps to Social Play

As noted in Chapter 4, early play of preschool children usually involves **solitary play,** or play that does not require peer interaction. Play in these early years usually centers around objects rather than people. Toddlers often enjoy playing by themselves with blocks. Role-playing toddlers may play "mommy" or "daddy" to toy "families" of doll babies. Later as children learn to interact with others, their play more and more frequently includes other people. By the time they reach four or five years old, children in free-play situations usually exhibit much more interest in their peers than they do in toys (Scholtz and Ellis 1975).

Social play, which involves playing with peers rather than toys, has its beginnings at about two or two-and-one-half years of age in what is called **parallel play.** Children engaged in parallel play do not directly involve themselves with others. Instead, they may play side by side with their peers, observing them, obviously enjoying the fact that they are present, but not directly interacting with them.

The next step after parallel play is **associative play,** in which children not only observe their playmates but also imitate their behaviors (Hurlock 1972). This imitation occurs most often when the children playing together differ in age or ability. Younger children tend to imitate the behaviors of older children.

Cooperative play develops after age three, when children learn to interact cooperatively with each other. Cooperative play involves learning to seek help from peers and to provide help for others. Children may take turns at such activities as pushing each other on the swings. In cooperative play involving role playing, one child usually plays a central model figure while others play satellite roles. Children "playing school," for example, often play teacher and students. The child who plays the teacher in this game is likely also to play the mommy or daddy when the children "play house."

In comparing the play of children of different ages, psychologists have noted that the amount of reinforcement children give each other increases with their ages. Four-year-olds, as compared with three-year-olds, exhibit much more positive attention, social approval, and affection toward one another. By the end of the fourth year, simple leadership patterns develop in small-group play. Other not-so-positive behaviors also develop, including peer rivalry and bullying (Cratty 1979).

MORAL DEVELOPMENT

The ways that children change, both in their responsiveness towards one another and in the rules they use to govern their interactions, have been studied extensively by stage-dependent theorists, particularly Jean Piaget and Lawrence Kohlberg.

Piagetian Theory

Piaget, in *The Moral Judgment of the Child* (1932), discussed the development of social and moral rules. Much of his theory was based on his observations of children playing marbles in the environs of his laboratory at Geneva. He noted what he called

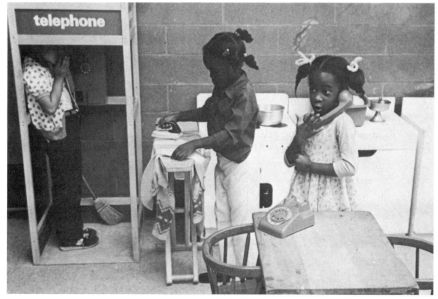

Preschool play assumes many forms, from pure physical fun to modeling adult behaviors.

clear developmental changes in the ways that children of different ages played and also in the ways that they viewed the rules of the game.

According to Piaget, the development of social rules occurs in a stage sequence essentially similar to that observed in cognitive development. The first stage, which he called the **presocial egocentric stage,** is characteristic of children in the preschool years, until approximately age six. At this stage, the only rules and regulations that govern preschool social activity are those set for them by adult caregivers. Thus three-year-olds who refrain from biting their playmates do so most probably because their parents have told them not to bite, not because they understand that their friends will feel pain if they are bitten.

Preschool children, according to Piaget, consider the rules they follow almost as made by God—unchanging and unchangeable. Instead of concerning themselves with learning rules, the children Piaget observed at marbles were preoccupied with learning control of their bodies and manipulation of the marbles. "Who won?" was a common question at the end of a game. Apparently, these children were much more interested in determining ways to make the marbles go where they wanted them than they were in winning a competition.

Preschool children take great pleasure in imitating the ordered doings of their elders and in identifying with them. According to Piaget, however, they neither know nor care why they are behaving this way. When they play, it is strictly for themselves.

Kohlberg's Refinement of Piaget's Approach

Lawrence Kohlberg (1969) extended the description of the stages of moral development advanced by Piaget and found a positive relationship between age and stage. Kohlberg described two stages typical of Piaget's presocial young children. The first stage, orientation to punishment and reward and to physical and material power, is descriptive of the behavior of younger preschool children whose guiding purpose is either to receive rewards or to avoid punishments. Children at this stage make decisions specifically based on whether they will receive praise or blame. Physical punishment and the possibility of material rewards are very important to them.

A second more advanced stage follows this very early stage: hedonistic orientation with an instrumental view of human relations. At this stage, children still make decisions on the basis of the rewards or punishments they may receive. They have learned, however, that if they provide reinforcers for others, they may receive reinforcement in return. Young children learn that their peers are capable of providing reinforcers. The specific age at which this occurs varies considerably from child to child. Children at this stage of development respond to many reinforcers other than physical power, love, and affection. They may respond positively, for example, to praise or to sharing toys with their peers. The five-year-old child may share a favorite toy with a friend. According to Kohlberg, most preschool children share not because sharing is intrinsically good but because they have beginning notions of reciprocity with emphasis on the exchange of favors. They fully expect to receive a favored toy in return.

INDIVIDUAL DIFFERENCES IN DEVELOPMENT

Just as it is true that each infant develops at his or her own pace, it is also true that there is considerable variation in the development of preschool children. Differences in the rates and style of sensorimotor development, language and cognitive development, and social–emotional development can be influenced by a variety of different factors, including socioeconomic status, birth order, and physical or mental handicaps.

Developmental Differences and Socioeconomic Status

A number of developmental differences have been found to be related to socioeconomic status. Babies born into poor families tend more frequently than others to be at risk (that is, they are more likely to suffer from birth defects and to have physical or mental disabilities). Preschool children from poor families frequently continue to experience these problems unless special care is provided to remedy them. The effects of inadequate nutrition either prenatally or during infancy often are long lasting. Perkins (1977), for example, found that intellectual deficits due to early malnutrition sometimes continue through at least the sixth year of life, even if proper nourishment is provided after infancy.

Poor children are more likely than middle-class children to be deprived not only of proper nourishment and material well-being but also of stimulation necessary for normal cognitive development. As a result, many people blame poverty for the fact that lower-class children of many different cultural backgrounds often test lower on IQ tests than children of middle-class families. Many psychologists believe that these differences are superficial and that their lower IQ scores are probably due to culturally biased test instruments (see, for example, Cole and Bruner 1972). But even though the IQ differences may have little meaning, many children from lower socioeconomic groups, especially those from minority groups, learn dialects different from that typically used by middle-class children. These children later find it difficult to learn in schools, which, of course, are usually staffed by middle-class teachers.

Children from lower socioeconomic groups also learn to express their feelings in ways somewhat different from middle-class children. Children whose low-income mothers work outside the home and whose days are spent in communal preschools, for example, may learn to cooperate and share at earlier ages than middle-class children reared at home in relative isolation from other children (Bronfenbrenner

Socioeconomic status can have a significant effect on rates of development.

1970). These same communally reared children only infrequently exhibit either hostile or instrumental aggression. Bellack and Antell (1974), in a study of German, Italian, and Danish preschool playground activity, found that children raised in a country where parents tend generally to act aggressively toward their children (Germany) tend to exhibit much more aggression in playground activities than do children raised where parents tend to be more affectionate (Italy and Denmark).

Aggression also has been linked by some authors to socioeconomic status. Poor children generally are more aggressive toward their parents than are children from more affluent socioeconomic backgrounds. Similarly, McKee and Leader (1955) found that three- and four-year-old children from lower socioeconomic backgrounds tend to be considerably more aggressive as well as more competitive in their peer interactions than are children from higher socioeconomic backgrounds.

Developmental Differences and Birth Order

It is now generally accepted that birth order is an important component of the child's environment and affects both personality and behavior. In general, younger siblings speak later than do older siblings. Psychologists attribute such delayed speech and lowered scores on tests of other abilities in younger siblings to a lack of parental attention at early ages; parents with more than one child are likely to have less time to devote to each child (Zajonc 1976). The fact that singletons (children with no siblings) speak earlier than do children raised in larger families appears to provide evidence for this position.

Developmental Differences and the Handicapped Child

We noted in Chapter 4 that physical handicaps and deformities noticeable at birth can affect developmental progress later on. A good example is Down's syndrome. Children with Down's syndrome exhibit specific physical facial characteristics associated with the defect. These include slanting eyes, broad skulls, and short fingers. Infants and young children with Down's syndrome exhibit extremely slow developmental progress and mental retardation. Other mentally retarded children who might not have been readily identified as such when they were infants because they appeared physically normal are noticeable by their developmental lags by the time they reach the preschool years.

Children with physical handicaps that keep them from interacting with others tend to lag behind socially as well as physically because a great deal of social development of the preschooler is learned through social interaction, identification, and imitation. Any handicap that serves to decrease social interaction also tends to slow social development.

THE CASE OF MARY-LYNN—A CHILD OF DIVORCE: A CASE STUDY FOR CLASS DISCUSSION

I. Identification and Sources of Information

Name: Mary-Lynn Solomon

Address: 14 Oak Lane, Denver, Colorado

Race: White

Age: Five years

Sources of Information

1. Interview with Mary-Lynn
2. Interview with Mary-Lynn's mother
3. Interview with Mary-Lynn's pediatrician

II. Family History

Mary-Lynn is the five-year-old daughter of Dr. and Mrs. Philip Solomon. The Solomons were divorced three years ago, when Mary-Lynn was two years old. Since that time, Dr. Solomon, a cardiologist, has lived in another state. Last year, he remarried. Mary-Lynn's mother is twenty-nine years old. She had married Dr. Solomon seven years ago; the divorce was initiated by him. One year ago, Mrs. Solomon became interested in another man, whom she is now planning to marry. Her fiance, Bob, also is divorced and has a

Continued

THE CASE OF MARY-LYNN *(Cont.)*

son, Billy, age six. Billy and his father occasionally visit the Solomon home and spend the weekend.

Dr. Solomon, since his remarriage, has not visited Mary-Lynn. Mary-Lynn visited her father once just prior to his marriage. In order to make the trip, her mother sent her alone on an airplane. Although her father and his fiancee met Mary-Lynn in the airport in the city where they live, Mary-Lynn complained a great deal about her fear of the flight. Her father has not invited her since, although he did write that they might plan a Christmas vacation together this year.

III. Case History

Mary-Lynn's pediatrician reported that Mary-Lynn was born without complications after a short labor. She developed normally during her first year. During her second year, her parents began to have serious marital difficulty. Her father began spending increasing periods of time away from the house. Her mother reported having "severe depressions." Mary-Lynn was left for extended periods of time with a baby sitter while her mother "rested in bed." When Mary-Lynn was almost three, her father moved from the house permanently. Her mother began several years of psychoanalysis. Mrs. Solomon has recently stopped her treatment on the advice of her analyst.

When Mary-Lynn was two, her mother first reported behavioral problems to the pediatrician. For one thing, Mary-Lynn, who had been toilet trained by eighteen months, began wetting her pants continually. The pediatrician suggested that this behavior is not uncommon in times of stress and that it probably would be resolved gradually if ignored. When Mary-Lynn was almost four, however, she was still having "accidents" on a regular basis.

Mrs. Solomon first took her daughter to a mental health specialist when the child was five years old. Mrs. Solomon was frantic about her daughter's behavior. Mary-Lynn, according to her mother, was extremely difficult to manage, was wetting the bed, and

was also wetting her pants daily. In addition, she was extremely rude to Mrs. Solomon's boyfriend.

Mrs. Solomon reported that she had returned to school to complete a master's degree in business administration and recently planned to begin work the following year. She said that she was "sick and tired of having to depend on Phil" (her ex-husband). "He only sends money after I ask and ask, and then he makes me document every last item I buy either for me or for Mary-Lynn. You'd think a physician would be a bit less chintzy than that. But then, he always was that way, making me count pennies on what I'd spend for food when he was bringing in more than $75,000 a year. Since he remarried, he's worse than ever. I told Mary-Lynn that she couldn't have a lot of toys for Christmas this year because her father was late again on his payments. Then Phil forgot even to send her a Christmas present himself! Next year, I probably will remarry. Then my alimony will stop, and even with the child support that Phil sends, it'll be important for me to work."

Bob's son, Billy, has lived with his mother since his parents' divorce. He sees Bob on weekends. When Bob (Mrs. Solomon's friend) and his son started spending increasing amounts of time at the Solomon home on weekends, Mary-Lynn started to act out more seriously than she had earlier.

Mary-Lynn complained in her interview that her mother used to spend more time with her. Now according to the child, "Mommy likes work and Bob and Billy, not me. I think she even likes Billy more than me; she's nicer to him." Mary-Lynn remembers spending lots of time with her mother in the past three years but thinks that "now Mommy always goes out." After the divorce, Mrs. Solomon let her daughter sleep with her. Mary-Lynn no longer is allowed in her mother's bedroom when her fiance is there. Mary-Lynn had no difficulty expressing hatred toward Bob or toward his son. She called them both "pigs." She became very clinging toward her mother and reported that "Mommy is the bestest person. I love her

THE CASE OF MARY-LYNN

very much." When asked about her feelings about her father and his new wife, Mary-Lynn became vague. "Daddy lives in another city," she said, and changed the subject to a new toy Bob had brought her. She threw the toy across the room angrily.

IV. Present Status, Diagnosis, and Prognosis

Mary-Lynn is excessively dependent on her mother and incapable of expressing the anger she feels. Her father's absence seems to have contributed largely to her feelings. Her toilet accidents began at the time that the Solomons' marriage dissolved. They got worse when Mrs. Solomon began thinking of remarriage and Mary-Lynn's father took a new wife. Mary-Lynn suffers greatly from insecurity and fears being abandoned. Because the loss of her father has left Mary-Lynn in a state of disequilibrium, any changes in her environment make her coping more difficult. If Mrs. Solomon is to work out a successful marriage and still help her daughter, both she and her new husband will have to give considerable support to Mary-Lynn in adjusting to the changes in her environment. They can do this most effectively by trying, at least in the first year, to keep the child to the most normal schedule possible. It may be important to change Mary-

Lynn's sleeping habits. Mary-Lynn can no longer share her mother's bed. But her mother and stepfather can do their best to keep other aspects of the environment as familiar as possible. This includes familiar foods and routines and her own belongings. No stress should be placed at this time on toilet demands. Mary-Lynn and her family all will need continued assistance from the mental health clinic if the child is to adjust and eventually develop a normal repertoire of socially acceptable responses.

Questions for Thought Concerning Mary-Lynn

1. It seems clear that some of Mary-Lynn's current behavior results from problems her mother had in adjusting initially to her divorce. How could Mrs. Solomon have behaved differently so as to make adjustment easier for her daughter?

2. How has Mary-Lynn's mother's attitude toward her ex-husband probably affected her daughter's view of the divorce and of Mrs. Solomon's new boyfriend?

3. Do you think Mary-Lynn's adjustment to her father's rejection is more difficult for her to experience than if her father had died? Why?

SUMMARY

Sensorimotor development increases rapidly during the preschool years. Children improve both their gross and their fine motor skills, with one set of skills building on another. Piaget suggested that preschool children increase their abilities to think and to understand by characterizing all new experiences according to past experience. He described specific stages of preconceptual thought in the cognitive development of young children. The early stage, symbolic representation, involves increasing interest in ability to use signs and symbols to represent objects in the outside world. The later stage, intuitive responding, involves learning to use these signs and symbols to test new methods of dealing with these objects. Symbolic play and fantasy play appear during this stage.

A number of different theories explain language development. Some learning theorists attribute it to reinforcement by caregivers; others suggest that modeling and imitation of caregivers play a major role; still others believe that language is primarily culturally determined. Linguist Noam Chomsky proposes that we cannot explain language fully without hypothesizing an innate characteristic inherent to the human mind that enables children to process language, construct language, and understand complex speech.

Much of preschool personality development takes place through imitation of and identification with model figures. Sex-role identification begins early, with preschool children learning sex-typed behaviors from peers and other models as well as from their parents. By age three, boys in our culture tend to exhibit significantly more aggressive behavior at play than do girls. Preschool children in the United States exhibit a variety of aggressive behaviors. Angry or hostile aggression seems to occur for its own sake; instrumental aggression is directed toward the achievement of what actually is a nonaggressive goal.

Two types of dependency have been studied in preschool children: instrumental dependency, which is a direct appeal for help or approval; and emotional dependency, which includes indirect attention-getting behavior. During the preschool years, children learn fear and either initiative or guilt, depending on the amount of freedom given to them by their caregivers. They also gradually become aware of their genitalia. According to Freud, mishandling of sexual feelings and behavior at this stage of development can lead to later sexual problems.

The learning of behaviors acceptable to society is called socialization. Compared to mothers raising their children in tribal societies where many caregivers share the childrearing load, American mothers tend to be stricter, more punitive, and more rigid. Discipline affects children differently depending on its nature (for example, love-oriented vs. power-assertive discipline or restrictive vs. permissive discipline), the consistency with which it is given, and the personalities of the parents. Child abuse is prevalent in our society. Characteristics of child abusers include low self-esteem, personal–social isolation within the family and community, fear of rejection, and low frustration tolerance. Changing family styles caused by increased divorce and separation and mothers working away from home have led to a variety of problems for preschoolers. The effects depend on the individual situations.

Television has significant modeling effects, even on preschool children. Researchers have pointed out a number of problems associated with widespread TV watching by preschoolers; evidence also shows that TV can have positive effects. A great deal of socialization is learned through peers and play. Psychologists have shown that peers can play important compensatory roles when adequate caregiving from adults is not available.

The development of social play occurs in a series of stages. Early play is solitary, without peer interaction. Social play consists first of parallel play, then of associative play, and finally of cooperative play. The development of social rules in play has been studied extensively by stage psychologists. Piaget noted that it occurs in a stage sequence similar to that of cognitive development. Preschool children vary considerably in rates and syles of development. Developmental differences can be influenced by a number of factors, including socioeconomic status, birth order, and physical or mental handicaps.

FOR FURTHER READING

Cole, M., and S. Scribner. *Culture and Thought: A Psychological Introduction.* New York: Wiley, 1974. The relationships among language, thought, and culture are given careful consideration in this text. Effects of different types of environments on cognitive and language abilities are described. Excellent examples from a variety of cultures provide interesting reading.

Jordan, T. *Development in the Preschool Years.* New York: Academic Press, 1980. An exceptionally thorough longitudinal study, *Development in the Preschool Years* describes and analyzes the psychological, social, and educational development of some 1000 children in the St. Louis area. Using biological, social, family, and maternal information, the author examines the physical, motor, intellectual, linguistic, and social development of the children. The sample includes black and white children, both inner-city and suburban, ranging in background from very poor to wealthy.

Preview Questions

- What are four major advances in the physical and motor development of middle childhood?

- How is the child's reasoning related to real objects during the concrete operational stage?

- Can you give examples of the following cognitive advances of middle childhood: decentration, conservation, seriation, classification, class inclusion?

- What are four major facets of personal and social development that change during middle childhood?

- How does the moral reasoning of children in this stage differ from that of preschoolers, and how are these changes influenced by parents?

- Can you explain how childrearing styles, social class, and television influence children's interaction with their peers?

- What are Gibson's four basic steps in learning to read, and how does reading skill influence a child's feelings of industry or inferiority?

- How does our educational system usually affect creativity, and what can teachers do about it?

- Can you explain how bilingualism affects children's success in school?

- What are the major functions performed by standardized intelligence tests and some precautions to be observed in their use?

- How does peer influence change during middle childhood?

- Can you describe some school-related problems that are caused by poverty, physical handicaps, mental retardation, learning disabilities, and hyperactivity?

6

Middle Childhood: The Years from Five to Eight

Because most studies of child development have involved children under the age of six, much more is known about infancy and the preschool years than about the period of middle childhood. The school years, however, particularly from kindergarten to grade three, are critical in the development of social behavior. During this period, interests, attitudes, and capabilities expand with the child's environment, and children gain more opportunities for socialization by interacting with others outside the family. The school exerts an increasingly strong influence on development in all areas. During the first several years of formal schooling, physical and mental abilities, body maturation, and perceptual-motor coordination increase, even though the rate of growth begins to slow and continues at a slower rate than during the preschool years. Thinking skills also develop, usually to the point at which children are able to handle many new cognitive tasks required at school. These newly developing skills enable youngsters to interact with others in increasingly complex ways and generally to adjust to the new life of the school years.

PHYSICAL AND MOTOR DEVELOPMENT

Physical growth and development in the primary school years are characterized by a gradual decrease in fatty tissue with a concurrent increase in bone and muscle development. The building of muscle is generally more rapid in boys, while girls continue to retain thicker layers of fat. Girls, on the other hand, soon equal boys in height. Although the average girl may be as much as three-quarters of an inch shorter than the average boy at the age of six, by ten years she has caught up and has often surpassed him.

Substantial improvements in motor skills are typically achieved during middle childhood. Children gradually perfect their control of their large muscles and improve control over their small muscles. Children in kindergarten can not only skip, but they can also stand on one foot for prolonged periods of time, more than eight seconds. By age seven, there is noticeable improvement in both their gross and fine motor coordination; children usually can throw balls in a more advanced manner (a "grown-up" throw with proper weight shift and step) and balance on each foot alternately, even with their eyes closed. They can walk a two-inch-wide balance beam, hop and jump accurately into small squares, and execute accurate jumping-jack exercises. They can tie their own shoelaces. By the time they are eight, they can engage in alternate rhythmical hopping in two-two, two-three, or three-three patterns. They are stronger and can participate in a wider variety of games requiring motor skills.

The drawing ability of first graders shows marked improvement over their earlier efforts. The circles they draw are rounder than at age five, and they often can draw squares and rectangles in one continuous stroke. About half of six-year-olds can write the numbers from one to twenty and the letters of the alphabet. The letters

By middle childhood, most children have improved significantly in their motor coordination.

they draw are smaller than those they drew at five, much more legible, and are drawn in clear alignment on the page. By seven years, children exhibit good hand–eye coordination: They can draw triangles accurately from the top downward and can copy diamond shapes. When asked to draw a person, they can put in many fine details, such as hands, neck, or articles of clothing. By eight, they still lack perspective in their drawing, but their drawings of people contain arms and legs represented by two parallel lines rather than the stick figures of previous years, a rudimentary kind of three-dimensional representation (see Fig. 6.1). Most eight-year-old children can perceive the differences among letters of the alphabet that have similar basic structures. The confusion that exists for most preschoolers among b, p, d, and q is gone for the vast majority of eight-year-olds (Watson and Lowrey 1967; Cratty 1979).

It is important to remember that children grow at their own rates and that there are wide individual differences in the ages at which various motor skills are mastered. This is as true for the years of middle childhood as it is for the preschool years. Researchers have shown that children who are able to perform many motor tasks well tend to have more positive self-images than children who perform less

Fig. 6.1   By the age of eight, children's drawings of people contain full arms and legs with width.

well. Hardy and Nias (1971) reported that children who learned most easily to swim also tended to be extroverted, a characteristic associated with high self-esteem. Platzer (1976) found that perceptual–motor ability was important to the self-concepts of young children. Poorly coordinated children who were trained to improve their perceptual–motor skills gained more positive self-images.

 COGNITIVE DEVELOPMENT

By the end of the preschool years, children have developed the ability to solve increasingly complex problems. They still, however, lack the ability to perform mental operations without the aid of concrete examples. Piaget called this period the concrete operational stage of cognitive development.

Concrete Operational Stage

When traditional techniques are used with children at the concrete operational stage, teachers use concrete examples of all new concepts to help them grasp fully the concepts being taught. Children at this stage are unable to perform mental operations that require abstractions. Children at the stage of concrete operations might, for example, be able to count two blocks set before them but they would not be able to solve the abstract problem $1 + 1 = 2$.

When young children at the concrete operational stage of development are presented with concepts that adults deal with abstractly, such as the concept of God, they tend to recreate the concept in language at a concrete level. First and second graders, for example, often talk to God as another human being subject to all the feelings and emotions they themselves experience. Following is an example of the concrete thinking characteristic of this age level (Marshall and Hample 1966):

Dear God:
We are going on vacation for two weeks Friday so we won't be in church. I hope you will be there when we get back. When do you take your vacation? Goodbye.

Donnie

First grade teachers in the United States have found that an effective way to teach children at the concrete operational stage such concepts as $2 + 2 = 4$ is to present to the class a number line or a series of objects, such as blocks that the children can count. Children learning to read also learn rapidly if learning materials are presented in concrete form. For example, the Montessori method of teaching reading uses concrete stimuli matched to the cognitive level of the students. Montessori (1914) used colored letters cut out of sandpaper. Children learning the alphabet were encouraged to pick up each of the letters and handle them as they learned their names and sounds.

Children learn to understand jokes, as long as they are matched to their level of cognitive development (McGhee 1976). Six-year-olds enjoy the joke about what one little daisy says to another. Only when they are much older will they appreciate political jokes dealing with such abstract issues such as war and peace.

Children at the concrete operational stage are able to focus their attention on several different dimensions of a situation simultaneously, an ability Piaget called **decentration.** An example of this is their awareness of the principle of **conservation**—that is, that certain properties of objects, such as volume or mass, remain constant (are conserved) despite transformations in the appearance of the objects. They understand, for example, that a ball of clay smashed flat on the table is still the same amount of clay as when it was round. They can also see that a quantity of liquid poured from a short, fat container into a tall, thin container is still the same quantity of liquid. Their ability to do this shows that they can focus on both the height and width in relation to each other. According to Piaget, however, to understand this, children at this cognitive level still need to touch or see the object in front of them; they are unable to understand it without being able to use their senses to explore the objects before them. After concrete experiences, the children's ability

During the concrete operational stage, children learn best when concrete objects
are used to present concepts. These Soviet children are learning to count by
watching their teacher and using cut-out pieces to match the numbers in
the story she is telling.

to remember and visualize the actual objects in front of them helps them in their
problem solving.

Children at this stage learn also to differentiate between parts and wholes.
Schoolchildren will not accept a cookie broken into two parts as two cookies, as
some preschoolers will. By the time they reach school age, children know that a
cookie broken in half consists of two parts of the same cookie.

Conceptual Abilities

Other conceptual abilities are mastered gradually, often before the child has mastered the concept of conservation. **Seriation** involves the ability to order a series of
objects along some dimension. Children at the concrete operational stage can learn

AN EXERCISE TESTING PIAGETIAN-TYPE TASKS   HIGHLIGHT 6.1

When Piaget conducted his research, he often used tasks that could easily be performed at the kitchen table. The following Piagetian-type tasks were used by an educational psychologist at the University of Pittsburgh with American children (Vasudev 1976). To try these tasks, find two children, one aged five or six and the other aged eight or nine. Ask them, one at a time, to perform the following tasks. Write their responses to your questions. When you are finished testing both children, answer the questions that follow the tasks.

Task 1: CONSERVATION OF MASS

Step 1: Take two balls composed of equal amounts of clay or dough. Show them to the child and ask, "Are they both the same?" (If the child does not think that they are the same, allow sufficient opportunity for manipulation of the balls to demonstrate that this is the case.)

Step 2: Roll out one of the balls, in view of the child, into a "hot dog." Ask the child, "Is there the same amount of clay in the ball as in the hot dog?"

Step 3: Ask the child to explain his or her answer.

Task 2: CONSERVATION OF CONTINUOUS QUANTITY

Step 1: Take two glasses and fill them with the same amounts of water. Ask the child, "Is there the same amount of water in both glasses?" (If the child does not think that they are the same, demonstrate that this is the case.)

Step 2: In front of the child, pour the contents of one glass into a glass that obviously is taller and slimmer. Ask the child, "Do the tall glass and the shorter glass have the same amount of water?"

Step 3: Ask the child to explain his or her answer.

QUESTIONS FOR THOUGHT

1. Did the children respond differently to the questions you asked them? If yes, describe these differences fully.

2. Look back to descriptions of Piaget's stages of cognitive development described in this chapter and in earlier chapters. According to these descriptions, at what level of development is each of these children responding? What evidence can you give to support your answer?

to pile blocks according to size, the largest block on the bottom and the smallest block on top with blocks of gradually decreasing size in between. **Classification** involves the ability to sort objects according to some quality. Younger children learn to classify according to such concrete attributes as color or size. **Class inclusion** involves the ability to recognize that some classes of objects are subsets of other more inclusive classes and that an object may belong both to the subset and to the more inclusive classes. Thus they know dogs are a subset of the class of animals and puppies belong to the subset dogs as well as to the more inclusive animal class.

As we have pointed out before, Piaget contends that children pass through the stages of cognitive development in a specified order. In order to reach the concrete operational stage of middle childhood, they first pass through the earlier preoperational stage. Similarly, in order to reach the formal operational stage characteristic of the later school years, they first pass through the concrete operational stage (Piaget 1952b; Piaget and Inhelder 1964).

At any given stage, children tend to learn concepts in a specific order (Dimitrovsky and Almy 1975). For example, they generally master the concept of conservation of quantity before they learn conservation of weight. Studies have shown that the ability to perceive part–whole differences develops in a regular progression. This is also true of the ability to understand conservation of mass, weight, and volume; the additive composition of classes; and the concepts right and left (Elkind 1961a; 1961b; 1961c; Elkind et al. 1964).

Children learn a variety of concepts by the time they reach first grade. For example, they usually know their right from their left hands and can verbally identify many more parts of their bodies, including even their middle and ring fingers. Psychologists believe that the order in which concepts are learned can be affected by experience: More commonly experienced objects and concepts are assimilated into the child's cognitive structure before less commonly experienced objects and concepts.

PERSONALITY DEVELOPMENT AND SOCIALIZATION

During the primary school years, a major developmental task of children continues to be learning to relate socially and emotionally to peers. Socialization now, as in earlier years, involves channeling emotional expression into behaviors acceptable to society.

Development of Sharing, Cooperation, and Generosity

Relating emotionally to peers in socially acceptable ways requires sharing, cooperation, and generosity. In addition, it sometimes requires inhibiting expression of socially unwanted emotions, such as jealousy. Of course, both cooperation and sharing

Children in the early elementary school years learn that in order to enjoy many activities, they need to cooperate with others and share the work effort.

are fostered when adults reward children for those behaviors. By the time they reach six or seven, most children are ready to share favored possessions, like candy, with other children who do not have any (Hull and Reuter 1977). Developmental studies, with rare exceptions, indicate that the incidence of generosity increases with age. Jealousy, an emotion not conducive to successful peer interaction, occurs when one child desires the attention or other reinforcement given to a peer. Those children who have been provided with consistent loving attention are less likely to exhibit jealousy.

Defense Mechanisms

Sometimes children, no matter how hard they try, have difficulty expressing their emotions in socially desirable ways. Often these are children who have frequently been punished or ignored. As a result, they often experience high anxiety. According

HIGHLIGHT 6.2 **LEARNING COOPERATION**

A few years ago, a New York City public school project was designed to teach cooperation through games (Vidal 1976). After a year of "literally playing games," fifth and sixth graders enrolled in P.S. 75 and P.S. 101 displayed significantly greater ability to cooperate, to communicate with others, and to resolve group conflicts.

The program leading to these behavior changes involved a forty-five-minute weekly game period in which all children learned to create new responses to old situations through creative skits and games, such as "Simon says" and "know your orange."

Project games were designed to develop skills that could help to reduce the likelihood of classroom conflict and competition. In "Simon says," for example, all competition was eliminated by allowing children who did things that Simon did not say to remain in the game. Instead, group cooperation and the individual need to listen were stressed. In "know your orange," class members sat in a circle. Each child was given an orange. Children were given five minutes to study their own oranges and later were asked to identify them from among a batch of oranges. The message in this game was simple: Oranges, like people, are not all alike.

QUESTIONS FOR THOUGHT

1. When teachers give children messages, like the one in "know your orange," that people are not all alike, should they assume that children will understand that they should therefore treat different people in different ways?

2. How do you think these games improve abilities to communicate and cooperate?

to Sigmund Freud (1905), highly anxious children are likely to develop **defense mechanisms**, unconscious strategies designed to reduce the anxiety. Many different mechanisms have been described by psychologists. One mechanism commonly used by preschoolers involves substituting acceptable behavior for unacceptable behavior. This mechanism is called **sublimation.** The hostile child discussed earlier may learn gradually that aggressive behavior will not lead to desired goals. Such a child may learn to redirect this behavior by becoming proficient at some activity, thereby regaining social approval and attention.

Another defense mechanism, **denial,** involves explaining away or refusing to acknowledge the existence of anxiety-producing stimuli. Children whose parents are in the process of a divorce may reduce the anxiety they feel by denying that they care about their parents or by denying that the parents are getting a divorce.

Projection, another defense mechanism, reduces anxiety by permitting a child to attribute unacceptable behavior to the outside world. Some children constantly initiate fights with other children, then accuse these victims of their own bad behavior. When this happens, we say that these children are projecting.

Sometimes children feel hostile toward an adult or toward another individual perceived to be powerful. Because they are afraid to act aggressively toward this person, they sometimes displace their aggression to a weaker person. A child whose teacher has just been highly punitive may immediately turn around and knock down a smaller child. Such behavior is an example of **displacement.**

Sex-Role Development and Sex Differences

Sex-role adoption, we learned earlier, refers to the degree to which children regard themselves as male or female. **Sex typing** refers to the selection of behavior that is considered socially acceptable for a given sex.

Sex typing begins well before the school years. By the time they reach primary school, boys and girls are remarkably similar in their ability to identify socially accepted sex-typed behaviors (Maccoby 1974). Williams *et al.* (1975) showed picture stories to young boys and girls from kindergarten through second grade, asking them to identify the picture characters with known adult sex-typed stereotypes, such as aggressive for masculine sex typing and dainty for feminine. As both boys and girls grew older they tended to give responses increasingly similar to these adult sex stereotypes. For example, male characters in the picture stories were more often described as aggressive, strong, or adventurous, and female characters were more often described as gentle, emotional, or appreciative.

Boys develop sex-role preferences earlier and more consistently than do girls. On measures of sex-role preferences—for example, on the IT Scale for Children, which asks children to select either male- or female-stereotyped toys—girls tend to fluctuate between male and female choices until about age ten, when a rapid shift to femininity occurs. School-age girls tend to fluctuate in their preferences more than do boys (Hetherington and Parke 1975). This ambivalence has been attributed by many psychologists to elementary school girls' increasing awareness of greater privilege and prestige associated with the male role in our society.

Attitude and Value Development

An important aspect of personality and social development during middle childhood is the development of attitudes and values. **Attitudes** refer to fairly consistent orientation toward difference aspects of the environment and toward oneself.

Attitude development begins at home and reflects the individual problem-solving activities, emotions, and perceptions of each child. Different socialization experiences produce different attitudes. A child constantly exposed to ridicule in the classroom, for example, may develop a poor self-image as a student as well as a negative attitude toward school; a child who receives praise in school is likely to develop a positive self-image and a more joyous attitude toward learning.

Values can be defined as evaluations of the acceptability or unacceptability of things and behaviors. Values are the criteria by which children judge their own responses and their environments. On the basis of values, they decide what is good or bad, what should be desired, and what sorts of actions to take. Values, like attitudes, are consistent. The child who is apathetic toward school may well have learned at home from parents that school learning is not to be highly valued. Such children can be expected to be very unhappy in school, for they are caught in a value–attitude clash between home and school.

School-age children perceive attitudes and values quickly and tend to develop attitudes and values similar to those of people they encounter in their play and other activities. In our own society, attitudes, values, and behaviors toward others change somewhat with age. As children progress through the elementary grades, they gradually become less selfish, less domineering, less approving of asocial behavior, and more inclined to value large numbers of friends (Guilford 1974).

Cross-cultural researchers have noted that attitude and value development are related to the pervasive attitudes and values expressed by the larger society. Communist societies, for example, place high value on conformity to conventional rules. Children growing up in these societies exhibit behavior that conforms more to those around them than do their age counterparts in Western nations (Shouval *et al.* 1975).

The Developing Self-Concept

An individual's attitude toward herself or himself as a person is called a **self-concept.** Self-concept often is expressed in learned roles or prescribed patterns of behavior. Preschool children have little or no understanding of self. They can identify themselves on the basis of their names or sex. They also can state that they perform such behaviors as drinking, running fast, or eating, but they do not yet perceive themselves as entities separate from their environments. It is now, during the school years, that children first express interest in who they are and what they can do.

The self-concepts of children, once they reach the school years, are a complex blend of attitudes shaped gradually by each child's individual learning experiences. As children grow older and learn from their interactions with others, they gradually develop more clearly defined pictures of their abilities and limits. Children who have learned, for example, that they can manipulate their environments successfully by adopting socially accepted sex-role behaviors are likely to maintain those behaviors and to perceive themselves most easily in these sex roles. Children who have not been reinforced for particular sex-typed behaviors are not so likely to develop these perceptions.

MORAL DEVELOPMENT
Theories of Moral Development

Piaget, you will recall, studied the social rules involved in the children's game of marbles. According to Piaget, preschoolers playing marbles are interested primarily in learning to coordinate their arms and hands to shoot the marbles, rather than in establishing social rules for group play. At this age, children believe that the rules of the game should be determined by authority figures and accepted unquestioningly. By the time they are seven years old, however, children consider winning the game to be a major reward. Now, for the first time, they are interested in learning rules for the purpose of winning. Piaget called this the stage of **incipient cooperation.** Table 6.1 describes the developing self-concept in relation to outstanding characteristics and social and family relationships of this age group.

In a series of experiments aimed at measuring the development of moral reasoning, Piaget told stories to young children in which other model children performed morality-relevant acts. Piaget's subjects then were asked to judge these acts on the basis of their acceptability. Preschool children tended to regard as unacceptable acts that had the most serious consequences in physical damage. For example, models who broke fifteen cups accidentally were judged naughtier than models who very deliberately broke one cup. Only children nine years or older, who had already developed the capacity to empathize or to participate in the feelings or emotions of other people, were likely to take motive into consideration and judge as more serious deliberately performed actions.

Piaget obtained similar results when he studied children's attitudes toward lying. He discovered that what preschool children felt to be most unacceptable were "bad words," words their parents had said were unacceptable for them to use. By the time they reached school age, children disapproved also of clearly falsified statements. It was not until they reached nine or ten years old, however, that they consistently disapproved not so much of untruths but of untrue statements made with specific intent to deceive (Flavell 1963; Berndt and Berndt 1975).

Studies similar to those conducted by Piaget have obtained similar results: As school-age children grow older, they grow increasingly sensitive to the intentionality of an act (see, for example, Keasey 1977). Psychologists believe, however, that school-age children are rarely concerned primarily with the moral issues involved. Aaronfreed (1968) suggested that young children often confess that they have behaved badly simply because it is advantageous for them to do so, not because they really

Table 6.1

The Developing Self-Concepts, Outstanding Characteristics, and Social and Family Relationships of Children Aged Five to Eight

Age	Self-Concepts	Outstanding Characteristics	Social and Family Relationships
5 years	Begins differentiation of self by alternately opposing, then making overtures toward, parents	High physical activity, boisterous, self-centered	Verbally aggressive but sensitive about being called names, dawdles, is impatient with others, difficulty relating to parents and siblings, forms erratic friendships
6 years	Develops self-differentiation		
7 years	Less self-centered, more concerned with others' reactions, sensitive, often ashamed of self	Greater mental activity, almost brooding as compared to 6-year-old	More polite, likes to help at home, has close peer friendships
8 years	Critical and self-evaluative, demanding and critical of others too, likes to compare self with others	New outgoingness, avid curiosity, not as comfortable with the world as when younger	General backsliding in home relationships, highly critical of parents, poor sibling relationships, peer friendships within same sex very important

Note: Adapted from Elkind (1971).

believe that they have done wrong. According to Aaronfreed, the internal control of behavior that allows children to say the right thing to their parents does not necessarily require what parents often think of as conscience. In many cases, he contends, children who appear to be acting according to their consciences really are considering the potential reward or punishment likely to be meted out in the situation. Children who are not likely to get praise from their parents for saying, "It was an accident!" or "It just happened—I don't know how" may decide to apologize because their parents respond with much more warmth and affection to an apology.

Lawrence Kohlberg has done considerable research in the area of moral development. He has focused particularly on the question of the ways children think about moral issues. Kohlberg suggests that moral reasoning, like cognitive ability, progresses in stages (see Chapter 1 for details of Kohlberg's theory). For example, the moral reasoning of children is less complex than that of most adolescents. Support for this position is suggested by a study by Suls and Kalle (1979), which found that kindergarten children who were told stories about people who were hurt tended to judge those people as "bad." The children apparently believed that when the story characters hurt themselves, they must have done something to deserve it. Adolescents who were told the same story, however, tended to base their judgments of "good" and "bad" on other qualities of the characters.

Aaronfreed (1968) suggests that this change in reasoning is not simply a function of growing older. He contends rather that a complex learning process is actually taking place. Children gradually change their own reasoning processes because of the ways they see others, usually their caregivers, solve problems and because their caregivers do or do not reward them for using more advanced problem-solving methods.

Moral Development and Parental Behavior

Psychologists agree that childrearing methods have an important effect on the ways children solve problems related to moral issues. They have long been aware, however, that morality is not taught directly through lessons on "how to be moral." Hartshorne *et al.* (1927) reported in a classic study on this topic over fifty years ago that simply teaching what is "right" or "wrong" behavior in school in no way guarantees children's behavior later in life. More recent research suggests that the behavior and attitudes of parents toward moral issues are a much better indicator of the kind of morality to expect of children than is the child's knowledge of right or wrong. Hoffman and Salzstein (1967) found that children who scored highest on scales of moral reasoning tended to have parents who also scored highest.

Parents influence moral reasoning in a variety of ways. Perhaps most important, they serve as role models. In addition, the childrearing techniques they employ influence their children's sense of morality. Research has demonstrated that parents who tend not to capitalize on their own power and authority in childrearing ("Do it because I say so") but who instead focus on the consequences of their children's actions on others ("If you do that, it will probably hurt Janie's feelings badly") tend to have children who are most advanced in levels of moral reasoning (Hoffman and Salzstein 1967).

One way of promoting moral reasoning is through social reinforcement. Approval, attention, and affection are usually used by parents to encourage desired social behavior. Parents who choose selectively to reinforce social behavior that demonstrates concern for the consequences of actions increase their children's abilities to solve moral problems in more advanced ways. Holstein (1969), for example, found that parents who reinforced their children for high moral reasoning tended to have children who scored highest on scales of moral reasoning.

Democratic parents encourage autonomy in their children while at the same time establishing firm guidelines for behavior.

THE CHILD IN THE HOME

Parental Styles

Although no two sets of parents interact in precisely the same way with their children, certain general dimensions of parental behavior have been found to be important in influencing the way that school-age children adjust to peers and school. One major dimension is acceptance-rejection. Accepting parents are warm and affectionate; rejecting parents are hostile and aloof. The closer parents fall to the rejecting end of the dimension, the more difficulty their children have in getting along with their peers, learning in school, and behaving appropriately. The rejected child often is aggressive and hostile (Anthony and Benedek 1970; Chwast 1972).

A second dimension is control-autonomy. Controlling parents establish and enforce rules for their children, but in so doing, they also attempt to restrict expressions of autonomy and individuality. Parents believing in autonomy are more likely to reward independence and individuality. In some cases, they are completely permissive and nondemanding (Baumrind 1972). Parents who are permissive, allowing their children to behave in any way they want, and who do not set guidelines for what is and what is not appropriate behavior, sometimes find that their children learn from others to exhibit behaviors that are not socially acceptable. Moderation is an advisable guide for parents. Parents who are too permissive often promote socially unacceptable behavior. Parents who are overly controlling tend to promote infantile, dependent behavior in their children. These children often are the subject of ridicule and teasing by their peers outside the home and frequently have adjustment problems in school (Armentrout and Burger 1972).

The ideal parental behavior pattern has been termed a **democratic parental pattern.** Democratic parents are accepting and warm, and they allow their children freedom and autonomy. At the same time, they are firm in their rule making. When little Johnny comes in to do his homework, they supervise and send him out to play only when it is done. When he gets into a fight with the new boy down the street, they are likely to give him a hug, talk with him about handling the situation, then send him outside to play and to work out his differences with the new boy.

Democratic parents tend to have children who are outgoing, self-assertive, independent, friendly, and creative, with positive self-concepts and low hostility (Kagan and Moss 1962). This is an ideal set of qualities for children who are to succeed in school (Kagan and Moss 1962; Rogers, Smith, and Coleman 1978).

Social-class Differences in Parental Behaviors

Psychologists who have compared the behaviors of poor and middle-class parents in this country have found a number of differences in the ways parents of different social classes interact with their children. According to early studies, methods of disciplining children vary according to social class. Hess and Shipman (1967) and Kamii and Radin (1967) found, for example, that working-class mothers more often controlled their children by appeal to parental authority. Discipline frequently included admonitions like "Don't talk to your mother like that!" or "Wait until your father comes home! He'll make you do it right!" Middle-class mothers more frequently appealed to guilt feelings with remarks like "Do you want me to feel bad?" or "Don't you want daddy to be proud?" Many early studies reported the working-class mothers tended to be more strict and to demand more conformity from preschool children than did middle-class mothers. At the same time, they provided school-age children with greater freedom. Masland *et al.* (1959) reported that working-class children often were "turned loose" by busy caregivers at earlier ages than

How do parents maintain a democratic style and, at the same time, set guidelines for what is and what is not appropriate behavior? Susan Isaacs (1968), in a popular manual for parents, provides simple directions. First, parents should realize that it is necessary to establish rules for behavior. Rules should be simple, easy to understand and easy to follow. Next, parents need to teach preschoolers what they must do to obey the rules. According to Isaacs, parents should fully expect the child to obey, in some things and for some purposes. But the careful caregiver needs to decide specifically what obedient behavior is important and why. Obedience, Isaacs cautions, should never become an end in itself.

Children need to have freedom and choice in addition to being obedient if they are to develop socially desirable independence and responsibility when they are older. Even the very little child needs some measure of real responsibility. Where do we draw the line? What behaviors are important? Isaacs divides the activities of children into three basic categories: (1) behaviors essential for health and socialization, (2) behaviors interesting to the child but not damaging either to health or to proper socialization, and (3) contingent behaviors not falling into either of the preceding categories. Let us look carefully at each and decide what to do about them.

Behaviors Essential for Health and Socialization

These include such behaviors as going to bed at certain hours, eating proper foods, not eating certain foods, washing hands before meals, and behaving in play activities in ways that do not hurt playmates. Isaacs suggests that these activities be regulated by rules established by parents. They are sufficiently important not to be left to chance. But rules should be clear and consistent! For example, rules for play should be the same, regardless of the playmate. It may be necessary to establish special rules for playing with younger playmates, like much smaller siblings. But these new rules apply to all younger children, not just to the one in your house. This should be made clear.

Behaviors Interesting to the Child and Not Damaging to Health or Socialization

This category includes very different sorts of behavior from those included in the first grouping. These behaviors do not require either rules or obedience, according to Isaacs. Children are capable, for example, of arranging furniture in their rooms in the manner that is "nicest" for them. Selecting room arrangements hurts neither health nor ability to interact with others, even if the arrangement is not aesthetically appealing to the parent. This particular activity provides useful learning experiences that will help in developing independence.

Contingent Behaviors

This category also should never be made part of rules or obedience prescriptions, according to Isaacs. Into this category Isaacs places friendly and generous behaviors, pleasant activities that are taught not through rules but rather through long-term imitation and modeling of adults. Other, less desirable behavior, like nail biting and stammering, are behaviors often symptomatic of other problems. Nail biting and stammering, Isaacs cautions, are far best left alone until psychological help can be obtained. They are not reduced by the development of rules.

QUESTIONS FOR THOUGHT

1. Allowing children to arrange furniture in their rooms is an example of a way to foster independence. Why do you think that arranging their own rooms is important to elementary school children?

2. Can you think of other ways that parents might foster independence while still keeping consistent rules for behavior?

were middle-class children. Less assistance was provided them by caregivers once they were able to care for their own physical needs.

More recently, Erlanger (1974) and Gecas and Nye (1974) concluded that although there are differences in parental behaviors among social classes in this country, these differences are far less important than researchers previously thought. Erlanger, for example, agrees that working-class mothers are more strict and spank their children more than do middle-class mothers. Gecas and Nye point out that working-class mothers tend to use spankings for most misbehaviors of their children, while middle-class mothers use physical punishment primarily as a response to behaviors associated with loss of self-control, as with losing one's temper or throwing a tantrum. All of these researchers concluded, however, that the differences in parental behavior noted are not very great. Furthermore, they suggest that the consequences of these different parental behaviors may be far less important to the development of school-age children than are the consequences of peer interactions.

Psychologists have also related social class to the type of verbal stimulation given young children (Robinson *et al.* 1973). In these studies, the parental behaviors often had more direct effects on children's behaviors. Bernstein (1960), in a detailed analysis of working-class and middle-class language styles, showed that middle-class mothers use more complex and abstract language in their verbalizations to their offspring than do working-class mothers. Middle-class mothers, according to Bernstein, also make more use of verbal problem-solving activities with their children than do working-class mothers. Children of these middle-class mothers are able to respond to problems requiring verbal skills with far greater ease than children of mothers who do not provide as much verbal stimulation.

The Continuing Influence of Television

If preschoolers spend a large portion of their days in front of the TV, many primary school children spend less time only because some of their day is spent in school. Much of the concern that has emerged in recent years about children's TV watching is related to the question of the impact TV has on children's behavior.

We discussed in Chapter 5 evidence that demonstrates that children who watch successful aggressive models on TV tend to imitate those models in new situations. Many researchers have found that TV can encourage a tolerance for aggression (see, for example, Eron *et al.* 1972; Lefkowitz *et al.* 1973; Sprafkin, Liebert, and Poulos 1975; Thomas and Drabman, 1975). Children who already exhibit problem behavior tend to be more affected by TV violence than are children who initially do not exhibit problem behavior (Feshbach 1970). School-age children scoring lower on tests of cognitive ability tend to be more affected by TV violence than children who get higher scores (Fouts and Liikanen 1975).

Friedrich and Stein (1973) demonstrated that prosocial TV programming can teach social behavior. Bryan and Walbek (1970) noted that the programs that use prosocial models who are warm and friendly and who openly express enjoyment at helping others tend to teach children to behave in this manner. The effects of TV are not limited to observational learning in which children imitate what they see on the screen. Bandura (1977) noted, for example, that children transfer much of what they see to new situations and new tasks. Thus, children who learn to be altruistic by watching altruistic models will probably find new ways to demonstrate this type of behavior, as by helping friends or relatives in new situations.

The effects of TV on children's behavior range beyond the effects of prosocial or aggressive models. Children at play often enact social roles they have seen on TV. Feminists suggest that TV sometimes serves as a rigidly conventional influence in portraying women's roles as being essentially home- and children-centered and that children learn from TV that it is "feminine" to maintain these qualities. Men's roles on TV tend to be more aggressive, dominant, and active. According to feminists, children learn from TV that it is important to maintain these qualities in order to be "masculine."

An important concern in recent years of psychologists regarding the increasing influence of TV in the American home is the effect that TV has on the social interactions with the family. Keniston (1975, p. 58) called the TV set a "flickering blue parent" that occupies more of the waking hours of American children than any other single interest. Keniston suggested that children of disinterested parents are the ones who watch most frequently and learn passively from what they see. Finally, studies have related TV to passivity and lack of tension. Rosenblatt and Cunningham (1976) suggested that in crowded households in which parents and children spend a great deal of time in the same room, the TV set may be used as a tension-control device. Children and parents watching the TV set passively, according to Rosenblatt and Cunningham, are less likely to fight.

THE CHILD IN THE SCHOOL
Industry vs. Inferiority

During the school years, children first become deeply concerned with performance at academic tasks. Lillie, who learned to read in kindergarten, cannot wait for reading period in first grade so that she can show what she can do. The teacher has divided the class into reading groups. Lillie is in the "robin" group, the top group in the class. Billy, on the other hand, is not so anxious for reading period to come. The teacher put him in with the "sparrow hawks." Billy knows that that group reads more slowly than any of the others, and he is ashamed. Billy hates to come to school.

Erik Erikson, the stage theorist, described the first several school years as a time when children develop feelings characterized as industry vs. inferiority. According to Erikson (1953), successful learning leads to industry, whereas continued failure leads to feelings of inferiority. Lillie is an excellent example of a child who has a sense of industry, whereas Billy is a child whose self-image is marked by inferiority. All children are not equally ready to be academically successful, of course. Even so, the successes and failures of the primary school years set the tone for the rest of a child's academic career.

What factors contribute to developing industry or inferiority? Why is Lillie so enthusiastic about school and Billy so negative? Early preparation may be a key factor. Lillie is probably a child whose parents spent a great deal of time helping her learn to read before she encountered the task in school, so that she is likely to feel positive about it. On the other hand, children whose parents do not expose

According to Erikson, success at school tasks will lead to feelings of industry.

them to books may not be as enthusiastic about reading. Another factor that might have affected Lillie and Billy differently is the length and the organization of the school day. In kindergarten, children spend only perhaps two and one-half hours in school, and they spend that time with one teacher and one group of children in a single setting. The change to the traditional first grade can be abrupt. For the first time, children join a larger group and spend most of the day in school. They eat lunch in the school cafeteria and play during recess with many other children. They learn to use a lavatory away from the classroom, and they learn to follow a host of new rules.

Some children, like Lillie, react to this pressure by working hard to tackle what is required. Others, like Billy, have a variety of adjustment problems. Children who are making difficult adjustments may cry frequently, have trouble eating their lunches, or have toilet accidents. They may become cross, rebellious, and disruptive. They may be unable to concentrate on the tasks before them. Teachers need to be alert to such signs if such children are to be able to develop a sense of industry.

Reading: A Vital Skill

Reading is a skill necessary for all later learning in school. Reading requires a discrimination ability more complex than the perceptual discrimination that preschoolers need to make in order to distinguish people and objects in their environments.

According to reading specialist E. Gibson (1965; 1969), in order to learn to read, children must first learn perceptually to differentiate among the many letters of the alphabet. Later, they learn to identify specific aspects of the printed word that are critical to meaning. Reading without meaning is obviously of little use. In fact, most psychologists and educators suggest that reading, by definition, must involve comprehension.

To answer the question "What does a skilled reader do that an unskilled reader does not," Gibson (1968) analyzed the process of learning to read. She derived from her analysis a hierarchy of four basic steps that must be learned in a prescribed order. More advanced steps require previous mastery of earlier steps:

1. *Learning to speak.* This is the first prerequisite to learning to read and normally takes place during the preschool years. Without use of language, it is impossible for reading to acquire meaning.

2. *Learning to discriminate among printed letters.* This step requires the ability to perceive differences in shapes of the individual letters. Children who have spent a great deal of time looking at storybooks while their parents read to them have an easier time with this task than children who have not.

3. *Learning to decode letters to sound.* This step is particularly difficult in learning to read English, because unlike phonetic alphabets, our alphabet does not have a one-to-one spelling–sound correspondence. The job requires effort and concentration at any age level.

4. *Learning to perceive higher-order units and to make rapid visual discriminations among different words.* This final step is, according to Gibson, the step that discriminates good readers from poor readers.

Learning to decode letters to sound presents special problems for students who are members of minority groups, because these groups often speak languages or dialects different from those of white, middle-class students. Communication difficulties between students and teachers or between students and their textbooks often occur because of discrepancies in speech patterns or environmental differences. Varieties of special compensatory education programs have been designed for these children.

Creativity

Creativity is the ability to solve new and different problems in new and innovative ways. The creative child is flexible, willing to try out new courses of action, and willing to experiment with ideas. Creativity seems generally to decrease as children get older. Psychologists believe that age and culture together account for this decline. Maslow (1959) suggested that the potential for creativity is common to all babies at birth. As children grow older, however, this potential decreases with enculturation.

Creative output tends to occur in spurts. During the first three years of school, most children increase their creativity. Some psychologists suggest that this might be true because teachers in the primary grades tend to allow more freedom of expression. After grade three, however, a sharp drop in creativity occurs, followed by a gradual decrease during the remaining elementary and middle school years (Bernard 1973).

Is declining creativity related in some way to our educational system? Marx and Tombaugh (1967) suggest three possible links. First, teachers frequently discourage creativity because it disrupts lesson plans. Second, school tests tend to measure rote learning rather than new or innovative types of responding. Third, social stereotypes fostered by our society, such as rigid sex-typed vocational expectations, frequently lead to stereotyped and noncreative student responses. Peers, teachers, and family all contribute in various ways to this stifling of creativity. "Curiosity killed the cat!" may be told to too many schoolchildren too often.

Can we make corrections? Can we teach children to think and behave creatively? Guilford and Torrance, two psychologists who have studied child creativity extensively, have suggested that we can. Guilford (1950; 1962) has suggested teaching in ways that allow for greater divergence of answers. The discovery method of teaching, in which teachers provide examples in order to let children "discover" the solutions, is one way to do this. Torrance (1972) suggests that allowing children to work in small groups and to learn by themselves to make decisions might be another effective approach.

Bilingualism

Today in America, many children learn and use more than one language to communicate with others. If they learn two languages or two dialects of the same language with equal facility, we call these children **bilingual.** Frequently, however, children learn to be only partly bilingual. Many Hispanic children living in the United States, for example, learn a combination of Spanish and some broken English. More recent arrivals to the United States from the Soviet Union, Korea, Cuba, and a host of other countries speak a foreign language in their homes and English in the schools and on the streets. Many black children, although both they and their parents were born in the United States, speak black English, a dialect that differs from standard white English. All these children frequently have problems learning in schools in which standard English is the means of communicating. Some of the ways in which children using a black dialect and children using a white dialect use the word *be* explain that communication can be difficult (see Table 6.2).

Does learning to be bilingual affect the ways that children think? Imedadze (1967) suggests that bilingual children learn to associate a specific language with

Table 6.2
Ways that the Word *Be* Can Be Used in Black Dialect and in Standard English

Black English	Standard English
Deletion	Contraction
She the first one.	She's the first one.
He be bad.	He's bad.
We at school.	We're at school.
He gon' stay home.	He's going to stay home.
You got to be good.	You've got to be good.
He the teacher.	He's the teacher.

Source: Adapted from Labov (1969).
Note: Where it is possible to contract in standard English, it is possible to delete in black English.

both the person who first taught them that language and with the subject matter learned in that language. Thus a child first learning to talk, who speaks Spanish with the mother and English with the father, may well continue in the same language with the respective parent throughout life. If the mother teaches something (counting, for example) in Spanish, the child may tend to have some difficulty understanding arithmetic later in English, even if the father has frequently discussed other subjects in English.

Researchers have shown that learning two languages simultaneously reduces the number of words spoken in both languages. Bilingual children, however, tend to show more advanced processing of verbal material, more discriminating perceptual distinctions, and more capacity to reorganize their perceptions in response to feedback (Ben-Zeev 1977). Being bilingual can be an asset to school learning as long as the child is fluent in the language in which school subjects are taught. For this reason, one often-successful approach to helping the child who speaks a language different from "school language" is bilingual education. In bilingual education, regular instruction of basic subjects is given in the home language, and lessons are given in English as a second language until English is mastered.

Intelligence Testing

Earlier in this chapter, we discussed the ways that elementary school children increase in their abilities to think and to solve problems as they get older. We also discussed the ways in which a child's environment can affect these abilities. Many psychologists look at cognitive ability from a different perspective. Rather than charting the progress of children over time, they are interested in comparing the abilities of many different children of the same age. The instruments they have developed to make these age-group comparisons are **intelligence (IQ) tests.**

IQ tests used today for schoolchildren make use primarily of problem-solving tasks similar to those presented in classroom situations. One reason is that most tests have been modeled after the Stanford-Binet scale of intelligence. The first Binet Scale of Intelligence was designed by Alfred Binet in 1905 for the purpose of identifying slow learners in the Paris schools and detecting individual differences among them in degrees of retardation. In order to select items for his scale, Binet observed children in classrooms to see what they did. He decided that to learn successfully in school, children have to learn to use language, to memorize, to comprehend the problems being discussed, to make reasonable judgments, and to solve certain types of problems. He then developed a scale to measure all of these abilities. Binet's early scale was revised for use in this country and has become the Stanford-Binet Scale of Intelligence (Terman and Merrill 1937; 1960). Items similar to those found on the Stanford-Binet are shown in Table 6.3.

The developers of the Binet and Stanford-Binet Scales assume a **general-factor theory of intelligence**—that is, they accept the approach of early theorists like

Table 6.3
Stanford-Binet Test Items

Age	Test Items
2 years	Shown a board with holes into which various shapes, such as square and circle, can be fitted, the child places the correct blocks in the holes.
	Shown pictures of common objects, such as a table or ball, the child correctly calls them by their name.
3½ years	Shown a card with a picture of a large and a small object, the child points to the larger one when asked.
	Shown a picture of an animal, such as a cow, the child can find another picture of a cow from among various animals.
5 years	Shown a picture of a person with some parts missing (for example, arm or leg), the child can tell what is missing.
	Asked to define simple words, such as table or hat, the child can give correct definition.
6 years	The child answers correctly such analogies as "a dog *walks;* a bird _____?"
	The child defines more difficult words, such as envelope.
	The child identifies numbers by giving the tester the number of blocks requested.
8 years	The child can define more difficult words, such as eyelash.
	The child can tell how two objects, such as football and apple, are similar and different.
	The child can name the days of the week and knows the correct order.

Note: These examples are similar to those used in the Stanford-Binet test (Terman and Merrill 1937) but are not exact duplicates.

Spearman (1904) who suggested that intelligence is a general factor that increases a person's capability to do anything. For developers of the Stanford-Binet Scale, this means a single intelligence quotient that reflects a composite of responses to many different types of problems. Since school learning requires language, a large number of questions on the Stanford-Binet measure verbal ability.

Some psychologists believe the general-factor theory of intelligence is too simple. They take note of researchers like Thurstone (1938) who hypothesized that intelligence is composed of many different nonoverlapping abilities. One intelligence test that measures two abilities, verbal and performance, separately is the Wechsler Intelligence Scale for Children (WISC). The WISC separates questions that require verbal ability from questions that deal with symbols, pictures, blocks, and jigsaw puzzles and that require nonverbal or performance ability (Wechsler 1949). The WISC can be used to obtain a general IQ score from a composite of the child's answers. It also can be used to obtain two separate verbal and performance IQ scores developed from answers on the verbal and performance parts of the test.

Both the Stanford-Binet Scale and the Wechsler Scale are known as **individual tests of intelligence.** They are administered on an individual basis to children by a trained tester who asks the child questions, writes down the responses, and then computes an IQ score from the number of correct answers. Children administered individual tests of intelligence do not have to be able to read.

Intelligence tests have also been designed to be administered by teachers in group situations. Public schools use these tests in order to determine as inexpensively and as rapidly as possible the IQs of groups of children. Two tests administered frequently by public schools in the United States are the Lorge-Thorndike Intelligence Test and the California Test of Mental Maturity (Gibson 1972). Most of us who have been educated in the public schools can remember **group tests of intelligence:** Questions are provided in test booklets, and children are required to read each question and then answer by filling in the appropriate box on a computer-scored answer sheet. Clearly, more rapid readers have a decided advantage over slower readers.

Most group tests of intelligence have been designed to measure the same abilities as those measured by individual tests, yet different types of intelligence tests, as well as specifically different tests, all ask different questions. Some tests have been designed to measure special abilities. The Arthur Point Scale, for example, is a performance test that measures ability to solve problems dealing with mazes, geometric puzzles, cubes, picture completions, and stencil designs. It is useful for measuring the abilities of children not fluent in language. The Terman-McNemar Test of Mental Ability asks questions dealing with information, synonyms, logical selection of words, word classification, analogies, and word opposites (Gibson 1972). Clearly, children taking this test need to be fluent in the English language in order to receive high scores.

What does a score obtained on a given test mean? IQ scores can range from mentally defective (usually considered to be IQs of 69 or under) to very superior (IQs of 131 and above). The classifications used most commonly for all standard intelligence tests are shown in Table 6.4.

The size of a child's IQ score depends on more than just the number of correct answers. It depends also on the way these answers compare with those of the **standardization population,** a sample population of children who have taken the same test. If Johnny receives more correct answers than most children of his age in the sample population, he will receive a higher-than-average IQ score; if his correct answers are fewer than those of children of his age in the sample population, he will receive a lower-than-average score. The standardization population is very important to IQ determination. As we know, learning experiences play a major role in determining ability to speak and to perform problem-solving tasks. Thus for the IQ score of any child to be a meaningful indicator of ability, it is necessary that the children in the standardization sample have learning experiences similar to that child.

Designers of intelligence tests do their best to get standardization samples truly representative of the populations for whom the tests are designed. Test standardization, however, is a time consuming and expensive task. It has proven less costly for testers to select standardization samples from urban areas, so that many children can be tested at one time. It often is simpler for testers to get permission from middle-class parents to test their children than to get the permission of parents of lower-income backgrounds. Most urban, middle-class children are both white and Protestant; most standardization samples are composed primarily of white, urban, middle-class, Protestant children.

Psychologists tell us that the IQ, on even the best of tests, is not very reliable—that is, children who take the same test repeatedly are not likely to get the same score each time. Scores can rise or fall, depending sometimes on the experiences

Table 6.4
Commonly Accepted Intelligence Classifications

Classification	IQ
Mentally defective	69 and below
Borderline defective	70–79
Low average	80–89
Average	90–110
High average	111–120
Superior	121–130
Very superior	131 and over

of the children being tested and sometimes on natural fluctuations inherent in the tests themselves. IQ scores have been known, in some cases, to vary as much as thirty points in a single year, even when the same test was used.

PEER RELATIONSHIPS

During the school years, peers play an increasingly important role as models. This is true whether peers exhibit socially acceptable or socially unacceptable behavior. Children whose behavior is reinforced in some way as through teacher approval or even teacher attention given to unacceptable behavior, are likely to be imitated by other children in the class. Children whose behavior is reinforced through peer approval at play are likely to be imitated by others as well.

What makes some children find it easy to get along with others and become the models that others imitate? As we saw earlier, parent–child interactions strongly influence a child's responses to school and to social interactions. Children whose parents have fostered independence, self-assertion, and prosocial behavior, for ex-

Affection and support from peers helps to encourage prosocial behavior.

ample, are likely to get along better with peers than children who are overly dependent on their parents and who have not learned to control their hostility in group situations. Children whose parents have not fostered behavior conducive to social interaction tend often to be lacking in self-confidence when they enter school. Often, these children's negative feelings are expressed in signs of defiance and lack of self-control as the school year continues (Spivack and Swift 1977). Children with family problems at home (for example, family tensions or impending divorce), lack of intellectual stimulation, economic difficulty, and personal strife tend to have greater school difficulties and fewer resources to cope with them than do children coming from homes with fewer problems (Felner and Francis 1978).

Primary school children gradually become less dependent on their parents and more dependent on their peers. At this stage, children play with others of the same sex more than with those of the opposite sex. For some children, the opinions of playmates or teachers may hold far greater weight than those of parents. The value placed on peer opinion increases as children grow from six or seven years of age to nine or ten.

SCHOOL-RELATED PROBLEMS

Many deficiencies in the development and learning abilities of children are especially pertinent to school success or failure in the primary school years. These include developmental effects of poverty and handicaps of various sorts, including physical handicaps, learning disabilities, and hyperactivity.

Problems of Poor Children

The bottom fifteen to twenty percent of our population in income and educational level has been labeled by sociologists the "lower-lower social class" (Havighurst and Neugarten 1967). The population is characterized by absence of steady employment, low level of education and technical skills, dependence on assistance programs, and isolation from other segments of the population. It is not characterized by any single race or minority group but includes whites, blacks, Hispanics, native Americans, and, most recently, a variety of other new immigrant groups. The children of this population, according to experts, have one major factor in common: They grow up in a "culture of poverty."

The children of poverty encounter problems even from birth. A problem of major proportions is inadequate nutrition. Seventy-five percent of poor children seen in free clinics during the 1960s suffered from nutritional deficiency anemia (Citizens' Board of Inquiry 1968). In 1966, the federally legislated Child Nutrition Act established a free school breakfast program for poor children in order to alleviate what researchers know to be the negative effects of hunger on school learning. Although children in the breakfast programs improved both their school performances and attendance records (Morrell and Atkinson 1977), many of these programs were cut back by 1980 because of lack of funding.

Diseases and environmental poisoning, such as lead poisoning, are also frequent among the poor. Poor children exhibit considerably more problem behavior both in and out of school than do children coming from more affluent homes. Many suggest that these problem behaviors are caused by the early learning of values and behaviors that later turn out to be out of place in middle-class schools (Karnes, Zehrback, and Jones 1971; Langner *et al.* 1974; Evans 1975; Taylor 1976). The result often includes defensive responses inappropriate to the school setting in which children spend the major portion of each day. Children who have learned, for example, that it is acceptable to come and go from their homes at times that vary according to what is happening that day, suddenly find that it is inappropriate to be even two minutes late to school in the morning. Children of some minority groups, who have learned to speak one language or dialect in the home, suddenly find that this speech is considered inappropriate in the new school setting. The psychological cost often is high and may include feelings of low self-esteem, powerlessness, and worthlessness, signaled by low motivation, inappropriate social behavior, and lowered intellectual functioning (Rosenham 1969).

Studies have also shown that poor children often have problems in learning to read, particularly when phonemic analysis of words is required. Wallach *et al.* (1977) report that these problems stem from inadequate skill in listening to different sounds of words, probably because these words are not used at home. As we noted earlier, reading is central to virtually all other school tasks. Thus children who are unable to master reading are unlikely to have either the motivation or self-esteem necessary to succeed in school. Many poor children eventually give up and drop out of school, thus setting in motion a continuing pattern of poverty.

Psychologists have suggested that public schools in the United States are particularly adept at "programming kids for failure" (Havighurst 1970; Richmond 1970). What do they mean? For one thing, they mean that teachers often do not take into consideration the past learning experiences of children. They tend often to select reinforcements that have been proven effective among middle-class children; then if poor children do not respond to these reinforcers, teachers assume they are incapable of learning. According to critics, the main problem in schools today often is misunderstanding. Havighurst (1970) reported the case of a substitute teacher entering a classroom of second graders who, according to school records, could not count. The substitute teacher tried an interesting experiment. It was Valentine's Day, and she came prepared with boxes of candy hearts. She suggested to the children that they each could have as many candy hearts as they could count. One child who was reported in the school records to be unable to count above three, counted to fourteen and received an equal number of candies!

Educational tests have been another contributor to the learning problems of poor children. One of the ways that some school systems elect to place students in appropriate groups for learning is by ability. Children who can learn most quickly, it is reasoned, should be placed in groups with other bright youngsters. Similarly, children who require more help in learning should be placed together.

One difficulty with this approach is that children are quick to discern whether that are in the "smart" group or the "dumb" group. Children in the lower tracks may be conditioned to feel they cannot learn, simply by virtue of the group to which they have been assigned. Their self-esteem and motivation may therefore be reduced, and their performances may suffer.

Another difficulty with the practice of tracking by ability is the ability tests themselves. Standardized tests used to set norms for ability have been criticized as culturally biased in favor of white, middle-class children. These culturally biased tests, it is argued, give invalid estimates of the abilities of children from other than middle-class background. In addition, tests that make use of verbal skills taught in middle-class homes also are biased against children who have not been taught standard English at home. Attempts have been made to develop **culture-free tests** (tests free of cultural bias), as well as **culture-fair tests** (tests fair to a particular society or group). For example, the Culture-Fair Intelligence Tests require no language skill. The Raven Progressive Matrices test uses abstract drawings instead of language to test general intellectual ability. Yet despite these efforts, there seems to be no effective way to measure the abilities of children who are not familiar with standard English.

Problems of Physically Handicapped Children

Difficulties in school are sometimes related to physical handicaps that impede children in seeing, hearing, or physically getting about. Some children with slight visual problems often can be helped by such simple aids as glasses. The crucial first step is for parents or teachers to identify the problem so that it can be remediated. Other children are not so lucky. Even with corrective glasses, they still cannot see or hear well enough to use the same learning methods as other students. Children who are blind or partially blind need to learn to use braille. Some children with slight auditory handicaps often can be helped by hearing aids once the handicap is identified by a physician. Children whose handicap cannot be helped by a hearing aid often have difficulty learning to speak.

Children often have problems of articulation, such as omissions, substitutions, distortions, and additions of sound. Voice and pitch defects are the second most prevalent problem. The child's voice might be too high, too low, or monotonous, or it might have unpleasant nasal quality or hoarseness. There are also rhythmic defects such as stuttering or stammering. Speech therapists can help children with all of these problems by providing speech instruction. Without help, the communi-

A speech therapist helps a deaf student learn to pronounce words by watching lip movements in a mirror.

cation problems that result are often complicated by the ridicule of other children, who sometimes can be insensitive to children who are different in any way.

Some children have neurological or orthopedic handicaps, such as physical deformity or paralysis. Some are crippled by accident or by disease, such as cerebral palsy, muscular dystrophy, scoliosis, or infantile arthritis. Some of these children use crutches or wear braces; others are confined to wheelchairs.

The physically handicapped child experiences the world differently from the child who is healthy, vigorous, and fully functioning. In addition to the difficulty of getting around in the world, the handicapped child often misses such normal activities of everyday life as joining a ball game in the school yard. In the past few years, we have become more aware of the difficulties of being handicapped. In 1978, the Education for All Handicapped Children Act was passed by Congress to help provide better opportunities and basic rights to education for handicapped children. Public

Law 94-142, as it is called, provides for the right to a "free and appropriate" public education in which children who are capable of learning in regular classrooms are taught there, together with other students. Public Law 94-142 also provides for the right to due process, nondiscriminatory testing and labeling, and confidential handling of school records and files.

What has Public Law 94-142 done to help the handicapped child? Specifically, it requires local school districts to establish individualized programs to meet the needs of students with handicaps that make it difficult for them to learn. To help in **mainstreaming** handicapped children into regular programs as mandated by law, public schools have provided facilities that make it easier for handicapped children to learn and simply to get around. Most schools today are equipped with ramps or elevators for wheelchairs. Special resource rooms provide elaborate equipment, such as braille typewriters, tables of appropriate heights for wheelchairs, and speakers to magnify sounds. Such special supportive services as counselors, psychologists, physical therapists, speech therapists, and occupational therapists are sometimes provided to assist teachers. Often, counselors are provided to assist teachers and class to bridge communication gaps and to help both the handicapped child and the classmates learn to deal in class with the problem.

Problems of Mentally Retarded Children

Mental retardation is a relative classification of ability to adjust to the environment and is made on the basis of average rate of developmental progress. Children who are unable to learn sufficiently to meet the standards of personal independence and social responsibility expected of their age and cultural group are placed in this category. Such children are said to have "impaired adaptive behavior" and require special training or education (Florida State Department of Education 1974).

Causes of mental retardation vary considerably. We discussed early in the text some of the genetic factors that cause retardation. Down's syndrome, as we noted, is caused by a chromosomal defect. Genetic factors, however, are less common than other factors, such as certain maternal diseases, malnutrition during the fetal period, brain injuries due to birth trauma, infections, disease, or metabolic disorders.

Degree of retardation usually is described by the help necessary for these children to adapt. The **profoundly retarded** are children who require lifelong care. They are characterized often by considerable central nervous system impairment and gross physical abnormalities. Frequently, they are blind and/or deaf. They tend to exhibit patterns of repetitive behavior, such as head banging or rocking movements. Such children are incapable of learning even the most basic self-care skills and often are bedridden. Most profoundly mentally retarded are institutionalized, so that the extensive medical and nursing services they require can be provided. Families that choose to keep the profoundly retarded child at home must drastically alter

WHAT IS MAINSTREAMING?

The term *mainstreaming* has been used frequently and in different ways during the last few years. As a result, there is some confusion regarding what the term really means. While there may not be a definition that is universally understood, some basic themes can be looked to for an understanding of the intent of mainstreaming.

Mainstreaming is

Providing the most appropriate education for each child in the least restrictive setting

Looking at the educational needs of children instead of clinical or diagnostic labels, such as mentally handicapped, physically handicapped, or hearing impaired

Looking for and creating alternatives that will help general educators serve handicapped children in the regular setting. Some approaches being used to help achieve this are consulting teachers, methods and materials specialists, itinerant teachers and resource room teachers.

Uniting the skills of general education and special education so that all children may have equal educational opportunity.

Mainstreaming is not

Wholesale return of all handicapped children in special classes to regular classes

Permitting children with handicaps to remain in regular classrooms without the support services they need

Ignoring the needs of some children for a more specialized program than can be provided in the general education program

Less costly than serving children in special, self-contained classrooms.*

QUESTIONS FOR THOUGHT

1. What seem to be the most important advantages provided handicapped children by mainstreaming?

2. Can you think of any disadvantages of mainstreaming?

---

*This material is provided as a service from the Council for Exceptional Children, 1920 Association Drive, Reston, Virginia 22091. Reprinted from *Exceptional Children* 42 (1975):174.

normal family routine to accommodate the extremely time-consuming day-to-day care that the retarded child needs.

Severely retarded children also are totally dependent during their lifetimes, although these children, with intensive and prolonged training, can learn many of the basic self-care skills, such as toileting and dressing. Severely retarded children often are multiple-handicapped. Some, because of organic brain damage, are difficult to control. Because of the intensive training necessary for these children, they often are cared for in institutional settings, although they may be adequately cared for at home.

Trainable retarded children are children capable of learning such self-help skills as toileting, feeding, and bathing. These children usually are considered moderately retarded in comparison to other children. They tend to have fewer additional handicaps when compared to the profoundly or severely retarded. Their motor abilities tend to approach normalcy. Trainable children can score between twenty-five and fifty IQ points on Wechsler or Stanford-Binet IQ tests. With special help, they can live within family settings and often adjust quite acceptably to community living.

Educable retarded children are more capable of learning than children falling in any of the other categories listed. The educable mentally retarded can score between fifty-one and seventy-five on a Wechsler or Stanford-Binet Scale of Intelligence. They are slower than most children in developmental progress. Both their physical appearances and their motor development, however, are close to normal. The poor learning abilities of these children usually are first noted together with their inability to learn at the same rate as others in school. They often can be mainstreamed into regular classes. Educable children can be given much more freedom than can children with lower levels of ability. They often can be taught skills sufficient for satisfactory adjustment to the outside world. They can learn to care for themselves in their own living quarters and can hold simple jobs. Because the educable mentally retarded tend to have some difficulty managing their own affairs, they still may have special problems and require help in interacting with other children.

Learning Disabilities

Many children with average or above-average IQ scores experience learning difficulties when they enter school. Frequently these problems are identified in preschool. In many cases, when this happens and special help is given, children can enter primary school and do very well (Wooden, Lisowski, and Early 1976). For ten to fourteen percent of school-age children, however, the learning problems first become apparent when they begin to learn to read and write in first grade. These problems, if left uncorrected in the primary school years, can handicap the child's entire school career.

Among the learning difficulties that have been identified are poor ability to combine vision and movement, poor listening ability, poor grasp of sequence and rhythm, and difficulty in processing information from several sensory channels at the same time (Golick 1970). Other symptoms include confusion in orientation in time and space. Learning-disabled children frequently confuse such concepts as yesterday and tomorrow, left to right, up and down, and so on. Many of these children also exhibit poor memory and motor coordination as well as disruptive behavior (Bradbury 1972). Some children have problems understanding written and spoken language. Because all of these problems result in learning difficulties, many of these children have, in the past, been incorrectly identified as retarded. Of course, for some learning-disabled children, psychological and physiological tests do indicate a minimal amount of brain damage. For others, however, there seems to be neither mental retardation nor any indication of cause.

The most common category of learning disabilities is called **dyslexia,** a term derived from the Greek roots *dys* meaning *difficulty* and *lexia, pertaining to words.* Dyslexic children exhibit a range of symptoms. They may have difficulty in developing spatial relationships, often confusing left and right or up and down. They may make letter reversals in reading and in writing, confusing letters like p and b and numbers like 6 and 9. Dyslexic children may reverse or rearrange letters in a group, thus mistaking spilt for split, god for dog, or not for ton. Further, they might not be able to discriminate among geometric shapes and designs. Dyslexic children can be found at all IQ levels. Sometimes dyslexic children have sufficiently high mental abilities that their difficulties are not very noticeable in the classroom; at other times, regular teaching methods seem sorely inadequate.

Ever since dyslexia was identified late in the nineteenth century, it has been studied and debated. What causes dyslexia? Researchers still are not certain. Many feel that there are a variety of different causes related to similar symptoms. These researchers feel that the label *dyslexia* tells little about the cause of the disorder and thus is misleading.

What can be done for learning-disabled children? Some experts suggest that the first step should be to drop the classification *learning disability* altogether. They point out that use of this label might actually cause some children to have more difficulty learning. Learning disability often is misunderstood as a disorder for which there is no known cause or cure. The label, many psychologists fear, may cause the frightened child and/or parents simply to give up (Silberman 1976).

Another important step is to identify learning-disabled children early. Once the problem has been identified, specific help tailored to each individual child is recommended. Small-group learning for children with learning disabilities seems to work quite effectively. Teachers and parents who are patient in evaluating and planning instruction have the best results. The most effective teachers are those who like children, take small steps, and provide a great deal of reinforcement (Haring 1970; Woestehoff 1970).

Hyperactivity

Some children classified as learning disabled actually suffer from **hyperactivity,** a behavioral problem characterized by extremely high levels of activity. Hyperactive children, most of whom are boys, often have difficulty simply because they cannot sit still long enough to learn. They tend generally to be impulsive and aggressive and may often have temper tantrums. Antisocial behaviors, such as lying, stealing, or cruelty to animals, are not uncommon among these children (Stewart 1970).

Hyperactive school-age children often have histories of restlessness, tantrums, and inability to relax. During the preschool years, they are considered "difficult" children; in school, they often are considered "impossible." Faced with angry teachers, they become increasingly aggressive and often hostile.

The causes of hyperactivity still are largely unclear. Some researchers suggest that hyperactive behavior may result from homeostatic mechanisms that allow some children to acquire additional needed sensory stimulation through more active behavior (Zentall 1975).

What can be done for the hyperactive child? One controversial method to treat hyperactivity has been drug therapy. Amphetamines, such as Ritalin and Dexedrine, used with other people as stimulants, have been found frequently to reduce hyperactivity (Bradbury 1972). There has been much controversy concerning the use of drugs with hyperactive children. Concerns have been voiced over the safety of the children; some fear negative side effects, such as further behavioral abnormality or addiction. Further, the qualifications of those administering the drugs in school have been challenged. Many psychologists as well as medical experts agree that drugs have been misused (Cole 1975; Stewart 1970; Weithorn and Ross 1976).

Many parents claim that their hyperactive child has been helped by following a diet that calls for eating only certain foods and eliminating food additives, artificial flavors, and artificial colors that are believed to contribute to the disturbance. This is known as the Feingold diet (Feingold 1975a; 1975b). Researchers are quick to point out, however, that even if changing the diet does decrease the symptoms, it does not necessarily follow that a particular food component has caused the hyperactivity. The cause could be an underlying metabolic or other type of defect. Thus some professionals remain skeptical about diet as the cause (Divoky 1978). Other researchers believe that the child's behavior improves on the diet because of changes in the attitude of the parents. Parents who put their child on the diet apparently pay more attention to their child. Nevertheless, the state of California has revised public school menus so as to reduce food additives. Feingold (1975b) and others have urged that all food packages should bear labels stating the presence of food additives.

Another method of treatment involves training hyperactive children in improved self-control. Simpson and Nelson (1974), for example, used breathing techniques and other body controls to help hyperactive children control various motor behaviors and maintain concentration. The research findings suggest that such training can indeed help hyperactive children develop better self-discipline.

THE CASE OF ARNOLD IRWIN—A HYPERACTIVE CHILD: A CASE STUDY FOR CLASS DISCUSSION

I. Identification and Sources of Information

Name: Arnold Irwin

Address: 14 Fifth Avenue, New City, Ohio

Race: White

Sex: Male

Age: Seven years

Sources of information

1. Personal observation
2. Interview with Arnie
3. Interview with Arnie's parents
4. Interview with Arnie's first grade teacher
5. Pediatric records

II. Family History

Arnie is the only child of Robert and Alice Irwin. Arnie's father works as a postal clerk. His mother worked full time as a dental hygienist before Arnie was born and she returned to work part time last fall, when Arnie entered the first grade.

Mr. and Mrs. Irwin had been married for six years when Arnie was born. They had tried to have a baby before that time, but all attempts had resulted in miscarriages. Arnie was delivered by caesarian section, and Mrs. and Mr. Irwin decided not to have any more children afterward. Both Mr. and Mrs. Irwin have siblings, all of whom live in New City, as do Arnie's maternal and paternal grandparents. The families socialize frequently, and family members all spend a great deal of time together. Arnie has two first cousins his age, both of whom live in his neighborhood and attend his first grade class.

III. Case History

Arnie was deliverd by caesarian section because of difficulties his mother was experiencing with birth. Mother and son were both reported in excellent con-

dition immediately after the birth. Arnie weighed seven pounds and one ounce. Both Mrs. Irwin and her baby son remained in the hospital a full week after the delivery. The Irwins had a great deal of help in the house to take care of both mother and baby when they came home. Mrs. Irwin's mother stayed in the baby's room and took care of night feedings so that her daughter could recuperate as quickly as possible from the surgery.

According to pediatric records, Arnie developed normally. He had chicken pox at age three but had no other childhood diseases. He was always an extremely active baby and became very difficult to take care of during his preschool years, according to his mother's reports. Mrs. Irwin stated, "From the time that Arnie learned to walk, he began to run. From the time he learned to talk, he began to yell continually. He was always getting into things and breaking them. It was impossible to leave him alone for a minute."

When Arnie was four years old, Mrs. Irwin decided that she had to get out of the house "at least for a few hours a day—to get my composure." She decided to return part time to her job and enrolled Arnie in a preschool program. Mrs. Irwin liked her job, and Arnie reported that he liked school. But within a few weeks, the principal of the school telephoned the Irwins and suggested that they find another placement for the child. "We have too many children to take care of to give Arnie the time he needs and to keep him from being destructive. We have obligations to all of the children in the program, and what can we say to other parents when Arnie punches them or tears up their papers or spills his juice on them deliberately?" The principal suggested that the Irwins find a child psychologist to help out and that perhaps he would do better at school the next year.

The Irwin family held a conference and decided that the principal was wrong. "Why, there's nothing the matter with Arnie," Mr. Irwin argued irately. "What do they expect? He's just a little more active than the

Continued

THE CASE OF ARNOLD IRWIN *(Cont.)*

others." Mr Irwin's sister, who had a son Arnie's age, offered to baby sit while Mrs. Irwin was at work. The family tried this arrangement but gave it up after two weeks when Arnie, in a fit of excitement, pulled the dining room chair out from under his cousin, and the little boy broke his leg. Mr. Irwin's sister apologized and said that she would be glad to baby sit for Arnie after her son recuperated. At that point, however, the Irwins decided that probably Mrs. Irwin ought to stay at home with Arnie herself. Mrs. Irwin quit her job.

Arnie had a difficult time when he began kindergarten. The teacher complained to the Irwins that "there are twenty-five children in my class, and all twenty-five heard the fire engine go down the street. All twenty-five stayed where they were, except Arnie. Arnie ran to the window, screaming, 'fire engine! fire engine!' He knocked over a bottle of poster paint that one of the children was carrying to his desk on the way." Arnie's teacher called the Irwins a number of times during the year. When spring came, the teacher sent Arnie in for tests to measure his readiness for first grade learning. Arnie did very well on reading readiness and prearithmetic tests, and although his teacher had reservations about his social behavior, it was recommended that he enter first grade the following year. Arnie was six and one-half years old when first grade began.

Arnie's first grade teacher required all children to remain in their seats except during specified breaks for exercise and play. Arnie had difficulty staying in his seat and was frequently punished for his misbehavior. He complained to his mother that the teacher used to make him stand behind the door whenever he was "bad," which was at least once a day and often more.

In October, the teacher slapped Arnie's hand after Arnie had jumped up and down and dug his heel into the teacher's ankle. Arnie bit the teacher and was sent immediately to the principal's office. The principal recommended that Arnie be placed in a special education class because he was not learning his regular subjects and because he was so disruptive. Mr. and Mrs. Irwin objected. The school brought in a psychologist, who tested Arnie; his IQ was 121, above normal. The test showed no reason that he was doing so poorly in his subjects. "Probably so much childishness that he doesn't have time to learn," Mr. Irwin said. Mrs. Irwin arranged her work hours so that she was home every day when Arnie got home from school and began systematic tutoring every afternoon. Arnie quickly learned to read and write under his mother's tutelage.

At the end of the first grade, Arnie had learned all the required subject matter for the year. The teacher reported that if he could "calm down," he ought to do well in school next year. Arnie, however, has become increasingly aggressive in school and hostile both to his teachers and other students. He played fairly well under his mother's supervision, but Mrs. Irwin had to keep calming her son down. The Irwin family finally consulted with their pediatrician about the problem. He recommended first trying the additive-free diet recommended by Dr. Feingold. He pointed out that the diet works in some cases, although the reasons are not yet clear to researchers.

IV. Present Status, Diagnosis, and Prognosis

Arnie has been on the Feingold diet for three months, with little noticeable change in his behavior. The Irwins' pediatrician has suggested that if the change in diet does not produce noticeable results in the next few months, he will begin drug therapy. The educational and developmental prognosis, he points out, is unclear at this point. Arnie can be expected to remain hyperactive for the primary school years if none of the experimental therapies work. He can be expected to have a great deal of difficulty mastering the primary school subjects. This lack of mastery, in turn, may well cause him difficulty in later school years.

THE CASE OF ARNOLD IRWIN

Questions for Class Discussion

1. Has Arnie's pediatrician suggested all possible remedies? Is there anything else that might be tried to help Arnie as well as his family get through some difficult periods?

2. Arnie's treatment did not begin until the teacher's complaints in the first grade forced the Irwins to seek professional treatment. Do you think Arnie might have been better off if treatments had begun when he first started having noticeable problems? In what ways might this have been helpful for his education? In what ways might it have helped him psychologically?

3. Is there any evidence in this case history that Arnie's behavior is not simply "childishness," as Mr. Irwin suggested? How does it differ from normal development? Is there evidence that it could have been prevented?

SUMMARY

The early school years are critical in the development of social behavior with the school itself exerting an increasingly strong influence. During middle childhood there is a gradual decrease in fatty body tissue with a concurrent increase in bone and muscle development. Substantial improvements in large and small motor skills are typically achieved during this period.

Most children during the primary school years are in what Piaget terms the concrete operational stage—that is, they learn new concepts when presented with concrete examples. During these years, they improve their understanding of concepts by learning through conservation, seriation, classification, and class inclusion. Socialization during the primary school years continues to involve channeling emotional expression into behaviors acceptable to society. Children who have difficulty expressing their emotions in socially desirable ways develop defense mechanisms, such as sublimation, denial, projection, and displacement. By primary school age, both boys and girls are able to identify socially acceptable sex-typed behavior. Boys, however, develop sex-role preferences earlier and more consistently than do girls.

An important part of middle childhood is the development of attitudes and values. School-age children tend to develop attitudes and values similar to those of people they encounter in their play and other activities. Children develop self-concepts during the school years; that is, they perceive themselves as entities separate from their environments. As primary school children grow older, they grow more sensitive to the intentionality of acts. True conscience, as we understand it, takes time to develop. Child-rearing methods have an important effect on a child's sense of morality.

Certain general dimensions of parental behavior are important in influencing child behavior; among these are acceptance–rejection and control–autonomy. The ideal parental behavior is democratic; democratic parents are warm and accepting and allow their children autonomy without being overly permissive. Although social-class differences in parental behaviors do exist in this country, they are far less important than researchers previously thought. Television continues to influence children during the primary school years. Television violence is related to aggression among school-age children; at the same time, prosocial TV programming can teach social behavior. Television also affects attitudes and social interactions within the family.

Success or failure at learning tasks in the primary grades shapes the learning process for years to come. Reading, a perceptual skill necessary for most other school-related tasks, comes more easily to some children than to others. Creativity seems generally to increase in the first three years of school, after which there tends to be a general decrease.

Psychologists have developed intelligence, or IQ, tests to compare the abilities of many different children of the same age. These can be administered on an individual or group basis. For the scores on these tests to be meaningful indicators of ability, the children being tested must have learning experiences similar to those of the children in the standardization sample.

Primary school children gradually become less dependent on their parents and more dependent on their peers. Parent–child interactions strongly influence a child's response to both school and social interactions with peers. Many deficiencies in background and development are pertinent to school success or failure. Poor children are hindered by inadequate nutrition, disease, and environmental poisoning, cultural misunderstandings, low self-esteem, and the bias inherent in standardized tests. Physically handicapped children experience difficulties in seeing, hearing, or physically getting about. Mentally retarded children require special education and training. Finally, learning-disabled children, such as dyslexic and hyperactive children, have learning problems that if left uncorrected in the primary school years, can handicap their entire school careers.

FOR FURTHER READING

Becker, W. *Parents Are Teachers: A Child Management Program.* Champaign, Illinois: Research Press, 1976. Becker's manual provides practical information for the parent who wants to turn the home into an environment supportive of educational and social growth.

Felker, D. *Building Positive Self-Concepts.* Minneapolis, Minn.: Burgess, 1974. This is a very practical how-to-do-it book for parents and teachers. It deals primarily with the self-esteem of young children but also considers behaviors associated with esteem.

Robertiello, R. *Hold Them Very Close, Then Let Them Go.* New York: Dial Press, 1976. This short primer for parents is written by a psychiatrist who views discipline as a very important form of parental love. Many of Robertiello's suggestions match closely the findings cited by Coopersmith.

Preview Questions

- What are two premises upon which motor theory is built, and how have they been used to improve children's learning?

- Can you describe the major cognitive advances that appear in later childhood and relate them to the type of humor that emerges during this period?

- How are personal and social development during these years related to the type of fears children develop?

- What are some characteristics of children who are most often chosen as friends, and how do friendship groups influence behavior?

- Can you show how a child's self-concept is central to his or her development and explain the effects of divorce, parental absence, and abuse on children?

- What are some major school-related factors that are connected with achievement motivation, and what is its relationship to sex-role development?

- What are several dimensions of cognitive style, and how are these related to a child's performance in school?

- How do grading systems, adult expectations, and social success influence the self-esteem of children in this age range?

- What can teachers do that will enhance children's moral development and decrease their misbehavior in the classroom?

- Can you explain how being poor, handicapped, or from a minority group can cause problems for youngsters in later childhood?

- What are four types of emotional problems that some children may have, and how should each be handled in school?

7

Later Childhood: The Years from Nine to Eleven

Children in the upper elementary grades (four through six) continue to develop and refine the interests, attitudes, and capabilities begun in earlier years. They are able to interact with others in extremely complex ways. They have learned a variety of complex cognitive and social skills. They have adjusted, either satisfactorily or with some problems, to the day-to-day regimen of school life. In addition, achievement motivation, the motivation to succeed at a variety of school and other competencies, assumes considerable importance to most children of this age group. Achievement motivation is expressed in different ways and to different degrees, depending in large part on past experience. This motive and other aspects of adjustment, to a large extent, are influenced by children's levels of sensorimotor and perceptual development, cognitive development, and personal–social development.

DEVELOPMENT IN LATER CHILDHOOD

Sensorimotor and Perceptual Development

By the time they reach fourth grade, children can perform a variety of skills requiring both gross and fine motor coordination that they were unable to perform before. Their speed in running, for example, is considerably faster: Fourth grade boys can run sixteen and one-half feet per second; girls reach this speed about a year later. Most nine-year-old girls can jump up in the air eight and one-half inches; their male counterparts can jump several inches higher. Coordination is much more finely tuned than in the primary school years: Children can intercept balls thrown from a much greater distance than they could when they were younger. About fifty percent of nine-year-olds can copy numbers and letters in neat horizontal alignment. By ten, they can draw three-dimensional objects accurately. Linear perspective appears in their artwork. Children's estimates of their own performances are extremely accurate by age ten or eleven (Cratty 1979).

Educators developing methods to increase learning in the primary grades have developed a model that emphasizes the role of sensorimotor and physical development. **Movement theory** describes the movements through which a child must go in order to make a learned response. All learning, according to this approach, requires movement, from very young children's early reaching and touching behaviors to see how the world differs from themselves to much more complex responding, such as written and verbal communication in the elementary school grades.

Movement theory is based on the distinctive characteristics of motor learning and on the premises (1) that readiness results from early learning of specific prerequisite motor skills and (2) that children need instruction in the motor skills prerequisite to other types of academic learning. In learning to print, for example, children must first learn to make their arms go where they want them to go. Then they must learn to control the muscles of their fingers so as to hold the pencil properly. Then and only then are they ready to learn to print. Once readiness has been learned, each of the little components required in the complex skill of printing can be taught (Gentile 1972; Hunter 1972).

Children in the Soviet Union are taught to draw and to print using essentially this same principle. They are taught first to use the muscles of their fingers to hold very fine hairline brushes and pens. According to their teachers, this is "to learn to make small movement with small hands." American children, on the other hand, usually are given extra large crayons to use. The reason for large crayons, according to most American teachers, is that children have not yet developed the readiness to make such fine movements. One result that researchers have noted is that the hand-writing skills of Soviet children are usually far more developed that those of American children (Gibson and Vinogradoff 1981).

Cognitive Development

Children entering the fourth grade usually still think and solve problems at the concrete operational stage of development—that is, they still need concrete stimuli to assist them in solving problems and coming to conclusions. By this time, they have mastered the perceptual skills discussed in Chapter 6, including conservation, seriation, classification, and class inclusion.

A very significant landmark during the upper elementary school grades is the emergence of what some psychologists have thought of as a scientific approach to learning and thinking (Powell 1979). Children may no longer accept without question everything they are told. The *why* and *wherefore* become important. Their ability to use visual symbols for reading and writing becomes a prominent feature of their repertoire of responses. At this time, language begins to dominate conceptual thinking, as children use more complex grammatical constructions to communicate more complex thinking. Children who are successful at mastering the basic cognitive skills can integrate new concepts. For example, they can think about time by reference to the clock and calendar—that is, in hours, minutes, seconds, days, or time of year (Friedman 1977). They can begin to understand the concept of space as a void between two different things. Children who have learned to read well now enjoy reading immensely and can read with great absorption. They like to listen to stories and also to tell their own.

The Development of Humor

Psychologists have studied the ways that children joke. In early elementary school, with increased abilities to think, to solve problems, and to use language in problem solving, children develop an awareness that many words are ambiguous in meaning, and they use this ambiguity to experiment with the language. A typical joke for this age group, studied by McGhee (1979), is: "Call me a cab." "You're a cab." According to Sutton-Smith (1975), a favorite form of humor for children at this stage of language development is the **riddle.** He defines the riddle as a puzzle that has within it a word, term, or letter that is presented in one way and later reclassified in another way.

Schultz (1974) and Schultz and Horibe (1974) have classified verbal jokes and riddles according to the type of ambiguity of language that they demonstrate. These involve lexical (word formation) ambiguities and phonological (speech sound) ambiguities. They also involve ambiguities in grammatical structure, including what Schultz and Horibe call **surface structure** (ambiguity that results from regrouping of words in a sentence to give two different meanings) and **deep structure** (ambiguity that results from the possibility of two different sets of structural relationships between the key nouns and verbs in the sentence). Table 7.1 gives examples of jokes and riddles fitting each of these classifications.

When five- to eight-year-olds make up their own riddles, their answers tend to be either realistic or completely nonsensical. Some children learn the form of a riddle. If they do not understand the ambiguity of the language that makes the riddle funny, they may substitute another response that provides an illogical conclusion. In

Table 7.1

Jokes and Riddles of Elementary School Children, Classified by Type of Language Ambiguity

Type of Ambiguity	Joke	Riddle
Lexical	"Order! Order in the court!" "Ham and cheese on rye, please, Your Honor."	"Why did the farmer name his hog 'Ink'?" "Because he kept running out of the pen."
Phonological	"Waiter, what's this?" "That's bean soup, ma'am." "I'm not interested in what it's been, I'm asking what it is now."	"Why did the cookie cry?" "Because its mother had been a wafer so long."
Surface structure	"I saw a man-eating shark in the aquarium." "That's nothing. I saw a man eating herring in the restaurant."	"Tell me how long cows should be milked." "They should be milked the same as short ones, of course."
Deep structure	"Call me a cab." "You're a cab."	"What animal can jump as high as a tree?" "All animals; trees cannot jump."

Source: Adapted from Shultz (1974) and Shultz and Horibe (1974).

the previous example, such a riddle might be worded as follows: "What animals can jump as high as a tree?" "Elephants, because they're so big." Between grades three and five, children often are endlessly preoccupied with riddles and may laugh over and over again each time a riddle is repeated.

Personality Development and Socialization

By the upper elementary school years, children are concentrating on beginning to become more independent of their parents. They have a more realistic view of their parents than they had earlier, and they begin to have their own opinions and make some decisions. The time of blind obedience to authority is past. Their relationships with their parents are both complicated and subtle: They want to know what their parents think, but they do not always accept their opinions. They often become extremely sensitive to criticism; at the same time, they really want parental approval. As they grow older, most children become more responsible, more independent, and more trustworthy. They tend to show far greater ability to accept criticism than before, and they can be self-critical. Nine-year-olds tend to have fewer fears than younger children. Some still are resolving fears that were conditioned during the early school years, such as fear of storms or the sight of blood, but for the most

Well-adjusted ten-year-olds are often described by parents and teachers as happy, companionable, friendly, and open.

part, children are now ready to conquer these fears and become self-reliant in both actions and thoughts. By ten, most children's early fears are gone and forgotten.

Ten-year-olds tend to be a happy lot. Parents and teachers often are surprised at the emergence of "nice, happy, casual, unselfconscious, straightforward, sincere, relaxed, companionable, poised, friendly, frank, and open" children at home and in class (Powell 1979, p. 194). There are worries, of course. Ten- and eleven-year-olds are beginning to become more involved in their studies, and this may cause them occasional worry. Sometimes, but not frequently, they explode into anger, but this is usually short lived. Many ten- and eleven-year-olds are beginning to think of the future: "What shall I do when I grow up?" "Whom will I marry?" "What will I become?" Girls frequently begin to show strong emotions for their fathers and may be devastated when their fathers express disapproval. The social pressure is for boys to begin acting like "men" and girls like "women." Although our society allows girls to be "tomboys" until puberty, more pressure is on boys to be "masculine" in most interests and activities. Table 7.2 describes the development of social and family relationships, self-concept, and outstanding characteristics for children nine to eleven years old.

Table 7.2
The Development of Social and Family Relationships, Self-Concepts, and Outstanding Characteristics of Nine- to Eleven-Year-Olds

Age	Social and Family Relationships	Self-Concepts	Outstanding Characteristics
9 years	Better relationships at home as the child becomes less critical, very close peer friendships	Still self-evaluating but more at ease with self, can admit mistakes without feeling threatened	Outgoing, curious, very involved in personal interests, self-confident
10 years	Likes almost everyone in family. Closer peer friendships, with sex differentiation (boys in larger groups, girls in small groups), likes organized clubs	Less self-evaluative, more self-satisfied	Stable, at ease with the world, sex differences emerging
11 years	Challenges parents and all adults, conflicts with siblings, peer friendships very important	New doubts and tensions as adolescence approaches, moody, sensitive, full of self-doubt	High physical activity (also big appetite), intense curiosity, no longer quite at ease with self and others

Source: Adapted from Elkind (1971).

The Development of Fears

Researchers have shown that the objects of children's fears change with chronological age. The greatest fears of preschool children are associated with imaginary creatures and with loss of caregivers. Barnett (1969), in a study of the fears of seven- to twelve-year-old girls, discovered that as children continue in elementary school from grades one to six, fears related to personal safety (for example, being placed in danger if one's parents were lost for a period of time) and of imaginary creatures decline. At about the age of nine, children begin to increase their fears associated with school and social relationships. Sometime between eleven and twelve years, this fear becomes a major importance to the child. Figure 7.1 illustrates the shift in importance of fear with chronological age, as demonstrated by Barnett.

Because, as they grow older, children spend increasing periods of time in school and in social relationships with peers, it is not surprising that fears associated with these activities should increase. Researchers believe that most fears are not irra-

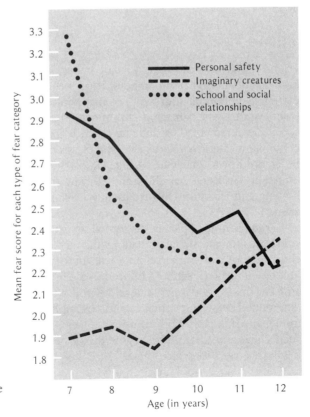

Fig. 7.1 **Changes in the fears of elementary school girls with chronological age (Barnett 1969).**

tional: Children who experience fear usually have had unhappy experiences associated with the objects of these fears. Flaste (1977) noted, for example, that children who are afraid to go somewhere alone also say that sometime in the past, they were hurt when they were out alone. Children who develop strong fears of social relationships typically have not been successful in learning to get along with others. Fraiberg (1959) suggests that in this sense, fear serves a self-preservation function in that children learn to anticipate aspects of their environments that might be dangerous to them, and they prepare for the danger by means of fear.

CHILDREN AND THEIR PEERS

As children spend less and less time at home interacting with their immediate families, the peer culture takes on an increasingly important role in their socialization. By the upper elementary school years, children form friendship groups based on goals or motives. These groups are one of the crucial factors in helping the child develop a sense of affiliation with others outside the family.

Friendship Groups

Friendship groups can have a major impact on the personal–social development of both members and nonmembers. Participation in a friendship group serves as an extremely important source of positive reinforcement. On the other hand, exclusion from a group can damage a child's self-esteem and limit opportunities for healthy social development. Research has shown that friendship groups are an important component of normal and successful classrooms and that they cannot or should not be ignored by teachers or parents (Root 1977). Such groups often provide the first "we–they" referents for children, allowing the "we's" to experience a sense of belonging and affiliation and frequently leaving the "they's" feeling lonely and alientated.

Friendship groups can be formal as well as informal. In either case, they provide bases for the social affiliations that are extremely important to the developing child. School clubs, for example, can be organized according to student interests. Among elementary school children, sex often is used as the basis for both formal and informal groups. Separate clubs for boys and girls usually engage in socially determined sex-typed activities—for example, the girls' sewing club and the boys' model airplane club. With more recent emphasis on non-sex-stereotyped behavior, such clubs and sports are beginning to be coeducational, with girls more often joining the boys than vice versa.

Elementary school children tend to base their informal groupings on commonalities of background. Among urban poor children, informal groups frequently form along ethnic or racial lines. These groups are used through the school years increasingly to fulfill affiliation needs; the distinction between the "we's" and the "they's" becomes more and more magnified.

Although members frequently vow undying fidelity, friendship groups are not perpetuated indefinitely. As children progress through school, their interests change, and they frequently leave one group to join another with more attractive goals.

The Peer Culture

Friendship and Popularity. **Popularity** refers to approval and acceptance by the group; popular children tend to serve as models for their peers. Research has shown that popular children provide more reinforcement to their peers, are better able to make friends, and are better able to identify emotions from the facial expressions of others than are unpopular children (Gottman *et al.* 1975). Popular children have been found to score higher in measures of academic achievement, intelligence, and interpersonal adjustment than unpopular children (Bailey and Pierce 1975).

According to Goslin (1962), popular children are able to **socioempathize**—that is, they have learned to perceive correctly the feelings and attitudes of others in their social group and therefore are able to respond in appropriate fashion. Unpopular children, on the other hand, have not learned to interpret the communications of their peers or, in turn, to communicate with others. Generally, popular children are considered to be friendlier, more sociable, and more outgoing.

Physical attractiveness seems to have some bearing on popularity, a fact that is reflective of the values of our society as a whole. Children who are physically attractive tend to have better relationships with their peers and, at the same time, get higher marks from their teachers on academic ability and adjustment than less phys-

Table 7.3

Reasons Given by Nine-, Ten-, and Eleven-Year-Old Children
for Selecting Certain Children as Friends

Age	Reason for Selecting Friends
9	Acceptance
	Admiration
	Prior interaction
10	Loyalty and commitment
11	Genuineness
	Friend as receiver of help

Source: Adapted from Bigelow and LaGaipa (1975).

ically attractive children (Lerner and Lerner 1977). By fifth and sixth grades, physically attractive girls tend to be more successful than their less attractive counterparts at interacting with boys. Physical attractiveness at this age, however, seems to be less important to boys in their relationships with one another. Unattractive boys actually are more effective than their more attractive counterparts at developing friendships with their same-sex peers (Dion and Stein 1978).

The reasons that nine-, ten-, and eleven-year-old children give for selecting certain children as friends rather than others are given in Table 7.3 (page 267).

Friendship Groups and Conformity. Figure 7.2 shows the steady increase in conforming behaviors of children from seven to eleven years of age. Upper elementary school children tend to conform to the behaviors of their peers. When it is popular to wear red sweaters to school, everyone wears red sweaters. When it is popular to carry lunch bags to school instead of buying hot lunches, everyone carries a lunch bag.

According to Piaget (1932), conformity and age are directly related. The relationship is curvilinear—that is, preschool children are relatively uninfluenced by peer behavior, whereas older children are highly influenced by their peers. Conformity to peer-group behavior begins with elementary school and increases steadily until age eleven or twelve.

Much has been written about the conformity of nine- and ten-year-olds. The behavior has been jokingly described as "herd instinct." But to the ten-year-old intent on looking like, talking like, and acting like his or her peers, it is serious business indeed! Pressure to conform is intense at this age. Children are afraid that nonconformity will bring rejection by the peer group. Because this peer group is increasingly important as children gradually spend more and more time with peers and away from family, fear of rejection also increases. Children are afraid to accept any opinions that differ from the friendship group.

In a classic study of conformity to group pressure performed more than thirty years ago, Berenda (1950) showed that children, when asked to estimate the length of a line presented to them, gave estimates similar to those already provided by other children in the class, even when doing so meant estimating incorrectly. Some statements typical of Berenda's subjects follow:

> *I know they were wrong, but it was like a jury—we were nine and I was the only one against eight. The majority wins. Besides, how could I prove I was right?*
>
> *I had a funny feeling inside. You know you are right and they are wrong, and you agree with them. And you still feel you are right, and you say nothing about it. Once I gave the answer they didn't give. I thought they would think I was wrong. I just gave their answers. If I had the test alone, I wouldn't give the answers I gave (Berenda 1950)*

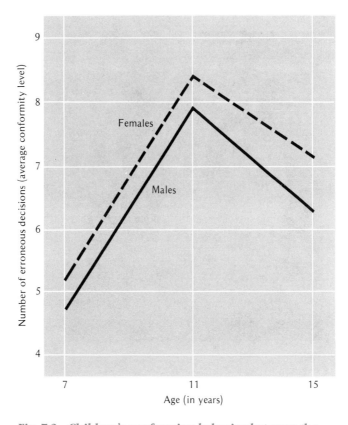

Fig. 7.2 Children's conforming behavior between the ages of seven and fifteen years. In this study, children were given problems to solve and erroneous answers to these problems given by peers. They were then asked to solve the problems themselves. Responses chosen as conforming were erroneous answers that matched those provided (Costanzo and Shaw 1966).

Egocentric thinking, according to Piaget, is thinking based on immediate perceptions and lacking the consideration of alternative points of view. **Sociocentric thinking** involves ability to recognize and respond to the attitudes of others. Tierney and Rubin (1975) showed that elementary school children measuring high in egocentric thinking tend to conform to group pressures more than do children who are sociocentric in their thinking. This probably happens because children at this stage of thinking are concerned primarily with the effects on themselves of conforming or not conforming. Later, after age eleven, many develop **empathic thinking;** they are able to participate in the feelings and emotions of others and are far less

During later childhood, youngsters usually choose friends of the same sex who have similar interests.

likely than before to conform to external peer pressures that contradict what they believe is right about other people or behaviors.

Social psychologists have related conforming behavior in elementary school children both to self-esteem and to achievement. Low-achieving children are more likely to conform to group pressures than are higher achievers (Sams 1974). This probably happens because these children have less self-confidence than do higher achievers.

CHILDREN IN THE FAMILY

Self-Concept and Self-Esteem

Childrearing methods and parental behaviors are related directly to self-esteem. Self-concept, you will remember, is the individual's perception of himself or herself as a person. When this perception is given a value judgment, we call it **self-esteem.** Coopersmith (1967) found that he could predict the self-esteem of ten- to twelve-year-old boys more accurately by the behaviors and attributes of their parents than

HOW DO CHILDREN SELECT THEIR FRIENDS?   HIGHLIGHT 7.1

Children of different ages frequently list different reasons for selecting friends. In one study (Bigelow and LaGaipa 1975), teachers asked elementary school students to think about their best friends of the same sex and to write essays about what they expected from these friends that was different from what they expected of other acquaintances. The choices made were similar whether the essays were written by boys or by girls. Requirements for friendship, however, tended to increase with the grade level of the children writing the essays. Children in the second grade, for example, tended to think of their best friends primarily as "help givers who share common activities." Third, fourth, and fifth graders added a number of additional requirements, such as stimulation provided in play activities, social acceptability, and loyalty. Seventh and eighth graders thought of their best friends as providing for all of these needs. In addition, they stressed similarity of interests and values and the potential for some form of intimate relationship.

The authors of the study related their findings to what they called a transition from "egocentric to sociocentric and sociocentric to empathic" views of children.

QUESTIONS FOR THOUGHT

1. In Chapter 6, we talked about Piaget's description of social development of school-age children. How do these findings relate to that description?

2. How do you think the reasons that children use for selecting friends differ from those of college students?

by factors more commonly assumed to be related to self-esteem in school children, such as physical attractiveness, intelligence, or motor ability.

In Coopersmith's longitudinal study of middle-class, ten- to twelve-year-old boys, those rated high in self-esteem described themselves as "worthy human beings." These boys tended to be more secure and less anxious than boys with lower self-esteem. In addition, they tended to be more inquisitive, more interested in activities around them, less afraid to question the teacher, and more creative than those with lower self-esteem. They also tended to be less physically aggressive toward their peers. Boys with lower self-esteem either reported that they were unsure of their self-worth or, more sadly, that they were unworthy.

Parents of boys with high self-esteem interviewed by Coopersmith tended to rate higher in self-esteem and emotional stability than did other parents. Mothers tended to be happier in their parental roles, and both parents tended to be significantly more attentive to their children. Although both parents were employed outside the home in many of the families, these parents, when they were home, consistently spent some of their free time with their children.

Parental behavior clearly serves as a model for the behavior of children. It is well known, for example, that highly aggressive parents tend to have aggressive children (Eron *et al.* 1974). Coopersmith suggested in his study that parents of the boys with high self-esteem served successfully as models for behaviors associated with high self-esteem.

What behaviors did these parents exhibit? Their parental style fit our description of "democratic parents" (see Chapter 6). They tended to be more strict than were the parents of boys with lower self-esteem. They established clear-cut rules of behavior for themselves and for their children and administered these rules consistently. They rewarded approved behavior consistently and only rarely administered punishment; when punishment was necessary, it was not inappropriately harsh. Parents of boys with high self-esteem tended also to use reasoning in their disciplinary methods, an approach consistent with nonauthoritarian methods of upbringing discussed earlier in this book. One way to interpret these findings is that parents of boys with high self-esteem taught their children by rules consistent with operant approaches to behavior. As a result, they were highly efficient at teaching desired behavior.

Self-esteem of school-age children has been studied by a number of other researchers as well. Their results, for the most part, complement those of Coopersmith. Miller (1975), for example, reported that self-esteem is related to the educational level and profession of the mothers. Miller found that the employment of both parents seems to be related to self-esteem. Mothers of low income and low educational level who were employed out of necessity tended to have children whose self-esteem was lower than did those who were more highly educated and who were employed by choice. In this study, the self-esteem of mothers probably was the factor most important to the self-esteem of children.

Woods (1972) found that the effect on school-age children of mothers employed outside the home is dependent to a great extent on what kinds of supervision are provided. Supervised children in Woods's study were more self-reliant and more independent; children left unsupervised tended to develop cognitive and social problems. In general, children who are provided high-quality supervision tend to be much better adjusted than those who are not.

Effects of Divorce

One tendency, supported to some degree by research, is to relate juvenile delinquency and other problem behaviors to single-parent homes and parent absence (Marino and McCowan 1976). The dynamics of divorce, however, are far too complicated to support such broad generalizations. Too often in the past, the research has not attempted to isolate certain extremely significant factors, such as the quality of the childrearing prior to and following a divorce, whether the divorcing parents behave amicably toward one another, how well the custodial parent adjusts to the divorce, and the like. Researchers have found that when divorcing and divorced parents make sure that their children are receiving proper attention and emotional support, when they are amicable toward one another, and when they adjust emotionally to the divorce in satisfactory ways, their children do not exhibit excessive problem behaviors or academic problems (Bachman 1970).

Although divorce causes temporary distress, there is no evidence that children whose parents are divorced suffer more emotional problems in later life than children from intact homes. Many parents report that after some initial anxiety, their children adjust to the new situation faster than the parents themselves. This is especially true when the parents, despite their own problems, make an effort to show that they are capable of managing their postmarital situation, of being good parents, and of keeping family life relatively free from stress.

How do children perceive themselves and the situation at the time of divorce? Generally, upper elementary school children develop slightly fewer problem behaviors or academic problems than their younger siblings (Kelly and Wallerstein 1976). But many strong reactions still occur, including crying, feelings of sadness, and longing for the absent parent (Bernard 1977). Many children are afraid that they too will be rejected or feel that they are the cause of the divorce. Frequently, they express anger toward the custodial parent, particularly if that parent initiated the divorce. Anxiety is particularly strong when the parents continue to fight after the divorce. One ten-year-old visiting a psychologist's office described her reaction this way:

> In a way, I thought that it was all my fault. Maybe I'd acted mean to my mother and my brother, and God was punishing me. So I tried to be really good by doing my homework and making my bed, and I hoped that maybe God would see I changed and make it all right. Later, I got mad at my mother and decided that it was really her fault. She made my father mad and leave us, and then she acted like a teenager—dancing and dating other men. It's been two years, and I'm used to it all now, even though, when I wish on a star, it's always to make things go back to the way they were before. Even when I know in my head that it wasn't all good, there are still so many beautiful things to remember—even make-believe ones.

Children aged nine to twelve years often are realistic about their situations but wish they could change things: "I wish my parents were married. I wouldn't mind so much that they're not if I just could see Daddy more." The following response of a fourth grader to her therapist, when asked what she would tell another child whose parents were getting divorced, is also not an uncommon one: "I would never say it will be good because it just won't."

HIGHLIGHT 7.2 IT WAS SCARY!

The following conversation took place between a psychologist and Mikey, a ten-year-old boy:

Mikey: Yes, it was real bad at first . . . it was scary, Mom taking off like that without even saying anything to me. I couldn't believe it in the beginning. I knew some kids didn't have a Dad, but I didn't know any kids whose Mom had gone off . . . .

Psychologist: What did you think?

Mikey: I began to wonder, you know, why is she doing it? To punish me? In the beginning I don't think I was mad, just scared. Like I didn't know how Dad and I would get along . . . after a while, I guess I got mad.

Psychologist: What did you get mad at?

Mikey: Well, who did she think she was anyway? Dad said she didn't hate me or anything. But I didn't believe him. He said she wanted to build a life without him. And she couldn't do it here. He said that someday she would come and see me—maybe just get on the telephone one day. But I kept thinking she must be mad at me. I must've done *something* wrong . . . like always making noise on Sunday morning when she used to like to sleep late.

Psychologist: But your Dad told you that she wanted to build a life without him. Didn't you believe him?

Mikey: He tried to make me think that was true. And I know he missed Ma. But they never had fights or anything. He cried the day she left—it was the only time I ever saw Dad cry. But she never used to get mad at him—only at me because I was

Apparently, no straightforward relationship exists between the intensity of a child's suffering at home and his or her reaction to divorce as observed in the school setting. Sometimes children who exhibit serious problem behavior at home may appear totally happy in school, where no painful associations are present. Other youngsters whose parents are divorcing have trouble in school—acting out their anxiety and displaying aggression (Felner 1977).

Special Effects of Parental Absence

A primary problem for upper elementary school children dealing with divorce is living without one parent. For one thing, the dynamics of the one-parent home differ considerably from the home as it used to be. Perhaps Mom used to be home every

always doing something bad. I guess she just couldn't take me anymore, so she had to leave both of us.

Psychologist: You said it was scary at first. Are you still scared?

Mikey: Not so much any more. Don't tell anybody, but I had a couple of months in the beginning where I actually wet my bed! It was awful. I felt like a little kid. But Dad said it would go away, and it finally did. I guess I'm still scared of wetting my bed, even though I don't do it anymore. And I get real scared if Dad is late coming home from work. I guess I'm a real pest.

Psychologist: Why are you afraid of that?

Mikey: I guess I'm afraid, you know, that he won't come at all, that I'm just too big a pest.

Psychologist: Didn't your Dad tell you you're silly?

Mikey: Yes, he always says that. Like when he takes me to a girl-friend's to visit and I don't want to go. He says I have to go; we're a team. He's the driver, and I'm in the back, riding shot-gun. I know it's silly to be afraid. It only happens now some-times. It's not so scary anymore.

QUESTIONS FOR THOUGHT

1. Mikey was confronted with a problem that some children of divorced parents face today: a mother who had decided to leave the family. What special problems does this situation present Mikey that might differ from those of other children?

2. Mikey lists a number of symptoms of anxiety. How might his parents help him alleviate these symptoms?

day after school to do things and to see how things went during the day, and now she comes home at five and just asks, "Did you do your homework?" Perhaps Dad used to have a few minutes to play ball every evening while Mom made dinner, and now, on the every-other-weekend visit, he rarely even thinks of it.

The vast majority of single-parent homes in the United States today are headed by mothers, although about ten percent are headed by fathers. Studies have shown that fathers who are single heads of households are generally more concerned than mothers with developing sex-typed behavior in their sons (Lynn 1976). For example, fathers are more apt to take their sons out for a ball game or other "masculine-typed" play activity than are mothers who are heads of households.

What happens, both to boys and girls, when the father is absent? The development of male and female sex roles is related to self-esteem and social adjustment and is affected by the presence or absence of parents who can serve as models. Female children tend to identify more closely with the feminine role; their lack of experience with a father figure may lead to difficulty in the formation of male–female relationships after puberty unless other adult male friends and family members serve as models. Research indicates that male children who lose opportunities to identify with a male model may develop slightly more "feminine" attributes, such as nurturing instead of competitive behaviors (Mickleson 1976; Heilbrun 1978).

One study shows that extended father absence may influence children in a variety of complex and often indirect ways, the most important of which has to do with the child's total environment. Father absence may, for example, influence maternal attitudes toward childrearing, which can, in turn, affect the child in many different ways. Mothers who adjust well to father absence tend to have more positive attitudes than do mothers who remain depressed or angry (Biller 1969).

Teachers report that fatherless boys tend to be retarded in their moral development and show more social deviation (Santrock 1975). In studies of boys whose fathers were absent because they were in the military service, boys with older sib-

The great majority of single-parent homes in the United States are headed by mothers.

lings tended to be more aggressive. First-born boys, however, did not exhibit this behavior (Hillenbrand 1976).

With the exception of a few such studies, the limited research available actually shows few measurable differences between children who have both parents living at home and children who live in single-parent homes with one parent absent. Contrary to many of our prejudices, single-parent families that give adequate amounts of love and attention can provide satisfactory environments for childrearing. Rutter (1974) suggests that it is the quality of children's relationships with their parents that matters much more than the fact of divorce.

Special Needs of Children in Single-Parent Homes

In general, the needs of children in single-parent homes in this country do not differ significantly from those of other societies. Basic needs include a warm and supportive environment, attention from a loving caregiver, and opportunity to develop in a fashion similar to other children. In order to meet these needs of their children, single parents require a sufficient income to provide adequate care. Children, as well as their caregivers, need opportunity to remain in the mainstream of social life. This includes, for elementary school children, opportunity to attend adequate day care after school, so that they will have adequate attention while their parent is at work, as well as opportunity to attend after-school educational and social programs. It also includes opportunity to receive counseling and rehabilitation services when needed. In a report to governmental agencies in Canada concerned with helping single-parent families and with reducing social problems (Guyatt 1971), a series of recommendations was made to meet these needs.

Because the greatest common problem of one-parent families is financial need, more adequate public support was recommended. Because both single parents and their children often are kept out of the social mainstream because of lack of opportunity to gain access to many day-care, education, and social programs available to two-parent families with more income, subsidized day-care, educational, and social services were recommended. Counseling, rehabilitation services, and additional volunteer programs to bring case-work services to needy families are very important; they were recommended to help prevent further family breakdown. In the United States, where many of these services were provided in the 1970s, financial cutbacks have reduced them in the 1980s.

Child Abuse

In Chapter 5, we discussed child abuse in relation to abuse of preschool children. Here we will consider the problem as faced by elementary school children. Physical abuse of elementary school children occurs more frequently among the poor than among more affluent groups. This should not be surprising, considering the many stresses that usually face poor families. Some researchers have related child abuse to neighborhood conditions. Families who live in poor socioeconomic neighborhoods also have access to a low level of material and social resources. Where families often are transient, both parents and children have little opportunity to gain help from neighbors, and they tend more frequently to be abusive (Garbarino and Crouter 1978).

Family violence directed at elementary school children, like that directed against younger children, increases in times of stress, such as that caused by divorce and increased unemployment (Gelles and Straus 1979).

The problem of abuse of the upper elementary school child is complex. It is not surprising that battering parents tend to use physical violence against older children less frequently than against younger children. Older children can fight back, and they often do. A 1979 survey showed that among children from three to nine years of age, eighty-two percent had been hit by their parents that year; sixty-six percent of children between ten and fourteen years, and thirty-four percent of fifteen- to seventeen-year-olds had been physically struck in the same time period (Gelles and Straus 1979).

School-age children often are abused in nonphysical ways. Abusive parents may ridicule their children and treat them in ways to lower their self-esteem and make them feel worthless (Giovannoni and Becerra 1980). Abused children, in turn, often act in "worthless" ways: They usually do poorly in school; they exhibit aggressive behavior and have difficulty getting along with peers and teachers. The parents frequently are called into school because of the child's disruptive behavior and learning difficulties, which often lead to further abuse. A vicious cycle often ensues; it may consist of school-related and behavior problems, parental abuse, and increased aggression in the classroom due to displacement of the child's anger. Chronic school difficulties add to the abused child's damaged self-esteem (Green 1978).

Another type of abuse inflicted on upper elementary school children is sexual abuse. Rape and molestation are sadly on the increase, at least as measured by the number of children in this age group requiring treatment for sexually transmitted diseases (Sgroi 1977). Sexual abuse, however, does not have to mean rape. It may mean sexual victimization, a term coined to refer to many different sexual activities that combine elements of dependence and exploitation, affection and taboo, deception, self-deception, and collusion, which occur as a result of family dysfunction (Brant and Tisda 1977; Finkelhor 1980). An incestual sexual relationship fostered by a parent or other relative and characterized by that person as a "love relationship that must be kept secret" is one example.

Most victims of sexual abuse are girls. The abusers tend to be men in the family, usually very domineering fathers or stepfathers who look to these children for companionship and affection that they cannot receive from their wives. Often the wife is very passive and suffers from such medical, physical, or social problems as depression or alcoholism. The relationship that ensues often involves bribing the child and

RESOURCES AVAILABLE FOR INCEST VICTIMS AND THEIR FAMILIES

Help for incest victims and their families can be found by consulting child protective services in communities, rape crisis centers, or women's centers. In general, the most effective programs to deal with the personal–social–emotional problems resulting from incest incorporate the following principles:*

1. When a child complains to anyone—a friend, a relative, or a teacher—of sexual abuse, therapists believe the complaint. Researchers report that false complaints are exceedingly rare. This is true even when children, under pressure, deny what they have previously revealed.

2. Professional therapists within programs always report suspected child abuse to the authorities responsible for protecting children, as required by law in all states. Nonreporting of suspected cases is not only illegal, but is tantamount, in most cases, implicitly to taking the abuser's side and convincing the child victims that they are trapped in the situation and have no recourse.

3. Immediate measures are taken to strengthen the relationship between the victim and the nonabusing parent. The child needs to be assured that she or he is not responsible. The child needs to be praised for coming forward and assured that further abuse will not occur. The nonabusing parent needs psychological assistance and support in order to serve as a more assertive and protective parent.

4. The abuser should receive treatment under court order. Researchers suggest that successful programs for treating addiction can serve as effective models in providing tight structures with rewards and sanctions. Group meetings with other offenders where confrontation is balanced with support have also been found to be effective.

QUESTIONS FOR THOUGHT

1. Why do you think that most incest victims have difficulty complaining about their abuse? What do these principles do to alleviate the situation? Can you think of additional ways programs can increase the ease of reporting incest?

2. What specific measures can you think of that might be taken to strengthen the relationship between the incest victim and the nonabusing parent? What other measures might be used to help the victim?

Source: Adapted from *The Harvard Medical School Health Letter*, March 1981, p. 3.

manipulating the child's need for affection; it does not necessarily require physical force. Usually the sexual interaction includes fondling or masturbation, which may proceed to intercourse over the years. The results of this relationship, both for the child and for family members, can be psychologically disastrous. For the child, it usually involves shame, guilt, and fear, as well as serious difficulties later in establishing normal adult sexual and emotional relationships.

CHILDREN IN THE CLASSROOM

In the upper elementary school years, social comparisons become more important; children want to do as well as or better than their peers at a variety of learning tasks and other skills (Feld, Ruhland, and Gold 1979).

Achievement Motivation

Psychologists note that nonhuman animals seem to need to explore their environments. Some suggest that there is a related need in human beings to master the environment. Such mastery leads to feelings of competence (White 1959). Motivational theorists tell us that some children strive more than others to obtain this mastery and to gain feelings of competence both in problem solving and in interactions with others. Such children are said to have a high need to achieve or high **achievement motivation.** It is these children who have been found to have the greatest success at learning.

Children who have high achievement motivation are more likely than are other children to be challenged by the personal effort required in solving problems. They also are more likely to persevere longer at learning tasks. Children who have a high need to achieve usually are not gamblers: They are more likely to use logic in solving problems than to take wild guesses without thinking. They tend to select goals that have intermediate possibilities of success—that is, goals that they can accomplish but that still present learning challenges. Students lower in achievement motivation tend to be more erratic: They more frequently select either unrealistically high or unrealistically low goals (Mouly 1970). Children with high levels of motivation have high levels of aspiration as well—that is, their expectations of themselves and predictions of future goals (such as grades desired or expected in school) usually are higher than those of children with lower motivation to achieve.

Why are some children motivated to achieve while others are not? Psychologists suggest that children with high needs to achieve have developed a clear understanding of the specific goals to be obtained through achieving. Through early successes, they have been able to observe self-improvement first hand. Equally important are their social environments, which are highly supportive of their efforts (McClelland 1965). The behavior of motivated children is much like that of the boys with high self-esteem described by Coopersmith (1967).

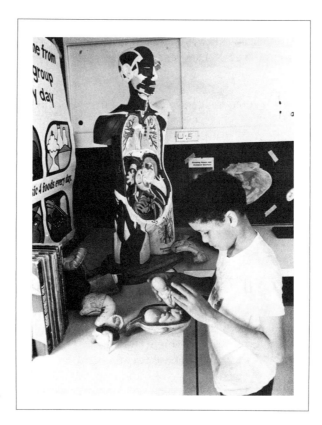

Children with high achievement motivation tend to select realistic goals—goals they can accomplish but that still present a challenge.

Level of aspiration is known to be affected by previous success or failure. In a classic study, Child and Whiting (1949) showed that children who performed successfully raised their goals and increased their self-confidence. Children who failed at the same tasks tended to lower their levels of aspiration. The effects of failure, however, seemed to be more variable than those of success: Children either gave up or, in some cases, unrealistically raised their reported expectations, almost as if the hope of success alone would bring success.

Factors Related to Achievement Motivation. Parents who are more democratic in their style of childrearing tend to have children with higher achievement motivation than do parents who are highly restrictive and punitive in their childrearing. McClelland (1972) performed an experiment involving young school-age boys who were blindfolded and then asked to stack irregular blocks with their left hands. McClelland found that boys whose mothers estimated in advance that they would do well and then encouraged them persevered at the task much longer than did boys whose parents were more prone to order the boys to perform the task properly and to try harder when they failed. The more successful boys also were found to be more highly motivated to achieve.

Psychologists have for some time related high need for achievement to methods of discipline. McClelland *et al.* (1953) showed that mothers of children with high need to achieve often use guilt-inducing methods of discipline (for example, suggesting that bad behavior makes their parents unhappy) to make their children maintain achievement standards. This was not found to be true of mothers of children with low needs to achieve.

Socioeconomic background also appears to be linked to variations in the achievement motivation of children. One study showed that parents higher on the socioeconomic scale have higher educational and occupational aspirations for their children than do parents in lower socioeconomic brackets. Presumably, their aspirations and corresponding encouragement affect their children's aspirations (Brook *et al.* 1974).

Sex-Role Socialization and Achievement Motivation. Although girls tend to out-perform boys academically during the first four years of elementary school, their academic achievement later falls relative to that of boys. How can this be explained? Although there may actually be multiple causes for this difference, psychologists have noted that, in the higher grades of elementary school, both the motivation of girls to master their school learning and their expectations of success tend to decrease considerably (Parsons and Ruble 1977). According to Kagan (1964), this decrease in achievement corresponds to an increase in fear of success and of competitiveness that appears even in the upper elementary school years. Although this fear may also occur in boys, Kagan and other psychologists have noted that it is more frequent in girls (see for example, Brook 1976). In order to obtain the best grades in schools, girls generally feel they must "defeat" their peers. The competitiveness this requires is clearly incompatible with girls' socialization, which fosters non-aggression and compliance.

As we have noted, childrearing for girls in our society differs greatly from that of boys. Emphasis tends to be placed at very early ages on the development of social skills rather than assertive behaviors. Girls are taught early that social approval is important for them, whereas boys learn that mastery is important for them (Harter 1975). McClelland (1958) pointed out that training in independence and mastery is necessary to high achievement motivation; girls in our society are taught to be dependent, boys to be independent. Furthermore, boys are taught directly that achievement is important; girls are not. Masculine identification has long been known to be related consistently to high IQ, creativity, and superior problem-solving ability (Milton 1957; Maccoby 1966). Feminine identification is not related in similar fashion to intellectual and academic tasks.

What about educational and occupational aspirations? Parents' aspirations for their offspring differ according to the sex of their children (Brook *et al.* 1974). Vocational roles more often associated with men are also generally associated with aggressiveness and competition, but not with social skills. The message for girls is quite clear. A study of female TV characters showed that female job holders in male-dominated fields were portrayed usually as unmarried or unsuccessful in their marriages (Manes and Melnyck 1974). The range of different occupations to which girls aspire is considerably narrower than that of boys (Hewitt 1975), presumably because girls have observed fewer successful women in a narrower range of outside activities. In addition, as they get older, girls may increasingly fear social rejection for high achievement at intellectual tasks. Horner (1972) suggested that this might mean that the higher the motivation to achieve, the higher the simultaneous fear of success.

Horner's theory proposes that academically successful girls can be expected to be very fearful of success. More recent data show, however, that this is not always the case (Condry and Dyer 1976). Today, society is more willing to recognize achievement as appropriate for females as well as males. Social pressure against achievement for women gradually is decreasing (Frieze 1974). Female children more and more often are able to observe mothers who combine successful professional careers with happy, well-adjusted personal lives. In recent years, studies have shown that children of successful professional mothers have higher academic and vocational aspirations than do children of either mothers not working outside the home or dissatisfied working mothers (Etaugh 1974). In one study of the motivation to avoid success in female children between grades five and eleven, only four percent of the girls studied were highly motivated to avoid academic success (Romer 1975). Similarly, high-ability female sixth graders tended to be as assertive as males in achievement, even though their female counterparts with lower IQs tended to be less assertive (Hedrick and Chance 1977). These data may suggest a relatively permanent trend toward encouragement of achievement motivation in girls.

Cognitive Styles

Differences in the ways children organize what they learn, categorize concepts, and employ problem-solving strategies are called **cognitive styles.** Because cognitive styles are indicative of different approaches to learning, they sometimes are referred to as **learning styles.** Psychologists have suggested that cognitive styles are shaped by early life experiences and that by the time children enter school, their learning styles are in large part already determined. By upper elementary school grades, their cognitive styles are well established. Researchers have measured the ways that differences in learning approaches among children are related both to personality and to motivation. They have also measured differences in the ways children make sense of the world and extract "pieces" of it to use in order to solve problems. Wittrock (1978) described these differences according to the different ways in which the child's brain operates—that is, in which the brain admits information, processes information, and uses what it selects.

Riessman (1966) categorized children's learning styles into three basic groupings: (1) the **visual learning style,** in which learning is accomplished most easily through reading, (2) the **aural learning style,** in which learning is accomplished most easily through listening, and (3) the **physical learning style,** in which learning is accomplished most effectively through touching, feeling, manipulating, and doing. Different children, because of habits acquired in early learning experiences, tend to use one or another of these approaches and learn most effectively through that one approach. Nations (1967), using a different analytical method to describe cognitive styles, identified two categories: the **response mode** or the manner in which children learn most effectively (for example, alone or in a group) and the **thinking mode,** or the way in which children approach each individual problem (for example, by gathering details first for later organization or by looking for the overall picture first and then supporting it with details). Nations's research suggests that teachers should examine the manner in which children solve problems most effectively and then adapt their teaching methods accordingly.

Many different cognitive styles have been described by researchers. One example is field dependence or field independence. Field dependence and independence are two different approaches to the perceptual organization of information. **Field-independent** children make fine discrimination in what they see before them and isolate items of importance from the surrounding material. We say that these children can discriminate figures from ground or background. **Field-dependent** children, on the other hand, often are overwhelmed if the materials presented to them appear in a complex context, for they have difficulty distinguishing figures from ground. Such children often are called unanalytical. Field-dependent children have more difficulty solving the types of problems usually presented in the classroom than do field-independent children. At the same time, they tend to be more socially oriented and to enjoy working in team situations more than do their field-independent peers (Messick 1970; Witkin *et al.* 1977).

Another dimension of cognitive style is **impulsivity or reflectivity.** Reflective children tend to take time in solving problems; they think over all possible alternatives before arriving at an answer. Reflective children may, because of this approach, make fewer errors along the way than do impulsive children. At the same time, they often take longer to solve problems than do impulsive children. They tend to persist for relatively long periods of time at different tasks and hold high standards for intellectual performance. Impulsive children, on the other hand, apparently have greater desire for quick success. They tend to solve problems quickly. They sometimes, however, test hypotheses too quickly and, as a consequence, come up with wrong answers.

In the classroom, teachers tend to rate impulsive children as "less attentive" and more often "hyperactive" than reflective children (Ault *et al.* 1972). They also rate impulsive children as less "task oriented" and "less considerate." Teachers tend to rate school-age boys as more impulsive and more distractible than girls, thus possibly initiating a self-fulfilling prophecy (Kagan, Moss, and Sigel 1970; McKinney 1975).

What cognitive styles are most conducive to intellectual performance? According to Swan and Stavros (1973), problem-solving methods that allow children to listen carefully before making use of information presented to them, to try new approaches to problems when old ones do not work, and to take risks lead to greater intellectual performance and classroom success. Problem-solving methods that keep children from interacting successfully in group-learning situations or that lead to uncontrolled behavior, distractibility, or apprehension all lead to diminished academic success.

Factors Related to Cognitive Styles

Many factors that are related to personality development and motivation are related also to cognitive style and problem solving. For example, the attention span of children is related directly to the ways in which they approach problem solving. Children who are hyperactive, for example, tend to have short attention spans and to jump from one problem to the next without necessarily completing the first problem. Children who are highly motivated tend to spend more time at problem solving than children who are less motivated to do well (Shumsky 1968). Some children need continual monitoring to continue attending to a long problem, yet others continue to work at a problem until it is solved.

Some children also have a greater capacity for independent work than do other children. Such children are able to work independently at solving problems without encouragement from others, but others need more praise and encouragement to keep from getting discouraged, particularly if a task is difficult. The latter are helped by a great deal of individual attention from teachers and peers in class and from parents at home. Peer teaching for these children can provide powerful daily rewards and exert strong influences on academic aspirations and classroom and playground behavior (Schmuck and Schmuck 1975).

Children also differ in learning rate; some take longer than others to solve the same problem, even though they are equally capable of coming up with the correct answer. Messick (1970) described individual differences in children's memories. Some children, who have not had practice in differentiating between present and past, for example, tend to confuse time in describing what is taking place. Others the same age have difficulty seeing similarities between what they experienced last week and what is happening today.

Children differ in general work habits, the attitudes with which they approach tasks, and their choices of tasks most interesting to them. Elkind (1971) points out

Researchers have described a number of dimensions of cognitive style among school children. These different styles are influenced by such factors as attention span, dependence or independence, and learning rate.

that although work habits are learned, we can predict a great deal about the work habits of children through their chronological ages and grades in school. Table 7.4 describes what can be expected of work habits of children in grades one through six.

The School and Self-Esteem

We learned earlier that the behavior of parents is crucial to the development of feelings of self-esteem. School also plays a major role in determining the quality of a child's self-concept. Children's attitudes toward and perceptions of their academic and social skills are determined by a number of factors during the school years. These include success or failure at school tasks, rewards or punishments meted out during the learning process, and expectations of success held by both children and their teachers.

Table 7.4
Work Habits of Children in Grades One Through Six

Grade	Work Habits
1	Works and plans in spurts, does not know when to stop, tires easily
2	Persistent and careful with work, better perspective of how much can be done
3	Social interests may interfere with school work, self-criticism may discourage work ("I can't spell")
4	Very persistent, self-absorbed, academic achievement very important
5	Likes school, has responsible work habits
6	Personal and social interests overwhelming, often has difficulty sustaining interest in schoolwork

Source: Adapted from Elkind (1971).

Effects of Grading Systems. Some children are motivated to achieve in school in order to develop feelings of competence; others are motivated to achieve in order to receive praise and social reinforcement. One method used in schools to provide social reinforcement is grading. It is assumed by many teachers and parents that students are positively reinforced with good grades and negatively reinforced with bad grades. Unfortunately, it is not that simple.

While it is true that children who are positively reinforced by high grades will strive harder for even better grades on the next report card, children who receive low grades are likely to have more variable types of responses. Giving up and unrealistic striving can both follow failure. Self-punitive behavior is an equally possible result (Ames, Ames, and Felker 1977). Educators and psychologists have been increasingly concerned over the sometimes severe anxiety that grading pressures create. A doctor in a midwestern state created quite a stir when he reported what appeared to be an alarmingly large number of first through fourth grade children with stomach ulcers. In discussing the report, educators suggested that these children were the victims of a "competitive, unreasonable, and demanding life . . . " (Georgiady and Romano 1971). They suggested that in spite of all we know about the shortcomings and inconsistencies of most grading systems, report card grades are accepted too frequently as the "indisputable measure of success or lack of it."

Grading systems also appear to have a negative effect on creativity. If children are indeed reinforced by high grades, they will learn to make the kinds of responses required for those grades. Too often, according to the critics of grading, these responses require primarily rote learning rather than new or innovative responding.

On the other hand, most parents today want to keep grades, if only to know how well their children are doing as compared to others in their community and to national norms. In our mobile society, many parents ask, "If we move to Kansas (or Alabama or California, etc.), will my children be in their regular class, or will they be put back (or ahead)?"

Teacher and Parent Expectations. Many critics of the educational system believe that teachers' attitudes toward their students, particularly toward students of minority and impoverished backgrounds, contribute to poor self-esteem in these children (Braun 1976; Rist 1976). These critics point out that too often, teachers have the attitude that poor kids are dumb and cannot learn. Parents' expectations play a role in this process. When both parents and teachers believe a child cannot succeed, this may contribute both to failure and to lowered self-esteem. Smith, Zingale, and Coleman (1978) found, however, that the effects are much more significant among children from high socioeconomic backgrounds than from low. They reason that parents' and teachers' expectations for children of higher socioeconomic backgrounds are usually high. When a child from such a background fails to meet expectations, it is this large discrepancy that results in problems of self-esteem for the child. These researchers report that children from lower socioeconomic backgrounds experience less decrease in self-esteem as a result of academic failure because the discrepancy between adult expectations and child performance is comparatively small.

One's concepts of ability and self-esteem, once learned, are difficult to change. Once children develop strong beliefs about what their abilities are, they tend to reject all new information inconsistent with these beliefs.

Social Success. Success at school social tasks, being liked and admired by one's peers, also has important effects on self-esteem. Children who are physically attractive tend to have better relationships with their peers and, at the same time, are judged more highly by their teachers on academic ability and adjustment than are less physically attractive children (Lerner and Lerner 1977). By fifth and sixth grades, physically attractive girls tend to be more successful at interacting with boys than their less attractive counterparts. Physical attractiveness at this age, however, seems to be less important to boys in their relationships with one another: Unattractive boys actually are more effective at developing friendships with their same-sex peers than their more attractive counterparts (Dion and Stein 1978).

The School and Moral Development

The learning of morality becomes more complex during later childhood, as children's ability to reason becomes more sophisticated. In school, teachers have the potential for helping children develop their moral reasoning through the same informal processes begun by parents.

According to Kohlberg, one way that teachers can increase the abilities of students to reason about moral issues is to give them practice at solving moral problems. Kohlberg and his colleagues have recommended providing students with educational experiences that reflect real-life moral issues and concern them directly, either individually or collectively, as members of a society. They have recommended also that moral reasoning be facilitated by presenting to children models who operate at higher levels of moral reasoning than do the learners.

Implications for elementary school education seem obvious: If school experience is to develop the ability of the child to reach qualitatively higher levels of moral reasoning, teachers must provide classroom experiences in solving morally relevant problems. They should themselves provide appropriate model figures. In socialist countries, this method of teaching moral reasoning already has been formally set into practice. Children begin group practice at solving moral dilemmas at early ages. Peer teachers are selected often on the basis of their abilities to share and to help others, behaviors considered to be of prime importance in moral upbringing (Bronfenbrenner 1970).

In the United States today, American parents and educators are questioning whether the goals of moral education fall within the realm of the school or family. Such questions as "Should teachers help children to pray in school or to learn about birth control?" are being asked. Questions about sexuality that used to be debated by high school teachers and the community are increasingly issues of concern for middle school and elementary schools.

Discipline

One of the most difficult tasks for teachers is to discipline students fairly and effectively. According to learning theorists, **punishment** is the attempt to eliminate an undesirable behavior by following it with an aversive stimulus (something unpleasant). If Johnny talks back to the teacher, the teacher may make him stay after school. Punishing Johnny is an attempt on the part of the teacher to keep him from talking back again. Researchers have shown that unpleasant results do not always wipe out the unwanted behavior (Hilgard and Bower 1975). Johnny *may* stop talking back if the punishment is strong enough, but researchers point out that it is not clear how strong the punishment must be to be effective. If it is too strong or occurs too frequently, Johnny may become too anxious to learn effectively.

Negative reinforcement, as discussed in Chapter 1, is the removal of an aversive stimulus and is designed to change a child's behavior by strengthening an escape response (Hilgard and Bower 1975). If Johnny talks back to the teacher, perhaps the teacher will ask him to stand up until he can be quiet. When he is quiet, Johnny can sit down and escape the embarrassment of having to stand in front of his classmates. Negative reinforcement can be effective in teaching if appropriate escape responses are available. Researchers believe that when reasoning and explanation are used together with negative reinforcement, learning of appropriate behavior is more rapid than under other conditions (Leizer and Rogers 1974).

Most psychologists believe it is preferable to discipline children by means other than punishment or negative reinforcement. Research shows that when parents or teachers do not adequately teach children to avoid the negative reinforcer or when they are inconsistent in its use, they often teach other unwanted behaviors instead. Punitive disciplinary techniques, in most cases, are far less effective in eliciting desired behaviors than are techniques that favor positive reinforcers (Wood 1977). For example, such reinforcers as free time for good behavior are probably more effective in teaching than any of the more punitive techniques.

Many factors account for the frequent failure of classroom discipline. Some teachers, attempting to make children behave in desirable ways, use punishments that range from ridicule to sarcasm to paddling and incarceration. In situations where the teacher's attention is divided among many students, discipline too frequently is inconsistently applied. For example, sometimes when the teacher sees that Jane is disruptive, the teacher will respond quickly and harshly; at other times, when the teacher is busy, the same misbehavior will go unnoticed and uncorrected. As a result, Jane will not learn that her disruptive behavior is wrong. She will learn instead that sometimes it is fine to behave this way, while at other times it is not. She may or may not learn when she will get away with this behavior. Students used to classroom punishment describe it in a variety of ways: "It made me feel like a nurd." "I felt disgraced and embarrassed." "I felt just terrible." "I don't care—nothing in school is really important."

From " McGuffey's First Eclectic Reader."

During the nineteenth century, it was common to punish students to get them to behave. Psychologists today contend that harsh discipline leads to a variety of negative outcomes.

Teachers cannot always control all of the contingencies in using behavior management in the classroom. For example, the teacher might want to extinguish misbehavior (for example, a child's making jokes while the teacher is talking) by ignoring it. At the same time, the other children may reinforce the same behavior by laughing. In many cases, particularly in large classes, discipline may be delayed well beyond the time period most optimal for learning. The teacher may, for example, have to wait some time to take the misbehaving child to the principal's office for disciplining. When this occurs, discipline may not be as effective.

Unwanted behaviors associated with inconsistent and harsh discipline range from fearful withdrawal and low creativity to aggression and other maladaptive behaviors representing resentment against school. These behaviors have been associated with feelings of low self-esteem as reported by boys in the Coopersmith study (1967).

In 1971, *The Nation's Schools* polled administrators in fifty states. Seventy-four percent of those who responded said that they used corporal punishment in their districts; well over half felt the practice was an "effective educational instrument in assuring discipline." As the incidence of misbehavior in elementary schools, particularly in urban areas, has increased in recent years, so also has the request by teachers' groups for increased use of corporal punishment. Disciplinary codes and procedures have been established at teachers' requests in many communities. As most psychologists would have predicted, where corporal punishment has been administered, there has been an increasing incidence of socially undesirable student behavior. Clearly, the issue is complex and involves the larger question of high levels of violence in our society as a whole. Nevertheless, responding to undesirable behavior with corporal punishment does not appear to be a promising approach.

PROBLEMS OF LATER CHILDHOOD

Many problems of later childhood have their roots in earlier periods of development and were therefore discussed in earlier chapters. Here we will review briefly some of these problems and discuss their effects in later childhood.

Children from Minority and Impoverished Backgrounds

Children from these backgrounds often have difficulty learning from kindergarten through grade three because of health problems, difficulties in communicating with teachers, and differences in behavior, attitudes, and values from the middle-class population. By the time they reach grade four, many of these children have fallen hopelessly behind academically. Research has shown that children who do not learn successfully to read and to write in grades one through three have increasing difficulty in higher grades in keeping up with their peers. As children go from grades four to six, the gap between achievers and nonachievers considerably widens (Cole

1977). Compensatory education programs designed for grades four through six are often unsuccessful because of the lower self-esteem that leads many of these children to respond in increasingly unsocial or aggressive ways.

Handicapped Children

Children who have serious physical, sensorimotor, or mental handicaps, such as mental retardation or learning disabilities from early ages, often have a particularly difficult time when they reach the upper elementary school years, when peer socialization becomes very important.

At home, parents and other family members usually have time to learn ways to deal with their handicaps. In the outside world, however, these children often meet adults who know little about their handicaps or ways best to help them adjust. As we learned in Chapter 6, Public Law 94-142, passed in 1975, was designed to provide the most appropriate education for each child in the least restrictive setting. For many handicapped children, this meant learning to cope in a world of nonhandicapped people. All handicapped children are not placed in regular classrooms in order to learn in the least restrictive setting. Figure 7.3 describes a variety of learning environments for the handicapped graded according to the severity of handicap.

Many handicapped children are mainstreamed into regular classes for the first time in grades four to six. Many of these children spend their first several years of schooling in nonmainstreamed special education classes or in special schools organized to help with special problems (some examples are schools for the blind, schools for the deaf, schools for the mentally retarded, and the like). As these children develop ways to adapt to regular classroom situations, more and more of them are mainstreamed. Especially for children whose parents helped them to adjust in positive ways to their handicaps, mainstreaming has been for the most part successful with children from nine to eleven years. For children of this age group whose psychological adjustment problems are severe or whose teachers are not equipped adequately to deal with their handicaps, mainstreaming has been less successful (Gibson 1980).

Emotional Problems

Some children have learning problems that cannot be explained by intellectual, physical, or sensorimotor deficiencies. Often these problems begin to become apparent during the preschool years. According to research, preschool children who tend to be disobedient, to have temper tantrums, to suck their thumbs, or to wet their beds often continue a pattern of general disobedience through the elementary school years (Sours 1978). Some of these children may exhibit much fearful behavior that impedes their socialization and their classroom learning. Others may have trouble building relationships because their behaviors consistently antagonize others

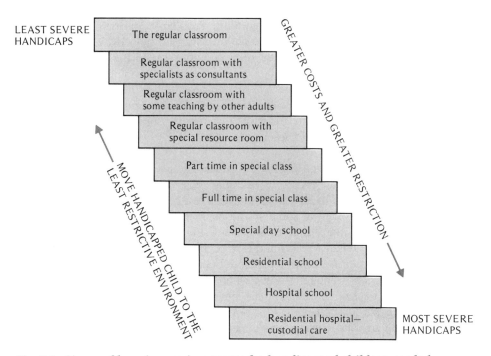

LEAST SEVERE HANDICAPS

GREATER COSTS AND GREATER RESTRICTION

MOVE HANDICAPPED CHILD TO THE LEAST RESTRICTIVE ENVIRONMENT

The regular classroom

Regular classroom with specialists as consultants

Regular classroom with some teaching by other adults

Regular classroom with special resource room

Part time in special class

Full time in special class

Special day school

Residential school

Hospital school

Residential hospital— custodial care

MOST SEVERE HANDICAPS

Fig. 7.3   Types of learning environments for handicapped children graded according to restrictiveness of environment, cost, and severity of handicap. From *Johnny's Such a Bright Boy, What a Shame He's Retarded* **by Kate R. Long. Copyright © 1977 by Kate R. Long. Reprinted by permission of Houghton Mifflin Company.**

or are inappropriate for given situations. Children with these sorts of behaviors are referred to as emotionally disturbed children or children with problem behaviors.

What causes problem behavior? According to many psychologists, problem behavior occurs when children have difficulty learning behaviors that are appropriate in helping them get along with others, in making friends with peers, and so forth. Often when these children discover that their behavior is not effective in helping them make friends, they become anxious. In order to reduce this anxiety, they resort to excessive use of defense mechanisms unacceptable to others. The behavior that results deviates considerably from acceptable behavior and is said to be maladaptive behavior—that is, it is ineffective in helping the child reach the desired goal of satisfactory interactions with others (Sarason 1972).

Many physically or mentally handicapped children, because they feel different from others, have difficulty adjusting to peers and often exhibit problem behavior. Other children who are average in all other respects exhibit behavior that interferes with their attaining desired goals. This happens in some cases when caregivers have not taught appropriate methods of responding. Problem behavior of this type can often be reduced. In many cases, these children can be helped by understanding adults who positively and consistently reinforce appropriate behavior. Home and school environments that provide stable and consistent caregiving help reduce problem behavior. In some cases, however, professional help is needed. According to the National Institute of Mental Health, some ten to twelve percent of elementary school children exhibit problem behaviors that require some form of professional therapy (Rogeness, Bednar, and Diesenhaus 1974).

Anxiety. **Anxiety** is a general feeling of uneasiness, apprehension, or fear, particularly in anticipation of an event. An example of an anxiety-producing event for many children in the nine-to-eleven age range is test anxiety, the fear of test taking. Apprehension is appropriate in some situations, as when a child is unprepared for the test, but many children fear tests even when they are prepared and know what is expected of them. When tension and fear occur without apparent cause or with broad self-doubt, anxiety becomes a problem behavior.

Anxious behaviors frequently occur when children have had past experiences in which a great deal of punishment has been used. Children who are punished severely by their parents or teachers for not doing well in school, for example, are likely to develop anxious reactions that generalize to all situations. Generalized anxiety reactions associated with school, when severe, lead to what is known as **school phobia,** or extreme fear of school. Children with school phobia often experience severe symptoms such as nausea, trembling, or vomiting. Hetherington and Martin (1972) note that children with school phobia often have parents who have overprotected them and reinforced their fears.

Children may develop anxiety attacks or panic reactions to certain situations that are extremely frightening to them. For example, a child who is frightened by a large dog in the playground or who sees a large dog attack another child, may develop a panic reaction because of seeing a dog free on the streets. In other serious situations, the anxiety becomes chronic, does not let up, and it is not so easy to discover the causes.

Drugs reportedly have been administered mistakenly to children suffering from anxiety. The results in many cases have been ineffective or have worsened the problem. In many cases, when the cause of anxiety can be discovered and "talked out" through interpretive therapy in which the children are encouraged to tell specifically what bothers them to the therapist, the therapist can use this information to help them find solutions to their problem.

Behavior management, in which therapists consistently reinforce desired responses incompatible with anxiety, also has been shown to produce good results when the specific situation causing the anxiety can be identified (Cooper 1973). Behavior management can be effective in reducing fear of specific objects or events, such as fear of dogs, by systematically reinforcing responses that are incompatible with anxiety reactions. Such a child first would be reinforced by the therapist for exhibiting physically relaxed responses without the dog's being present. Later, the behavior would gradually be shaped by continuing the reinforcement for the relaxed behavior as a toy dog is brought closer and closer. The final steps of this process, called **deconditioning,** would involve continuing the reinforcement in the presence of a live dog brought closer and closer to the child.

Depression and Withdrawal. Children who exhibit regularly general feelings of sadness and extremely quiet behavior are said to be depressed. **Childhood depression** sometimes leads to **withdrawal,** a psychological retreat from others. Withdrawn or depressed children tend to spend large amounts of time both at home and at school daydreaming and fantasizing instead of interacting with those around them. Excessively withdrawn children appear to be fearful, secretive, and apathetic. Frequently, they dislike interacting with others so much that it becomes painful for them to go to school. In such cases, hypochondriacal symptoms are not at all uncommon, with children complaining of headaches, stomachaches, and other ills that appear just as they are ready to depart for school. Sometimes the hypochondriacal (or sometimes real) physical symptoms keep the withdrawn child at home and away from school altogether.

Asthmatic coughing, high blood pressure, skin disorders, and gastrointestinal disturbances are all physical ailments that, in many cases, may be **psychosomatic** illnesses—that is, illnesses associated with tension and extreme emotion rather than with physical causes only. Children with severe school phobia, when required to attend school, may simply refuse to go. If physically forced to go to school, they may spend most of the time either mute or crying. Sadness and deep depression are not uncommon in withdrawn children (Freedman and Doyle 1974).

Researchers have noted that depressed children too frequently are not noticed by anyone, including their families and teachers. Unless they do something to draw attention to themselves, such as in acting out in school, they often are not even considered behavior problems (Harper 1974). Unfortunately, depressed children rarely act out. More often they do not draw attention to themselves until their withdrawal becomes so severe that they are no longer able to deal with reality. Such children sometimes use threat of suicide as an attempt to get attention. Others use suicide as a way to escape their problems (Toolan 1978). We will discuss this problem in Chapter 8.

Help can be provided for depressed children, provided that their problem behavior is noticed by the adults who interact with them and an appropriate diagnosis is made (Costello 1980). Therapists dealing with depressed behavior have found that consistent reinforcement for behavior that requires involvement with others helps. Depressed children need to be convinced that they are worthwhile human beings. Group-centered therapy approaches in which trained therapists provide acceptance

---

HIGHLIGHT 7.4 REDUCING PROBLEM BEHAVIOR

Many parents write to the Department of Health, Education and Welfare to ask for help in handling their children's problem behavior. They often ask the same questions. Some of the most commonly asked questions addressed to the Public Health Service and their answers follow:

Q: If I do seek help, where would I go?

A: You could start by contacting your local community mental health center. More than 500 of these centers in different parts of the country have been funded by the federal government and are being operated by state and local groups and agencies.

Q: I don't have any hospitalization coverage; where would I get the money to pay for all this?

A: The cost of any of the services should depend on what you can afford to pay. So if you have no money or very little, services are provided free at these centers.

Q: What goes on in these places? What's their treatment all about?

A: A specially trained staff member will talk with your child.

Q: Talk? I can talk to anyone for free. Why pay a doctor?

A: You're quite right. If your child has a wise and understanding friend who is willing to listen to these problems, the child may not need professional help at all. But often that's not enough. Children may need a professionally trained person to help dig out what's really bothering them, and they sometimes need medication.

---

and encouragement and in which depressed children learn that their problems are similar to those of others and that they are not alone, have also been effective (Harper 1974).

Unsocialized Aggression. Children characterized as expressing **unsocialized aggression** are quickly spotted by teachers and families alike. These children are hostile, disobedient, and destructive. Like hyperactive children, they may have frequent temper tantrums. They tend also to be both verbally and physically abusive toward others. Assaults on people or property are not uncommon. Unsocialized, aggressive children tend frequently to lie, steal, and vandalize. Teachers are particularly aware and highly critical of aggressive children and tend to consider this behavior as much more serious than withdrawn behavior. Unfortunately, teachers and especially parents often respond to the aggressive child with aggression of their own, which frequently increases rather than reduces the unwanted behavior.

Psychologists offer many explanations for children's aggressive behavior. Children may first learn aggression by modeling the behavior of punitive caregivers.

HIGHLIGHT 7.4

Q: How can just talking make problems disappear?

A: When you're talking to someone who has helped many others with problems similar to yours, that person is able to see the patterns that have led to unhappiness. In therapy, the job is to help your child recognize those patterns and then try to change them.

Q: Does therapy for mental and emotional problems always work?

A: Sometimes it does, and sometimes it doesn't. It depends on your child and the therapist. The child may not "click" with a particular person, and someone else or some other method may be more suitable for your child. You can ask your therapist for a referral to another mental health professional, or if you prefer, you can call a mental health association for the names of other therapists.

QUESTIONS FOR THOUGHT

1. Have you known many children whose parents have sought mental health services for their problems? If so, what kinds of services provided seemed to be most helpful?

2. Many children fear therapy because they think that other children might laugh at them. How would you make a child who needs therapy feel more comfortable about receiving it?

Source: Adapted from U.S. Department of Health, Education and Welfare (1975).

Hostile aggressive behavior has long been associated with extreme frustration (Miller and Dollard 1941; Miller 1948). Not surprisingly, children who tend to exhibit unsocialized aggression in their interactions with others tend also to be unhappy children who are frequently and easily frustrated.

Parents, teachers, and cooperative siblings and peers can help frustrated children to learn a few needed helpful skills. Competence leads to reduced frustration and higher self-esteem. A positive cycle of development begins, and maladaptive behavior is reduced. Another method of helping these children is carefully and systematically to provide nonfrustrating environments in which positive reinforcement can be given immediately following appropriate behavior. This involves, in therapeutic learning situations, placing children in small groups where a great deal of attention can be given (Culbertson 1974). Group-centered therapies, of the type used for withdrawn children, can be useful with aggressive children as well. Therapists and others dealing with these children must be extremely careful, however, not to respond to aggression with aggression and thus unwittingly provide models for imitation.

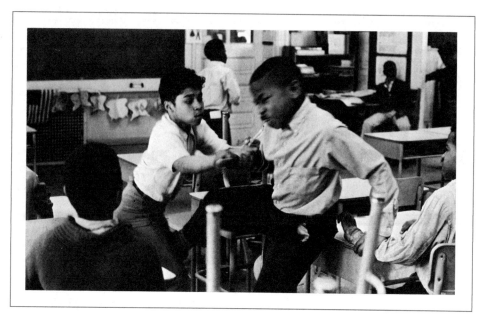

Unsocialized aggression is frequently demonstrated by disruptive behavior in the classroom.

Autism. Thus far, we have been discussing children who are able to function in society with problem behaviors, although they may do so with some difficulty. They are in touch with reality. Other children exhibit behaviors that suggest that they are cut off from what we normally consider reality.

Autism is a disorder characterized by extreme withdrawal and avoidance of contact with others. Often, it is first exhibited at extremely early ages; parents of autistic children often report that their babies appeared unresponsive even in the first year of life, while being fed and held. Children later diagnosed as autistic frequently have histories of crying day and night in infancy. As they grow older, they exhibit such repetitive behaviors as head knocking, do not speak, and appear totally uninterested in the world around them. Autistic children do not appear to be interested in communicating and do not become socialized to the world around them. Some psychologists suggest that this behavior is a defense mechanism that allows these children to shut themselves off from the rest of the world. Thus far, however, little is known of the causes of autism. For this reason, therapy related to this disorder has been less successful than for some of the other problem behaviors discussed. One of the most successful methods of providing help for autistic children has been extensive use of behavior-management techniques. Behavior management designed for autistic children sometimes uses positive reinforcement for desired behavior together with negative reinforcement for unwanted responses (Sage 1975).

Childhood Schizophrenia. Another serious behavior disorder of childhood is **childhood schizophrenia.** Childhood schizophrenics may exhibit a wide variety of symptoms, including extremes of activity, sudden mood changes, verbal disturbances, regression, or apathy. As yet, this disorder is not well understood. For this reason, there is considerable debate concerning the most effective therapy. Therapy of many different sorts has been used with these children, with varying degrees of success. Many psychologists believe that in severe cases, childhood schizophrenia is treated most successfully by removing the child from the family and providing full-time therapy.

THE CASE OF CLAIRE FRAZIER—A HIGH ACHIEVEMENT-MOTIVATED FIFTH GRADER: A CASE STUDY FOR CLASS DISCUSSION

I. Identification and Sources of Information

Name: Claire Frazier

Address: 101 Shady Lane Avenue, Westbury, Ohio

Race: White

Age: Ten years

Sources of Information

1. Interview with Claire
2. Interview with Claire's parents
3. Interview with Claire's teacher and with the psychologist at Claire's school

II. Family History

Claire is the older of two daughters born to Mr. and Mrs. Fred Frazier. Mr. Frazier is employed as an electrical engineer at a large company in their town; Mrs. Frazier is employed as the town librarian. Claire's younger sister, Phyllis, is five years old and attends kindergarten at Claire's school.

Mr. and Mrs. Frazier agreed, at the time of their marriage, to have two children. Although Mr. Frazier,

in particular, had wanted very much to have a son, the parents decided that two children are a sufficient financial expense and decided to stop at two. "Just think," Fred Frazier commented, "what it costs to send a child to college these days. And we want our girls to have the best educations available—Myra and I will have to go without a lot of things we planned on at this rate. If we were to have three children, it would really be rough."

Both Claire and Phyllis had normal deliveries. Claire was six pounds, nine ounces at birth; her younger sister was somewhat larger. Mrs. Frazier was in delivery an average length of time for both girls. Both children were healthy infants, with only a few of the normal childhood diseases and no complications.

Mrs. Frazier began teaching Claire to read when she was three years old. By the time she entered kindergarten, she was able to read the usual "see Spot run" books, and she was already able to do basic arithmetic. Her father was particularly proud of Claire's preschool ability to solve problems. He remembers enjoying showing off his little daughter in front of friends by giving her arithmetic problems to solve in

Continued

THE CASE OF CLAIRE FRAZIER *(Cont.)*

her head. "She used to be like a regular computer," he said. He had visions of a daughter who would go on, after a bachelor's degree in mathematics, to graduate work in theoretical math. "It's unusual, but not impossible for a girl, you know," he told the interviewers. "And from what Claire has shown, she certainly has as much capability as any male."

When Claire was in preschool, her mother stayed home full time. Mrs. Frazier went back to work when Phyllis was two years old. Phyllis therefore spent her preschool years in a preschool center. Mr. Frazier pointed out that Phyllis had not had as much practice in reading and numbers as her older sister had. "But when she entered kindergarten in September, she could do better than most of the other kids. I don't think she's really as interested as Claire is, though. My guess is that Phyllis will go out for something more feminine—maybe literature—like her mother." So far, Phyllis is enjoying kindergarten and doing well.

III. Case History

Claire excelled at all her classes in grades one through four. She was at the top of her class in reading and math and was selected for the all-city spelling bee. Although she did not win (she missed the word *algorithm*), she came out a semifinalist. On the standardized achievement tests, though, her best scores were in math, and she was delighted to receive the praise that was always forthcoming from her father when she brought her grades home. In fifth grade, however, something seemed to happen to Claire's achievement. Her report card remained high; she brought home all As almost every time, but her "citizenship" grade went down. Claire's teacher complained that when Claire was supposed to be working on arithmetic problems in class, she was instead often passing notes to her girlfriends.

By midyear, although Claire continued to receive high scores on her standardized tests, she began to get lower grades on her teacher-prepared class

tests. Claire confided to the school psychologist that she was "embarrassed" at being the top student all of the time, and she preferred to be "like the rest of the kids." When one of the boys in the class got a copy of a science test the day before the exam, and offered it to Claire to see, Claire looked at the questions. She told the psychologist that she was ashamed at having cheated. "But Bobby is a popular student, and he thought he was doing me a favor. I didn't know how to say no." The psychologist pursued the matter further. "Did the test questions help you do better?" "Oh, no," said Claire. "I already knew all the answers. I think I did worse on the test because I was so frightened that the teacher might have found out that I had cheated that I didn't read the questions carefully when I went to take the test. And I left out two answers I knew." Claire did not tell her friends that cheating did not help. She said she did not want them "to think I'm a snob."

The interviewers asked Claire what she wants to be when she grows up. "Daddy wants me to be a mathematician, and I guess that would be all right. But I don't know anyone else who wants to be a mathematician. Maybe a dog trainer. I like animals, and it would be fun to work in a circus. Of course I don't think Mom and Dad would like that very much. Sometimes I daydream that I will be a great ballet dancer, but that's silly, because I'm as clumsy as anything. I know I want to be a mother and have at least two children. Mom takes care of us and has fun at her job at the library. That's really what I probably will end up doing. Lots of times we play librarian at home. I always play the librarian, and Phyllis comes and takes out books. Sometimes I make her take out math books, and she always complains and says she wants the fairy stories."

IV. Present Status, Diagnosis, and Prognosis

Claire admitted the cheating to the school psychologist, who agreed to keep the information in confi-

THE CASE OF CLAIRE FRAZIER

dence and not report it to the science teacher. The psychologist had a long discussion with Claire about her reasons for cheating, and they talked about different ways to deal with similar situations if they come up in the future. Claire decided to tell her friends that she was afraid to cheat and that not only did she not want to, but she also did not need to cheat because she knows her work so well.

Claire fears greatly doing significantly better than her classmates because she is afraid that she will lose her close friends and that they will not like her any more. She thinks that she would like to have a career and knows many adult women who, like her mother, have successfully combined marriage and children with a career. But she recognizes that her father wants to fit her into a mold that will be, at the least, difficult. She currently is rebelling at his ideas of working hard in fields that "boys are supposed to like." If her feelings persist, she is likely to draw away from math and science courses and head into more "female-oriented" courses. Claire and her father both need to face the problem that although Mr. Frazier wanted to have a son, Claire is a little girl and wants to remain one. Unless Mr. Frazier stops trying to force her into his mold, she can be expected to become more rebellious and less successful at school during the next several years.

Questions for Class Discussion

1. Horner's theory proposes that academically successful girls can be expected to be very fearful. What evidence does Claire's case present that this is true, at least in some aspects? Just what is Claire afraid of? Why?

2. What are some of the reasons, which Claire suggested, that she would like to be a ballet dancer? How can this be explained by what we know of achievement motivation?

3. Do you think that the psychologist handled the problem of Claire's cheating in the best possible fashion? Why?

4. Do you expect similar or different academic records for Phyllis and Claire? Why?

SUMMARY

Children from ages nine to eleven can perform a variety of new skills requiring both gross and fine motor coordination. They have begun to question, to think conceptually, and to become more independent of their parents. Fears associated with school and social relationships increase. During later childhood, peers take on an increasingly significant role, and friendship groups have a major impact on personal–social development. Popular children serve as models for their peers; they tend to score higher in achievement, intelligence, and interpersonal adjustment. Children of this age are highly conforming and are affected strongly by peer-group pressure. Researchers have related conforming behavior in this age group to self-esteem, which is in turn related directly to childrearing methods and parental behaviors.

Research shows few measurable differences between children who have both parents living at home and children who live in single-parent homes. Single-parent families that give adequate love and attention can provide satisfactory environments for childrearing. Physical abuse of elementary school children occurs more frequently among poor than among more affluent groups, and it increases in times of stress. School-age children are also victims of such nonphysical abuse as ridicule, and some suffer sexual abuse.

Children with high achievement motivation have been found to have the greatest success at learning. Achievement motivation has been related to social environment, the childrearing styles of the parents, parental methods of discipline, and socioeconomic background. Girls tend, after the fourth grade, to decrease their achievement motivation. One theory suggests that they have a fear of success related to stereotyped sex roles in our society.

By the upper elementary school years, children have established fixed styles that are not likely to change. These learning styles are related to many factors, including attention span, capacity for independent work, learning rate, field dependence or independence, and impulsivity or reflectivity. Some problem-solving methods make it easier to learn in school than others. School, like parental behavior, has a strong effect on the self-esteem of children. Grades, teachers' attitudes, and success at school social tasks are all significant factors in a child's self-concept.

The learning of morality continues through the school years and can be aided by teachers who provide classroom experiences in solving morally relevant problems. Psychologists recommend using methods other than punishment or negative reinforcement for disciplining children, primarily because these methods can lead to a variety of unwanted behaviors.

Many problems of later childhood have their roots in earlier periods of development. The problems of children from minority groups and the problems of poor children intensify in the upper elementry school years because of their lack of learning in the primary school years. Physically and mentally handicapped children need to learn to interact with other children in normal settings; they are not getting that opportunity through Public Law 94-142, the mainstreaming law designed to provide the most appropriate education for each child in the least restrictive setting.

Some learning problems are related to such emotional disturbances as anxiety, depression, withdrawal, and unsocial aggression. More severe emotional disturbances include autism and childhood schizophrenia; these children exhibit behaviors that suggest they are cut off from what we normally consider reality.

 FOR FURTHER READING

Baker, B., A. Brightman, L. Heifetz, and D. Murphy. *Steps to Independence: A Skills Training Series for Children with Special Needs.* Champaign, Illinois: Research Press, 1976. This test provides how-to-do-it help for anyone working with parents of children with special needs. It deals primarily with early, intermediate, and advanced self-help skills, as well as behavior problems.

Coopersmith, S. *Antecedents of Self-Esteem.* San Francisco, California: Freeman, 1967. Coopersmith's longitudinal study of youth in America and his findings concerning the relationship between school and familial variables and self-esteem are particularly valuable to parents or prospective parents.

Skolnick, A. The myth of the vulnerable child. *Psychology Today,* February 1978, 65, 56–60. This provocative article provides a look at child involvement in the family. The point is made that many studies claiming to show parents' effects on children can just as well be interpreted as showing children's effects on parents. Although Skolnick does not address child abuse, the parent–child relationship is viewed with a newly developing perspective.

Adolescence

Part IV

Preview Questions

- What are the two main features of physical development in adolescence, and how do boys and girls differ with respect to each?

- What problems are caused by the great physical variability among individuals of both sexes?

- Can you describe five characteristic behaviors that show adolescents to be different from children?

- Why is the question of identity so important to adolescents, and what are some negative effects of role confusion?

- Why is it so crucial for adolescents to belong to friendship groups, and what are some consequences of nonacceptance?

- Can you explain how traditional sex-role expectations influence the school success and occupational choices of adolescents?

- Why is sexual experience increasing among adolescents, and what factors influence the rate of teenage pregnancy?

- How does the thinking of adolescents in Piaget's formal-operations stage differ from that of children in the concrete stage, and how do these differences influence their idealism and goal-setting behaviors?

- Can you compare the moral reasoning of adolescents in Kohlberg's stages 3, 4, and 5 and show how it is influenced by both cognitive and psychosocial development?

- How is the moral development of adolescents related to their political thought, and what cautions should be observed in interpreting the stage of moral decision making at which they are operating?

8

Adolescent
Development

Adolescence is the period from about age thirteen to age nineteen that marks the transition between childhood and adulthood. It begins with **pubescence,** a term referring to the rapid physical growth that occurs at this state and maturation of reproductive functioning. Adolescence begins and ends at different ages for different individuals. By age eleven, for example, some girls have reached the beginning of pubescence. Some boys do not reach pubescence until as late as seventeen years of age. In similar fashion, adulthood is reached at different ages for different individuals. In this chapter, we will consider developmental changes in the six years that approximately encompass this period. The next chapter considers adolescents in their environments.

Adolescence is marked by profound psychological as well as physiological changes. A restless transition is common, marked by temporarily increased exposure to conflicts and a foreshadowing of the developmental tasks and problems that are just around the corner. While many young people go through the adolescent period in relative calm, pursue courses of study approved by their parents and teachers, and generally develop in happy, socially acceptable ways, many others have social–emo-

Adolescence is a period of physical and psychological change, often marked by increased preoccupation with appearance and developing identity.

tional problems that they did not have before. Adolescence is often regarded as "no fun," by both young people and adults. The delicate issues that arise have led educators and psychologists to plan specially for young people. As an increase in problem behavior among this group has developed in the past two decades in this country, specialists have begun experimenting with methods designed to deal with the problem before it arises.

PHYSICAL DEVELOPMENT
The Growth Spurt

The beginning of pubescence is signalled by a sudden spurt in growth, which occurs about two years prior to **puberty,** or full sexual maturity. The growth spurt typically begins about two years earlier for girls than for boys. For girls, this means between nine and twelve years of age, and for boys, between ten and fifteen years of age. The growth rate during this period often is extremely rapid. Tanner (1971) points out that early adolescents (individuals from about age eleven to age fourteen) grow at a rate that they last experienced when they were about two years old. For a year or more after the growth spurt begins, rate of growth approximately doubles. The spurt lasts about two years. During this time, girls grow about six to seven inches and boys about eight to nine inches in height. Figure 8.1 shows graphically the

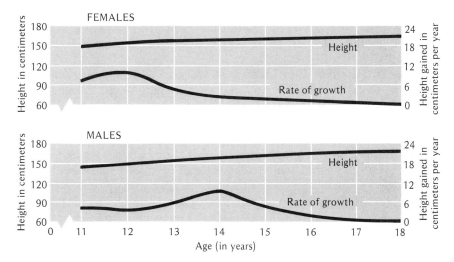

Fig. 8.1   Height and growth rate increments in height gained from one age to the next for individuals between the ages of eleven and eighteen. (From J. M. Tanner, Growing up, in _Scientific American_, September 1973. Copyright © 1973 by Scientific American, Inc. All rights reserved.)

typical height gained during the growth spurt for boys and girls between the ages of eleven and thirteen and the height gained after that until about age nineteen, as well as the rate of growth during these periods.

Sexual Maturation

In addition to changes in stature, pubescence is marked by a number of other changes. The pituitary gland contributes both to rapid growth and to the secretion of the sex hormones, testosterone and estrogen. For both males and females, changes in skin texture occur, usually during the high school years. Acne and skin roughening become a source of distress for some teenagers of both sexes, although these problems are more common in boys than in girls. Glands in the underarm and genital regions develop rapidly for both sexes and are manifested by changing body odors.

Girls and also probably boys mature earlier than they did a century ago. The average age, for example, of **menarche,** the onset of menstruation in females, at that time was seventeen years. Today, researchers tell us that the average age of menarche is twelve and one-half years. Research evidence of the age of puberty in males one hundred years ago is less accurate. Today, it usually begins at about thirteen, also earlier than assumed one hundred years ago (Rienzo 1981). Although some evidence shows that the trend toward earlier puberty in females is decreasing in industrial nations (Winter, Faiman, and Reyer 1978), the age at which girls reach puberty continued to decrease in just the past four decades. Tanner (1971) reported, for example, that British girls begin to menstruate a full two years earlier than they did only forty years ago. Researchers attribute this earlier sexual development to improved nutrition and decreased childhood illness.

Changes in Females after Menarche. Puberty is usually measured in girls by menarche. Once menarche occurs, the growth spurt slows. Considerable change continues, however, in body proportion marked by rapid development of the sexual organs. In girls, the breasts increase in size with an increase of glandular cells and the formation of fatty and connective tissue. Pigmented areas around the nipples become elevated at what is known as the bud stage of breast development at about ten or eleven years. Hormonal secretions begin to produce increased fatty and supportive tissue in the buttocks and hips, and pubic and axillary (underarm) hair begin to develop. Menarche usually occurs following this development. Early menstrual periods tend to be irregular. About twelve to eighteen months after the first menstrual period begins, ovulation takes place (Hafez 1973).

Changes after Male Puberty. The onset of puberty is usually measured in boys by the first appearance of sperm in the urine at about twelve or thirteen years. When this takes place, there is accelerated growth in the testes and scrotum. This is the time when pubic hair begins to develop at the base of the penis. At the same time, the penis gradually lengthens and thickens. The larynx enlarges, causing the male voice to deepen. About two years after pubic hair begins to grow, axillary and facial hair make their appearance. Muscle mass increases in males at puberty, at the same time that shoulders and rib cages begin to expand. Although there are many differences in developmental rate, after about fourteen years of age, the prostate gland produces fluid that is ejaculated during orgasm. Mature sperm are not present until about a year later. At about fifteen years, boys begin to have "wet dreams," nocturnal emissions of semen during sleep.

Sex Differences in Physical Development

The advanced development of girls as compared to boys is dramatic, particularly during the early adolescent years. As we learned, girls often have a two-year physiological lead on boys, noticeable in height and rate of sexual development. At any one time, some girls aged eleven, twelve, and thirteen will have reached sexual maturity, whereas boys may not mature until age thirteen, fourteen, or fifteen.

An important physical change in later adolescence (from about age fourteen to age eighteen or nineteen) is boys' dramatic increase in muscular strength as compared to girls. Until puberty, boys and girls are fairly similar in muscular strength. At about age fourteen, however, after puberty, boys tend to develop greater muscular strength than girls with particularly strong increases occurring in their hands and forearms. The rapid increase in muscular strength of boys occurs because of major physical differences: They have larger hearts and lungs than girls relative to body size; they have higher systolic blood pressure, lower resting heart rate, a greater capacity for carrying oxygen in the blood, and a greater capacity for neutralizing chemical products of muscular exercise (for example, lactic acid). These changes account not only for boys' physical strength but also for their increased athletic ability (Malmquist 1978).

Variability in Rate of Development

Although physical changes in development are generally predictable both in sequence and in time of occurrence, the sequence does not hold true for all individuals or for different aspects of physical development. Figure 8.2 demonstrates that wide variations in adolescent growth and sexual maturity between persons of the same chronological age can be dramatic.

The adolescent often experiences **asynchronous growth,** variations in the developmental sequence for various parts of the body. For example, feet suddenly grow more rapidly than other parts of the body, as do ears. Asynchronous growth sometimes leads youngsters to worry about their body images. Girls worry about having a good figure and boys about having an athletic physique. Boys with athletic physiques tend to have more positive perceptions of themselves than boys who are

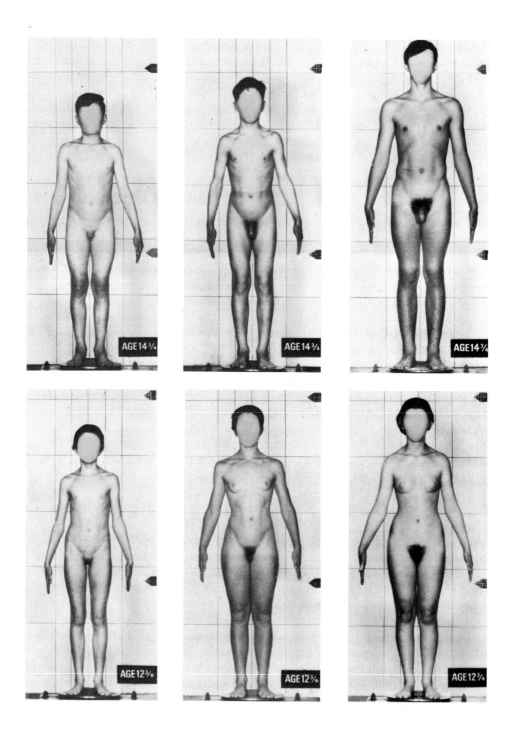

either skinny or chubby. In early adolescence, boys who succeed in athletics often have higher status.

Development of secondary sex characteristics also has a major impact on self-images of the adolescents. Jones and Bayley (1950) suggest that physically accelerated boys are usually accepted and treated by adults and peers as more mature. Physically immature boys, on the other hand, tend often to exhibit many immature behaviors, perhaps because others tend to treat them as immature. A fair proportion of physically immature boys tend to strive for attention or else withdraw, perhaps as a way of counteracting their physical disadvantage.

The anxiety associated with the physical changes of adolescence seems to be related to the high variability among individuals in developmental rate. It is not only the individual differences in the ages at which physical changes take place that affect the adolescent's self-image but also the change rate and unpredictability of the changes for any individual once the sequence begins (Malmquist 1978). Part of the problem with unpredictable growth is the adolescent's need to conform to the peer group. Puberty seems to be a pivotal event for the reorganization of the adolescent's body image and sexual identity (Koff, Rierdan, and Silverstone 1978). For girls to conform to the peer group, development must come in time near to that of the others in the group. Goldings (1979) described an eleven-year-old girl who insisted (at a time that bras were still fashionable among adolescents) that her mother get her a bra at the first notice of breast development and well before there was any true "need." The girl wore the bra day and night for a week. Then she took her allowance money and went out to buy weight-lifting equipment.

Because it is important at early adolescence to be like everyone else, an early-maturing girl might be embarrassed in front of her friends because of her maturity; a late-maturing girl might be equally uncomfortable because she feels she looks too childish. For boys, however, early maturation is more beneficial. A late-maturing boy might feel that he has a handicap with respect to athletic competition, as well as a problem with respect to social interaction with girls.

PSYCHOSOCIAL DEVELOPMENT

The period of adolescence was not recognized as a special and separate stage of development until fairly recently. It was not until the early 1940s in this country, in fact, that adolescents began to consider themselves and to be considered by others

◀ Fig. 8.2 Descriptions of adolescent growth and sexual maturity as shown in body shapes of three girls, each the same age (twelve years) and three boys, each the same age (fourteen years). (From J. M. Tanner, Growing up, in *Scientific American*, September 1973. Copyright © 1973 by Scientific American, Inc. All rights reserved.)

The recognition of adolescence as a special stage of development is a relatively recent phenomenon, dating back only to the 1940s.

as a special group, characterized by specific patterns of interests, attitudes, and behaviors. During World War II, when many fathers were away at war and mothers began to be employed on a regular basis outside the home, adolescents began to band together to pursue common activities and interests. The peer culture and independent establishment of values that resulted caused observers finally to see adolescence as an important life stage characterized by very specific behavior (Lowe 1972).

What specific behaviors mark adolescents and show them to be different from the children they were only the year before? For boys in early adolescence, the noticeable activity associated with the changes in bodily function preoccupies them. This activity is expressed among early adolescents in humor related to bodily functioning, particularly elimination. Games related to elimination abound; a good example is the common competition among boys for the length and strength of the urinary stream against the wall of the school building. In organized sport, young adolescent boys excitedly display team spirit.

Early adolescent girls enjoy many of the same jokes about bodily functions as do their male counterparts. They also display team spirit. In addition, they often develop more intense relationships with other girls than their counterparts do with other boys. In later adolescence, humor gradually increases in sophistication. Jokes and games related to elimination give way to jokes related to sexuality, increasingly a focus of interest.

Adolescent boys and girls both tend to exhibit impulsive and unpredictable behavior. Many adolescents channel their energies into socially accepted areas, such as becoming coach of a Little League team. Some, however, fantasize and daydream, sometimes to the extent of interfering with their school work.

Most early adolescents idolize famous people. For example, in 1980, a national poll of teenagers in middle school and high school listed as their heroes Abraham Lincoln, Eleanor Roosevelt, Albert Einstein, Jonas Salk, and Elvis Presley, among others. Many early adolescent girls also select their heroes on a far more personal basis. Often, adolescent girls only a few years older become the object of intense and sometimes lavish identification. This schoolgirl crush is soon outgrown.

Many adolescents look to music as an emotional outlet. Popular music often expresses many of their conflicts and desires, and popular musicians frequently become adolescent folk heroes. To many adolescents, such figures represent consistent ideas and values not found in the adult culture. When parents ridicule the heroes ("How can you like a singer who can't sing?"), so much the better. Teenagers identify with their folk heroes, their "poor" voices, and their unconventional appearances. After all, they themselves are just learning about their own strange voices and appearances.

Puberty is interpreted by adolescents as a signal that childhood is over and what they consider to be babyish attitudes, beliefs, and behaviors must stop. Sometimes, giving up earlier behaviors is difficult and poses more conflict for the adolescent. Kagan (1971a) described a girl recalling her first menstrual period: She suggested that the real meaning to her was that she was finally too grown up to ride her bicycle. Puberty is interpreted also as a means of sex typing. Adolescents, deeply interested in their bodily changes, are increasingly concerned with conforming to the image of their peers. In order to do this, adolescent boys feel the necessity to be more autonomous, active, and independent. Girls feel the need to be more socially sensitive and passive. These behaviors are consonant with culturally defined masculinity and femininity and strongly shape the behavior of this age group. Feelings, attitudes, motives, and wishes become sex typed as never before as adolescents do their best to emulate what they view as the important behaviors of their male and female peers.

Adolescence in our society has been called a period of "storm and stress," a stage of "being part way." Entertainer Judy Garland once described female adolescence poetically as "just an in-between—too old for toys, too young for boys." Adolescents today, unlike those of Judy Garland's era, no longer feel themselves too young for many adult activities. Adults often disagree, with resulting conflict.

Identity in Early Adolescence

Adolescence is a period when individuals try to determine who they are. Boys and girls worry about what their changing bodies mean to them and often spend a lot of time in front of the mirror studying their appearances. Girls spend hours combing their hair; boys develop studied casual looks. Many keep diaries that attest to their new feelings of self-importance. Early adolescents' extreme interest in their bodies and themselves has led many psychologists to refer to them as egocentric.

Identity in Later Adolescence

Erik Erikson described the fifth, or adolescent, stage as one of crises and potential turning points. According to Erikson, beginning at about age thirteen or fourteen, adolescents are most interested in answering the question "Who am I?"

"Who am I" is a complex question that is thought about but not answered in early adolescence. According to psychologists, to answer the question, adolescents must understand the physical changes that take place at the time, define their external environments, and define their roles within those environments. Adolescents are concerned also with making explicit their own personal positions in relation to the values of the world around them. Erikson* (1968) believes that in our own society, unlike some others, there is a period during adolescence in which individuals are allowed to delay answering this question. Instead, they are allowed to experiment with different roles and explore different dimensions of life without choosing any one of them. Often, they stop or postpone steps toward answering their question of identity and wait until additional information is gained from their experiences.

Tome (1972) studied adolescents' views of themselves, and suggested that adolescents have two self-concepts. The first is their own ideas of themselves, formed

---

*Erikson (1950) considers adolescence the period from ages thirteen to twenty-two and breaks this period into two stages: the stage of early adolescence (ages thirteen to seventeen) and the stage of later adolescence (ages eighteen to twenty-two). His fifth stage, the stage of early adolescence, encompasses what in this book are called both the stage of early adolescence and the stage of later adolescence. In this book, we refer to the period from about eighteen to twenty-two years as the period of youth, using the term devised by Kenneth Keniston (1972). The periods of youth and young adulthood are discussed in Chapter 10.

The realization that childhood is over makes the young adolescent stop to ask, "Who am I?" "Where am I going?"

by incorporating the opinions expressed by parents, teachers, and peers into their own belief systems. Adolescents gradually develop awareness of others' unexpressed judgments of themselves because of their slowly increasing ability to take in a variety of outside judgments. This ability leads them, according to Tome, to a social self-image that is made up of impressions they think they are giving to other people. Adolescents tend to be sensitive about what they perceive to be the views of others and worry endlessly about the images that they present. Tome found that this sensitivity leads them often to have more exacting views of the ways their parents perceive them than their parents have of their children's perceptions of them-selves.

According to Erikson, the crisis of adolescence involves finding an answer to the question "Who am I?" If adolescents are able to establish clear senses of who they are, they are then equipped to commit themselves to other people as well as to meaningful kinds of work or other goals. In the high school years, individuals are freer than before to begin functioning, at least in some cases, as adults and to "try on" new roles. High school students are more able than their younger peers to assess realistically future possibilities and their current potential.

The early adolescent is concerned deeply with approval of peers; group identity also is important. Early adolescents experience considerable pressure to ally themselves with a peer group. The pressure may begin from both the family and the school. Some parents feel that the popular child is the successful child. The peer group itself also exerts considerable pressure. Children of middle school or junior high school age spend much more time away from home than they did in elementary school; often, they spend time after school with friends or in school activities. Only toward the end of the middle school years do they begin to question more specifically the composition of the group to which they belong and what this group represents.

Feelings of **role identity,** one's role in society, develop gradually through the adolescent period. At first, in early adolescence, role identities are diffuse and fluctuating. This is the period, according to Erikson, that youngsters are often at sea with themselves and with others. At this time, Erikson believes, many young adolescents overcommit themselves to peer groups.

As they get older, teenagers gradually develop clearer definitions of who they are and what they want. When teenagers understand that the roles they expect or want to assume in society as they grow up may be impossible to attain, the knowledge is painful. One result is **role confusion.** Because choice of future occupation assumes major importance during the high school years, role confusion often is associated with occupation. Many adolescents develop role confusion by observing a standard of living on TV and in the mass media that far surpasses anything available in their real world, and they plan unrealistically to attain that standard of living for themselves. In some instances, the adolescent simply cannot decide what to do. Some adolescents at this point simply stop in their tracks in confusion and seem unable for a time to make any decisions. At the point at which they need to decide what college they should apply to, for example, or whether or not they should consider going to college at all, they may become so indecisive that they simply escape decision making by going to a party instead. When such a period of indecision lasts weeks or months, we say that the high school student is suffering from role confusion. A variety of other unwanted behaviors common to this age group can also result from role confusion; such behaviors include excessive daydreaming, role playing, and acting out of subconscious wishes (Erikson 1963).

The question "Who am I?" must be answered in order that later development not be hampered, according to Erikson. The student who cannot resolve role confusion sufficiently to decide the next step toward reaching a goal, such as applying to a college or taking up a job, will not continue to mature until this problem is solved. Ability to make a decision and to decide what steps should be taken next does not require that the student resolve all unresolved issues at earlier stages of development, according to Erikson. Although Erikson's stages are a logical sequence, they are not hierarchical, as are cognitive stages. For example, the students described here need not have resolved the trust vs. mistrust conflict of an earlier age to be able to deal with the problem of choosing a career. They must, however, develop ability to assess possibilities open to them, evaluate them, and choose from among the choices on the basis of the value they place on each.

Life for adolescents presents a variety of conflicting possibilities and choices. Deep down, they are not yet sure that they know who they are, what they want to be, how they appear to others, and whether they really are capable of providing satisfactory answers to these extremely important questions. It is resolution of these questions that brings what Erikson referred to as identity instead of role confusion and the beginning of adulthood. Resolution can be found both by adolescents who fail to reach desired goals and who elect to change their goals at this point in their lives and by those who are happy with their choices and are able to reach these desired goals.

According to Erikson, adolescence is a crucial turning point, during which development must move in one direction or another, toward either positive or negative identities. For adolescents to build positive identities, they must arrive at satisfactory role commitments. Whereas earlier their concerns revolved around immediate successes or failures, these concerns now are more far-reaching, involving future occupation and life-style. High school students selecting colleges are making decisions related not just to what they will be doing for the next four years but, in many instances, to what they will be doing for the rest of their lives. High school students electing to apply to engineering schools, for example, are making choices that directly affect their choice of life careers, both what they can do and what they cannot do in the future. Teenagers who elect at this point to begin to commit themselves to other people, as do teenagers who elect to marry before their educations are complete, also restrict personal choice of life-style later on.

The answer to the question "Who am I?" differs very much for the adolescent failure and the adolescent success. The adolescent failure is left with feelings of low self-esteem; the adolescent successful at reaching a desired goal is much more likely to develop feelings of high self-esteem. The adolescent unable to answer the question at all remains mired in confusion and self-doubt.

Conforming to the Peer Group

Conforming to the peer group is a central factor in the development of the early adolescent, for acceptance or rejection by peers has profound implications for shaping the young person's self-image. Carson McCullers (1946) in her novel *The Mem-*

ber of the Wedding, underscored the importance of friendship groups in the following description of a twelve-year-old's feelings of nonmembership and alienation:

> *The long hundred miles did not make her sadder and make her feel more far away than the knowing that they were them and both together and she was only her and parted from them, by herself. And as she sickened with this feeling a thought and explanation suddenly came to her, so that she knew and almost said aloud: They are the "we" of "me." Yesterday, and all the twelve years of her life, she had only been Frankie. She was an "I" person who had to walk around and do things by herself. All the other people had a "we" to claim, all others except her. . . . All members of clubs have a "we" to belong to and talk about. The soldiers in the army can say "we," and even the criminals on chain-gangs. But the old Frankie had had no "we" to claim." (McCullers 1946)*

Adolescents are deeply involved with their peers. They enjoy being with friends, often much more than being with their families. Girls are more socially oriented than boys and tend to be far more dependent on the views of others for their self-images. Many adolescents of both sexes have difficulty withstanding social peer pressure to behave in certain ways and to do certain things, even if these behaviors meet with the disapproval of family or teachers.

Adolescents' friendship groups, interests, and even styles of dress are extremely important to them because they contribute to a sense of being accepted by the group. One reason for the importance of the peer group at this age level is that it provides security. As members of particular peer groups, adolescents feel they have more influence on the world than they would have as individuals. The group expands feelings of self-worth and protects adolescents at a time they often feel lonely. When conflicts develop at home, the peer group offers comfort and intimacy. To receive these rewards, many adolescents pay the price of suppressing their individuality. More mature teenagers, however, those who are developing a clear, consistent sense of who they are, are able to move beyond the peer group in making major choices and decisions.

The composition of friendship groups is based on many factors. Children who value academic achievement often group together; other groups form on the basis of fun or common interests, socioeconomic group, church affiliation, similar neighborhoods, and the like (Cohen 1979). Early adolescent friendship groups are often still all-girl or all-boy. Now, however, the two groups interact and are interested in each other. Popular pastimes include "hanging out" with the group at a pizza parlor or on the street and doing very little other than chatting. Between eleven and fourteen, friendship groups demand increasing loyalty, conformity, and intimacy. This is especially true for girls' groups. Boys more often are less expressive of feeling or intimacy, which are considered female sex typed in our society (Douvan and Adelson 1966).

MY STRONGEST DESIRE

The following essay was written by an eighth grade girl whose physical handicap keeps her in a wheelchair.

My Strongest Desire

My strongest desire is to be like everyone else in class. I would like to look like the other girls and not have to wear my leg brace. I would like to be able to get together with the other kids in my class after school and not have to have anyone push my wheelchair. I would like to take gym with the other students. I would like to be able to walk. I would like to feel as if I belonged.

I have another desire. I would like to be a teacher. I suppose that this desire is more important than my first desire, but it will take me a long time to reach this goal. When I become a teacher, I will spend a lot of time helping handicapped kids like me. I will make sure that they have the opportunity to join groups even though they usually have to go to and from school separately from the other students. I will call on them in class so that the others will get a chance to see how much they know about things. When they're frightened, I'll do my best to help them get over their fears.

I'll teach the other children in class that handicapped kids have the same feelings as everyone else and want to be included as much as anyone. This might be the most important thing I could do as a teacher.

Phyllis Doherty, English I
Ms. Philips

QUESTIONS FOR THOUGHT

1. What sorts of problems does Phyllis face at school? How are these related to her particular stage of psychosocial development?

2. What do you think Ms. Philips could do to help Phyllis feel that she belongs?

Popularity is a central concern for all. Children who are accepted by peers into the group have higher self-esteem and are more sure of themselves than those who are not so popular. Popularity is particularly important to youngsters because of their egocentricism at this stage of development. Elkind (1967) suggests that adolescents feel most of the time as if they are being watched by the group. Reactions of peers then become terribly important. The egocentricity of adolescents, according to Elkind, makes them far more concerned with being observed than of observing others.

Popularity and conformity to group norms that adolescents believe to lead to popularity are terribly important to adolescents. Psychologists have proposed a number of explanations for this. For one thing, the adolescent in American society is increasingly alienated from the adult world. Many theorists have related alienation from adults and dependence on the peer culture to permissive, inattentive child-rearing. It has also been suggested, as noted earlier, that this alienation may have its roots in parental attempts to develop independence in their children and that these attempts often are viewed by children as rejection. Other psychologists suggest that what appears to be parental rejection is actually just a matter of too little time: American parents are so busy with their own concerns that they simply do not pay enough attention to their children. Fathers and, to a great extent, mothers are less available to their children because of work commitments. Many adolescents thus grow up in households with little parental supervision and attention. They look to their peers for the love and acceptance they feel are missing at home. Conforming adolescents feel that nonconformity will reduce this acceptance (Bettelheim 1971; Bronfenbrenner 1972).

Other factors that have been identified as contributing to the adolescent's feeling of alienation and need to conform to a group are the lack of continuity in our society, conflicting values, and lack of personal security (Thornburg 1971). These

Ethnic background is sometimes a factor in the formation of adolescent peer groups, especially in areas with high concentrations of minority groups.

factors, all associated with rapid social and economic change of twentieth-century Western society, may lead many adolescents to fear that society does not place enough value on human life. It is clear that concern for the meaning of life is important in the peer culture; group identification reduces loneliness and gives some meaning to existence.

Perceived membership in an ethnic group often is a major factor in determining peer and friendship groups. Particularly when young adolescents are members of minority ethnic groups whose values may differ from those of the larger American society, conflicts of allegiance may develop. Black and Hispanic young adolescents often belong to friendship groups consisting only of others with their own ethnic backgrounds. The group provides assistance in answering such questions as whether or not to try to succeed in the white society, whether or not it is better to preserve the heritage of the ethnic group or to accept the values of the larger culture. Often, the ethnic peer group reinforces group conformity by pointing out the differences between group values and values of society and strictly reinforcing the group values.

According to Piaget (1972), adolescents stop conforming when they learn to develop their individual modes of responding. This begins to occur in the later high school years. At the same time, they develop the ability to accept the opinions of others, even when these opinions differ from those of the friendship group. They begin to use rules as devices for meeting individual rather than group ends and goals.

Decisions That Will Affect Later Occupational Choices

During middle childhood and early adolescence, most children add to their information about the job market. For many children who do not go on to college, the first choices that affect eventual occupational choice take place in the early adolescent years, often when the youngsters are not even aware that they are making decisions. We learned earlier that many adolescents observing a standard of living on TV that far surpasses anything available in their worlds, plan in childhood to attain that standard of living for themselves. Elementary school children who are failing in school may report that they plan to be doctors or lawyers, but by the time they reach middle school, they are beginning to think seriously about what it might really mean to become a doctor or a lawyer.

Beginning at early adolescence, boys develop understanding that they are expected to become serious students and to develop ways to take care of themselves so that later they will be able to take care of their own families. Girls learn frequently, at the same time, that they are expected to be "feminine" and attract boys. It is not surprising therefore that during this period of time, boys begin to do better in their schoolwork than do girls. Boys excel particularly in such "masculine" subjects as mathematics and science. Girls tend to excel at more "feminine" subjects, such as art. It is interesting that girls have excelled at math problems when these problems are placed in a socially accepted feminine context, such as problems involving recipes (Kagan 1964).

Both the courses that adolescents select in school and their academic performances during this period clearly affect later career possibilities. Children from eleven to twelve years of age, when asked, tend to select prospective occupations on the basis of current interests. By thirteen to fourteen, they begin to take their aptitudes into consideration. Seventh graders may not yet feel ready to make occupational choices through their course work but often find themselves in the position where they must do so. Sixth, seventh, and eighth graders, however, who do not succeed at advanced work in math are not likely to be accepted later to advanced math classes in high school. These same students will not qualify for occupations later that require advanced mathematics training.

By fifteen to sixteen, teenagers consider personal values and goals as well. Only after age seventeen do most adolescents begin to make realistic decisions regarding future occupations. By this time, a combination of feedback from school grades and advice of parents and school counselors has usually helped to provide information necessary to make realistic decisions.

 ## PSYCHOSEXUAL DEVELOPMENT

Freud (1905) called the period from puberty on the **genital stage.** This term refers to the maturing young person's renewed interest in sexual expression, focused on the genitals. As discussed in Chapter 1, Freud proposed that during most of childhood the individual is in the period of latency—that is, once the Oedipal and Electra complexes have been satisfactorily resolved, sexual impulses to a great extent lie dormant. The hormonal changes that accompany puberty, however, give renewed impetus to the sexual urges. At first these urges are usually expressed through masturbation (Kagan 1971a; Mitchell 1974). Later, however, the young person becomes more outer directed, focusing his or her interest on heterosexual activity.

Much of Freud's research was based on his own case studies of young people who were growing up in Europe at the turn of the century. Today, individuals growing up in America have many experiences different from those described in Freud's case studies and have different interests that relate to those experiences. Developing a value system with regard to sexuality is difficult in our society. As children, most of us are taught about sexuality in negative ways, often through prohibitions. Adolescents who have learned as children that masturbation is evil or dangerous will probably still masturbate, but they may also experience guilt, fear, and conflict. Although their parents are likely to convey the idea that sex is appropriate primarily within the context of marriage, or at least of a loving relationship, they receive a very different message through the mass media. There, the sexual side of life often is portrayed as being of central importance, and attractive "with it" people are shown having casual sexual relationships outside marriage. Thus young people may learn that many of the moral rules regarding sexuality that they were taught as children do not apply to adult behavior. They may begin seriously to question sexual as well as other basic values.

Sexual Behavior

Erikson suggests that in anticipation of adult sexual intimacy, adolescents engage in a variety of behaviors designed to define what it means for them to be males or females. Sexual behavior among adolescents includes many different kinds of experimentation, from masturbation to kissing and petting to sexual intercourse. Among

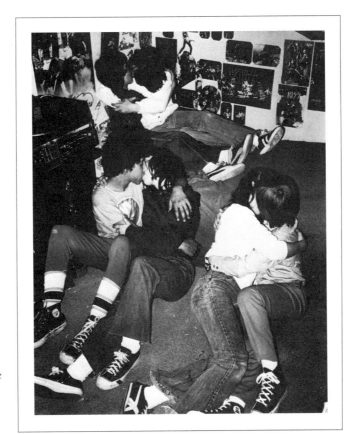

Sexual experience among American adolescents is occurring earlier than in the past.

young adolescents, there is often a great deal of anxiety about many different kinds of sexual expression, but researchers point out that this anxiety tends to decrease with age and that older adolescents are more likely than their younger counterparts to agree that sex brings them pleasure (Diepold and Young 1979).

Masturbation occurs among early adolescents of both sexes and increases in high school, particularly among boys. Even with the old myths surrounding the feared consequences of masturbation (for example, mental retardation or insanity), most boys have engaged in masturbation by age fourteen. Almost all males masturbate to orgasm during their teens (Diepold and Young 1979). Boys and girls now begin kissing at earlier ages than in past years, with many beginning well before high school. By the end of high school, researchers report that it is a near-universal phenomenon (Diepold and Young 1979). High schoolers engage in both light and heavy petting, with more girls at each age level involved than ever before.

Researchers have found a clear trend toward earlier heterosexual experience among both male and female adolescents. In the midseventies, some fifty-nine percent of all males and forty-five percent of all females between thirteen and nineteen reported that they had already had sexual intercourse (Vener and Stewart 1974). About one-fifth of thirteen- and fourteen-year-olds report that they have engaged in sexual behavior, and it is likely that many more experiment sexually and do not report it (Hopkins 1977). This represents about four million teenage girls and seven million teenage boys.

Why is sexual experience increasing among this age group? For one thing, the lowered age of puberty increases interest in sex among younger people. For another, increased sexual freedom within the society as a whole provides models for adolescents to emulate. Rienzo (1981) suggests that most adolescents have more difficulty than adults in deferring instant gratification. At a time when movies present younger and younger sex symbols as models to emulate, it is very difficult for adolescents to understand why they should not experiment. Another reason for increased sexual experimentation among adolescents is peer pressure. Girls tend to discuss their sexual activities more openly than a few years ago. While adolescents often rebel against traditional values, they tend to be fiercely conformist within their peer circles. Some seventh graders report that if they have not had sex with their boyfriends, they pretend they have "in order to be like everyone else."

Adolescent Pregnancy. Together with earlier sexual maturity and more adolescents than ever before engaging in sexual intercourse before graduation from high school and, in increasing numbers of cases, from middle school, the pregnancy rate of adolescents is increasing. Researchers report that in the United States each year, some 30,000 girls under fifteen years of age become pregnant. Many of these girls are as young as eleven or twelve (Kapp, Taylor, and Edwards 1980). According to one report (Ryan and Dunn 1979), the United States has the second highest pregnancy rate in the world.

What are the factors that are related to this high pregnancy rate? For one thing, race and socioeconomic status are associated with teenage pregnancy. Black students have a higher rate of teenage pregnancy than white students. Typically, it is poor adolescents who begin at earlier ages and who experience more heterosexual activity than middle-class students. By late adolescence, however, poor and middle-class students tend to engage in intercourse about as frequently (Diepold and Young 1979).

Kantner and Zelnik (1972*a;* 1972*b*) reported two reasons for the racial differences observed in teenage pregnancy. For one thing, more white students than black use birth control at the age that intercourse begins. For another, for many black teenagers, pregnancy is considered socially acceptable by peers and adult family members as well. In addition, more white teenagers than black have a generally accurate understanding about the time of greatest risk of pregnancy. For both black and white teenagers, lack of knowledge about their sexuality is important in deter-

The factors in teenage pregnancy are complex, but at least some young women become pregnant because they are looking for purpose in their lives.

HIGHLIGHT 8.2 RELUCTANT FATHERS: THE OTHER SIDE OF THE TEENAGE PREGNANCY STORY

The mass media provides this country with a great deal of material regarding teenage pregnancies. There are more than a million of these annually, costing taxpayers more than $8 billion a year in welfare and other expenses. A lot is written and spoken about the young mothers, why they got that way, what can be done to help them, and what might be done in the future to prevent such cases. But for every teenage mother, there is another person not so often discussed, the teenage father.

Who are the teenage fathers? One researcher (Jensen 1980) reports that in one sample studied, eighty percent are unemployed; fifty percent cannot read or write; forty percent cannot understand basic reading materials; and fifteen percent have no plans for the future. According to Jensen, ninety percent know nothing about the reproductive process. Like teenage mothers, they are younger than they were a few years ago; most are only one to three years older than their girlfriends. They may not like a certain contraceptive device or do not want their girlfriends to try another. Maybe neither they nor their girl-

mining who becomes pregnant. Many pregnant teenagers offer such explanations as the following to explain why they thought they would never get pregnant: "I thought that if you had sex on Sunday, you could never get pregnant." "He said I had to be seventeen to get pregnant." "If you have sex relations standing up, it's hard to become pregnant." "If you dance around after intercourse, it's almost impossible to get pregnant."

It might seem difficult to understand why so many young girls become pregnant, given the wide availability of contraception. The fact is, however, that many teenagers are ambivalent about sex even when they are involved in sexual activity. These youngsters hesitate to ask for information, and many do not use birth control, even if they know how, because to do so would be to admit that they were having sex. Adolescents frequently avoid using contraceptives even when they are not uncomfortable discussing sex with each other. Chesler (1980) suggests that the general behavior patterns of adolescents are incompatible with systematic use of contraception. For one thing, she reports, they tend to have patterns of erratic, infrequent, and spontaneous sexual encounters. In addition, they are often held back from obtaining adequate information about contraceptive services because of feelings of guilt or ambivalence in front of adults. Finally, there frequently is little verbal communication about sex or anything else between sexual partners.

Many teenage mothers—about one quarter of them—become pregnant because they want to. These girls feel that a baby will provide for them what they lack most, purpose in life and someone who will love them.

friends think about contraception. Maybe they wanted a baby to prove their manhood, without thinking of the consequences. Most fathers are not around for the consequences, even when girls provide information to authorities as to who they are.

Jensen's research shows that many teenage fathers, like teenage mothers, never finish high school. They are not in a position to take care of their offspring even if they want to. Many have more than one child and accept responsibility for none.

QUESTIONS FOR THOUGHT

1. How do you think that teenage fathers are affected by adolescent pregnancy?

2. Can you think of some ways to help provide solutions to the increasing numbers of adolescent pregnancies by working with high school boys?

The price of adolescent pregnancy to society is high. One study estimated that the financial cost in welfare and other expenses in 1980 was $8.3 billion a year. Rienzo (1981) points out three types of costs: medical, psychological, and social. Medical costs include higher risk of stillborn infants; increased infant mortality, premature births, and pregnancy complications; and increased chance of maternal mortality. Some of the psychological costs include increased risk of postpartum psychiatric symptoms and increased risk of attempted suicide. Social costs include permanent disruption of education, decreased economic opportunity, stigma, and increased divorce rate.

Perhaps the incidence of adolescent pregnancy can be decreased through appropriate counseling and education. To be effective, this education would have to be provided *before* heterosexual activities begin, one important reason that many people today are promoting sex education in middle school or earlier. Both pregnant teenagers and young girls of child-bearing age also need to learn about proper diet, for young mothers and their babies are at greater risk than mothers who have their babies in their twenties.

Homosexuality. Homosexual activity usually has its beginnings before high school in both girls and boys, with both masturbation and mutual masturbation. During adolescence, according to researchers, the majority of homosexual youngsters date members of the opposite sex, both to experiment with intercourse and to test their conflicted orientation in order to help them determine sexual preference and sexual identity. The overall incidence of homosexual contacts during adolescence decreases with age (Diepold and Young 1979). What influence the gay liberation movement will have on the reporting of homosexual behavior is not yet clear.

COGNITIVE DEVELOPMENT

From about age eleven on, children begin to be able to evaluate the world around them without relying on information gathered from concrete objects. According to Piaget, they now enter the **formal operational stage.** Children at the stage of formal operations gradually develop the capacity to reason through the use of abstractions. When given information, they can start making logical deductions without first turning to concrete examples.

The Development of Thinking

It is important to realize that the stage of formal operations does not arrive in a single step. Many young adolescents beginning to develop from the concrete to the formal operational stages go through part but not all of the transition. There are great individual differences in development. Most eleven-year-olds are unable to solve any problems presented to them at the formal operational level. Later, many early adolescents will develop ability to solve some problems correctly, particularly if those problems are related to topics about which they have had a great deal of experience. Thus adolescents who have had a lot of opportunity to solve mathematical problems will probably be ready long before other adolescents to take on the abstractions required in algebra. Still later in the course of development of formal operations, according to Flavell and Wohwill (1969), adolescents may be able to solve problems correctly on the basis of newly developing logic but still often make errors because they have not yet learned sufficient performance skills. Youngsters at this stage of development may be able, some of the time, to play complex chess games that require a great deal of abstraction, but because of low attention span or practice at the game itself, they may often make errors. Only after considerable practice at the game will they reach the true stage of formal operations, when they are sufficiently sure of themselves to run through games quickly without errors. In fact, only a little more than half of adolescents will eventually reach this stage.

Adolescents who reach the formal operational stage are able to understand why, in order for an equation in algebra to retain its meaning, canceling figures on one side of the equation requires canceling figures on the other. Number lines and blocks are no longer needed. Adolescents gradually develop ability to solve other new types of problems as well. They can imagine several alternative explanations of the same phenomenon by now and are no longer bound by one solution to a problem. They can operate with symbols that have abstract definitions, and they can operate with metaphors. At this point in their cognitive development, they can begin to understand and enjoy political cartoons. As adolescents enter a world of new ideas and contemplation and begin to hypothesize about relationships, the better thinkers take logical systematic approaches to problem-solving. An example of the type of answer given by an adolescent as compared to a younger child was described by Kohlberg and Gilligan:

> *An example of the shift from concrete to formal operations may be taken from the work of E. A. Peel. Peel asked children what they thought about the following event: "Only brave pilots are allowed to fly over high mountains. A fighter pilot flying over the Alps collided with an aerial cableway, and cut a main cable causing some cars to fall to the glacier below. Several people were killed." A child at the concrete-operational level answered: "I think that the pilot was not very good at flying." A formal-operational child responded: "He was either not informed of the mountain railway on his route or he was flying too low. Also his flying compass may have been affected by something before or after take-off, thus setting him off course causing collision with the cable."*
>
> *The concrete-operational child assumes that if there was a collision the pilot was a bad pilot; the formal-operational child considers all the possibilities that might have caused the collision. The concrete-operational child adopts the hypothesis that seems most probable or likely to him. The formal-operational child constructs all possibilities and checks them out one by one" (Kohlberg and Gilligan 1971, pp. 1061–1062).*

In another comparison of adolescent thinking and thinking of younger children, a psychologist studying self-concept asked adolescents and younger children to describe themselves. Adolescents responded with their personal beliefs, motives, and interpersonal characteristics, all new ideas that involve ability to deal with formal operations. Younger children responded at the concrete operational stage of development with such concrete characteristics as physical appearance, possessions, and play activities (Montemayor and Eisen 1977).

Hypothesizing New Solutions to Problems

The period of formal operations, as Piaget described it, sets the thinking of adolescents apart from that of younger children in a number of other respects. Now that adolescents are beginning to develop the ability to think in abstractions—that is, outside their realm of concrete experience—they can begin to think of ideas and possibilities that have not occurred in their own lives. Adolescents become very interested in hypothesizing new solutions to problems they have heard their parents discuss, as in "What should the United States government do about an arms agreement with the Soviet Union? Should the United States decrease its armaments or increase them?" Adolescents are likely to develop such idealistic solutions to the problem as planning meetings with youth from all over the world to help find world peace in ways that adults have not been able to do.

The developing ability of adolescents to hypothesize or imagine the consequences or possible solutions to different kinds of questions, such as the social questions around disarmament, is extremely important both to the academic work required of them if they are to succeed in school and to the development of identity. The social world becomes an organic unit with laws and regulations and roles and social functions only when formal operational thought is reached. Personality development, once this stage of reasoning is reached, depends on an exchange of ideas by social intercommunication and a sense of equality rather than submission to adult or peer authority.

Adolescents caught up in the development of idealistic solutions to problems are systematic, often to the point of placing their ideals before values possessed by their parents. They continue to search for internal consistency and restructure their

Adolescents may lend their idealism to various social and political causes such as the antinuclear movement.

thoughts and attitudes in the direction of greater self-consistency—that is, they try to demonstrate their values in all of their behaviors, not simply in those that are rewarded by their parents, teachers, or peers. They tend more than ever to conform to a group norm, a new image, or some other cognitive model, and they do their best to be consistent in their conformity. Adolescents' interest in theoretical ideas leads them often to propose utopian solutions to world problems. As adolescents develop increasing ability to think of new ways to end human suffering and social inequity, the result often is conflict. Adolescents may be infuriated when they observe their parents or teachers being inconsistent in their own values and behaviors and when they hear their parents tell them to "do as we say, not as we do."

Adolescents' new freedom in forming hypotheses, however, often makes it more difficult for them to reach decisions. They tend to doubt their own judgments and many hide their self-doubt by challenging authority figures to prove that other views are more consistent than their own. Often they believe their parents are wrong but lack the self-assurance to prove their beliefs in a systematic way. The result frequently is more conflict.

Developing Long-term Goals

Young adolescents have more mature senses of time than do children. With an increased ability to conceive of the distant future, they are able for the first time to set realistic long-term goals for themselves and to plan for activities that may come in the next semester, the next year, or longer away in time.

Intelligence

Campbell (1976) points out that adolescents are beginning to reach their peaks in many abilities associated with school success, such as memory. Many adolescents experience a slight decrease in IQ. According to Campbell, this decrease is true more often for girls than it is for boys. Boys more frequently increase their scores slightly during this period. What does this mean? An increase or decrease in IQ score does not mean that an individual is increasing or decreasing his or her level of cognitive functioning. An increased or decreased score reflects instead the fact that the rate of increase of cognitive development is increasing or decreasing. Apparently, the rate at which cognitive development proceeds is increasing for boys and decreasing for girls. One explanation for this difference might be that at adolescence boys learn that acceptable behavior involves succeeding at school-related tasks. Girls, on the other hand, often learn that it is "not feminine to be smart." Girls often begin at this period to put less emphasis on their schoolwork. Campbell reports that among those adolescent boys whose IQs declined, he found fewer who accepted the masculine stereotype that males are supposed to be more successful at school-related tasks than females.

MORAL DEVELOPMENT

In Chapter 6, we described Lawrence Kohlberg's theory of the development of moral reasoning. As we saw in that chapter, stage one, orientation to punishment and reward, and stage two, hedonistic orientation with an instrumental view of human relations, are the levels at which most children in middle and later childhood respond. Stage three, "good-boy/good-girl" orientation, and stage four, orientation to authority, law, and duty, both are characterized by choices made in response to concern for group values. These stages constitute the "conventional" level at which most adults and some adolescents operate.

Kohlberg's third stage, in which the individual's behavior focuses on obtaining the approval of others, is the first stage of conventional moral reasoning. Adolescents at this stage are beginning to reason according to the expectations that others hold for them. Morality is defined in large part by ties to particular peer groups. Adolescents feel social pressure to win approval of their peers by living up to the expectations that the others have—that is, by conforming. Adolescents solving moral dilemmas at this level of moral reasoning conform more than do adolescents who have reached higher or lower levels. Adolescents at lower stages are much more interested in solving problems that satisfy their own personal needs than in what others think of them. Adolescents at higher levels of moral development might often solve the same moral problems in ways that differ significantly from their peers and not care, as long as they believe that their decisions are based on a higher principle than their peers offer (Saltzstein, Diamond, and Belenky 1972). Adolescents at stage-three reasoning tend to be concerned primarily with the intent of behaviors rather than the outcome. If a person "means well," then that person is OK. The high school football player who gives the following reason for cheating is probably operating at stage three: "I did it because I didn't want to let the team down. The coach said he wouldn't let me play the next game if I didn't pass that course, and that was the only way to do it. I would really have hated if I would've let the guys down. What would they have thought of me?"

Adolescents at stage-four reasoning tend to be concerned primarily with what they should do, according to what duty requires. It is no longer satisfactory for a person "to mean well," if the behavioral outcome is unlawful. Adolescents at this stage of reasoning are likely to say that although they do not want to go into the army, it would be their duty to their country to do so in the event of a draft. They are also concerned with the lawfulness of behavior. As one adolescent at this stage of cognitive development put it, "I might be opposed to joining the army because I don't believe in killing people. On the other hand, if the law required it, of course it would be wrong not to go."

At stage five, Kohlberg proposed, moral decisions are reached on the basis of a person's internal ethical principles rather than concern over societal views of right and wrong. Those few morally precocious adolescents who reach this stage try to develop idealistic solutions to the problem of morality and ethical principles and try to put this into practice by making their behaviors match their ideologies. Adolescents at stage-five reasoning are no longer concerned with the importance of law or duty, if law or duty interferes with their internal principles. Thus the adolescent who believed in the universal wrongness of killing might decide to resist a draft, even if that resisting leads to prison. The same adolescent who believes in the universal immorality of lying would tell the truth even if doing so would lead to pain for other people.

The development of moral reasoning requires a parallel level of cognitive and psychosocial development. The development of abstract reasoning in adolescence makes it possible to consider logically the possible outcomes that can occur from different responses to a situation. This cognitive ability is necessary to moral reasoning. Miller (1978, p. 243) points out that individuals do not move into conventional reasoning until they can view moral dilemmas from multiple perspectives and thus incorporate the feelings of others into moral decision making. Ability to view problems from this perspective develops during the formal operational stage of cognitive development.

The development of moral reasoning is also related to the development of **empathy,** the ability to experience the feelings of another person. Empathy is significantly related both to adolescent moral development and to parental socialization practices. The warmer and more empathic the parental models and the warmer and more democratic the socialization practices, the higher the level of moral reasoning of children (Eisenberg-Berg and Mussen 1978).

Finally, moral development is related to adolescents' ability to deal with the identity crisis that faces them at this period of life. Muuss (1976) concludes that in order to effectively question the conventional morality of one's society, one must have previously questioned one's own identity. One conclusion that may be drawn here is that people going through an identity crisis are more unstable and inconsistent in their moral reasoning.

Thus the same teenager who agrees that it is morally right to respect elders may at the same time become so emotionally engrossed in the development of a personal value system that he or she responds in hostile or rude ways to his or her parents. Many high schoolers, still grappling with Erikson's question "Who am I?" are unable to remain consistent in their attitudes toward others, even when they try their best. Youngsters at this stage often become unable to cope with the concerns of others in some situations when they are able to deal with them in others. The same teenager may have a reasonably polite discussion about politics with his or her parents on one day and the next day may become upset at the position that the parents are taking and may storm out of the room in anger.

Development of Political Thinking

The development of political thinking and interpretation of political ideologies go hand in hand with the development of moral reasoning. Adelson (1975) interviewed over 1000 adolescents in order to determine the ways their political thinking developed with age. He concluded that the most important change in political thinking was related to the development of cognitive reasoning. Among young adolescents, political thinking usually takes the form of beliefs of "rightness" or "wrongness" according to their concrete results, as with the "wrongness" of killing because it causes innocent people to die. Later, as adolescents refine their ability to think abstractly, decisions concerning the "rightness" or "wrongness" of political positions are based more and more on abstract concepts of the notion of freedom, equality, or human rights. Older adolescents may think of "rightness" or "wrongness" in historical causes or implications for future decisions or events, as in the "wrongness" of expecting people to obey the law if the law is not systematically administered to everyone.

Interpreting Moral Decision Making

When observers see adolescents making moral or political decisions in which they reject inconsistent or hypocritical societal theories, they often conclude that these young people are operating on the basis of principled moral reasoning (stage five). Kohlberg and his colleagues suggest that while this may well be true of some adolescents, observers should be cautious in making such assumptions. Many adolescents make decisions based on considerably lower levels—for example, Kohlberg's stage two, hedonistic orientation, or stage three, "good-boy/good-girl" orientation. While the behavior may appear to be motivated by the same reasoning as stage-five behavior, because the adolescent is rejecting societal values, the moral reasoning may actually be at a lower level (Kohlberg and Gilligan 1971). Thus if Anne stays in study hall and prepares for a test while the gang cuts class and goes out for pizza, she might be doing so because she believes that it is the "right" thing to do based on her own ethical standards (stage-five morality). It is equally likely, according to Kohlberg, however, that she stays in study hall in order to receive approval, in this case from the teacher (stage-three morality).

Unacceptable Moral Decision Making. Not all early adolescents solve problems so that they behave in socially approved ways. Many employ unacceptable methods even when they want to reach socially acceptable goals. For example, adolescents at Kohlberg's stage three or stage four often cheat on examinations in order to get grades that will get approval from their parents. Cheating among adolescents creates a problem not only for themselves but for other students whose grades are determined on the basis of how everyone in the group has done. Surprisingly perhaps, most students who cheat do not cheat to keep from failing but do so in order to protect high grades (Fisbe 1975).

Although the grading systems used in our schools are rewarding for some students, they can be anxiety producing for others. Anxious students are often less able to obtain high grades than are students who are less anxious and pressured. Students particularly affected are those who are beginning to plan for their futures and who realize the importance of their grades in helping them become what they want.

Often, these are also students whose parents are concerned that they receive high grades. Psychologists suggest that strong parental pressure for high grades is one factor that leads to student cheating. Children who are unable to do well in school but who have parents with high aspirations for them experience the greatest pressure. These children cheat more frequently than others (Pearlin, Yarrow, and Scarr 1967).

Many students whose parents do not pressure them to do well also cheat. Some students report that they cheat because their friends cheat, and their friends "would laugh at them" if they did not. For the peer-oriented adolescent who reports "*everybody* cheats in Spanish class," it is difficult to provide a convincing argument that cheating is wrong. If the peer group does it successfully, why not? If the adult world provides additional successful cheating models, it makes it that much harder *not* to cheat.

THE CASE OF CHERYL GURNEY—TEENAGE PREGNANCY:
A CASE STUDY FOR CLASS DISCUSSION

I. Identification and Sources of Information

Name: Cheryl Gurney
Address: Harlem, New York City
Race: Black
Sex: Female
Age: Fourteen years
Sources of Information
  1. Personal interview with Cheryl
  2. Interview with Cheryl's mother and two sisters
  3. Interview with Cheryl's teachers
  4. Interview with the school social worker

II. Family History

Cheryl is the middle child with two sisters, ages twelve and fifteen. All three girls live in a two-room apartment with their mother. Cheryl's older sister, Ruby, gave birth last year to an illegitimate son who lives with the family. Cheryl's father deserted the family five years ago. Since that time, Cheryl's mother has supported the family through occasional employment as a cleaning woman.

When Ruby's baby was born, Ruby applied and received additional welfare payments for herself and her baby. She contributes half of this money to the household and saves the rest for herself. Ruby feels it gives her "freedom." Ruby dropped out of school at the time of her pregnancy and did not return. She spends most of her time at home with her mother and the baby, although she frequently leaves the baby with someone in the house to go to a neighborhood bar or to go dancing. Cheryl's younger sister, Sarah, has been going steady for a year. It is her ambition to be the first of the sisters to get married. She is envious of her sister's pregnancy and says she would like to have a baby of her own too. Cheryl and Sarah both are still attending public school, although Cheryl has repeated a grade twice and Sarah has repeated one grade. Ruby had just finished sixth grade when she had her baby last year.

III. Case History

Cheryl's teacher reports that Cheryl seems to have a great deal of potential as a student. Throughout her school career, whenever she attended classes regularly, she received average grades, but Cheryl cuts

Continued

THE CASE OF CHERYL GURNEY *(Cont.)*

classes quite frequently. Teachers have noted that whenever Cheryl has received a particular low grade on a test, the grade will be followed by a period of low class attendance and still lower grades, a vicious cycle. Cheryl has always been popular. She has had a series of boyfriends and reports that she has gone steady "on and off" with a number of them since she was ten years old. She visited the school counselor during her fifth month of pregnancy to announce her decision to withdraw from school. The counselor informed her at that time of the programs in the city available to her that would allow her both to receive a prenatal education and continue her regular studies while she is pregnant. Cheryl has not yet made any decisions as to whether or not she will enter the program. She has instead begun cutting classes at the regular school more and more frequently.

In an interview with a school social worker who came to her home to talk, Cheryl said she did not think that she needed any prenatal education. She received a lot of information watching Ruby's pregnancy, and she was sure she knew what to expect. She was unhappy about not seeing much of her friends from school, but she thought that "probably, after the baby is born, lots of them will come around." Cheryl said that she is looking forward to having a baby—"just like lots of my girlfriends"—and that she will never consider abortion. She told the social worker that she knows who the father of the baby is, but that she is not going to tell anyone, "including my mother." "Him and me—we're not interested in each other anymore. And besides, he has a new girlfriend." Her mother reports no idea of who the father is.

Cheryl has never been caught with any illicit drugs, although Ruby was once expelled from school for smoking marijuana. Cheryl admitted to the school social worker that she has used "all the usual stuff" at parties. "You know—hash, a little Mexican mud (that's what we call heroin), and coke—whenever it's around *and* somebody has the money." Cheryl's mother said, "None of my girls has ever been in-

volved with anything heavy—just what everybody else does—nothing more." "Cheryl," she hastened to add, "has never been involved in selling anything, anyways."

The social worker interviewed Cheryl at some length about her knowledge of the effects of diet and drugs on prenatal development. Cheryl's thinking is limited to her conviction that "it isn't good for the baby if I don't eat enough. Now I'm eating for two, and I have to be sure that I'm not hungry." As for drug use, Cheryl reported hearing of alcohol- and drug-addicted babies being born. "But that was to addicts—not to anybody like me. I only use the stuff socially," she reported.

The social worker gave Cheryl published information about dietary requirements for pregnant women as well as a manual on the effects of drugs on the unborn infant. She also gave Cheryl a pamphlet describing the program in the city for pregnant girls. She expects to follow this initial visit with another in two weeks' time.

In an interview at her home one week after the social worker's first visit, Cheryl said that she has not yet read the materials that the social worker left. She has also not been to school for the past week because she feels embarrassed in front of her classmates. Cheryl reported that she has "been thinking more and more about the special school—it might be fun to be in classes with a bunch of girls just like me." Ruby never attended the special school, although the social worker had told her about it. Ruby reported that she was not sorry—"It was fun staying home—just watching TV. Ma was with me a lot, and there never was no hassle—you know," she added. Mrs. Gurney does not think that there is any real reason for Cheryl to go to school. "If she thinks she's going to go back and get a high school degree and leave me or the others with the work of another baby in the house," the older woman reported, "she's got another guess. I got all this cooking and cleaning to do already. And there isn't any room in such a small

THE CASE OF CHERYL GURNEY

apartment for any privacy. When I want a social life of my own, I have to go out to have it. Who would look after the baby if Cheryl stayed in school? Ruby is going out more and more now . . . . . She wouldn't do it. It sure wouldn't be fair to dump on Sarah—even if she thinks she'd like it." Cheryl listened during the interview with an expression of complacency. "Maybe I'll stay in school at least 'til the baby is born," she mused. "After that, we'll see what'll happen."

IV. Present Status, Diagnosis, and Prognosis

The probability is very great that Cheryl will formally drop out of public school in the next few weeks and will not take advantage of the special program for pregnant girls. Even if she does, the probability is still great that she will not continue to attend school after her baby is born or that she will ever study nights for her GED (the equivalent of a high school diploma offered by examination).

Teenage pregnant girls in Cheryl's socioeconomic bracket tend to have the highest proportion of infants at risk, and Cheryl is no exception. The social worker is particularly concerned about Cheryl's nutrition and drug intake during her pregnancy. Although Cheryl never goes hungry and there is plenty to eat in the Gurney household, most of it is junk food. Cheryl munches on potato chips all day and, after five months of pregnancy, has already gained eighteen pounds. Cheryl has not thrown away the materials given her by the social worker, but she has not read them either. The odds are in favor of a baby at risk and later of a young mother incapable of doing the best job of caring for her youngster.

Questions for Class Discussion

1. What are the most serious dangers facing Cheryl and her unborn baby?

2. If you were an educator planning a program for pregnant girls, just what would you include in the curriculum in order to help reduce these dangers? Why?

3. If you were a social worker trying your best to entice girls like Cheryl into entering such a program, what specific steps would you take?

SUMMARY

Adolescence, the period from pubescence to adulthood, is marked by profound psychological and physiological changes. The beginning of pubescence is signaled by a sudden growth spurt occurring about two years earlier in girls than in boys, which slows when puberty is reached. Growth and development in adolescence may be asynchronous; the high variability among individuals in rate of development can produce embarassment and anxiety.

Specific psychosocial behaviors mark early adolescence and differ somewhat between the two sexes. Both boys and girls exhibit impulsive and unpredictable behavior. Feelings, attitude, and motives become sex typed as never before. In adolescence, individuals begin to try to determine who they are and where they are going and to make explicit their own personal positions in relation to the values of the world around them. Group identity is of major importance to early adolescents and leads to a great deal of conformity to the group. According to Erikson, adolescence is a turning point during which identity crises must be resolved if identity confusion is not to develop. Role confusion can occur when the adolescent seeks particular roles in society that are impossible or difficult to attain.

The importance of popularity and conformity to group norms that characterize adolescence has a number of explanations in our society, including alienation of adolescents from the adult world, lack of continuity, conflicting values, and lack of personal security. Group identification reduces loneliness and gives some meaning to existence. The first choices that affect eventual occupations and careers are made in adolescence. During this time, boys begin to do better in schoolwork than do girls, particularly in "masculine" subjects.

The hormonal changes that accompany puberty give renewed impetus to the sexual urges. Children in our society receive conflicting messages about sexuality and may begin to question sexual as well as other basic values. Adolescent sexual behavior includes many different kinds of experimentation, from masturbation to intercourse. Researchers have found a clear trend toward earlier heterosexual experience; the accompanying increase in adolescent pregnancy carries a high price to society.

According to Piaget, children from about eleven on are ready to begin thinking and solving problems through the use of abstraction. Once they reach this formal operational stage, they can reason through use of hypotheses. Their search for internal consistency often leads to conflict with adults. Adolescents are beginning to reach their peaks in abilities associated with school success.

Most adolescents operate at Kohlberg's third and fourth stages of moral development. Adolescents at stage three tend to be concerned primarily with the intent of behaviors rather than their outcomes; those at stage four are concerned primarily with what they should do, according to their concepts of duty. The development of moral reasoning requires a parallel level of cognitive and psychosocial development.

Often when adolescents appear to be making decisions on the basis of principled moral reasoning, they are, in fact, behaving in this way to receive social approval. Many early adolescents exhibit a great deal of behavior such as cheating, that society does not consider moral. Some reasons for this include parental pressure for good grades and social acceptability of cheating according to the peer and adult cultures.

FOR FURTHER READING

Elkind, D. *Children and Adolescents: Interpretive Essays on Jean Piaget.* Oxford, England: Oxford University Press, 1981. This is a new edition of a collection of essays on child and adolescent cognitive development. Included is an extended discussion of adolescent education as an embodiment of Piagetian theory.

Erikson, E. *Identity, Youth, and Crisis.* New York: Norton, 1968. Erikson's book remains one of the most extensive analyses of adolescent conflict based on the stage-dependent approach to development. His discussion of identity should be read by anyone expecting to work with, and sensitively deal with, adolescents during their careers.

Preview Questions

- What are some major conflicts that develop between parents and their teenagers, and what factors influence their seriousness?

- How does the home influence the values of the adolescent, and what special precaution must divorced parents take in this regard?

- Why are "middle-school" youngsters so difficult to teach, and how will demands on them change in high school?

- Why does achievement become so important for adolescents, and what differences appear between the academic records of boys and girls?

- What are some factors that have caused achievement to decrease in American schools, and what differences are attributed to socioeconomic and ethnic backgrounds?

- Can you explain why classroom discipline becomes more difficult to maintain at this age and show how the problem is related to peer relationships?

- What are six major problems found among adolescents, and what are some factors that are believed to cause each?

- What are some major causes for adolescent depression and suicide, and what can parents and teachers do to prevent them?

- Can you list and describe four kinds of help that are available for teenagers who are in trouble?

9

Adolescents in Their Environments

Adolescence, as we have learned, is a period of rapid physical and mental development. At the same time that sudden changes affect the physical appearances and capabilities of adolescents, new thoughts, experiences, and opportunities to interact with others affect the ways they experience the world. As young people experiment and try new roles, they frequently find themselves in conflict with those in authority. The adolescent strives to be independent, yet, in our society, is still socially and economically dependent. The conflicts that develop are reflected in relationships with parents, teachers, peers, and others in the community.

Adolescents must also learn to take responsibility for their achievements or lack of achievement. Performance at school becomes especially important during this period, for opportunities later in life will be shaped by the choices the adolescent makes at this stage. Behavioral and emotional problems during this time are often related to the adolescent's friends, activities, use of drugs or alcohol, and attendance and behavior at school. A few teenagers exhibit such severe problems that special interventions and strategies are necessary to help solve their problems. Chapter 9 explores the ways adolescents interact with parents and other family members, teachers, and peers in their homes, at school, and on the street.

 ## FAMILY RELATIONSHIPS

Parent–Child Conflicts

Many American parents report that they have difficulty understanding their teenagers and that family conflicts develop whenever their teenagers are present. Most parents take some comfort in believing that in this country at least, the problem is almost universally shared by parents of teens. Loving parents who want their children to develop into happy, healthy young adults experience frustrations and anxieties they never anticipated when their children were small. They are shocked when they feel that their youngster is pretty hard to like and equally disturbed to realize that they do not even like their own reactions toward their children.

Is conflict between parents and adolescents a necessary part of growing up in all societies, or is it a reflection of the particular learning experiences of children in our own culture? Cultural anthropologists, such as Margaret Mead and Ruth Benedict, have pointed out that adolescence is not a period of difficulty in all societies or in all environments. In some societies in which the rules of adulthood are clearly prescribed and in which there is not much freedom of choice for the adolescent, parents and children tend more easily to share the same values and make similar decisions (Benedict 1938; Mead 1949; Mead and Heyman 1965). Bronfenbrenner (1977) and Gibson and Vinogradoff (1981) reported that children in many other present-day societies, as in the Soviet Union, for example, share the values of their parents during this period more readily than do American children.

What accounts for these differences? First, the behavior of adolescents growing up in cultures where their future roles are largely predetermined differs markedly from the behavior of adolescents who have a great deal of choice as to which roles they will take. In industrial societies that provide more opportunity for choice of occupational roles, parent–child tensions during adolescence seem to increase. Levy (1949) reported that with greater urbanization, increased ability of young people to find employment outside the home, and less dependence of young people on their immediate families in the People's Republic of China, adolescent Chinese began long ago to develop patterns of parent–child conflicts. More recently, studies of urban-area Australian adolescents also showed conflict patterns essentially similar to those of American children (Collins and Harper 1974).

One major complaint of both adolescents and their parents is that there is no real communication between the generations. Thirteen-year-olds cannot seem to tell their parents what the problem is. "Why bother trying?" said one disgruntled adolescent. "My mother can't even remember that she was ever young—she probably wasn't." Adolescents complain also that their parents have no understanding of what young people want or why they want it. Often, this is due to adolescents' preoccupation with their bodies and themselves; they are too self-absorbed to be aware of the interests and needs of their parents. Continues the same teenager, "My mom seems to *know* when I want to read a book or write in my diary. That's when she calls me to do the dishes. Other times, when I want to help her, she doesn't notice or call."

One reason for the lack of ability of teenagers to understand what is expected of them and why, according to cultural anthropologists, is the absence in our society of a specific **rite of passage,** or initiation experience in which adolescents are symbolically divested of childhood and invested with adulthood (Benedict 1938; Eisenstadt 1962; Knepler 1969). American society particularly seems to be very ambivalent about the social status of adolescents and often is inconsistent in its behavior toward them. This leaves adolescents with the impression that there is no real place for them in the adult world. On the one hand, parents might suggest to adolescents that they are old enough to take some responsibilities around the house, like cleaning the kitchen, mowing the lawn, or emptying the dishwasher. At the same time, they might point out that adolescents are too young to borrow the family car or to stay at a party overnight. It is true that American adolescents are given much more freedom than children from many other societies in their opportunity to interact with their peer groups. At the same time, however, in such common situations, they are treated in many ways as children longer than children in other societies (Kandel and Lesser 1969).

Parents also complain frequently that their offspring are not "responsible." A father will tell his son, "When I was your age, I had a paper route and was giving my mother all my pay. We needed it to buy food. Now you complain because we

The bar mitzvah for Jewish boys represents one of the few rites of passage in our society. For the majority of young people there is no initiation experience whereby they symbolically enter adulthood.

don't have a big enough color TV. I just don't understand your values. They certainly didn't come from me." This father's conclusion needs further exploration. Frequently, the same father who complains that his son does not take responsibility forgot that he never gave him an opportunity to be responsible. Without this opportunity to be responsible, the son has no clear status and therefore does not know how to respond. If he had made a suggestion to his son that he would help him get a better TV set if his son earned some of the money to pay for it, perhaps his son in turn would have exhibited more responsible behavior.

Adolescents often are inconsistent in their responses toward their parents, so that it may be difficult for parents to know what to expect. One day the teenage daughter will be delighted to talk with her mother about her boyfriend. The next day, she will appear very secretive and complain that her mother asks too many questions. One reason for inconsistent behavior among adolescents is that many who are still grappling with Erikson's question "Who am I?" are unable to cope with the concerns of the other people around them. They respond therefore to their inner feelings and seem sometimes to be completely unaware of adult feelings.

Youngsters at this stage frequently hurt their parents' feelings with sudden inability to understand the problems that their parents are going through. "Just wait till you're my age and see how you feel!" is the common complaint of the parents who feel that their children are so self-centered that they seem to be unaware of their parents' needs. At the same time, the same youngsters depend on their parents and assume that it is proper to expect their parents always to be available to help.

Parental attitude clearly has an effect on adolescent behavior. Researchers have shown both that parents who are warm and attentive tend to have adolescent children who have less difficulty in adjusting to the changes of this age period and that parents who are detached and hostile tend to have adolescent children who are more likely to get in trouble and to exhibit hostile rather than trusting behavior (Robinson 1978). One explanation of the relationship between parent and child behavior is that even at the same time that they appear to be uninterested in their parents, adolescents still are using their parents as models in their day-to-day behaviors.

Dependence and Independence

As adolescents grow older, they also grow increasingly independent from the family. High schoolers are usually much more independent than middle schoolers. They are away from home and family interactions more than ever before. Often, they spend their school evenings and weekends as well with friends, dating, or at school functions. Many sixteen-year-olds today learn to drive; the family car provides a vehicle high schoolers can use to increase peer contact. At the same time, it increases the time that high schoolers spend away from their families. With the resulting increased feedback coming from peers and the decreased opportunity to provide feedback from family members during this time, these other people play increasingly important roles in helping teenagers develop independent identities. Adolescent striving for independence is important to the development of positive identities. At this age, individuals define themselves by their abilities to succeed socially on their own without their parents' assistance.

Some theorists suggest that adolescent independence develops primarily because our society exhibits extreme concern with activities rejecting dependence and promoting independence in young people. They further suggest that it is this rejection of dependence that often leads to adolescent frustration (Hsu 1972). During adolescence, individuals learn that adult status comes only through work and self-sufficiency, yet most adolescents have no way to be self-sufficient because there is no real place for them in the labor market. It has been suggested that frustration associated with this inability to be taken seriously provides the major impetus for the adolescent's rejection of adult values.

Parents of high schoolers often complain about a number of changes that result in the family setting from the increased independence of their offspring at this stage of development. For one thing, there is often difficulty planning meals and other family events because of high schoolers' independent outside activities. Parents seem at this period to have more difficulty guiding their children in part because they see them less often. They frequently complain, in addition, that although they still try to serve as proper role models for their children as they did when their children were younger, the same children act independently and often simply disregard their parents' advice. Worried parents often ask what their children feel are obtrusive questions now: "Who went with you to the movies last night?" "That boy John you double-dated with, is he the son of that woman who runs the florist shop? Aren't his parents divorced?"

Home: A Place to Learn Values

Researchers have shown that learning "right" or "wrong" behavior in no way guarantees an individual's behavior in solving moral problems (Hartshorne *et al.* 1927). Devereux (1972) demonstrated that a far better indicator of adolescent values is the behavior and attitude of parents toward moral issues. Simply put, teenagers watch their parents very closely and tend to emulate what their parents do far more than what they say that their children should do. Parents who reinforce their children for high moral reasoning tend to have children who score highest on moral-reasoning scales (Holstein 1969). At the time in their lives in which they are deciding what values to take seriously in their adult lives and what ideals are important in incorporating into the self-images they are developing, most teenagers turn to their parents as model figures. At this time it is particularly important for parents not to teach that cheating is appropriate adult behavior by demonstrating that they can get away with cheating on their income taxes. Because part of the identity that the adolescent develops deals with male and female roles, parents who present happy, well-adjusted models who interact in satisfactory ways with one another tend to have children who find it easier to develop satisfactory sex roles for themselves. Divorced parents of adolescents have particularly to be careful to demonstrate to their children that although they have decided that marriage (to each other) is not a satisfactory role solution for them, they have respect for one another and can interact on necessary matters in satisfactory ways.

ADOLESCENTS AND SCHOOL

Most adolescents make a satisfactory adjustment to the new demands of the middle school or high school environment. Some, however, experience difficulty in school, perhaps for the first time. The physical changes that accompany adolescence may make it harder to concentrate on academic matters. In addition, many youngsters are so absorbed with their peers that learning takes a back seat. Teachers who have learned to expect a great deal from these children based on their earlier records may be surprised at their poor performances.

Middle School

In the past fifteen years, many American cities have developed special middle school programs for sixth, seventh, and eighth grade students. Unlike the older junior high school concept, in which a special school was provided to bridge the gap between the sheltered elementary school and the larger, freer school, the middle school does more than provide a miniature high school program. The middle school was designed to meet the separate and special needs of the pubescent and early adolescent years. Advocates of the middle school concept remind us that all adolescents are not the same and that the period we call adolescence can be broken into smaller substages, each characterized by certain degrees of physical, social, emotional, and cognitive development. Different sorts of problems arise in early pubescence and in the later years of adolescence. Ideally, the middle school can provide special programs that cater particularly to the needs of less socially assured early adolescents. These include help with some of the learning problems that develop as well as help with developing sexuality, interest in values, and interest in peers. The success of these programs, and indeed of the middle school concept, is still to be determined. Successs of each individual middle school is dependent on the particular programs established in it. Informality in teaching, flexible schedules, small classes, and extra guidance usually contribute to success.

Teaching the middle schooler is not always easy, for a variety of reasons. Early adolescents vacillate frequently and unpredictably from adult behavior to child behavior. Adolescents typically demonstrate increased self-awareness and the ability to generate more possible alternatives to problems than they did in the elementary school years, but they often are so engrossed with their own complex metamorphoses that they cannot pay adequate attention to what is going on around them. They assume that others are as fascinated by them and their behaviors as they are. Parents and teachers complain that early adolescents fail to distinguish between objects of concern to themselves and the subjective attitudes of others.

Without special guidance, the period in which they attend middle school is not fun for many youngsters, even when it was fun for them in elementary school. Serious study is a difficult adjustment, and helping a student to study often requires a great deal of attention and reinforcement from teachers and parents. The former "all A" student may actually cut class and stay with the gang in the hall smoking a cigarette. The early adolescent, used to praise and approval from doting teachers in earlier grades, may now be far more concerned with obtaining the approval of peers.

HIGHLIGHT 9.1 **TEACHING VALUES AND DECISION MAKING
TO ADOLESCENTS**

A bomb has been dropped, and the only ten people alive in the world are in a bomb shelter. However, food and oxygen available can accommodate only seven of the survivors until fallout has reached a new level. These seven will have to create a new society. Which of the ten people should be selected? (Beatty 1977, p. 1).

This task is one of a number in New Model Me, a program designed to teach relations to others, to discover something about beliefs and why we have them, to develop value systems, to understand the human motivations underlying behavior, to realize the ways resources and physical and social environments influence behavior, and more generally, to learn effective ways to solve problems (Beatty 1977). Teenagers working at the tasks are asked to decide an answer to each problem unanimously.

The project is designed to focus on adolescents with behavior problems. Because these adolescents frequently suggest that they have difficulty communicating with their parents, the tasks are used by counselors or social workers. The students who come to work on the tasks are placed in special groups to receive help because they are either terribly withdrawn or terribly aggressive in regular school classes. Many want to drop out. The tasks provide opportunity to learn to communicate with others and, at the same time, to accept responsibility.

In another group, a counselor posed a practical problem that most students face at one time or another:

High School

By the time adolescents reach high school, most are ready to take on the serious work activities involved. High school is the place that the first tentative decisions are made concerning future life work. Both the courses students choose and their academic performances may affect all later career possibilities, and students know this. While many middle schoolers begin to take their aptitudes into consideration in their first thoughts about their futures, high schoolers tend to consider personal values and goals as well. It is at this period that budding scientists or creative artists begin to plan their college educations or their vocational school training and that popular student body officers begin, perhaps, to think seriously of using their administrative skills. Only after age seventeen, however, do most adolescents begin to make realistic decisions regarding future occupations.

> Let's say that you value school and there's a gang of kids on the corner who are taking off for the day. They might say to you, "That's dumb to go to school." What would be your decision? (Beatty 1977)

Students and counselor together weighed the possibilities, discussed the advantages and disadvantages of each, allowed each member of the group to share thoughts, and then came to a group decision.

Some of the participants' comments about the decision-making process were as follows:

> Man, it was hard work trying to get the guys to see what I meant. Finally, I saw what they were thinking and knew they were right, and it was easier to decide to go along with them.

> I guess if you know something's right, it don't matter what the others think . . . if you know it's right.

> Nothing's dumb if it's right. I'd go to school. (Beatty 1977)

QUESTIONS FOR THOUGHT

1. In New Model Me, counselors take the place of parents in helping adolescents with behavior problems learn to make positive value decisions. What might parents do to reinforce the learning of the group?

2. Why do the participants in this group need to listen to each other's ideas in order to learn to make decisions?

Achievement

For a variety of reasons, academic and nonacademic, school achievement becomes particularly important during adolescence. Gordon (1971) suggests that achievement is symbolically validated performance that can be compared with a socially defined standard of excellence long before adolescents can prove themselves in the adult field of work. Achievement or lack of it forms a major base for the development of self-esteem among adolescents. It also is an important determinant of popularity.

The Importance of Achievement. Exploring new interests and abilities and selecting an occupation are adolescent developmental tasks. Sex typing plays an important role here. Many adolescents have trouble determining the roles that they can and will play in life. Sixth, seventh, and eighth graders are just beginning to

Whereas high school boys tend to excel in math and science, girls do better in subjects like English and art. These differences appear to be related to their different socialization.

understand that if they do not do well in math, they will not be able to take advanced math courses in high school and prepare for careers requiring mathematical abilities. Some high schoolers must meet the disadvantages of not having done well in the middle school years. Even those who have succeeded may be concerned by the decisions facing them that will affect their futures. This may be true because they are still without adequate direction. The resulting role confusion can lead to a variety of behaviors, both desirable and undesirable. For example, in their attempts to define themselves, many adolescents fall in love and attempt to develop new identities through the perceptions of their boyfriends or girlfriends. Many, as we learned, become idealistic and devote their energies to religious or political causes. If these adolescent behaviors allow them to continue pursuing socially acceptable goals, they can be useful in resolving the identity crisis. Some behaviors, however, do not help the adolescent achieve a sense of integration. Daydreaming and acting out are common examples.

Sex Differences in Achievement. In their achievements, the records of high school boys and girls differ. Boys tend to excel at "masculine" subjects, such as mathematics and science. Girls tend to excel at traditionally "feminine" subjects, such as art and English (Eme, Maisiak, and Goodale 1979) and to do less well at math and science. Much of the reason for girls' poorer performance in math and science may be related to their awareness that males will find them less attractive if they pursue "masculine" subjects in school.

Other differences in orientation toward achievement seem to be related to differences in social-class background and parents' occupations. Achievement-oriented girls tend to come from lower-middle-class homes. These girls use achievement as a means of mobility. Girls with professionally successful mothers also tend to be more highly achievement motivated than girls whose mothers do not have outside careers. Today, more and more adult women are entering previously male-dominated professional fields. With women gradually moving out of accepted sex-typed occupations, corresponding changes can be expected in the attitudes, behaviors, and choices of adolescent females.

Decreasing Achievement in American Schools. All students, of course, are not high achievers. For these students, high school can contribute to role confusion and negative self-esteem. Some experts, however, believe that even good students today learn less than students did a few decades ago. Teachers contend that the quality of reading and writing has decreased considerably, and evidence shows that achievement, as measured by standardized test scores, is decreasing. Studies by the College Entrance Examination Board and others suggest a general malaise, both in the motivation of young people and in the lessening of the role of their families in the educational process. Added to this, they suggest that TV has played a role in decreasing reading in the home, that there has been an increase in elective as opposed to required courses in school, and that the importance in our society of academic scholarship has diminished (Kellaghen 1977; Shane and Wirtz 1977; Trotman 1977).

The lower-income student traditionally has done less well in school than have middle-class counterparts. Just as achievement of middle-class students has fallen, achievement of lower-income students has also fallen. Poorer adolescents often suffer from serious role confusion and negative identities as a direct result of poor learning in school. This problem leads many to give up and drop out. For those who do not drop out but who stay on and finish high school, most tend to have far lower levels of aspiration than their middle-class counterparts (Elder 1968).

The following statement made by a black, teenage school dropout is typical of many such statements heard by counselors:

I don't care what happens to me, man. Nothing I do turns out anyway. I never made the grade, and I don't care. When I had to go to that school, I learned that it wasn't worth a try. I couldn't do no better than last place. And then, when I got out, man, then it really was bad. All's I wanted was a job and some break, man. But I couldn't do it; I ain't no good.

The decreasing achievement of young people of all socioeconomic backgrounds affects them when they enter the job market or go to college. These topics will be discussed in Chapter 10.

Discipline

Discipline can be a particularly difficult task for teachers of adolescents. Often, individuals at this stage are especially boisterous and enjoy gaining the attention of peers. It is very important for adolescents to be able to identify with their teachers as appropriate models of adult behavior. Adolescents whose parents and teachers understand them, communicate their understanding, and at the same time, communicate their values tend to have fewer teenage disciplinary problems than others.

A typical disciplinary problem in both middle school and high school is acting out, behavior in which students, typically low achievers, make jokes or otherwise draw attention to themselves. Their goal usually is to get reinforcement from peers, when they cannot get it from teachers. For some, even negative attention from teachers can be reinforcing.

Gibson and Vinogradoff (1981) point out that many of the behaviors that occur frequently in American schools do not appear at all in schools in some other countries. In the Soviet Union, for example, where most parents and peers alike provide a great deal of reinforcement for such adult-accepted behaviors as studying and engaging in organized after-school activities, there is far less student behavior that is not related to study or other socially desired activity. Fourteen-year-olds are usually far more concerned with doing well on their examinations so that they will be allowed into the next level of schooling than they are in smoking in the hallways, although there is some acting out behavior in Soviet schools.

In general, teachers who treat their students with dignity, who use humor, but not ridicule, to maintain order, and who understand that their students at this age are especially sensitive are more likely to be able to maintain an environment that is most conducive to learning.

Adolescents and Their Peer Groups

We learned in Chapter 8 that adolescent peers pressure each other to band in groups. First, a peer-group social structure usually is well established in high schools. Students who become members of any group are more acceptable to all peers in the social structure than those who choose to remain aloof and isolated.

Social pressure to belong to a peer group comes also from the school itself. Teachers, both passively and actively, encourage organization of students into peer groups. They usually accept passively, for example, the groups that exist and do little to encourage members of one group to join another. The high school cafeteria often becomes a meeting place for friendship groups, with different groups occupying different areas to sit and chat. Teachers probably have the most influence on the organized clubs and activities. Teachers reinforce characteristics of particular clubs by selecting certain students for monitoring or for assisting in record-keeping functions. They also reinforce group formation when they organize such academic clubs as the honor society or the French club. Newman (1976) points out that school facilities also encourage separation of students into cliques. This occurs when, in the interests of efficiency, unrelated activities are located in separate areas. A common example is that in many high schools, vocational education facilities are located in different wings from academic facilities. This has the effect of isolating students into "vocational" and "academic" groups.

Social pressure to belong to a peer group comes finally from parents, who try to encourage some relationships that they consider favorable. To the extent that peer

The peer group increasingly replaces the family as a source of support for many teenagers.

groups reflect parents' values and goals, there is minimal conflict. When adolescents join groups that do not reflect parental values, they often experience conflicts and anxiety at home. Sometimes the result is that they spend more time with some group outside the family (Newman and Newman 1976). Parental views are extremely important to high schoolers, even though they may not act on these views and often appear to rebel against them. Niles (1979) reported, for example, that although adolescent girls at an urban high school tended to conform to the behaviors of the peer group, their general attitudes toward their mothers were actually more favorable than toward their peers.

Conformity to peer pressure seems to have a curvilinear relationship to age. Children become increasingly conformist through the middle school years and into high school. Sometime in high school, as they begin to acquire strong self-concepts and feel more secure about their identities, the need to conform begins to decrease. In the later years of high school, students are more apt to make decisions because they agree with the idea involved rather than because they think that is the way their friends would respond. When this occurs, young people are ready to make decisions on their own, an important step toward adulthood.

 ## PROBLEMS OF ADOLESCENTS

Adolescence is a time of change and experimentation. While most young people are able to handle the pressures of this period of life, some encounter problems along the way. Some insecure adolescents who have self-esteem problems become extremely shy. Adolescents who have been inadequately socialized may engage in delinquent behavior. Although many teenagers experiment with drugs and sex without serious consequences, others lack a clear value system on which to base their behaviors in these areas.

Some adolescents are troubled by severe pathologies as well, including intense anxiety and depression, which are reflected in a rising suicide rate among this age group.

Extreme Shyness

Extreme shyness is a problem that confronts adolescents as well as younger students. If individuals do not learn to deal with shyness by the time they reach adolescence, they often are unable to develop satisfactorily in the interpersonal relationships with others that are so important at this level. Often, extreme shyness interferes with academic work as well. Zimbardo, Pilkonis, and Norwood (1975) reported in a survey of high school students that forty percent of those interviewed said that extreme shyness has accompanied and affected their interpersonal reactions throughout their growing-up periods. One interviewee reported that he could remember as far back as four years of age exhibiting behaviors specifically designed to hide from interactions with others. He would look the other way when seeing people he knew, in the hope that they would not notice him. He never raised his hand to answer teachers' questions in class. These behaviors were accompanied by blushing, excessive perspiring, and having "butterflies in the stomach" whenever he was forced into social interactions. One result was that this student was not only socially a loner but also a low achiever. He did far less well than his ability level as measured by his IQ would have predicted he would do.

Researchers believe that the development of extreme shyness may be related to the type of parenting exhibited in the home (Robinson 1978). Parents who are consistently warm and affectionate to each other as well as to their children tend to have adolescent children who are not shy and withdrawn but who are outgoing and sociable instead. High schoolers whose parents are warm and affectionate are more likely to be unafraid of talking about themselves freely to others, even to the extent of comfortably confiding intimate details without discomfort (Snoek and Rothblum 1979).

Delinquency

Delinquency among younger as well as older adolescents is increasing at an alarming rate. According to learning theory, delinquent behaviors are accompanied by reinforcement in the form of attention from the peer group and frequently in the form of punishment from the adult society. This serves to set in motion a vicious circle: more delinquent behavior in return for more reinforcement from the peer group, catalyzed by more punishment from the adult society and more anger on the part of the adolescent. Price, Price, and Toomey (1980) suggest that the problem behavior of adolescents occurs because of poor self-concept. We learned earlier that teenagers from unstable environments in which parents provide socially inappropriate models are much more likely to emulate these models. In addition, they are more likely to have poor self-concepts because of their histories of little reinforcement at home and to look to the friendship group as a source of substitute need satisfaction.

Students who have trouble learning in school often band together with peers who have the same problems. These often are the students who exhibit aggressive and destructive behavior in school. In the late 1970s, seventy-three percent of the nation's schools were reporting more than one major crime in a single semester. FBI reports showed that at the time, more crimes were committed by this age group than by adults. Motives reported by adolescents for school-related destructive behaviors include outright rebellion and peer acceptance as well as school failure (Sabatino *et al.* 1978).

In urban schools today, teaching has become a dangerous profession, because of the high incidence of serious crimes, including shootings by teenagers and teenage gangs.

Younger Adolescents. Violent crimes are not the primary activities that make young adolescents delinquent. The most common delinquent behavior, particularly in middle school, is vandalism: breaking into a school and damaging classrooms, spray painting the walls of the school building or elsewhere, cherry bombing mailboxes, breaking light bulbs. Other behaviors regarded as delinquent are habitual disobeying of parents or teachers, habitual truancy from home or school, endangering the health or morals of the young person or others, patronizing what are considered disreputable places, or associating with immoral persons.

Students in middle school vandalize to a far greater extent than do older adolescents. One study of middle-class youngsters (Richards 1979) showed that nearly half the adolescent students in the study in grades below the tenth admitted to at least one incident of school damage, and nearly one-third admitted involvement in at least one incident of school defacement. Surprisingly, girls in this age group were found to vandalize more frequently than boys. Richards reports that the degree of vandalism among the students studied was related most directly to vandalizing behavior of friendship groups and also to anger toward parents. Apparently, the friendship group serves as the model and reinforcer for vandalizing behavior; anger toward the adult culture probably serves as a catalyst.

It is often a source of anger to many young adolescents that many behaviors that make them delinquent and result in punishment are behaviors that would not be considered delinquent if the perpetrator were an adult. The habitual truant, for example, is what is called a **status offender,** one who is delinquent by virtue of his or her age. The adult who goes to a bar instead of to work might be frowned on by neighbors or might lose a job but would not be placed in a detention home, as may be done to the habitually truant youngster. Clearly, categorizing such behaviors as truancy with more serious behaviors contributes to the difficulties of helping troubled youngsters.

Older Adolescents. How does high school delinquency differ from that of younger students? As just noted, younger adolescents engage most often in vandalism. Older delinquents are more likely to become involved in serious crimes, including shootings and muggings. There has been a 200 percent increase in the rate of homicides among adolescents over the past twenty-five years (Wynne 1978). Today in some states, juvenile offenders in their early teens are required to stand trial as adults, with the possibility of life in prison.

Drugs and Alcohol

The problem of drug use by young people has been discussed at great length by educators and the general public since the 1960s. Although many students get through the adolescent years without getting involved with drugs, use of such illegal drugs as marijuana, LSD, stimulants, depressants, and narcotics is still a serious problem among adolescents.

Alcohol. Surveys have shown, however, that among students from seventh grade onward, use of alcohol actually is more prevalent than of any other substance (see Fig. 9.1). Over eighty percent of students surveyed in several New York state schools, for example, admitted to drinking alcohol, while only one-third used marijuana (Lipton *et al.* 1977). In another study, twenty-three percent of a national sample of thirteen- to eighteen-year-olds reported being drunk at least four times (Wynne 1978). In many cases, they are simply trying to be more grown up.

Because three-quarters of all adults in this country drink alcohol, and one-tenth are problem drinkers, it is not surprising that young adolescents try drinking. A

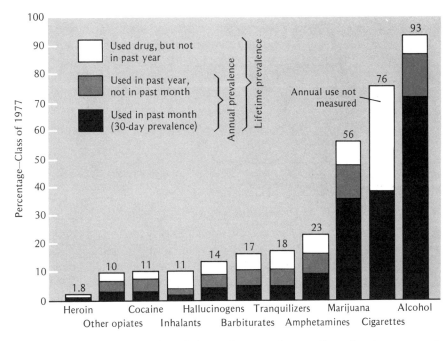

Fig. 9.1   Lifetime, annual, and thirty-day prevalence of use (and recency of use) for eleven types of drugs, class of 1977 (N = 17.087). (Johnston, Bachman, and O'Malley 1977).

HIGHLIGHT 9.2 HELPING THE TEENAGE ALCOHOLIC

What can be done to help the teenage alcoholic? Keep in mind the tremendous amount of denial that the teenage alcoholic exhibits, and consider some basic guidelines that can be followed (Dykeman 1979):

1. *Establish concern.* Talk with the alcoholic and convey your love and concern over the changes in his or her behavior.

2. *Reflect the behavior.* There will be changes in the alcoholic's behavior. You can do much to facilitate the alcoholic's awareness of his or her condition by reflecting on such changes in attitudes, values, and behavior.

3. *Do not accept excuses.* Alcoholics often develop excuses and rationalizations to avoid talking about their problem. Do not fall for it. Keep on the topic.

4. *Confront the alcoholic.* It is possible to reject the behavior of the alcoholic while, at the same time, to accept him or her as a person. You can convey love and concern while not condoning drinking behavior.

5. *Seek professional help.* Enlist the aid of a professional. Most communities have a council on alcoholism that can provide a professional counselor. Alcoholics Anonymous offers assistance to those in need.

QUESTIONS FOR THOUGHT

1. Why is it particularly important for the teenage alcoholic to know that he or she is accepted as a person?

2. Does Alcoholic Anonymous in your community offer special services for teenagers? Why?

*Reprinted from Dykeman, B. Teenage Alcoholism: Detecting those Early Warning Signs. *Adolescence,* Summer, 1979, 14(54), 251–3. Used with permission.

---

related factor is the attraction provided by the media. People who drink are consistently portrayed as popular, beautiful, and sophisticated. The message conveyed is that the developing youngster will be equally appealing if he or she drinks.

Psychologists have listed special characteristics to identify adolescent alcoholics. Dykeman (1979) suggests that adults look particularly for the following symptoms, which can be more readily identified with the teenage alcoholic:

Failing grades at school

Sudden decrease in handwriting skills

Shortened attention span

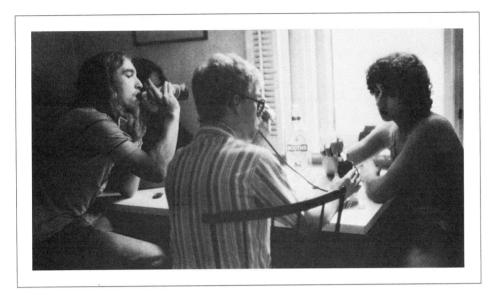

Alcohol is the most widely used drug among high school students.

Absences and tardiness at school

Inability to cope with frustration

Constant changes in the peer group

Irritability with family members and previous friends

Suspiciousness of friends, other students, and teachers

Rebelliousness

Giggling and giddiness

Low capacity to persevere

Lying to parents and teachers

Impulsive behavior

Frequent trips to the doctor or school nurse

Promiscuous behavior

Drugs. The desire to keep up with peers, to be one of the gang, is another reason that adolescents turn to alcohol or to illicit drugs. Pope reported

A little while ago, there was an article about drug use among younger kids in some magazine. The article had a photograph of a bunch of fifth or sixth graders sitting around smoking dope. The picture was probably simulated; probably none of the kids in the picture had even seen any dope. But the effect of the picture was that sixth graders all around the country looked at that article and said, "Gosh! I'm really getting behind. Here I am turning twelve years old and I haven't even smoked dope yet!" And so, of course, he smokes dope a lot sooner than if he'd never seen that picture. . . . Two seventh graders started doing dope just because they had seen that article. Of course the article said in words, "Isn't it terrible, all these little kids doing dope," but on another level it was saying "Hey, kid, this is where it's at. It's time that you get with it" (Pope 1971, p.1).

Experimentation with drugs and alcohol does not necessarily lead to serious problems. Usually when youngsters become dependent on drugs, they are having difficulty coping in many areas of their lives. Adolescents who become heavy users of many illicit drugs, however, tend to have strong feelings of **anomie,** or separation

Some teenagers use marijuana to increase intimacy and intensify social interactions.

of themselves from the norms of society, and alienation. They report often a lack of authentic meaningful relationships with others, including their peers. They tend to have confused senses of identity and frequently feel inferior or powerless. Often, they are fearful of independence (Coleman and Broen 1972).

Some drugs, such as marijuana, frequently are used by adolescents in groups for the purpose of increasing intimacy and intensifying awareness. For this reason, Goode (1969) classified marijuana as a **sociogenic drug,** a drug that stimulates social activity.

Regular marijuana users usually began by conforming to a peer group that uses marijuana. Even though regular marijuana smokers often smoke alone, novices first learning tend to do so in groups. The friends might be gathered together at a party or in the park. The students who have the marijuana are expected to share it. Given a hypothetical situation in which some member of the group did not pass a joint, one informant exploded, "It just doesn't happen. Nobody would let it happen; they'd just take it away from him" (Zimmerman and Wieder 1977, p. 201). Students report, "You can't help but get stoned. It's really hard to turn the thing down in front of the other kids." Smoking pot, like many other adolescent behaviors, is reinforced by the peer group, with peer-group members serving as models.

Drug Addiction

What is the adolescent addict like? More often, the addict is male rather than female. The addict's behavior is likely to be quiet, polite, easily influenced, and withdrawn. Although addicts have probably smoked marijuana, they generally have few friends among their peers, unlike social marijuana smokers. Withdrawal and alienation from adult and peer society increases with drug addiction. The early adolescent addict usually has obtained drugs from an acquaintance of the same age in school, rather than from an adult pusher. The fact that parents and the law are more concerned with the often-nonexistent adult pusher rather than the real people in this narrowing world makes the addict feel even more alienated from adult society (Jalkanen 1973). The young addict today is often a middle-class youngster who began the habit in early adolescence. The initial motivation may have been social, and the addict may never have wanted nor expected to develop an addiction.

Sexually Transmitted Diseases

Sexually transmitted diseases (STDs) have reached epidemic proportions in the United States over the past several decades (see Fig. 9.2). They are a growing problem among middle schoolers, although the problem is more prevalent among the high school- and college-age groups. Teenagers account for twenty-five percent of the one million reported gonorrhea and herpes cases each year (Rienzo 1981). Unfortunately both STDs and pregnancy often occur before students really understand

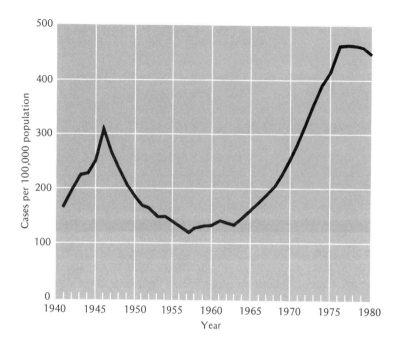

Fig. 9.2   Reported civilian case rates of gonorrhea in the United States. (Center for Disease Control 1979).

their sexuality. Psychologists stress the importance of sex education courses for early adolescents so that they can learn to take care of their bodies (Yarber and McCabe 1981). As long as many parents and children do not discuss sex openly while the peer group does, educators suggest that sex education offered by the schools may be the best prevention. The problem of STDs is common across many Western industrial countries, and sex education is compulsory in many countries today, including Denmark, Sweden, Czechoslovakia, and East Germany. In the United States, where control of the curriculum lies within each school district, we have no national program. According to many psychologists, too few schools offer sex education, and when they do, they often do not explore students' feelings about their sexuality. Discussion of sexual values would seem to be as essential in the education process as explanations of physiology and hygiene.

Runaways and Castaways

Running away from home frequently is triggered by many of the same factors that cause teenagers to be truant from school. Some of the specific reasons given by runaways for leaving home are feelings of alienation, parental abuse, parental alcoholism, and school problems. In the second half of the last decade, researchers began to take note of a subgroup of runaways, called **castaways** or **throwaways.**

The term *castaway* was coined by Gullotta (1978) and refers to young people who do not willingly choose to leave home but, for whatever reasons, are kicked out of their homes by the parents and then reported either by parents or police to be runaways. In one study done by a large volunteer shelter program, twenty-four percent of runaways were found to be castaways (Gullotta 1978).

Runaways face serious dangers when they leave home. Usually, they have no money or work skills and quickly turn to prostitution or drug dealing. Their inability to support themselves in legal jobs makes them easy targets for unscrupulous adults. The number of adolescent girls and boys engaged in prostitution has never been adequately estimated, because arrest and juvenile court statistics do not include those who do not get caught, but the increasing number of female adolescent runaways is rapidly dropping the average age of prostitutes who are arrested. In the 1970s, arrests of prostitutes under age twenty-five in New York jumped from twenty-four percent to seventy-four percent. Brown (1979) reported that in Boston, the average prostitute is only twenty years old, and in Miami, the average age is only eighteen.

Dropping Out of School

Some problem behaviors are unique to the high school years. Dropping out of school, for example, although it can occur illegally in earlier years, is legal for sixteen-year-olds in this country. Dropping out is a behavior that presents many problems to adolescents, whether they drop out legally or illegally, and it continues to be a major problem in the Unites States. The reasons that adolescents give for leaving school are varied and are generally related to continued failure to learn. But dissatisfaction with achievement is generally part of a larger picture of discontent. Dropouts report that they feel "useless"; they often leave school in order to get relief from unbearable conditions, only to find that conditions away from school are equally unbearable.

Pathologies of Adolescence

Early adolescents sometimes exhibit a variety of problem behaviors that require the help of a psychologist. As in earlier years, boys show a greater prevalence of problem behaviors than girls, particularly in the areas of adjustment, antisocial behaviors, gender identity, and neurotic and psychotic disorders (Eme 1979). Boys tend more often than girls to suffer from **enuresis** (nighttime bedwetting), sometimes until high school. Enuresis has been related to tension and anxiety (Sours 1978). Young adolescents of both sexes tend to be more disobedient in school than they were in earlier years. At the same time, many young adolescents are so conscientious about doing well and, at the same time, getting along with peers that they become very anxious.

HIGHLIGHT 9.3 ANOREXIA NERVOSA

Phyllis seemed to be the ideal teenager: a high achiever, well mannered, and smart. At seventeen, she was a member of the Honor Society, president of the French Club, and secretary of the Junior Class. Phyllis was also attractive, at least until she began to lose weight. At five feet, four inches, she weighed 115 pounds in September. By April, she was down to 91 pounds. Her parents took her to a series of physicians who gave her repeated medical examinations. Their conclusion: Phyllis seemed to have no medical problem that they could diagnose. Phyllis had a dangerous habit, one that finally was diagnosed properly and that led her to a psychotherapist's office and to years of therapy to work out the problem.

The cause of Phyllis' weight loss: **Anorexia nervosa,** a pathological loss of appetite typically accompanied by deficiency symptoms and emaciation. Phyllis simply could not eat. The taste of food made her nauseous. When she succumbed to pressure from her parents to eat, she could get a little food down, but most often she regurgitated it a half hour later.

Phyllis began her syndrome convinced that eating really was not good for her, that she had a terrible figure, and that she would be far more attractive if she could just lose a little weight. She told her mother about her feelings at the time but did not think that her mother took her seriously. "Mother only worried that I wouldn't be able to do my schoolwork if I went on a real diet," she told the therapist later. "So what I began doing was the easy way out. I ate a little when she really forced me. Then I ran to the bathroom when no one noticed and threw up." Phyllis quickly developed a dangerous, humiliating habit that she could not stop when she tried. Eating became a horror for her. Her parents' nagging became more of a horror, and she began to make more and more excuses to stay in her room and away from her parents who, she felt, just did not understand. Before it was over, Phyllis was in the emergency room of the local hospital being fed intravenously. From there she went to a halfway house for victims of anorexia nervosa for three months. At nineteen, she was able to resume her schoolwork, a shaken young woman who still had years of psychotherapy ahead of her before she was safe from the dangers of the illness.

Anorexia nervosa was a little-known illness just ten years ago. Then college and high school counselors began to be aware of the increasing numbers of girls who seemed to be losing weight for no known reason. In severe undiagnosed cases, anorexia nervosa victims have died of malnutrition. For increasing numbers like Phyllis, therapy is begun soon enough to help.

What causes anorexia nervosa? Psychologists say that the victims like Phyllis usually begin their problem behavior at seventeen or eighteen. Many are talented and attractive girls who are depressed or under stress because of school or home tensions. Most are perfectionists who are always afraid that what they are doing is not good enough. Because they are ashamed of their "habit" and hide it from family members, accurate numbers of anorexia cases are hard to determine until they become severely ill like Phyllis. But anorexia, like its counterpart illness, **bulimarexia,** in which forced vomiting is interspersed with massive overeating, is a serious and spreading disorder affecting thousands of teenagers and young adults today. Many hospitals throughout the country have established eating-disorder clinics to provide psychotherapy to help these young people. Treatment begins with diagnosis; therapy involves learning to stop the dangerous behavior, which for anorexia victims is like addiction, and at the same time, learning to deal with the anger, frustration, or loneliness that brought it on in the first place (Langway 1981)

QUESTIONS FOR THOUGHT

1. Anorexia nervosa seems to be increasing in our society. What might be some of the particular tensions facing this age group at this time that initially bring on unwanted behaviors of this sort or another (for example, alcohol or drug addiction)?

2. What particular role do you think that the premium on thinness in our society plays in the development of this disorder? What might we as a society do about it?

As noted earlier, most adolescents engage in fantasies and daydreams. Fantasies permit privately indulging in the new wishes and hopes that emerge during adolescence. Used in a realistic manner, fantasies can provide the impetus toward achieving positive goals. A girl who dreams of becoming a physicist might ask her science teacher for books to read that describe what it is really like to be a physicist. Sometimes, however, fantasies are a response to high levels of anxiety, and they are experienced by young adolescents as feelings of estrangement from their own bodies or surroundings. When indulged to the extent that the adolescent begins to feel "flat" or "like I'm dead," fantasies may indicate serious depression.

Depression. Serious depression, accompanied by suicidal fantasies, is characterized by such symptoms as sadness, feelings of helplessness, loneliness, feelings of loss, unspecified feelings of "being bad," negative self-esteem, feelings of being unable to help others, inability to be liked, expectations of being used by others, feelings that the situation will not change, and feelings of being wicked, hated, and justly punished (McConville, Boag, and Purohitt 1973). For most early adolescents, feelings of depression come and go. They are affected in part by biological forces acting on all adolescents and in part by personal experience. Day-to-day and hour-to-hour changes in mood are not uncommon. Each adolescent responds to these changes in his or her own way, depending on the personal meaning of the events. For better-adjusted early adolescents, periods of depression are few and not very severe. For the disturbed adolescent, they are more frequent, more severe, and in some instances, lead to self-destructive behavior.

In later adolescence, simply because of the greater independence that high schoolers have, pathological behaviors more often take serious turns. Antisocial behaviors become more dangerous as boys and girls become physically more capable of doing more damage. Seriously depressed early adolescents frequently become seriously depressed older adolescents. Those who exhibit these symptoms frequently and in severe form sometimes commit self-destructive acts.

Depression and Suicide. Adolescent depression and suicide always have existed. In recent years, however, the incidence of suicide has been rising. According to the National Center for Health Statistics, more than 1000 children between the ages of ten and fourteen committed suicide in the 1970s, an increase of 32 percent from the previous decade (Jerome 1979). The suicide rate among adolescents between fifteen and nineteen years old increased 171 percent from 2.8 deaths per 100,000 to 7.6 deaths per 100,000 in the past two decades. Suicide ranks as the second most common cause of death in this age group (Rosenkrantz 1978; Wynne 1978).

Adolescents make three times as many attempts at suicide as do adults. Psychologists concerned with the large number of suicide attempts point out that these attempts can be interpreted as pleas for help and have proposed a number of explanations (Wynne 1978). For one thing, many adolescents have a great deal of difficulty resolving identity problems associated with sexuality. Adolescents who are free to experiment sexually may experience great feelings of guilt at the same time and develop negative self-identities. For another thing, many adolescents have a great deal of difficulty developing the ability to be independent of their parents and to define their roles in the world. When the conflict between doing what they want in the world and doing what they perceive to be what their parents or other adults expect them to do becomes severe, they experience disorder, rage, and despair that frequently are self-destructive. Suicide may not be so much the outcome of societal pressure to develop proper roles, but pressure without social support to do so. Thus the adolescent may be aware of what he or she should do but does not know how to accomplish this goal and has no place to go for assistance. The result sometimes is a suicide attempt.

Suicide attempts of adolescents frequently are associated with loss. They occur most frequently, for example, after the death of a loved one or after a divorce of a parent. Adolescents who experience loss may respond with feelings of depression.

The rate of suicide is particularly high among adolescents.

Those whose parents divorce and remarry may feel not only loss of the divorced parent but also loss of the parent who has taken on a new spouse. Early adolescents are particularly vulnerable to the stresses of depression and feelings of loss because of the other physiological and psychological changes taking place within them. Increasing numbers of parents who are busy with jobs or do not spend enought time with their children may be a contributing factor in depression among adolescents.

Suicide attempts or suicide do not mean that a teenager has not been loved or physically cared for. They probably do mean that he or she was not needed by others in a tangible fashion. Some researchers point out that one result of the increasing numbers of personal interests and career aspirations of adults in our society in recent years has been an increasing psychological neglect of children and adolescents (Bronfenbrenner 1970). This neglect is manifested not only by teenagers' stress on peers as an attempt to reduce feelings of alienation but also by increased feelings of low self-esteem and depression.

Many adolescents are alienated within their homes from parents with diverse outside interests that keep them occupied. Researchers suggest that educational systems, which segregate adolescents from adults who used to support them and that supply instead less reliable sources of support in peers, foster the alienation that can lead to suicide. Instead of teaching adolescents to develop intimate relationships with others, Wynne suggests that "the present school system seems scientifically designed to teach students how not to handle intimacy and, consequently, how to fear and flee from it." "But," he continues, "wholesome intimacy is essential to satisfying life" (Wynne 1978, p. 313). It is those adolescents who do not develop intimacy with others and feelings of being needed who are most likely to attempt or commit suicide.

While the new social roles of adults in our society as well as the schools may contribute to problems of alienation in large part, adolescent depression and suicide have their roots in childhood depression that goes unrecognized. The majority of children and early adolescents who suffer depression are not diagnosed properly and do not receive treatment of any kind. From this group probably emerge the later adolescents or young adults who, during a further depressive episode, commit the final destructive act (Poznanski, Krahenbuhl, and Zrull 1976). For this reason, it is important to explore some of the reasons that adolescent depression often goes unnoticed and to examine some of the ways it is dealt with in our society.

Frequently, the depressed adolescent is not noticed either at home or in school, in large part because depressed behavior is not likely to disturb what is going on. The depressed adolescent, unlike the aggressive student, tends to withdraw. Busy parents and teachers frequently do not become aware of the problem because the teenager does not draw himself or herself to their attention. For this reason, one way that has been used to help the depressed teenager is parent and teacher education. Movies, magazines, and newspapers all have been introducing material in recent years on the symptoms and dangers of extreme withdrawal in this age group. Parents and teachers who are aware of students with these symptoms are encouraged to help through individual or group therapies. One type of therapy that is increasingly used and that seems to be effective is **family therapy,** in which trained therapists work together and separately with family members, helping them to recognize the feelings and concerns of both parents and children and helping them learn to express their needs to each other in ways that they all can understand.

HELP FOR TROUBLED TEENAGERS

In recent years, new programs have been designed to help troubled adolescents. For students with learning difficulties, new teaching methods are being explored. For example, teachers are seeking ways to increase student motivation. A variety of alternative schools have also sprung up to try new approaches to educating young people.

The open-classroom concept today is in use in both elementary schools and high schools. Open classrooms are based on the belief that students learn best when they themselves help design their learning experiences and when they are permitted to pursue interests independently and at their own desired pace. In most instances, the open classroom is not, however, a "free school"; the learning environment is carefully structured to engage the students' attention with many options and alternatives. Variations of the open classroom have been implemented with some success at the high school level, both in regular schools and in special programs for dropouts and potential dropouts. Little research on the results of this type of classroom has been done. Many parents feel that too little learning may be taking place, as evidenced by the pressure in many communities to provide "fundamental schools" where subjects are clearly and thoroughly taught. Other parents feel, however, that the open learning environment allows many of those adolescents who never would try to learn in a traditional classroom to make serious academic efforts.

Because one of the main goals of adolescence is to develop job skills and independence, another method under experimentation is skills training. Dropouts and potential dropouts are learning realistic work skills through work–study programs in which skills training is incorporated into work settings (Borrow 1973). Finally, although controversy still exists as to whether the proper place for sex education is in school or at home, there is almost no dispute that sex education in some form is necessary. A number of public school programs have also experimented with role-play courses in marriage. A high school in Portland, Oregon, has even designed a course in which students role play divorce and then work out the consequences of their decision together.

Alternative Schools

Large numbers of so-called alternative schools were opened in this country in the 1970s. Most are small, privately operated programs that attempt to reach young people who have been in trouble or who show signs of being in difficulty in the future. Schools that successfully motivate these students and that do not have discipline problems seem to have a number of characteristics in common: They are small; student schedules are flexible; there are rules; and there is frequent informal interaction between students and teachers (Duke and Perry 1978). These are characteristics that tend to allow students opportunity to model their teachers' behaviors closely and that allow the schools to provide reinforcement for behaviors other than grades.

Because of the increase of adolescent pregnancy in the past decade, many cities have developed alternative schools or classes for these young girls. In alternative schools, the general curriculum and prenatal education are provided together with guidance in caring for babies and, more generally, in managing households. High school academic courses are offered so that pregnant teenagers can qualify for regular high school degrees.

Crisis Intervention

Crisis intervention centers, places where teenagers can go for help when they feel that they are in states of crisis, have sprouted all over the country and in most urban areas. Counselors in these centers provide help for drug addicts, advice and shelter for runaways, and counseling for a wide variety of problems, including suicide. Most large cities today have crisis intervention centers that deal with drug abuse only. In these centers, young people are encouraged to come at any time that they need immediate help. Trained counselors as well as other young people who themselves have had involvement with drug problems are available to provide assistance. One method that has proved most effective uses therapy programs in which young people help each other. The helper-therapy principle works, according to its developer, because it provides support for both the drug abusers and the therapists (Reissman 1965; Jalkanen 1973). Drug users who are runaways are particularly helped by counselors who provide a great deal of social reinforcement. One reason is that runaways, who usually have a great deal of self-doubt, tend to manifest a readiness for counseling because of their need of reinforcement (Wolk and Brandon 1977).

Medical Strategies

Recognizing that adolescents not only have difficulty communicating their problems to others but also have special problems related specifically to their age, many physicians began in the 1970s to specialize in adolescent medicine. Adolescent pediatricians frequently are used as sounding boards by their patients, who want to talk about anything from acne to sexually transmitted disease, from weight control to birth control. Some large cities, such as New York, set up special medical clinics serving adolescents on an out-patient basis. Psychologists and psychiatrists established special adolescent practices to deal exclusively with adolescent problems. As the 1970s ended, it was possible in many cities for adolescents to receive birth-control information and to be tested for STDs or pregnancy through free clinics without their parents' knowledge.

Psychological Strategies

Psychological counseling and therapy today take a variety of forms. One experimental counseling program to try to deter adolescents from entering into serious delinquent behavior involved having inmates of a maximum-security prison give the youngsters straight talk about the grim realities of prison life.

Family counseling is based on the premise that the problems of the troubled individual are closely tied to the dynamics of the family as a whole.

Family counseling, in which troubled adolescents are counseled together with their parents and other members of their families, is being used increasingly as a method of helping teenagers who have trouble controlling their behavior toward others as well as teenagers who are anxious, depressed, or suicidal (Beal and Duckro 1977; Schomer 1978). Psychologists as well as psychiatrists advocating family therapy reason that it takes more than one person to cause a family crisis and that working with all members of the family rather than just the troubled youngster is likely to provide better solutions to the problem. The plan involves diagnostic family interviews (in some cases, the counselor observes the family in their interactions at home) and private consultations, depending on the situation. Family meetings are used frequently as one way to teach adolescents about sexuality and family life and to improve parent–child communication on this topic (Goodman and Goodman 1976). Psychologists and psychiatrists also provide important help in diagnosing learning problems and in individual therapy for these problems when necessary. Counseling services are available privately and through such public agencies as social services and other governmental agencies that deal specifically with adolescent problems. Rehabilitation counselors are helpful in providing vocational assistance.

When should help be requested from a psychologist or psychiatrist, and when from a counselor? There is a disagreement within the professions as to specific rules. Some researchers suggest that a good policy to follow is to make use of psychological or psychiatric help for involuntary referrals (as when the school principal sends an unsocialized, aggressive child for help) and that counseling be reserved for voluntary referrals (Nugent 1973; Taylor and Hoedt 1974). The most important attribute of the social worker is his or her ability to function as a liaison between the family and other service agencies. The social worker also is trained to understand the needs of people of different backgrounds, an important asset in dealing particularly with minority-group children and their families.

THE CASE OF RICHARD HARRIS—AN ANGRY HIGH SCHOOLER: A CASE STUDY FOR CLASS DISCUSSION

I. Identification and Sources of Information

Name: Richard Harris

Address: 7521 Bennett Street, Chicago, Illinois

Race: White

Sex: Male

Age: Sixteen years, two months

School: Hudson High School

Sources of Information

1. Personal observation
2. Interview with student
3. Interview with mother
4. Interview with teacher

II. Family History

Richard is the oldest of four children, all males. His three younger siblings are in grades five, six, and eight at Harrington Elementary School. All are in good health and doing well academically. Mrs. Harris appears to be interested in her sons, is an active member of the PTA, and is well known to the teachers both at Hudson and at Harrington because of the time she has put in doing lunchroom duty and helping in extracurricular activities.

Mrs. Harris is forty-five, a graduate of an exclusive "ivy league" college. She married shortly after graduating and has never been employed outside the home. Mr. Harris has a master's degree in business administration and is employed in a local brokerage house. Economic status of the family is high.

III. Case History

Richard was a good student throughout his years in elementary school. He got along well with his family and peers, seemed to make friends easily, and generally appeared to be a well-adjusted child. When he enrolled at Hudson, however, his behavior seemed to change abruptly. Richard still obtains moderately good grades, although his first two report cards in the tenth grade contained some Cs and a D, the first in his academic history. His parents were not as concerned about the grades on Richard's report as they were upset at the belligerent attitude Richard seemed to take about the grades. When his father suggested that he be punished, Richard became very angry, stormed out of the house, and stayed away from home through the dinner hour. When he finally returned home, he refused to talk with anyone in the house and locked the door of his room so that he could not be disturbed.

THE CASE OF RICHARD HARRIS

The Harrises decided to call in a psychologist when Richard's behavior had been hostile for several months. He refused to eat with other members of the house, often staying out with his friends until after nine o'clock each evening. His teachers reported that he attended classes regularly and did not misbehave there but that he seemed uninterested in anything going on around him.

In an interview with the psychologist, Richard reported that school was dull and uninteresting and further that his family was as dull as school. He said that he did not want to grow up and be "dull like them." He said also that many of the students in his class had experimented with drugs but that he had not as yet tried them. He did not see any reason why he should not experiment, however, because whatever he did, he knew in advance that his parents "would say it was wrong."

IV. Present Status, Diagnosis, and Prognosis

For the present at least, Richard is not in serious trouble. There is no reason that he should not be able successfully to complete the tenth grade if he tries. But according to the psychologist preparing the case history, Richard may well be in serious difficulty if he does not learn to communicate with his parents, and his parents with him. It is recommended that Mr. and Mrs. Harris and Richard come together for family therapy at the local guidance clinic. Because Mr. and Mrs. Harris have sufficient funds, they may decide instead to seek guidance from a private practitioner.

Questions for Class Discussion

1. What could be the major source of Richard's anger? Was there something that Mr. and Mrs. Harris probably could have done to prevent it?

2. Is the peer group playing an important role in Richard's behavior? What is your evidence for your answer?

3. The psychologist preparing this case history recommended that the Harris family undergo therapy in order to learn to communicate with one another. What is the prognosis if they do not go with the therapy, given what you know of the psychosocial development of high school students?

SUMMARY

Conflict between adolescents and their parents is widespread in American society and in other societies where adolescents have a great deal of choice as to which roles they will take. American society particularly seems ambivalent about the social status of adolescents. Adolescents are striving for independence, which may lead to frustration at the same time that it helps development of a positive identity. During this period, teenagers use their parents as model figures; parents' behavior and attitudes toward moral issues will be reflected in their children's behavior and attitudes.

The middle school was designed to meet the separate and special needs of the pubescent and early adolescent years. This can be a difficult period for many children, who at this age are often engrossed in themselves and pay inadequate attention to what is going on around them. In high school are made the first decisions concerning future life work, and school achievement becomes particularly important at this time. Evidence shows that achievement in American schools, as measured by standardized tests, is decreasing, both among middle-class students and among their poorer counterparts.

Peer-group social structures are usually well established by high school, and grouping is encouraged by teachers and parents as well as by peers. Some time in high school, as teenagers begin to acquire strong self-concepts and feel more secure about their identities, the need to conform begins to decrease. Among the problems that face adolescents is shyness, which can interfere with interpersonal relations and with school achievement. The development of extreme shyness may be related to parental attitudes and behaviors.

Delinquency among adolescents is on the increase. Researchers suggest that adolescent problem behavior occurs because of poor self-concepts caused by inadequate reinforcement at home. Younger delinquents often commit vandalism, a behavior probably produced by anger toward the adult culture and reinforced by friendship groups. Older delinquents are more likely to become involved in serious crimes. The use of drugs, particularly alcohol, is widespread among teenagers, and is encouraged by the media and by peer pressure. Although some drugs, such as marijuana, stimulate social activity, heavy use of most drugs tends to lead to alienation and withdrawal from adult and peer society. Sexually transmitted diseases are also a growing problem among adolescents. Educators suggest that sex education programs in the schools may be the best preventive.

Adolescents sometimes exhibit problem behaviors requiring professional help. The most common pathology is depression accompanied by suicidal tendencies. Although parental neglect as well as our educational systems may contribute to problems of alienation, adolescent depression and suicide have their roots in childhood depression that goes unrecognized.

Many new programs have been designed in recent years to help troubled adolescents. Open classrooms, for example, are structured to engage the student's attention with many options and alternatives. Skills training is being offered to dropouts and potential dropouts. Alternative schools attempt to reach and motivate young people who have been in trouble, including pregnant teenagers. Crisis intervention centers provide help for drug addicts, advice and shelter for runaways, and counseling for a wide variety of problems, including suicide. Among a variety of forms of psychological therapy now available is family counseling, in which troubled adolescents are counseled together with their parents and other members of their families.

 FOR FURTHER READING

Adolescence. Libra Publishers, Inc., P.O. Box 165, 391 Willets Road, Roslyn Heights, New York 11577. This quarterly journal is devoted entirely to issues dealing with adolescents. The journal attempts to represent all points of view on topics dealing with life between twelve and twenty. Many articles from *Adolescence* are discussed in this chapter.

Gagney, T. *How to Put up with Parents: A Guide for Teenagers.* Champaign, Illinois: Research Press, 1980. This paperback book brims with examples from Dr. Gagney's experiences as a school counselor. Written in an easy-to-read conversational style, the text guides teenagers in helping themselves and their parents toward happier, fuller lives.

Wilson, J. *The Rights of Adolescents in the Mental Health System.* Lexington, Massachusetts: D. C. Heath, 1978. This book explores the rights of adolescents receiving mental health services, placing particular emphasis on the respective rights of parents and children when parents voluntarily commit their offspring to mental institutions. In arriving at a model procedure for admission, treatment, and release, Wilson explores the constitutional dimensions of the relations among parent, child, and the state.

Early and
Middle Adulthood

Part V

Preview Questions

- How does the stage of youth differ from adolescence, and what factors cause this new stage to arise?

- Can you describe one important characteristic of young adults in each of the following aspects of their development: personal, social, and physical?

- How does the cognitive development of the young adult differ from that of the later adolescent?

- What differences does Kohlberg see between the moral reasoning of youth and that of young adults, and how does Gilligan's "love ethic" compare with Kohlberg's postconventional morality?

- How do college cheaters differ from noncheaters, and at which of Kohlberg's stages are most of the cheaters operating?

- Can you list four major developmental tasks of the young adult and describe some difficult problems associated with each?

- What are several reasons why marriages between partners who are under age twenty don't last as long as those between older adults?

- How do sex roles in two-income families differ from those in one-income families?

- What are some major reasons why people choose to remain child-free?

- Can you list and explain the seven major values that Hoffman and Manis found to be associated with having children?

- What factors have caused so much single parenting in our country, and what are some of the problems that often attend it?

- Can you describe the following alternative life-styles and compare each to a legal, heterosexual marriage: cohabitation, social-contract marriage, singlehood, homosexuality, communes, and group marriage?

10

Youth and
Young Adulthood

Youth and young adulthood together encompass for most the period roughly from eighteen to twenty-five years. These are stages in which most people stop rebelling against society. For some, these stages mean a transition from dependence to independence; for some, they involve a continuation of schooling and continued dependence; for most, they mean finally establishing an identity and thinking about, if not finally settling into, a career and a life-style.

During youth and young adulthood, individuals reach their full potentials, both physically and psychologically. Psychological research regarding these stages is oriented more toward life tasks and roles than toward age-related development. In other words, the study of adulthood is somewhat different from the study of childhood and adolescence. Once they become adults, people at the same age may be at different stages in the roles they have assumed.

YOUTH: A TRANSITIONAL STAGE

Erik Erikson (1968) described most of the period from eighteen to twenty-five years as late adolescence, a life stage in which individuals concentrate on the problem of determining their individual identities. Kenneth Keniston (1972) pointed out, however, that many characteristics of this age group differ significantly from those of adolescence. Individuals, often those of college and graduate student age, may no longer spend their energies rebelling against the adult generation. At the same time they cannot seem to "settle down" the way their parents did and are not ready to commit themselves to what are generally regarded as adult tasks, such as work and family roles. He referred to people in this situation as **youth.** Unlike their adolescent predecessors, youth are no longer struggling so hard with the problem of defining themselves. They have just begun to sense who they are, but they have not yet resolved conflicts that exist between the self and the outside society.

A good example of the difference between the stages of youth and young adulthood appears in the descriptions of John and Sally, two twenty-year-olds. John, at twenty years, is majoring in engineering because his parents always wanted him to be an engineer and not because he wanted to be one. John is vacillating between finishing school and dropping out. He may well decide at twenty-two to go to graduate school and study mathematics. Later, he may decide to study history. If so, he may continue to expect financial support from his parents and will not make a career decision that ties him down for a few more years. John is an example of a young man at Keniston's stage of youth, and he will remain at this stage until he is able to make some serious decisions about his life and what he wants to do with it.

Sally, at twenty years old, has resolved conflicts between the self and the outside world, conflicts that John is still dealing with. Sally has dropped out of college and begun a successful career as a photographer. Her parents are upset because they wanted her to get a college degree, but Sally knows that she enjoys her work and has had a first extremely successful year working as a free-lance photographer. She has had two photos accepted in national contests and has a contract to work for a popular magazine. Sally does not want to get married, which has upset her mother. Although she thinks she might want to go back to college some day, she feels that professionally it is best to be out in the field. She understands the reasons that her parents worry and hopes they will not worry too much. Even if they do, however, she thinks she has resolved her career problems in an appropriate way. Sally, in contrast to John, is a young adult.

During the period of youth, according to Keniston (1972, p. 128) "family tradition, family destiny, family fate, family culture, and family curse arise with full force." The question of whether to live one's parents' life, or to what extent to do so, becomes a real and active question. Youth often develop compulsive needs to live out for themselves the destiny of their parents, "as if to test its possibilities and limits, experience it from the inside, and (perhaps) free themselves of it" (Keniston 1972, p. 120). They may alternately try what they consider this destiny, then reject it, only to try it on again a few months or a year later.

Youth is a period, according to Keniston, best described as a state of flux in which feelings of estrangement from the world alternate with living within it and feeling the freedom to change or become anything one wants. Youth recognize that

In contrast to adolescents, who have not yet resolved problems of identity, young adults have defined their goals and are actively pursuing them.

they will become older and that aging will change their status in the world. They develop during this period the foundation for later commitments, but they are not yet ready to make them. Today, millions of young people from the industrial nations of the world experience this stage before going on to young adulthood.

How did the stage of youth emerge? One of the major factors seems to be the increasing complexity of modern society. Young people today must adjust to a rate of social change so rapid that it may render obsolete many institutions, values, and technologies within the lifetime of each generation. To find a place in our society often requires a high degree of education. As a result, it has become commonplace for college students to pursue graduate and postgraduate training, thus postponing, sometimes until their late twenties or early thirties, entry into the work force. Many young people who have not taken special training face a somewhat different problem in establishing themselves in satisfying jobs. Thus a common reaction for middle-class young people in this situation is to "drop out" for a while to travel or to explore other alternatives to settling down.

When youth resolve the conflicts that Keniston described, they move on to the next stage, young adulthood. Some young people go through this period quickly. Some take a great deal of time. Some extremely mature individuals omit the period of youth and go directly to young adulthood where they take on seriously the problem of defining the roles they must play in order to be independent. It is during the stage of young adulthood that young people select and adjust to their careers, lifestyles, and adult relationships in preparation for the years ahead.

Not all young people fall into the stage of youth or the stage of young adulthood. Some remain perpetual adolescents. Some remain in the stage of youth for a very long time and become sources of worry for the adults who love them.

 ## DEVELOPMENT DURING YOUNG ADULTHOOD

Keniston, in his description of youth, focused primarily on the problem of identity. Both youth and young adults can be described by other changes that take place in their development. Here we will focus on their personal, social, and cognitive development and on the tasks and moral concerns that characterize this period.

Personal, Social, and Physical Development

During young adulthood, interpersonal relationships assume a great deal of importance. A young person who has established a strong sense of identity learns to value dissimilarities as well as similarities in other people. Often, young adults develop a capacity to like their parents as individuals and to look at them more objectively than they were able to do during adolescence. Often, they become more concerned with family tradition.

One intimate relationship that has been the focus of recent study is that between young adult women and their mothers. In many cases, conflicts begin during the adolescent period. Adolescent girls often become jealous of their mothers at this time: They feel that restraints are being placed on them, and they resent the freedoms, sexual and otherwise, that they feel their mothers have. Mothers and daughters often do not begin resolving these problems until much later, in young adulthood.

Many young women who were at odds with their mothers during high school now begin to understand their mothers better. Friday (1977) pointed out, however, that many young women (and older women too) have difficulty developing personal characteristics that are different from what their mothers want. These women often are terribly fearful of behaving in ways that might cause them to lose their mothers' love. According to Friday, even when young women during the period of youth

During young adulthood, many women experience a better understanding of their mothers.

swear that they will never develop the personal characteristics that they think they dislike in their mothers, they usually develop many of the very same characteristics later in life. This is only logical. After all, their mothers usually were their models during the important years of childhood and adolescence.

For both women and men, a central concern of young adulthood is the establishment of intimate heterosexual relationships. For most, it is the beginning of a long period of learning to get along with an intimate partner and establishing a sexual and interpersonal relationship that is meaningful for both partners (Vaillant and McArthur 1972). Young men tend to be less concerned about finding a marriage partner and more concerned about first establishing themselves in desired life-styles or careers. Young women often are interested in finding mates, although this may not be as true of highly educated women as it is of less-educated women. In our society, early socialization teaches young women, but not young men, to read romance stories.

Youth and young adults usually are at their peak health, strength, vitality, and athletic ability. Women in their twenties are at the best age biologically for childbearing, even though many wait until their thirties when more problems (such as decreased fertility and birth defects) are more likely. Men are at their sexual peak in their twenties, whereas women reach their peak somewhat later. The twenties are a peak time for athletic achievement. It is at this period of life that men and women who have trained during their earlier years win major awards in athletic competitions.

Cognitive Development

As discussed in earlier chapters, during the stage of formal operations described by Piaget, individuals develop the ability to think and solve problems without concrete stimuli provided as aids, and they develop the ability to make hypothetical deductions, combine propositions, and isolate variables to test hypotheses. Piaget (1972) has suggested that the stage of formal operations is not necessarily attained in adolescence, although many adolescents do reach this stage. Rather, many postadolescents in the stage of youth are just developing the ability to think at the formal operational stage. Their growing awareness of the variety of ways of looking at issues may make it difficult for them to make decisions or accept the dominant social values. Not until later, when they mature to young adulthood, will the social world become an organic unit with laws, regulations, roles, and social functions into which they fit.

Young people develop gradually the ability to solve problems in ways that meet the needs of others as well as themselves. For example, it is during young adulthood that many young people first learn to compromise in their professional aspirations; some may select careers that are not as exciting to them as others but that allow them time to spend with their families.

Moral Development

Theories of Moral Development in Youth and Young Adulthood. According to Kohlberg, early adulthood is the period during which some people reach what are termed the postconventional levels of moral reasoning. The person operating at stage 5, social contract orientation, places value primarily on the individual rights of others. The individual operating at stage 6, morality of individual principles of conscience, is concerned primarily with deciding the morality of issues on the basis of individual conscience rather than societal laws.

Young adults may be ready to respond to moral issues at postconventional levels of moral reasoning, according to Kohlberg, although most youth in fact do not do so. Some research has suggested that students moving through high school and into college are able to reach higher stages of moral reasoning at more rapid rates than those who do not go on to college (Rest, Davison, and Robbins 1978). Other research indicates that a person's experiences as an adult are more important than specific educational programs in determining whether or not that person will reach the postconventional levels of moral reasoning (Papalia and Bielby 1974). It has also been found that those young people who continue their education in fields of study that emphasize moral reasoning (for example, philosophy) often are able to solve moral dilemmas at higher levels than those who do not concentrate in such areas (Kohlberg 1971).

A psychoanalytic critic of Kohlberg, Gilligan (1976), points out that for young adults, a more mature stage of functioning may exist beyond what most researchers consider postconventional morality. Gilligan suggests that understanding the reasons for feeling as they do and acknowledging realistically the reasons for their behavior is much more important to young adults than reaching the next level of Kohlberg's stages of morality. Gilligan calls this understanding a "love ethic." He suggests that adults who are able to love meaningfully meet their mutual needs in relationships most effectively out of psychological self-understanding rather than out of moral obligations in which they feel the necessity to sacrifice.

College Cheating. One issue of concern related to moral development of young people is college cheating. In recent years, it has become clear that the cheating that occurs so much among high school and early-grade students continues to exist openly among college students. Successful cheating can be observed in every sphere of scholastic and professional endeavor in the United States. Cheating on college campuses has become a lucrative and well-organized national enterprise grossing millions of dollars annually. Some outfits have coast-to-coast networks of franchises established to sell already-prepared term papers and theses; others prepare research papers to order. Cheating in the business and political worlds also is commonplace, and college cheating probably reflects this general acceptance of unethical behavior in our society.

The following classroom experience occurred at a major American university several years ago and provides a method of demonstrating the ease with which many college students choose to cheat.

In the fall quarter, Dr. James Smith (not his real name), Visiting Professor of Economics, strode into the principles of economics class and made the following surprise announcement: "You people have won. I'm going to sell grades. Grades will go to the highest bidder. If you people are so happy with the free-market process, why don't we just let the market system dictate who gets what?"

According to newpaper reports of the event, Dr. Smith then called in a colleague to "auction off the grades without prejudice." While a few students objected to the auction—some even complained to the dean and department chairperson—approximately ninety percent of the class participated. Professor Smith collected almost $1000, averaging $85 for an A in the course, $55 for a B, $35 for a C. Smith accepted IOUs from most of the students. One student, however, insisted on his accepting $80 in cash. Another student, observing the absence of several friends who were cutting class, bought extra Cs and Ds and tried to make a profit by advertising them for sale in the school newspaper.

All students participating in the auction were dismayed later to find that it was a hoax.

QUESTIONS FOR THOUGHT

1. If you were given the same opportunity to buy your grade as the students in Dr. Smith's class, what would you do?

2. Why do you think most of the students participated in this program rather than objecting to it?

What qualities characterize college students who cheat? Bushway and Nash (1977), in a review of the research on cheating behavior, describe the cheater as being somewhat lower in ability or school achievement than the noncheater and having more close friends and classmates who cheat than the noncheater. Students who cheat generally tend to be more extroverted, as well as more tense, irritable, and anxious than noncheaters.

Many situational factors seem to affect whether or not students cheat in any given situation. Steininger, Johnson, and Kirts (1964) reported that students who might not have cheated otherwise may do so if the professor leaves the classroom.

Clearly, the chances of success in cheating constitute a major situational determinant. Successful cheating that can be observed by other students leads to more cheating and less guilt by those watching the cheating models. Advertisements in student newspapers for prepared class outlines, lecture notes, and term papers, together with student models who respond to the advertisements, clearly encourage the situation.

Generally, students report that cheating is justified when what they call success or survival is in jeopardy. Students who cheat in order to stay in school may be responding at Kohlberg's stage 2, in which their behavior is designed to obtain rewards. Cheating for "good" causes, such as helping out a friend, is looked on more favorably than for personal reward (Savitsky and Babl 1976); individuals who cheat because they believe that they will gain respect of their peers and serve community welfare may actually be operating at a higher level (stage 5) according to Kohlberg's stages of moral development. In fact, however, most are operating at stage 2, seeking to avoid disapproval or dislike of peers. Bushway and Nash (1977) suggest that there are numerous reasons for cheating. This may explain why cheating is so widespread.

DEVELOPMENTAL TASKS OF YOUNG ADULTHOOD

Youth and young adults have a number of specific developmental tasks to meet if they are to become mature adults. According to Erikson, a young person must first establish a sense of identity. In addition, youth and young adults need to become independent of their families, to start planning careers, and to make decisions about the life-styles they will lead in the future and the partners with whom they might want to share their lives. Youth who refuse to "settle down" or who are unable to accomplish these tasks may not reach the next stage of development. As a result, they may never be able to form lasting relationships or serious commitments, no matter what their chronological ages. For those who enter into marriage during young adulthood, the tasks are "to achieve a balance between settling down and moving forward; growing new roots while striving for achievement; meeting new obligations in young adulthood toward spouse and perhaps children; and investing oneself in the lives of a few significant others to whom one will be bound for years to come" (Neugarten 1979, p. 890).

Establishing Identity

Although youth have begun to sense their identities, they are often still in a period of exploration. For some, this may mean dropping out of college to explore living in a youth commune, traveling, or trying different kinds of work. Some may stay at home and be supported by their parents. Others may want to be independent from their families but have not developed the skills that allow them to do so. Establishing an identity ultimately involves finding what one wants to do and what kind of lifestyle will be most satisfying. It means making commitments to others and discovering ways to fit into the larger society.

Developing Independence

Independence is an attribute reinforced by our society, desired by youth, and attained by most young adults. About fifty percent of young adults leave their parents' households by age nineteen and establish their own homes either as singles or as new marital partners (Hill 1977). Work is the most dominant force in establishing the split. Young men and women already in the work force account for most of those who leave home, although major differences between sexes are apparent in the ages at which leaving home and becoming independent occur. Young men are more likely to leave home when they find a job. Young women who do not go on to college are most likely to remain home until they marry. Young men, more than young women, are likely to strike out on their own if they have a large number of siblings also living in their parents' home. College students tend to leave home at later ages than young people who enter the work force right after high school. This probably occurs because higher education tends to increase economic dependence on families. In the 1960s and 1970s, when the number of individuals seeking higher education beyond the bachelor's degree was still increasing, many young people remained dependent on their families well past the age of twenty-five.

Occupational Planning

The world of work is important in the lives of adults. Careers, away from or inside the home, provide sources of identity both for men and for women and are important contributors to both positive and negative self-concepts. What we do to provide for ourselves and our families generally describes for us what we are. Careers that command a great deal of respect enhance positive self-concepts, whereas those that command little respect create negative self-concepts.

During the 1960s, many college students enrolled in liberal arts programs that were either marginally related or unrelated to specific careers. This pattern reflected both the affluence of the times and the orientation of young people toward individual development. In the 1970s and early 1980s, by contrast, college students have more frequently enrolled in programs that lead to specific jobs than in general liberal arts programs. In 1979, more than twice the number of students graduated from higher educational institutions with business and management degrees than with any other type of degree (Fact-File 1980). This trend appears to reflect current

Graduation from college is followed by one of the most important tasks of young adulthood: planning for jobs or careers and entry into the work force.

concerns about being able to achieve financial success in an uncertain economic environment.

Interests in career development and career choice differ considerably between young men and young women. Many young women still go into traditionally "feminine" career areas, such as education, nursing, or physical therapy. This is particularly true for those women who have been raised in traditionally oriented families and whose mothers encouraged a traditional sex role orientation. Salley (1977) found, for example, that young women who tend to compete in college in intellectual, athletic, and political arenas tend to be less oriented toward "feminine" interests and more oriented toward high achievement than their noncompetitive peers. In addition, these high-achieving women tend to have mothers who encourage the "masculine" competitive behaviors.

In another study, Crawford (1978) reported that young women who choose careers in traditionally "feminine" occupations tend to be more conservative with respect to marital relationships and obligations than their less-traditional peers. On the other hand, those who are more liberal in their vocational, educational, intellectual, and sexual behavior are more likely than the others to be found in male-dominated careers. Clearly, many women, both older and younger, are still traditionally oriented today. Hacker (1980, p. 14) suggests that it was the very large number of these women who felt threatened by changes in women's roles who opposed the Equal Rights Amendment. The ERA, according to Hacker, "was definitely a women's issue, with women dominating both sides of the struggle. . . . Women opposed the ERA because it jeopardized a way of life they had entered in good faith."

While women have become an increasingly important part of the labor force in the United States, the topic of career development for women still is ignored or given only cursory treatment by many schools. One result is that young women who already have traditional "feminine" role perceptions tend to choose traditionally "female professions" without ever learning very much about what other options are available to them (Crawford 1978). Young women who have learned through maternal models, for example, that math is "too hard for women—and, after all, jobs associated with math are for men. . . ." are much more likely to choose programs in college related to more "feminine" activities, such as education or speech therapy, than to more male-dominated activities, such as computer science or engineering.

For most young people who do not go to college, graduation or dropping out of high school is followed by entry into the work force. Some young people who go to work without benefit of higher education have feelings of low self-esteem. Many others, however, find good jobs in their areas of interest. Employment enables them to become independent of their families and to take on the roles of young adults. It is the young adults who fell at the bottom of the achievement ladder in high school who have the most serious difficulty adjusting to being in the job market. Without skills, they are not attractive to most prospective employers and find quickly that they are spending a lot of time in the unemployment lines or working at poorly paying, unskilled jobs. The current economic climate of high unemployment also poses problems for young people who have done well in school but who have not trained in areas where there are openings. Still dependent on their families for help, these young people regard independence as something to be feared rather than to look forward to.

Problems of Minorities.   For many American youth and young adults without higher education, a steady job is a distant hope. High unemployment has traditionally been the lot of young people, especially minority young from urban ghettos. Vander Zanden (1978) reports that white racism seems to be a factor contributing to high black unemployment, for the unemployment rate of white high school dropouts, at least in the 1970s, was lower than that of black high school graduates. Shirley Hufstedler, Secretary of Education in 1980, pointed to the extreme psychological burdens that lack of employment for developing young adults places on them, and she noted that unemployment for this group causes the nation as a whole to "pay a terrible price" (Guidepost 1980).

The armed services have provided good career opportunities for many minority youths who cannot find jobs in the cities.

Young people going to college delay for some years the job problem of less-educated youth. Those who enter college with poor records in high school are less likely than their high-achieving peers to do well in college and to learn skills that will be of use to them when they graduate, although many students do "find themselves" during their college years and are very successful.

Problems Facing College Graduates. A number of problems also face college graduates seeking to enter the job market. Increasing numbers of students are entering college without basic knowledge of reading, writing, and arithmetic necessary for success in college. In the late 1970s, a steady decline in standardized achievement test scores was noted for students applying to colleges during the past several years. Although in 1978, for the first time in a decade, the average verbal score of seniors taking the test for application to college did not decline further, the math score had gone down that year yet another two points. The result may be an increasing number of low-achieving college students who ultimately graduate from college but who still lack the skills that make them useful to potential employers. Many other higher achievers, because of economic problems in the society that are causing a restricted pool of jobs, find themselves in the same boat. Many Ph.D.s today, for example, cannot find work in their fields and are frustrated by conflicts between their expectations and reality.

Sex Differences in Career Choice. Young men and women still differ in the amount of higher education they receive, even though female enrollment in graduate programs has been increasing. Marini (1978) suggests that a primary reason fewer women than men go to graduate school is that young women today still are less career oriented than men and less concerned about the money they will earn. Even today, most college women tend to plan their adult lives in large part according to their husbands' careers rather than their own. When they opt for careers after marriage, their later social roles still are determined primarily by their husbands' occupational status.

A major reason for women's differing educational expectations seems to be related to a sex role prescription against high achievement in women (Stiver 1976). The young woman who is first in her college class may earn a fellowship to graduate school, but she might reduce her chances in the marriage market in the process. The woman who gives up the fellowship and chooses marriage instead may give up the opportunity for reaching full potential.

Women marry about two years earlier than do men (U.S. Bureau of the Census 1980). To the extent that they enter the work force immediately after completing their schooling, they are likely to begin their first full-time jobs somewhat earlier as well. College women generally still train in areas that are considered traditionally "feminine." Cerra (1980) noted that even though the number of female college graduates increased in the past two decades by almost 400 percent, the vast majority of degrees they earned were in six traditionally female-dominated areas: education, English and journalism, fine and applied arts, foreign languages and literature, and nursing and library science. For a variety of reasons, fields dominated by women have always paid less than fields dominated by men. This is one reason that the average female college graduate working full time earns only sixty percent of the salary earned by a man with the same education working full time. The gap in earnings is expected to remain well into the 1980s.

Job Expectations. In general, both young men and young women regularly change their aspirations as well as their jobs several times during the period from eighteen to twenty-five years. Many young people entering the work force find a great disparity between what they think they will be and what they are able to become. This is particularly true when they first start out. Gottfredson (1979) found that this disparity decreases, particularly for young men, with chronological age. In Gottfredson's study, approximately fifty percent of eighteen-year-olds working full time had aspirations vastly different from what they actually did on the job. Among subjects aged twenty-five, however, well over seventy percent of the verbal descriptions of career aspirations matched their actual jobs. Gottfredson suggests that two factors are responsible for this difference. First, as they begin to understand the job market, many young people adjust their aspirations to more realistic levels. Second, people often are better able to find jobs in their areas of interest as they gain more experience working. This view is supported by another study (Holland 1973), which found that twenty-five-year-olds hold significantly more jobs in fields related to investigative, social, and enterprising activities than eighteen-year-olds who want to work in these areas. The younger workers tend to hold jobs that require less thinking and more physical labor because they do not have the experience for the jobs to which they aspire.

Sexual Intimacy

Sexual Activity. Youth and young adults have more opportunity and much more freedom to engage in sex than do adolescents. Most young people who have not engaged in sex during adolescence do so between the ages of eighteen and twenty-five (Zelnick and Kanter 1972; Levin and Levin 1975). The extent of exploratory sexual activity during youth is correlated with the age of first sexual intercourse; those who have engaged in sexual intercourse at earlier ages tend to be most experienced at later periods of life. One study of 509 male and 476 female college students (DeLamater and MacCorquodale 1979) showed that seventy-five percent of college males and sixty percent of college females had experienced nonmarital coitus. These data point to an increase over time in incidence for both males and females. They also suggest that increasing numbers of female college students are engaging in nonmarital intercourse.

Data gathered in the 1960s and 1970s showed a dramatic change in both the sexual behavior and the sexual attitudes of college females. In the past, many males and females alike believed that although sexual freedom was permissible for males, it was not acceptable for females. This "double standard" was reflected in the views of both males and females concerning just who should engage in sexual intercourse. In one study (King, Balswick, and Robinson 1977), college males and females were asked in 1965, 1970, and again in 1975 to respond to the five following statements:

1. I feel that premarital sexual intercourse is immoral.
2. A man who has had sexual intercourse with a great many women is immoral.
3. A woman who has had sexual intercourse with a great many men is immoral.
4. A man who has had sexual intercourse with a great many women is sinful.
5. A woman who has had sexual intercourse with a great many men is sinful.

The results showed that among females, the view that premarital sexual intercourse with one or many people is immoral or sinful decreased significantly from 1965 to 1975. The same view among males also decreased significantly. Males, however, tended at the outset to be more liberal than females, and by 1975, there was virtually no difference in attitude.

These findings can be interpreted to mean that an increasing liberalization of male and female behavior seems to be approaching a single premarital sexual standard, at least for college youth. Youth who have left school and are out in the job market tend to express less liberal attitudes than their college counterparts, even though they engaged in greater amounts of sexual exploration at earlier ages. The double standard is more common among adults who are lower on the socioeconomic scale (King, Balswick, and Robinson, 1977). This fact might well account for the difference.

Intimacy vs. Isolation. Sexual activity by itself does not provide what Erikson (1968) termed intimacy, or the ability to be psychologically close to another person. We learned earlier that according to Erikson (1963; 1968), adulthood is the stage of life in which individuals either develop the ability to be intimate with another person or else suffer isolation. According to Erikson, the answer to the question "Who am I?" comes in part from the identity established by interactions with others. By young adulthood, individuals arrive at a sense of who they are, which is reaffirmed by others in their personal and social lives. Once a sense of self is sufficiently developed, individuals can begin interacting with others more intimately—that is, they can express their own feelings and interpret and experience the feelings and behaviors of others without being afraid of losing their own identities.

The young adult who can be intimate with another person experiences feelings of closeness in his or her encounters with that person. This process allows young adults who are able to be intimate to develop smoothly functioning personalities and sets the stage for still more intimate social interactions. Once their own identity issues are resolved, these individuals then can relate with others not

Table 10.1

Frequency of Reported Stresses between College and a Ten-year Follow-up: Interview of Sixty-three Postcollegiate Subjects

Stress	Frequency
Shattered love affair	25
Career development slow or disappointing	24
Parents' marriage broken by divorce or marked by conflict	24
Harassed by indecision about vocational choice	23
Long-continued financial dependence on parents after college	22
Relation to mother too close emotionally, too dominated by her, or too distant	22
Neuroticism in parent	19
Relation to father too close emotionally, too dominated by him, or too distant	19
Financial pressures (regardless of income level)	19
Financial stringency or insecurity in parental home	16

Source: Cox (1970).

solely for the purpose of helping themselves but also to know and sense the other person with whom they are intimate. Such individuals do not suffer from feelings of isolation.

Among youth and young adults who have not yet established permanent relationships, establishing and maintaining intimacy often is a source of stress. Cox (1970), in a study of young men and women in the first ten years after college, showed that shattered love affairs were listed more frequently than any other stresses. Other serious stresses related to intimacy included relationships with parents or between mothers and fathers. Table 10.1 lists the frequency of reported stresses in Cox's group.

According to Erikson, individuals who have not yet established their own identities are unable to experience intimacy with other people. Such individuals may suffer from feelings of isolation or anomie, as it is called, even while they are spending their time with many people or engaged in extensive close physical contact during sexual activity. Accordingly, some young people searching for intimacy try to use sexual encounters to reach their goal, but instead realize only isolation because they have not been able to resolve their own identity crises.

SELECTING A LIFE-STYLE

Young adulthood brings with it the possibility of choosing a life-style, which is the manner in which each individual chooses to pursue his or her day-to-day activities. Young adults may choose, for example, whether or not to pursue a married life-style and whether or not to have children. In our society today, although most people marry, they may also choose to live in any one of a variety of alternative living situations at least for a period of time. Among these alternatives are cohabitation with a member of the opposite sex, homosexual living, or single living. Their choices affect the ways they live, the people with whom they live, and their day-to-day contacts with others.

Sometimes, young people still in Keniston's stage of youth choose alternate life-styles in order to avoid making commitments. The life-styles of youth, unlike those of young adults, are recognizable by periods of flux and indecision. Youth are just coming to grips with the decisions that they must make in the future. They may decide, for example, to cohabit for a while before deciding to live alone. Later, they may decide to cohabit again with another person. For the time being, such youth are alternating their life-styles in order to experiment and to delay the decisions that ultimately must be made (Dyer 1979).

Young adults choose alternative life-styles for other reasons. Often, life-styles are not deliberately chosen. For example, a young adult may be forced by a divorce to be single. Some young adults remain single because they have not found a suitable marriage partner. Many other circumstances, such as divorces that are still pending, might force a young adult today to cohabit rather than to remarry. Some young adults today choose other alternative life-styles to meet a variety of individual interests, needs, and goals.

Marriage

Almost all Americans marry, most of them as young adults. Young women now marry later than their mothers did. In 1960, only twenty-eight percent of women aged twenty to twenty-four were unmarried. By 1974, this percentage had jumped to forty percent (Glick 1975). At the end of the 1970s, the median age for young women marrying for the first time was twenty-two years; for men it was twenty-four (U.S. Bureau of the Census 1980). More people under the age of thirty-five were single in the 1970s, pursuing various life-styles, than at any time since the turn of the century (U.S. Bureau of the Census 1980). Call and Otto (1977) point out three socioeco-

For many people, marriage is a rite of passage representing entry into the full responsibilities of adulthood.

nomic factors that affect the age of marriage. These include father's occupation, mother's occupation, and mother's education. Young people from lower socioeconomic backgrounds whose parents have had little education and whose fathers work at lower-status jobs tend to marry earlier than middle-class youth. These young people leave school earlier, enter the work force earlier, and feel themselves prepared for marriage earlier than their middle-class counterparts.

While women tend to be slightly younger than their husbands, most husbands and wives are similar with regard to both race and education. College graduates tend to marry college graduates with some exceptions; high school graduates tend to marry high school graduates. Men, more than women, tend to marry partners with slightly lower levels of education (U.S. Bureau of the Census 1980). For young women planning to go on to higher education or to earn graduate degrees, this fact sometimes poses a problem, for it may decrease the potential number of men available as future husbands.

Marital Stability. One of the most important variables affecting whether or not a marriage will endure is age at marriage. Considerable evidence shows that people who marry young are much more likely to have their marriages end in divorce. This is particularly true of couples who marry prior to age twenty (Lee 1977). Many explanations have been given for the difficulties of youthful marriages. These range from the immaturity of youth, escaping the anomie of youth (the feeling among some young people of alienation from the rest of society), and marrying just to spite parents to inability to choose the "right" spouse. One of the important factors contributing to marital difficulties among those who marry at sixteen or seventeen is premarital pregnancy. Many young women who decide to marry at this age because they are pregnant find that marriage does not provide the easy escape from their problems that they thought it would. The result often is divorce (deLissovoy 1973).

Another significant factor is economic problems. Because young people who marry before age twenty usually have entered the work force directly out of high school, they often encounter severe economic stress, especially if a child is involved and the wife cannot work. One study found that young married women are less unhappy with their objective standards of living than they are with their standard of living compared to their unrealistically optimistic expectations (Herrmann 1965). It is likely that young married men have similarly unrealistic aspirations of what they can expect in their standard of living. This would seem to result from insufficient preparation for marriage, work, and life. The high school football player who marries the class beauty queen the day after graduation may get stuck working as a clerk in a grocery store or may be selling used cars. This is a far cry from what he or his young wife expected of life while she rode in the queen's parade at the last football game during senior year. After two babies, life often is far more difficult than either expected.

For young people who marry in their mid twenties, the likelihood that their marriages will endure increases, as do their life satisfactions and realistic aspirations. These couples tend to be better educated, have smaller families, and be more mobile than younger couples. Wives under twenty-five years of age, more than any other age group, tend to be in the work force (U.S. Bureau of the Census 1980). Many of these young women put off having children for the time being; having children tends to discourage women from working outside the home for at least the first six years. The more education young wives have, the more likely they are to be working or looking for work. Only approximately one-third of young wives with high school educations are employed outside the home as compared to more than one-half of those who have completed college. For college graduates, not only has there been more time to prepare for an occupation, but there is also an objectively better chance to achieve a higher standard of living.

The Two-Income Family. Most young people who decide to get married today plan, at least at the outset, to have both partners work. In many cases, the reason for this is economic, but partners may also work to meet their needs of self-esteem. Some young married women, especially those who have planned for a career, look forward to long periods on the job, although in fact, the percentage of these women who remain employed after the births of their first children decreases by about sixty percent. For those who remain on the job, the percentage of working hours decreases, on average, by about the same amount (Cramer 1979). Leaving the work force to stay home and raise children decreases the economic opportunities for young married women and may make unrealistic their career aspirations. This is one important factor in the decision of increasing numbers of young married adults in the 1980s not to have children. Studies have shown, however, that wives still do most of the housework (Stafford, Backman, and DiBona 1977), although more young working couples than in the past are sharing many of the tasks formerly believed to be the domain of the wife, such as grocery shopping and preparing meals.

The growing number of young married women in the work force is causing many married couples to examine their attitudes toward themselves and their work. In a few marriages, partners have reversed traditional roles and have had husbands take over household duties completely and wives earn the family income. In some of these cases, husbands have taken over household duties while their wives continued their educations. (See, for example, Schwartz and Sullivan 1978.) In general, our society seems to accept rather then reject the role changes that are occurring.

Parenthood: To Be or Not to Be

The vast majority of married couples want to become parents. A study done in 1970 (Pohlman 1970) showed that more than ninety percent of American married women at that time wanted children. Estimates of childlessness among married people in this country varied from six to fifteen percent. It is not clear among this relatively low percentage just how many childless couples chose to remain childless or did not have children because of infertility.

Choosing to be Child-Free. Many married couples today, unlike those of a decade or two ago, are choosing not to have children. A small but growing number of young couples today, particularly those who are highly educated, do not want to become parents. Many of these individuals prefer to call their decision **child-free**, rather than childless, because their choice, they feel, is a positive rather than a negative one (Lind 1977). According to the Census Bureau, in 1978, six percent of wives aged eighteen to thirty-four expected not to have children, and one in six expected not to have any children or to have only one child (U.S. Bureau of the Census 1980).

Why is this so? One reason that an increasing number of young couples gave is their attitude toward the problem of increasing world population (Westoff and McCarthy 1979). Individuals with this concern indicate that the present rate of increase in world population is unprecedented in history. If sustained, in less than 700 years, there would be one person for every square foot on earth (Freedman and Berelson 1974). Demographic data on population rise has led the movement for "zero population growth" to campaign actively for smaller families.

Coupled with concern for overpopulation for many of these young adults is a pessimism related to political and ecological problems of today. The class speaker for the 1969 Mills College graduating class described this view in her statement: "Our days as a race on this planet are numbered. . . . I am terribly saddened by the fact that the most humane thing for me to do is to have no children at all" (Peck and Senderowitz 1974).

A more important reason than either of these seems to be the desire of wives who have outside employment, especially those pursuing careers, to remain in the work force. A number of researchers have found that decisions as to whether or not to have children are related directly to career decisions made at the time (Cain and Weininger 1973; Schultz 1973; Willis 1973; Turchi 1975). Some young couples are concerned about the opportunities, both economic and personal, that might be lost to them if the wife stops working to raise a family. The loss of income is, of course, an obvious concern. Some relatively affluent couples, however, are more concerned about restrictions on their freedom. The freedom to take vacations and to come and go as they please is restricted for married couples who become parents. Gars (1975) reported that one major concern of child-free wives is that their careers not be disrupted. Such women do not want to stop careers to raise children and therefore elect to be child-free. In interviews with eighty-nine voluntarily childless women, Fabe and Winkler (1979) found that many women reported that they felt that their own mothers were "burdened and oppressed in their roles as women." Each of these daughters felt that she wanted a different life-style that would afford her more freedom. Furthermore, Houseknecht (1979), in reviewing studies of voluntarily childless women, found that many of them remained childless because they tended to believe that children would disrupt their marriages and that the responsibility of motherhood was not what they wanted. According to Houseknecht, many of these women were highly educated career women.

In the past, voluntarily childless couples experienced considerable social stigma. Today, however, this option has become more acceptable. Articles presenting couples' personal reasons for deciding not to have children appear frequently in the mass media. Child-free is a term coined to negate the idea that "if one is without children, one is 'less'" (Peck and Senderowitz 1974).

Today, married families may select life-styles in which children play no part, with less pressure from family and friends to "fulfill their parental duty." The statement of one young professional woman typical of this new life-style follows:

> John and I decided before we were married that childrearing just wasn't our thing. I was interested in pursuing my own career, which involves a lot of traveling. And John just wasn't interested in staying home and changing diapers while I was on the road. We haven't felt that we've missed much. Compared to our friends with children, we lead a much more exciting life—we take more vacations, travel, and socialize. Many of our friends admit that they are envious.

Choosing to Have Children. Most married couples do still want to be parents. In some studies of women who already had had two children each, ninety percent reported that they had wanted the second child (Pohlman 1969a; 1969b). Why? Psychoanalytic theory proposes that childbearing is proof of a woman's feminity and a man's virility. Anthropologist Margaret Mead (1949) suggested that women have an "innate need" to have children. According to psychoanalytic theory, motherhood is a major source of feminine identity. The modern women who can fulfill both professional and maternal roles satisfactorily may well feel quite remarkable, perhaps even "superfeminine," although frequently physically tired. In this sense, having children not only helps mothers define their roles, but it also helps them receive the adult status they desire (Hoffman and Hoffman 1973). Having children helps fathers in the same sense prove their virility and their male role.

Studies done in many different countries show that in all of them, parents tend to feel that having children is a way of achieving a sense of immortality. Children provide a tie to the past and the future because they carry on one's genes (Hoffman and Manis 1979). Another reason people have children is social pressure. Such pressures are deeply rooted in the ancient Judeo-Christian tradition. Today, the popular media, while acknowledging women's changing roles, still depict the nuclear family as the ideal unit. Even though social stigma against voluntary childlessness is decreasing, young women who deliberately decide to remain childless still may be viewed by many people as being self-involved and neurotic (Rainwater 1965).

ECONOMIC COSTS OF PARENTHOOD

According to the Bureau of Labor Statistics, in 1975, the cost of raising the average baby to adulthood in the United States was $70,000. In round figures, parents spent an average of $2500 on recreation for each of their children, $4000 for medical expenses, $6500 for housing, $7000 for clothes, $13,000 for food, and $14,000 for miscellaneous expenses. The total cost of education for children through college in 1975 was $24,000.

Creeping inflation since the mid 1970s has made all of these figures significantly higher. By the end of the 1970s, researchers estimated that the cost of raising children to age eighteen, without including any of the costs associated with college, was an average of $56,000 for moderate-income families (Edwards 1979). By 1980, direct costs, or out-of-pocket expenses, had risen to $73,000. Basics, such as food and clothing, have increased drastically. The cost of medical care since that time has skyrocketed, as has the cost of college. Expenses involved in higher education since the late 1970s have made it impossible for large numbers of college-age students to enroll. If we include in the economic cost of parenthood the cost of sending a child to a public university, the cost of raising a child in 1980 was more than $85,000 (Espenshade 1980).

Even the basic cost of having a hospital delivery has skyrocketed, causing many young couples to look for other means of delivering their babies. In 1978, the cost of a hospital delivery in one large American city ran about $1500. Local doctors were charging between $300 and $600 for prenatal care and delivery. The cost for a four-day stay at a major obstetrical hospital was above $1140 (Sachs 1978). By 1979, the cost of hospital delivery in this country had risen to between $2170 and $2220 (Edwards 1979).

None of these costs includes the costs of nonemployment of parents or day care. When opportunity costs, income that a parent forgoes to stay home to care for children or money that pays for child care, are added, the cost of raising a child in 1980 was approximately $138,000 (Espenshade 1980). The 1980s costs exceed those of the 1970s by major proportions.

QUESTIONS FOR THOUGHT

1. Given the economic costs of parenthood, how likely is it that the numbers of child-free couples and couples with only one child will increase in the next decade?

2. Does this present any problems to our society in the foreseeable future?

Having children can decrease loneliness and alienation in families where young parents are not able to find enjoyment in satisfying employment, education, or other alternative rewarding roles. Most couples who want children report that they value a child as someone toward whom to express love and affection (Hoffman 1975; Hoffman, Thornton, and Manis 1978; Hoffman and Manis 1979). In some studies, wives separated from their husbands expressed a greater interest in having more children than did other wives (Pohlman 1969a; 1969b; Pohlman 1970). Apparently, these women used their children as sources of love and affection in place of their spouses.

Hoffman and Manis (1979) surveyed a representative sample of American married men and women, both parents and child-free couples, and identified seven major values that people associated with having children. The values that Hoffman and Manis found are described as follows, ranked in order of importance:

1. Children provide primary group ties and affection—that is, they provide love and companionship and act as a buffer against loneliness. This value appears to be more important to women, a finding that is consistent with the woman's traditional nurturing role.

2. Children provide stimulation and fun. Children are seen by parents as bringing stimulation, activity, and joy to life. Individuals referring to this value made such statements as "They bring happiness and joy" and "Just watching them grow— it's like a built-in change so that each year is different from the one before."

3. Having children provides expansion of the self. Children, in this sense, were perceived by individuals as fulfilling human needs to find meaning and purpose in life and to attain a sense of immortality by having a part of the self live on after death. Among the mothers responding, Jewish women mentioned this value far more often than Protestants and Catholics. The emphasis in the Jewish faith on children as a means of attaining immortality may account for this difference.

4. Having children provides adult status and social identity. Individuals reporting this value believe that parenthood is a sign of maturity and acceptance into adulthood. This value was reported more by less-educated and unemployed women and women who have a traditional view of gender roles. These individuals tended to define motherhood as their primary role in life and saw it as the role that gave them acceptance and status.

5. Children provide feelings of achievement, competence, and creativity. Individuals reporting this value felt that producing a child can give parents a feeling of creativity, and watching the child grow and develop contributes to a sense of parents' competence.

6. Children provide economic utility and security in old age. Children were valued by some individuals for the economic contribution they might make to the

Helping a child to learn provides a feeling of creativity and contributes to a parent's feelings of competence.

family and the security they can offer parents in old age. Not surprisingly, this was not a major value for Americans, probably because, as we have already observed, in this country children are an economic liability rather than an asset.

7. Having children provides a "moral" life-style. Raising children requires a sense of unselfishness that, according to some individuals, makes people feel the experience helps them become better as people. Most individuals responding to Hoffman and Manis did not rank this value highly. Some parents, however, did feel that having children had helped them become less selfish.

Clearly for many, watching a child develop from a helpless infant to a happy, healthy, responding youngster can be an exciting, rewarding experience in itself. The experience may be worth all of the costs discussed earlier and more rewarding than all the alternative methods of self-fulfillment available in our society. When a representative sample of Americans was asked by a researcher, "What are some of the things that you feel happy about these days?," more responses were related to children than to any other aspect of people's lives (Gurin, Veroff, and Feld 1960). As one married couple who decided to have children put it, "Mostly we wanted children because they are fun to watch and be with. And they give you an excuse occasionally to act like a child yourself. When there's a kid around, you can play with electric trains and make funny noises at the dinner table" (McGrath and McGrath 1975).

Adjustments of Parenthood. Whether or not individuals decide they want to have children, all parents are faced with many adjustments when children arrive. The arrival of even one child to a family reorganizes the life of every family member. Ryder (1973) points out that in some respects, parenthood competes with husbands' and wives' roles. Women who have a first child, Ryder reports, often feel that their husbands no longer pay as much attention to them. Russell (1974) reports that conflicts that never occurred before in relation to in-laws, fatigue, and money problems often occur after children arrive. At best, most married couples tend to feel that parenthood produces many new stresses with which they must deal.

Keeping Family Size Small. Because of the many advantages that couples feel children present and in spite of the many stresses related to the arrival of children in a family, many American couples today are deciding to be parents. At the same time, however, they are deciding to keep their family sizes small. More accessible public information about family planning has given couples control of the decision. Services provided in the last ten years by family-planning agencies through the Population Growth Act of 1970 have made birth-control information readily available to the public. Decreases in the United States birthrate have followed. With more family-planning information available, the percentage both of childless and one-child families in this country is expected to continue to increase.

Family planning has not been restricted to the use of contraceptive devices, such as diaphragms, birth-control pills, IUDs, and condoms. Today, do-it-yourself pregnancy tests are available. In New York State, where the most liberal abortion laws became effective as early as July 1970, and particularly in New York City, where major hospitals first performed free abortions, a sharp drop appeared immediately in the birth rate.

The effects of the 1980 rulings to disallow abortion payments by welfare agencies in many states, according to many analysts, may serve to increase the birthrate somewhat, although many researchers believe that it will serve only to increase the number of badly performed abortions. The next census should supply the answer. The United States has seen an increase in sterilization of both males and females. Between 1965 and 1970, the number of Americans requesting sterilization more than doubled (Osborne and Bajema 1972). By 1970, more than one in six couples who had had their desired number of children already had been sterilized. Nearly fifty percent more indicated that they would seriously consider sterilization to prevent future unwanted pregnancies (Kohli and Sobrero 1973).

Single Parenting. Married men and women are, of course, not the only people to be parents. **Single parenting**, or parenting by only one of the parents, constitutes an important life-style in the United States today because of the increase in recent years of both divorces and pregnancies among young unmarried women. For divorced people who raise their children alone, the costs—both direct out-of-pocket and opportunity costs—income, or career opportunities that are foregone in order to provide adequate child care are high. We will talk in later chapters about the life-styles that develop for parents who, because of divorce, raise their children alone.

Recent years have shown an increase also in the numbers of young women who have never married and who have chosen to raise their children alone. This increase reflects a new perspective on the part of single parents to keep and raise children without feeling the guilt that in the past was associated with illegitimacy.

Single, unmarried mothers, like divorced mothers, often have difficulty providing for their own economic needs as well as those of their children. Many of these mothers, as we have learned in earlier chapters, decided initially to keep their babies because they felt that being mothers would give them both purpose in life and someone who loves them. Unfortunately, many of these mothers did not take into consideration the problems with which they would have to deal in order to keep the family unit intact and raise their babies adequately. Some single mothers, of course, already have their educations and careers and seek the "total female experience," of which having a child with or without benefit of a husband, is one significant part (Eiduson 1974).

Cohabitation

One life-style that is common among today's youth and young adults is **cohabitation**, a full-time nonmarital living arrangement between a man and woman. Many researchers have reported that cohabitation is highly popular among young Americans, particularly college students (Peterman, Ridley, and Anderson 1974). Studies have shown that in the mid 1970s about twenty percent of young adult males described themselves as cohabiting (Clayton and Voss 1977). These researchers also found that fewer male college students (fifteen percent) than noncollege students had cohabited with a woman for as long as six months.

Other research has shown that one-quarter of cohabiting couples under twenty-five years of age included one or both adult members enrolled in college (Glick and Norton 1977). The U.S. Bureau of the Census reported that in 1970, 1.1 million couples in America stated they were cohabiting. By 1979, the number had risen to 2.7 million, with the sharpest rise in the "under twenty-five" category. Between 1977 and 1978 alone, the number of cohabitants increased by nineteen percent. By 1979, nearly three percent of all households with couples and nearly four percent of all unmarried adults lived in this type of relationship (U.S. Bureau of the Census 1980).

The trend, as these figures show, is toward more cohabitation in our society, especially if young adults are a guide. Glick and Norton (1977) point out that among people under twenty-five years old, the number of unmarried couples living together increased eightfold.

Exactly what is cohabitation? Cohabitation is both similar to and different from marriage. For some people, cohabiting may involve marriagelike commitments, although it does not legally obligate the partners. Unlike those involved in common-law marriages, most people who "live together" describe themselves as "not married" (Lewis 1973; Lewis *et al.* 1975). Cohabitation is seldom a permanent relationship. Partners change, often when apartments do not. Although most people who cohabit intend to marry at some point in their lives, they usually do not get married to each other (Newcomb 1979). Most cohabiting couples live together for a relatively short period of time. Glick and Norton (1977) report that sixty-three percent live together for less than two years before they either marry or separate. For many youth, cohabitation seems to be part of an emerging courtship pattern. Research suggests that it is not usually a "trial marriage." Rather it might be likened to steady dating of one partner. Most cohabiting partners experience no guilt about this arrangement. Companionship, sexual gratification, and economic gain serve to keep partners together for a time (Olday 1977).

Who cohabits? Clayton and Voss (1977) report that people who live in metropolitan areas cohabit more frequently than those from smaller cities or rural areas. They also found that level of education seems to be associated with cohabitation. The male cohabitants in their nationwide random sample were more likely to be nonstudents or high school dropouts than they were to be high school or college graduates. Those who select a cohabitation life-style tend, while they remain in it, to accept traditional gender roles. Couples must make many of the same decisions as married people; for example, they must decide whether to be monogamous or to have outside sexual partners. Many youth who want an opportunity for an experiment in living with a partner without requiring a longtime decision enter into a cohabitation life-style. Other young adults who, for a variety of reasons, do not want or are unable to marry also are among those who cohabitate.

Social Contract Marriages. Some adults choose to live together without legal marriage but in a way that commits them emotionally to one another and suggests more permanence than does cohabitation. Eiduson, Cohen, and Alexander (1973) called this life-style the **social contract marriage.** According to Eiduson, social contract marriages take place when young adults who feel that a bond of love and trust holds a couple together in far more important and stronger ways than the legal bond authorized by church or state make ideological commitments to one another. Individuals in social contract marriages differ in many of their attitudes both from individuals who select legal marriage and individuals who choose to cohabitate. Eiduson and Alexander (1978) found, for example, that individuals who select social contract marriages tend to be more idealistic in their values and less concerned with material possessions than individuals in either of the other two groups. They also found that fathers in social contract marriages tend to have more involvement with their young children.

The Single Life-style. Just as many young adults are choosing marriage more and more frequently without children, many others are choosing not to marry and to remain single at least for some period of their lives. Many unmarried choose to live with someone else; sometimes an apartment mate of the same sex is chosen, and sometimes the choice is cohabitation. Others choose to live by themselves. Young adults who opt for living alone, or single living, forgo many of the advantages of life long considered to fall within a family of one's own: status placement and emotional gratification (Almquist *et al.* 1978). Even so, evidence shows a marked increase in the number of individuals who, for a variety of reasons, have chosen this alternative life-style in recent years. Libby (1977) points out in his studies of single people that there are degrees of what he calls "singleness." Individuals who remain single, for example, might maintain their own households, but they spend varying amounts of times in close relationships with others. They may be single, later choose to cohabit or marry, and finally, return to a single status. The single life-style, like marriage, according to Libby, is not a lifetime commitment and may be replaced with a new life-style from time to time.

The numbers of single young adults have grown in our society; Glick (1975) reported that one in six American households consists of a single person living alone. As this change has occurred, single communities have grown up in most metropolitan areas. Today, there are "singles apartment complexes" and "singles bars." People who choose to remain single may lead active sex lives while maintaining greater freedom and independence than people who choose to marry or cohabit.

Not much research has been done on singles. Dyer (1979) points out that the future of singleness is not clear. Those who choose to remain single in their twenties might still choose to live in another manner at later periods in their lives.

The Homosexual Life-style. The idea of the homosexual life-style as an alternative to traditional way of life is highly controversial. For many generations, our society regarded homosexuality as "deviant." It was not until the mid-to-late-1970s that psychologists began to stop focussing on the causes and cures of homosexuality and began to focus on the descriptions of the homosexual life-style. Although many people today consider this life-style "alternative" rather than "deviant," many others still regard it as "deviant." When some people reach young adulthood, however, many who are homosexual elect to live with partners of the same sex. Homosexual couples live and interact with one another in most of the ways that heterosexual couples do. Bell and Weinberg (1978) pointed out, for example, that adjustment patterns in homosexual relationships are similar to adjustment in marriage. Homosexual women are more likely to cohabit than homosexual men because fewer questions are raised when two women live together (Bell and Weinberg 1978). Homosexual adults often are aware of their sexual preference during adolescence or even earlier. As young adults, they often have come to terms with their homosexuality, feel comfortable

In recent years more people have come to regard homosexuality as an alternative life-style rather than as deviant behavior.

with their sexual orientation, and have learned to function effectively in work and social roles. A growing acceptance of the idea of homosexuality as an alternative life-style has made it easier for homosexuals to establish permanent relationships.

Communes. Another life-style, popular among American youth in the 1960s and into the 1970s, was the youth commune. Initially, many communes were populated by the so-called hippies, youth estranged from what they considered to be the materialism and hypocrisy of American society. The hippie communes were characterized for the most part by open sexuality, transient commitment to the group rather than to a single partner, and an unprogrammed or even anarchistic structure. They were predominantly, though not exclusively, rural, and their members made pervasive use of drugs. By the late 1970s, virtually all the hippie communes had disbanded. The demise of the hippie communes coincided with the rapid increase of more personal sexual experimentation and cohabitation in couples rather than in groups. When communal living is tried today, it usually is in one of the more well-ordered and work-oriented collective settlements that began to spring up in the mid and late 1970s. Many collective settlements are religious in orientation; others may consist of young people in urban settings who lead otherwise conventional lives. Monogamy tends to be the rule, and drug usage either is limited or forbidden.

Group Marriage. Some young adults try, for a time, **group marriage**, an arrangement in which two married couples live together (Constantine and Constantine 1974; Duberman 1974). Typically, the couples have children born before the group-marriage arrangement (Constantine and Constantine 1974). The purposes of group marriage include a widened circle of sexual intimacy and the desire to share time and resources for the welfare of the larger group. Children in group marriages are sometimes raised communally with all adults in the extended family functioning as parents. One possible advantage of group marriage may be that individuals can be better parents when they are reinforced by the group rather than when they are alone. Group marriages typically are not long lasting, probably because of the many adjustments they require. Because group marriages are not condoned in our society, such arrangements are not widespread, and the likelihood is small that they will become a popular alternative.

THE CASE OF CARLOS DALAGO—A YOUNG MAN WHO HAD DIFFICULTY DECIDING WHAT TO DO WITH HIS LIFE: A CASE STUDY FOR CLASS DISCUSSION

I. Identification and Sources of Information

Name: Carlos daLago

Address: Los Angeles, California

Sex: Male

Ethnic background: Spanish-American

Age: Twenty-two years

Sources of information

1. Personal interview
2. Interview with Carlos's parents
3. Interview with Carlos's girlfriend
4. Interview with Carlos's counselor at the university

II. Family History

Carlos daLago is one of six children of Alfonso and Nina daLago. Mr. daLago brought his family to the United States from Mexico City twenty-five years ago. Carlos's two older brothers were born in Mexico City; Carlos and his younger sisters and brother were born in Los Angeles where Mr. daLago is employed as the manager of a supermarket. Both of Carlos's older brothers graduated from colleges in the area. His oldest brother, Alfredo, graduated last year from law school. Carlos entered UCLA with extremely high grades. He thought, in his freshman year, that he wanted to be a writer. To his parents' great unhappiness, however, he dropped out in his senior year and became instead an active member of a communal group in the hills just north of Los Angeles, Alfonso daLago told his son furiously that with three more children to send to college, he simply was unable to assist Carlos further, particularly if he were "messing up" his life. Alfonso told his son that if he wanted to remain at the commune, he did so without Alfonso's sanction. Only when Carlos wanted to return to school would Alfonso help.

(Continued)

THE CASE OF CARLOS DALAGO *(Cont.)*

III. Case History

Carlos described to his counselor in his junior year just how unhappy he was. "I think it's all meaningless—what's the point of working on the newspaper—spending all your time at the desk trying to think of something to write about—when everything you *really* need to know is out there—just waiting? You can't really write until you've lived, man!" The counselor discussed the job possibilities that might be available to Carlos if he would only "hang in." When Carlos was put on probation for bringing pot into the dormitory where he stayed frequently in his girlfriend's room, the counselor spoke up for him to the university officials. Carlos was not thrown out after the incident, in large part because the counselor described him as an intelligent, sensitive young man and said he had faith that Carlos would pull through if they gave him the opportunity.

But the next year, Carlos broke up with his girlfriend. After that, he became depressed. For the first time, he began to do poorly in classes. He did not drop an advanced writing course, but at the same time, he did not turn in any work. By mid year, he was failing that course as well as one in political science. Carlos began to spend more and more time away from the university and came out of his depression gradually after he met an entirely new group of friends. "They really know what they're doing," he told his parents. "They're sensing the world—through music and through meditation." Alfonso understood how much young people loved music, but try as he might, he could not understand meditation. He angrily told Carlos that he was lazy and would turn out to be nothing. "I worked my way up from nothing to get where I am," he thundered. "And what do I have? A somebody who wants more than anything to be a nothing!" Carlos's mother cried and begged her husband not to fight with Carlos.

In February of that year, Carlos left his parents' home. He had met, during the previous Christmas holiday, a young woman at the commune. She invited him to join her as a partner in the group. "You'll see how much you like it—there's such a feeling of satisfaction to know that you aren't building for just yourself, but for all of us as one," she crooned.

At the commune for four months, Carlos shared Ann's room in the old farmhouse. During the days, he worked the farm with the others. The group did not do very well, either with planting or with taking care of the animals. Mostly from the city, they depended on the members' getting money from their parents to pay for their food and rent. Carlos thought that that was a "cop-out" but could not think of any other way to get enough money. Carlos and Ann got along very well until Ann asked him to leave so that another man could sleep with her, "just for one night," she said. Carlos tried to accept the fact that no one belonged to anyone and that love was shared "for everyone and by everyone." Ann told him that it was the best way to live, and Carlos tried to rationalize his discomfort. He talked with the others at the commune for days about his "unhealthy jealousy." "Man, he was hung up on Ann, that was the problem. Any of the other chicks would have taken him, but he didn't want anybody—only Ann," one of the commune members commented. "That's why he finally left . . . . back to the school and to see his old girl."

Carlos visited his old girlfriend. She tried to persuade him to return to classes at the university. "It's too bad you can't get help from your father. But you could get a job and save up anyway. You'd be able to come back at least part time by September. You could work at the newspaper maybe. And if you do well, I'll bet your Dad will put up the tuition again." Carlos did not think so. And Judy, who was sharing an apartment by now with another young man, went her own way.

Carlos returned to his counselor. "You're really the only person who understands why I was unhappy. It's so hard to decide what to do." He told the counselor that he was thinking of hitchhiking across

THE CASE OF CARLOS DALAGO

the United States. "I've got to learn more about who I am before I take classes again. Maybe I'll be back in a few years. Who knows? Maybe I'll know where it's at, and then I can write about it . . ." Carlos told his counselor that he was not unhappy that he dropped out of school and lost his degree, only that he really could not communicate with his friends anymore. "And I wish my father understood that I didn't do all this just to hurt him, like he says." His father's feelings were terribly important, Carlos said, and some day Carlos would make it up to him. "Maybe I won't be a writer. Maybe I'll be a teacher . . . Who knows? It's just too much to decide now . . . ."

IV. Present Status, Diagnosis, and Prognosis

Carlos fits Keniston's description of "youth." He has not yet decided what or who he wants to be; he is unsure of himself in his relationships with women, although he is involved in continual experimental relationships. He still is sufficiently unsure to be confused as to whether the problem at the commune was related to Ann's infidelity or to his insecurity. Carlos is just beginning to understand his parents' points of view, although he cannot acquiesce to their demands. He is not really worried that he will always disappoint them, but he really is not ready to return to school yet and probably ought to look for a job for a year or so until he can make up his mind about what to do. His counselor has told him that he will help Carlos when Carlos is ready; if he wants to return to school and feels that this is the appropriate choice for him, the counselor is certain he will do well. Psychological counseling is recommended if Carlos wants it.

Questions for Class Discussion

1. Carlos clearly represents youth, as Keniston defines it. What makes Carlos different from adolescents or young adults?

2. What differences might be expected in the relationship between Carlos and his father if Carlos elects eventually to return to school? What might be expected if Carlos elects not to complete school but decides to begin instead writing short stories for publication in a literary magazine?

3. Did Carlos's relationship with Ann and the other commune members hinder or help Carlos in his attempts to reach adulthood?

SUMMARY

In the years between eighteen and twenty-five, most young people gradually stop rebelling against society, develop independence from their families, begin establishing their individual identities, and plan for the future. Some young people, in the transitional stage Keniston calls youth, have begun to sense their identities but are not yet ready to settle down. Youth is a period of alternating estrangement from the world and acceptance of it. When youth resolve their conflicts, they go on to the next stage, young adulthood. In this stage young people select and adjust to their careers, life-styles, and adult relationships in preparation for the years ahead.

Interpersonal relationships become very important during young adulthood. Often, young adults learn to view their parents more objectively than during adolescence. A central concern at this stage is the establishment of intimate heterosexual relationships. Young adults are usually at their peak health, strength, vitality, and athletic ability.

According to Kohlberg, few young adults are ready to respond to moral issues at postconventional levels of moral reasoning. Gilligan suggests that understanding one's feelings and the reasons for one's behavior represents a more mature stage of functioning for young adults. One issue related to moral development of young people is college cheating, which may reflect a general acceptance of unethical behavior in our society.

Erik Erikson has identified a number of specific developmental tasks that young adults must meet before they can go on to the next stage of development. These include establishing an identity, developing independence, choosing an occupation, and learning to become intimate with another human being.

Interests in career development and career choice vary considerably for young men and women. Many young women today still have traditional role perceptions and choose traditional occupations. In general, they are less career oriented than men and less concerned with how much they will earn. For a variety of reasons, fields dominated by women have always paid less than fields dominated by men. For many young Americans without higher education, however, a steady job is a distant hope. Young people from minority groups and urban ghettos are at a particular disadvantage.

Research shows an increasing liberalization of male and female sexual behavior that seems to be approaching a single premarital sexual standard. Sexual activity, however, does not by itself provide intimacy, which Erikson describes as the ability to be psychologically close to another person. Intimacy is not possible without the establishment of one's own identity. Although American youth today experiment with a variety of different life-styles, most marry at some point. Often, life-styles are not chosen deliberately but are dictated by circumstances.

An important factor in the stability of marriage is age at marriage. People who marry young are more likely to divorce; as young people approach their mid twenties, the likelihood that their marriage will endure increases. In most cases today, both partners plan to work outside the home, at least for a while. An increasing number today are choosing to remain child free. Some make this decision because of political and ecological concerns, others because of a reluctance to disrupt careers or alter life-styles. Most married couples still want to be parents. Children are seen as a way of achieving immortality, as a source of love and affection, and as providing a feeling of achievement, competence, and creativity. Although parenthood produces many stresses, most feel that raising a child is an exciting, rewarding experience that is worth the costs. Family planning has enabled parents to keep their families small.

An increasingly common life-style today among young people who do not choose to marry is cohabitation. Cohabitation does not legally bind partners and is often not a permanent relationship. Most cohabiting partners experience no guilt about this arrangement but are kept together by companionship, sexual gratification, and economic gain. Social contract marriage is a life-style chosen by some young adults who do not choose legal marriage but wish to make a stronger commitment than simple cohabitation. Still other alternative life-styles chosen by young people include remaining single, homosexuality, communal living, and group marriage.

FOR FURTHER READING

Carro, G. The wage earning mother—what working means to her marriage, her kids—her life. *Ladies Home Journal,* December 1978, XCV, 56–59, 164. This is a brief description of a study done by *Ladies Home Journal* and the A. C. Neilson Company and sponsored by Kentucky Fried Chicken. A cross-sectional study with a rather small sample ($N = 508$), it attempts to point out national trends.

Curtis, J. *Working Mothers.* Garden City, New York: Doubleday, 1976. This well-written and well-researched book contains interviews of two hundred women, their husbands, and their children, from various sections of the United States. Results confirm that family patterns are in a state of change. The quotes from the extensive interviews make the book very readable.

Keniston, K. Youth: A "new" stage of life. *American Scholar,* 1972, 109–127. Keniston's article, discussed in this chapter, describes the period of youth as a "new" stage that is presenting as many problems as adolescence for the adult generation. Keniston attributes the new stage as due in very large part to the changes that are taking place in our society. Considered by many a very important article, it has been reproduced in many books of readings.

Terry, M. *Couplings and Groupings.* New York: Avon Books, 1972. Megan Terry has interviewed a large cross section of young Americans: singles, couples, groups, nuns, priests, communards, heterosexuals, and homosexuals. These people talk about their feelings regarding life, love, and sex in a time of flux and uncertainty.

Preview Questions

- How does the importance of physical development in adulthood differ from that in earlier years?

- What are some special problems associated with infertility after thirty?

- What are some major trends in cognitive development that begin after thirty?

- Can you describe several personal–social changes that take place between thirty and forty?

- Can you describe two transitional periods that occur in the thirties and forties and explain some of the reasons for each?

- What are some new developmental tasks that emerge in the thirties?

- How does childrearing affect marital adjustment in the thirties?

- Can you distinguish between two-career and two-earner marriages and describe their impacts on parenting and marital roles?

- What are some trends and problems with reference to behavior over the course of a marriage?

- Can you describe the incidence of family violence in this country and explain some methods being used to avert it?

- What are some factors that bring about divorce and some problems that usually result?

- How successful is remarriage after divorce, and what problems arise for those who choose to remain single thereafter?

II

Young Adulthood
to Mid-life Transition

In the last chapter, we talked about the roles and tasks of young adulthood. Our particular emphasis was the transitional period of youth, which many young people pass through before taking on the tasks and roles of adult life. This chapter focuses on the period of adult development from about twenty-five to forty years. This is the period that includes the peak years of biological functioning, although evidence suggests that some physical decline begins, even in one's thirties. It is also the time when people either learn to live with an intimate partner or remain psychologically alone, what Erikson (1968) called intimacy vs. isolation. In addition, it represents the period Erikson called generativity vs. stagnation. Generativity may be expressed through having and caring for children or through active involvement in work or other creative endeavors. Stagnation may result if an individual is not able to develop a concern for succeeding generations and instead becomes excessively self-absorbed. During their twenties, most adults in our culture make relatively permanent choices regarding their life-styles, organize their lives in order to achieve their chosen goals, and finally begin at the mid-life transition, to evaluate and judge their accomplishments and failures (Buhler 1968).

DEVELOPMENT IN ADULTHOOD

Physical Development

Physical Changes. During the first twenty-five years of life, biological changes play an important role in psychosocial development. By adulthood, biological changes are not as important. Adult men and women normally are physically strong. Even in their late thirties, most are still near their peak capacities. Apart from impairments due to accident, illness, or not taking care of their bodies, they have not fallen much below their maximal level of physical ability. Visible cosmetic changes, of course, do occur and bother men and women in different ways, often because of the attention given them by our culture. Women are warned, for example, to remove their facial wrinkles and other signs of aging with special cosmetics. They are told to "keep that young look." Men are told of new methods to stop their balding. Both sexes, but especially women, are constantly reminded that to remain youthful, they need to keep in shape through diet and exercise. In our society, normal signs of aging symbolize for both sexes the loss of youth and the beginning of the middle years.

Infertility Problems after Thirty. Women who postpone child bearing into their thirties are more likely to have difficulty conceiving than women in their twenties, primarily because fertility generally begins to decrease in the thirties. The primary cause of infertility among women in their thirties is endometriosis, which refers to tissue adhesions that may permanently block the fallopian tubes. Three decades ago, one out of ten couples was believed to have difficulty conceiving a child; today, with

Many women, especially those with outside careers, are postponing childbearing until their thirties. A recent example is Boston newscaster Natalie Jacobson, who had her first child at thirty-seven.

more women postponing childbirth because of their careers, experts estimate that the figure is one out of six (Kleiman 1979).

Many infertile couples begin anguished searches to bear children. Why do they do so? Some report a difference between what one plans as a young adult and what one wants at thirty or thirty-five years. As one mother in her late thirties with a career outside her home put it, "I'm tired of the double life, but I suppose I wouldn't have had it the other way. Those in their thirties and forties who want children and still have the good life end up on the job physically exhausted and emotionally drained. But those in their twenties who think they have a lock on sanity because they've decided against having children and permanent attachments may wake up when they're fifty, if they haven't succumbed to a heart attack or lung cancer, to find themselves curiously empty." As many people like this approach mid life, they become particularly anguished because they realize that with each year of life, their child-bearing years become more limited.

Many men and women decide finally that the value of having children far out-weighs the burdens (Hoffman and Manis 1979). Fortunately, advances in fertility, such as those discussed in Chapter 2, are enabling more infertile couples to bear children, and others who are unable to solve their infertility problem may elect to adopt a child.

Cognitive Development

As described previously, Jean Piaget and his colleagues propose that the ability to think and solve problems increases in complexity with increasing chronological age. They argue, however, that the underlying maturational process that causes cognitive development stops with adulthood. Any increases in thinking and problem-solving ability after this time, they contend, are due to life experiences. Because different adults have different life experiences, Flavell (1963; 1970) suggests that it follows that the process of cognitive development differs for each adult. Because most intel-ligence tests, at least in part, measure learning of the sort that takes place in school, it is not surprising that adults who continue their formal education tend to do better than adults who stop their education.

Psychologists tend to agree that for most adults between twenty-five and forty, cognitive functions measured by IQ tests no longer increase at the rate they do during childhood. The tests that usually are used to measure cognitive development, however, may not be able accurately to measure the cognitive abilities that adults use in their day-to-day activities.

Alpaugh (1975) studied both creativity and verbal performance of adult school teachers and showed that their creativity scores dropped with increasing age, even though their verbal ability scores remained the same. For this group of adults, verbal ability was used every day on the job and remained at plateau. Creativity apparently was not such an important part of these teachers' jobs. Schaie (1977–1978) suggests that the most reasonable way to measure cognitive ability in adults is to measure the ways they solve tasks set for their age group. For those in their late twenties, this includes implementing role independence and assuming responsibilties. For those in their early and late thirties, it includes assuming responsibility for families intead of individuals.

Another way to look at cognitive abilities of adults is to consider the quality of creative results. Levinson and colleagues (1978) point out that some great artists who have continued to create after age forty have produced more profound works than before. Adults often continue to develop their ways of thinking and solving prob-lems, and with increasing age, they seem often to make their most effective contri-butions to politics, diplomacy, and philosophy. When this happens, it often is due to their experiences at work, which have increased their cognitive development. Adult creative scientists do more integrative theoretical work, and by their forties, they begin to set directions for the upcoming generation.

Personal–Social Development

Personal Relationships. The most important adult developmental changes prior to middle age are related to factors other than physical and cognitive abilities. They have to do with marital relationships, children, occupational and career decisions, and adjustments that take place when marriages dissolve. How well they handle these tasks determines how they will view themselves and their lives both in the present and in the future.

Young adults ordinarily form their preliminary adult identities while they are still in their twenties—that is, they make their first major life choices, usually involving marriage, occupation, and life-style. The mid twenties and early thirties are for many the time for having and raising children. The first several years in the lives of couples who have decided to have children tend to be somewhat stressful, for small children require parents to make many psychological and economic adjustments.

Men and women in their twenties and thirties also make serious decisions about occupations during this time. For those who are well educated, career paths begin to unfold that will have long-term effects on the individual and the family. Traditionally, young people in professional areas first establish themselves at junior levels and then advance along formal or informal ladders. Not all succeed, of course; many find themselves at forty having failed to accomplish what they had hoped and unable to change their careers. Others may decide that although they are succeeding, their career requires them to give up too much of their personal lives. This can be an increasing concern for married men and women who want to succeed but believe that their family is as important as career success. These people must sometimes make the choice of remaining at a middle-level job if they do not want to accept the frequent transfers of the longer hours required to rise in the ranks.

Relationships between the generations change considerably during this period. Adults in their twenties may already be fathers and mothers, yet at the same time, they may not have become completely independent of their parents. By their late thirties, their relationships with both their children and their parents often have changed sharply. Their children are growing up and becoming increasingly independent. Their own aging parents, at the same time, may begin to look to them for care and leadership. This issue becomes particularly prominent at mid life.

Reevaluating Occupational Goals. By age thirty in our society, young adults are expected to have chosen their occupations or careers and begun to carry out their occupational goals. Later at about age forty, adults often begin to reevaluate the choices they have made. Success at a career normally involves assuming what Neugarten (1969) termed **executive responsibility.** This means assuming responsibility and developing strategies for integrating complex relationships, the sorts of tasks often required by people successful in business or professions. For many adults, this involves overseeing and managing the work of employees or colleagues. Many adults

Occupational stress is an important factor in the decision of some individuals to change careers at mid life.

entering their forties decide that promotion to a managerial position is not what they want, perhaps because managing other employees is inconsistent with their personalities or because they feel it will not be as satisfying as their previous position. At this point, some change their careers rather than continue into what they feel would be a promotion into a stultifying position. The research has shown that adults who elect voluntarily to make major career changes in their forties or older tend to have a more stable work history than those who do not make a change during their mid-life transitions (Vaitenas 1976). Presumably, people who have been successful in carrying out their work responsibilities are more likely to feel confident enough to reassess their values and, if necessary, change the direction of their lives.

Another important factor that influences adults entering middle age to change occupation or career is stress. Some adults elect to move from stressful to less stressful positions at this time, such moves being particularly common among adults who have experienced severe illness and who become worried at mid life about the possibility of continuing illness shortening the lifespan. It is at this point that the professionally successful business executive may elect to forgo that next promotion and take on a less well-paying or prestigious job that is not so fast paced or demanding. The decision to move from stressful to less stressful jobs is also made by people in lower job echelons, although adults in lower-paying jobs frequently have less flexibility in deciding to change occupations because they cannot afford cuts in salary as easily as those in higher-paying positions.

Transitional Periods

Several transitional periods prior to middle age have been described by psychologists. During these periods, individuals normally take time to evaluate who they are, what they are doing, and where they will go next. For some, this period properly is termed a "crisis"; for others, it may be more passive, a period of thoughtful reflection before moving on (Gould 1972; Levinson *et al.* 1974; 1978). One important transitional period occurs for most in our culture at about age thirty. Levinson and colleagues (1978, p. 79) point out that by this age, our society expects adults to complete the shift from the position of still being dependent in many ways on their parents to adults with responsibilities of their own. By thirty, adults in our culture are also expected to have established identities and to have taken on the tasks of the adult world and adult relationships. To meet this goal, young adults must have explored the available opportunities, arrived at articulated definitions of themselves as adults, and made and accepted choices regarding occupations, love relationships, life-styles, and values.

For many young adults approaching their thirties, these tasks are formidable; for some, they are impossible. For these last, the period sometimes is called the **age-thirty crisis,** although the actual crisis itself may fall earlier or later than age thirty (Berman *et al.* 1977). Individuals passing through the crisis need to make decisions regarding their life-styles or values to their satisfactions and then change their lives to match these decisions if they are to adjust happily to later stages of life.

It is about age thirty that many people begin extensive periods of working out marital problems as well as previously unresolved personal problems, such as self-esteem. Enough people of this age group seek psychiatric help that therapists have been alerted to the specific problems of the thirties (Marmor 1975).

A second period of adult psychosocial transition falls normally at the end of the thirties or the beginning of the forties. Jung (1971) called this the **mid-life transition (mid-life crisis)** when what he called the "hidden parts of people often emerge, releasing new potential." According to Jung, at this period of life, people come more and more to accept the reality that they do not have forever to live, and many people make use of psychological resources to reach goals they have never even tried to attain before. This is the age that many women decide to return to college to complete their educations or to prepare for new careers. Many men at this same time decide to make changes in their careers or their personal lives, sometimes electing divorce and remarriage to change their life-styles. For those who do not try to develop their potentials at this stage of life, Jung believes, there is a danger that middle age may be characterized by acceptance of a rigid and ritualized existence, the middle age that our culture warns us in many different ways to fear.

Levinson and colleagues (1978), in a study of American men aged thirty-five to forty-five and drawn from different racial, ethnic, and professional groups, found the same period of psychosocial transition among this population. Levinson and colleagues note that this period of life brings a tumultuous struggle, particularly for people who have been up until this time concerned primarily with career development and who suddenly decide that other personal needs are equally important to them as career success. This period of adult psychosocial transition coincides for many with the resolution of Erikson's stage of intimacy vs. isolation. Individuals who have learned earlier in life to be intimate and to share themselves with others without fear of losing their identities often are less upset at this period than those who are psychologically isolated because their personal needs are not being met. For many people, according to Levinson and colleagues, aspects of their lives come into question, and they are upset by what they see. Many individuals become angry at themselves and decide to change their lives. The study reports that the result for many is a breaking out of the old career path and change of life-style.

Levinson and colleagues emphasized the importance of maintaining a sense of excitement and commitment for the mental health of the men studied. Men who at this period of their lives decide that their careers did not provide this sense are those most likely to develop the most serious problems and need for change. Figure 11.1 depicts Levinson's developmental periods as well as the transitional periods from young adulthood to the mid-life transition.

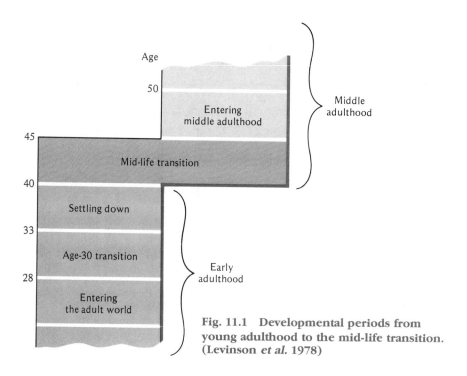

Fig. 11.1   Developmental periods from young adulthood to the mid-life transition. (Levinson *et al.* 1978)

Gould (1978), in studies of both women and men at the end of their thirties or beginning of their forties, found that many were troubled by a new understanding that life is not what they always thought it to be, and that for them, new conflicts are not easily resolvable. Parents who find that their children are not growing up to be what they wanted or that their children do not approve of their parents' behaviors or values are likely to turn their feelings of resentment inward and wonder whether they have done everything they could do as parents to raise their children properly. For many parents, the sudden realization that the sacrifices they thought they were making as younger parents did not produce what they wanted comes as a great disillusioning shock. Even those adults who seem to have been successful at achieving what they want, either personally or in their career experiences, tend to doubt their achievements at this period. Often, they feel confused or depressed. According to Gould, many begin to question the values that they chose as young adults.

Many adults at this stage of life begin new lives by learning to express new talents, strengths, and desires. The adult man or woman approaching forty no longer believes in magic. He or she recognizes that half of life may be over. Many decide that if they are ever going to change during their lifetimes, now is the time.

As noted earlier, not all adults in their thirties and early forties experience the transition to mid life as a crisis. Some adults pass their mid-life transitions recognizing that the nature of their lives is changing but without undergoing a painful process to reach the next stage. For the great majority, however, the transition is a difficult one: Adults prepare for the next stage of development by questioning nearly every aspect of their lives. Those who feel they cannot continue as before may require several years to form a new plan or modify the old.

Developmental Tasks

Developmental tasks change between the ages of twenty-five and forty, as life experiences change. The tasks of young adults in their late twenties may still involve exploring the possibilities for adult living and keeping their options open. In their thirties, the task is to create a more stable life structure, to "make something of life." Vaillant and McArthur (1972) view the thirties as the years for planning career development. With increasing age come increasing responsibility and pressure related to care of others, such as children and their economic needs. The shift from one set of tasks to another is indicated not only by chronological age but also by a crucial event, such as a major change in occupation or career, a divorce or extramarital relationship, a serious illness, the death of a loved one, or a move to a new locale.

For many couples, parenthood constitutes a major developmental task. Leifer (1977), in fact, calls motherhood an important developmental stage of life for women. Motherhood and fatherhood have been associated in our culture with a variety of stresses, not the least of which involves integrating the new baby into the family (Dyer 1963). Cross-cultural studies suggest that social factors play a significant role in the difficulties that American parents experience in assuming childrearing. Specifically, the isolation of the nuclear family in this country places tremendous responsibilities on parents.

 ## MARRIAGE AND FAMILY RELATIONSHIPS

Most American adults today choose to marry. More than seventy-seven percent of American families consist of husbands and wives or of husbands, wives, and children; only seven percent of Americans under sixty-five years of age live alone. Of the married couples, more than thirty percent contain wives working outside the home. At the end of the 1970s about three percent of American couples living together were unmarried (Friedan 1979).

Marital Adjustments

As we learned in Chapter 10, married couples need to make many adjustments for their lives and relationships to run smoothly. When married couples decide to have children, one adjustment that each partner needs to make is to accept or adapt to the other's beliefs about childrearing. Beliefs of adults about the best way to rear children are affected in large part by information made available in the mass media. Newspapers, magazines, television, and books all provide professional advice on rearing children. American couples today usually are aware, for example, of the work of Dr. Benjamin Spock, and many couples have selected and followed his advice. Dr. Spock, in recent years, has provided a great deal of advice for married couples raising children when wives are employed elsewhere. In general, psychologists report that the availability of information about child development has led to a greater awareness of the child's needs (Bronfenbrenner 1970).

Today, American parents are more apt to regard some behaviors as normal that in the past were considered unacceptable. For example, American parents often used to tell their children that it was "not nice" to be jealous of a baby brother or sister or even to express anger or jealousy overtly. Psychological research findings have helped parents to realize that these feelings are quite normal and that the best thing they can do is help their children find socially acceptable ways to express them. These findings do not mean, however, that both members of a couple agree as to exactly what should be done in the raising of children. Nor do they mean that parents are not anxious about making decisions that affect them and their children. Even when parents agree on a life-style and a particular style of childrearing, they often disagree on particular aspects. Belsky and Sternberg (1978) note, for example, that parents who agree on placing their children in day care often experience new tensions among themselves as their children develop new relationships with their caregivers and with them. Parents who were confident while a parent was at home raising the children may become less confident of their own decisions and their own relationships with their children when a third party is in charge.

In part because so much information is available on raising their children, increasing numbers of parents report high levels of anxiety associated with childrearing. Women who are working outside the home tend to have more anxiety than other women (Etaugh 1974). This is particularly true for overworked mothers who did not want to leave their homes or who were ashamed of their economic status. Many feel "less sure about the right thing to do." In their uncertainty, some parents tend to switch from one approach to another, never confident that they are acting properly.

One fundamental cause of this anxiety, according to Kagan (1975), is a lack of consensus on values. Parenting, says Kagan, means "implementing a series of decisions about the socialization of your child—what you do when he cries, when he's aggressive, when he lies, or when he doesn't do well in school." According to Kagan, childrearing decisions are harder to make today than they were thirty years ago, even though experts are ready and willing to give advice on child care, because "there is no consensus in America today as to what a child should be like when he is a young adult." Many parents in the 1980s, however, are looking seriously at their value systems, deciding what attitudes and skills are helpful in coping with adult life, and deciding what parental activities help children develop these attitudes and skills. They are increasingly conscious of the long-term effects of many early experiences.

Two-Career and Two-Earner Marriages

The decisions about raising children and adjusting to marriage in general are complicated in today's society in an increasing number of families in which women are marrying and are also establishing themselves in careers. Many careers involve positions that require a great deal of commitment, are personally rewarding, and demand long-term obligations. The marriages that result are referred to commonly as **two-career marriages.** An increasing number of women are also entering the job market before or during marriage, not because of commitment or personal reward but because of economic necessity. In **two-earner marriages** both partners are working in order to make ends meet or to increase their incomes to obtain material possesions. Two-earner marriages often imply less psychological "fulfillment" for the woman, because most women in today's job market are not in important or high-powered jobs. Two-career and two-earner families, however, face many of the same problems. These include excessive demands on each individual's time, energy, and

In some two-earner families, husband and wife are able to divide the child-care responsibilities by arranging their work schedules.

leisure; conflicts over family and job demands; and tensions that result when either partner brings work problems home. Reasearchers studying two-career and two-earner families report that these problems tend to take a greater toll on wives than on husbands (Heckman, Bryson, and Bryson 1977).

Parenting in Two-Career and Two-Earner Families. Women with careers on average tend to have fewer children than those without careers (U.S. Department of Labor 1980). One reason, as we have learned, is that these women and their husbands often decide to limit their families in order to keep open other opportunities. Women in two-earner families frequently go to work during periods of their lives in which it is economically necessary to do so and are less likely than those women with satisfying careers to decide to limit their families.

When children in two-career or two-earner families are young, meeting their needs often takes combined efforts of both parents. Hall and Hall (1979) describe these common solutions to the problems of childrearing: husbands share more responsibilities with their wives; husbands and/or their wives modify their work schedules to enable one of them to be with the children; or they hire outside help either at home or in day-care facilities.

Stockard and Johnson (1980) report that some husbands and wives today divide the responsibility of supporting the family by each working outside the home half or three-quarters of the time. This arrangement solves some of the problems of childrearing. The solution is used by two-career families in which both parents wish to remain in their careers during the time that their children are young so that their educations will not become obsolete and so that by the time their children are old enough for them to spend larger amounts of time away from the home, they will not have lost their positions on the career ladder.

The greatest difficulty facing most two-career and two-earner families is the rigidity and unresponsiveness of the workplace. **Flextime** is one of a number of new systems instituted by some American businesses to "preserve the quality of family life" and is often an asset to working parents. Flextime is designed so that everyone works during the mid-day core of hours, but each employee arranges starting, leaving, and lunch times according to individual needs (Friedan 1979). Some individuals working on flextime may start work later than others in order to have time in the morning to leave their children at day-care centers. Others may decide to skip lunch hour and leave at three o'clock in the afternoon to be at home when children come home from school. Married couples in which both partners are working on flextime can arrange their two schedules optimally to meet their childrearing needs.

New Roles in Two-Earner Families. According to some researchers (Schwartz and Sullivan 1978), the hallmark of the 1980s may be the growth of "fifty-fifty" marriages, those characterized by egalitarian role relationships. Increasing numbers of working couples regard flexibility in their jobs as a requirement for maximizing the happiness of the household. Whereas ten years ago, rising young male executives stood ready to go anywhere, anytime, for advancement, more married men today are declining jobs that require frequent transfers or out-of-town travel. By the late 1970s, according to one survey, sixty-six percent of major companies reported employees turning down transfers, nearly twice the number from five years earlier (Schwartz and Sullivan 1978). For these men, their families are clearly a higher priority than job advancement. Because of the importance of their jobs to family economics, wives working outside the home exert more decision-making power in the family.

Although husbands' incomes still largely determine the level at which families live, the fact that a wife is earning money strengthens her hand. Even if the wife's income is only half that of her husband, the power relationship may be egalitarian (Klemesrud 1980). In 1962, sixty-six percent of women participating in a long-term

---

A jingle for the perfume, Enjoli, "the eight-hour perfume for the twenty-four-hour woman," went like this:

> I can put the wash on the line, feed the kids, get dressed, pass out the kisses, and get to work by five of nine—'cause I'm a wo-man.

What kind of woman? Unlike the tireless temptress in the fatuous fragrance ad, most employed mothers rest because of exhaustion, before struggling through yet another workday marathon. Rapoport and Rapoport (1969) suggest that these women with children in two-earner families develop what is called **role overload.** They discover they are having to take on too many roles to perform them all satisfactorily and that the "double-duty" that results leaves them in states of exhaustion.

Although role overload is more common for women than for men, in families where both parents are employed, role overload can occur for both wife and husband. It is a major factor leading to reported marital dissatisfaction (Giele 1971). The following comment was made to a marriage counselor by a

---

research project felt that the major family decisions should be made by the man of the house. In 1980, when they were asked the same question, only twenty-eight percent agreed with the statement (Klemesrud 1980). Increasingly, husbands are expected to take on a more prominent role in the household tasks and in caring for the children. Psychologists suggest that our social structure may well eventually be transformed by these evolving marital roles (Schwartz and Sullivan 1978).

Sexuality during Marriage

Sexuality within Marriage. As we have learned earlier, a trend in our society has been one of earlier and wider expressions of sexuality among both males and females. Among young and single people, the rates of sexual intercourse have risen significantly in the past several decades. Gagnon (1977) reports that two-thirds to three-fourths of all women who marry today have experienced premarital sexual intercourse. Hunt (1974) indicates that about eight out of ten have experienced sexual intercourse prior to marriage.

In marriage, the need for sexual intercourse is normal and expected. Mancini and Orthner (1978) suggest that the priority given this need, as opposed to other personal and relational needs, tends to be high in early marriage, but it steadily drops over the years of marriage. Although major individual differences exist among couples, of course, on average, young married couples have intercourse about three

young women who was studying full-time and pursuing a Ph.D. degree in English literature while simultaneously caring for two small children:

> Sometimes I feel as if I am a workhorse instead of a human being. When I want to be reading Herman Hesse, I find myself washing diapers; when I think I need to spend a few hours extra time in preparing a term paper, one of the kids gets sick, and I spend the afternoon instead at the pediatrician's. Sometimes I feel as if I never should have gotten married or had children.

QUESTIONS FOR THOUGHT

1. The Enjoli jingle described above was extremely popular for some time. Why do you think American women enjoyed it so much?

2. Is your answer related to the fact that although women today recognize the disadvantages of role overload, they continue to try to emulate this model? If so, why should this be the case?

times per week. Over time, this rate declines so that by the time they reach forty, married couples tend to have intercourse about twice weekly.

Despite the change in frequency of intercourse with age, research shows that an overwhelming majority of couples consider their coital activity "pleasurable" (Hunt 1974; Sarrel and Sarrel 1980). These same researchers found, however, that not all people are completely satisfied. Some married people want more sexual activity; a few want less. Most often, it is the men and women who are not happy with other aspects of their marriages who want more sexual intercourse. Today, women's expectations for intercourse are more similar to men's than they were several decades ago, when women were not expected by society to have sexual desires that were nearly as strong as men. Unfortunately for women, their frustration with insufficient marital intercourse now equals that of men.

Recent research has shown that many myths abound concerning sexual behavior of American adults. Although many adults do not always achieve orgasm during intercourse, for example, Sarrel and Sarrel (1980) have found that seven out of ten women report that this does not keep them from feeling that they enjoy excellent sexual relationships with their husbands. At least ninety-five percent of men who feel that their sex lives are excellent have orgasms nearly every time they have sexual relations with their wives. The same researchers, however, tell us that so do ninety-five percent of the men who feel that they have bad sexual relationships.

Good communication has been shown to be closely related to a good sexual relationship.

Diamond and Karlen (1980) suggest that sometimes frustration with sexual intercourse results from boredom with techniques and positions that have become patterned and routine over time. Much of the excitement of sexual intimacy is lost when partners know each other so well that every move and feeling can be expected and no new sensations are explored. With increased discussion of sexuality in our society, however, has come increased open discussion of methods to stimulate one another. The variety of means used by men and women to arouse each other sexually has also increased. Diamond and Karlen suggest that it is now much more likely than in the past that precoital sexual play will result in greater sexual arousal for both partners, even after long-term marriages, and that this may account, at least in part, for the higher frequency of female orgasm reported today as compared to earlier decades.

Researchers report that good communication with one's partner seems to be the factor most strongly related to having a good sexual relationship. Sarrel and Sarrel (1980) point out that superior sexual communication skills are reported by eighty-five percent of the men and eighty-two percent of the women who report that they feel that they have excellent sex lives.

Sex therapy, psychological therapy designed to increase sexual satisfaction, has made a dramatic introduction into the methods being used today to solve marital sexual problems. Today, there are some 1200 certified sex therapists in the United States, many of whom have devised a variation of the treatment methods originally designed by sex therapists Masters and Johnson (1966; 1970).

Extramarital Sexuality. Extramarital sex refers to a sexual relationship with someone other than one's marriage partner. Hunt (1974) reported that approximately one-half of the married men and one-fourth of the married women have experienced at least one occasion of extramarital sexual intercourse. In a national study of 2000 married women (Bell and Lopsenz 1977), one-third of the wives who had never been involved in an extramarital venture reported that "it might happen" in the future.

Despite the frequency of extramarital sex, the attitudes of most Americans are disapproving. A 1978 Gallup poll reported that sixty-five percent of the adults polled felt that sexual relations with someone other than the marriage partner are wrong. Probably for this reason, most extramarital sexual arrangements are kept secret from spouses. Most experiences are not long-term affairs, but rather brief, noncommitted arrangements that are over before any great emotional involvement develops. Walster, Traupman, and Walster (1978) report that the more emotionally and sexually deprived a man or woman feels in a marriage, the more likely he or she will be to seek or fall into an extramarital involvement. Glass and Wright (1977) point out that divorce probabilities are higher among men and women engaged in extramarital sexual arrangements, even when their marriages had been thought to be satisfactory. It is difficult to determine, however, whether the outside relationship contributed to the breakup of the marriage or whether it occurred because the marriage was breaking up.

All extramarital sexual relationships are not clandestine. In a minority of marriages, husbands and wives agree together that it is appropriate to have extramarital sex. Francoeur and Francoeur (1973) describe the **sexually open marriage** as one in which both partners agree to accept each other as equals, friends, and partners. O'Neill and O'Neill (1972) stress that open marriages that are successful allow couples to decide at the outset whether or not to be open to a variety of types of outside relationships, not just sexual relationships. These authors suggest that the real search in open marriage is for intimacy, caring, and love with others, all of which can but do not necessarily involve sex. Researchers studying open marriages tend to report that couples choosing this life-style tend to be young (Athanasiou, Shaver, and Tarris 1970). Knapp (1976) found that the personality test scores of men and women choosing open marriage indicated much higher individualism and independence, higher achievement, creativity, and nonconforming values and behaviors than are normally found.

In addition to open marriages, another small percentage of married people involve themselves in **mate-swapping (swinging) marriages,** in which husband and wife participate together for short episodes of extramarital sex. Hunt (1974) reports that it is difficult to know the number of people who actually practice this form of marriage, but the estimate is about two percent of the marriages in the United States. Smith and Smith (1975) report that swinging couples usually are in their adult years rather than in their youth, usually well-educated, and otherwise fairly conventional. Gilmartin (1977) suggests that they often come from families in which they did not receive a great deal of emotional gratification and that they have learned from their earlier years to seek emotional gratification from large numbers, rather than from a few important people in their lives.

Family Violence

Family violence, including spouse abuse, is becoming a focus of increasing concern in our society. Straus, Gelles, and Steinmetz (1979) reported that sixteen out of every one hundred couples in the United States have violent confrontations of one sort or another in the course of a year. This may include kicking, biting, punching, or hitting with objects. About four of every one hundred wives are seriously beaten by their husbands. The incidence of marital violence that comes to the attention of the police or other professionals is highest among the urban poor, but violence occurs among the affluent as well. All in all, some 1.8 million women are battered each year by their husbands, according to a national survey (American Personnel and Guidance Association 1980). It is true also that wives beat husbands, although we do not hear as much about this as we do about husbands beating wives. Perhaps the reason is that husbands are ashamed to admit they are battered.

Many methods are being used to try to avert family violence. An Office of Domestic Violence, for example, established by the Department of Health and Human Services in 1979, began to coordinate many separate programs that can assist battered women. In addition, communities have set up their own shelters and hotlines. All of these programs seek ways to reduce family strife as well as help individuals to obtain health, social, legal, employment, and other services (American Personnel and Guidance Association 1980).

Various forms of family therapy have been helpful in treating family violence. Generally, husbands, wives, and children meet with therapists both together and separately to work out problems that involve them mutally (Schomer 1978). Many approaches have been used successfully in family therapy, from brief strategic interventions and short-term problem-oriented approaches to long-term extensive analysis of family dynamics.

DIVORCE AND REMARRIAGE

Despite the gradual evolution of new roles within marriage, the pressures facing today's families are intense. In 1980, when the federal government convened a series of conferences for a representative sample of the American public to explore ways of making public and private policies more responsive to family needs, nearly half of all Americans who attended reported that they thought that the "quality of family life" had deteriorated in the last fifteen years. Most agreed that family structure was under severe strain. The greatest pressures cited were the high cost of living, drug and alcohol abuse, and what many believed to be a decline of moral standards (Beck and Lord 1980). Many people criticized tax, welfare, health, and foster-care policies that ignored or undermined families. The government's insensitivity to these problems was a frequently mentioned issue, but economic pressures resulting from inflation, poverty, or unemployment ranked as most important by many (American Federation of Teachers 1980). One result was no agreement among the conferees about ways to resolve family strains that cause divorce. In 1978, the number of divorces was almost half the number of marriages (2.2 million). The Census Bureau projects that if these rates continue, the proportion of marriages ending in divorce over a lifetime will reach forty percent (Glick and Norton 1977).

We learned in Chapter 10 that marriages that take place for couples twenty-five years or older have greater chances of success than marriages of younger couples and that marriages of couples under twenty years of age have the least chance of success. According to Lee (1977), reasons could be that older couples have fewer financial problems to cope with and greater interpersonal understanding in developing their marital relationships.

What happens to a couple who decides that their marriage is unsuccessful? Nevaldine (1978) reported that fifty percent of a representative sample of divorced people defined themselves as "leavers," those who think that they first seriously considered divorce as the solution to marital conflict, first verbalized the suggestion, and filed the legal papers. Some "leavers" reported experiencing ambivalence but experienced a "last straw" event that precipitated the final decision. No sex differences were evident between "leavers" and "lefts"; as many females and males chose to leave relationships as to try to maintain them.

Divorce today is such a common occurrence that many institutions are starting programs to try to help before problems occur. Increasingly, for example, young couples are making an effort to avert divorce even before they marry. University of Wisconsin undergraduates, for example, can enroll in courses designed to teach them to assume multiple roles necessary for good family relationships: worker, parent, homemaker, and community member. The courses were taken by both male and female students. Although at this point, it is too early to determine the outcome, students reported that they felt that the courses might make life decisions easier and thus help avert divorce.

Factors in Divorce

Why do so many marriages end in divorce? One popular notion is that family tensions increase when the wife works outside the home. It is assumed that stress becomes particularly intense if the wife's job has a higher status than the husband's. The facts, however, do not seem to indicate that wives' careers are a problem. In fact, wives working outside the home with occupational prestige higher than their husbands have not been found to have higher marital stress and dissatisfaction in their marriages than other wives (Richardson 1979). Another study found that husbands of employed women evidence no more signs of marital discord or stress than do spouses of housewives (Booth 1977). A woman who is unhappy in her marriage and who feels she could support herself alone, however, is more likely than an unhappy nonearning wife to seek a divorce (Levinger 1979).

Many men and women both tend to divorce at times of developmental crisis, at about age thirty or again at about age forty. These people may use divorce

A number of factors have contributed to the high rate of divorce in our society. One social factor of significance is the increasing acceptability of divorce.

as a means of changing the directions of their lives and their developmental patterns. Among many other reasons for divorce are incompatibility, preference for another partner, family violence, and the increasing acceptability of divorce in our society.

Divorce Settlements and Custody

When efforts to avert divorce are unsuccessful, the next step is arranging the divorce settlement and, if there are children, determining custody. Frequently, these issues produce a great deal of stress both for the spouses who are terminating their marriage and for their children.

A basic issue addressed in the court settlement is the division of property. The aims of most state systems are that property be divided either equitably (fairly) or evenly, that children be adequately supported, and that when necessary, alimony be provided temporarily for a spouse while he or (more often) she prepares to enter the work force. In 1980, forty-four states and the District of Columbia required that marital property be divided equitably or evenly. Only about ten percent of divorced women were awarded alimony, and fewer than half the settlements provided child support. Thus divorce produces substantial economic strain on women who are awarded custody of their children, especially those women not employed outside the home during marriage (Quinn 1980).

Another difficult issue is that of child custody. The law requires that the parent or parents who are felt to be best able to see to the needs of the child be awarded custody. Although wanting custody of the child is not the overriding factor, it is an important one. With changing conceptions of the parental roles of men and women and with more fathers seeking custody of their children, the "tender years doctrine" historically granting child custody to the mother is fast eroding. State statutes in the past ten years have gradually adopted the view that the best interests of the child should govern who gets custody. Today, neither parent has an automatic right to children. Even so, the percentage of fathers with sole custody of their children is still very small.

One recent innovation in child-custody arrangements is joint custody or coparenting. This alternative was made possible by eight states in 1980, and most other states have approved it in appropriate cases. Shared or **joint custody** involves two areas: (1) the legal area, in which both parents share decision-making responsibilities for all important aspects of a child's life and (2) the physical area, in which both share caretaking responsibility for the child. The solution can only work for divorced parents who are able to put the interest of their children above their own and who are capable of working together amicably despite being divorced. Joint custody unquestionably is an attractive idea, for it allows both parents to retain central roles in the child's life. Because of expenses, however, joint custody today remains a middle-class phenomenon. One joint-custody expert estimated that at least twenty-five percent more income is needed to support two households (Quinn 1980). It is not yet clear whether joint custody is best for the child. Some parents think it is the best way to assure that a child retains close ties with two parents. Others say that children need one strong parental anchor after a divorce and that sharing custody can make this difficult. It seems likely that the success of this alternative depends largely on how well the situation is handled by the family involved.

Remarriage

Although men are somewhat more likely to remarry than women, the remarriage rates for both sexes are high. About five-sixths of divorced men and three-fourths of divorced women remarry (Furstenberg 1980). Glick and Norton (1977) report that younger people and childless people are the most likely to remarry and that they do so more quickly. Divorced childless women under age thirty, for example, re-marry after an average of only 2.6 years from the divorce, while women of the same age but with three or more children usually take over five years to remarry. It is possible that the responsibility of childrearing delays courtship for women with children. It is also possible that men are not as likely to marry quickly into already existing families as they are to marry childless women. Of those men and women who remarry, Glick and Norton report that some forty-four percent can expect to divorce a second time. Figure 11.2 shows graphically the odds for divorce following marriage and remarriage for American adults.

Remarriage presents new challenges and some new stresses not encountered in first marriages. Remarried couples encounter strain from stepparent–stepchildren

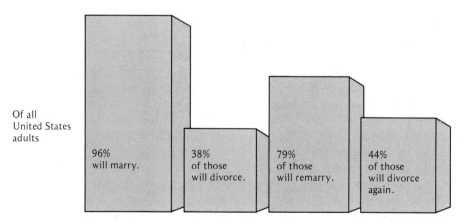

Of all
United States
adults

96%
will marry.

38%
of those
will divorce.

79%
of those
will remarry.

44%
of those
will divorce
again.

Fig. 11.2   Odds for divorce after marriage and remarriage for American adults (Glick and Norton 1977).

relationships, financial difficulties resulting from obligations to more than one family, and the fact that persons who are poor "marriage risks" generally carry their "risk factors for poor marriage" from one marriage to another (Rallings 1976). Goetting (1979) suggested that one important cause of tension is ex-spouses who sometimes interfere and cause resentments. This seems to be particularly true when children are involved. Another problem involves that of psychologically developing a new identity as a couple after having gone through the pains of giving up an old one. Fear of marital failure also seems to be more common among those who have already had experience in failing at marriage than among those who have not previously gone through divorce.

On the positive side, Furstenberg (1980) in a study of remarried couples reported more sharing of household tasks and decision making and more emotional interaction between husband and wife than was true in their first marriages. Furstenberg believes that the greater gender equality of remarried couples may be influenced by changing cultural expectations about the nature of marriage. Whereas first-married couples probably feel more bound by traditional ideas of marriage, remarried individuals are free to "modernize" their conception of marriage in line with the changing times and their particular needs.

A comparison of three surveys reporting marital happiness of remarried couples and couples in their first marriages revealed significantly greater marital happiness for women in their first marriages but not for men (Glenn and Weaver 1977). The researchers concluded that remarriages of divorced persons that do not quickly end in divorce probably are, as a whole, almost as successful, despite the additional stresses, as intact first marriages. One possible reason is that people entering second marriages may have had an opportunity to mature personally and socially since their initial relationships.

Single Parents

One result of the high divorce rate is the growing number of single parents in our society. In 1970, the proportion of children under eighteen living with one parent was eleven percent; by 1979, the proportion had increased to nineteen percent, almost one of every five families with children in the home (U.S. Bureau of the Census 1980). Single parenting can also occur because of other forms of family disruption. These include desertion, widowhood, out-of-wedlock pregnancy and the fact that women with children but no husbands are more likely today to remain independent rather than live with their relatives.

In many cases, desertion produces more stress than does divorce, partly because the decision to desert usually is unilateral and may not be expected by other family members. Financial as well as social problems complicate the lives of the deserted parents and are likely to affect in some way their interactions with their offspring. The widow or widower generally has one major advantage over the single

HIGHLIGHT 11.2 STEPPARENTING

Researchers estimate that about one child in ten lives in a **blended family**—that is, a family in which at least one of the spouses has a child by another marriage and in which at least one of the spouses is a stepparent. Families containing stepparents are often quite complex and may include children from the previous marriages of both husband and wife as well as children from the new marriage. Relationships among all the members of the new family can be very complex, with children of divorce having three or four parents instead of two; at least three sets of grandparents, and more aunts, uncles, and other relatives than most other children. Most important to the new family, however, seem to be the relationships that develop among parents, stepparents, and children.

No two stories of families living in these situations are alike, but some common concerns do emerge. Most important is the recognition that stepparenting is different from primary parenting. It can be just as satisfying, but it is different. Kompara (1980) notes that a major problem in the mutual adjustment of stepparents and stepchildren is that the children have been socialized by a different parent and that parent is still in evidence. This may contribute to the feelings of inadequacy reported by remarried people with respect to their parental roles. According to Kompara, one arena in which tension frequently develops between stepparents and children is in discipline. "For better or worse," says a stepmother, "it's self-conscious parenting . . . you're damned if you do and damned if you don't!"

Cohen (1978) writes of growing concern among some family professionals also over the lack of appropriate incest taboos between nonblood kin relations in remarried families. One stepfather reported, "I really wasn't seeking to become a father, certainly not to a beautiful fifteen-year-old girl with two sisters who are sure to be as beautiful as she is when they get a little bit older. But I fell in love with my wife, Janey, and there she was with her children. They came along as part of the package—along with their father whom they visit every other weekend. So we were married. It didn't take long before I discovered the package was ticking and likely to explode." Despite their doubts about their parenting, stepparents do not appear to have any greater difficulties with their family role performance than do first-married parents.

Research seems to show that despite the potential pitfalls of stepparenting, people in stepparent families, whether they are adults or children, seem to have almost no characteristics to differentiate them from people who grow up in regular families. Wilson and colleagues (1975) found that among a large group of children and adults surveyed, both adults and children seemed similar psychologically to adults and children in regular families. They concluded that stepparenting can be as successful as parenting. One stepparent pointed out that developing relationships similar to those that exist in regular families takes "some getting used to, but they can be made." At first, this stepfather tried to do everything with his new kids; he would take them to the zoo on the weekends they stayed home with their mother and him, and he would play softball with them after work. He felt himself watched by everyone in his wife's family and under great pressure to succeed, to measure up. But there were no cues to guide him. "You see, although I was old enough to be a father, I'd never had any kids of my own in my first marriage, and here were two little boys—fresh from a bruising divorce. At first, I thought they just hated me. Now I realize it's more complicated. We have to learn that we have ties through my wife with one another and build a different relationship on that."

QUESTIONS FOR THOUGHT

1. If the problems of stepparenting are far more complex than those of parenting, why do you think that researchers have found that people in stepparenting and parenting families seem to have the same psychological attributes?

2. What does the research cited here tell you about the adaptability of adults and children to new living situations?

parent: strong emotional support from family, friends, and community immediately following the loss of the spouse. After the period of bereavement, however, the widow or widower must confront and resolve the same day-to-day childrearing problems that other single parents face.

Parenting without a partner can be extremely stressful because of the additional burdens placed on the single parent. Particularly in the case of divorce or separation, the transition to a stable life can be difficult and prolonged. One study of parental adjustment to single parenting showed that several years elapsed before most single mothers felt that they had regained a sense of coherence and stability after divorce (Wallerstein and Kelly 1980). Even so, only about one-fifth of the sample of divorced men and women studied by Wallerstein and Kelly viewed their situations as totally negative five years after the divorce, and they still felt that they had not been successful in helping their children understand the divorce.

What are the particular pressures facing the single parent? For one thing, there is the realization that they and they alone are responsible for the care and protection of their children. Single parents, especially women, face severe economic problems.

About half of all children living in families with no father present live below the poverty line (U.S. Bureau of the Census 1980).

Social pressures abound as well. Single parents point out that schools have not yet accepted the fact that for many children, the "normal" family is a one-parent family. Schools continue to offer activities such as the annual "breakfast with Dad." Courses such as "family life" offered in some schools describe the "normal" family as having a natural mother and father and two or more children. The implication is that other family configurations are abnormal. Single parents sometimes are pitted against parents without custody in gaining access to school records. Although the regulations of the federal Family Educational Rights and Privacy Act of 1974 guarantee full parental rights with regard to school records to noncustodial parents and to surrogate parents, many schools today still continue to behave as if the law had

Single fathers usually do not have as serious economic problems as single mothers. Their major adjustment is often in learning the child-care and household tasks usually performed by the wife.

ONE SINGLE PARENT WHO "MADE IT": A WOMAN TELLS HER STORY OF ADJUSTMENT

"I was widowed when I was twenty-six and left with three children. Kevin was two months old, Joanne was three, and Shirley had just started school and was six. We'd just moved to Chicago a month before my husband died, and I didn't know anyone. I was lonely, depressed, and felt sorry for myself. For the first few months, I moped around the house—barely paid any attention to the kids except to go through the motions of feeding them and taking care of them. I just couldn't seem to get myself together. Here I was in a strange city with three small children, and the little money my husband left was running out fast.

"Well, one day I was down at the laundromat, sitting there waiting for the wash to dry and thinking about how it had been before Bob died and how on earth I was going to raise those kids by myself. I felt I just couldn't face the future and was almost on the verge of tears. Then this woman came over and asked me if I had some change for the machines. She was real nice and friendly, and I guess she could see I was at the end of my rope. We got to talking, and somehow it came out about Bob's death and all. Then she told me her husband had run off and left her with six kids a couple of years ago, and I thought, 'Wow, she's worse off than I am,' and I really felt sorry for her. But she didn't feel that way. She felt she had made a pretty good job of handling things without him. So I asked her how she did it. Maybe what worked for her could work for me.

"It didn't sound easy, but I knew I had to do something soon, so I decided to take her advice. Like she said, keep smiling and go to everybody who might help. Well, I didn't always smile. At first I was scared, but I forced myself to go to lots of agencies and talk to a lot of people. Some places, they told me I didn't qualify for their services because I hadn't been in the area long enough, but finally the Public Assistance helped me to get ADC (Aid to Dependent Children), and a church nearby took my two youngest ones into their day-care center. That was a big help because with the kids taken care of, I could go look for a job. I wasn't trained to do anything, but the employment office found a job for me waiting tables. The tips were good, and so were the hours. I could be with my children when they were home from school, and I started to take more interest in them. I guess I just hadn't realized before how rough it was on them without their father and with a mother who could only think about how much she was suffering. I gave them a lot of love and attention and tried to comfort them about losing their dad.

"Things were going pretty good for us, but I was still lonely for companionship. I talked to the woman I worked for at the restaurant about it, and she

Continued

invited me to join her bowling team. I'm still not much of a bowler, but I have fun, and I've made some good friends.

"I've even joined the PTA at Shirley's school because she wanted her teachers to meet me. At first I went just to please her, but I really enjoy it now. And would you believe it, last week I was elected chairman of the ways and means committee.

"It seems that the happier I am with myself and my life, the happier my children are. When I look back to four years ago, I'm amazed at how much I have accomplished for myself and for my children. The kids are doing well in school, and the future is looking brighter all the time. Oh, we have our ups and downs, but the older the kids get, the more they realize that we all have to work together. And we've become a very close family because of that.

"I'd say there are several things you have to do when you are left to raise your children alone. First, try to stop feeling sorry for yourself and that things are hopeless. Realize that the children need you more now than ever before. Make yourself get out and talk with people. Ask for their advice and help. And get help from any agency you can find. Most of all, don't give up. Keep working at it, and anyone can raise kids by themselves if they have to, and do a good job, and have some fun too."

QUESTIONS FOR THOUGHT

1. The young woman reported in this case history has dealt with a large number of problems related to being a single parent. Briefly, what are the most important of these?

2. What support that was *not* provided might have helped make the transition easier?

Source: U.S. Dept. of Health, Education and Welfare (1974).

never passed. For example, a mother who does not have custody of her child might call the school and request a duplicate report card, only to be told that it is against the school's policy to release the report without approval of the other parent.

Other problems in adjusting to being a single parent relate to balancing the roles of parent and independent adult. In some instances, it is difficult for the single parent to have a social life. Here there is a difference between the sexes. While single mothers are sometimes considered a threat to other married women because of their presumed interest in finding a husband, single fathers do not seem to encounter the same negative image. Handling sexual relationships is an area of concern among both male and female single parents. Views on dealing with this problem vary from maintaining sexual relationships or hiding them from the children to remaining celibate.

The increase in our society in recent years of divorced fathers obtaining custody of their children has prompted considerable interest in the phenomenon of single fatherhood. Although single fathers still constitute a small minority of one-parent families, over a half million men are now rearing their minor children alone (Mendes 1976). These fathers must make psychological and sociological adjustments that are somewhat different from those facing single mothers. Whereas a major problem for single mothers who have not previously worked outside the home is finding well-paying jobs, the task facing single fathers is to take on childrearing and household tasks. Today, single fathers are learning to cook and clean, to take care of babies, and to teach preadolescent daughters the facts of life. Studies of single fathers suggest that for many, meeting the demands of child care contributes to their own stability and personal growth (Keshet and Rosenthal 1978).

One researcher suggests that many of the pressures of raising children as a single parent could be alleviated by a variety of cooperative efforts, such as day-care centers that extend service into the evenings, child-care facilities in shopping centers, baby-sitting cooperatives, cooperative arrangements to transport children to and from day-care centers, classes on single parenthood, and female children becoming involved in the Big Sister organization, which provides a strong female role model in their family (Orthner, Brown, and Ferguson 1976).

Single Living After Divorce

Many divorced adults remarry. Carter and Glick (1976) found that the number of women in our society who remain single after divorce is considerably higher than the number of men. There are several reasons for this. After about age thirty, divorced females seeking new spouses face less favorable conditions than divorced males. One difficulty is that more women seek partners than the number of available adult males, because as a group, men do not live as long as women. Women also encounter the "double standard of aging" in which the value of the female declines with age, and the value of the male increases. Orthner, Brown, and Ferguson (1976) also point out that single-parent fathers tend to be in no hurry to remarry after divorce, although they tend to maintain active social lives. Many single adults, however, choose after a divorce to cohabit, an alternative that they feel affords them intimacy without the legal constraints of marriage. The percentage of adults who cohabit after divorce is, in fact, higher than the percentage of younger people who cohabit before marriage. Newcomb (1979) reports thirty percent more cohabitants in the twenty-five to sixty-four age group than in the below-twenty-five age group and that twenty percent of cohabiting couples live with one or more children.

THE CASE OF FRANCES LEE—A PEDIATRICIAN AND MOTHER OF TWO CHILDREN:
A CASE STUDY FOR CLASS DISCUSSION

I. Identification and Sources of Information

Name: Frances Lee

Address: York City, USA

Ethnic background: Chinese-American

Sex: Female

Age: Forty-three years

Sources of information

1. Personal interview with Frances Lee

2. Interview with Dr. Ann Pederson, colleague of Frances Lee

3. Interviews with the mother, husband, and two children of Frances Lee

II. Family History

Frances Lee was born in San Francisco's Chinatown, the daughter of a wealthy Chinese-American merchant in the city. She was the elder of two daughters, both of whom attended public school in San Francisco and then the University of California at Berkeley. Frances took premedical courses in college and then went on to medical school, where she met her husband. Frances's sister studied journalism and currently works as an editor for a major newspaper.

Frances was twenty-six when she completed medical school and married John Lee, then a resident in cardiology. When she was twenty-seven, her first daughter, Kim, was born. Later, after completing her residency in pediatrics, she gave birth to her son, Tommy. When she was thirty-three and Tommy was two years old, she opened her first office, together with Dr. Ann Pederson. The Lee–Pederson practice is a large one today and has added two additional pediatricians to the staff. The Lee family today lives in a suburb of San Francisco; a full-time housekeeper takes charge of the house while the Drs. Lee are at work. Kim is eleven years old; Tommy is seven. Both children have always done well in school. During the

past six months, however, Frances's mother, who has lived with the family for the last year since her husband died, reports that the children have been causing problems at home. Kim has been staying out late and is generally disobedient; Tommy got a D on his last report card. Frances's mother told us that Frances and John have been quarreling about what to do about the children.

III. Case History

Frances came in for therapy when she began to get headaches about a year ago, shortly after her father died. She reported that she was relieved that her mother had moved in with the family because "it's a big house, and I feel better knowing that she is there to watch over the children and that the children at the same time can offer her company." Frances reported not feeling very much loss at her father's funeral. "I think it was simply too difficult to believe that he'd died—he was only sixty-four years old, after all. I think I didn't quite believe it at the time. Gradually, though, I noticed I'd begun to think about him at odd times—in the middle of the night, which would make me wake up in a cold sweat. Or while I was in the middle of examining a child, or worse—when I was in the middle of surgery—an appendectomy once. It was quite scary. Then I began to get the headaches, and thought I'd better come in."

Frances's colleague, Ann Pederson, told the therapist that Frances was the hardest worker she had ever seen—"and that was true from medical school on." Frances was always in the office first in the morning, even before the secretary, and was to last to leave. She took house calls often because she did not want children who were seriously ill to have to go outdoors. She therefore rarely was home with her own kids. Ann Pederson did not think that Frances's workload bothered her husband; John Lee usually worked as late as his wife. But it did leave the housekeeper much of the responsibility for the kids. Ann

THE CASE OF FRANCES LEE

thinks that it was shortly after her father's death that Frances began to think about "the time lost" and "my kids growing up without me." She began more and more to talk about how short life really is. And when her mother moved in with the family, John Lee told us, "Frances gave up her house calls altogether. I was glad to see her do that," he said. "She'd been looking a little peaked for a long time; the kids had been acting up a little—not seriously or anything, but enough to make us both worry—and I know she wanted the time to be with her mother."

Frances's children were polite when we interviewed them. Kim told us that she was terribly sorry her parents were so upset about her behavior. Tommy was penitent about his bad grade. He told us he promised to do better the next time, and although he had not been studying much, he would do his best to be a better scholar.

IV. Present Status, Diagnosis, and Prognosis

Frances is in her late thirties, near the age at which Jung projected the mid-life crisis. The death of her father provided for her the event by which she could view the changes to expect in her world. The adjustments she had to make involved rethinking a great deal of what she has done in the past. It is a good thing that Frances has reduced her workload somewhat. It would be a wise idea for her now to reduce it still further, perhaps for a few months going to work part time or even leaving practice for a few months' vacation to give herself ample time to think things through, to regain her assurance, and to make certain for herself that she spends the next half of her life doing what would be best for her own development. That might well include reducing her professional work and spending more time with her children. Or it might mean returning to her work without guilt, knowing that she is doing the right thing. More therapy is suggested in the interim period, to help her raise and answer the appropriate questions.

Questions for Class Discussion

1. The professional life of Frances Lee passed through two potential crisis periods. What were these; what were the crises involved; and how were they resolved?

2. Do you think women electing to maintain professional lives have crises different from those of other women? Why? In what way?

SUMMARY

During the period from about twenty-five to about forty years of age, biological changes become less important than they were earlier, and most people are still near their peaks physically. Fertility does decrease, however, and women who postpone childbearing into their thirties are more likely to have trouble conceiving than women in their twenties.

Although the underlying maturational process that causes cognitive development stops with adulthood, the ability of many adults to think and to solve problems increases in complexity because of their life experiences. The most important adult developmental changes prior to middle age are personal–social, focusing on marital relationships, children, and occupational and career decisions.

Two important transitional periods occur prior to middle age. At about age thirty, the first transitional period, young adults are expected to have established their identities and to have taken on the tasks of the adult world and adult relationships. For those who have not met this goal, the thirties often represent a period of crisis during which they must make decisions regarding life-styles or values if they are to adjust happily to later stages of life. The second transitional period falls usually at about age forty, when adults normally begin preparing themselves for the next stage of life. For most, this is a difficult period, during which they question nearly every aspect of their lives. Many feel they must modify their lives and require several years to complete the transition to what they feel is a more meaningful way to live. Developmental tasks change between the ages of twenty-five and forty as life experiences change; for many, the most important developmental task is parenthood.

Most American adults today choose to marry. One of the biggest causes of anxiety among married people is childrearing. Decisions about raising children and adjusting to marriage in general are complicated by the increasing number of two-earner families in which both partners face excessive demands on each individual's time, energy, and leisure (particularly the wife's). Conflicts can be caused by family and job demands and tensions of bringing work problems home. The greatest difficulty facing these families is the rigidity and unresponsiveness of the workplace; a number of systems, including flextime, can be designed to help out. Also, husbands are now playing more important roles in domestic work and child care.

Most couples consider their sexual activity "pleasurable"; generally, it is people who are not happy with other aspects of their marriage who are dissatisfied sexually. Communication with one's partner seems to be the most important factor in a good sexual relationship. Most Americans still disapprove of extramarital sex, though a minority participate in sexually open marriage, mate swapping, or swinging marriages.

The pressures facing today's families are intense, and a large number of marriages end in divorce. Many men and women elect to divorce during periods of developmental crises, using divorce as a means of changing the direction of their lives. Issues of division of property and of child custody are sources of a great deal of stress during divorce, and the economic strain can be severe. Remarriage, though common, presents new problems and some new stresses not encountered in first marriages. Often-mentioned difficulties include the strains of stepparent–stepchildren relationships, the financial difficulties resulting from obligations to more than one family, and the fact that persons who are poor marriage risks continue to be so.

One result of the high divorce rate is single parenting. The transition to a stable life can be difficult and prolonged. Additional pressures on these parents include the knowledge that they alone bear responsibility for their children, economic problems, and social pressures not ordinarily faced by parents in nuclear households. Social and sexual adult lives can be difficult to maintain. In recent years, more and more fathers have been taking on single-parent roles.

FOR FURTHER READING

Atkin, E., and E. Rubin. *Part-time Father: A Guide for the Divorced Father.* New York: Vanguard Press, 1976. This book is concerned primarily with the difficulties fathers face in becoming "absent" parents following divorce. It also deals with part-time fathers' subsequent relationships with their children.

LeMasters, E. *Parents in Modern America.* Homewood, Illinois: Dorsey Press, 1977. This book focuses on what happens to parents trying to raise children in America and to incorporate the social changes of the past decade in doing so.

Scott, N. *Working Women.* Kansas City, Kansas: Sheed Andrews and McMeel, 1977. This book takes a look at the ways women today are coping with the problems of employment and motherhood in the United States. The book discusses the rearing of children by single parents, managing home and job responsibilities simultaneously, and many other topics.

Preview Questions

- Can you describe several physical changes that come about during the middle years?

- What are the three major causes of death in the middle years, and how does stress influence their frequency?

- What are some differences in the way the climacteric affects middle-aged men and women?

- How does sexuality change for men and women in their middle years?

- Can you describe the changes in crystallized and fluid intelligence that occur in middle adulthood?

- What is the mid-life transition and how is it related to Erikson's generativity vs. stagnation crisis?

- What are the four conflicts Peck believes middle-aged people must deal with, and how are these related to Bardwick's concern for commitment?

- How do career expectations and change differ for men and women in these middle years?

- How do parent–offspring relationships change after the children have left home?

- What happens to the marriage relationship of couples after their children have left home?

- How do middle-aged people respond to the needs of their aging parents?

- Can you describe five distinct styles of grandparenting that have been noted by Neugarten and Weinstein?

12

Middle Adulthood

Middle adulthood, commonly called **middle age** in our society, refers to that period of adult development roughly encompassing forty to sixty years of age. Some psychologists consider this period the most potentially productive part of peoples' lives. It is the time during which married couples complete the task of raising families and then launching their children into adulthood. It is also the period during which careers usually peak and during which most adults accept full responsibility for themselves and those around them (Neugarten 1979).

Development during the middle years brings with it a number of physical changes as well as changes in cognitive and social skills. Psychologists report that during middle adulthood, individuals go through transition periods in which they reassess their personal lives and their job or career expectations. For many, the mid-life transition leads to change in family and marital relationships and sometimes to career change.

People at mid life are often at the height of their power in their abilities to care for others and to take on important career positions. Middle adulthood is the period of life in which individuals often are at the height of their earning power as well. Those whose children are leaving home and establishing their own lives often have more economic freedom that allows them to do many things they could not afford when their children were younger.

At the same time, people at mid life often feel discomfort about their age. One major reason for this discomfort seems to lie in our society's negative view of aging that places major stress on visible cosmetic changes that take place during the middle years. Underlying an emphasis on youth in appearance, clothing styles, and even entertainment in America seems to be a pervading feeling that to be young, look young, and act young is good. Because of this, Americans, perhaps more than most people in the world, fear middle age and what follows. Many fear that as they and their bodies change, so do the perceptions of others who interact with them.

Bardwick (1978) gives another reason for dissatisfaction with middle age. Middle age, Bardwick points out, seems to be the time that people realize that the years are passing unpunctuated by events of great moment. The earlier years, by contrast, were marked by diplomas, births, buying one's first home, obtaining the first big promotion. Middle age is that time of growing awareness that one's everyday problems are not really unique but actually are the same as everyone else's. For some, middle age may be experienced as a period of mourning, for children who have left home, things that have not been done, roles that have not been tried, hobbies that have not been developed, or experiences that have been passed by.

DEVELOPMENT DURING THE MIDDLE YEARS

Physical Changes

Middle adulthood marks the beginning of a gradual process of physical aging, as the body slowly gives evidence of biological decline. Researchers have shown that middle-aged people often are as healthy as they were in their twenties and thirties (Friedman 1977). Still, the visible cosmetic changes that began to worry adults in their thirties do not go away in their forties and fifties but slowly become more and more noticeable and worrisome. Facial wrinkles and other signs of aging do not go away, even with all the modern creams and cosmetic surgery now available. Exercise gets rid of paunches, and forty- and fifty-year-olds often become extremely exercise conscious. But the sixty-year-old tennis player who can still beat the "young college punk" on the court can do so because of a forehand that is better controlled, not because a sixty-year-old is more powerful. Sixty-year-olds cannot win if college students keep them on the run. They no longer have the stamina.

For some people, physical changes have strong effects on both cognitive and personal–social development. For others, physical aging interferes very little with such important areas as occupation or intellectual judgments. The physical changes that occur from the forties to the sixties are noticeable in many different ways. Skeletal bone structures stiffen and even shrink a bit during mid life. The person attending a high school reunion may actually be slightly shorter than in reunions from years before. A loss of some elasticity of the muscles occurs, which is evident in facial wrinkling and looseness of the skin in some other parts of the body. Sensory abilities, such as visual acuity, begin to decline in one's late forties; bifocals become the sign of the middle-aged person who needs one type of prescription to see distance and another for reading. Many middle-aged people have less acute hearing, especially in the upper frequencies. Sensitivity to taste, pain, and smell also gradually diminish (Ebersole 1979). During the middle years, the likelihood of developing degenerative diseases increases. For example, although middle-aged people are less prone to cavities than younger people, often they are more likely to develop gum disease.

During middle age, other abilities also gradually decline. Biological functions, such as reaction time, slow down. Motor skills decline with age, but the rate at which they decline can be modified by practice. Internal changes occur also during this period of life. The nervous system begins to slow down. The heart pumps about eight percent less blood to the body for each decade after adulthood is reached. The size of the opening of the coronary arteries gradually decreases so that by middle age, it is about one-third less than it was in the early twenties. There is a corresponding decrease in lung capacity so that it is more difficult for middle-aged people to do hard physical labor than it is for younger people.

Individual differences, of course, are evident in the rates of these declines, just as individual differences are evident in other forms of development. Many middle-aged fifty-year-olds who have taken care of their bodies through diet and exercise look, feel, and act younger than many forty-year-olds. The middle-aged jogger who has run daily for the past ten years may well surpass someone two decades younger who is out of condition. But the fifty-year-old jogger will decline in skill rapidly without practice, and those who begin an exercise program at this time also find it more difficult than they would have ten years earlier.

Degenerative Disease. The incidence of two degenerative diseases, cardiovascular disease and cancer, increases sharply in mid life (Kimmel 1980). As the body ages, it becomes increasingly vulnerable to these diseases. Heart disease accounts for almost forty percent of deaths in the United States (U.S. Bureau of the Census 1980). Thirty-three percent of deaths of men between forty-five and fifty-four years of age are due to coronary arterial problems (Ebersole 1979). Women tend to have fewer heart attacks than do men, until menopause when estrogen is no longer produced by their bodies. Even after menopause, however, women tend to be less vulnerable to heart attacks than men, although with increasing numbers of women in stressful work situations, more women are experiencing cardiovascular disease. Reaction to serious illness such as heart attack seems to vary with chronological age. Denial of the seriousness of the attack is common at earlier ages; depression is common among those who are still in the work force but whose life-styles are changed by the attack. Cooperation with doctors is most common among older patients. Whatever the behavioral reaction to serious illness, the illness itself requires the person to make life-style changes (Rosen and Bibring 1968).

People do not as a rule suddenly develop heart trouble. Individuals who have a family history of heart disease have a higher probability of developing symptoms during middle age than those who have no such history. Those who live life-styles that promote heart disease (for example, those whose careers involve stress, those who do not get a great deal of physical exercise, and those who overeat) tend to develop symptoms more frequently than those who live healthier life-styles (Ebersole 1979).

Physical aging begins to be more noticeable in middle age, but a healthy life-style that includes exercise can slow down the development of degenerative diseases.

The second-highest cause of death in the United States is cancer (U.S. Bureau of the Census 1980). Like cardiovascular disease, cancer causes more deaths among men than among women at any age level. Middle-aged men tend to be more prone to lung cancer than are women; women tend to be more prone to breast cancer.

A third major cause of illness and death is diabetes. Ebersole (1979) reports that one-half of the three million diabetics in the United States are in their middle years. Diabetes, which tends to occur more frequently in women than in men, occurs in increasing rates and increasing severity at middle age. One of the serious consequences of diabetes is that it complicates other physical problems that develop at this period of life.

Stress and Degenerative Diseases. Stress as a factor related to degenerative disease among middle-aged adults has been studied extensively by researchers. As we already learned, individuals whose life-styles contain a great deal of stress tend to be more prone than others to cardiovascular disease. One reason for this relationship may be that both physical and psychological stresses have negative physiological effects on homeostatic mechanisms that maintain vital physiological balances in the body (such as the pH and sugar levels of the blood). Researchers believe that as these mechanisms begin to age, their efficiency is decreased, even without the addition of stress, and individuals become more vulnerable to many diseases. Stresses that can be easily tolerated in younger people begin to have seriously deteriorating effects on middle-aged people. By late adulthood, stress often becomes life threatening (Comfort 1964; Timiras 1972; Selye 1970). We will discuss the physiological effects of stress on the elderly in Chapter 14.

Rosenham (1974), in a study of 3400 men from age thirty-nine to age fifty-nine, compared personality style with incidence of coronary heart disease, in part to determine whether any relationship exists between ways in which individuals perceive stress and react to the world and the probability of their developing this degenerative disease. Rosenham subjected the individuals in his study to personality evaluations and typed them according to the ways they handled day-to-day activities. His subjects fell on a continuum. At one extreme was what Rosenham called the "Type A personality." **Type A individuals** tended to be highly competitive, aggressive, achievement oriented, hostile, and impatient. They tended to be tenser, to express feelings of urgency, and to speak a great deal. These individuals, according to Rosenham, by virtue of their personalities, tend to be more affected by external stresses than were other people. **Type B individuals,** at the other end of the continuum, tended to have the following characteristics: lack of aggression, lack of competitiveness and achievement orientation, patience, and a feeling of relaxation. Most individuals fall somewhere between Type A and Type B. Rosenham examined his subjects three times during a longitudinal study that took almost nine years to complete. At the beginning of this study, none of his subjects had experienced any symptoms of cardiovascular disease. By the end of the study, twice as many Type A individuals had developed cardiovascular disease or had suffered fatal heart attacks than had Type B individuals. This was true regardless of diet, incidence of cigarette smoking, and exercise regimens of the two groups.

Rosenham's study, of course, does not demonstrate that personality characteristics by themselves cause heart disease. Some individuals who fell on the continuum between personality Type A and personality Type B developed cardiovascular disease. We learned earlier that cardiovascular disease has also been related to dietary habits and exercise. Rosenham's study, however, provides a clear warning to the middle aged that stress may well play an exceptionally important role in increasing the possibility of cardiovascular disease.

Today, many middle-aged people are warned by their physicians to try to reduce stressful situations in their lives as much as possible in order to reduce the probability of cardiovascular and other degenerative diseases. Unfortunately, many stressful situations occur, regardless of the attempt of individuals to reduce them. Holmes and Rahe (1967) point out that the single life event that produces the greatest amount of stress for an individual is the death of a spouse. In order of decreasing amounts of stress, other important life events include divorce, marital separation, jail terms, deaths of close family members, and personal injury or illness. Many of these events that cause stress for an individual are not within his or her control.

Adjusting to Physical Changes. The qualitative drop in body functioning during middle age requires, for some, accommodation in style of living and social roles, especially with regard to work.

The professional athlete who gives up playing football at thirty has another ten years of adulthood to establish himself in another occupation before middle age. The athlete who continues playing football until his late thirties, however, may go through a more difficult period during his mid-life transition. Those who cannot alter their modes of work at this point often burn out and no longer function adequately (Levinson *et al.* 1978).

Knowledge of the bodily changes that are taking place is what often leads middle-aged people to the exercise room. By fifty, the issue is not simply to slim that waistline or to reduce the belly. It is to try to recoup the strength that one had as a young adult. Thus the forty- or fifty-year-old is likely to be exercising so that he or she will find it easier to climb the stairs without getting out of breath or to enjoy a day on the ski slopes without fear of overexertion.

Being "on-time" or "off-time" becomes a compelling basis for self-assessment of physical change in middle age. Neugarten (1979) points out that men and women compare themselves with their friends, siblings, work colleagues, or parents in deciding whether they have made good, but they always have a time line in mind. It is not that one reaches forty, fifty, or sixty that is important, according to Neugarten, but rather the question is, "How am I doing for my age?"

Menopause and Climacteric

A major physical change that is considered one of the major biological phases of life is the **climacteric.** This term refers to a group of hormonal changes that affect the reproductive system and the emotional effects that may accompany these changes. In middle-aged women, the climacteric is called **menopause** or "change of life." Menopause is the period of natural cessation of menstruation and production of eggs by the ovaries. Menopause is not an overnight event but occurs gradually over a period of years between forty-five and fifty-five years of age. Neugarten (1979) reports that menopause is occurring later for women now than it did in previous generations, although the evidence for this is uncertain. During menopause, periods become irregular and gradually cease. The vaginal walls become thinner because of declining estrogen levels, and women experience less vaginal lubrication. The ovaries and uterus also atrophy. A common symptom of menopause is hot flashes, which are bothersome for twenty to sixty percent of menopausal women. A wide variety of other symptoms may also occur, including insomnia, irritability, depression, headaches, dizziness, nausea, and constipation (Jones, Cohen, and Wilson 1972). Only about twenty-five percent of women, however, seek medical help for symptoms related to menopause (Novak *et al.* 1970).

Today, with more biological knowledge available to women about what to expect during menopause and with awareness of remedies for unwanted side effects (for example, lubricating jelly for vaginal dryness), most women do not experience menopause as a critical event. In fact, for most, cessation of menstruation brings some psychological relief (Brock 1979). As one middle-aged woman reported,

Even though it came as a shock to me when I realized I was really that old, and it was actually happening to me, I had to give a sigh of relief. I'm Catholic, and my husband and I have used abstention all these years. Still, it didn't always work. We had four kids, and that's certainly enough. At my age, I didn't want to be like some of my friends and have another baby! I suppose I would have loved it once it was born, but a mid-life child might have taken my last gasp. No, a sigh of relief—tinged with a bit of regret at the knowledge that I must admit I'm no chicken—just an old hen. That was what accompanied the knowledge that I have stopped menstruating. I think the same feeling was true for my husband.

The climacteric in men is not marked by the same sort of obvious and rapid changes that occur in women. Many men continue to produce healthy sperm into their old age. A gradual decline in production of the male hormone testosterone, however, causes a decrease in the frequency of erection and the amount of ejaculate as well as the force of ejaculation, a slight decrease in the size of the testicles, and enlargement of the prostate gland. Middle-aged men also find that they may require longer to achieve an erection than they did in their younger years (Brock 1979).

Researchers have found that many men report physical symptoms related to the male climacteric, among them impotence, frequent urination, and even some symptoms common to female menopause, such as hot flashes and headaches (Ruebsaat and Hull 1975). It appears that changes in hormonal levels may be related to some of these symptoms but that factors, such as stress at work or in the family, also play a large role.

Self-Concept

Middle age is the period of life in which most individuals take time out from their personal lives and their careers to assess themselves, their goals, and their accomplishments. For many, the assessment is a difficult one, leading to severe self-criticism. The fifty-year-old woman who is beginning menopause might ask herself whether she is still a woman and worry that the decrease of hormones in her system is leaving her sexless. The self-concepts of women are likely to be affected negatively if they view menopause as the end of their attractiveness and usefulness. Such feelings unfortunately are enhanced by our youth-oriented society. On the fortunate side, Neugarten and colleagues (1964), in a survey of post menopausal women, reported that only one-third of the subjects she studied were affected adversely and had diminished self-concepts at this period of life.

Men going through their climacterics also may be extremely critical in their evaluations of themselves and their accomplishments. Their resulting self-concepts might be very low, even when objectively, their accomplishments have been great. One reason is that at this period of their lives, men, like their female counterparts, tend to assess themselves as harshly as possible. With the coming of the climacteric is the clear-cut message that life is not infinite. Many individuals respond to this understanding with an attempt to stop evading sensitive issues and to be as realistic as possible.

Sexuality

Sexual activity and interest can remain high for both males and females in their middle years (Pfeiffer 1972; McCary 1973). Researchers point out that people in good health are capable of enjoying satisfactory sex lives during middle age (Levinson *et al.* 1978). Even so, for many, the frequency of sexual activity tends to decline in middle age. In one major survey, married people over forty-five years old reported that they had sexual intercourse about once a week, whereas men and women between thirty-five and forty-five reported having intercourse about twice a week (Hunt 1974). For some middle-aged people, there may be physiological causes for the decline in marital sexual intercourse. As mentioned previously, some middle-aged males take longer to have or maintain erections.

Many of the sexual problems that some couples encounter in middle age can be overcome if the couple has a desire to continue sexual intimacy.

For some females, reduced lubrication and elasticity of the vagina may contribute to discomfort during intercourse. Most sexual problems can usually be overcome if a couple is still interested in each other and the partners wish to continue sexual intimacy. Hunt and Hunt (1974) suggest that couples use lubricating oils when a woman's natural lubrication is insufficient. They also suggest trying different forms of foreplay to aid in sexual arousal. Continuing to have sexual intercourse regularly is another important contributor to enhanced sexual enjoyment.

For most middle-aged people with problems experiencing satisfactory sexual intercourse, the causes are at least in part psychologically based. The fear of losing sexual ability can become a self-fulfilling prophecy. Performance anxiety can become a major problem (Masters and Johnson 1970). Another psychologically based problem for longtime spouses is simpler: boredom. Some couples, even though emotionally satisfied with one another and with their lives, become bored sexually, particularly after long marriages, many years of which were filled with childrearing and other activities that have stifled sexual creativity. Hunt (1974) discovered that about forty percent of married men surveyed and thirty percent of married women were dissatisfied with their sexual activity. Lack of sexual satisfaction and self-doubts about personal attractiveness are probably some of the reasons that the so-called mid-life crisis in the early forties is so often punctuated by an extramarital affair.

Cognitive Development

The cognitive tasks faced by adults in their middle years differ in certain ways from those faced by younger adults. Schaie (1977–1978) suggested that cognitive development at this stage of life is best described as the completion of a transition to the responsible stage. Middle-aged adults, more often than any other age group, tend to be the individuals in our society who hold power in family situations and on the job. It is they who, based on their own experience, tend to give advice to younger people and who tend at this point in their lives to hold positions of responsibility in their careers. The ability to be responsible at these tasks, according to Schaie (1977–1978, p. 134), requires "a pattern which facilitates integrating long-range goals as well as consequences for one's family unit in the solution of real life problems." It is the middle-aged person who can use the experiences gained in earlier stages of life to assess the value of seeking particular long-term goals. The middle-aged parent, for example, can more easily than the child see the "wisdom" of staying in school for that next academic degree, regardless of today's costs, because "in the long run, it will pay." The ability to work at achieving goals implies increased skills in relevant problem-solving tasks and shifts in cognitive style to greater flexibility and lessened field dependence.

Neugarten (1969) pointed out that people in the middle years of their lives require "executive abilities" that enable them to deal with complex relationships within the family and on the job. Clearly, middle-aged people often make effective contributions in fields requiring these abilities, such as politics, diplomacy, or management. All of these areas are dominated by people in their middle years. Adult creative scientists often do more integrative theoretical work in their middle years than in their earlier years and frequently set the direction for younger colleagues. Table 12.1 shows the percentage of total works created at each age level between twenty and eighty years in a study of creative productivity of individuals in a variety of professions. It is clear from this table that the highest percentage of works by the individuals studied occurred when they were in their forties, fifties, and sixties.

Many middle-aged people worry that their cognitive abilities, as measured by tests of intelligence, are not as high as in young adulthood. Middle-aged people often joke nervously about not remembering as well as they once did. For example, a middle-aged professor joking about her memory points out, "there are three things to remember about middle age: The first is that physiological decrements take place; the second is that visible cosmetic changes take place; and I can't remember the third." Regardless of this concern, most people in their middle years continue successfully at complex reasoning tasks that require memory. In fact, intelligence as measured by IQ tests, does not, in general, decrease during the middle years. Longitudinal studies have shown that individuals tend to keep the same general IQ scores as well as scores on reasoning, verbal ability, and questions on general information from early adulthood through middle age (Owens 1966).

Table 12.1

Percentage of Total Works Created at Each Age Decade from the 20s to the 80s by Individuals Engaged in Scholarship, Sciences, and Arts

| | *N* | *N* | \|Age Decade\| | | | | | |
			20s	30s	40s	50s	60s	70s
Scholarship	*People*	*Works*						
Historians	46	615	3	19	19	22	24	20
Philosophers	42	225	3	17	20	18	22	20
Scholars	43	326	6	17	21	21	16	19
		Means	4	18	20	20	21	20
Sciences	*People*	*Works*						
Biologists	32	3456	5	22	24	19	17	13
Botanists	49	1889	4	15	22	22	22	15
Chemists	24	2420	11	21	24	19	12	13
Geologists	40	2672	3	13	22	28	19	14
Inventors	44	646	2	10	17	18	32	21
Mathematicians	36	3104	8	20	20	18	19	15
		Means	6	17	22	21	20	15
Arts	*People*	*Works*						
Architects	44	1148	7	24	29	25	10	4
Chamber Mus.	35	109	15	21	17	20	18	9
Dramatists	25	803	10	27	29	21	9	3
Librettists	38	164	8	21	30	22	15	4
Novelists	32	494	5	19	18	28	23	7
Opera Comp.	176	476	8	30	31	16	10	5
Poets	46	402	11	21	25	16	16	10
		Means	9	23	26	21	14	6

Source: Reprinted by permission of *The Gerontologist/The Journal of Gerontology.* Taken from W. Dennis, Creative productivity between the ages of 20 and 80 years, *Journal of Gerontology,* 1966, 21, 1–8.

Some intellectual abilities improve with chronological age through middle age. **Crystallized intelligence,** or those abilities that require processing and recording of information, includes verbal abilities, vocabulary, comprehension, and some abilities related to spatial perception. Neugarten (1976) reports that these abilities continue to improve as long as individuals remain alert and are able to take in new information. When middle-aged people are tested for these abilities, they frequently do better than they did when they were twenty-five years younger (Dennis 1966). It is therefore not surprising that many academics are more productive in their middle age and later years than they were at any other time of their professional careers.

Some researchers, however, have found decrements in late middle age on some specific isolated skills, particularly those that involve speedy responses (Bischof 1976). This may be due to a general slowing down of the central nervous system's ability to process information. It is important to note, however, that this does not diminish the ability of middle-aged people to remember ideas or to integrate theories, both skills required for success at Neugarten's "executive tasks" and Erikson's generativity tasks.

Schaie (1977–1978) reminds us of the loss of particular fluid abilities at middle age or older. **Fluid intelligence,** as these abilities are called, refers to abilities that require speed and effectiveness of neurological functioning. They include such abilities as those used in developing motor speed, induction, memory, and figural relations. Fluid intelligence is required in developing new perceptions and in recognizing and learning to deal cognitively with new information. Neugarten (1976) points out that although fluid intelligence declines somewhat among middle-aged people, this decline normally brings these abilities back only to the level that they were in mid adolescence. Apparently, there is so little decrease in fluid intelligence that it hardly has any effect on the thinking of middle-aged people. Moreover, fluid intelligence is not usually related to the experiential demands of people at this stage of life or to Neugarten's "executive responsibilities." For this reason, some loss would have little effect on the behavior of people at this stage of life.

 ## THE MID-LIFE TRANSITION

Much has been written about the **mid-life transition,** or the **mid-life crisis,** as it is sometimes called. Psychoanalyst Carl Jung (1971) believes that the change in thinking of people at this stage of their lives comes from what he calls a shift in control. Jung points out that the mid-life transition for most people is essentially a transition from the first to the second half of life. In the first half of life, individuals exercise control over themselves and their environments in a conscious manner. They decide what they want to do with their lives, often set specific goals, and set out to achieve these goals. At the mid-life transition, however, they begin, often for the first time, to recognize the many factors over which they have no control. At this point, they begin to face personal limitations and the limitations that mortality places upon them. This is the stage, Jung suggests, at which individuals often begin to confront their unconscious feelings for the first time. They become far more reflective and inner directed than they were at earlier stages of their lives. Jung believes that the mid-life transition occurs as they learn gradually that the source of control in their lives has shifted. Figure 12.1 shows the **mid-life transition** as it occurs with other developmental periods of middle age.

Many individuals pass through the mid-life transition with few noticeable external differences. Others face deep emotional crises as they attempt to interpret their

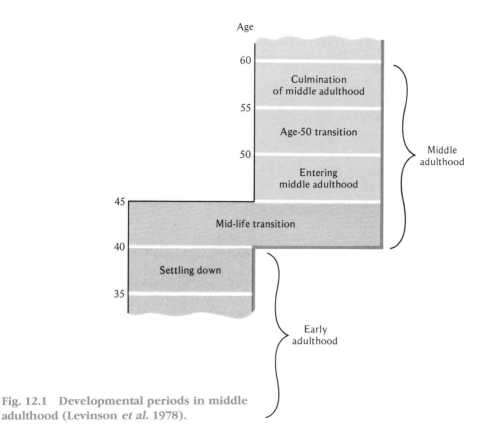

Fig. 12.1   **Developmental periods in middle adulthood (Levinson *et al.* 1978).**

new thoughts. Gould (1978) points out that for some, the mid-life transition forces people to face realities repressed in earlier life. Those who adjust to these realities adjust also to middle age.

Personality Development

Middle age often begins with review of progress. Middle-aged people ask, "What have I done with my life? Where am I now? Of what value is my life to me or to anyone?" People who, at the mid-life transition, have failed to meet their expectations must come to terms with the failures and arrive at a new set of choices around which to rebuild their lives. Levinson and colleagues (1978) point out that it is here that middle-aged people either make or break their futures. As they attempt to reappraise their lives, they often discover that much of life has been based on illusion. It now is their task to "deillusion" themselves. If they succeed, they then must consider the meaning and value of their success.

The seventh stage of adult development proposed by Erik Erikson is of special relevance here. The crisis of this stage is referred to as **generativity vs. self-absorption.** According to Erikson, middle-aged people who express generativity assume responsibility for new generations of adults. Levinson and his colleagues, building on Erikson's theory, suggest that generativity involves finding ways of combining authority and mutuality in dealing with younger adults, those with whom the middle-aged adults live or work, instead of treating them as children under the benign control of the middle-aged (Levinson *et al.* 1978). As senior members of the adult world, middle-aged people need to be able to relate to younger adults as junior but fully adult members who will soon succeed them. To become generative, many people at mid life try to make some changes in their lives. The individual who has been very involved previously in work may become more involved with family, or the housewife might choose a career. According to Levinson and his colleagues (1978, p. 3), this change helps individuals avoid a "sense of not growing, of being static, stuck, drying up, bogged down in a life full of obligation and devoid of self-fulfillment." Levinson's approach assumes that once people experience the mid-life crisis, they must move beyond their life-styles or learning experiences in some way and find wholesomeness and meaning.

Vaillant and McArthur (1972), in reviewing the personality characteristics of middle-aged men described in the Grant longitudinal study of adult development at Harvard University, point out that men between the ages of forty and fifty are more likely to be concerned about others close to them than they were in the past. Specifically at age fifty, in discussing their jobs, they are far more concerned about those who work with them or for them than they were when they were younger. For this group of men, Erikson's term *generativity* goes beyond caring only for the young; it means achieving responsibility for other adults as well.

Generativity is not achieved by all people in middle age. Some middle-aged individuals maintain adaptive styles reminiscent of adolescence (Vaillant 1972). They have not developed a capacity for love and intimacy with others. This inability to love is a major contributor to poor adjustment in marriage and to marital instability. Vaillant and McArthur point out that those adults who measured low in generativity account for most divorces in our society.

Erikson's descriptions of adult development include, as we have learned, the stage of generativity vs. self-absorption. This stage is followed in later life by the stage of integrity vs. despair in which individuals look back over their lives and either decide that they are satisfied with what they have done or despair that they have not satisfactorily accomplished their major goals.

Peck's Description of Personality Development. Peck (1968), a psychologist concerned with expanding and elaborating both of these stages of development, suggests that during the middle years, there are four major conflicts or issues. These conflicts or issues must be resolved satisfactorily during middle age so that individuals first resolve the crises involved in the stage of generativity and self-absorption and then, later in life, develop the ability to look back on their lives with satisfaction. Peck suggested further that individuals who adjust satisfactorily to middle age develop important new skills and values to deal with these conflicts. The four issues or conflicts with which middle-aged people must deal, according to Peck are **valuing wisdom vs. valuing physical powers, socializing vs. sexualizing, emotional flexibility vs. emotional impoverishment,** and **mental flexibility vs. mental rigidity.**

During middle age, people tend to shift a good part of their energies into mental rather than physical activities. According to Peck, those individuals who learn to

According to Peck, adjustment to middle age is enhanced when individuals learn to value wisdom more than the physical powers of earlier years. For example, the man whose greatest pleasure used to come from winning at tennis now gains as much satisfaction from instructing his children in the sport.

value wisdom as opposed to physical power adjust more easily than those individuals who try to retain their youth by doing their best to continue to excel at those physical skills that they performed well when they were younger. Thus according to Peck, the middle-aged man who used to enjoy winning at tennis but who now derives more pleasure from instructing his son at the game may enjoy this period of his life far more than his counterpart who still spends all of his time and energies trying to maintain the physical strength and dexterity that he gradually must lose anyway. This is not to say, of course, that the middle-aged individual ought to stop trying to increase strength and maintain athletic abilities. Instead, it suggests that individuals can continue their athletic activities recognizing at the same time that their abilities must decline with age and placing emphasis on other aspects associated with these abilities.

Second, according to Peck, men and women who want to adjust satisfactorily to middle age need to find a new balance between "socializing" and "sexualizing" in their human relationships. Many people at this stage of life adapt by stressing companionship over sexual gratification in their relationships. Those who were sexually competitive in their younger years tend to become less so. This adjustment is one imposed not only by the biological changes that occur at this age in relation to sexuality but also by social constraints. The middle-aged person in our society is simply not expected to behave aggressively in relation to "sexualizing." To adjust satisfactorily to this stage, he or she needs to learn to develop skills at socializing.

Third, successfully adjusted middle-aged people need gradually to develop emotional flexibility to adjust to the changes of mid life. This is necessary, according to Peck, for people to be able to deal satisfactorily with the various adjustments that they need to make at the period of their lives in which their children are growing up and leaving home and old interests stop being their central focus.

Finally, successfully adjusting middle-aged people need to develop mental flexibility and use this flexibility in fighting the inclination to become too set in their ways or too distrustful of the changes they see occurring around them. The conflict that must be resolved is increased by the threat imposed by our technological society that increases steadily the rate of change. Peck cautions that this is not a simple task for many people; it is often easier to become mentally rigid and to judge change on the basis of what was correct or incorrect earlier in life than to examine closely new ideas and judge them on the basis of their utility at the present.

Bardwick's Concern for Commitment. Many researchers have discussed the personality adjustments that must be made for middle-aged people to adjust satisfactorily to this period of life. Bardwick (1978), for example, adds to Peck's interpretation the notion that it is important for middle-aged people to develop new commitments. Individuals who are aware of their own aging, Bardwick points out, need to be able to create new senses of future in order to make the next portion of their

MIDDLE AGE AND A SENSE OF FUTURE

"Is the normal developmental phase of middle age always a crisis? For some, surely, there will be a realization that at least some of the promises of youth have been realized. Some will be at the height of their creative productivity, some will be wise rather than merely smart, humane instead of egocentric, the mentor rather than the student. Yet when we think about middle age we tend to ignore the constructive aspects and concentrate on the negatives. Middle age seems to be a period when people mourn for the things they have not done, for the roles they have not participated in, for the experience they have not had. I think that is because for most Americans middle age is the first intimation in the experientially real sense that they will die, and it is reasonable that experiencing your mortality, acknowledging your restricted alternatives, and understanding the permanence of decisions you make now, provokes psychological crises. In other cultures where death is less feared and age and experience are venerated and life's rhythms are repeated, flowing from one generation to the next, then one could imagine that someone's fortieth birthday would be as full of promise as the twenty-first is for us. In a culture of rapid social change that is much less likely.

"It may be useful to conceptualize adult phases as periods when one attempts to create new existential anchors. Existential anchors are roles or commitments such as work, marriage, and parenthood that literally anchor you to your present reality because they force you to cope with real tasks and people. Existential anchors have the inherent capacity to focus effort and provide feelings of growth as the nature of the tasks change. Anchors are central organizers in one's present time. . . .

"Sadly, technological societies threaten members by dint of the very rate of change within the society. Individuals within rapidly changing societies are those most in need of anchors. If one's world is in a vortex of change at least one's own identity ought to remain stable, like the eye of a storm. Yet that is exactly what cannot happen because the definitions of what constitute anchors are themselves being changed. A decade ago, for example, the existential anchor for women was to be found in the family relationship. Today, in the radical ideal, that anchor is rejected in favor of anchoring within the self and there is the specific rejection of finding one's existential anchor or identity within relationships. For women the anchor of parenthood is rejected, in the radical ideal, for the anchor of work. For men, the anchor of competitive success is rejected in favor of family or individual self-sufficiency.

"The people who will emerge more mature and stronger from the crisis that is the awareness of their aging will be those who have been able to create Continued

HIGHLIGHT 12.1

a sense of future. It seems necessary for people to be involved in a commitment which is real. It seems necessary to believe that it will be a good, that is, a moral thing for you to achieve what you do. It seems necessary to experience yourself as initiating and controlling change, for then change for its own sake is perceived as exhilarating. It seems necessary to experience yourself as coping and as becoming as you work toward your future which is also your present. Those who experience the crisis of middle age as a developmental or growth phase are those who are able to create an existential anchor which fills their present time and creates a reality which extends endlessly forward and thereby creates a future."

QUESTIONS FOR THOUGHT

1. How do Bardwick's proposals solve the conflicts that Peck describes as important to middle-aged people?

2. In a practical sense, what specific kinds of commitments do you think would be most effective in helping people adjust to middle age?

Source: Reprinted from Judith M. Bardwick, Middle age and a sense of future, Merrill-Palmer Quarterly of Behavior and Development, 1978, 24, 129–138, by permission of the Wayne State University Press.

lives meaningful. To do this, Bardwick suggests making new commitments. Women who spent the earlier portion of their lives committed to raising their children and caring for their families now need to develop new commitments, perhaps to an outside job. Men who might have been committed primarily to their careers might elect at this point to develop new interests, new ways to interact with their families, or new hobbies.

Gould's Description of Resignation and Mellowing. Gould (1972) views the middle-age years first as years in which individuals become increasingly resigned to the realities that they have already developed their personalities and that with the limitations of time, they are not likely to create great change. Later, according to Gould, are years in which people mellow and become more accepting of themselves and others close to them. The early middle years therefore often are bitter to accept because of a new understanding of time limitations. Many individuals become more relaxed during this period as they accept that they can no longer create change as they could when they were younger. Gould points out that many middle-aged individuals whom he and his staff tape-recorded in group discussions seemed to have little concern for either the past or the future. Gould attributed this lack of concern to a greater acceptance of mortality. Individuals who reach this stage have passed successfully through the mid-life transition and have learned the changes necessary to adjust to their new feelings and to the needs and desires of those around them.

Career Expectations and Career Change

Some people realize at the midpoint in their lives that the routes they chose in earlier adulthood have helped them to grow into a creative and meaningful middle age. Yet to reach this point, these individuals are likely to have experienced a time of questioning and reassessment. Gould (1972) suggested that self-scrutiny and questioning of goals and values at this stage of life are the norm. Middle-aged people ask themselves, "Have I done the right thing?" and "Is there time to change?" For many, work is seen as offering the last hope that dreams can still be realized. For some, however, work may become an escape from asking the hard questions about life.

Whether or not an individual continues to grow after mid life or settles into a pattern of stagnation depends to a great extent on that person's response to the mid-life crisis. For example, the forty-five-year-old engineer who decides to quit a stressful job and, with his wife and children, to move to a rural region to "get back to the earth" will probably lead a more personally satisfying life than the high school biology teacher who realizes at forty that she hates her job but decides to stay on because she does not want to face making a major life change.

As discussed earlier, a person who has successfully handled the crisis of middle age is characterized by Erikson as having achieved generativity, the ability to care for the succeeding generation and help young persons develop. In addition, according to such developmental theorists as Levinson, the middle-aged person who has passed this transitional point successfully has learned to adjust in certain ways to what he or she does daily on the job (Levinson *et al.* 1978). At the mid-life transition is an emerging feeling that the ultimate message of overall career success or failure is about to be delivered in the form of recognition and advancement, on the one hand, or job dissatisfaction on the other. Doubts about life-style often express themselves in questioning whether the present career can help fulfill and express all important aspects of the self. Mid-life career changes often are due to lack of satisfaction on the job and desire for advancement (Doberstyn 1978). Middle-aged blacks have been found to be much more conservative than whites in their approach to job or career changes and are less likely in their forties and fifties to change what they are doing (Doberstyn 1978). This may be due in part to fewer opportunities for blacks.

What happens to people who decide, at their mid-life transitions, that they are not doing what they want to do with the rest of their lives and want to make a change? Some, of course, have these feelings but give up and experience a sense of failure. Others change the direction of their careers. Vaitenas and Weiner (1977) suggest a clear difference between career changers and those who do not change their career directions at mid life. Career changers, for one thing, tend to be less consistent in their interests. They also tend to have more emotional problems. Some middle-aged men who change careers do so because they were never sure what they wanted to do in the first place. Some select careers that are less threatening to self-esteem. A good example from a psychologist's files is the business executive who spent the first twenty years on the job striving to become president of the corporation. In his mid forties, after he was bypassed for promotion to vice-president, he quit and took a job as director of a much smaller corporation. "I didn't want to sit back and watch younger men pass me by," he said. "I saw it happen once, and I didn't think I was up to being hurt again. This new position will never lead to what my old one might have, but it is a secure, safe job, and I won't be under stress to get ahead here. I'm at the top, maybe a big fish in a small pond, but at least a safe fish."

Those who select new careers at mid life sometimes do so to have more opportunity to express their feelings of generativity. An example from a psychologist's files is the professor of medicine who resigned from his position after a heart attack at age fifty to go to an Indian reservation and take on a general practice. Vaitenas and Wiener (1977) found that middle-aged men changing their careers usually did not behave exactly as this man did and did not tend to select new careers with more potential for social service in their vocational interests. Instead, they tended to select a variety of different interests. Apparently, career changers tend to make the choices they do because of a wide variety of interest changes.

Job Satisfaction. Because jobs and careers are so crucial to middle-aged people's feelings of satisfaction with their lives, this area has been studied in some detail. Clausen (1976) reported recent follow-up studies of middle-aged men who were subjects in a long-term longitudinal research program at the Institute of Human Development at Berkeley. Roughly three middle-aged men in ten from working-class and middle-class backgrounds in Clausen's report said that they believed that they were doing professionally what they "really" wanted to do. Nearly half said that their careers had been "approximately" what they wanted, even though not ideal. Only about one-fourth indicated serious dissatisfaction. Fifty-year-olds, more than forty-year-olds, tended to report dislike of working long hours and tension on the job. By the time men reach their fifties, according to Clausen, their aspirations for advancement seem to subside, and most men come to terms with the jobs and careers they have.

Careers and the Woman at Mid Life. For middle-aged women in the Berkeley study, career practices and expectations differed considerably from those of middle-aged men. When they were interviewed at age thirty-eight, only about one-fourth of the women studied were working outside their homes. The remaining three-quarters were involved in domestic duties and childrearing. Of those working outside their homes, only a few had a heavy investment in their jobs. When interviewed at age forty-eight to fifty, however, nearly half the women reported working part time, and a third were employed full time. Apparently, by this age, many of the women had launched their families and wanted to make use of other skills and interests. In another study, Livson (1976) found that moving out of the mother–housewife roles is particularly beneficial to the psychological health of "independent" (as opposed to traditionally feminine) middle-aged women. By independent, Livson means women who had personal ambitions outside the mother–housewife roles. These women often tended to have some discomfort during the childrearing years because they wished to be using other skills and pursuing other interests. Apparently, the psychological health of "independent" women improves when disengaging them from

Today, more women who spent their younger years at mothering and home-making tasks are deriving satisfaction from pursuing outside careers at mid life.

mothering frees them to develop more assertive job-related skills. Traditionally feminine women, on the other hand, those who are less ambitious and less intellectually oriented from youth, have an easier time through their mother–housewife years. According to Livson, although they may work outside the home after their children are grown, either for personal or economic reasons, they tend to prefer being a "second earner" in the family rather than aspiring to a career that requires commitment and promises personal fulfillment.

Independent, self-assertive women approaching fifty years old today are usually newer at their careers than their husbands. They tend to be far more interested in getting ahead than men are at this age, and they tend to have higher aspirations. Presumably, the difference between these middle-aged men and women lies in the very different activities with which they were involved during their earlier adult years. It is probable that these differences will not appear at middle age for the current young generation of working husbands and wives.

MARRIAGE AND FAMILY RELATIONSHIPS

The Berkeley Growth Study sheds some light on marital relationships and the changing prominence of various aspects of interpersonal family relationships at mid life. Clausen (1976) reported that at both forty and fifty, companionship and understanding tend to be ranked as the most important aspects of marriage for both men and women. Men rate sexual relations next, just a bit above "being a parent," while women rate parenting before sexual relations. Although sexual relations are ranked a bit lower by the fifty-year-olds, the shift is not great. For both sexes, intimate personal ties were ranked as more important than the comfort and security afforded by family life.

Departure of Children from the Family

One transition that many middle-aged people fear is the departure of grown children from the family. Some research shows, however, that most middle-aged couples in one study report that they expect their children to leave home and further that departure is a "natural and expected" process. Researchers suggest that many middle-aged parents still feel anxious about departure, particularly for the first child who is leaving home. Today's society stresses the importance of allowing children to depart and considers it unhealthy psychologically for parents to try to hold onto their children. Anxieties that develop frequently come from parental fears that their children might not do well when they are out on their own. A second fear is that **postparental** families (families in which children have grown up and left home) will not do as well as family units once the children are gone. The transition is made easier when there are several children and they leave individually over a period of time. Families that have allowed children to experience temporary separations, such as going off to camp or away to school, often find the transition easier than families that have remained close without many separations.

Even after children have left the family to go out on their own, of course, relationships between parents and children can remain close. Well-adjusted middle age, however, requires changes in these relationships. The person who has achieved generativity in mid life has learned to be intimate with others and to accept responsibility for others. This includes colleagues, friends, children, siblings, spouse, and parents. This may be because today's parents who successfully deal with this transition tend to shift their parental roles toward support and availability and away from direction or coercion. Parents who learn to listen to what their grown children have decided to do find themselves in closer relationships with them than do those who try to dictate life-styles. Contact and exchange often continue between middle-aged parents and their children. The quality of this contact depends in large part on the type of parenting relationships that have evolved over the years. Parents who are able to phase out parental responsibilities gradually and develop relationships with their children as adult friends as well as parents are likely to make the best adjustment to separation.

Although the makeup of the American family has changed a great deal in the past several decades, sociologists have found that American adults have tended to maintain close contact and interdependence with family members (Troll 1971). When parents and children live far apart, they usually maintain contact through the mail and by telephone.

Middle-aged Americans who have the means tend to provide continued economic support for children still in the stage of adolescence or youth. Even when children reach young adulthood, develop careers, and become economically self-sufficient, many parents continue economic support through gifts or services, such as babysitting. Frequently, gifts from parents mean the difference between living comfortably and having difficulty getting established. As one married woman in her late twenties put it,

> *I never realized just how much help Mom and Dad really were when John and I got married. Our first baby was born in our second year of graduate school, and we thought we were supporting ourselves on our teaching assistantships. When the baby was born, though, Mom and Dad gave us a gift of the crib, carriage, high chair, and even a washing machine. Without those and the other presents they brought whenever they came to visit, life would have been awfully barren. It's really funny to think of it now—we were so proud that we were self-sufficient. And we weren't, really.*

The same woman had an amusing picture of the graduate student housing complex where the young couple had lived:

The apartments were all tiny—two rooms each. And they were terribly dingy. Most of the students had furnished them with used furniture. But outside every apartment that had a baby was a brand-new baby carriage. And although kids might have bought their dining room tables at Good Will, most had good china and, of course, a new TV set . . . again, presents from mommas and daddies who were helping out on the side.

The decade from forty to fifty can be troublesome for many adults who have difficulty learning to accept in their own children the difficulties that they themselves faced as youth and young adults. "Why does Bobby have to make it so hard on himself?" grumbled one father about his nineteen-year-old son. "We are not wealthy, but we certainly have enough money to send him to a good school. He could be off on a campus, enjoying dormitory life and learning about anything he wants. Instead, what is he doing? Insisting on living here in the city, working at a gas station, and living in a slummy apartment. *Next* year he says he'll go to college. Who knows if next year will ever come?" The same father was reminded that he had dropped out of college himself at twenty and joined the navy. "Well, I suppose I understand now why my parents were so upset. They couldn't have known what I'd do next. But that doesn't mean Bobby has to be stupid—just because I was!"

Weaning youth and young adult children from their dependence is an important task of the middle-aged parent. Youth, those young people in their twenties who still have made no commitment to permanent life goals, often cause more worry for the American parent than all the physical changes and declining abilities associated with the middle years put together. Parents who see other people at their age level relaxing and enjoying life worry about whether or not their own chilren, when they reach middle age, will be able to have a satisfactory life for themselves. Middle-aged parents who are aware of their own aging begin to worry that time is runnng out for their children who have not been able to decide their life goals. They also worry that they might not be able to provide support for their children if their children need it.

Sometimes, children select their life goals and leave their families but remain economically dependent. This generally occurs primarily among young people who go to graduate school. Many of these young people remain dependent on their middle-aged parents into their late twenties and sometimes longer. The freedom many middle-aged parents have is severely curtailed by dependent youth, and this may be another source of stress in the middle years.

Many mothers and fathers become upset when their offspring choose life directions that seem inappropriate to the parents. Hill (1977) reported that about fifty percent of young people leave their parental households by about age nineteen to establish their own homes either as single people or as parts of married couples. When this break takes place without parental acceptance, it can be a source of stress for all family members. Children who decide that they do not want to continue in school and decide to settle for occupations lower on the socioeconomic ladder than their parents want or who marry individuals with less education or from families with lower or different socioeconomic status sometimes find themselves in serious conflict with their middle-aged parents.

Postparental Marital Relationships

The launching of children into independent lives leaves the original marital unit, the husband and wife. Because families tend to be smaller now than they were several generations ago and because the average lifespan now is longer, many researchers suggest that this period of life represents a new major portion of the lifespan (Glick 1955; Cavan 1963). For most adults today, the postparental marital relationship is one that consumes a far longer period than it did for couples in the past. American middle-aged men and women often can look forward to another four decades of life together interacting with one another without the interference of children.

Studies of attitudes of middle-aged couples have shown that although there are individual differences, marital relationships and satisfactions often are perceived as better after children have grown up and left home. Deutscher (1964), in interviews with postparental couples, found that the vast majority felt that the "empty nest" stage of life was a good one, and for more than half, it was better than all preceding stages. Why? The reasons given varied from couple to couple. Many felt they had a "new freedom" to do things together that they could not do when they were raising their children. For the women in the study, the launching of their last child meant freedom from a great deal of household work that they used to perform, more freedom to pursue their own interests, and freedom from always acting as a model for the children. Husbands and wives reported a great amount of freedom from financial responsibilities once the children were self-sufficient. As one father put it, "We can have candle-light dinners alone now or go out to a good restaurant without worrying about what we are depriving the children of. It's our turn now."

Although most postparental couples find this to be a satisfying time of life, Deutscher (1964) found that approximately five percent of individuals in his study felt that this period was worse than what came before. Some of the women complained about the unpleasant side effects of menopause, and some individuals of both sexes were distressed about physical disabilities associated with aging. Some people felt that they had failed at major developmental tasks, such as careers or childrearing. A few individuals, particularly women who had never worked outside the home, felt an inability to fill the gap left when their children departed. Finally, some couples were unhappy with their life together. These tended to be spouses who reported that they had remained in the marriage "for the sake of the children."

Lower-middle-class couples in Deutscher's study tended to respond more negatively toward these problems of postparental life than did upper-middle-class couples. The reason for this is probably that upper-middle-class people, because of their

Contrary to the popular perception that they are unhappy, most postparental couples look forward to the pleasures and greater freedom available when their children leave home.

relative affluence, have more freedom from economic worries. Their higher educational levels may also leave them with greater opportunity to make use of their free time in more enjoyable ways and to participate more fully in new experiences.

Bardwick (1978) gave another reason that many middle-aged people, regardless of their income and educational level, feel dissatisfied with relationships during postparental life: boredom. Individuals who have been extremely busy in their earlier years handling many details related to care of children, homes, and careers now find that there is less to do at the same time that they have developed a lifetime of habits that make it easier to perform these tasks. They also have less to talk about.

Pineo (1978), in a study of disenchantment in marriage after twenty years, points to some other causes for feelings of dissatisfaction with marriage relationships in middle age. He points out that individuals often feel that they have lost some inti-

Table 12.2
Indices of Marital Satisfaction in Which Statistically Significant Decreases
Occur for Both Husband and Wife from Early to Middle Years

Index	Decrease in Scores of Marital Satisfaction	
	Husbands	Wives
Marital adjustment	4.63	5.42
Love	2.01	2.87
Feelings of permanence	2.12	2.64
Consensus of opinion	2.26	2.37
Sharing of interests and activities	3.84	4.56
Frequency of sexual intercourse	2.31	2.13

Source: Pineo (1978).
Note: Scale of marital satisfaction by Pineo. $N = 400$.

macy. More people at this period of life report feelings of loneliness in marriage than do people in earlier periods. One reason might be that the amount of sharing of activities sometimes decreases at the same time that the frequency of sexual intercourse decreases. Some of the results of Pineo's study in which he measured the change from the early to middle years of marriage for indices of marital satisfaction, marital type, and personal characteristics are shown in Table 12.2.

The Middle Aged and Their Aging Parents

One of the ironies of middle age today is that just when couples have launched their children, they may find themselves facing the responsibility of caring for aging parents. Neugarten (1979) called middle age the age of "parent caring." Because of increased longevity, many middle-aged children have living parents in their seventies and far older. Whereas the adult children once looked to their parents for help, they now may be responsible for assisting their parents in many areas of their lives, from decisions about health to financial support. Lieberman (1978) suggests that for middle-aged children parent caring is becoming the major task of family life and a major source of family stress.

Contrary to popular myths, most middle-aged children do not neglect their aging parents. Rather they offer support in a variety of different ways. Troll (1971) reported that approximately thirty-three percent of aging parents live with their children. In most of these situations, middle-aged adults take in a widowed parent (usu-

Middle-aged children often have closer ties to their parents based on a mature appreciation of one another.

ally female) when it no longer is possible for the parent to support or care for herself or himself. When a parent finds it appropriate to live alone, middle-aged children may offer different kinds of support, such as shopping, visiting frequently, or managing their parents' financial affairs.

Middle-aged Grandparents

One of the most pleasant familial relationships for many middle-aged people is with their grandchildren. Grandparents often find that interactions with their grandchildren are free of the stresses that accompany interactions with their own children. One reason for this is that most grandparents do not feel they have the responsibility for their grandchildren that they had for their children. Reports a proud grandmother in her forties:

There's nothing like my daughter bringing little Mindy over to visit. We have a lovely afternoon together, and then my daughter takes her home, dirty diapers and all. I can enjoy Mindy without all the work I used to have with Charlotte (Mindy's mother) when she was a baby—no staying up all night during teething, no taking care of her through the chicken pox. Mindy is all the pleasure and none of the work.

This grandmother, even though she works full time, baby sits for her granddaughter fairly frequently, about once every two weeks. But she feels free to say no when her daughter and son-in-law ask.

Some middle-aged couples are uncomfortable about becoming grandparents, particularly those who become grandparents while still in their forties. These individuals probably fear that the status of a grandparent somehow ages them more rapidly. This is particularly true for middle-aged people seeking new life-styles following mid-life crisis. "What will everyone in the office think when they realize I'm old enough to have a son who is a father himself?" worries a forty-five-year-old man who recently divorced and married a twenty-eight-year-old woman.

Robertson (1977) studied the attitudes of a group of 125 women, most of whom were grandmothers. She found that most grandmothers enjoyed their new roles. In particular, they enjoyed being grandmothers to young children with whom they could play and who loved the attention of their elders. Many enjoyed this role more than being a parent. Following is a list of some of the role behaviors of grandparents, as judged by the women Robertson studied. The role behaviors indicate these women's perceptions of what grandmothers should do and the roles they should play:

Providing gifts

Baby sitting with grandchildren

Home recreation

Zoo and shopping trips

Drop-in visits

Relating family history

Teaching sewing

Helping with emergencies

Taking grandchildren on vacations

Taking children to church

Providing advice on personal problems

Providing advice regarding work

Providing advice regarding religion

Teaching native language

HIGHLIGHT 12.2 ON BEING A GRANDMOTHER

Grandmothers learn about what it is like to be a grandmother from a variety of sources long before they take on the role themselves. For example, Robertson (1977) points out that they learn informally from reading the *Ladies Home Journal* or the "Dear Abby" column. They learn from TV and fairy tales, which depict grandmothers usually as playing very important and usually loving roles in the eyes of their grandchildren. Grandmothers are usually portrayed in stereotypical ways: jolly, bespectacled, white haired, lovers of children, and bringers of presents.

Robertson sent questionnaires to 125 women, most of whom were grandmothers, to determine what they thought of the grandparenting role. She found that not all looked forward to becoming grandmothers, in part because they did not perceive themselves in stereotypical ways and did not think they would receive feelings of satisfaction. For those who wanted to have grandchildren, grandmothering offered pleasures that these same women as young mothers never had the opportunity for. Grandmothers reported that it was a satisfaction to watch the children of their own children grow up. At the same time, grandparenting did not take the tremendous effort that childrearing did, so that it was even more enjoyable.

Many grandmothers in Robertson's study suggested that they enjoyed the role of being grandmother because being a grandmother alleviated loneliness. An example of this view was given by Mrs. D:

> I'd like to have them (my grandchildren) come and see me often. I'd like them to take me for rides, to visit with me, and help me keep up my morale. They are good grandchildren. I know they will come.

The same theme was echoed by another woman:

> I'd be awfully unhappy not to have my grandchildren. As I look at some of my friends who have no one, it's terrible. There are so many people alone. . . . The more people you have to think about, the less you worry about yourself.

Many middle-aged grandmothers, however, were so busy with their own post-parental roles that they did not perceive grandmotherhood as a primary source of satisfaction, even though they did report that they like the role. The following comments by a fifty-four-year-old married employed grandmother are typical:

> I really wasn't too happy at first because I felt I was much too young for that. But now as I look back, my grandchildren have enriched our lives. . . . I'm glad to be young and healthy enough to do things with them when I can; I don't have much time though. . . . I work, and we have so many things to do ourselves, and so do the kids these days. . . . They don't have time for us either.

Grandmothering seemed a particularly enjoyable role to grandmothers when they could make of it what they wanted and not feel bound to the stereotypes they had of what they should do. Grandmothers particularly enjoyed their role when their grandchildren's parents did not burden them with too many duties.

QUESTIONS FOR THOUGHT

1. As more and more middle-aged women spend longer periods of time in the postparental years back in the job market and out on new careers, how do you think the stereotypes of grandmothers in our society will change?

2. How do the comments of the women reported by Robertson fit your own perceptions of yourself as a grandmother or grandfather?

Neugarten and Weinstein (1964), in a study involving seventy grandparent couples, found that grandparenting styles differ greatly. They identified among the subjects of their study five distinct styles. Grandparents who play formal grandparenting roles follow prescribed rules in establishing relationships with their grandchildren. They avoid offering unsolicited advice on childrearing and, in general, agree that it is the parents' role to raise the children. Formal grandparents may visit and baby sit their grandchildren, but they follow the directions of the grandchildren's parents in childrearing. These grandparents tended to be older than those who assumed other grandparenting styles.

Neugarten and Weinstein referred to fun-seeking grandparenting as a tendency to behave in a different manner. Fun-seeking grandparents regarded their grandchildren as sources for enjoyment and spent far more efforts at establishing relationships. These grandparents felt far more comfortable taking charge and giving advice, and they tended to be younger than the first group, usually under sixty-five years of age. "Reservoirs of family wisdom" was the category given grandparents, typically grandfathers, who attempted to maintain positions of authority within the family, including children and grandchildren. These grandparents, often first-generation Americans, gave formal approval or disapproval of childrearing methods. "Distant-figure grandparents" were those who had little to do with their grandchildren's day-to-day lives, often because they lived in cities distant from their grandchildren. Many of these grandparents accepted the role of gift givers on birthdays and holidays. Young grandparents in Neugarten and Weinstein's study who were not fun seeking tended to take on distant-figure grandparenting styles.

A last category of grandparenting style described by Neugarten and Weinstein was "surrogate parent." These usually were grandmothers who assumed full responsibility for raising their grandchildren while their daughters were working else-where. Grandmothers who become surrogate parents are often mothers of daughters who have two-career or two-earner marriages. They also often are the mothers of girls who have had babies before they are capable of caring for them themselves. Mothers of teenagers who become pregnant and decide to keep their babies often fall into this role. More of these grandmothers are black than white; most are from poor economic backgrounds (National Center for Health Statistics 1977; Diepold and Young, 1979). For these women, grandparenting really means becoming a parent all over again. At a time that other women are finding more time for themselves, middle-aged "parenting grandmothers" are performing the tasks that their own children cannot easily do; these include night feedings, care of sick babies, and household tasks. It is not surprising that stress tends to be high in these households (Rienzo 1981). Ironically, many teenage mothers report that they decided initially to have the babies in order to have what they lack most, a purpose in life and someone who loves them.

Many grandparents are able to enjoy the pleasures of parenting without having to worry about the responsibilities.

THE CASE OF DR. FRANK MALONE—A UNIVERSITY PROFESSOR: A CASE STUDY FOR CLASS DISCUSSION

I. Identification and Sources of Information

Name: Dr. Frank Malone

Address: Chicago, Illinois

Race: Black

Sex: Male

Age: Fifty years

Sources of information

1. Personal interview with Dr. Malone

2. Interviews with Dr. Malone's immediate family, including his wife, father-in-law, and daughter

3. Interview with Dr. Malone's dean

II. Family History

Frank Malone was born in New York City, the youngest son of a public school custodian. His mother, who worked nights as a cleaning woman, had two daughters by a previous marriage. She and Frank's father also had two additional children, a set of twins two years older than Frank.

Frank attended New York City public schools and then City College of New York. He was the third member of his family to go to college but the only one to complete more than one year of school. He majored in history, then continued graduate studies through a Ph.D. in history at Columbia University. He was the only black student in his class at the time of his graduation.

Frank's brothers and sisters currently all live in New York City and are employed as a bus driver, barmaid, and waitress. One sister is married to a candy store owner and works with her husband in the store.

Frank married Alice Robinson in his third year of graduate school. Alice is the daughter of a black mother and white father; she grew up in New York City and was studying journalism when she met Frank.

Alice worked for a while after the marriage. When Frank received an offer as assistant professor at the university, she quit her job. One year after the family moved to Chicago, Alice gave birth to a daughter. Alicia, now twenty years old, is in her senior year at college. She is majoring in engineering and expects to enroll in graduate school when she gets her B.A. Her mother has been working for the past three years as an editor in a small publishing firm in Chicago. Alice is very excited about her job and often brings work home from the office.

Three years ago, when Alice's mother died, her father came to live with the Malone family. Mr. Robinson is retired from his job as a postal clerk. He spends most of his time at home, taking care of the small garden behind the Malone house, watching television, and reading. A stroke last year left his left arm partially paralyzed, but he is still able to take care of himself and still enjoys his gardening activities. This year the family bought a dog, and Mr. Robinson often goes on walks with Bruiser. Mrs. Malone explained, "It gives Dad an opportunity to get outside and exercise. He has to accompany the dog in the city for its walks. And it also provides him a protecting companion. Dad was afraid of getting mugged—I guess we were all worried that he might be hurt—and somehow, we all feel safer that Bruiser is out with him on the street."

III. Case History

Dr. Malone has been a member of the history department in his university for more than two decades. When he first arrived at the university, it was his ambition to become the "first and best black full professor and maybe dean." He thought that he would spend his early career writing and then "when the time was right, move on . . . maybe back to New York . . . maybe somewhere else." The main goal was to make a big name for himself. The first part of

Continued

THE CASE OF DR. FRANK MALONE (Cont.)

the plan was accomplished rather easily. When Frank Malone was thirty-three years old, he published his first book, a history of the American Civil War, the thesis of his doctoral dissertation. When he was thirty-eight years old, he had already published three books, and was well known throughout the country for his research. Many students came to the university to work with him. He became a full professor the following year.

When Frank was forty years old, the dean of arts and letters made him department chairman. Frank kept the appointment for three years and gave the position up only to take a sabbatical and work on a new book. In the meantime, Alice's mother became ill, and Alice went to New York frequently to stay with her after her many hospital stays. The illness dragged on, and when the elderly woman finally died, the Malones brought her husband to stay with them. "It's strange," Frank remembers now. "I always thought that I was ambitious. But all those years with Alice running off to New York thinking that this visit might be the last has left me much less interested in getting ahead than I was when I was younger. I can remember those nights explaining to Alicia why her mother was gone and why we were eating alone and thinking, 'it's foolish to waste a lot of time trying to get somewhere when we're all going to end up the same way anyway.'"

Last year Frank received the offer that he had always wanted: a deanship at a good college in New York City. He turned the position down. Frank's dean told us how glad the administration at the university was to be able to keep him. "We thought we'd certainly lose one of our best professors," he said. "And even though we were able to come up with a salary that compensated in some ways, we never thought he'd stay on. Frank has always been ambitious, and we knew he wanted to go back to New York one day."

We asked Frank why he had turned down the job he had been planning for twenty years. "It began

with my mother-in-law's death," he explained. "But there was a lot more. My own father died the following year, and my mother went to live with my sister. Alice took on a job and was really happy at getting back to work after all of those years. Taking on the position in New York would have disrupted a very comfortable life-style for all of us. With our remaining parents as old as they are, it's hard not to remember always that we might not have so very much time ourselves. And why should we disrupt what we have here?" Frank paused. "We have a lot . . . friends, interesting things to do at our respective positions, family with us. Alice's Dad doesn't think so well as he used to. And he's comfortable in the neighborhood now. Disrupting him wouldn't help him clear his head. It would be hard. And Alicia has another year of school. I suppose she could live in the dorms. But it's much nicer this way. I know I surprised everyone at the university. But I really didn't surprise my closest friends and my family who know me best. They saw my ambition drain away. But they also saw a contented man evolve . . . . a man who wants to hang onto those things closest to him and keep them near and well just as long as he can."

IV. Present Status, Diagnosis, and Prognosis

Frank can be described as a contented man, but one with the concerns of most middle-aged people. He probably will stay on at this university until his retirement. He might accept an administrative appointment, but only if he is pressured by his colleagues. He enjoys his work and is busy on some new research that probably will take his free time for the next few years. Frank is extremely close to his family; he can expect a number of traumas in the next few years as his mother and father-in-law get older and sicker. It probably will be difficult for him to adjust next year to his daughter's leaving the city to attend graduate school. He advised her to go elsewhere because she could get better training, "but it still hurt

THE CASE OF DR. FRANK MALONE

knowing that we probably have just one more year with our girl. Once she leaves, it'll only be short visits . . . the kind we gave our own parents. It's still hard to believe how fast it all went."

Questions for Class Discussion

1. Explain the ways that the development of generativity affected Dr. Malone's attitudes toward his

family and his career. Explain specifically the reasons for his attitude changes over the past twenty years.

2. Dr. Malone alluded in his interview to the importance of his wife's career. Why do you think Mrs. Malone's career is increasingly important to her at exactly the time when Dr. Malone is becoming less ambitious about his own career?

SUMMARY

Middle age, the years from about forty to sixty, can be the most productive period of people's lives. Middle age does, however, carry negative connotations, usually associated with concerns about physical changes. During these years, people go through transitional periods in which they reassess their personal lives as well as their career expectations.

Many physical changes mark the middle years. These include stiffening and shrinking of bone structures, loss of muscle elasticity, decreasing motor skills, and increasing sensory defects. The probability of degenerative disease, such as heart disease or cancer, increases during this age period. Research shows that cardiovascular disease in particular may be related to stress, and physicians urge middle-aged people to reduce stressful situations in their lives as much as possible, although many of these situations are not within an individual's control.

A major biological change that occurs in middle age is the climacteric. In middle-aged women this change is called menopause; during this time menstruation and production of eggs by the ovaries cease. Although men do not undergo such obvious changes, there is a gradual decline in production of the male hormone testosterone. Some men also report physical symptoms similar to those experienced by women during menopause. The climacteric is frequently accompanied in both men and women by a difficult period of self-evaluation, during which they may be extremely critical of themselves and their accomplishments. Sexuality need not decline for middle-aged people. Nevertheless, the frequency of sexual activity does tend to decrease, often for psychological reasons.

People in the middle years assume "executive responsibility" and develop cognitive strategies to deal with complex relationships within the family and on the job. Contrary to the fears of many middle-aged people, many cognitive abilities, such as crystallized intelligence, continue to increase through middle age. People in middle age undergo a mid-life transition that for some causes deep emotional crises. Jung believes that this transition occurs as people learn that control of their lives has shifted from themselves to factors that are outside their control.

People who successfully handle their mid-life crises achieve what Erikson calls generativity. These people can be intimate with and accept responsibility for others. Peck identifies four conflicts that people must resolve before achieving this stage: valuing wisdom vs. valuing physical power; socializing vs. sexualizing; emotional flexibility vs. emotional impoverishment; and mental flexibility vs. mental rigidity. Successful middle-aged people have learned to adjust in many ways to their career successes and failures. Some, at their mid-life transitions, choose to change careers. These people usually have a history of inconsistency in their interests and tend to have emotional difficulty dealing with middle age. Some people take on careers that are less threatening to their self-esteem than their old careers; others make changes that give them better opportunity to express their generativity.

The career expectations of middle-aged women differ from those of their husbands. The change from mother–housewife roles when entering the work force is particularly beneficial to the psychological health of women who are independently oriented (as opposed to traditionally feminine). Well-adjusted middle age requires changes in the relationship between parents and children as the children leave home to be on their own. Parents who deal with this transition successfully tend to shift their parental roles toward support and availability and away from direction or coercion. Many continue to provide economic support, although one of their primary tasks at this age is to wean their children from dependence.

Marital relationships and satisfactions are often perceived as better after children have grown up and left home because of more freedom, less work, and greater economic independence. Postparental couples who do not adjust well to their children's growing up complain of a number of factors, including boredom with one another. Ironically, this is also a time when many middle-aged couples face the responsibility of caring for their own aging parents.

One of the most pleasant familial relationships for middle-aged people is their grandchildren. Grandchildren can provide all the joys of children without the stresses and physical strains. Some grandparents are uncomfortable about grandparenting; these are usually people who have difficulty adjusting to aging and who feel that grandchildren make the aging process more rapid.

FOR FURTHER READING

Neugarten, B. Time, age, and the life cycle. *The American Journal of Psychiatry,* July, 1979, 136 (7) 887–893. This article presents an overview of Neugarten's developmental theory and an excellent description of what takes place as individuals increase in age through the adult years. Neugarten points out clearly how, in our society, the timing of specific events is becoming less regular, how specific chronological age is losing its customary meaning, and how the trends suggest a "fluid life cycle."

Sheehy, G. *Passages.* New York: Bantam Books, 1977. Sheehy's book was on the best-seller list for adult reading for several years. Although not a psychologist herself, Sheehy based her book on interviews with a large number of developmental psychologists and psychiatrists concerned with adulthood. She also interviewed a large number of adults. Descriptions of these interviews makes the book readable and interesting.

Later Adulthood

Part VI

Preview Questions

- What are some major physical changes that take place during the young-old years, and what are some problems that each causes?

- Can you describe four different theories of aging and estimate the acceptance that each has among experts in development?

- How is sexuality related to other factors in later adulthood?

- What are some cognitive changes that appear in the young-old years, and how are they related to the activities and attitudes of older people?

- How is the self-concept of a person in later adulthood related to life satisfaction and morale?

- Can you describe four different theories that explain one's adjustment to aging and estimate the credibility each has with the experts?

- How does Peck expand Erikson's description of the integrity vs. despair crisis in later adulthood?

- What are some factors that seem to be related to satisfaction with retirement, and how are these related to Miller's identity crisis theory?

- Can you explain why inflation has caused special problems for retired people?

- What happens to the marital relationships of young-old couples, and what are some differences in the responses of men and women to the death of a spouse?

- How do the leisure-time activities of young-old adults compare with those of their earlier years?

- Can you explain why retirement communities have become so popular in the last decade?

13

Later Adulthood: The Young-Old Years

Continuous improvements in health care, diet, and living conditions in our society have increased the lifespan so that today, far more individuals live to later adulthood, past sixty years of life, than ever before. In 1900, 3.1 million individuals over 65 lived in the United States; they were 4.1 percent of the population. By the end of the 1970s, this population was more than 23 million, or more than 10.5 percent. More than 5000 Americans reach their sixty-fifth birthdays each year (Harris 1978).

What is old age? Many myths and stereotypes persist about this stage of life. Contrary to some beliefs, later adulthood does not necessarily bring with it senility. Many older people continue to be bright and competent and to lead productive lives well past their sixties and seventies. Old age today is a relative category that can vary considerably from individual to individual, depending on the number and timing of role transitions that each undergoes in earlier stages of development. Hirschhorn (1977) pointed out that in recent years the timetable of the life cycle has become more and more fluid, with social acceptance of wide age discrepancies in marriage (as characterized by May–December marriages), career changes that bring adults at mid life to the beginning of new life-styles, and early retirement for middle-aged people who are financially secure.

One way of distinguishing the elderly is by determining whether they are what Neugarten (1974; 1979) termed "young–old" or "old–old." Neugarten devised the category **young–old** to refer to adults in their sixties to about age seventy-five who, because of retirement, have a good deal of leisure time. These older people are relatively healthy, relatively comfortable financially, well-educated, politically active, and important consumers of goods and services. They are distinguished from what Neugarten termed the **old–old** partly by their health and vigor and partly by their successful adjustment to aging. Individuals who have reached what Neugarten describes as the old–old years are no longer so healthy and are becoming increasingly limited by their aging. This chapter deals with the development of the young–old; Chapter 14 will deal with the old–old period of life.

The young–old is a new concept in America and in other parts of the modern industrial world. Not only are adults living longer in these areas, but living longer also enables them to have productive years after retirement. Because the young–old are relatively affluent, they are able to maintain enough economic and psychological freedom to continue developing their life-styles in ways they see fit.

Some new developmental tasks arise during the young–old period: adapting to loss of the work role and possibly to the death of friends and spouse, yielding of some positions of authority, adjustments in relationships with adult children, and evaluation of past achievements and failures. The young–old period brings with it a greater awareness that life is passing quickly. For those who adjust successfully to growing old, life can provide a sense of enjoyment and meaning. Neugarten (1979, p. 891) pointed out that most persons who reach sixty do not wish to be young again, even though they may wish to feel young: "They want instead to grow old with equanimity and with the assurance that they will have had a full measure of life's experience."

Neugarten describes the young–old as those individuals in their sixties to mid seventies who are in good health, are reasonably comfortable financially, and have made a successful adjustment to aging.

DEVELOPMENT DURING THE YOUNG–OLD YEARS
Physical Changes

The gradual physical decline that occurs during mid life increases with increasing age. **Senescence,** or the biological aging of the body, is a continual process. Figure 13.1, indicating some of the biological and physiological decline that normally takes place with increasing age, demonstrates substantial declines in many functions and tissues. Because these declines take place over several decades of life and because our bodies gradually adapt, changes in functioning are not sudden.

One of the most apparent changes in the young–old years is in the skin, which becomes thinner, dryer, and less elastic. Brown spots of pigmentation, called "liver spots" appear, and warts may appear on the face, scalp, and body. Many of the changes in the skin are attributed to changes in collagen, a component of connective tissue found throughout the body. The amount of subcutaneous fat and muscle bulk begins to decline so that skin may hang in folds and wrinkles on all parts of the

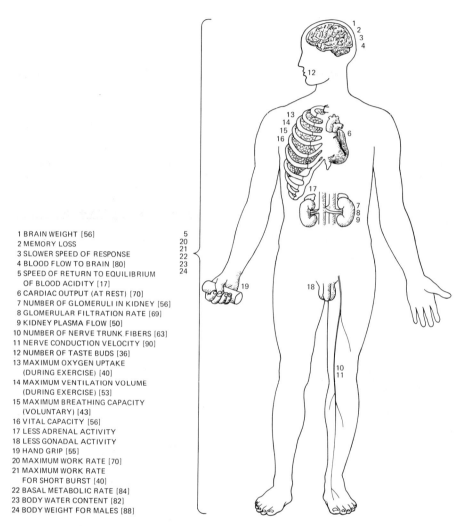

1 BRAIN WEIGHT [56]
2 MEMORY LOSS
3 SLOWER SPEED OF RESPONSE
4 BLOOD FLOW TO BRAIN [80]
5 SPEED OF RETURN TO EQUILIBRIUM
  OF BLOOD ACIDITY [17]
6 CARDIAC OUTPUT (AT REST) [70]
7 NUMBER OF GLOMERULI IN KIDNEY [56]
8 GLOMERULAR FILTRATION RATE [69]
9 KIDNEY PLASMA FLOW [50]
10 NUMBER OF NERVE TRUNK FIBERS [63]
11 NERVE CONDUCTION VELOCITY [90]
12 NUMBER OF TASTE BUDS [36]
13 MAXIMUM OXYGEN UPTAKE
  (DURING EXERCISE) [40]
14 MAXIMUM VENTILATION VOLUME
  (DURING EXERCISE) [53]
15 MAXIMUM BREATHING CAPACITY
  (VOLUNTARY) [43]
16 VITAL CAPACITY [56]
17 LESS ADRENAL ACTIVITY
18 LESS GONADAL ACTIVITY
19 HAND GRIP [55]
20 MAXIMUM WORK RATE [70]
21 MAXIMUM WORK RATE
  FOR SHORT BURST [40]
22 BASAL METABOLIC RATE [84]
23 BODY WATER CONTENT [82]
24 BODY WEIGHT FOR MALES [88]

Fig. 13.1 The biological and physiological decline that takes place with increasing age. Percentage figures at the right of each category indicate the percentages of functions or tissues that remain in an average seventy-five-year-old man from optimal functioning at age thirty. (From Nathan W. Shock, The physiology of aging, in *Scientific American*, January 1962, p. 101. Copyright © 1962 by Scientific American, Inc. All rights reserved.)

body. Bromley (1974) suggests that hair loss that begins for many males in the middle years may be caused by the gradual decline of secretion in the adrenal glands. By the young–old years, lower blood circulation in the scalp may also contribute to hair loss in males and females both.

Of all the changes that take place in the skin at this time, the most serious for the functioning of young–old people is in the ability to regulate body temperature. With increasing age, individuals lose their ability to respond adequately to changes in external temperature. Because of a marked reduction in sweat glands and a resultant inability to sweat freely, heat exhaustion can occur more easily. Young–old people also are more susceptible to the cold because of the loss of insulating layer of subcutaneous fat (Rossman 1976).

With advancing age, the chemical composition of the bones changes, perhaps because of changes in calcium metabolism. As the bone structures stiffen, the risk of breakage increases. Broken bones take far longer to heal than during earlier periods of life. The skeleton also reflects previous damage or disease. Although diseases of the joints, such as arthritis, can occur at many different stages of life, they often become more problematic at this stage because of continued wear and other age-related changes in the bones (Kimmel 1980).

Increasing age has an effect on an individual's height because the invertebral discs in the spine and the cartilage between the disks decrease in size and strength. Other factors, such as gradual loss of muscle tone that causes older people to develop a stooping posture, further suggest the appearance of decreasing size. Age also has an effect on the health of teeth. Tooth decay increases in the old–old period for a number of reasons, including a reduction in the amount of saliva of the young–old and increased incidence of periodontal (gum) disease.

Sensory impairments, particularly in vision or hearing, tend to become more pronounced after age sixty. Crandall (1980) reports that about seven percent of those sixty-five to seventy-four are blind or have serious vision impairments. Vision accuracy for near and far perception, adaptation to light and dark, and ability to adapt to glare decreases with chronological age. Decline in vision develops at this period because of gradual atrophy of the optic nerves, a gradual yellowing and loss of elasticity of the lens, and a gradual decline in the size of the pupil that does not allow it to admit as much light as previously. About thirteen percent of those in the young–old years also have serious hearing problems (Crandall 1980). In addition, others experience gradual degrees of decline. A great deal of hearing loss at this age is due to gradual atrophy of the nerve tissue of the ear, calcification of the bones of the inner ear, and accumulated disease or accoustical accidents. Both visual and hearing impairments affect the life-styles of individuals because they restrict the ability to communicate with others.

In the sixties and seventies, other senses, such as the sense of smell, gradually become less acute. The speed of reaction time and fine motor coordination decrease as a result of the slowing of central nervous system functioning (Botwinick 1970). In the young–old years are distinct decreases in efficient functioning of the heart and cardiovascular system (Roberts 1976; Kohn 1977). Researchers report that the heart circulates less blood through the system. It gradually becomes irregular in its beating pattern and loses the ability to accelerate to high levels. Once a rapid heartbeat is established in a young–old person, it takes longer to decline in speed. Because of a buildup over time of waste materials in the system, arteries become clogged, and the heart must pump more to move blood through the circulatory system.

The lungs of the young–old individuals inhale less new oxygen than those of younger people and are less capable of absorbing the oxygen that has been inhaled. This gradually decreasing ability to obtain and use oxygen brings about a gradual decrease in metabolic rate (Bromley 1974). Young–old people tend to spend more time in light sleep than in earlier years, to waken more easily, and to have more difficulty in falling asleep. Because it is during deep sleep that the body regenerates and repairs itself, the corresponding decrease in deep sleep leads to less opportunity for body repair (Prinz 1977).

In part because of these physical changes, there is a noticeable increase in the number of serious illnesses in older people. Even the young–old who are generally in good health experience more frequent aches and pains. Among the major impairments are arthritis, rheumatism, high blood pressure, heart disease, cancer, endocrine dysfunction, and defective vision or hearing. Depression and other emotional distresses are also common. About eighty percent of deaths after age sixty-five are attributed to three major causes: (1) such cardiovascular diseases as heart attacks and strokes, (2) cancer, and (3) accidents. Heart disease and cancer are the two primary causes of death and impairment of young–old adults. Men have higher rates of death and impairment than women in this age group. One result is an increasing number of widows in the sixty to seventy-five age group (Kimmel 1980; U.S. Bureau of the Census 1980).

It is important to recognize that there are individual differences in the rates of senescence among adults in the young–old period, just as there are among adults in their middle years. The sixty-five-year-old who exercises daily may look, feel, and act younger than many fifty-year-olds. But the sixty-five-year-old must exercise regularly, for retaining a high level of fitness is far more difficult than it was even five years earlier. Senescence is a factor that young–old people cannot ignore. Their physical condition affects their abilities to get along in the world and to interact with others. It also affects their perceptions of themselves and their outlooks on life. Neugarten (1979) notes that for the young–old, goals for physical skill are of necessity far lower than that of previous years, no matter how much exercise is applied. For this reason, young–old people who judged themselves on the basis of their performance for their age will have a far better adjustment to this period of life than those who continually mourn lost abilities.

Theories of Aging

We all agree that people age with time. Although no researchers to date have proven a cause of aging nor produced a remedy to stop this process, a number of theories do explain just why senescence takes place. Finch (1976) suggests what he terms the **wear-and-tear theory of senescence.** He hypothesizes that the body is similar to a machine and that over time it simply wears out. All organs in the body are not subject to wear in the same way, however, and organs that do age vary from individual to individual. The wear-and-tear theory of senescence does not take into consideration the human body's ability to repair itself, nor does it take into consideration that exercise often increases longevity rather than decreases it. Evidence that seems to demonstrate that aging is not due simply to wear and tear finally comes from the little-known disease, **progeria,** that ages individuals prematurely, stunts growth, weakens the body, hardens the arteries, and generally leads to death in the mid teens. Progeria ages the body without the usual time requirement for wear and tear. Doctors do not know the cause of progeria but assume that it has something to do with the inability of the body to control whatever mechanism ages the body.

A second theory explaining senescence, the **hormone theory of senescence,** proposes that hormones have a major impact on aging and that with increased age, the body decreases its ability to produce these hormones. Prehoda (1968) reports that hormonal therapies of various types have been used to alleviate some of the symptoms of aging. To date, however, researchers have been unable to isolate specific hormones directly related to senescence and thus are unable to prove the theory.

The **collagen theory of senescence** proposes that collagen, a substance found in connective tissues that exist in more than half the body and that give the body support, becomes increasingly rigid with chronological age. It is possible, although no researchers have yet been able to prove conclusively, that this rigidity may make both the ingestion of nutrients and the expulsion of waste products more difficult and thus increase the aging process in the body.

Another theory is the **autoimmunity theory of senescence.** This explanation of senescence assumes that with increasing age comes increasing mutations in cell division. The body responds to these mutations as it does to foreign bodies, and it produces antibodies. In the resulting response, called the autoimmune response, the body essentially destroys itself. Crandall (1980) reports that studies have shown that life expectancy is increased if the autoimmune responses are slowed down. This approach, like the other approaches, does not explain the reasons that exercise decreases the rates of many aspects of senescence.

Sexuality

In most societies today, it is assumed that sexuality decreases or ceases altogether as the aging process continues. These attitudes to the contrary, sexuality remains an important part of life throughout all stages of development, including later adulthood. Pfeiffer (1974), in a study of older individuals with a mean age of sixty-eight years, found, in fact, that eighty percent were interested in sex and seventy percent were "sexually active."

Many psychologists feel that it is these individuals who have reached older adulthood who are most in need of giving and receiving sexually (Weg 1975). Sexuality may be expressed at this stage of development in a variety of behaviors and

Stereotypes to the contrary, many older people are capable of continuing to have fulfilling sexual relationships. For a large number, the biggest obstacle is lack of a partner.

expressions, including holding, touching, flirting, verbal discussion of sexuality and affection, masturbation, and sexual intercourse. Some theorists suggest that opportunity for touching is particularly important to the emotional development of individuals. Weg (1975), for example, emphasizes that sexual expression among older adults is important in reducing serious depression.

In Chapter 12, we noted that the climacteric is accompanied by some physical changes that may contribute to sexual difficulties. Masters and Johnson (1970), for example, point out the decreasing ability of some older males to have or maintain erections. In general, the older male requires more stimulation in order to maintain an erection. He is able, however, to control ejaculation more effectively than when he was younger, and therefore may be more able to satisfy his partner (Masters and Johnson 1970). After menopause, females have less vaginal lubrication and less elasticity of the vagina. The walls of the vagina become thinner with age. The vagina shortens in length and width, and much of its ability to expand decreases. Weg (1976) indicates that the orgasmic stage tends to be shorter and less intense in older women and may sometimes be painful.

Although these problems can generally be overcome if a couple wishes to continue a fulfilling sex life, some psychologically based sexual problems may become more prominent during the young–old years. Performance anxiety, for example, can become a major problem for males when this was not the case during the middle years (Masters and Johnson 1970). Fear of rejection may become an important problem for many young–old adults who are aware that the physical changes of aging are making their bodies less attractive. This can be a particular problem for some young–old people who have lost spouses, remarried at this period of their lives, and might be shier in front of a new spouse than in front of the person with whom he or she has lived intimately for long periods of life. For both aging males and aging females, the maintenance of effective sexuality is directly related to continuing active sexual expression: The more an aging couple continues to engage in sex, the greater the ease and enjoyment of future sexual activity (Masters and Johnson 1978).

Young–old individuals who are single tend, in general, to have less opportunity for sexual activity than married individuals. For example, Sviland (1975) reported that while seventy percent of healthy married couples were sexually active and engaged in sexual intercourse with a frequency of 0.9 times per week, only seven percent of single older individuals reported that they were still sexually active. Wasow and Loeb (1978), in a study of the elderly, found that most individuals who reported that they were no longer sexually active gave health problems, inability to perform, or lack of a partner as the reason. Table 13.1 details specific reasons given by the subjects in the Wasow and Loeb study. McCary (1973) points out that masturbation is one frequent alternative form of sexual expression for many individuals who no longer engage in sexual intercourse.

Table 13.1
Reasons for Discontinuation of Sexual Activity

Reason	Percentage of Males	Percentage of Females
Poor health	16.7	16.3
Lost interest	10.0	27.9
Sex not appropriate	6.7	7.0
No partner	30.0	39.5
Inability to perform	16.7	10.0
Celibate	6.7	2.3
No answer	13.3	2.3

Source: From *Sexuality and Aging,* Robert L. Solnich (ed.). Lexington Books, Lexington, Mass., D.C. Heath and Company, copyright 1978, The Ethel Percy Andrus Gerontology Center. Reprinted by permission of the publisher.

Cognitive Changes

Cognitive Tasks. Cognitive tasks faced by young–old adults differ considerably from those required during middle age. Young–old adults usually no longer require the executive abilities that are so important to middle-aged people. Schaie (1977–1978) suggests that cognitive development at the young–old stage of life is best described as a **reintegrative stage,** in which individuals become more reflective, look inward, and interpret their lives in very personal terms. This stage completes "the transition from the 'what should I know' through the 'how should I use what I know' to the 'why should I know' phase of life," according to Schaie (1977–1978, p. 135), as the individual's concerns gradually come to center on more and more personal issues. The reintegrative stage occurs at a time when role requirements are reduced because of retirement from careers and fewer responsibilities for children. Because of these changes, the cognitive structure demands simplification.

Young–old adults, because they have more leisure time, can give more selective attention to cognitive demands that remain meaningful or attain new meaning. Problem solving now has purpose within the more immediate life situation of the individual; it is no longer a response to the need to exhibit competence and gain recognition at work or family tasks. The sixty- and seventy-year-olds who attend sculpting class do so not for the purpose of achieving eminence as sculptors. They do so instead to achieve new skills that demonstrate to them their new capabilities and understanding of the arts. Even those who go on to serious study tend to do so usually for personal fulfillment rather than for external recognition.

Cognitive Functioning. It has generally been assumed that old age is accompanied by mental decline. But is this really the case? Research has shown that the specific decrements in fluid intelligence that first show themselves in middle age become more noticeable in the young–old years. (See, for example, Botwinick 1967; Bischof, 1976.) Some researchers have found age-related deterioration in some aspects of cognitive functioning that increase at this stage of life (Horn 1976; Reese 1976; Arenberg and Robertson-Tschabo 1977). Young–old adults tend to be slower at recall and ability to deal with figural relations, both skills that require speed and effectiveness of neurological functioning. Even though this is the case, the aged still tend to compare equally with younger adults on vocabulary parts of intelligence tests, and verbal abilities and stored information of the aged tend to decrease relatively little if at all with increasing age (Botwinick 1977).

Apparently, while some aspects of memory have been found to decline with age, others have not. Perlmutter (1978) showed, for example, that, although sixty-year-olds have more difficulty than twenty-year-olds with the same level of education on tests that involve the ability to recall and recognize words they have seen before, these same sixty-year-olds do as well as their younger peers on overt tests requiring them to think of words through free association. They even do better on problems involving recall and recognition of factual material. Granick (1971) showed that some aspects of cognition, including skill at answering vocabulary and verbal items on IQ tests, increase during the young–old years. Men in their seventies in his study actually increased their general IQ scores over the previous eleven years.

A number of theories have been proposed to explain the age-related decrements that do exist in some aspects of cognitive functioning. For example, the fact that older people have longer periods of time and larger numbers of opportunities to store large numbers of facts in the memory increases the possibility that this stored information will interfere with newly stored information and cause decreased or slower recall (Craik 1977). General decay of cognitive functioning is another explanation. Some researchers suggest that decrements in fluid intelligence at this stage of life are due to a general slowing down of the central nervous system (Hooper, Fitzgerald, and Papalia 1971).

Some researchers indicate many conditions other than a natural deterioration of the brain that can lead to decreased cognitive performance in the young–old years. Granick (1971), for example, hypothesized that increasing age itself does not cause decreased cognitive ability and that medical status might well be a factor affecting older people's scores on tests of cognitive functioning. Any study of cognitive skills of the aging, he suggested, is surely affected by the fact that few elderly are free of at least some physical pathology. Specific pathological conditions also seem to be associated with decreasing intelligence and are frequently found among older people. For example, a damaged cardiovascular system or arteriosclerosis may reduce the blood flow to the brain and thus cause changes in cognitive ability. Finally, Prinz (1977) notes that the sleep patterns of the aged, characterized by increased periods of wakefulness and light sleep, may decrease opportunity for the brain to rest and may be responsible for brain changes that lead to reduced cognitive ability.

Some evidence shows that general physical well-being increases the ability of young–old people to perform cognitive tasks. Schaie and Gribben (1975), for example, note that people with fewer physical diseases and with relatively low blood pressure do better on tests of cognitive ability than do individuals of the same age with a greater incidence of disease and higher blood pressure. In addition, young–old individuals who get a sufficient amount of physical exercise tend to do better at cognitive tasks than those who are more sedentary.

In addition to physical factors, a number of psychological factors have been isolated by researchers and seem to be related to ability to perform cognitive tasks in the young–old years. Schaie and Gribben (1975) point out that many older persons are so afraid of decreasing cognitive skill that they tend to make mistakes at cognitive tasks and at tests of cognitive skill because of nervousness. In addition, because they expect to do poorly and tend often at this age to have lowered self-concepts, many older people may in fact, perform poorly. Carey (1958) points out that the individuals who tend to be hardest on themselves and, in addition, have the

Older people who continue to exercise regularly tend to do better at cognitive tasks than those who do not exercise.

lowest self-concepts are women. Some researchers suggest that lack of ability in the aged to solve cognitive problems may be related to an increased rigidity of mind set. Meichenbaum (1974) suggests that elderly who cannot solve cognitive problems because they tend to be rigid in their methods of finding solutions can be given special training to improve their ability to organize information and generate alternative solutions. Providing increased opportunity for intellectual stimulation is another way of increasing ability to perform cognitive tasks. Blum and Jarvik (1974) noted that individuals with higher amounts of education who maintained their intellectual pursuits in later adulthood tended to maintain their ability to perform cognitive tasks to a far greater extent than did individuals who had had less education earlier in their lives and who tended to remain less intellectually active.

Quite clearly much more information is needed before a complete explanation of changing cognitive functioning in the later years can be given. Tests need to be devised to measure skills that are required of people in this age group, not simply skills required of younger people, most of whom are in the work force performing activities different in many ways from those of people in their retirement years. Even though some early researchers devised tests to measure cognitive skills of the older age group (see, for example, Demming and Pressey 1957), changing life-styles of the American young–old have, for the most part, rendered these attempts invalid. At this time, psychologists have yet to devise a method adequate to measure the specific capabilities of the young–old. The task, according to Schaie (1977–1978), is at least as great as that faced by Binet in initially measuring the intelligence of schoolchildren.

Creativity. Dennis (1966), in a survey of creative productivity between the ages of twenty and eighty years, showed that for many scientists, scholars, and people working in the arts, creativity continues well past seventy years. Dennis reported that the least productive period for creativity is early adulthood, when most people still are novices in their fields. The highest rate of output, in numbers of creative works, is middle age. After age sixty, creative output tends to decrease, although many excellent works in all fields of endeavor are created by people in their seventies and older. Why does output diminish? For one thing, physical strength diminishes with age. Some researchers also believe that cognitive decrements that occur in the young–old years might well make many tasks more difficult for young–old persons than they are for younger adults. As noted previously, an age-related deterioration occurs in some aspects of memory. Researchers suggest that some cognitive functions slow because of a general slowing of the central nervous system. The medical status of this age group also may contribute to a decline in creative output (Granick 1971). Finally, it can be hypothesized that many young–old scholars may actually continue their creative thinking and living but that they may simply be tired of recording their achievements for society in the form of works that can be measured. This attitude is shown in the words of one retired composer who reported,

> *I've been composing a little just for myself in the last few years, not taking time to write it down, you know, but tape-recording it and listening to it myself with Janie (my wife). I don't want to compose for the public anymore. Getting others to listen, finding the right group to play, and so forth, is work I just don't feel like doing anymore. I'm too tired. But I do enjoy composing a little and playing—just for Janie. The rest of the time, I listen to music. I never could get enough of that when I was younger. Now there's time. And there is an excellent symphony here in town.*

PERSONALITY DEVELOPMENT AND ADJUSTMENT
Self-Concept, Life Satisfaction, and Morale

The ways in which individuals perceive themselves affect the ways in which they perceive their lives and their morale. Individuals in late adulthood tend frequently to view themselves and the aging process harshly. This is particularly true for young–

old women who, researchers say, hold more negative feelings about aging than do their male counterparts (Riley *et al.* 1968; McTavish 1971). Young–old women may view the aging process negatively because, in our society, so much more emphasis is placed on remaining young. As we learned in Chapter 12, femininity is associated by many people in our society with youth. This may well make it difficult for young–old women to maintain positive self-concepts as they perceive the aging process in themselves. Of course, young–old men also perceive the aging process in themselves, but because their masculinity is usually less threatened by these perceptions, the same effect on self-concept does not take place.

Two concepts related to the self-concept of young–old people that have been examined by researchers are life satisfaction and morale. **Life satisfaction** refers to the attitudes that individuals hold about their pasts, presents, and futures. **Morale** refers to the emotional component of life satisfaction. Individuals who have high self-concepts tend frequently to have high levels of life satisfaction and to have high morale—that is, they feel happy about their lives and circumstances. Researchers studying life satisfaction and morale frequently ask individuals to react to positive and negative statements about their lives and feelings. Table 13.2 shows the percentage of people sixty-five years and older and the percentage of under sixty-five in one study who agree with statements related to life satisfaction. Many similarities are evident between the two age groups in both positive and negative life satisfaction about the present and past. The largest differences appeared in individuals' views of the future. The older adult population was less likely to think of late adulthood as the best years of their lives and more likely to think of them as the most dreary than was the younger population. Although the differences between age groups do not seem to be very great, research data seem to show that the ways in which individuals perceive themselves and the satisfaction they derive from their lives tend to be lower in later adulthood than they were in earlier periods of life (Harris *et al.* 1975)

Theories of Adjustment to Aging

The personal concerns of the young–old differ in many ways from the concerns of people at mid life. Jung (1933, 1971) proposed that aging people become more introverted and that they reorganize their value systems. According to Jung, the elderly become more preoccupied with themselves, their health, and their own personal interests and less preoccupied with the concerns of former years: jobs, the lives of their children, and the like. Because rising on the career ladder is no longer an issue for the retired person and because adult children are capable of taking care of themselves, it is not surprising the young–old adults turn to what Buhler (1962) called "goal restructuring," the developing of new goals for living that relate most frequently to personal rather than group needs.

Table 13.2
Percentage of People 65 Years and Older and People Under 65 Reporting
Activities at Which They Personally Spend a Great Deal of Time

Activity	Percentage 18–64	Percentage 65 and over	Net difference
Socializing with friends	55	47	−8
Caring for younger or older members of the family	53	27	−26
Working part time or full time	51	10	−41
Reading	38	36	−2
Sitting and thinking	37	31	−6
Gardening or raising plants	34	39	+5
Participating in recreational activities and hobbies	34	26	−8
Watching television	23	36	+13
Going for walks	22	25	+3
Participating in sports like golf, tennis, or swimming	22	3	−19
Sleeping	15	16	+1
Participating in fraternal or community organizations or clubs	13	17	+4
Just doing nothing	9	15	+6
Doing volunteer work	8	8	—
Participating in political activities	5	6	+1

Reprinted from *The Myth and Reality of Aging in America,* a study prepared by Louis Harris and
Associates, Inc., © 1975, p. 57. Published by The National Council on the Aging, Inc., Washington, D.C.

An example of the older person's growing inner-directedness is illustrated by
the young–old parent who used to be terribly concerned that his daughter complete
her college education but who seems to show little interest when she finally achieves
the hard-earned goal. "Dad," telephoned one forty-year-old woman, "I'm calling to
tell you that I finally finished the dissertation, and I've got a good job lined up. What
do you think of that?" "Oh," responded the father. "That's nice, Dear. Your mother
and I are fine, except that I've had a bad cold for the past week. Nothing to worry
about, I don't think. The weather's been good here . . ." Neugarten and colleagues
(1964) suggest that what is taking place actually is a change from "outer-world" to
"inner-world" orientation that they call increased "interiority" or "psychological disengagement."

The idea that people adjust to aging by becoming increasingly detached from
their former social roles is embodied in the **disengagement theory** proposed by

Cumming and Henry (Cumming and Henry 1961; Cumming 1964). On the basis of cross-sectional studies of aging people conducted in Kansas City, these researchers found a marked decline in social interaction and ego investment in current roles and a withdrawal from former role activity with increasing age. They hypothesized that the decreased role activity represents a process of normal and successful aging, a process they termed "disengagement." More specifically, Cumming and Henry hypothesized that as individuals age, they simultaneously are released from social roles and withdraw psychological energy from social ties. Such events as retirement and widowhood provide increased opportunity and social sanction for disengagement. Cumming and Henry posited that ideal aging results from mutual disengagement of the individual and society simultaneously. Disengagement, according to this view, is accompanied by increased feelings of placid, detached contentment and a centering of self that will help the aging person prepare for inevitable death.

Most researchers today disagree with the disengagement theory. Maddox (1963; 1970), for example, proposes that the aging person's morale is highest as long as he or she remains active. The successful young–old person, according to Maddox, is one who has changed roles, not reduced roles. He or she has replaced the roles of the work years with new and exciting retirement hobbies and activities. Neugarten, Havighurst, and Tobin (1961) believe further that two phases of disengagement actually take place. Psychological disengagement, reflected in decreasing concern for care of others, precedes a decrease in social role activity. While many young–old persons decrease their worry and concern about others in their late fifties and early sixties, they do not usually decrease their social role activities significantly for another ten years or so, until their late sixties or their seventies.

According to Maddox's **activity theory,** older persons tend as long as possible to try to maintain the activities of middle age and to find substitutes for those activities that they are forced to relinquish. Individual differences appear, of course; some young–old people remain more active and interested in the outside world than others. Some have more difficulty coping with the aging process than others.

Neugarten, Havighurst, and Tobin (1961) found in studying the life satisfaction of the elderly that satisfaction with life for the young–old is more directly related to role activities than it is to chronological age. Those people who are most innovative in developing new roles tend to be most satisfied with life, another finding that refutes Cumming and Henry's theory of disengagement. It follows that social change in the past several decades that has opened opportunities for young–old people to participate in social institutions (for example, community colleges that offer free courses to senior citizens) simultaneously has increased the opportunity for the young–old to increase their life satisfaction (Bentson, Kasschau, and Ragan 1977).

Another theory of aging, called **continuity theory,** suggests that people cope with aging by increasing the amount of time they spend in roles they played at earlier stages of their lives. For example, the retired college professor may choose to use her increased free time writing textbooks. The woman who spent most of her adult life taking care of the home and family may spend increasing amounts of time at this period of life as a volunteer at a hospital.

Atchley (1975b), a proponent of continuity theory, points out that older people tend to stick with tried and true ways rather than experiment. Atchley suggests that young–old people want their lives to be as much as they were before as possible, even though there is a gradual reduction of all activity. Obviously, this theory does not fit all young–old people, even though it may fit the majority.

Psychological Issues in Later Adulthood

According to Erikson (1963), individuals during their later years undergo the crisis of ego **integrity vs. despair.** Young–old adults who experience ego integrity are those who regard their lives as meaningful and useful on the whole. They have accepted the life they have lived with all its successes and failures and use this life as a basis for productive living in their later adult years. These are the individuals who, in the young–old years, are most likely to try new hobbies, adapt most easily to changes in life-style due to decreasing physical ability, and in general, have feelings of contentment. By contrast, those who experience despair tend to regard themselves and their lives as failures. They tend to reject their past lives as well as the present and future as useless and meaningless.

By the time they reach the old–old period of development and experience increasingly debilitating physical decline, elderly people who feel their lives have meaning have qualitatively different life-styles from those who give up, those whom Erikson described as "despairing." It is the former who tend to accept impending death, as well as life, most easily, and it is the latter who are most likely to experience serious emotional depressions and withdrawal from the activities of life (Erikson 1963).

Peck (1968), expanding on the work of Erikson, suggested that, just as specific crises are associated with the middle years, specific crises are associated with old age. Each of these crises must be satisfactorily resolved for the elderly person to be psychologically healthy. The first of these is **ego differentiation vs. work-role preoccupation.** People who have defined themselves in middle age entirely according to their work or family roles may have difficulty adjusting in their young–old years when many of these roles must be relinquished. The young–old person needs to learn new roles related to a conception of self as opposed to the ability to take care of children, household tasks, or job. The person who is able at this stage of life to develop meaningful hobbies can transcend this crisis more easily than one who cannot develop new interests. A second issue is **body transcendence vs. body preoccupation.** The young–old person who is able to avoid preoccupation with the aches, pains, and physical disabilities that accompany old age adjusts far more effectively than one who is preoccupied with his or her body. Outside interests are important in dealing with this crisis, just as with the earlier crisis. A third

Peck suggests that an important issue in adjustment to aging is the ability to get beyond preoccupation with one's self and become involved in the upcoming generation.

issue, which Peck suggests is important to adjustment in these years, is **ego transcendence vs. ego preoccupation.** This crisis deals with the same issues Erikson calls ego integrity vs. despair. People who age successfully are able to accept the prospect of their own deaths by becoming involved with the younger generation who will outlive them.

RETIREMENT

Retirement marks an important transitional point for the young–old person. Whether or not this transition leads to a well-adjusted old age seems to depend on a number of factors particular to our times, our society, and to ourselves personally.

Factors Associated with Satisfaction in Retirement

Barfield and Morgan (1978) interviewed retired auto workers and found that satisfaction with retirement among this group was associated primarily with health and income. Those who said they were happy with retirement had in common the following factors: having retired for reasons other than poor health, having remained at least as healthy after retirement as they were before retirement, finding life as they expected, having a retirement income of at least sixty percent of what they had when they were still employed, having suffered no unexpected savings decrease since retirement, and enjoying a standard of living after retirement that did not fall when they left their jobs.

Retired workers who expressed dissatisfaction with their lives often were concerned about poor health. Their unhappiness was reflected by statements similar to the following: "I'm just not happy. I don't feel like a man anymore. Why, I don't have strength enough in my arms even to lift anything. My wife has to do everything now." "There's not much to think about anymore now that I'm not working—except that pain in my gut and the idea that I might not be around too much longer."

Another factor associated with satisfaction in retirement is economic. Retirees who had high incomes before retirement and who now are relatively well off economically and have a cohort of economically affluent retired friends tend to accept their full-time leisure as legitimate and have more positive self-identities than those who are less well off and whose friends are still in the work force.

Adjustment to Retirement

Many researchers have characterized personal–social adjustment in the young–old years according to adjustment of personal–social goals to retirement. Miller (1965) characterized retirement as a crisis that can lead to a breakdown in a person's self-esteem and sense of identity. According to Miller's **identity-crisis theory,** individuals who have worked all of their adult lives come gradually to derive their personal identities primarily from what they do for a living. For example, the psychology professor thinks of herself primarily as a psychologist, rather than as a fifty-year-old woman, mother, and so forth. At retirement, there is often a sudden and drastic reduction in group belonging with one's former colleagues who are still working. The concept of the retired person is ill defined in comparison to the concept of the psychologist, postal worker, or steelworker.

According to the identity-crisis theory, the retired person is no longer sure who he or she really is. It is this feeling that causes the crisis. Miller suggests that retirement, if it is to work to the benefit of the retiree, involves reorganization of the hierarchy of personal goals. If a retiree's career is very high on his or her list of personal goals, a satisfactory adjustment might involve continued work in a similar field. The retired professor might begin writing a book; the retired steelworker might go into a part-time business.

The identity-crisis theory implies a strong work orientation that often is manifested in resistance to retirement. Not all people, of course, carry this work orientation into the young–old years. If a retiree's career is low on the list of personal goals, a satisfactory adjustment might involve increased leisure time activities, community involvement, or other activities. Figure 13.2 describes graphically the possible effects of retirement, depending on the personal goals of the individual.

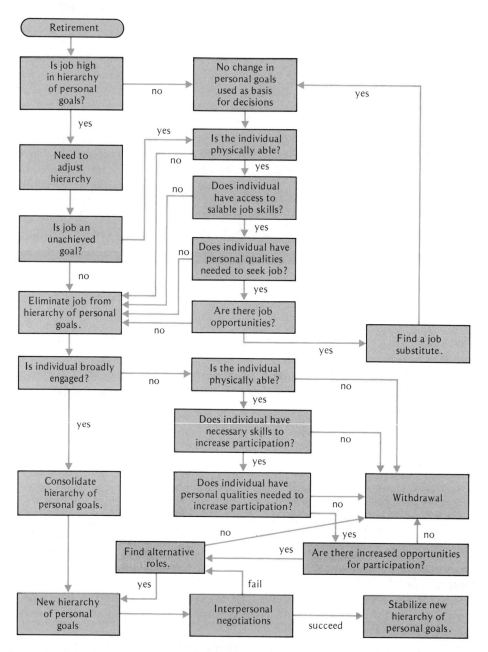

Fig. 13.2 Effect of retirement on personal goals. The personal goals of retired people are affected in a variety of ways, each of which depends on the responses to boxed questions in this sequence and the consequent routing to new steps leading to adjustment. (From R.C. Atchley, Adjustment to Loss of Job at Retirement in *The International Journal of Aging and Human Development,* 1975, vol. 6 (1) 17–27. Reprinted by permission of Baywood Publishing Company.

Individuals who retire voluntarily and who, like this couple, have saved enough money to do something they enjoy, are likely to make the best adjustment to retirement.

The identity-crisis theory suggests also that change from the young adult and middle-age work life to the young–old leisure life carries with it a need to redefine oneself according to the new people with whom one now interacts daily and according to the new goals that need to be set. Atchley (1971) suggests that young–old persons who feel that they are maintaining their self-respect during their retirement years tend to be those who are both healthy and who are still able to engage in a number of pursuits.

An important factor in ability of young–old people to adjust to the retirement crisis is planning. Retired persons who planned during their early adult and middle years to make the best use they could of their financial resources and who, at the same time, remain active have tended to adjust more satisfactorily to retirement than those who tried never to think about old age and who did not engage in activities before retirement that they could continue to enjoy when they were no longer working (Glamser 1976). A supportive spouse is an important factor as well: Husbands and wives who look forward to new activities and additional leisure time with each other contribute to positive attitudes about the future and experience greater retirement satisfaction (Fengel 1975; Kimmel 1980).

Researchers have shown also that people who retire voluntarily are likely to adjust better than those who are forced to retire before they planned. Peretti and Wilson (1975), for example, found that involuntary retirement caused by illness, phasing out of jobs, or the like, is related to lowered emotional satisfaction, feelings of being useless, lowered self-image, and lowered emotional stability. Voluntary retirees, on the other hand, tend to have more feelings of contentment, a higher sense of worth, more self-confidence, and fewer emotional problems, such as feelings of failure. Voluntary retirees tend finally to have more daily social contacts and activities. Presumably, people who are forced to retire are less likely to have planned adequately, a fact that leads to greater problems.

The Economics of Retirement

To some extent, people can improve their chances of maintaining their health and strength through proper diet and exercise, and until recent years, people who planned for retirement by savings and investment could be reasonably confident that they would not experience severe economic problems in their retirement years. Unfortunately, this situation has been changing over the past decade. A study in 1980 by the President's Commission on Pension Policy showed that many retirees today are beset by economic problems that they simply did not (and perhaps could not) anticipate before they retired. One in seven Americans over the age of sixty-five today lives at or near the poverty level.

Why did this happen? For one thing, American working adults did not anticipate the inflation that has affected this country in the past decade. People putting money into private pension plans assumed that what they would receive at retirement would be adequate for a comfortable life. By 1980, however, living costs had jumped at a 7.4-percent annual rate for the past decade, and the purchasing power of the private pensions of those who had retired in 1970 had already been slashed more than fifty percent. Today the dent is even larger (*Business Week* 1980). Inflation has also affected many who planned for retirement through private savings and investment. Flint (1980) suggests that fewer Americans today are saving for old age or for anything else. People seem to feel that it is advantageous to buy today instead of tomorrow when the price is certain to be higher.

Those retirees with neither private pensions nor savings are totally dependent on Social Security, a fact that economists feel is the main weakness of the American retirement system. Social Security was never intended as the sole means of support of retirees, but rather as a means to bolster whatever other retirement arrangements had been made. Because the benefits most elderly people receive are so low, thousands of old people, primarily widows and divorced women without private pensions, live at or near the poverty level.

The lowered birthrate in the United States for the past several decades has added another complicating factor: The proportion of younger working people paying into the Social Security system is decreasing at the same time that the proportion of elderly is increasing. In another forty-five years, it is estimated, those over sixty-five will constitute twenty-two percent of the population, double what it is today (Kreps, 1970). Social Security taxes paid by today's workers make up the payments given to today's retirees. With a smaller proportion of workers in the future to a larger proportion of retirees, an economic crisis seems to be in the offing unless some changes are made (Flint 1980). The future of the Social Security system in the United States is still uncertain.

What are the effects of this economic situation on today's retirees? For one thing, some people who in the past might have taken an early retirement are afraid to do so, and more people are staying on the job in order to add to their retirement savings. One senior vice-president of a large bank explained,

> *I don't want to be like my friend Phil. Phil retired ten years ago, when he was sixty-two, from his appointment as senior vice-president. He looked forward to what he thought would be a comfortable retirement based on his income from Social Security, savings, and a sizable pension from the bank. Today, however, his private pension check seems considerably smaller than it did ten years ago. He worries about money constantly; even the electric light bill and oil bill make him nervous. I don't want that. My wife and I thought we'd retire when I turned sixty-two and get a condominium in Florida. I have a heart condition, and the doctor told me I'd do better in a warmer climate. But we're going to try to hang on until I'm at least sixty-five. It'll make a big difference.*

Financial matters are a constant worry for some retired persons, and many have been forced to adjust their standards of living downward. The problems of the retired bank vice-president, for example, did not seem very important to a retired Western Union employee. As a seventy-year-old widow who had worked for thirty-three years as a teletype operator when she retired a decade ago with a pension of $126.38 a month, her problems were more immediate. She complained,

> *Inflation is just killing me—I almost never eat meat anymore. If it weren't for Social Security, I'd be dead. And that certainly doesn't give me a whole lot. I had to depend on my children to help me with the fuel bills this winter, and it was humiliating.*

It is important to stress, however, that for the majority of retirees, leaving the work force does not mean a life of severe deprivation. Many retired persons find ways to supplement their income during their later years.

HIGHLIGHT 13.1 RETIREMENT EDUCATION

Because of the complexities involved in planning for retirement in the 1980s' inflationary period with its rapidly changing laws regarding retirement and health benefits, gerontologists suggest that educational programs teaching retirement planning should begin early, optimally before adulthood. Interest and thought about what happens in the last third of life can be introduced in the school years, perhaps through social studies courses in high schools, to stimulate interest in young people to think ahead in economic planning. They should continue to be available to all adults through community-sponsored workshops or community college programs, in part to teach adults to deal with the specific planning steps that need to be taken at each level (for example, how, when, and where pension and savings investments can be put to best use for retirement) and in part to keep people informed of current legislation affecting retirement planning and retirement. Such programs already are in existance in many American communities today (Fillenbaum 1971; Glamser 1976; Bynum, Cooper, and Acuff 1978).

Another type of program important for retirement planning and available today to adult American workers as well as retirees involves training in leisure skills. Psychologists indicate that many retirees are able and ready to take on many new activities about which they had no time to learn during their working years. Senior adult education is important in teaching young–old people things they can do to fulfill themselves and make their lives worthwhile (Bynum, Cooper, and Acuff 1978). Friedan (1979) suggests that this is particularly important for women retirees, many of whom today have never been in the work force and have never had an opportunity to interact on a daily basis in the workaday world.

A positive orientation toward retirement in the United States should involve long-term formal programs to teach retirement planning and to reduce uncertainties about what is involved. The following program shows the implementation of such a plan in a series of steps that begin as far back as the adolescent years:

1. *High school.* High school programs should include, possibly as part of the social studies curriculum, initial orientation as to the need for retirement preparation. This should include both economic and psychological needs.

2. *Early adult education.* Formal programs should be made available in community colleges for young adults on financial planning for the "after-sixty-five years." It is important to encourage young adults to participate in these programs while they are still sufficiently young to counteract inadequate financial planning and to take appropriate steps to ensure their savings.

3. *Later adult education.* More adult education programs should be made available by communities to adults five years or less from retirement to provide planning information to help solve the immediate economic problems involved with retirement. Programs for this age group should include information concerning legal aspects of retirement, health services available to retirees, housing and work opportunities, and more planning and economic information to update what was taught in earlier programs. Training for leisure skills also can be an important aspect of retirement planning.

4. *Postretirement Education.* Adult education should be made continually available to retirees learning to cope with new laws, new economic situations, and new psychological situations. Postretirement programs run by communities and community colleges may include methods of counteracting negative stereotypes of retirement and adjustment to work and leisure skills. They should also provide continuing training in leisure skills.

QUESTIONS FOR THOUGHT

1. The program explained here is a formal way of dealing with retirement education. Can you think of informal methods that might be used to meet the same goals?

2. Researchers believe that concern about the adult retirement years can begin with programs in the school years. How can high school students be taught to address the economic and psychological needs of the retirement years?

Retirement of Women

Women, on the whole, tend to adjust more satisfactorily to retirement than do men. This is particularly true of professional women, more of whom retire voluntarily than their male counterparts (Jewson 1978). Many explanations are suggested for this. First, in our society, women frequently are younger than their husbands. Many professional women choose to retire when their husbands do. It is also possible that many professional women do not invest as much of their self-concepts into their work because they have spent so much time in their lives in other roles as wives and mothers.

Jaslow (1976) examined the morale of different categories of women and found that employed women had the highest morale, followed by retired women. Women who had never worked outside the home had the lowest morale. One reason for these findings seemed to be that the women working outside the home were younger, healthier, and in a better financial position than the other categories. Retired women were better off financially than those who had never been employed. The women who were never employed were the oldest group and had the lowest levels of income and the poorest health.

Many professionally working women are married and bring additional pension benefits to the family on retirement. These women and their husbands have fewer economic problems, on the whole, than men and women in homes where the wife never worked outside the home. Because professional women are often younger than their husbands, they frequently work at part-time jobs after a couple's retirement. Even when they are not employed, they often keep active in their professions through continued acquaintances with their colleagues, attendance at conferences, and the like. Of course, the majority of employed women are not in professional careers. Jewson (1978) found that poorer women usually work at jobs that they do not wish to continue after retirement.

MARITAL AND FAMILY RELATIONSHIPS

As discussed in Chapter 12, research has shown that marital satisfaction tends to increase once children have left home. In general, the postparental years seem to offer spouses an opportunity to renew their ties to each other as intimate partners. According to Deutscher (1964), couples in the young–old years are more likely than not to say that they have never been happier together and that the best time of their lives together is retirement. Some studies have shown that from young adulthood through middle age, many couples experience a certain loss of intimacy as measured by confiding, kissing, and reciprocal settlement of disagreements (see, for example, Pineo 1978). By the time a couple reaches the young–old years, however, much of this disenchantment seems either to be forgotten or to have dissipated.

Marital satisfaction in the young–old years is positively related to morale. Happily married young–old men and women report more satisfaction with their way of life and more positive feelings about what the future will bring than do young–old men and women whose marriage relationships are not satisfactory. Lee (1978) reports further that the relationship between marital satisfaction and morale in this age group is much stronger for women than for men. This finding is consistent with the typically greater involvement of women in family and marital relationships during their younger years.

Relationships with Other Family Members

During the young–old years, women particularly tend to renew old family ties that might have been limited during the middle years by work and childrearing responsibilities. Many researchers feel that the development of family ties is what makes

Couples in their young–old years often report a high degree of marital satisfaction. This couple has been married over half a century.

adjustment to the retirement years easier, on the whole, for women than for men (Jewson 1978; Friedan 1979). The elderly who live far away from their children maintain close ties through letter writing, telephoning, and periodic visits. Many brothers and sisters who have lost contact over the years visit more frequently with one another and review old memories together. Many young–old parents and their adult children reestablish their relationships on new grounds, with adult children acting as a source of psychological and sometimes economic help.

Roughly eighty percent of those young–old women who become grandmothers enjoy what researchers term the pastime of grandmothering (Robertson 1977). Grandmothering may include a variety of activities, and Robertson reports that grandparenting styles at this age can be predicted from previous life-styles. Grand-mothers who liked to lavish attention on their grandchildren during middle age usually continue to enjoy their grandchildren as they grow older.

Whereas the young–old today often have large numbers of relatives to rely on, the young–old in the near future are not likely to be so fortunate. Decreasing family size in the United States may mean that some older people may not have an adult child to call for financial help, caretaking, and emotional and personal support (Shanas and Hauser 1974).

Marriage and Remarriage in Later Life

Most men in their young—old years tend to be married. Butler and Lewis (1973) report, however, that only one-third of women sixty-five years of age and older are married. Some possible reasons for this discrepancy are that, on average, women live longer than men, that women tend to marry men older than they are, and that following death of a spouse, women are far less likely to remarry than are men. Burnside (1979) discovered in a study of aged people that men are eight times more likely to remarry than women.

As we learned earlier, marriages that last until later life tend to be satisfactory for both partners. Yarrow and colleagues (1975) found in one study that up to one-third of marriages in later life had some problems, although older marriages, those that have lasted longer than three to five years, are more likely to end because of death of one spouse than because of divorce.

Some young—old people do marry at this period of their lives. Marriages that take place in the young—old years are not subject to the stresses of young or middle adulthood, when first many other family members play major roles in the day-to-day life of the married couple and later couples learn to adjust to decreasing family size and to children's growing up and leaving home. By the time that young—old people marry, most are adjusted to their children's growing up and are accustomed to living as a two-person marital unit. New stresses affect relationships of the married couple at this age. These include all the stresses that accompany the young—old years (for example, illness, loss of physical strength, decreased income, and so on).

Single Living

Although many young—old people who are not married are happy and adjust satisfactorily to their new way of life when they become single, many single young—old people have problems adjusting to life at this stage of development. Glenn (1975) and Gubrium (1974), for example, showed that older married people tend to score higher on measures of morale, psychological adjustment, happiness, and life satisfactions than do widows and widowers in the same age categories.

Isolation can be a major problem for some young—old single people. This problem seems to affect men to a far greater extent than it affects women. Curran (1978) suggests that one reason this might be the case is that women throughout their lives have tended to maintain close ties with family and friends. Friedan (1979) points out that, after the death of a spouse, widows in the young–old group tend to adjust more easily than widowers, probably because during their younger years they invested their energies in family connections and human relationships, whereas men tended to invest most of their energies in job or career. Friedan suggests in this respect that childrearing experiences of women probably help them make the transition to their later years.

The social problems of single living differ for men and women, although both may feel uncomfortable in social groups once they are single. Both males and females adjust to the discomfort of loneliness in different ways. Men are more likely to develop new heterosexual relationships and to remarry than are women. Women's ability to develop social relationships and to find companionship with other widows or with family members may reduce the stress of adjustment to single living for them. Still researchers point out that many women become disorganized and have difficulty defining their self-identities and their lives after their husbands' deaths. Lopata (1973), in a study of widows, found that it was those women who were the best educated, who were middle class, and who were involved heavily in their roles as wives when their husbands were alive who had the greatest difficulty adjusting as widows. Lopata hypothesized that these women were more involved with their husbands when they were alive than were poorer women who tended frequently to live in sex-segregated worlds and spend much of their socializing time with relatives and friends of the same sex, or were women with careers who were immersed in many activities in addition to interacting with their husbands. Lopata concluded that adjustment to widowhood varied with the degree to which wives were involved in their husbands' lives and activities when they were alive.

Some researchers indicate that adjustment to widowhood and widowerhood depends on factors external to the marital couple as well as previous interactions with one another. Harvey and Bahr (1974), for example, pointed out that ability to adjust is related to socioeconomic status and that long-term adjustment problems often have to do with socioeconomic deprivation as much as they have to do with single living itself.

LEISURE AND THE YOUNG—OLD

The leisure activity of people after retirement is related to their attitudes toward their lives. Those who have positive outlooks are much more likely to enjoy their leisure time and make good use of it. A number of factors affect the ways older people spend their time; these include physical health, economic status, and marital status, to name a few of the most important. Our discussion will focus on the activities of the young–old who, as we noted earlier, are people who are in good health and are relatively comfortable financially.

HIGHLIGHT 13.2 THE OSCAR ROSE JUNIOR COLLEGE SENIOR ADULT EDUCATIONAL PROGRAM

Many gerontologists point out that senior adult-education programs can be very beneficial for young–old people just entering the retirement years. Such programs can provide information dealing with a variety of issues crucial to people at this age level, including the economics of retirement and dealing with new economic problems caring for health problems associated with aging, making best use of leisure time, and developing new leisure skills.

One such program has been the Oscar Rose Junior College Senior Adult Educational Program near Oklahoma City (Bynum, Cooper, and Acuff 1978). The program used the faculty, administration, and the physical plant of the Oscar Rose Junior College campus to offer a wide variety of tuition-free courses. The only entrance requirement was that enrollees must be permanently retired.

Investigation of the program showed that it did indeed have a positive effect on enrollees, as the researchers had expected. Nearly fifty-five percent of those who completed courses reported that they felt they had learned new skills that they could use in retirement; over seventy-three percent mentioned that they had made new friends and now spent more time socializing, a factor equally important to this group; nearly twenty-three percent felt that the program had given them information that had helped in making new decisions about their lives; and forty-five percent emerged with new plans for the future.

For those who enrolled, the Oscar Rose Senior Adult Education Program *did* appear to function successfully as anticipatory socialization to ease role

After retirement, young–old adults in American have opportunity to spend large portions of their time in what Kelly (1972) described as "unconditional leisure," leisure that has as its purpose pure enjoyment and is undertaken for its own sake. Unlike the time of their working years, when much of their nonwork time had to be spent in leisure activities related in some ways to their careers or other responsibilities, young–old retirees have sufficient time free of other commitments to do what they want.

What do young–old adults do with this time? Some continue to spend their time on activities related to those of their work years. Retired teachers may volunteer their expertise, for example, working with exceptional children or teaching reading. Some people go back to work part time; others do volunteer work or become involved in church and community activities. Nonprofessional retired workers are likely to have more difficulty coordinating their new free-time activities with their previous

transition and reorientation, but it is important to note that the program did not reach important segments of the elderly population. The enrollees were typically middle and upper class, white, female, and Protestant. They were also mobile, autonomous, better educated, and more affluent than the average person in the community. Finally, they enjoyed better health than the average retiree sixty-five and older in the community near Oscar Rose Junior College. The program did not attract many minority groups or poor people. In addition, it tended to attract people who had already, at previous times of their lives, attended some college courses. Apparently, the program attracted people who felt comfortable in college environments.

The challenge for adult-education programs would seem to involve attracting elderly people who need the skills offered but are unikely to feel comfortable in a college setting.

QUESTIONS FOR THOUGHT

1. The same program might not be for everyone. How might you go about developing a senior adult-education program that would be attended by more segments of the population in this age group? What incentives would you use to entice these senior citizens to come?

2. What basic elements should the curriculum contain? Do you think it should differ from group to group? If so, how?

occupations, although some continue to work part time at jobs related to their old jobs. As one retired bus driver reported, "I use my car for a taxi service now. I pick up a few bucks taking relatives back and forth to the airport usually, and often I take groups to the supermarket. The extra money pays enough to keep my car in gas. But mostly, I like getting a chance to be with people during the few hours a day I work."

Not surprisingly, most young–old people continue the leisure patterns they developed while they were younger. Gardening and watching television are favorite activities of many elderly people. In recent years, many have been taking courses. Sports activities, such as golf and tennis, are also very popular, not simply because they are enjoyable but because they help maintain health and longevity. In communities where many people in this age group live, tournaments often are held just for them. Men and women in their sixties, seventies, or eighties compete on the courts or on the courses with their own age groups. Table 13.3 illustrates the various activities reported as commonly practiced, in a Harris poll, by people sixty-five years of age and older and people under sixty-five.

Unfortunately, many Americans, young and old, have difficulty planning their recreation and leisure activities in meaningful ways. Since Americans, compared to people from less affluent countries, have more leisure time throughout their entire lifetimes (Robinson and Converse 1972), this fact is both surprising and dismaying.

Table 13.3
Percentage of People 65 Years and Older and Percentage Under 65 Who Agree with Statements Related to Life Satisfaction

Statement	Percentage of Public 18–64	Percentage of Public 65 and Over	Net Difference
Positive statements			
I expect some interesting and pleasant things to happen to me in the future.	86	57	−29
As I look back on my life, I am fairly well satisfied.	85	87	+2
Compared to other people my age, I make a good appearance.	85	83	−2
The things I do are as interesting to me as they ever were.	82	72	−10
I've gotten pretty much what I expected out of life.	80	82	+2
I have made plans for things I'll be doing a month or a year from now.	71	53	−18
I am just as happy as when I was younger.	68	56	−12
As I grow older, things seem better than I thought they would be.	67	64	−3
I have gotten more of the breaks in life than most of the people I know.	59	63	−4
I would not change my past life even if I could.	56	62	+6
These are the best years of my life.	56	32	−24
Negative statements			
My life could be happier than it is now.	49	45	−4
In spite of what some people say, the lot of the average person is getting worse, not better.	37	34	−3
When I think back over my life, I didn't get most of the important things I wanted.	24	32	+8
I feel old and somewhat tired.	21	46	+25
Compared to other people, I get down in the dumps too often.	14	13	−1
This is the dreariest time of my life.	13	23	+10
Most of the things I do are boring or monotonous.	12	14	+2

Reprinted from *The Myth and Reality of Aging in America,* a study prepared by Louis Harris and Associates, Inc., © 1975, p. 57. Published by The National Council on the Aging, Inc., Washington, D.C.

**Retirement communities have become extremely popular in the United States.
In addition to providing many services to residents, these communities offer a
pleasant environment and opportunities to meet others who share
similar interests.**

Gerontologists suggest that one solution for the period of retirement, as well as for
the earlier years, is recreation and leisure planning. Neulinger and Raps (1972) suggest that the most important goal of such planning is the development of the attitude
that leisure is worthwhile. This requires learning "how to leisure by acquiring the
'right' leisure attitude" (Neulinger and Raps 1972, p. 206). Although leisure is increasingly coming to be accepted as a worthwhile life goal, a strong element in our
society still regards work as the only legitimate source of identity. Developing the
"right" leisure attitudes then would require placing less emphasis on work as a
primary value.

LIVING ARRANGEMENTS: RETIREMENT COMMUNITIES

The young–old years in America bring, for many, new kinds of living arrangements. Retirement communitites that cater to people fifty-five and older are a particularly American phenomenon. Such communities have sprouted in states where the climate is warm year-round, but such communities also exist in most major cities in colder climates. Retirement communities meet the needs of many older Americans in a number of ways. For one thing, they provide living quarters away from the noise and confusion associated with the raising of young children. For another, the communities afford opportunities to meet other older people with similar interests. Many other services may also be provided, depending on the needs of the residents. Those designed for the old–old age group, for example, often have doctors and nursing staffs in residence and cafeterias or dining halls where meals can be taken by people who would prefer to eat in the company of others rather than alone in their apartments and still not have to bother with cooking. Most retirement communities are near shopping centers or have stores on the premises where staples can be purchased.

While most adult entertainment in our society is aimed at attracting young adults, entertainment organized in retirement communities is intended expressly to meet the needs of the elderly. The older adult who vacations at a mountain lodge frequented by young people might spend time relaxing in the sauna or reading a book alone, while the younger people go outside. But the entertainment planned for the recreation area of the Florida retirement condominium complex involves bridge, bicycling, and a list of other activities chosen by the retirees who live there. Recreation and the company of other young–old people are two reasons for the popularity of retirement communities in the United States today.

THE CASE OF MARY GATSBY—AN ARTIST–WIFE–MOTHER–GRANDMOTHER: A CASE STUDY FOR CLASS DISCUSSION

I. Identification and Sources of Information

Name: Mary Gatsby

Address: New City, Arizona

Race: White

Sex: Female

Age: Sixty-nine years

Sources of information

  1. Personal interview

2. Interview with Phil Gatsby, Mary's husband; and Rachel, Mary's daughter

II. Family History

Mary Gatsby was born the youngest child of a family of seven. She completed high school in her home town in Wisconsin and then completed one year of secretarial school there before marrying Phil Gatsby, a sales representative for a large corporation. The

THE CASE OF MARY GATSBY

Gatsbys have one daughter, Rachel, who is married and has two children now in high school. Mary was a housewife for most of her life, although she worked as a secretary for four years while Rachel was in college "to supplement the family income and to help out with extra costs." She left her job after Rachel graduated in order to stay at home and help her mother who, at the time, was quite ill. When her mother died, Mary did not return to work. Mary is close to her daughter who now lives in New York and is also close to her brothers and sisters who still live in Wisconsin. Although the family does not get together very frequently, they talk to one another regularly on the phone. Ever since Mary and Phil moved to Arizona, they became the household that vacationing members of the family visit regularly. At least one of Mary's siblings spends a week or so visiting the Gatsbys each winter. Rachel visits regularly also. Mary feels that family ties are stronger than they were when she and her brothers and sisters were growing up. She worries a great deal about her oldest sister, Sarah, age seventy-nine, who has not been well the past year. Mary has been trying to talk Sarah into moving to a warmer climate, but thus far Sarah has not wanted to leave her old neighborhood.

III. Case History

Mary and Phil moved to New City nine years ago when Phil retired from his job. They sold their old home in Wisconsin and bought a two-bedroom house in a new retirement community in central Arizona. Mary was extremely pleased with the move from the beginning. She had been having difficulty with her arthritis, especially during the winter months. Shortly after the move, she noticed that many of the aches and pains she had come to take for granted had gone away. She began to participate in some of the sports activities available in the community and soon found herself taking swimming lessons at the community pool. For Christmas the first year they were in Arizona, Phil and Mary bought each other bicycles. They quickly began to spend much of their time on excursions together and with groups of friends they met.

At first, Phil had more difficulty adjusting to his new free time than Mary did. He found himself waking early every morning and began to fix breakfast regularly. After a few months, one of the neighbors suggested that Phil join him at golf. One year after the Gatsbys moved, Phil was spending most afternoons on the golf course. This was the first time he remembers really enjoying retirement.

Five years ago, New City's community college opened a new program. They made regular courses available free of charge to senior citizens whenever their classes were not filled. Mary enrolled in classes in oil painting and weaving. She was delighted. "You see, I always wanted to study art when I was young. Somehow, like lots of other things that happened, I just never got around to it." Mary became very interested in her painting and soon gave up thoughts of other classes. She turned one of the bedrooms at home into a studio and began to work at home as well as in the community college studio. Sometimes now, she can get very busy with a painting and remain in her studio all day. Often, she and Phil "make a quickie sandwich and have it with a beer" or go out to eat so Mary can get back to finish something she's started. Phil reports that he is very happy with Mary's accomplishments. "Last year she won first prize with an abstract she did. We went out to celebrate at a restaurant, and there were people there who pointed us out and said, 'There's the artist who won the state prize!' I don't need to tell you how we felt!"

Mary thinks she spends more time at her work than she has ever spent at any one thing during her entire lifetime, except perhaps, taking care of Rachel when she was small. Mary gets tired sometimes but thinks it's a "good tired feeling." She worries that she may not be giving Phil the attention he needs, but

THE CASE OF MARY GATSBY *(Cont.)*

Phil has also become busy with a number of activities himself, including becoming president of the local home owners' association. Phil is using his business techniques from his working days to try to keep some of the community costs down. He discovered this year that the presidency takes up a great deal of time. "If I want to get really good bids on getting a job done, like reapplying asphalt to the driveways, I need to visit the local people in the business, examine the work they've done on other jobs, and make sure they're good. It all takes time."

Mary and Phil feel that they are enjoying their marriage now more than they ever remember enjoying it. "We have some fights," Mary explains, "but these come only rarely. They always have to do with silly little things, like who did the dishes last. But Phil has taken over lots of the household duties, and he really is very helpful in the kitchen."

Rachel reports that her parents seem to be in good health and well adjusted. They are always glad to talk with her when she phones but never seem to miss her very much when she does not. "It's a very funny feeling," Rachel reports. "Ten or fifteen years ago, when I was younger and used to call my folks, they'd always spend a lot of time asking me what my husband and I were doing and then worrying about whatever I'd tell them. Now when I call, they're always anxious to tell me what *they're* doing. And I think they don't worry anymore about us. At least they don't let on if they do . . . . The conversations we have always end up with their telling me something good that's happened. Last week Mama won a prize in a major competition."

Mary told us about the prize. "You know, I couldn't believe it . . . I was so proud I thought I'd burst! Phil took me to dinner that night to celebrate. I never realized that life could be so much fun. I hope it stays like this for a long time. We really have no worries, and we are enjoying life so much. We do worry that one of us might get sick, like so many of our neighbors. But thus far, we've been very fortunate. Phil is going to be seventy-five next year; it's really hard to believe."

IV. Present Status, Diagnosis, and Prognosis

Mary Gatsby, like many women her age in her economic circumstances, is making an excellent adjustment to the retirement years. Phil made a good income during his working years, and his company had an excellent pension plan to help out. Now, Mary has learned new skills that she is using to make her leisure time useful and meaningful to her. She has maintained close family ties, which are another help in her adjustment to this period of her life. Mary no longer worries about Rachel or her family; she knows that she has given Rachel an excellent start in life and expects that Rachel will be able to cope with whatever follows. She enjoys visits from her grandchildren but is much more concerned about her life with Phil and her new-found artistic ability than she is with very many other things.

Questions for Class Discussion

1. Which of the theories of development—the disengagement theory, the activity theory, or the continuity theory—explains the changes in Mary Gatsby's behavior from preretirement to the retirement years? Why was it probably easier for Mary to adjust initially to retirement than it was for Phil?

2. How was Rachel's role changed in her relationship with her young–old parents from ten or fifteen years ago? What are the probable reasons for these changes?

3. What are the most important problems that Mary and Phil are likely to face in the next five to ten years?

SUMMARY 𝒷2

The biological aging of the body continues during the young–old years. Some of the important physical changes are in the skin, bones, teeth, and senses. There are distinct decreases in efficient functioning of the heart and cardiovascular system, and a noticeable increase in the number of serious illnesses. A number of theories explain the reasons that senescence takes place. These include the wear-and-tear theory, the hormone theory, the collagen theory, and the autoimmunity theory. None of these approaches, however, explains the reasons that exercise decreases the rate of many aspects of senescence.

Sexuality remains an important part of life in later adulthood. Although the climacteric is accompanied by some physical changes that may contribute to sexual difficulties, these can generally be overcome. For both men and women, the maintenance of effective sexuality is directly related to continuing active sexual expression.

Young–old adults no longer require the executive responsibilities needed during the middle-age period. Cognitive development for young–old adults has been described as a reintegrative stage in which cognitive structures are simplified and role requirements are reduced. Although certain cognitive skills, such as some aspects of memory, show age-related deterioration, others remain the same or actually increase during the young–old years. A number of theories have been proposed to explain age-related decrements in cognitive functioning, including both physical and psychological factors, but much more information is needed before a complete explanation can be given.

Individuals in later adulthood tend to have lower levels of life satisfaction and morale than they did in earlier periods of life. The personal concerns of the young–old differ in many ways from those of middle-aged people. Jung described a gradually developing introversion. Neugarten suggested a change from "outer-world" to "inner-world" orientation, what she called "psychological disengagement." Several theories have been developed to explain the preoccupations of older people. The disengagement theory proposes that older people simultaneously are released from social roles and withdraw psychological energy from social ties and that this disengagement is a normal and successful aging behavior. The activity theory proposes that older people tend as long as possible to find substitutes for activities they are forced to relinquish. The continuity theory proposes that young–old people spend increasing amounts of time in roles they played earlier in life and that they tend to stick with tried and true methods rather than experiment.

According to Erikson, individuals during their later years undergo a crisis of ego integrity vs. despair. Peck, expanding on Erikson, suggested several other crises that elderly people must resolve to be psychologically healthy; ego differentiation vs. work-role preoccupation, body transcendence vs. body preoccupation, and ego transcendence vs. ego preoccupation. Whether retirement leads to well-adjusted old age depends on many factors. Those who are happy with retirement tend to have good health and are relatively well off economically. Voluntary retirees tend to be more satisfied than involuntary retirees. According to the identity-crisis theory, retirement calls for redefining oneself according to the new people with whom one interacts daily and the new goals that need to be set. Successful retirees tend to be those who are both healthy and still able to engage in a number of pursuits. A study of the economics of retirement shows that inflation has had a major detrimental effect on satisfaction with retirement in the past decade. Women, on the whole, tend to adjust more satisfactorily to retirement than do men.

Marital satisfaction tends to be high among the young–old and is strongly related to morale, particularly for women. Women also tend to strengthen other family ties during these years. Far more men than women in their young–old years are married. People in this age group who are married tend to score higher on measures of morale, psychological adjustment, happiness, and life satisfactions than do single young–old people. Single young–old people have a number of problems, including isolation and loneliness. Successful adjustment to single living in later life depends heavily on socioeconomic status.

After retirement, Americans have opportunities to spend large portions of time at unconditional leisure. Some spend time on activities related to those of their work years; most continue the leisure patterns they developed when younger. Many unfortunately have difficulty planning recreation and leisure activities in meaningful ways and need to learn to see leisure as worthwhile.

 ## FOR FURTHER READING

Atchley, R.C. *The Sociology of Retirement.* New York: John Wiley and Sons, 1976. This is an excellent book that provides a conceptual framework through which retirement can be viewed as a complex and evolving social phenomenon. It also summarizes the research literature on retirement.

Finkelhor, D. *The Triumph of Age.* New York: Follet Publishing, 1979. The easy-reading style of Finkelhor's book might lead readers to believe that the author is a professional woman describing ways to get ahead. She is, but she describes ways to do it in your seventies during retirement. The book describes the personal experiences of Finkelhor and her husband in dealing with age, getting along with one another, and in planning new recreational and professional activities.

Shanas, E., and D. Hauser. Zero population growth and the family life of old people, *Journal of Social Issues,* 1974, 30, 79–92. This article presents a comprehensive look at the American elderly of the future if zero population growth occurs in this country. The article presents tables and figures showing predicted size of the sixty-five-and-over population group, as well as its characteristics. A comparison is made between current family life and family life projected for the future. Solutions to some of the problems cited are discussed.

Preview Questions

- What are some major physical changes that create problems for the old-old adult?

- Can you describe some basic personality changes that accompany later adulthood and the effects that life satisfaction has on their seriousness?

- What are some functional mental health problems that become more prevalent for old-old adults?

- Can you describe some organic disorders that cause mental problems for people in later adulthood?

- How does senility differ from organic brain dysfunction, and what are three types of isolation that may produce the former?

- What are some normal cognitive changes that take place in later adulthood, and how are these related to longevity?

- Can you compare the disengagement and continuity theories with respect to the way they explain adequate adjustment of the aged?

- What are some reasons for the economic concerns of the aged, and how are they related to socioeconomic status and ethnic background?

- Can you characterize the attitudes of medical personnel toward old-old patients who are in the hospital?

- What are several types of living arrangements that are made by old-old adults, and what are some advantages and disadvantages of each?

- Can you describe the stages of mourning that follow the loss of a spouse and explain the differences in the way men and women adjust to this trauma?

14

Later Adulthood:
The Old-Old Years

Increasing longevity and the decreasing birthrate in this country have produced significant changes in the nation's demographic structure. In 1960, nine percent of the population was elderly. Today the figure is twelve percent (U.S. Bureau of the Census 1980). In the year 2000, it is possible that twenty-three percent of the total population will be composed of people sixty-five and older. Of this group, about thirty-five percent should be aged seventy-five or older.

In recent years **gerontologists,** those researchers who examine the aging process, have focused extensively on the changes that take place in older people during the last stage of life. The old–old period described by Neugarten (1979) often begins in a person's mid seventies or early eighties, although individual differences are great and for many this period occurs somewhat earlier. In contrast to the young–old period, which is characterized by an active interest in life, the old–old years are often characterized by decreasing abilities, passive modes of responding, ill health, depressed or paranoid behavior in some individuals, and mourning.

During the old–old period, people experience a series of losses: loss of friends and loved ones, loss of ability to interact with the environment, and finally loss of

Celebrating one's one-hundredth birthday is a time to reminisce about the past and about what contributions one has made.

life. Neugarten (1979) believes that the ways in which aging people respond to these losses need to be considered in relation to their changed physical conditions and the types of interactions they are able to have with the environment. Lieberman (1975) suggests further that the traditional views of psychological health do not apply to aged persons. Older people, often of physical necessity, must use different mechanisms to cope with their environments than they used when they were younger. Thus passive modes of responding may be adaptive rather than unhealthy. Lieberman is in agreement with the views of Busse (1959), who proposed some years ago that the psychodynamics of depression in the aged are probably quite different from those in younger people because they are based on mourning and loss, whereas depression in younger people often stems from aggression turned inward. For some old–old individuals, passivity and depressed responding are appropriate responses that help people prepare for impending death.

DEVELOPMENT DURING THE OLD–OLD YEARS

The developmental changes that occur in one's seventies and eighties are affected in even greater ways than in the sixties by the physical decline that takes place during this period. Most of the old–old experience a steadily narrowing environment because of increasing physical disability and the loss of loved ones and close acquaintances.

Physical Changes

Physical decline increases rapidly during old age. Already, deep wrinkles become deeper; loss of skin elasticity increases so that loose skin often seems to hang; extensive hair loss is common, and what is left turns white. The skeletal structures become increasingly brittle so that a major problem of the elderly is falling down and breaking bones. Now, bones that used to take a long time to heal sometimes will not mend at all. This, of course, can severely limit mobility. A fall is the most common event leading to hospitalization for the elderly. As is true at early stages of life, general physical decline can be slowed with appropriate diet and exercise. A balanced diet combined with a consistent program of such simple exercise as walking has been shown to help control hypertension, improve cardiovascular function, increase flexibility and decrease depression. At the same time, exercise should be tailored to the individual's general physical condition, for overexertion can be dangerous.

Physiological decline from about age thirty to over seventy-five has been charted systematically. Blood flow to the brain decreases approximately twenty percent from age thirty to age seventy-five; kidney plasma flow decreases fifty percent; the kidneys and liver function less efficiently; actual brain weight decreases forty-six percent. A decline in heart function by thirty percent permits the average old person's heart to pump only about seventy percent as much blood as at age thirty. Hand grip grows weaker; lung functioning shows marked decline (Shock 1962). (See Figure 14.1 for a description of the decrease in lung capacity with age.)

The old–old are far more susceptible to all kinds of illnesses than when they were younger. Serious illnesses account for rapidly increasing mortality in this age group. Men have much higher rates of death and impairment than do women, so

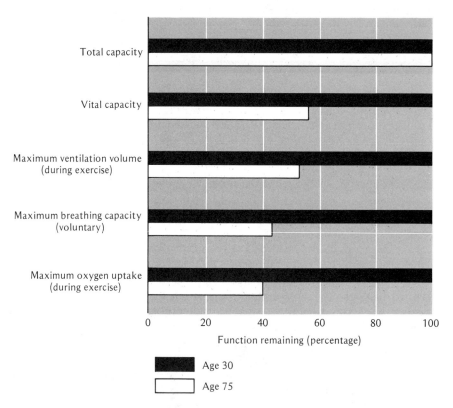

Fig. 14.1 Changes in lung capacity with age. Functions of the lung show marked decline with age. Total capacity is the amount of air the lungs can hold; it does not decrease. Vital capacity is amount of air forcibly expelled in one breath. Maximum ventilation volume during exercise represents involuntary movement of air. Maximum breathing capacity is the amount of air that can be moved in and out of the lungs voluntarily in fifteen seconds. Oxygen uptake is the quantity of oxygen absorbed by the blood from the lungs for transportation to the body cells. (From Nathan W. Shock, The physiology of aging, in *Scientific American*, January 1962, p. 108. Copyright © 1962 by Scientific American, Inc. All rights reserved.)

that only thirty-eight percent of people seventy-five and older are men (U.S. Bureau of the Census 1980). About eighty percent of elderly people have several chronic diseases (Kimmel 1980). Disabilities, whether in the form of symptoms or actual loss of functioning, however, should not be written off casually as aging. In many cases, specific diseases can be identified for which there are treatments. More than forty percent of old–old people have significant impairment in eyesight or hearing, for example. The first noticeable symptom sometimes is depression or withdrawal due to sensory deprivation. When the cause of the depression can be identified as related to sensory decrements, it can often be alleviated by treating the physical problem. Forty percent of the elderly have arthritis, the symptoms of which can sometimes be eased by medication. Some thirty percent or more have noticeable signs of cardio-vascular disease, for which there are also helpful medications. More than fifteen percent have diabetes, which can be managed medically. Finally, falls caused by giddiness, loss of balance, fainting or tripping often are the first symptom of other diseases (Exton-Smith and Evans 1977).

The principle cause of death of elderly persons is cardiovascular disease (Havighurst and Sacher 1976). More than forty percent of elderly people die of cardiac disease, and twenty percent more of cerebrovascular diseases. Symptoms common to this age group include cardiac rhythm disturbances that cause rapid, irregular heartbeat, palpitations, and fainting; hypertension (high blood pressure), and congestive

HIGH BLOOD PRESSURE

Hypertension, or high blood pressure, is a disease that commonly affects old people. This ailment may carry with it no obvious symptoms. People with high blood pressure may feel well, even though their conditions are serious enough to require medical treatment. For this reason, many old people do not receive treatment when it is needed. If left untreated, high blood pressure can lead to very serious conditions, including stroke, heart disease, and kidney failure. High blood pressure can be detected by readings that measure the pressure of blood against the blood vessel walls. Typical causes of the condition are obesity and diets high in salt.

High blood pressure cannot usually be cured, but it can be controlled by continuous treatment. If doctors find that an elderly person has high blood pressure, they may recommend that he or she lose weight, eat a salt-free diet, or get more exercise. In some cases, hypertension may be controlled by making these simple changes in daily habit. In other cases, drugs are needed to control high blood pressure. But even when drugs are prescribed, doctors may still recommend that the elderly person follow careful guidelines on weight, salt intake, and exercise.

Continued

HIGHLIGHT 14.1

When blood pressure is lowered by medication, it can rise again if the patient forgets to take the medication regularly. Some elderly people are forgetful and need to be monitored. For this reason, those who learn to take their medication at the same time every day and who establish a regular and easily remembered routine are more easily treated. Older people who understand the reasons and the methods for treatment are more likely to remember to take their medication.

QUESTIONS FOR THOUGHT

1. Why is it particularly important to explain in detail to elderly patients just what their medications are and why they should use them?
2. Can you propose a plan to assist elderly people who live alone with handling medication?

Source: U.S. Dept. of Health and Human Services (1980).

heart failure. Diseases of the vascular system that cause sudden blockages in the veins can lead to heart attacks or strokes. Although most cardiovascular diseases cannot be cured, medications may reduce symptoms considerably.

Mental Health

Researchers point out that the elderly tend to have personality characteristics that make them distinct from younger age groups. For example, Neugarten (1977) and Botwinick (1973) report that elderly, on average, are more preoccupied with their inner lives, more introverted, less willing to deal with complicated or challenging situations, and more conformist than are younger people. This does not mean, however, that individuals go through sudden personality changes as they reach old age. To the contrary, Bischof (1976) points out a continuity in personality throughout the developmental stages and indicates that most personalities are consistent from one stage to the next. Thus individuals who have been political radicals in younger years may move to the right in their thinking as they age, but they still remain distinctly liberal.

Life satisfactions and morale of people in the old–old years are affected by health conditions. Old–old people who are healthy and active tend to have far higher levels of life satisfaction and morale than the elderly who are sick and incapacitated (Toseland and Sykes 1977; Markides and Martin 1979). Individuals higher on the socioeconomic scale get higher life-satisfaction scores (Wolk and Telleen 1976). Individuals whose families provide economic and psychological support in an environment that allows them as much freedom as possible tend finally to have high levels of life satisfaction and morale.

Mental Health Problems

Emotional problems, such as depression, loss of self-esteem, loneliness, anxiety, and boredom, are common behavior patterns among elderly people. Usually, these are people who have experienced the deaths of others close to them and other crises and feel they have little control over their lives. A relatively high proportion of elderly people seem to have mental health problems requiring that they be confined to mental hospitals. Lawton and Gottesman (1974) report that about thirty percent of individuals in mental hospitals are over sixty-five years of age. Some researchers suggest that this high percentage is due primarily to psychologists' lack of awareness of the special needs of aged in testing situations, so that the aged sometimes score as mentally ill when they are not and that many responses to personality tests that appear "abnormal" for young people are, in fact, "normal" for the aged individual (Schaie 1977–1978).

Unfortunately, just because the elderly are placed in hospital situations does not necessarily mean that they are receiving adequate treatment for their symptoms. Kucharski, White, and Schratz (1979) found that elderly people are much less likely to have psychological treatment recommended for them than younger people, even when their psychological symptoms are the same as younger people. Many elderly people with mental health problems are given custodial care rather than treatment for their symptoms.

Although the aged are overrepresented among age groups hospitalized in mental hospitals, fewer elderly individuals than individuals in any other age group seek or receive treatment from community mental health facilities. Kramer, Taube, and Redick (1973) report that only about two percent of out-patients at mental health clinics are aged. One reason for this might be that elderly patients often are not seen by psychologists or psychiatrists until their mental health problems are so severe that hospitalization is required.

Functional Disorders. One of the primary causes among the elderly of **functional disorders** (disorders for which there is no discernible physical or organic cause) that require treatment is an inability to deal with the changes that occur at this stage of life.

The most frequent functional disorder is **depression.** Depressed individuals appear sad, lonely, guilt ridden, withdrawn, and sometimes hostile. They often experience insomnia or lose their appetites. As we have learned, some depressed individuals attempt suicide. Vickers (1976) points out that although depression is a functional disorder, it can be effectively controlled in many cases through drug therapy and counseling. Some elderly individuals who are unable to deal with the changes in their lives exhibit **manic behaviors,** and they move and talk in rapid and sometimes incoherent ways. Langley (1975) reports successful use of drug therapy with the manic elderly, although the cause of manic behavior, like depression, is not known.

Many elderly people develop **hypochondriasis.** Because of the fear of loss of bodily functioning, these individuals become overly concerned with their bodies to the exclusion of the world around them. Many hypochondriacal patients lose some of their fear when doctors or family members take the time to explain to them the reasons that their bodies are changing as they are and just what the doctors and their medications can do to help.

Feelings of **paranoia** are another functional mental disorder experienced by some elderly people. Those who develop paranoia are convinced they are being persecuted, feel that others are avoiding them, avoid others in turn, and eventually cause a self-fulfilling prophecy. Feelings of paranoia often are the result of isolation and fear. Paranoid elderly are the people Erikson (1963) termed "despairing" in contrast to those elderly who have developed what he called "integrity." The de-

Sometimes mental disorders of the elderly occur because of physical damage to the brain; in other instances, social isolation or inability to adjust to old age may be contributing factors.

spairing spend their time at activities that seem meaningless and have no apparent psychological goal.

Individuals classified as having **psychosis** develop more serious distortions of reality than do neurotic individuals. Psychoses are more incapacitating and more difficult to treat than neuroses. Psychotic elderly may suffer from hallucinations or delusions, which in turn trigger depression or paranoia. Sometimes, the elderly develop psychotic symptoms in which there is mood disorder, such as extreme mania or depression.

Organic Disorders. Some mental disorders of the elderly have organic causes. In **organic brain syndrome** impairments of intellectual and cognitive functioning develop because of physical damage to the brain. In about ten to twenty percent of elderly people with organic brain syndrome, symptoms are reversible (Pfeiffer 1977). Some organic brain syndrome, however, is irreversible. We will discuss both temporary and permanent symptoms of organic brain syndrome in the sections that follow.

Senility

Senility is an all-too-frequently used term that refers generally to mental incapacities, such as forgetfulness or confusion, that may be caused by a variety of different factors associated with increasing age. Senility is not a medical diagnosis but refers instead to a series of particular intellectual impairments. After eighty years of age, about one out of every five people exhibits some signs of impaired mental functioning, which is often called senility. Loss of orientation, forgetfulness, more severe memory loss, and inability to carry out many cognitive tasks are typical symptoms of impairment. These symptoms can be the result of a variety of general conditions that affect the entire body. Some examples are anemia, kidney dysfunction, dehydration, infections of the urinary tract, and others. In addition, the impairments caused by organic brain syndrome are referred to as senility (U.S. Department of Health and Human Services 1980), but as we shall see, many other causes of symptoms are similar to those caused by organic brain syndrome and other illnesses.

Organic brain syndrome itself may have different causes. Omenn (1977) describes one cause as atrophy of some of the brain cells of the cerebral cortex. Atrophy of this sort, called **senile psychosis,** can lead eventually to irreparable impairment of both short- and long-term memory, inability to remain oriented to the environment, impairment of judgment and comprehension, unpredictable expression of emotions, and inability to carry out sequential tasks. Organic brain syndrome caused by senile psychosis leads eventually to death because of cessation of some vital activity of the brain. Another cause of organic brain syndrome is **cerebral arteriosclerosis**, a disease in which a cerebrovascular accident, caused by hardening of the arteries of the brain, leads to interruption of blood flow to a part of the brain and results in death of brain cells because of disruption of the oxygen supply. Some of the symptoms that result include hallucinations, incoherent speech, sleep-lessness, apathy, depression, anxiety, and a lack of ability to think clearly—all symptoms frequently characterized as senility. The onset of senile behavior because of cerebrovascular disease differs from that caused by atrophy in that impairment is sudden. Cerebrovascular disease symptoms may include other impairments in addition to those associated with intelligence and cognition, such as neurological impairment causing paralysis of some parts of the body. In some cases, individuals can recover their abilities after cerebrovascular accidents. In other cases, damage is irreparable. Repeated episodes may lead to cumulative and irreparable impairment of cognitive and other types of functioning and eventually death.

Many symptoms of senility may be alleviated to some extent by special care of the patient. Butler and Lewis (1977) note, for example, that even when a large part of the damage caused by organic brain syndrome is irreparable, patients often can be helped to adjust to their handicaps through physical and emotional support. For example, elderly patients who seem to be unable to cope with their environments without assistance may do far better at dealing with the tasks at hand if they are surrounded by a familiar environment and family members who assist them in sensitive ways.

Elderly patients who exhibit transient impairment of mental functioning after cerebrovascular accidents, metabolic malfunctions, heart failure, infection, or some other traumas also may be helped through physical and emotional support. In many instances, such patients can relearn some or all the lost skills through opportunity to practice them.

Many elderly patients exhibit symptoms associated with senility that are not due to organic causes. Selye (1956) noted that stressful situations common to the lives of the elderly, such as the death of a spouse, are related to increased forgetting and memory loss. Isolation can be a major cause of many symptoms of senility. Ernst and colleagues (1978) report that, for elderly people who exhibit confused or disoriented behavior and impaired ability to comprehend and to make judgments, three kinds of isolation are playing a role in producing the behavior: (1) emotional isolation in which the person rejects friends, withdraws from social activities, and becomes apathetic, (2) social isolation in which the deaths of others close to the person leave that person alone, and (3) physiological isolation caused by sensory difficulties, such as impaired hearing and sight, and impaired motor ability, which serve to restrict the person's ability to communicate and get around. Isolation can also exacerbate depressive reactions: The elderly who find it difficult to interact with others because of emotional, social, or physical isolation often have fewer people, in turn, attempting to interact with them and thus increase their loneliness and confusion.

Another cause of symptoms of senility that is not organically based includes overmedication of tranquilizing drugs commonly used to calm anxious elderly patients in hospitals or nursing homes. Often, the supposedly senile old person is simply drugged. These patients often return to a normal mental state when the drug is no longer administered.

Normal Cognitive Changes

During the old–old years, the extent of societal involvement gradually decreases as aged people adjust to increasing infirmities and as biological changes impose increasing constraints. For this reason, most elderly people are involved in different types of cognitive tasks from those required in their younger years. Schaie (1977–1978) described this period of life as the "final phase of cognitive function." For both the young–old and the old–old, this involves a "reintegrative stage" in which individuals increasingly are affected in their thinking by motivational and attitudinal factors. They are no longer motivated by social stimuli to the extent that they were when they were younger, and they spend increasing periods of time in quiet contemplation. The anxieties and frustrations of earlier periods of life are forgotten; the older adult's attitude toward life tends increasingly to be more accepting. Figure 14.2 portrays the change from earlier stages to Schaie's reintegrative stage.

Most elderly people give increasingly selective attention to cognitive demands that attain new meaning in their lives. With their diminishing ability to deal with

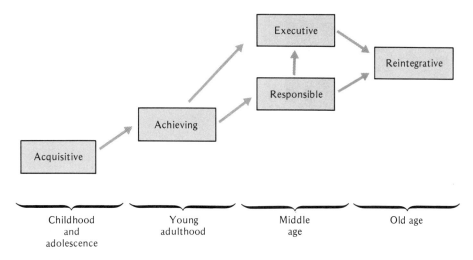

Fig. 14.2   Schaie's stages of cognitive development. (From K. Schaie, Toward a stage theory of adult cognitive development, in *The International Journal of Aging and Human Development*, 1977–78, vol. 8 (2) pp. 129–138. Reprinted by permission of Baywood Publishing Company.)

problems, such as competing professionally, or even with day-to-day concerns, such as shopping for food, the elderly tend to focus more on their immediate life situations. For the old–old person, day-to-day problem solving might concern itself with such issues as whether or not the temperature outside will be warm enough to allow leaving the house sometime during the day or whether food in the house is sufficient to cook dinner. Illness becomes a major focus of attention at this period. For an elderly woman at home with her sick husband, for example, this immediate life situation might involve caretaking activities that require few new cognitive demands. For an elderly person who is still active in the community, however, the problem-solving tasks might resemble those of earlier years.

As is true of the young–old period, there are no tests of cognitive ability that can measure accurately the functioning of the old–old age group. A body of evidence, however, is accumulating and suggests that qualitative intellectual functioning, as measured by scores on standardized tests of intelligence used with adults, is related to expect longevity of the individual. Specifically, a sharp decline in scores on standardized IQ tests may signal the approach of death in the individual (Granick 1971). Of course, the elderly who survive the longest tend also to be in better health than other elderly people, engage in more physical and social activities, and have more positive psychosocial attitudes.

For elderly people who remain actively involved in the community, problem-solving tasks are similar to the cognitive tasks of earlier phases of the lifespan.

A longitudinal study of elderly people at age seventy and of the same people eleven years later showed that their visual motor coordination and their speed and flexibility of responding, as measured on standardized tests, decreased considerably during this period (Granick 1971). As is true during the young–old years, some aspects of memory also decline (see, for example, Horn 1976; Reese 1976; Arenberg and Robertson-Tschabo 1977).

Impaired mental functioning caused by environmental conditions often can be reversed. With training, the elderly often can achieve greater relative improvement in their ability to recall names and facts than can younger people. As with younger adults, intellectual performance can be influenced by education or physical disabilities.

It is important to remember, of course, that not all old–old people suffer from seriously impaired mental functioning. Frequently, scholars and artists who were creative in their younger years continue to produce outstanding works well into old age, although the number of works for this age population decreases (Dennis 1966).

Although many people think that forgetfulness is associated with senility, slight confusion or occasional forgetfulness at this stage of life, just as at any other stage, may only signify an overload of facts in the brain's storehouse of information. Some impaired mental functioning common to the aged is due to gradual loss of brain

---

INTELLECTUALLY PRODUCTIVE ELDERLY   HIGHLIGHT 14.2

Many individuals ninety years and older have demonstrated that they can lead highly productive intellectual lives regardless of their ages. Some nonogenarians, as these people are called, are known to all of us. Albert Einstein and W. Somerset Maugham are two examples. Einstein and Maugham began their famous productivity in their earlier years and continued it through to the old–old period. Other famous nonogenarians, such as Grandma Moses, began to produce in the later years. The following list of individuals compiled by Apple (1979) demonstrates a wide variety of skills and creativity exhibited by other famous nonogenarians. Many elderly people, like these but less famous, continue to live with interest in their day-to-day activities and demonstrate motivation to continue in roles important to them and to their families.

Sir Adrian Boult	Conductor who founded the BBC symphony and at age ninety published the book *Music and Letters*
Lord Noel Baker	British Quaker and winner of the 1959 Nobel prize who celebrated his ninetieth birthday by addressing the Royal Institute of International Affairs in England on the "unending struggle for world peace"

Continued

HIGHLIGHT 14.2

Elizabeth Craig	Famous chef who, at age ninety-six, published one of her numerous books
Sir Robert Mayer	British patron of music for young people, who shortly after his one-hundredth birthday, set off on an American lecture tour

QUESTIONS FOR THOUGHT

1. The individuals listed here all engage regularly in activities that stimulate the intellectual processes; this is one reason that they remain so able to deal with new thoughts and ideas. What ways might other not-so-famous elderly people use to stimulate their mental problem solving?

2. Can you think of some ways that local universities or other institutions might help to develop programs to increase intellectual productivity of elderly citizens? Explain.

cells. This leads, according to researchers, to memory loss. Slight confusion is often associated with repetition of thoughts.

Researchers studying memory are not sure just how memory occurs, or what exactly is lost when memory is lost. Hebb theorizes that both repetition and slight confusions might result from loss of inhibitory neurons in the brain. These neurons in earlier life, he hypothesizes, inhibited extraneous ideas. With their loss, the elderly more frequently have extraneous ideas pop into their heads and cause slight confusion (Cohen 1980).

PERSONALITY AND ADJUSTMENT

Theories of Adjustment

The theories of adjustment to aging have been used to describe the ways that elderly change and adapt in the old–old years. The theory of disengagement (Cumming and Henry 1961; Cumming 1964), discussed previously, views normal aging as a process of progressively withdrawing from former roles. The term *disengagement* accurately describes what happens to many of the elderly. As they become more isolated because of physical problems or loss of spouse or companions, they spend less time interacting with the outside world. Activity for this age group tends to be far more inner directed than for people in the young–old years.

Whether this withdrawal represents successful aging or is simply the result of enforced isolation has been debated by researchers. Neugarten, Havighurst, and Tobin (1961), for example, contend that life satisfaction is more directly related to role activities than it is to chronological age. According to this view, the elderly who are likely to be most well adjusted are those who have been able to continue some of their former roles. More recent work by Atchley (1975a) supports this position, suggesting that adjustment is enhanced when old people are able to continue in roles they used in earlier periods of their lives. Theorists taking this position point out that for the old–old individual to adjust most satisfactorily to aging, that individual must replace many of the old roles or relationships that are lost with new ones.

Havighurst (1961) points out that in describing individuals in the old–old period of life, this theory may be too simple to describe the behavior of many people who, of necessity, are adjusting to many different kinds of loss. Some people who are able to maintain a highly intimate and stable relationship with another person, for example, are better able to adjust to aging than others (Lowenthal and Haven 1968). For many elderly, apparently, happiness is not maintained simply by staying active. Many old–old individuals prefer sendentary lives to the strain of trying to maintain activity levels that were easy for them in earlier years.

Apparently, what leads to most successful adjustment for one individual may be very different from what leads to successful adjustment for another. Although some people are happy with few roles and low levels of activity, it is necessary for other aging people to develop new roles for their personal adjustment to this stage of life. A good example of one older person who changed his life-style to find new activities that better met his needs at this stage of life is psychologist Donald Hebb, who at age seventy-five retired as a psychologist because he felt he was "not as smart as I used to be." He became involved in full-time care of the farm to which he had retired. Observation of his own behavior led him to conclude that he had undergone not a *loss* in motivation but a *change* in motivation (Cohen 1980).

Hebb's example represents one form of successful adjustment to the aging process. Other old–old people may exhibit other types of responses to aging depending on a number of factors, such as past life experiences and the individual's reaction to these events, as well as individual differences in personality. Physical health factors as well as certain life stresses common in old age have also been found to affect the personality of elderly people. As we already discussed, older people tend, on the whole, to have many more health problems than younger people. At the same time, they experience the death of peers and relatives more frequently. Their social world tends to shrink as they get older because of their progressing infirmities. Tallmer and Kutner (1969) studied 181 adults from age fifty to age ninety and discovered that increasing withdrawal is not related directly to increasing chronological age but rather to stresses associated with the aging process. Old–old people who experienced fewer of these stresses tended to be less withdrawn; those subjected to more stresses tended to be more withdrawn, regardless of chronological age. The work of Levinson and colleagues (1978) supports Tallmer and Kutner's argument. These researchers found that when a person experiences physical decline and ensuing social deprivation, life can lose all meaning. When health and social interaction are good, however, psychosocial development continues.

Developmental Tasks

What developmental tasks are required of old–old people? Some old–old people continue to be active in a variety of activities. At the same time, at the end of the life cycle, they must come to terms with the inevitability of dying and prepare for their own deaths. At the end of earlier periods of life, development involved taking on new kinds of responsibilities. By their eighties, however, people must yield earlier roles to those younger than they. They must make their peace with the loss of spouse and friends. Personality development continues to the extent that they are able to view their lives as meaningful and accept the inevitability of death. Kubler-Ross (1969) points out that this is a time of life that individuals tend to reminisce about the past and the contributions they have made to life. Those who are unable to do so are likely to feel a sense of despair. Old–old people fortunate enough to feel that their lives have had meaning and order may feel satisfied with themselves (Neugarten 1977), and provide others models of wisdom and self-worth as well.

ISSUES AFFECTING THE ELDERLY

The "graying" of America has focused increased attention on a number of issues of particular concern to older citizens, including economic conditions, health care, and living arrangements.

Economic Concerns

The amount of income available to the old–old determines to some extent the quality and length of their lives. Crandall (1980) points out that the aged are one of the most economically deprived groups in our society today and that more than fifteen percent live below the poverty line and another twenty-five percent are at a "near poor" level, defined as one hundred twenty-five percent of the poverty level. Personal income for elderly sixty-five years of age and older is shown in Table 14.1.

The elderly rely on several sources of income. About ninety percent of the aged receive Social Security payments. The major problem with Social Security for the

Table 14.1
Personal 1973 Income* for Public 65 and Over

Income	65 and Over	65–69	70–79	80 and Over	White	Black
	Percentage of Public					
Under $1,000	3	2	3	4	2	7
$1,000–$1,999	10	8	10	15	8	26
$2,000–$2,999	14	10	16	16	13	24
$3,000–$3,999	15	13	14	22	15	15
$4,000–$4,999	14	15	14	12	14	9
$5,000–$6,999	14	15	15	12	15	8
$7,000–$9,999	14	17	13	7	15	4
$10,000–$14,999	9	12	8	3	9	3
$15,000–$19,999	3	3	3	2	3	—
$20,000–$24,999	1	2	1		1	†
$25,000 and over	1	2	1	1	1	†
Not sure/refused	24	24	24	26	24	22
Median income (in thousands)	$4.5	$5.1	$4.4	$3.5	$4.6	$2.6

Source: Reprinted from *The Myth and Reality of Aging in America,* a study prepared by Louis Harris and Associates, Inc., © 1975, p. 235. Published by The National Council on the Aging, Inc., Washington, D.C.
*Income for people 65 and over who are heads of households and their spouses includes total household income. Income for people 65 and over who are neither heads nor spouses of heads includes only the income that is available to them and their spouses personally to spend and not income that belongs to other members of the household.
†Less than 0.5%.

elderly is that it has not been designed as a system to provide their total income. For that reason, payments are often very low. Social Security payments with no additional source of income maintain individuals at poverty level. Supplementary Security Income (SSI), instituted by the federal government, guarantees the elderly a certain income each month. If Social Security payments and other income add up to the figure below the specified amount, the individual can receive the difference through SSI. This is of particular benefit to those sixteen percent of the elderly who receive reduced Social Security benefits and to those who receive no benefits at all. Harris (1978) showed that in 1975, the average SSI payment to the aged was ninety-one dollars per month. At that time, only seven percent of the aged were receiving SSI. Many others were not eligible because of the requirements established by the government in the form of an assets test.

Some elderly people hold private pensions, although the number currently who have access to these funds is not much more than about one-third of the elderly

About fifteen percent of the elderly live below the poverty line. In many cities, charitable organizations provide hot meals for elderly people who would otherwise be poorly nourished.

population (U.S. Bureau of the Census 1980). Most of those who do have private pensions derive small amounts of income from them. In almost all cases, this income is not adjusted for cost-of-living increases. Today, savings account for only a small percentage of the income of elderly people because most who are aged did not have an opportunity in earlier life to accumulate much savings.

Elderly people often feel that their low incomes do not allow them to live in the manner they would like. Peterson (1972) asked a group of elderly people about the adequacy of their retirement income. Most individuals responded that to live comfortably, they would need about thirty-three percent more income.

Old–old elderly women tend to experience the greatest economic difficulty. One reason for this is that elderly women greatly outnumber elderly men because of women's greater longevity. Another reason is that unlike elderly men, few women in this age group have contributed toward pensions or Social Security. Those who have generally have retired with fewer benefits because they worked outside the home for shorter periods of time and earned lower salaries than their male counterparts. Women living alone, whether they are widowed, single, or divorced, tend to be much more dependent on Social Security than are couples or men living alone. This is true because so many elderly widows today have never worked out-side their homes. For these women, Social Security payments on the average make up about seventy percent of their income. Widows over seventy who have never worked receive about one-third less on average than widows or widowers who have worked full time for most of their adult lives. The economic impact on elderly women is immense: Their poverty rate is sixty percent higher than it is for men (U.S. Bureau of the Census 1979).

Black and other minority elderly people also experience considerable eco-nomic difficulty. The black elderly have been and still continue to be below the poverty line three times as frequently as the white elderly population (Harris 1978). (Table 14.2 lists selected characteristics of aged individuals below the poverty line.) Even though the black elderly are so much less affluent than the white elderly, Williams (1977), in a survey of black elderly people, reported that the majority of respondents seemed satisfied with their financial status, despite economic problems and substandard housing, often in areas of unusually high crime rates. One reason for this might be that these elderly people have always lived under substandard conditions and do not feel that this period of their lives has brought with it de-creased standards to the extent that many previously more affluent individuals might feel.

Table 14.2
Selected Characteristics of Persons 60 and 65 Years Old and Over Below Poverty Level: 1959–1977

Age, Family Status, and Race	Percentage Below Poverty Level				
	1959	1970	1975*	1976*	1977*
Persons 60 and over	(NA)†	21.3	14.2	13.7	12.9
Persons 65 and over	35.2	24.6	15.3	15.0	14.1
White	33.1	22.6	13.4	13.2	11.9
Black	62.5	47.7	36.3	34.8	36.3
In families	26.9	14.8	8.0	7.9	7.8
Heads of families	29.1	16.5	8.9	8.9	8.6
Male heads of families	29.1	15.9	8.3	8.0	7.8
Female heads of families	28.8	20.1	12.7	14.4	13.7
Other family members	24.6	13.0	7.0	6.6	6.7
Unrelated individuals	61.9	47.2	31.0	30.3	27.3
Male unrelated individuals	59.0	38.9	27.8	25.9	23.6
Female unrelated individuals	63.3	49.8	31.9	31.5	28.4

Source: U.S. Bureau of the Census (1978).
*Not strictly comparable with earlier years due to revised procedures.
†NA = Not available.

Health Care

As noted previously, chronic illness and growing infirmities are the hallmark of the old–old period. Most elderly people require more medical care with each succeeding year of life. Concern about health care revolves about two main issues. The first has to do with whether they can receive the care needed to maintain the most comfortable life possible for their age group. Government-subsidized health care for the aged is provided under Titles XVIII and XIX of the Social Security Act. Popularly known as Medicare and Medicaid, these programs ensure the availability of medical care and treatment both for people retired at fairly substantial incomes and for the poor.

Even with Medicare and Medicaid, many researchers point out that the elderly patient is in a rather dubious position in the medical world. LaSagna (1970) has noted that the quality of medical treatment varies according to the age of the patient. He maintains that the medical charts of the aged are more likely to be marked "NTBR" (not to be resuscitated) than are the charts of younger patients. A number of possible explanations are offered for this medical approach to the aged. First, Crandall (1980) points out that very few physicians or nurses specialize in geriatrics medicine or geriatric nursing because geriatrics has traditionally been a low-status specialization. Kalish (1972) notes further that in our youth-oriented society, a geriatric patient's death is not considered a social loss and that for this reason, medical personnel tend to provide as little as possible in the way of time and resources to assist the elderly. According to Glaser (1966), many medical personnel rationalize what he terms "social death" by such statements as "She's too old to resist the disease," or "People at his age often get this illness, and there is nothing more to do for them," or "The individual has led a full life and has nothing more to live for."

Many elderly become extremely anxious about their health. Old people living in retirement communities, nursing homes, and the like regularly see illnesses around them that lead to hospitalization or death. Fears frequently develop that symptoms indicate serious illnesses. Many elderly people become anxious that they might not remember to follow doctors' directions for use of medications. This is a real concern, for many of the elderly do in fact have difficulty remembering to follow directions for using medications. The elderly regularly take several different medications simultaneously. One study of elderly residents in long-stay institutions found that these old people took or were administered an average of about four different drugs daily in their later years (Spasoff *et al.* 1978). Because medications have different effects on the elderly than they do on young people, the elderly experience many more undesirable side effects from medications than do younger people. Often, elderly people receive no explanation from physicians about the ways their medications work and the possible side effects. This can be very frightening, especially for those who have never had to take medications before and now find themselves increasingly dependent on something they do not fully understand.

Living Arrangements

Making living arrangements appropriate to their needs often is a problem for the elderly, particularly when they are no longer able to care for themselves. Most elderly want to remain independent, and although they prefer to live close to their families, few want to live with relatives other than their spouses. Elderly people with sufficient incomes who are able to maintain independent households separate from their children usually do so (Shanas and Hauser 1974). Many try to remain independent even when their health would indicate that they need outside help. Elderly married or cohabiting couples and elderly who live with a sibling or friend often can maintain considerble independence in the face of infirmities by nursing one another or by reallocating household duties. Concerns about living arrangements usually develop when one spouse dies and the other is not sufficiently healthy to care for himself or herself alone.

Cohabitation. Even though widows receive less in Social Security benefits than do married couples, widows and widowers who combine their Social Security benefits actually receive larger monthly allotments than do married couples. These statistics might be one cause of an interesting phenomenon among American elderly in recent years. Glick and Norton, in a 1977 study, reported that 1.3 percent of men over sixty-five years old, or 85,000 men, were cohabiting, living with a woman without marrying. This statistic represents a 300-percent increase over those in their middle years. Newcomb (1979) suggests a number of benefits of cohabitation for elderly Americans in addition to the financial benefits. These include reinstatement of the role of spouse, companionship, and for some, sexual gratification. More research is needed before we can determine conclusively the reasons that cohabitation has increased among this age group.

Living Alone. Whether single people can continue to live alone is often determined by their health. Some support services are available for the single elderly, including services that provide for someone to visit, clean, fix a hot meal, and assist at tasks that are particularly difficult. "Meals-on-Wheels" and "Dial-a-Ride" are additional services designed to increase the elderly person's independence and mobility. At some point, however, such services may no longer be sufficient. Although many elderly remain mentally and physically able to care for themselves well into the old–old period, many others must give up their independence when they still have many years to live. Sometimes the elderly are forced to leave their old neighborhoods

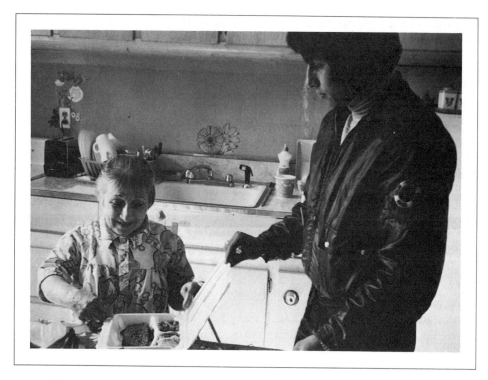

Most elderly people prefer to remain independent as long as they can. Programs, such as "Meals-on-Wheels," help many old people to continue to live in their own homes or apartments.

when these neighborhoods become too dangerous to live in. Often, the elderly leave because they can no longer care for themselves.

A number of different types of living arrangements have been developed to care for elderly people who are infirm. These include various types of institutional settings that provide caretaking and medical assistance. Although a large number of elderly are eventually placed in institutional settings for at least some period of time, many others live with their adult children.

Family Settings. About thirty percent of elderly Americans who have adult children move in with them (Johnson and Bursk 1977). Generally, a widowed woman in poor health is the most likely to live with her adult children. In many ways, living with adult children is a satisfactory solution to a number of problems of the elderly, especially the problem of isolation. Contrary to the notion that younger Americans show little concern for aging parents, research has shown that adult children provide

SWEDEN'S OPEN-CARE SYSTEM

The Swedish model for care for the aged involves a system of services that support community living. The Swedish open-care system is characterized by flexibility. Whenever possible, the elderly are encouraged to remain independent. This means living at home if possible. Elderly citizens also have the option of living in a residential hotel with many other elderly people, where an array of services is provided. Medical help and long-term residential care are available when necessary (Little 1978).

Sweden is one of the first modern Western countries to make explicit policy decisions not to build any more old-age homes. Instead, the government supplies as many special services as needed to meet the requirements of the elderly and still allow them as much independence as possible. Allocation of resources for home help is a major aspect of the Swedish program, with services that provide for meal distribution, occupational activities, chiropody services, transportation facilities, and the like. Home helpers and other agencies provide a variety of special services, including hairdressing, bathing, and snow removal in the winter. According to official statistics, Sweden maintains a ratio of 923 home helpers to 100,000 population, making available more home-help services than other countries reporting to the International Council on Home-Help. Table 14.3 compares this ratio to that of other selected countries.

Swedish elderly in urban areas often live in special apartment buildings where added features include recreation, therapy, and special services. Most have cafeterias or restaurants and built-in security devices, such as a switchboard that lights up when a resident has failed to flush a toilet for twelve hours or more. Special services include care of clothes, foot care, and housekeeping, referrals to social clubs and hobby groups, and provision of such technical aids as hearing aids or eyeglasses. Meals brought to their homes are available to the homebound. In rural areas where large numbers of elderly people live today, many of the services provided by special-service programs in the cities are handled by the post office. Rural postal employees are involved in contact and alarm services, delivery of goods, home visits, and other special duties.

Sweden's program is part and parcel of its social-service system. The bulk of the program costs are carried by the government. Most services are free to pensioners whose retirement income is based solely on government pensions. Those who retire with more income pay on a sliding-scale basis.

The result of the Swedish system is that more elderly Swedes than elderly in other countries remain independent for longer periods of time at an economic cost the government believes will be lower in the long run than long-term residential care. More data are still needed, however, for a comprehen-

Continued

HIGHLIGHT 14.3

sive evaluation of cost effectiveness and the degree of coordination between health and medical services and social and environmental services in comparison with other models of care.

QUESTIONS FOR THOUGHT

1. This description of the Swedish programs lists a number of major advantages for the elderly of programs of this sort. Can you think of any major disadvantages?

2. Sweden is a small country with a socialistic system. Do you think that it would be possible in a country as large as the United States and with a less socialistic economic system to have a program like Sweden's? Why?

Table 14.3
Ratio of Home Helpers per 100,000 Population in Selected Countries—May 1973 and December 1976; Number of Working Hours per 1,000 in December 1976

Countries	May 1973			December 1976				
	Total population (millions)	Number of home helpers	Ratio per 100,000 population	Total population (millions)	Number of home helpers	Ratio per 100,000 population	Number of work hours	Ratio per 1,000 population
Australia	12,296	30	0.2	12,500	2,747	21.97	—	—
(Box Hill)				3,254.6	2,747	84.5	—	—
Austria	7,373	355	5	7,525	340	4.5	—	—
Belgium	9,581	4,018	42	9,957	8,661	87	9,934,150	998
Canada	21,377	5,000	23	22,000	3,290	15	4,110,000	510
Finland	4,688	4,556	97	4,500	6,073	135	8,115,000	1,800
France	49,756	7,144	14	50,000	7,144	14.3	—	—
W. Germany	58,653	11,203	19	60,000	12,685	22	—	—
Gr. Britain	48,988	67,439	138	49,000	129,724	265	—	—
Israel	2,879	273	9	3,300	350	10.6	300,000	91
Italy	53,978	50	0.1	54,000	50	0.1	—	—
(Milan)				1,750	50	3.0	19,313	11
Japan	107,372	9,220	9	111,934	8,706	7.7	—	—
Netherlands	12,878	52,130	405	13,800	82,700	599	68,765,000	5,000
Norway	3,851	22,231	577	3,988	33,478	840	38,135,280	9,560
Sweden	7,968	65,700	825	8,220	75,900	923	59,000,000	7,170
Switzerland	6,150	2,060	33	6,000	2,505	41.7	—	—
United States	203,166	30,000	15	209,000	60,000	28.7	—	—

Source: International Council on Home-Help Services (Utrecht, The Netherlands, February 1978).

substantial physical, emotional, social, and economic support to their often chroni-cally ill elderly relatives (Brody, Poulshock, and Masciocchi 1978). Family satisfaction and solidarity are apparently still strong even in our mobile and rapidly changing society. Older people report being especially satisfied with their family relationships and do not feel abandoned and neglected, as the stereotypes of the elderly imply (Seelbach and Hansen 1980).

Demographic and social factors, particularly in the past several decades, have presented a number of problems to American families caring for an elderly parent. First, because people are living longer, the very old in greatest need are often cared for by offspring who are young–old themselves. Middle-aged children caring for aging parents have other concerns. Most middle-aged men and women are part of the work force and must devote considerable energy to their jobs and their children. Thus they have difficulty finding time to care for their parents. Also, because family size is shrinking, fewer family members are available to share the support task. The burden of caring for infirm parents tends to fall on women primarily and is espe-cially hard on women who work outside the home. The future promises little relief from the problem, for every indication shows that families will remain small (Treas 1977). Finally, although elderly who are still vigorous may be able to provide help in the household with various tasks, parents who are infirm can require consider-able attention. Treas (1977) reported that two-fifths of children caring for aged par-ents in their own homes spend the equivalent of a full-time job in this custodial activity. One solution to this problem currently being tried in many urban areas is day-care for the elderly. This service is designed to free the family from custodial activity during the work day and at the same time provide a setting for social inter-action for the elderly. Currently, however, such programs are not widespread.

It is clear that additional support systems are necessary to reduce family stress resulting from care of the elderly. One result of excessive stress is the phenomenon of abuse of the elderly. A special report on elderly abuse found that some 2.5 million elderly are victims of physical or psychological abuse. Physical abuse included beat-ings, being deprived of food, and the like. Psychological abuse included threats and verbal assaults. Most victims were female, over seventy-five, and with disabilities that made them dependent. Most abusers were relatives, usually children (McCormack 1980).

Private Residential Care. Many religious and ethnic groups provide residential care in institutional settings for elderly people from particular cultural backgrounds. These facilities usually are voluntary, nonprofit institutions and often are run by church or cultural groups with federal assistance. In some instances, the homes provide settings in which it is possible for the residents to speak languages other then English learned in their youth or to eat ethnic foods to which they became accustomed when they were young. In most cases, the social life of these homes centers around the ethnic background of the residents. For many of these elderly people, living in a residential setting is made easier because the residents share a common background.

One example of private residential settings is the Stephen Smith Home for the Aged, founded by Afro-American groups. Through the founding of old-age homes like this one, Pollard (1977) reported, Afro-American groups have found an outlet and expression for their veneration of their old. At the same time, the home provides a facility in which elderly black people are provided opportunity to spend their time interacting with others who have had common experiences.

Nursing Homes. The elderly housed in long-term care institutions in the mid 1970s averaged eighty-two years of age, and about twenty percent or more were ninety years of age or older (Office of Nursing Home Affairs 1975). Nursing homes are facilities that provide long-term medical care. They have a full-time nursing staff in residence and phsyicians on call. What are known as **skilled nursing facilities** provide services under the supervision of registered nurses. **Intermediate-care facilities** are designed for less serious medical problems and provide less intense nursing.

The research indicates that being placed in long-term care often has negative consequences for the elderly. For one thing, residents tend to become passive and

One of the problems of nursing homes is lack of sufficient stimulation. This situation can lead to withdrawal and apathy.

lose interest in the outside world (Spasoff *et al.* 1978). Most are very fearful before going, although once in nursing homes, they tend to complain little about conditions affecting their lives there. Figure 14.3 describes the attitudes toward the move into an institutional setting of a group of elderly people in one study. Psychological problems have been associated with institutionalization. These include fears of being abandoned and vulnerable to physical and psychological deterioration (Tobin and Lieberman 1976); they also include depression and apathy.

One elderly woman whose family was trying to arrange a place for her after she fell down the stairs and broke her hip put it this way, "I would rather go back to my own house than any place else they want to send me. I don't want to go to that nursing home. I feel as if I would be sitting 'on hold,' just putting in my time, you

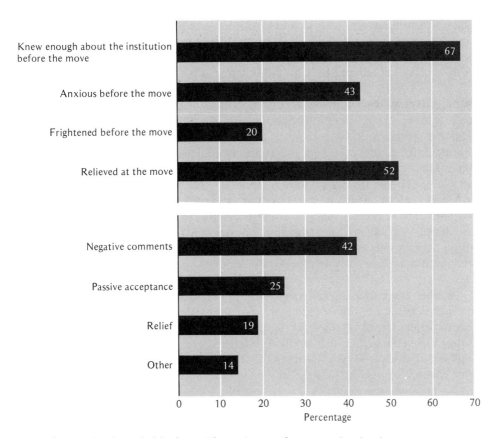

Fig. 14.3   Attitudes of elderly residents in one long-stay institution (From Spasoff *et al.* 1978).

know, until they're ready to put me underground. Now if they let me go home, I'm sure it would be different. I *know* I'm alone at home. And there *are* the stairs. But still, if someone would just spend a little time, maybe shopping for me, I wouldn't have to get put away like a worn old bag."

Four months later, the same woman gave in to her family and allowed herself to be placed at a nursing facility. She spoke again, "Well, I'm here, and I guess it's not too bad. The food's all right, I suppose. And the nurses are good to me. But I sit here all day and wait for my daughter to call or my son to visit after work. I feel so useless and bored. But I suppose it doesn't really matter any more *where* I am actually as long as I can't walk. I just sit and watch TV."

One reason that the elderly fear institutional care, either in nursing homes or in other institutional settings, is that they are afraid that they will be left there permanently. Another fear is that they will die there. This latter fear is realistic: Although it is a commonly accepted notion that approximately five percent of the aged population live in long-term care facilities, research has shown that in the early 1970s, some twenty percent of the elderly did in fact die in extended-care facilities (Kastenbaum and Candy 1973). This proportion had increased to some thirty percent by the late 1970s (Lesnoff-Caravaglia 1978–1979).

Other Alternatives. A living arrangement that has the potential to meet the needs of some elderly people is boarding houses. Elderly boarders could provide additional income to low-income urban families who need additional money. At the same time, the family accepting the boarders could provide opportunity for companionship with a family setting. Today, however, most boarding houses that accept elderly people do not provide a family environment. More often, they house many poor elderly living on small incomes and offer few services. In some urban areas, the elderly remain at night in the boarding houses and go to day-care facilities during the day. While boarding houses are a promising arrangement, it will be necessary to ensure that these facilities and the families involved are interested in the welfare of the elderly and not just in the income they can provide.

Another alternative living arrangement in which individuals share housing and expenses is being used by some elderly people in the United States. The **Share-A-Home** concept (Streib 1978) was first developed in Forida where a group of elderly arranged to live together as a family in a large house managed professionally. The members of share-a-home pool their money, use the same kitchen, and help each other whenever possible. Kellogg and Jaffee (1977) point out that the concept provides a number of advantages for the elderly, including increased ability to lead more autonomous lives at a much higher standard of living than if they lived independently or in a nursing home and increased ability to establish close personal relationships with others who share their age and interests. These authors report that more share-a-homes are planned for the future.

WIDOWHOOD

Over the age of seventy-five, about twenty-four percent of men and seventy percent of women are widowed (U.S. Bureau of the Census 1980). For most elderly people, one of the most difficult losses that occur with age is loss of a spouse. Because women outlive men by an average of ten or more years, it is not surprising that there are about three times as many widows as widowers after age seventy-five. What specific concerns do the elderly have about widowhood, and what issues do they face in adjusting to their new status?

Bereavement

Bereavement generally progresses through a series of stages and may occur in varying degrees. Researchers suggest that the process of mourning begins with an initial stage of denial, followed by depression, then final acceptance, and finally entry into new social roles. This process typically takes a year or somewhat longer (Hardt 1978–1979).

Depression may last for some time. Although the bereaved person appears to have adjusted to the loss, he or she may continue for a long time to question it inwardly and to long for the dead spouse. Although the memories tend to be of happier times, dwelling on the past can create barriers in coming to final acceptance of the loss. The elderly who adjust best to the death of a spouse are those who eventually are able to see the loss as something that is now behind them. Acceptance involves a sense of relief in having worked through grief and a readiness to accept a new set of roles (Bowlby 1974).

For the elderly, depression after death of a loved one often is greater than it is for younger people. One reason might be that the elderly are often more dependent on their spouses when they are alive than are younger people. For younger people, acceptance of loss may be the impetus for planning a future life to live. For the elderly, however, it usually means resigning oneself to a new situation and accepting more passively what is to come next.

Adjusting to Widowhood

Research has shown that the elderly and widowed tend on the whole to adjust more satisfactorily to being widowed than do people who lose their spouse unexpectedly in early adulthood or middle age. The reason for this is probably that the elderly know that their lives are coming to an end, and this forewarning allows them to be better able to accept that they or their spouse may die. A major concern of the widowed elderly is fear of what life will be like without the spouse—that is, how they will care for themselves, and how they will deal with loneliness (Carey 1979–1980). Religion seems to play little part in adjustment for widowed people. Widowed

Widowhood may be less difficult for women than widowerhood is for men because women have often established roles independent of their husbands as well as close personal ties with friends and family.

people who are religious have not been found to adjust more easily than widowed people who do not have religious orientations (Carey 1977). In general, elderly widows and widowers who live alone for other reasons tend to have lower morale than elderly who are married (Lee 1978).

Widowhood brings many changes in the roles of both the male and the female elderly. Research shows that these changes tend to be far more difficult in general for men than for women (Berado 1970; Troll 1971). Many possible reasons might explain this. For one thing, women usually have had a life history of taking care of domestic chores and are less likely to require assistance at these tasks than are men whose feelings of helplessness might increase when they become widowers. For another, women tend to remain closer to family and friends and are less likely than men to feel cut off and isolated.

Elderly widows and widowers have a much higher rate of suicide than elderly married people (Bock and Webber 1972). This fact is probably due to the high number of widowed individuals who lose reason to live when they are isolated. We will discuss suicide among elderly in Chapter 15. Research shows that the effects of widowhood cannot be fully understood without examination of a number of related factors. Morgan (1976), for example, found that morale scores of widowed women were not different from nonwidowed companions when groups were equated for health. According to Morgan, the health of widowed people is an important determiner of adjustment. Shulman (1975) found, in addition, that widows or widowers who have fewer roles to replace or who quickly reestablish lost roles suffer fewer adjustment problems than those who are unable to make role substitutions or role adaptations. Atchley (1975*a*) shows finally that economic variables play an important role in adjustment for widowed people. Individuals with higher incomes and fewer economic concerns have easier times adjusting to this trauma, just as they have less difficulty adjusting to other traumas in their lives.

THE CASE OF SAMUEL HARRIS—A GERIATRIC PATIENT: A CASE STUDY FOR CLASS DISCUSSION

I. Identification and Sources of Information

Name: Samuel Harris

Address: University Nursing Home

Race: White

Age: Eighty-seven years

Sources of information

1. Personal interview with Mr. Harris

2. Interviews with Mr. Harris's children

3. Interviews with Mr. Harris's physician

II. Family History

Samuel Harris is the oldest of three siblings. He and his family grew up in Boston. Samuel attended college, where he studied economics. He married his wife, Sarah, now deceased, when he was thirty-six years old and working as a high school teacher. Sarah never worked at an outside job for the forty-four years that they were married, and she did all the cooking and cleaning until she became ill at age sixty-five. Samuel and Sarah had four children: Tom, now fifty-seven years old; Bob, fifty-five; Peter, fifty-three; and Agnes, fifty. Samuel retired from his job at sixty-five, and he and Sarah moved to Florida where they lived for ten years. When Sarah died of cancer, Samuel mourned for a year and then gave up his Florida home to move in with Agnes and her husband. The family, who had suffered terribly at the loss of their mother when she was so young, was delighted to be able to help their bereaved father. For seven years, Mr. Harris helped Agnes and her husband take care of the house and the children. He reported that for the first time since Sarah died, he felt "needed." Agnes took a job as bookkeeper for a small corporation a year after her father came to live with them, and everyone in the family agreed that Samuel helped a great deal at that time. One of the things he was able to do was to provide adult companionship every day when the children came home from school. He often helped them with their homework.

Continued

THE CASE OF SAMUEL HARRIS *(Cont.)*

Five years ago, Mr. Harris fell and broke his hip. Agnes quit her job to stay at home with him for the first several months. Later, Agnes's brothers chipped in to provide a full-time nurse at the house. Last year, the family decided that they could not provide adequate care for their father at home. When none of Samuel's sons could take him in, the family arranged for placement in University Nursing Home.

III. Case History

Samuel Harris appears to have adapted fairly well to the nursing home. The family has been able to find a home that had a private room suitable to his needs. Agnes's brothers arranged to have some of the furnishings that were in Mr. and Mrs. Harris's old home in Florida brought to the nursing home; Agnes cut the draperies to fit the new windows. Although Agnes's brothers and their families live some distance away, they visit several times a year. Agnes and her family are able to visit weekly.

Although Samuel's spirits seem to be high, his doctors report that he is becoming discouraged by a chronic physical condition. Since his first fall, he has been confined to bed or a wheelchair. His legs are no longer able to support him. Several operations did not aid with the healing. Now in the home, Samuel gets around in a wheelchair. He is helped to and from bed and the toilet and shower by the nursing staff.

Mr. Harris's children worry that their father seems to have lapses of memory in which he cannot remember their names. These lapses seem to be increasing as Mr. Harris gets older. Sometimes, in the middle of a conversation, he changes the topic to something none of them know anything about. Often, the topic is changed to early experiences of Mr. Harris when he was in college before any of his children were born.

Mr. Harris reports that he expects to be able to get up and walk, even though his physician tells him that this will not be possible. He is friendly and polite to the staff at the home and tells them that he expects to recuperate because he is following their directions. He misses his wife and keeps her picture on his dresser. He has been spending increasing amounts of time with an elderly widow who has a room down the hall from his. The two often eat their meals together at the cafeteria. Once when the woman was kept in bed because of a cold, Mr. Harris requested visiting her and was angered when the head nurse told him that she was not allowed to have visitors. He enjoys the visits of his children but tends to become quiet and depressed when they leave. Often, when they get up to go at the end of a visit, he wheels his chair to the door and says jokingly, "Now, be a good son, and wheel me right down that ramp." When no one responds, he says, "What kind of a boy are you? Didn't I teach you to obey?"

Mr. Harris's attitude toward death is common to people of his age. He expects it, accepts it philosophically, and in the course of his daily activities, thinks of it periodically, although he tries not to dwell on it. "I don't want to get like some of the loonies you see in here, always moaning and crying. I just want to get myself stronger and get out of here and back with my grandkids. It just seems to be taking so long; I get a little discouraged now and then. I suppose it will be a long time before I die . . . I don't know."

IV. Present Status, Diagnosis, and Prognosis

Samuel Harris's physician reports that he does not expect that Mr. Harris will be able to walk or leave the home. Every time weight is put on his leg, a new bone crack occurs. Eventually, Mr. Harris will be confined full time to his bed. The memory lapses noticed by his children at this point are common to his age group. These lapses and ensuing confusion can be expected gradually to increase with the aging process. Mr. Harris can be expected to have increasing problems both with his physical health and his ability to adjust to it. One way to increase his morale is to increase his opportunities to socialize. To that

THE CASE OF SAMUEL HARRIS

end, it would be useful for the nursing staff to encourage his friendship with his female acquaintance and also with other people in the nursing home.

Questions for Class Discussion

1. Mr. Harris is somewhat unusual for this age group because it is far more common for a woman to outlive her spouse than for a man to do so. What changes were made in his life-style that were particularly different from what he was accustomed to when his wife was alive? How did these changes, at least when he was still living with Agnes and her family, help him?

2. Mr. Harris, who was always rather authoritarian as a younger man, seems to be exhibiting in his older years more dependent types of behavior toward his children. How does he exhibit this dependency?

3. Does the disengagement theory explain Mr. Harris's adjustment to aging? Explain your answer.

4. How will the eventual adjustment on the part of his family toward Mr. Harris's death probably differ from that experienced by these same people when Sarah died? Why? How can we expect Mr. Harris's attitude toward death to change in this next period of his life? Why?

SUMMARY

The development of the old–old, those individuals in their mid seventies and beyond, is characterized by physical decline, a steadily narrowing environment due to increased physical disability, and a narrowing of acquaintances. Physical decline involves all the body functions, and serious illnesses account for rapidly increasing mortality. Emotional problems are common, and a high proportion of elderly are confined to mental hospitals. Some elderly people who are unable to deal with the changes that occur at this stage of life develop functional disorders, such as neuroses, depression, manic behaviors, hypochondriasis, paranoia, and psychoses.

Symptoms of senility, such as loss of orientation, memory loss, and inability to carry out many cognitive tasks, appear in about one of every five people over eighty. Sometimes, these disorders are organic in origin, as in organic brain syndrome; in other cases, symptoms of senility are caused by stressful situations, isolation, or overmedication. In many cases, these symptoms can be alleviated by special care and by physical and emotional support.

During the old–old years, people enter the final phase of cognitive function, a reintegrative stage in which societal involvement gradually decreases and concerns tend to focus more on immediate life situations. Declines in mental functioning tend to occur in hand–eye coordination, in speed and flexibility of responding, and in some aspects of memory. Although no tests can measure accurately the functioning of this age group, evidence suggests that qualitative intellectual functioning is related to expected longevity of the individual.

The disengagement theory of adjusting to aging views normal aging as a progressive withdrawal from former roles. Other researchers believe that the most active old–old people are the best adjusted. The continuity theory suggests that adjustment is best when people continue the roles they played earlier in their lives. Some people adjust by changing to new roles to match their abilities. Adjustment is highly individualistic and is closely correlated with physical health and life stresses. At the end of the life cycle, people are coming to terms with the process of dying and preparing for their own deaths.

The amount of income available to the old–old determines to some extent the quality and length of their lives. Old–old women tend to experience the greatest economic difficulty, partly because they greatly outnumber men, because of their greater longevity, and also because fewer have contributed to pensions or Social Security.

The growing infirmities of the old–old period require increasing medical attention. Although Medicare and Medicaid ensure the availability of health care for both the aged and the poor, the quality of medical care for the aged has been questioned. Many elderly people are anxious about their medical care and about the increasing number of medications they must take. Finding suitable living arrangements with adequate care is a major concern of the elderly. As long as they remain married and are not seriously ill, the elderly often are able to take care of themselves and each other. Widowhood, together with increasing infirmities, produces new problems. Many elderly Americans move in with adult children. As families become smaller and people live longer, however, arranging housing in family settings becomes more difficult. Also, economic and social stress are placed on families caring at home for elderly relatives. Many elderly are compelled to live in institutional settings, primarily nursing homes. Researchers note that institutionalizing elderly people may lead to isolation, fear of dependence, fear of being abandoned, and depression. Alternative living arrangements with potential for some elderly include boarding houses and share-a-homes.

Married elderly often have to deal with the death of a spouse. Bereavement among the elderly often follows a process similar to that of younger people except that the elderly realize that death may occur and have more opportunity to prepare themselves. Men tend to have a harder time adjusting to widowhood than do women. Also, individuals with higher incomes adjust more easily, just as they do to other traumas in their lives.

FOR FURTHER READING

Hall, E. Acting one's age: New rules for the old. *Psychology Today,* 1980, 13, 11–60. This brief article is an interview with Bernice Neugarten, a major authority on the psychology and sociology of the aging. Neugarten, appointed as 1981

Chairperson of the White House Conference on Aging, argues that age is not the best predictor of the ways elderly people live today. She presents compelling reasons for her position.

Manard, B., R. Woehle, and J. Heilman. *Better Homes for the Old.* Lexington, Massachusetts: Lexington Books, D.C. Heath, 1977. This book provides a clear picture of old-age institutions in the United States and of what it is like to live or work in them. The authors identify some of the new problems that have developed in old-age institutions in the era of federal support, and they also suggest ways of solving them.

Preview Questions

- How have the major causes of death changed over the past 200 years, and how are these changes related to aging?
- What is meant by speaking of death as a cultural reality, and how has this changed in the twentieth century?
- Can you describe several signals that are predictors of impending death and explain why they are reliable?
- What are three different support systems for the dying and some advantages and disadvantages of each?
- How does the meaning of death for children change as they grow and develop into adults?
- Why do middle-aged people fear death more than either young people or the elderly?
- Can you describe Kübler-Ross's five stages of adjusting to death and compare her views with those of other researchers?
- How do active and passive euthanasia differ, and what is their relationship to the *Living Will?*
- What are some symptoms of grief from bereavement, and what three stages does a bereaved person usually pass through?
- Can you describe three functions that can be performed by death education and several approaches that have been used to accomplish them?
- Why is death easier for the old-old adult to accept than it is for younger people?

15

The End of Life

Elizabeth Kübler-Ross (1975) defined the period of death and dying as "the last stage of growth." It is only recently in the history of human beings that the end of life is expected to follow the stage of old age. Only 200 years ago, most people lived through only the stages of infancy and childhood, and thirty percent of human deaths occurred before age twenty-five years (McKeown 1977). Today in the United States, only five percent of reported deaths happen to people who have not yet reached adulthood, and babies born now can expect to live to an average age of seventy-three.

COMMON CAUSES OF DEATH
Disease

Historically, when most human deaths took place in infancy or childhood, the most common causes of death were infectious diseases, such as smallpox, tuberculosis, and pneumonia. Increasingly adequate health care and development of modern medicine in the past 200 years have reduced most early deaths due to communicable or infectious disease. Today, smallpox has been eradicated everywhere in the world. Cures have been found for diseases like tuberculosis and pneumonia. Such infectious diseases are still common causes of death in young people in developing and impoverished countries where health and medical care is poor and among poor people in more affluent countries. With the delay of death until the middle years or old age for most middle-class people in the United States, however, more and more deaths occur because of degenerative diseases, such as heart disease, cancer, and stroke (Lerner 1976). Heart disease, which ranked fourth as cause of death in the United States in 1900, now ranks as the most common cause of death, with cancer and stroke ranking second and third.

Stress-Related Causes

Today, together with an increase in the age at which individuals can anticipate the end of life, we have seen an increase in the relative incidence of deaths attributed to diseases suspected of being stress related. A growing body of research (see, for example, Dohrenwend and Dohrenwend 1974; Ruch 1977) shows that many degenerative diseases, such as heart disease, stroke, and cancer, are related in one fashion or another to sources of life stress. These include such crises as job loss, divorce, forced retirement, physical incapacity, or deaths of loved ones.

We have learned that numbers of these stresses are associated with increasing age. Eisdorfer and Wilkie (1976) suggest that these stresses may accelerate the aging process or lead to increased physical illness that, in turn, increases degeneration.

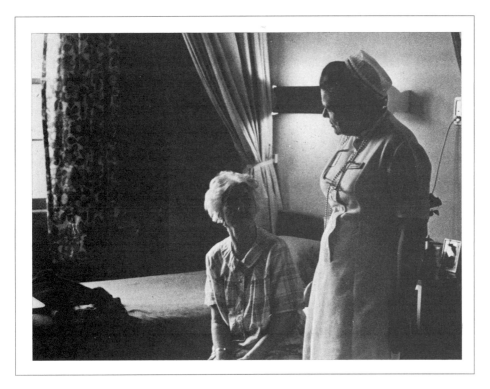

Among the stresses that can increase the likelihood of death is relocation to a new environment, such as a nursing home.

Working in this fashion, stress may impair the elderly person's capacity and make it more difficult to combat disease. For some people, the loss of a spouse is related to increase in the risk of death during the first year of bereavement. Rowland (1979) reports that the increased mortality of men following death of a spouse can be understood through increases in diseases of the vascular system. Bereavement also leads often to social changes that can predispose the elderly to death. Lack of assistance in restructuring lives is one factor that is important here. Psychological factors include guilt, anxiety, and a preoccupation with the deceased (Lopata 1973).

Finally, relocation of elderly from their own homes to homes for the aged is also related to increases in the likelihood of death. The crisis caused by leaving a familiar environment is believed to cause stress and anxiety. The aged who have no alternative but to move into institutions suffer a higher death rate than those who have alternatives open to them (Schulz and Brenner 1977).

Suicide

Suicide, we have learned, is one of the ten most common causes of death in the United States. The elderly make up between ten and fifteen percent of the United States population. Data show, however, that they comprise more than twenty-five percent of the suicides. Researchers point out that this figure, composed of proven suicides, is conservative (Patterson, Abrahams, and Baker 1974). Because death in old age is anticipated, suicide is rarely expected or considered as a cause of death. Miller (1978) points out that suicide attempts by the elderly are more successful than attempts by younger people, and he offers two explanations. First, the methods used by the elderly tend to be more lethal, most probably because the elderly who attempt suicide really want to die while many younger people who attempt suicide want to draw attention to their problems. Second, the elderly generally are physically weaker than younger people. Attempts at suicide that result in physical conditions that are lethal to older people may not be lethal for younger people.

Many factors discussed earlier contribute to the high incidence of suicide among the elderly. These include such traumatic events as widowhood. Bock and Webber (1972) point out that the widowed aged have a significantly higher suicide rate than the married aged. As many as eighty percent of elderly persons who are predisposed to suicide, according to researchers, are subject to psychopathological symptoms of depression (Benson and Brodie 1975), and as many as sixty percent have severe, debilitating physical illnesses.

Researchers describe two types of suicide among the elderly. The first is a single overt act, such as taking an overdose of pills or leaving the gas on in the stove without lighting the burner. The second consists of general neglect of physical and mental well-being, referred to as **benign suicide,** also called "subintentional," or "passive" suicide. Burnside (1976) suggested that many elderly who refuse to take medication or who take too much or too little medication often are viewed as senile or confused, and for this reason are not considered potential suicides.

Accidents

Another leading cause of death among the elderly is accidents. Although the aged constitute only slightly more than ten percent of the population in the United States, they are involved in twenty-four percent of accidental deaths (U.S. Bureau of the Census 1980).

Several reasons explain why the elderly have so many accidents. First, with their diminished sensory abilities, they are less likely to hear fire alarms, to see oncoming traffic, or to feel the pain of a cut or sore until the problem has intensified. Slower reflexes and reaction times make it more difficult for elderly people to respond immediately to dangers. With greatly reduced strength and weakened bone structures, once accidents occur, the elderly have far more difficulty recuperating than do younger people. An accident that is debilitating for a younger person often is lethal for an elderly person.

DEATH AS A CULTURAL REALITY

Historian Philippe Aries (1981) argued that regardless of the specific cause of death, the end of life is as much of a cultural reality as a biological reality in the human lifespan. According to Aries, twentieth-century men and women do their best as long as possible to deny this last stage of development. Denial as a psychological defense against facing the reality of death is particularly noticeable among the elderly who are closer to death than most of their younger counterparts. Bentson, Kasschau, and Ragan (1977) reported that elderly discuss fear of death far less frequently than do younger people. Jeffers and Verwoerdt (1969), in a study of 140 elderly Americans, noted that five percent denied that they ever even thought of death.

In the past, according to Aries, when deaths occurred more frequently among young people, death was considered a natural, normal part of life. The concept of death as a topic that should be disguised, hidden, and seldom mentioned began its transformation in Western society in the 1860s with the rise of the funeral industry. Prior to the development of this industry and prior to extensive use of hospitals and nursing homes to care for individuals with degenerative diseases, most people died at home and were kept there until they were buried. As health codes became stricter and medical procedures were developed that kept many individuals alive who would have died previously, death and dying were removed from homes to hospitals, nursing homes, and funeral parlors. What was 200 years ago a natural normal process has made death and dying for the twentieth-century American a strange, mysterious process.

Views of Death

In Western society today, from a scientific perspective, death means the end of existence. It is this reality that is denied by Americans when they employ a variety of techniques, such as lying to the dying or reporting about how "well" they look. Religion helps many to ease the crisis. From the religious perspective of most Western peoples, the soul continues to exist after the death of the body. More than fifty percent of the Western elderly report that they believe in some form of afterlife (Kalish and Reynolds 1976).

All societies today do not deny death to the extent that we in modern, Western industrial society do. Societies that offer philosophies that make it easier to deal with mortality seem to have individuals who adjust to death without needing to resort to such severe psychological defenses as we do. In the religions of some primitive societies, such as the Tanala of Madagascar or the Tlingit of Alaska, death is accepted with calm or joy (Grof and Halifax 1977). Long (1975) pointed out that some of the world's major religions, such as Hinduism and Buddhism, maintain that individuals can accept the traumas of life only by accepting death and finding identity and unity with God.

In Hinduism, individuals learn that the body passes through childhood, adulthood, and old age and that at death, the soul assumes another body. In this sense, death is a normal part of life rather than a topic that must be denied.

Changing Western Views

According to clergy, counselors, and others, Americans, as other Westerners, are gradually changing in the ways they deal with death and dying and the ways they grieve for their dead. Because of the increased mobility of today's society, together with increased concern about spiraling costs of inflation, fewer people today plan the traditional funeral ritual of a generation ago, and more and more choose less-expensive, less-ritualistic ways of commemorating the importance of the death of a relative or close friend (Lindsley 1980). More and more people, including the elderly, discuss death more openly today than they did only a few decades ago.

 ## PREDICTORS OF IMPENDING DEATH

Psychologists for a long time have been interested in describing those factors that can be used to predict impending death or long life.

General Well-Being

Palmore and Stone (1973) interviewed more than 900 elderly persons. Then five years later, they returned to do follow-up studies of those still alive and to determine which of their initial interviewees had died. Studies of the initial interviews showed that the most important factors studied as possible measures of longevity were physical and psychological health and the ability to care for themselves. Those elderly people who were most physically and psychologically healthy and able to care for themselves at the initial interview tended to be most healthy at the second; those who had died by the second interview tended to be least healthy and least able to care for themselves at the first.

Education and Occupation

Other factors related to longevity in this study were education and occupation. Elderly people who had had the greatest amount of education and who had better jobs during their adult working years tended to live longer on the whole than peo-

Morale plays an important role in longevity. The warmth of family ties can help the aged person to retain a positive outlook.

ple who had had less education and lower-paying jobs that usually required harder physical labor. Substantial evidence suggests, according to Palmer and Stone, that both education and job roles during adulthood, together with socioeconomic status provided by education and jobs, affect longevity by affecting peoples' abilities to solve day-to-day problems, to adapt to crisis and strain throughout their lives, and to provide safer and better working conditions, income for health care, nutrition, and housing. Clearly, the better-educated individual has opportunity for job roles and socioeconomic status that makes available all of these factors.

Morale

Another factor related to impending death among the elderly is degree of morale or will to live. Dubos (1981) points to the existence of healthy, vigorous centenarians (individuals who have lived one hundred years or more) who remain involved in affairs around them until the end of their lives. This involvement, Dubos implies, is related to their longevity. Ellison (1969), in a study of elderly retired steelworkers, showed that socially isolated elderly people had far less will to live than the elderly who maintained the ability to interact with others. Ellison demonstrated also that the poorer the health of these elderly people, the less was their will to live. Sickness for the elderly not only means pain and discomfort; it also means isolation. Sick, immobile elderly people have lower morale than healthy, mobile elderly. The sick and immobile also tend to die earlier.

 ## SUPPORT SYSTEMS FOR THE DYING

In a study by Lesnoff-Caravaglia (1978–1979), at least thirty percent of the elderly in America today die in the nursing homes or other extended-care facilities, presumably where they were brought because of serious chronic illness. Another fifty percent die in hospitals where they were brought because of more sudden serious illness, and only about twenty percent die at home. Table 15.1 shows the place of death by sex and race for individuals in Lesnoff-Caravaglia's study.

Institutional Help

Examining the nursing and hospital programs available has led psychologists to question their provisions to care for the social, spiritual, and emotional needs of the dying elderly. Both extended-care facilities and hospital settings are designed to provide support systems for the living rather than the dying.

Even when medical staffs are given special training in dealing with geriatric patients, most still are unprepared for the final stage, dying and death, when the patient often is no longer able to communicate his or her needs and fears. Gerontologists complain that the result, too often, appears to be a lack of compassion. What it might also be is simply an inability to meet the very particular needs of the dying person.

Table 15.1
Place of Death by Sex and Race for Persons Aged 65 and Older in Springfield, Illinois, 1975

	Group	Total	Nursing Home	Extended-Care Facility	Hospital	Private Home	Other
Women	Black	15	2	3	9	3	0
	White	380	90	136	194	50	0
	Other	0	0	0	0	0	0
Men	Black	28	2	4	13	10	1
	White	354	50	89	206	51	8
	Other	0	0	0	0	0	0
Race	Black	43	4	7	22	13	1
	White	734	140	225	400	101	8

Source: G. Lesnoff-Caravaglia, The five percent fallacy, *The International Journal of Aging and Human Development* 1978-1979, vol. 9(2) pp. 187–192. Reprinted by permission of Baywood Publishing Company.

The Hospice System

A new setting used more and more frequently in the United States to care for the dying is the **hospice,** an institution that specializes in caring for the dying. The concept of the hospice originated in Great Britain where doctors and other medical staff have developed homelike settings where extraordinary personal care can be provided to dying patients without extraordinary medical cost. Stoddard (1978) reports that the lower cost is possible partly because hospices do not contain the life-prolonging machines that hospitals provide. Lower costs are maintained also because often family members participate in the patient's care. The emphasis is on making the dying process free from pain and as comfortable as possible for the patient.

In 1980, the United States Department of Health, Education and Welfare announced an experiment in the hospice concept in the United States. Those behind the movement, inspired by similar work in England, contend that hospitals and nursing homes have been unable to meet the needs of the terminally ill and their families. Particularly for dying elderly patients, being placed suddenly in strange places and attended by strangers can be very frightening. Hospices provide what their proponents hope will be a dignified, pain-free, and more comfortable death. To achieve this goal, hospices have experimented with social activities for those who are still able to respond, around-the-clock visits by relatives, and strong drugs to alleviate pain as much as possible. The main goal is to keep patients free from pain. The drug most frequently used in Great Britain is heroin (Stachell 1977). Families work together with physicians and specially trained nurses in caring for the patients so as to keep faces as familiar as possible and to provide the feeling that the patient is not alone. Even when family members help in patient care, the nurse–patient ratio in a hospice is usually one to one.

Today, more than 200 organizations and groups in the United States are operating specific hospice programs. A national hospice organization has been formed and is seeking recognition as the policy-setting and accrediting body for hospice programs. The goal, as in British hospices, is to develop programs that allow death to occur in as familiar and comfortable place and with as little pain as possible. Some hospices allow patients to bring their own furnishings. All allow them their visitors whenever they want. For those dying elderly who are not so infirm that they have already lost all ability to interact socially, this last opportunity for companionship can be of utmost importance in accepting impending death. For the dying, who are about to lose forever all ability to interact with others, last visits may ease many remaining concerns. The wife of an older patient who died in a hospice reported:

The visiting hospice team gradually opened the door for Jacob. He trusted them because they provided the medication to control the pain. They made him comfortable, but he was still in reality. We talked a great deal about his death. He talked about some of the things that were bothering him. And when

Hospice benefits have been cited, not simply by patients and their families but by insurance providers as well. Doggett (1980) reports that most Blue Cross plans already have some kind of home care benefit and that it is entirely possible that in the future, the cost of providing hospice care may be totally underwritten by health insurance agencies. According to Doggett, Blue Cross in 1980 began a three-year study of hospice care to determine just how economical it is. They found that instead of someone's staying in a hospital for, say sixteen days at $200 per day, that person can stay in the hospital for four or five days and then go for home or hospice care at $22 to $50 per visit by medical staff. A national committee is working on studies of whether hospice care will be included as a separate benefit, as part of present insurance programs, or not at all.

According to Doggett's interviews of insurance officials, there is probably a potential for reducing costs but a lot of policy must be worked out.

QUESTIONS FOR THOUGHT

1. Many patients feel safe in a hospital with round-the-clock medical staff and life-saving machines near to protect them. If insurance companies elect to provide full benefits for hospice care, which would you choose for yourself—a hospice or hospital? Why?

2. Which would you choose for your parents or your spouse?

he was finished, he said he could die in peace. I think my husband finally died not quite happy but at least calmly resigned. He had some fear at first, not of death itself but of the cancer pain. But the closeness of the family and learning how much we loved him helped make the difference.

In the end, Jacob needed so much medication that he slept continually. When he died, it was in his sleep.

All elderly do not remain clearheaded through most of the dying period as Jacob did. But like younger dying people, whether they always are in contact with reality or not, they still can be helped to be more comfortable and less afraid in more familiar settings with familiar people.

Dying at Home

The ultimate hospice is the patient's own home. Today, some fifteen percent of deaths of elderly take place at home (Lesnoff-Caravaglia, 1978–1979). Many of these deaths are sudden and occur in such short time that it is impossible to move the dying person to another setting. Those who die of long-term or chronic conditions usually are cared for at home under conditions similar to those in hospices, with a nurse in attendance. Dying at home presents for many elderly the least disruption of normal day-to-day living and the possibility to remain in contact with this life as long as possible.

THE MEANING OF DEATH

Both death and dying have different meanings for different people. Death has a meaning for the bereaved very different from the meaning for the dying person, for example. For the bereaved, death involves loss of a loved one and often loss of a life-style. For the dying person, death means loss of family, friends, ability to interact with the environment, and ability to continue life. Death has different meanings also, depending on the age at which impending death occurs.

Children and Death

Preschoolers up to the age of five or six in our society usually have little experience with and little understanding of death. Most children at this age are unable to differ-

By the age of ten, children are able to comprehend death in a manner similar to adults.

entiate between a person's being away and being dead. Koocher (1975) describes a typical response of preschoolers to being told that someone close to them has died. The response is a series of questions, such as, "Where did he go?" or "When will he be back?" Because of this association of death with separation, the fear that preschoolers report most about death is separation, not being able to be with one's parents.

By the time children reach seven to nine years old, they begin to understand that death is the end of life. Dying children at this age level are especially concerned about any accompanying physical injury or mutilation. Spinetta and colleagues (1973) found, for example, that children who were dying leukemia victims at this age were far more afraid of hurting themselves than were chronically but nonfatally ill children. Nagy (1948) suggests that death is personified for this age group. For some children, death may be an angel; for others, it may be an evil, frightening monster who comes in the night to take children away. Waechter (1971) found that among this age group, children are likely to understand that an illness is life threatening even if they have not been told they are likely to die. In Waechter's study, children who were fatally ill talked more about death and dying when asked to make up stories about pictures presented to them than did children who were healthy or sick with brief illnesses. Beginning at the age of ten, children gradually develop realistic views of death that match their adult conceptions.

Adults and Death

Although, as we have learned, there is a strong tendency in our society to deny the personal reality of death, adults tend to recognize that death is a final and inevitable stage of life as we know it. The dying person faces loss of his or her entire world. A premature death, one that comes before the individual has had a chance to meet the goals he or she intended to meet, carries with it strong feelings of denial and anger.

Middle-aged people in the United States often first develop their own personal experience with death and dying. This happens as parents and friends of middle-aged people begin to die. At this period of life, their career goals as well as the personal goals they hold for children or other close family members often have not yet been met. Many middle-aged people begin to worry about the shortness of life and fear the possibility that they will not live long enough to reach their goals. For these reasons, it is not surprising that middle-aged people tend to think about and fear death more than either young people or the elderly (Riley 1970).

The Elderly and Death

Kübler-Ross (1969) pointed out that before individuals develop ability to accept death, they first experience feelings of denial and anger. With time, they gradually come to accept reality. The elderly, who have more time and forewarnings than any other age group that death is imminent, have more opportunity than younger people gradually to come to grips with their concerns. Elderly people, more than younger people, have faced the deaths of spouses, friends, or family members. As they grew older, they often became more resigned and depressed and tended less and less to express denial or anger. Unlike younger people who often are much more shocked and bereaved at a sudden death when they have not had time to adjust, the elderly often demonstrate the same feelings of bereavement whether a spouse dies suddenly or after an extended illness. Sanders (1979–1980) suggests that the reason that this is so is that loss is always expected in the aged. One elderly woman put it this way: "Oh, it's so good to see you. And it's so good to feel well enough today to enjoy seeing you. Sometimes when I get up, I am surprised that I'm still alive. I'm so tired that I expect one day soon I won't wake up."

DEALING WITH THE DYING PROCESS

Elizabeth Kübler-Ross (1969) was one of the first researchers to examine the process of death and dying in America in the same fashion that other developmental psychologists have studied the process of living: by defining its stages. Much of her research describes the time when people first realize that death is imminent. Through interviews with 200 terminally ill patients of many ages, she identified five separate and predictable stages in the process of adjusting to death through which, according to Kübler-Ross, 197 of her subjects passed. According to Kübler-Ross, the five stages do not last any definite length of time. Some dying patients go through the stages more rapidly than others. Some progress to the next higher stage or may be in several stages at one time. For all patients, hope permeates all the other stages until shortly before death—that is, almost all dying patients express hope for another chance to live.

Kübler-Ross' Stages of Death and Dying

The First Stage: Denial and Isolation. The initial response, according to Kübler-Ross, of patients who have just discovered that they have a terminal illness and that death will soon follow is denial. The **denial stage** is characterized by intense feelings of isolation. Denial is particularly important to younger people who need the time to adjust to the reality of the diagnosis. While the elderly may have longer time to adjust to their conditions, other factors that we discussed earlier, such as loss of such sensory abilities as sight and hearing, have already begun to contribute to feelings of isolation.

The Second Stage: Anger. In Kübler-Ross' studies, only three out of four hundred patients maintained the denial mechanism until death. Gradually, most dying people replace denial with feelings of resentment, anger, or rage, according to Kübler-Ross, and they enter the **anger stage.** The younger person often has more difficulty dealing with these feelings than the elderly. Visitations with spouses or loved ones often become settings in which the dying person vents his or her frustrations, hates, and fears. This occurs less frequently with the elderly. One reason may be that the younger, terminally ill person has more frustration because more of the lifespan is being taken away. For the elderly, less is lost.

The Third Stage: Bargaining. Younger people who pass through the anger stage gradually develop a desire to bargain with God for more time or for time free of pain. In the **bargaining stage,** they also turn to those around them for help: their families, their clergy, and their doctors or nurses. It is no accident that elderly frequently turn to religion at the end of their lives.

The Fourth Stage: Depression. As time runs out for the dying person, according to Kübler-Ross, hopelessness and depression take hold. In the **depression stage, reactive depression** first comes about as patients react to past loss of health and independence due to their illness. Later, **preparatory depression** occurs. Kübler-Ross describes this as a depression that is, in fact, preparation for death. It anticipates loss of everything that has been important during life. Death brings for the dying person loss of all that he or she has ever known.

The Fifth Stage: Acceptance. Given sufficient time to adjust, most (although not all) dying people gradually come to accept their fate and enter the **acceptance stage.** After a long illness, the dying person is, at the end, often silent and uncommunicative. He or she is usually very weak, tired, and often heavily drugged. Some communication still can take place, in the form of handholding or simply having a visitor in the room. This stage, according to Kübler-Ross, is devoid of feelings and emotions. Kübler-Ross suggests that the lack of responsiveness represents a return to the state in which the person existed at the beginning of life. In this sense, death is bringing the dying person full circle, to closure.

Other Research on Death and Dying

Kübler-Ross's descriptions of the stages of death and dying have done a great deal to eliminate some of the myths and mystery about just what dying entails. Some researchers, however, point out that Kübler-Ross' stages are based on the impression of one individual with no attempt to control or systematize the interview data or check the reliability of the observations (see, for example, Schulz 1978). Kübler-Ross also does not provide data on the percentage of dying individuals who do not make the transfer from one stage to another before they die. Nor does she explain the reasons for transitions from one stage to the next.

While some people who are dying withdraw from activities, others use the time remaining to them to accomplish desired goals. Cancer victim Terry Fox, shown here, ran halfway across Canada to raise money for cancer research before succumbing to his illness.

Other researchers (Weisman and Kastenbaum 1968; Kastenbaum and Weisman 1972) used what they reported to be more objective methods than did Kübler-Ross to plot the feelings and behavior of dying patients. The procedures of these researchers involved what they called "psychological autopsies," conferences with doctors, nurses, and family of recently deceased patients in which the psychosocial context of the death was discussed. These researchers found that according to those near them, some patients seemed to be aware of death, to accept impending death, and to withdraw from activities well before the end. Others, who also seemed to be aware of impending death, vigorously engaged in as many activities as possible.

Kastenbaum (1974) suggested from these data that there appears to be no one fixed universal stage that is appropriate for all individuals and that the behavior of any dying individual may be defined by any one of many stages. Schulz (1978), in surveying the research on the dying process, concluded that while Kübler-Ross's stages are important in beginning to describe the behaviors and attitudes of the dying, they should be viewed as hypotheses rather than as classical guides for policy formulation for all dying patients.

Issues Related to Death

More and more Americans in recent years have questioned traditional American medical policy of maintaining life as long as possible, regardless of the quality of the life that remains. Today, just as more and more people are changing in their responses to rituals for death, many dying as well as healthy people are responding to the medical approaches used to keep them alive when death is inevitable.

Engelhardt (1976) suggested that the issue of maintaining life too long is similar in many respects to premature death. Just as we do not want to die before we are ready to do so, he pointed out, we do not want to extend the scope of life by medical technology until life no longer has any meaning. In America, many elderly people are kept alive beyond this point, leading to situations in which elderly who are so senile that they can no longer respond to their environments may be kept alive through technology, such as pacemakers.

Euthanasia. Many elderly, as we discussed earlier in this chapter, choose to end their lives themselves by suicide before life becomes meaningless or intolerable. Some individuals close to dying patients elect to help these patients die before they reach the point where life is meaningless or intolerable for them. The word **euthanasia** refers to the act or practice of killing for reasons of mercy, popularly called "mercy killing." Schulz (1978) distinguishes between two types of euthanasia: passive euthanasia and active euthanasia. **Passive euthanasia** refers to situations in which individuals die because available preventive measures are not used to keep them alive. In passive euthanasia, treatments may be withdrawn or withheld so that the patient will die earlier. **Active euthanasia** is something deliberately done to shorten an individual's life, such as administering poison. The moral, ethical, and legal distinctions between these two types of euthanasia are not always clear. Nor does everyone believe that they are medically or morally different or that any type of euthanasia should ever be practiced on human beings. Today, the law still does not recognize the "mercy" aspect of mercy killings, and most euthanasia cases are tried as murder cases, although juries tend to be very sensitive to motives and are reluctant to convict (Schulz, 1978). In a 1973 Gallup poll, fifty-three percent of the total population surveyed and forty-eight percent of the Catholic interviewees reported that when a person has a disease that cannot be cured, doctors should be allowed by law to end the patient's life by some painless means if the patient and family request it. A similar poll conducted in 1969 with members of the American Physicians' Association revealed that eighty-seven percent of physicians replying at that time approved of passive euthanasia and eighty percent admitted practicing it.

The Living Will. Many dying people today are seeking the right to die with dignity. One expression of their concern is the **Living Will,** a document requesting that should the person signing it fall victim to any terminal illness from which there is no hope of recovery, the physician in charge be instructed not to prolong life by artificial means. Adults who have elected to sign these documents give them to their physicians, clergy, lawyers, and family members. The Living Will does not give anyone permission to end the life of another by active euthanasia. The Living Will, an example of which is shown in Fig. 15.1, is subject to different interpretation in different states and should be examined by a lawyer before being put to use.

BEREAVEMENT

Death and dying have special meaning for the bereaved. For aged husbands and wives, death of a spouse means a loss of both companionship and a life-style. It means increased isolation and knowledge that death, for them, is also not far off.

To My Family, My Physician, My Lawyer and All Others Whom It May Concern

Death is as much a reality as birth, growth, maturity and old age—it is the one certainty of life. If the time comes when I can no longer take part in decisions for my own future, let this statement stand as an expression of my wishes and directions, while I am still of sound mind.

If at such a time the situation should arise in which there is no reasonable expectation of my recovery from extreme physical or mental disability, I direct that I be allowed to die and not be kept alive by medications, artificial means or "heroic measures". I do, however, ask that medication be mercifully administered to me to alleviate suffering even though this may shorten my remaining life.

This statement is made after careful consideration and is in accordance with my strong convictions and beliefs. I want the wishes and directions here expressed carried out to the extent permitted by law. Insofar as they are not legally enforceable, I hope that those to whom this Will is addressed will regard themselves as morally bound by these provisions.

Signed _____

Date _____

Witness _____

Witness _____

Copies of this request have been given to _____

_____

_____

_____

(Continued)

Fig. 15.1   The Living Will. (Reprinted with permission of Concern for Dying, 250 West 57th St., New York, New York, 10019.)

To make best use of your LIVING WILL

1. Sign and date before two witnesses. (This is to insure that you signed of your own free will and not under any pressure.)

2. If you have a doctor, give him a copy for your medical file and discuss it with him to make sure he is in agreement.

   Give copies to those most likely to be concerned "if the time comes when you can no longer take part in decisions for your own

future". Enter their names on bottom line of the Living Will. Keep the original nearby, easily and readily available.

3. Above all discuss your intentions with those closest to you, NOW.

4. It is a good idea to look over your Living Will once a year and redate it and initial the new date to make it clear that your wishes are unchanged.

IMPORTANT

Declarants may wish to add specific statements to the Living Will to be inserted in the space provided for that purpose above the signature. Possible additional provisions are suggested below:

1. a) I appoint _____
      to make binding decisions concerning my
      medical treatment.
                    OR
   b) I have discussed my views as to life
      sustaining measures with the following who
      understand my wishes
      _____.
      _____.
      _____.

2. Measures of artificial life support in the face of impending death that are especially abhorrent

to me are:
   a) Electrical or mechanical resuscitation of my heart when it has stopped beating.
   b) Nasogastric tube feedings when I am paralyzed and no longer able to swallow.
   c) Mechanical respiration by machine when my brain can no longer sustain my own breathing.
   d) _____

3. If it does not jeopardize the chance of my recovery to a meaningful and sentient life or impose an undue burden on my family, I would like to live out my last days at home rather than in a hospital.

4. If any of my tissues are sound and would be of value as transplants to help other people, I freely give my permission for such donation.

Fig. 15.1 (continued)

For bereaved children, death of a parent has a different message. This is, for many, knowledge of the fact that the parent is no longer in acute discomfort. It is also knowledge that another generation has reached the last stage of development. The message to a son burying his father is, "You are next." Once a parent dies, it no longer is possible *not* to acknowledge the fact that the children also will die.

Dealing with Bereavement

The bereaved deal with death in the same stages that dying people do, progressing from Kübler-Ross's (1969) first stages of denial and then anger through bargaining and depression to final acceptance. The elderly tend to accept the loss of others with increased resignation. One reason is that as they grow older themselves, the elderly have increased opportunity to deal with deaths of others.

Symptoms of Grief from Bereavement

Grief expressed after the death of someone close has been studied in depth by psychologists. Lindemann (1944), in a study of 101 patients suffering extreme grief from death of others close to them, observed a number of common physical symptoms:

Somatic distress occurring frequently

Feelings of tightness in the throat, choking, and shortness of breath

Loss of muscular power

Empty feeling in the abdomen

A need for sighing

Psychological and behavior symptoms included:

Preoccupation with an image of the deceased

Feelings of guilt

Hostility toward friends and relatives

Restlessness

Inability to complete tasks

Parkes (1972) and Glick, Weiss, and Parkes (1974) divided the normal grief response described by Lindemann into three phases. The first phase begins, according to these researchers, when death occurs and continues for a few weeks after the funeral. The bereaved reacts with shock and reports feeling numb, dazed, and confused. After several days, an all-encompassing sorrow takes over, expressed often by extended periods of crying or weeping. Glick, Weiss, and Parkes (1974) reported that many widows express fear of "not making it," "losing their minds," or "breaking down." Free-floating anxiety is common. After several weeks of bereavement, these symptoms decrease.

The second stage of grief occurs at the time when the bereaved must confront reality of daily living. For a bereaved spouse, this often means facing the world alone. During this stage, the bereaved frequently engages in what Schulz (1978) calls an "obsessional review," a recounting of the period just prior to the death. Often, this review uncovers feelings of guilt for what might have been done to change events. Parkes (1972) points out that in some cases, at this time, the bereaved talk and think a great deal about the dead person and feel his or her presence. Some widows have illusions at this time of having seen their dead husbands. With time, these obsessional reviews pass, and death is accepted.

The third phase, recovery, starts about the beginning of the second year after death, often preceded by a conscious decision that the past is gone and life must

HIGHLIGHT 15.2 EPITAPHS AND WHAT THEY SAY ABOUT US

Although many people in our society have difficulty discussing death, they have less difficulty later in discussing the deceased. One format for this discussion, from the beginning of the seventeenth century, has been the epitaph. Sones (1980) reproduced highly personal epitaphs from a tombstone from the seventeenth century:

> Here lyes ye precious dust of
> Thomas Bailey
> A painful preacher,
> An eminent liver,
> A tender husband,
> A careful father,
> A brother for adversity,
> A faithful friend,
> A most desirable neighbor,
> A pleasant companion,
> A common good,
> A cheerful doer,
> A patient sufferer,
> Lived much in little time
> A good copy for all survivors.

Epitaphs of more recent years read

> Honey, I will miss you
>
> Together always
>
> Too well loved to ever be forgotten
>
> We will meet again
>
> This was a woman

Sones suggests that these epitaphs demonstrate a need to memorialize what once was but is no more.

QUESTIONS FOR THOUGHT

1. At what stage of grief do you think the writers were when they composed these epitaphs?

2. What needs, in addition to memorializing, might these writers have been meeting?

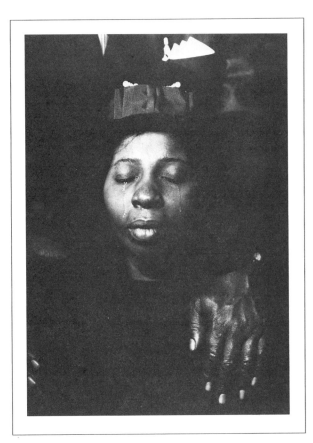

The process of grief seems to occur in stages. Most people recover and resume an active involvement in life after about a year's time.

proceed. The amount of grief expressed at bereavement varies depending on the relationship of the dead person to the bereaved. Sanders (1979–1980) reported that measures on an inventory developed to measure amount of grief demonstrated that death of a child is usually mourned more heavily with significantly greater grief than death of a spouse. Table 15.2 lists the types of grief expressed as well as the amount of grief described as means on Sanders' Grief Inventory Scale. One reason often given by mourners for feeling so much grief at the death of a child is that death of a child is unanticipated, unnatural in the scheme of things. "It should have been me," grieved an old woman whose fifty-year-old daughter died of cancer. "Children aren't supposed to go first. She still had a long life to lead and many things to do. My life is almost finished anyway. Why did it have to be this way? I'll miss her so much."

Table 15.2

Types of Grief Expressed and Measures of Extent of Grief Shown as Means on the Grief Experience Inventory for Death of a Parent, Spouse, and Child

Scale	Means*		
	Death of Parent	Death of Spouse	Death of Child
Denial	2.32	4.74	2.71
Atypical responses	3.91	5.31	6.57
Despair	6.71	7.72	11.65
Anger	3.97	3.33	5.36
Loss of control	5.26	4.76	6.07
Somatic behavior	4.79	6.52	9.14
Death anxiety	5.71	4.28	6.14
Loss of appetite	.59	1.22	1.64
Physical symptoms	2.62	3.11	4.79
Optimism/despair	1.18	1.65	3.07
Loss of vigor	2.53	2.69	3.11

Source: C. Sanders, A comparison of adult bereavement in the death of a spouse, child, and parent, *OMEGA—Journal of Death and Dying,* 1979–80, vol. 10:4, 1979–80, pp. 303–322. Reprinted by permission of Baywood Publishing Company.
*Higher mean scores indicate greater amounts of expressed grief associated with the death of the relative cited in the table.

Death Education

In order to make bereavement easier to deal with and in order to make the impact of death predictable and controllable both to the dying and to the bereaved, Schulz (1978) suggests what he calls death education, educational programs designed to prepare individuals for dealing with death.

Death education, according to Schulz, can be carried out formally or informally. It can offer practical information for people who interact with the dying. It can ease the psychological stress of the dying and bereaved. Finally, it can give individuals opportunity to confront and express feelings about death. For the elderly and terminally ill, opportunities for death education are more limited than for other age groups, many of whom have access to death education offered in schools, universities, and medical schools. The type of death education offered for the elderly and terminally ill is designed to serve therapeutic functions. The type of interaction Kübler-Ross provided her patients when she conducted the interviews that led to her stages of death and dying (1969) is a good example of this type of death education. Her goal was to give her patients the opportunity to express their feelings about the impending death. In addition to this approach, other informal methods have been used to provide death education to the elderly and terminally ill, including discussion groups for the dying, psychoanalysis, and drug therapy.

Death: The End of Life

For most old people, loss of those closest to them has come gradually. As middle-aged and young–old people, they have lost their parents. Later, if they live to the old–old years, they bring with them the experience of mourning the loss of siblings and spouse. Resignation is a typical response of the old–old to these losses. Resignation gives rise eventually to a quiet waiting for death. For the extremely old person, his or her own life is the last thing to be taken away.

THE CASE OF MARY BROWN—A DECISION TO MAKE ABOUT DEATH AND DYING: A CASE STUDY FOR CLASS DISCUSSION

I. Identification and Sources of Information

Name: Mary Brown

Address: 132 Reed Street, Johnsville, Ohio

Race: White

Sex: Female

Age: Eighty-eight years

Sources of information

1. Interview with Mary Brown
2. Interview with Mary Brown's daughter
3. Interview with Mary Brown's physician

II. Family History

Mary Brown was the youngest of six siblings, now all dead. She was born in the United States in the small town in which she still resides. Both parents are buried in the town cemetery. Three children, all in their sixties, still live in the town. Mary and her husband had seven children. The oldest died as an infant. Mr. Brown died ten years ago, at the age of eighty-two, of cancer. Mary, who was deeply devoted to her husband, lived with her eldest daughter for eight years after his death. Two years ago, because of increased infirmity, she entered a nursing home. She is still close to her children and sees them frequently.

III. Case History

Mary Brown entered the nursing home complaining of a series of ailments with which her daughter was incapable of dealing at home. She had lost the sight of one eye because of a cataract several years earlier. About three years ago, she began to lose the sight of her other eye. At the time she entered the home, she was almost totally blind and had lost a great deal of her hearing. A kidney infection had left her incontinent. It was at this point that she agreed to be placed where she could have nursing care around the clock. Her three children who still live in Johnsville visit several times weekly, so that she rarely goes more than a few days without a visitor. Mary's daughter reports that until her most recent illness several months ago, she was alert a great deal of the time.

Mary's physician reports that she made a good adjustment to the home, considering her infirmities. She has a number of symptoms of depression. Until recently, visits by her family tended to reduce the symptoms somewhat. For the last several months, however, Mary seems to have lost interest in company. The physician is not certain that she is able any longer to recognize her children.

Three months ago, Mary woke up in the middle of the night. Instead of calling a nurse, she attempted to get up by herself. She slipped on the floor and broke her hip. She underwent surgery, and the surgeon put a steel pin in her hip to promote rapid healing. Progress has been slow, and the doctor has confined Mary since that time to her bed. At first, Mary tried to fight the restraints that forced her to stay in a prone position. After a few days, she ceased her struggles and lay quietly in her bed. Mary's

Continued

THE CASE OF MARY BROWN *(Cont.)*

daughter reports that she is no longer responsive to visitors.

Last month, the nursing home telephoned Mary's daughter to report that Mary had suffered a heart attack. It had occurred, fortunately, at a time when Mary's physician was making his rounds, and he had her sent immediately to a hospital. The doctor requested permission to have a pacemaker installed. Mary's daughter tried to contact her younger brother, but he was not immediately available. She gave permission for the surgery.

When Mary was returned to the nursing home after the pacemaker was installed, she appeared far less alert than she had been prior to the surgery. She remained quietly in bed and stopped all speech. She was capable of some responding and ate when food was placed in her mouth. She also responded to a handclasp with a faint return squeeze.

IV. Present Status, Diagnosis, and Prognosis

Mary Brown has been back at the nursing home for ten days. There has been no noticeable change in her behavior. Her physician reports that her hip injury is continuing to heal very slowly. The pacemaker is working, and there seems to be no immediate concern that her heart will stop. The physician reports, however, that Mary is far more frail than she was prior

to this last series of problems and that any new illness may prove fatal.

Mary's daughter has contacted her siblings who live in distant cities as well as those who live in Johnsville. The family agrees that she made the proper decision when she agreed to have the pacemaker installed. Family in the immediate area have agreed to visit daily and to watch Mary's responding. No one is certain whether Mary is aware of her condition or not or whether she is aware of who is visiting. The family has agreed that if a long period goes by during which Mary ceases to respond, they will request that, at the next serious illness, the physician agree to use no extraordinary measures to keep Mary alive. They agree that although they all love their mother, continuing her life when it no longer is meaningful is not what she would have wanted. It was a difficult decision to come to and leaves them all grieving.

Questions for Class Discussion

1. Mary Brown's family and physician are faced with a moral dilemma in deciding what type of treatment to give Mary during her next illness. What specifically are the issues with which they are dealing?

2. What would you have done in Mary's family's place? Why?

SUMMARY

Today, with the increase in longevity brought about by medical advances, heart disease is the most common cause of death, followed by cancer and stroke. Evidence now shows that many degenerative diseases are related to sources of life stress and that the numbers of life stresses tend to increase with age. Among the elderly is also a disproportionate incidence of suicide. Another leading cause of death among the elderly is accidents, which occur more frequently and tend to be more debilitating than among younger people.

Death is a cultural as much as a biological reality. Today, with death largely removed from the lives of all but the elderly, death has become a hidden, mysterious topic. Societies and religions that offer philosophies to make it easier to deal with mortality tend to have individuals who adjust to death more easily than do most people in Western society.

Studies show that the most important factors relating to longevity are physical and mental health and the ability to care for oneself. Other important factors include education, occupation, and morale. There is growing awareness today of the inadequacy of most nursing homes and hospital programs in meeting the emotional, social, and spiritual needs of the dying elderly. One solution that is being used with increasing frequency in the United States is the hospice program, the goal of which is to allow death to occur in as familiar and comfortable a place and with as little pain as possible. The ultimate hospice is the patient's home.

The meaning of death varies with age. Children do not generally develop realistic views of death until around the age of ten, and it is not until middle age that most people begin to develop their own personal experiences with death and dying. Middle-aged people tend to think about and fear death more than any other age group. The elderly, who have more forewarnings of death, have more opportunity to come to grips with their concerns. They often become more resigned and depressed and less apt to express denial or anger.

Elizabeth Kübler-Ross identified five separate and predictable stages through which most people pass in the process of adjusting to death: denial and isolation, anger, bargaining, depression, and, finally acceptance. Although her descriptions of these stages have done a great deal to eliminate some of the mystery surrounding dying, other researchers caution against using these stages as guides in forming policy for all dying patients.

More and more Americans are questioning the traditional medical policy of maintaining life as long as possible, regardless of the quality of that life. Some individuals advocate euthanasia, or mercy killing, where patients are helped either passively or actively to die before life becomes meaningless or intolerable to them. Many dying people are signing a document called a living will, requesting that in the event of terminal illness their lives not be prolonged by artificial means. The moral, ethical, and legal issues surrounding euthanasia and such documents as the living will, however, are not at all clear.

Like dying people, the bereaved deal with death in stages. Researchers have divided the normal grief response into three stages. The first stage, that of confusion and shock, occurs immediately after death and continues usually for several weeks. The second occurs as the bereaved confronts the realities of daily living. The third phase, recovery, usually begins about the second year after death. The intensity of grief varies depending on the relationship of the dead to the bereaved.

Individuals can be helped to prepare for death through programs in death education. Such programs can offer practical information for people who interact with the dying, can ease the psychological stress of dying and bereavement, and can give individuals opportunity to confront and express feelings about death.

FOR FURTHER READING

Aries, P. *The Hour of Our Death*. New York: Alfred A. Knopf, 1981. A historian who wrote a classic description of childhood at different times in history *(Centuries of Childhood)* focuses attention in this book on death and dying. He describes in vivid detail the ways that society accepted this stage of development at different periods in the history of the human race and particularly the ways and reasons we accept it as we do today.

Kübler-Ross, E. *On Death and Dying*. New York: Macmillan, 1969. This classic has been described as a profound lesson for the living about dying. It was written initially to make known what the dying have to teach doctors, nurses, clergy, and their own families. Kübler-Ross deals specifically with loss and the process of mourning and discusses death, not just among the old but among people of all ages.

EPILOGUE

LOOKING BACK: AN INTERVIEW WITH AN OCTOGENARIAN

I interviewed Mr. Duffy at the St. Vincent Nursing Home on the afternoon of his eighty-fifth birthday. The home had held a birthday party, complete with a cake and candles, in his honor earlier in the day. Later, Mr. Duffy took his regular place in his wheelchair in front of the television set in the first floor lounge to watch a quiz show. He sat in his chair, already lined in a row together with several other elderly men and women. Mr. Duffy's attention, however, was not on the set but on the strap of his wrist watch. I had to tap him on the shoulder several times before he noticed my presence.

"Well, you've finally come to see me. I guess this really is a special day for me after all. First, my son sends me a new wrist watch to replace the one I lost. Then a birthday cake. Now a real live visitor!"

"What do you expect?" I replied. "How often do I get a chance to celebrate an eighty-fifth birthday?" Mr. Duffy chuckled.

"Well, I suppose birthdays are more a novelty for you than me. I've had so darned many of them; one more doesn't seem like so much!"

"It certainly is special! That's why I brought a present. I hope you like it." I handed the old man a small package, and helped him untie the ribbon.

"Thank you. My fingers don't work as well as they once did. Oh! A pair of sunglasses. Somebody must have told you I lost mine! I seem to be losing everything these days! Thank you very much."

I suggested we go somewhere to talk.

"How about my room?"

"Good idea!" I pushed the wheelchair down the long corridor. We passed the chairs where the elderly sat nodding and then passed the nurses' station.

Mr. Duffy's room was on the first floor. It was large enough to house a worn easy chair in addition to the regular bed, dresser, straight chair, and footstool. The furniture, with the exception of the easy chair and a photograph in a gilt frame on the dresser,

belonged to the nursing home. A TV set sat on a shelf on the wall. The photo was of Mr. and Mrs. Duffy on their fiftieth wedding anniversary.

I asked Mr. Duffy to talk about his life. On such an important occasion as an eighty-fifth birthday, I suggested, he might enjoy listing what he thought were the most memorable events.

Mr. Duffy: Memorable events? I guess I've had a lot of those. Let me think some. I've lived a long time in this country . . . raised my family here . . . watched some die here. An awful lot of things have happened to me and mine. It's hard to know how to begin.

Me: Why not begin at the beginning and go from there?

Mr. Duffy: The beginning? OK. That was in the old country, Ireland. I was only sixteen years old when I left. I hid out on a boat with another boy . . . thought we'd never get here. They caught us six days out but decided to look the other way after we begged. The captain was not a bad guy. He must have known the cook was giving us some food, but he pretended he never saw.

My cousin Bill lived in New York in those days, and I went straight to him when we got in. Course, there was a time when I wasn't sure I'd make it . . . when I had to jump overboard to get past the customs official. But that worked out all right. There I was, one soaked lad still wet behind the ears, having the adventure of his life.

I arrived at my cousin Bill's with nothing in my pocket but his address. Only the Good Lord knows what would have happened if he'd moved or anything . . . Bill got me a job loading freight, and

EPILOGUE

I was on my way. Loaded freight the rest of my life here.

Me: Your wife was born in Ireland too, wasn't she? Did she come over at the same time you did?

Mr. Duffy: Goodness, no! Annie was two years older than I was. She had come over with her mother and father six years before. When I met her, she was working in a saloon making big money, I thought. In those days, anyone with a full-time job seemed rich. We met, courted, and finally married about five years after I came. We got a two-room apartment on the east side. The next year, that was the year my boy Jim was born, and the next year Bill. Annie had to stop work then . . . and it was hard to live. For awhile, we took in Annie's sister Jane, and she helped with the rent. But then Jane took sick and died.

Me: What did Jane die from?

Mr. Duffy: Who knows? In those days, young people died more easily, and fewer people asked questions than today. It seems to me the clinic doctor said she had consumption . . . later, that's what the doctor said killed our Bill too. But Jane just worked too hard. She wasn't even twenty years old, but she had a cough that used to keep her up all the nights. I think it finally just tired her out so she couldn't fight any more . . . you know, I can still hear that coughing. Annie and I slept just the other side of the wall from her bed. After she died, the quiet was terrible.

I promised myself in those days that when my children grew up, they'd have an easier life . . . no working themselves to death. That's why we came to America in the first place after all . . . to have a better life. My Jim and our other two boys and my daughters too are educated. I don't mean just reading and writing. All of them graduated from high school, and my youngest boy had three years of college. Jim is retired now. He used to own a gas station. His brothers both own their own houses. And my two girls . . . why, both of them married right out of high school and never even had to work like their mother. Their husbands have good jobs, and they live well.

Me: Has life here been as good for you as it has been for your children?

Mr. Duffy: Well, that's a little harder to answer. I always loaded freight . . . I was a laborer. But I liked it. I suppose that what's good for the children is good for me. Of course, it's not the same anymore now that Annie is dead.

Me: How long ago did she die?

Mr. Duffy: Let's see now. It was seventeen years ago come August. But it still seems like yesterday. Annie and me, we did everything together. Even the nights when I'd go out with the men, I'd know just what she was doing—sitting at home, watching the kids, and waiting for me. I just couldn't imagine living without her, you know. After she died, I used to come to the kitchen in the morning for breakfast, look at her empty chair, and I'd just bust out crying.

Me: I know you must miss her terribly. Can you tell me some of the things you and she used to do together?

Mr. Duffy: Why, everything. I remember once taking her on the roller coaster at Coney Island. We were married less than a year, and she was already pregnant with Jim. If I had known she was pregnant, I wouldn't

EPILOGUE

have let her go, but the little imp never told me. Oh, there were so many good times in all those years. I remember when Jim graduated from high school. I sat there in the audience with Annie, proud to death. We knew then that our family was going to make it the American way.

I watched Annie hold our first grandchild . . . You know, she looked young enough to be his mother instead of his grandmother. She was already fifty years old and putting on weight, but she didn't have a wrinkle.

If Annie could see the family now, she'd be right proud. The oldest grandson, he's finished college and is going to law school! My children—and their children—they've made it good. Nobody worries about having enough to eat, not like when Annie and I were kids. Life has treated the Duffys good. How can I separate myself from that?

Me: Do you think this came about because you came to this country?

Mr. Duffy: What else? If only my own mother could have seen her greatgrandson in college! You know, my mother couldn't read or write. She was a farm girl. She wouldn't believe it!

My mother died the year after I came here, so she never got a chance to know anything about us. In the old country, almost nobody ever lived to be an old codger like I am . . . at least not in those days. They all died off earlier . . . from sickness or just getting too tired . . . like Jane.

Me: Are there any things you did that you would change if you could?

Mr. Duffy: Oh, Lord, yes. But I don't think I should tell you about things like that. I always

told Annie that what she didn't know couldn't hurt her. I suppose, if I could, I'd keep some of the old ways. The new ways made me do things a lot differently. Look at me here in the nursing home. In the old country, do you think I'd ever have agreed to be sent off to a place like this so far from my boys? It's the moving that did that and made me decide to come here. America's the most moving country I ever saw!

Me: I don't understand. What do you mean?

Mr. Duffy: It's simple. Everybody's always moving somewhere. Everybody's living some-place different. If they're here today, they move tomorrow.

My sons all used to live here in this city. Now my oldest boy went to Florida to retire, and the other boys moved off to other cities to work. My two girls are still here. But the youngest one expects to move next year because of her husband's job. Of course, they all have better jobs than I ever had because they got more education. I was a laborer. And the better jobs always seem to be away from here.

Me: Isn't that the reason you came here in the first place . . . for a better job?

Mr. Duffy: To work, yes. But not for a better job . . . for a *job!* There was *no* work in the old country. But I expected to keep near my family here. I came here to my cousin Bill. The plan was that as soon as I got a job, I would start to bring over my brothers. I did bring some, two of my brothers. But my parents died before I saved enough to bring them.

I expected work and good pay. I usually had work, even during the bad years. But I didn't expect the traveling.

I suppose the young folk don't mind it. Otherwise they would stay put, even if they didn't like their jobs.

Me, I wish they were all close by. But I wouldn't go with them.

My boy Jim and his wife wanted me to come to Florida and stay with them in their trailer. But then I'd be so far away from everyone I ever knew, I thought I'd just die. I didn't want to leave the city where Annie lived for fifty years. Then I had my heart attack and my stroke. And here I am. I couldn't get out too much to see my old friends, even if they were alive. Most of them are dead or dying off now. And the girls come in and see me all the time.

It's so lonely without Annie. Sometimes at night she talks to me. "James," she says, "James, stop your grumping. I'm waiting for you." She is too. I know it.

Me: What do you think most about?

Mr. Duffy: Well, I wonder how long I'll be here. I don't suppose I'll have too many more birthdays, with the old ticker the way it is. I'm ready. I think about how tired I am, and how good it will be finally to rest and be with Annie.

I hope it won't be too hard to let go when the time comes. I was sitting by Annie when she died. It was cancer, and she suffered terribly. But she didn't complain much. I kept thinking, looking at her, that it was too hard for her to suffer like that. I prayed to the Lord to let her go. Finally, she just closed her eyes, and it was done. I hope I can go as well when my time comes. I hope I can let go without fighting. I'm too tired to fight much. I'm content, but it's not right to live so long that you can't do anything for yourself. I've lived a good life and done things . . . most things at least . . . so that my boys and girls have a better life. Sometimes now I think there's no more reason for me to wait. The feeling comes on at night when I get lonely or when I'm sick. The Lord knows I'm luckier than most people, but I do get tired of the aches and pains and downright hurts. Well, forget about me for a moment. There's other things to think about. I think it must be getting time for me to take my nap.

The nurse came in then. "You've had a long day, Mr. Duffy," she said and smiled. "It's time for your pill and your nap so that you'll be ready for your company. Your family will be here to visit soon." I left the room.

Postscript: James Duffy suffered his second heart attack two months after this interview was completed. He survived just long enough for his sons to come from three states to be at his bedside. They and their sisters were with him when he died.

Glossary

Acceptance stage Kübler-Ross's fifth stage of death and dying, in which dying patients gradually come to accept death.

Accommodation The process of equilibration through which one either modifies existing behaviors or adds new behaviors to one's repertoire of responses to the environment.

Achievement motivation According to motivational theorists, the need to obtain mastery and feelings of competence in solving problems and in interactions with others.

Active euthanasia Mercy killing in which an act is deliberately performed to shorten life, such as administering poison.

Activity theory Maddox's theory that older adults tend as long as possible to maintain the activities of middle age and to find substitutes for those activities they are forced to relinquish.

Adolescence Freud's fifth stage of development, involving a resurgence of instinctual sexual drives, a desire to lessen parental attachments, and a variety of conflicts.

Adulthood The period of life in which individuals make life commitments, define roles, and develop adult relationships.

Afterbirth The final stage of the birth sequence, during which the placenta, remaining amniotic sac, and what is left of the cord are expelled.

Age-thirty crisis A period of transition that occurs often at about age thirty, in which individuals evaluate themselves and their relationships as adults and frequently decide to change their psychosocial developmental directions.

Aggression Behaviors intended to harm another individual.

Alienation A subjective feeling of lack of meaningful relationships with others.

Altruism Apparently unselfish behavior with no observable external reward.

Amniocentesis The procedure involving the removal of fluid surrounding a fetus *in utero* to study the fetal cells it contains.

Amniotic sac A fluid-filled cavity serving as a protective device for the embryo.

Anaclitic identification Identification occurring during infancy and used to explain attachment to the primary caregiver.

Anal stage The Freudian stage concerned with developing control of the child's environment, often through the bladder and bowels.

Anecdotal record Account of a student's behaviors recorded by a teacher on a regular basis.

Anger stage Kübler-Ross's second stage of death and dying, in which patients express rage over impending death.

Anomie A subjective feeling of separation of oneself from societal norms.

Anorexia nervosa Mental illness characterized by a pathological loss of appetite, typically accompanied by deficiency symptoms and emaciation.

Anoxia A condition, sometimes occurring during the birth process, in which the full oxygen supply is not absorbed into the bloodstream; effects can vary from irritable behavior to death.

Anxiety General feeling of uneasiness, apprehension, or fear, particularly in anticipation of an event.

Anxious attachment An attachment response in which a great deal of anxiety is displayed at separation from the primary caregiver.

Anxious-avoidance attachment An attachment response in which avoidance of the primary caregiver is displayed on reunion after separation.

Apgar scale Scale used to check health and vital signs in newborns, such as pulse rate, muscle tone, skin color, reflexes, and responsiveness to the environment.

Artificial insemination A medical process in which a syringe containing semen is inserted at the opening of the uterus during a woman's peak fertility period and the semen is deposited.

Assimilation The process of equilibration through which one responds to novel stimuli by using already-existing modes of behavior.

Associative play Play in which children both observe their playmates and imitate their behavior.

Attachment The psychologically close relationship between an infant and its primary caregiver, usually the mother.

Attitudes An individual's relatively permanent orientations toward factors in the environment; considered to be learned.

Audition The ability to hear and discriminate among sounds.

Aural learning style Cognitive style in which learning is accomplished most easily through listening.

Autism A severe behavior disorder characterized by extreme withdrawal or unresponsiveness to others and often, in more serious cases, by self-destructive behaviors.

Autoimmunity theory of senescence Theory that proposes that increased mutations occur with aging and that senescence is due to the antibodies developed to respond to mutation.

Autonomy vs. doubt A stage described by Erikson that, depending on the success of the individual's attempts to control the environment, can result in that individual's developing either positive or negative feelings about competence.

Babinski response A reflex found in neonates in which the toes fan up and outward when the sole of the foot is stroked.

Bargaining stage Kübler-Ross's third stage of death and dying in which dying patients bargain for more time.

Benign suicide Suicide that takes place when an individual neglects to take proper medication or follow a doctor's directions; also called subintentional or passive suicide.

Bilingual Having the ability to use two languages or two dialects of the same language with equal facility.

Birthing room Hospital facility that provides homelike qualities and, at the same time, technology and other back-up services; birthing rooms are used for family-centered delivery.

Blastocele A cavity that forms in the zygote as it descends the fallopian tubes during the period of the ovum.

Blastocyst The term describing the zygote during the period of the ovum.

Blended family Family in which at least one spouse has a child by another marriage and in which at least one spouse is a stepparent.

Body transcedence vs. body preoccupation Crisis of the young–old defined by Peck in which people either learn to adjust to their changing bodies or develop preoccupation with their decreasing abilities.

Bonding Formation of attachment between infant and primary caregiver.

Breech presentation A delivery in which the infant is born with buttocks entering the vagina before the head.

Caesarian section A medical procedure for delivering an infant in which both infant and placenta are removed from the uterus through an incision made in the mother's abdominal wall.

Caregiving The feeding, cleaning, caring for, and protecting of an infant or a child.

Castaway Term that refers to young people who do not willingly leave home but are kicked out by their parents.

Centenarian An individual who has lived one hundred years or more.

Centration According to Piaget's theory, the tendency of preschool and early school age children to concentrate on a single aspect of an event during problem solving.

Cephalo-caudal principle The principle that growth and development proceed from head to foot.

Cerebral arteriosclerosis One cause of organic brain syndrome; due to cerebrovascular accidents.

Child abuse The physical or psychological abuse of children by their primary caregivers through either direct administration of punishment or withdrawal of satisfaction of basic needs.

Child free The voluntary decision of two married people not to have children.

Childhood depression Feelings of sadness and extremely quiet behavior that frequently lead to psychological withdrawal.

Childhood schizophrenia A serious behavioral disorder characterized by changing styles of behavior, extremes of activity, and mood and verbal disturbances.

Chromosomes Rod-shaped bodies in cells containing the genes.

Class inclusion The ability to recognize that some classes of objects are subsets of other, more-inclusive classes and that an object can belong both to the subset and to the more-inclusive classes.

Classical conditioning Learning that occurs when a response associated with an unconditioned stimulus becomes associated with an initially neutral (conditioned) stimulus paired with the original stimulus.

Classification The ability to group objects along one or more dimensions.

Climacteric Term referring to a group of hormonal changes that occur at middle age and affect the reproductive system; also implied are the emotional effects that may accompany these changes.

Cognition The process of thinking, understanding, and problem solving.

Cognitive structure The term used by Piaget to describe the coherent organization of information to solve problems.

Cognitive styles Individual preferences in organizing learning, thinking, remembering, and problem-solving.

Cohabitation A full-time nonmarital living arrangement between a man and woman.

Colic A general term for excessive crying and irritability in an infant.

Collagen theory of senescence Theory that proposes that the collagen in the connective tissues of the body becomes more rigid with age and that this leads to senescence.

Concrete operational stage A stage of thinking described by Piaget in which children still require the presence of concrete objects to solve problems.

Conditioned response (CR) In classical conditioning, a response elicited by a conditioned stimulus; in operant conditioning, a response reinforced by a particular stimulus that follows it.

Conditioned stimulus (CS) A previously neutral stimulus that, through pairing with an unconditioned stimulus, comes to elicit specific responses previously elicited only by the unconditioned stimulus.

Conditioning Learning that occurs through association between stimuli and responses, as in classical or operant conditioning.

Conservation The Piagetian concept that, regardless of changes in shape or disbursement, the original amount of a substance remains constant.

Continuity theory Theory suggesting that older people cope with aging by spending more time in roles they played at earlier stages of life.

Continuous reinforcement schedule A learning schedule in which reinforcement is provided after every single desired response.

Control subject The subject in an experimental study who, while matched with the experimental subjects' relevant characteristics, is not subjected to the independent variable.

Conventional morality Piaget's second stage of the development of moral reasoning, in which moral decisions are based on the attitudes of others toward the activity.

Cooperative play The highest form of social play, in which children rely on each other successfully to complete a period of play.

Creativity The ability to solve problems in new and innovative ways.

Crisis intervention centers Centers for providing assistance during crises; help to resolve problems while reducing the immediate effects on the people involved.

Cross-sectional design A research design in which groups of individuals of different ages are evaluated and then compared.

Crowning The instant during the delivery of a baby in which the head first becomes visible in the mother's vagina.

Crystallized intelligence Those abilities that require processing and reordering of information, including verbal abilities, vocabulary, comprehension, and some spatial abilities.

Culture-fair test A test that is fair to a particular society or group in that the items being measured appropriately reflect the background of the group.

Culture-free tests Tests free of cultural bias.

Decentration According to Piaget's theory, the ability to focus attention on several different dimensions of a situation simultaneously.

Deconditioning A behavior-management process in which individuals are reinforced for exhibiting a behavior incompatible with the behavior that the therapist is attempting to remove.

Deep structure Grammatical structure defined by relationships between nouns and verbs in a sentence.

Defense mechanisms Behaviors developed to decrease anxiety.

Defensive identification Identification processes through which individuals internalize the prohibitions of a model figure.

Democratic parental pattern A child-rearing pattern characterized by acceptance, warmth, allowance of freedom and autonomy, and firmness in making rules.

Denial A defense mechanism characterized by refusal to acknowledge an anxiety-producing situation.

Denial stage Kübler-Ross's first stage of death and dying, in which patients deny impending death.

Deoxyribonucleic acid (DNA) A nitrogen-based compound that forms genes.

Dependent variable In experimental design, a change that takes place as a result of experimenter-controlled manipulation of the independent variable.

Depression Functional disorder in which individuals feel sad, lonely, and withdrawn.

Depression stage Kübler-Ross's fourth stage of death and dying, in which patients begin to feel hopeless.

Descriptive method Developmental research that occurs in natural settings; conditions are not manipulated by the researcher.

Development The process in which an individual changes from a simple to a complex, highly structured organism.

Developmental readiness The collection of growth and/or maturational competencies, as well as specific learned skills, that enable individuals to learn more efficiently.

Developmental stages Descriptions of sequences of age-related behavior and changes in behavior that take place as individuals grow, and that are the result of a combination of maturation and learning.

Developmental tasks Tasks that, according to Havighurst, must be mastered at proper and accepted developmental stages in order that individuals develop normally.

Discipline The class of behaviors for which the primary purpose, strictly speaking, is to teach new behaviors or to teach control of an individual's actions.

Discrepancy hypothesis The hypothesis that stranger anxiety develops from an infant's awareness of the discrepancy between the expected (the mother or other primary caregiver) and the unexpected (an unfamiliar person).

Discrimination In language development, the ability to apply linguistic rules to appropriate words.

Discrimination learning Learning that requires the ability to perceive and act on differences among stimuli.

Disengagement theory Cumming and Henry's theory that people adjust to aging by becoming increasingly detached from their former social roles.

Disequilibrium A state of cognitive unbalance that must be resolved for successful interaction in the environment.

Displacement A defense mechanism characterized by hostility toward persons or objects weaker than the actual object of the aggression.

Dominant gene A gene capable of determining the appearance of a certain trait in an individual, regardless of the contribution of the second gene.

Down's syndrome A genetic abnormality resulting from the acquisition of forty-seven rather than the normal forty-six chromosomes per cell.

Drive An internal state, resulting from needs, that compels an individual into a state of activity. work roles.

Dyslexia A common learning disability involving a variety of perceptual or organizational difficulties.

Ectoderm The outer layer of embryonic cells; it gives rise to the skin, some mucous membranes, and the central nervous system.

Educable retarded The least severe level of mental retardation; the educable mentally retarded are capable of learning skills necessary to hold relatively simple jobs.

Ego (self–other) differentiation Erikson's term for the psychological separation of the self from other people and objects in a person's experiences.

Ego differentiation vs. work-role orientation Peck's crisis in which young–old individuals either define themselves according to their own egos or develop difficulty adjusting to decreased work roles.

Ego integrity Erikson's eighth stage in which young–old adults either develop the ability to regard themselves and their lives as meaningful and useful or experience despair and depression.

Ego transcendence vs. ego preoccupation Crisis of the young–old defined by Peck, in which people either adjust to their impending deaths or become preoccupied with their problems.

Egocentric play The solitary play of infants. Before about age two, infants express little interest in the play of other children around them.

Egocentric speech An early form of speech seemingly intended to serve one's own purposes rather than to communicate information to others.

Egocentric thinking In Piagetian theory, thinking seemingly based on immediate perceptions and lack of ability to consider alternative points of view.

Electra complex Freudian concept in which female children feel sexual love for their fathers and hostile rivalry toward their mothers.

Embryo Term applied to the developing organism between the third and seventh week of prenatal development.

Embryonic period The stage of prenatal development normally between the third and seventh week of pregnancy.

Emotional dependency Feelings associated with those behaviors normally demonstrating strong attachment, such as separation anxiety or approval seeking.

Emotional flexibility vs. emotional impoverishment A conflict with which middle-aged people deal, according to Peck.

Empathetic thinking Thinking that is characterized by participation in the feelings and emotions of others.

Empathy The ability to participate in the feelings or emotions of others.

Enactive mode of responding Bruner's term for describing the way young children habitually use one mode of responding to a variety of stimuli.

Endoderm The innermost layer of the embryonic area, which develops into lungs, bladder, alimentary mucosa, pancreas, and liver.

Enuresis Nocturnal bed-wetting.

Equilibration In Piagetian terms, a balanced set of ideas, caused by the interplay of assimilation and accommodation, that can be organized to solve problems effectively.

Equilibrium A state of cognitive balance usually resulting in the demonstration of social adjustment.

Euthanasia The act or practice of killing for reasons of mercy, popularly called "mercy killing."

Event sampling A research method in which specific events in the life of an individual are studied.

Executive responsibility Term coined by Neugarten to describe the assuming of responsibility and development of strategies for integrating complex relationships, a task most often accomplished in the late thirties or early forties.

Experimental method Research in which aspects of the environment are manipulated to measure resultant behaviors.

Experimental subject The subject in an experimental study who is presented with the independent variable in an experimental design.

Exploratory drive According to some motivational theorists, a need of living organisms to explore the environment.

Extinction The operant-conditioning procedure that causes termination of a learned response after reinforcers are no longer presented.

Extramarital sex A sexual relationship with someone other than one's marriage partner.

Failure-to-thrive syndrome (FTTS) A behavioral disorder in which babies fail to achieve normal growth although no physiological disorder is apparent; behavioral symptoms include passivity and lack of attachment.

Family therapy A group process in which trained therapists work together and separately with family members to recognize concerns and feelings of individuals and to help express needs.

Fantasy play Play in which children's imaginations allow them to transcend the limits placed on them by reality.

Fear of success According to motivational theorists, a desire not to succeed, which results in decreased achievement motivation.

Fetal alcohol syndrome Term used to characterize syndrome affecting newborns of alcohol-dependent mothers who, in turn, are alcohol dependent themselves.

Fetal period The third phase of prenatal development lasting from approximately the eighth week of pregnancy through birth.

Fetus Term used to describe the developing organism from eight weeks after conception until birth at approximately forty weeks.

Field dependence An approach to the perceptual organization of information in which it is hypothesized that individuals may be overwhelmed by the context within which a problem occurs; this often results in problem-solving difficulties.

Field independence An approach to the perceptual organization of information in which it is hypothesized that individuals can isolate easily the important bits of information from the total context in order to solve a problem.

Fixation In Freudian terms, the arresting of the normal process of development because of unfulfilled basic needs.

Fixed schedule of reinforcement Schedule in which a reinforcer is provided only after a specified period of time has elapsed or a number of responses has been emitted.

Flextime One of a number of new systems established by some American businesses to make working hours flexible so as to help employees better to meet family needs.

Fluid intelligence Those abilities that require speed and effectiveness of neurological functioning; includes motor speed, induction, memory, and figural relations.

Fontanels Six soft spots on the neonate's skull at which the bones have not yet ossified, or hardened.

Forceps delivery Delivery of an infant in which the obstetrician uses forceps to help pull the infant from the mother's vagina; used most often with breech deliveries.

Formal operational stage The Piagetian stage in which thinking can occur at an abstract level; the child no longer requires the presence of concrete objects for problem solving.

Function words Words consisting of verbs and adjectives that explain the way action is carried out.

Functional disorders Mental or physical disorders for which no discernible physical or organic causes are evident.

Gametes Sperm and egg cells.

Gametogenesis The process through which gametes are produced.

Gene The carrier of genetic information.

General factor theory of intelligence The theory that intelligence is a general, pervasive ability that facilitates a person's capability.

Generalization The process hypothesized by learning theorists, through which stimuli or responses are associated with other similar stimuli or responses.

Generativity vs. self-absorption A stage described by Erikson and occurring during child rearing and middle years, in which the individual is concerned with dealing with the concerns of others or exhibits excessive self-concern.

Genital stage Freudian stage characterized by the desire to obtain pleasure through adult sexual gratification.

Genotype Characteristics or traits due to the individual's genetic makeup.

Gerontologists Researchers who study the aging process.

Group marriage A life-style in which two or more married couples live together to share time and resources for the welfare of the larger group.

Group tests of intelligence IQ tests that can be administered simultaneously to a group of individuals.

Group-centered therapies Therapy methods in which therapists interact with small groups of patients, providing attention and opportunity for interaction.

Growth Quantitative changes in size and number of responses or abilities.

Habituation The process resulting from prolonged stimulus presentation, by which one ceases to attend to the stimulation.

Holophrastic speech An early form of speech in which single words are used to express complete thoughts.

Hormone theory of senescence Theory that hypothesizes that decreasing ability to produce hormones is the cause of senescence.

Hospice An institution that specializes in medical and psychological care of the dying.

Hostile aggression A common form of aggressive behavior in which children display hostility directed toward others, often to reinforce "tough" images of themselves.

Hyperactivity A condition characterized by erratic, restless behavior.

Hypochondriasis Functional disorder characterized by fear of ill health and disease.

Iconic mode of responding (image representation) Bruner's term for image-based representation built on partially complete concepts.

Identification A learning process through which children internalize both the behaviors and the standards of a model.

Identification with the aggressor Identification with model figures who possess power or authority.

Identity confusion Erikson's term for an unresolved identity crisis that results in adjustment problems; most common during the adolescent period.

Identity crisis theory Theory that explains adjustment to retirement as related to the possibility of a crisis that can lead to a breakdown in identity.

Identity vs. role confusion A stage described by Erikson in which individuals either come to know who they are or remain uncertain of the roles they are able to or wish to play during their lifetimes.

Image-based thinking Piaget's term for the ability of individuals to represent to themselves both events that have occurred in the past and objects that are no longer in their view.

Imitation Learning by observing models.

Imprinting A form of learning that occurs in a young animal and involves recognition of and attraction to its mother or adopted mother figure.

Impulsivity A characteristic of cognitive style in which individuals respond quickly to a problem without first analyzing its components carefully.

Incipient cooperation Piaget's stage in which children first desire to learn rules in order to win at a game.

Independent variable In experimental design, that which is manipulated in some manner by the experimenter.

Individual test of intelligence IQ tests administered on an individual basis.

Industry vs. inferiority A stage described by Erikson in which conflicts may arise between the individual's attempts to win recognition through production and any inadequacies in these attempts, which may produce discouragement.

Initiative vs. guilt A stage described by Erikson in which conflicts may arise between the desire to exhibit newly discovered skills, such as motor control, and their consequences.

Inner speech Vygotsky's term for children's ability to guide their behavior without verbalizing what is happening or should happen.

Instrumental aggression A common form of aggressive behavior in which individuals resort to antisocial behaviors to attain desired objects if less-aggressive means are not successful.

Instrumental conditioning Synonym for classical conditioning.

Instrumental dependency Behaviors initiated to receive attention from others.

Integrity vs. despair A stage described by Erikson during which adults, if they have not yet developed a sense of order and meaning in their lives, feel a profound sense of despair over not having succeeded at this task.

Intelligence (IQ) test A measure of cognitive ability, usually composed of problem-solving tasks.

Intermediate-care facilities Facilities in nursing homes for patients with minor medical problems who do not require registered nurses.

Interval schedule A schedule of reinforcement in which reinforcers are given at specified times.

Interview A method of data collection consisting of orally administered questions that require oral responses.

Intimacy vs. isolation A stage of early adulthood described by Erikson during which individuals strive to establish emotional relationships; conflicts may arise if these relationships are not established, resulting in withdrawal and isolation.

Intuitive stage Piaget's stage of thought involving image-based thinking and perceptual centration.

In vitro fertilization A medical technique in which an egg is surgically removed from the mother's body and fertilized outside the body; later, the fertilized egg is implanted in the mother's uterus.

Joint custody Child custody arrangement in which both parents share legal custody of their child.

Karotyping A procedure for studying the number, form, and size of chromosomes in the fluid surrounding the fetus *in utero*.

Kernel (elementary) grammar Chomsky's term for the earliest, simplest linguistic utterances.

Labor The three-stage process by which a baby is expelled from the uterus through the vaginal canal.

Labyrinthine reflex Reflex that appears in infants at about thirty days and that allows them to right themselves when held downward.

Latency stage Freud's stage during which people outside a child's immediate family become primary love objects.

Learning A relatively permanent change in behavior resulting from interaction with the environment.

Learning disability Term used to describe difficulties experienced by children when they begin to learn to read or write; unrelated to intelligence.

Learning styles Term for cognitive styles or strategies for problem solving.

Leboyer method An alternative childbirth procedure that includes dimming delivery room lights, allowing the mother to hold the infant immediately after birth, and leaving the umbilical cord intact for up to six minutes after birth.

Life satisfaction Attitudes that individuals hold about their presents, pasts, and futures.

Living will A document requesting that if an individual is ill with no hope of recovery, life will not be prolonged by artificial means.

Longitudinal design Research design in which a group of individuals is evaluated periodically in regard to any specified characteristic over a period of time.

Love-oriented discipline Discipline using positive interpersonal behaviors, such as affection, as tools for teaching children.

Mainstreaming Placing children with special needs in regular classrooms with regular teachers, when appropriate.

Manic behaviors Symptoms of a functional disorder in which individuals move and talk in a rapid and often incoherent manner.

Marasmus A condition of some institutionalized infants that sometimes results from lack of adequate contact; consequences range from listlessness to death; also called "hospitalism."

Masturbation Erotic stimulation involving the genital organs, commonly resulting in orgasm achieved by manual or other contact exclusive of sexual intercourse.

Mate swapping See Swinging marriages.

Maternal attachment See attachment.

Maturation Development that occurs regardless of environmental influences.

Meiosis All division that takes place during gametogenesis, in which reproductive cells are produced.

Menarche The onset of menstruation.

Menopause The period of natural cessation of menstruation and production of eggs by the ovaries at middle age.

Mental combinations stage In Piagetian theory, the stage in which a child is able to perceive relationships and solve problems without direct manipulation of materials in the environment.

Mental flexibility vs. mental rigidity A conflict with which middle-aged people deal, according to Peck.

Mesoderm The middle layer of cells within the embryonic area; cells of the mesoderm develop into blood, muscles, bones, and certain organs.

Middle age The middle-adulthood years, roughly encompassing forty to sixty years of age, also called mid life.

Middle school A school specially designed for sixth, seventh, and eighth graders.

Mid-life transition (mid-life crisis) A transition, according to Jung, from the first to the second half of life in which individuals often reassess themselves and their lives.

Mitosis The process of cell division for all cells except the gametes.

Modeling behavior Imitating the behavior of a model figure.

Morality The overt expression of social attitudes and values.

Moro (startle) reflex A neonate's rapid reaching upward and jerking of the arms; results from withdrawal of physical support.

Motivation Inferred internal processes measured by goal-directed behavior.

Motivational theory The attempt to describe internal processes in order to explain behavior.

Movement theory Theory describing the specific movement behaviors through which a child must proceed in order to make a learned response.

Naturalistic Observation See Descriptive method.

Need An internal condition of the individual, the reduction of which produces satisfactory adjustment to the environment.

Negative reinforcers Stimuli that an organism ordinarily seeks to avoid or stop, resulting in the strengthening of escape or avoidance responses.

Neonate Term used to describe the infant during the first two weeks of life.

Object-oriented discipline Discipline that uses objects as tools for teaching children.

Object permanence In Piagetian theory, the ability to recognize that objects exist when not in one's visual field.

Oedipal complex Freudian concept that male children feel sexual love for their mothers and hostile rivalry toward their fathers.

Old—old stage Stage of life in later adulthood, defined by Neugarten, in which people become increasingly limited by the aging process.

Olfactory sense The sense of smell.

Open classroom concept Concept of teaching whereby children are encouraged to pursue interests independently and at their own pace and design their own learning experiences.

Operant conditioning Learning in which a response is followed by a reinforcer that increases the probability that this same response will occur again under similar circumstances.

Operant response In operant conditioning, the response that operates on the environment to produce a desired outcome.

Operational stage The Piagetian stage during which children are first successful at solving problems through direct manipulation of materials in their environment.

Oral stage Freud's first stage, in which activities revolve around the mother, the nipple, and the thumb.

Organic brain syndrome Organic disorder of the elderly that leads to impairment of intellectual and cognitive functioning.

Organic disorder Mental or physical disorder with organic causes.

Orienting responses A form of attention in which an infant focuses its sensory mechanisms on particular stimuli.

Overgeneralization In language development, the tendency of young children indiscriminately to apply linguistic rules inappropriately, resulting in common errors in speech.

Overt speech Vygotsky's term for verbalizations, ordinarily following what he called "inner speech."

Palmar grasp A flexion response in which a neonate will grasp an object placed in the palm.

Parallel play A form of children's social play characterized by playing alongside others but with no direct interaction.

Paranoia Functional disorder characterized by fear that others are about to do one harm.

Passive euthanasia Euthanasia in which individuals die because of lack of preventive measures.

Perception The process of interpreting stimuli sensed in the environment.

Period of the ovum The phase of prenatal development lasting until the second week after conception during which the zygote lives off its own yolk.

Permissive discipline A method of discipline in which a great amount of freedom is provided.

Phallic stage Freud's developmental stage in which the child becomes aware of genital differences and the pleasures associated with them.

Phenotype The observable expression of the interaction between the genotype and the environment.

Placenta An area of the uterine wall through which food, oxygen, and waste pass between mother and fetus.

Polygenic traits Those characteristics determined by a number of genes in combination.

Positive reinforcers Stimuli following a response that result in an increase in the probability of that response's occurring again.

Postparental families Families in which parents are middle aged or older and in which children have grown up and left home.

Power-assertive discipline Discipline involving the use of parental power and authority.

Preconceptual thought Piaget's early stage of thinking characterized by reliance on only partially complete concepts to solve problems.

Preconventional morality Piaget's first stage of moral development, in which moral reasoning is based on the consequence of any given action, regardless of the intent behind the action.

Prehension The ability to grasp objects.

Preoperational thought According to Piaget, the thought processes of children aged approximately two to seven years and characterized by egocentrism and perceptual domination.

Preparatory depression Depression that, according to Kübler-Ross, is preparatory to death.

Prepared childbirth Childbirth involving special exercises and a minimum, or nonuse, of anesthetics.

Presocial egocentric stage According to Piaget, an early stage in the development of children's conception of rules; characterized by adherence to adult authority.

Primary caregiver That person with primary responsibility for feeding, cleaning, caring for, and protecting an infant or child.

Primary circular reaction stage. In Piagetian theory, an early circular reaction stage involving the repetition of simple behaviors; an early form of cognitive development in which children discover relationships between behaviors and consequences.

Primary needs Those internal conditions necessary for physical survival that can be met by reinforcers such as food or water.

Primary reinforcers Stimuli necessary for physical survival, such as food or water.

Profoundly retarded The most extreme level of mental retardation; the profoundly retarded are helpless and require lifelong care.

Progeria Disease that causes senescence prematurely and that generally leads to death in the midteens.

Prohibition learning The learning of a society's "don'ts," often taught through identification.

Projection A defense mechanism characterized by attributing one's undesirable behavior to other people.

Proximo-distal principle The principle that development proceeds from the central nervous system to the body's extremities.

Psychoanalytic theory Freud's theory describing the development of personality and social interactions as a function of meeting the individual's needs for food, love, warmth, and security.

Psychosis Mental disorder in which individuals develop more serious distortions of reality than do neurotic individuals.

Psychosocial Descriptive term for Erikson's developmental theory describing children's orientations to themselves and their social world.

Psychosomatic illness An illness that is associated with psychological factors such as emotion and stress rather than with physical causes alone.

Puberty The period of full sexual maturity.

Pubescence The state of arriving at or reaching puberty.

Punishment An unpleasant event immediately following a behavior that is designed to obliterate the behavior.

Questionnaire A method of data collection through which an individual can either orally or through writing indicate responses to a variety of written questions.

Ratio schedule A learning schedule in which reinforcement is provided based on the number of desired responses produced.

Reactive depression Feelings of depression that are related to past loss of health and independence.

Recessive genes Genes that must be paired during fertilization of the ovum with other, corresponding recessive genes if the individual is to exhibit any given trait determined by those genes.

Reflectivity A characteristic of cognitive style in which individuals consider carefully all the components of a problem before posing a solution.

Reflexive responses Involuntary motor responses.

Reflexive stage A substage of Piaget's sensorimotor period during which reflexive behaviors become more efficient.

Reinforcement In operant theory, any stimulus that increases the immediately preceding response.

Reinforcement schedule The procedures by which reinforcers are presented.

Reintegrative stage Final phase of cognitive function described by Schaie, in which individuals are no longer as motivated by social stimuli as they were earlier and spend more time in contemplation.

Reliability Extent to which individuals taking the same test repeatedly are likely to get the same score.

Response mode Cognitive style in which children learn most easily, either in a group or alone.

Restrictive discipline A form of discipline characterized by attempts to dominate and control children's behavior through frequent planning and criticism.

Rh factor Genetically determined condition in which substances present in the red blood cells cause maternal and fetal blood to become incompatible.

Riddle A puzzle that has within it a word, term, or letter that is presented in one way and later reclassified in another.

Rite of passage Initiation experience defined by society in which adolescents are symbolically divested of childhood and invested in adulthood.

Role confusion The knowledge that a personally satisfying role is not available to an individual coupled with that individual's desire not to accept anything less than satisfactory.

Role identity The understanding of one's self, including one's strengths and limitations.

Role overload The taking on of too many roles to be able to perform them all satisfactorily. Occurs frequently in two-career or two-earner families and more often to women than men.

Rooting response A typical behavior of neonates in which stimulation near the mouth results in movement toward the source of the stimulation.

Runaway A minor who leaves home without parental permission.

Schema See Cognitive structure.

School phobia The fear of being in school.

Secondary circular reaction stage In Piagetian theory, a later circular reaction stage, in which an infant's responses are made apparently in order to reexperience cause–effect relationships.

Secondary reinforcers Stimuli that are not necessary for reducing primary needs yet still influence behavior (for example, social approval or money).

Secure attachment An attachment response in which the infant uses the caregiver as a secure base from which to explore the world.

Self-concept One's perception of one's individuality.

Self-esteem The value judgment given to one's self-concept.

Senescence The biological aging of the body.

Senile psychosis Senility due to atrophy of the brain cells of the cerebral cortex.

Senility A nonmedical, frequently used term to refer to mental incapacities of the elderly, such as forgetfulness or confusion.

Sensation Awareness of stimuli in the environment; made possible through the receptor organs.

Sensitive periods of development Those times during development when certain interactions with the environment must take place if development is to progress normally.

Sensorimotor stage Piaget's first stage of development, during which infants learn to respond to their environments through the senses and through mastery of motor development.

Separation anxiety An infant's fear of separation from the mother or object of attachment.

Seriation The ability to sort objects in a series along one or more dimensions.

Severely mentally retarded Those mentally retarded individuals who, with intensive training, may be able to learn some self-care skills.

Sex typing The individual's learning of socially acceptable behaviors for his or her sex.

Sex-role identification The process by which individuals internalize the roles considered appropriate to their sex and reactions characteristic of those roles.

Sexually open marriage Marriages in which both partners agree to accept each other as equals, friends, and partners and to allow both partners freedom to establish independent relationships in addition to the marriage relationship.

Sexually transmitted diseases (STDs) Diseases, such as gonorrhea, syphillis, and herpes, that are transmitted through sexual intercourse.

Shaping In operant conditioning, the step-by-step reinforcement of behavior, the result of which is the establishing of a new behavior; also referred to as the method of successive approximations.

Single parenting Parenting performed by only one parent because of death of the other spouse, divorce, or separation.

Skilled nursing facilities Facilities in nursing homes that provide registered nursing care.

Social contract marriage A full-time living arrangement between a man and woman without legal marriage but in a way that commits them emotionally and suggests permanence.

Social contract orientation The fifth post-conventional stage of Kohlberg's stages of moral reasoning, in which the individual places value primarily on the rights of others.

Social play An advanced form of play involving more than one child in direct interaction.

Socialized speech A form of speech designed to communicate information accurately to another person, often taking into account the listener's point of view.

Socializing vs. sexualizing A conflict with which middle-aged people deal, according to Peck.

Sociocentric thinking The ability to socioempathize or to recognize and respond to the attitudes of other members of a group.

Socioempathy Ability to perceive correctly the feelings and attitudes of others in a social group.

Sociogenic drug A drug, such as marijuana, that stimulates social activity.

Solitary play An early form of play characterized by interactions with inanimate objects, such as blocks or toys, rather than with other people.

Standardized population The sample of people whose scores on a standardized test determine the norms against which all people taking the test are compared.

Standardized tests Tests administered to large samples of people from which norms that can be used to compare individual scores are determined.

Status offender An individual who has committed an act that is judged delinquent by virtue of his or her less-than-adult age.

Stranger anxiety An infant's fear of unfamiliar people.

Sublimation A defense mechanism characterized by substitution of acceptable behaviors for unacceptable ones.

Sudden infant death syndrome (SIDS or crib death) A condition of uncertain origin that results in the sudden death of infants from three weeks to six months of age.

Surface structure Grammatical structure defined by grouping of words in a sentence.

Swinging marriages Marriages in which both partners participate voluntarily in extramarital sex with other couples.

Symbolic play Piaget's term for imitative play in which an object represents its real counterpart in the child's mind.

Symbolic representation (image-based thinking) Piaget's term for the preschooler's ability to use signs and symbols to represent objects in his or her experience.

Syntax Grammatical structure of language.

Tactile sense The sense of touch.

Tertiary circular reaction stage In Piagetian theory, a final circular reaction stage in which the infant makes a response to draw attention.

Thinking mode Cognitive style in which children approach problems either by gathering details or looking for organization first.

Throwaway Term that refers to young people who do not willingly leave home but are kicked out by their parents.

Time sampling A research method in which small samples of time are used to periodically gather information.

Toxemia A condition of pregnancy characterized by rising blood pressure, fluid retention, and other symptoms.

Trainable mentally retarded The level of mental retardation in which the individual can learn sufficient self-care skills to live successfully in the community rather than in an institution.

Trophoblast The part of a blastocyst that gives rise to the amniotic sac and the yolk sac.

Trust vs. mistrust Erikson's first psychosocial stage, during which an infant either does or does not develop basic confidence in the environment; this stage influences later social and emotional relationships.

Two-career marriages Marriages in which both partners are establishing themselves in careers that ordinarily require commitment and that are personally rewarding and demand long-term obligations.

Two-earner marriages Marriages in which both partners work outside the home to meet financial needs.

Type A individuals People whose personality and general behaviors are characterized by stress, as categorized by Rosenham.

Type B individuals People whose personality and general behaviors are characterized by calmness and lack of stress, as categorized by Rosenham.

Umbilical cord The structure that carries food and waste products between mother and fetus.

Unconditioned response (UCR) In classical conditioning, a response that occurs spontaneously upon presentation of a given stimulus.

Unconditioned stimulus (UCS) In classical conditioning, a stimulus that, without benefit of learning, produces a given response.

Unsocialized aggression A behavior problem of children characterized by hostility toward others, expressed by physical and verbal abusiveness, lying, and the like.

Values Individuals' criteria for evaluating their environments according to their acceptability or unacceptability; values remain relatively constant over time.

Valuing wisdom vs. valuing physical power A conflict with which middle-aged people deal, according to Peck.

Variable A factor in the environment that, in an experiment, is allowed to vary in some way.

Variable schedule of reinforcement A schedule in which the reinforcer is provided at intervals that the subject cannot predict.

Vestibular sense Sense of movement and balance.

Visual learning style Cognitive style in which learning is accomplished most easily through reading.

Volition According to Bruner, the voluntary control of the body in order to obtain a desired outcome.

Wear-and-tear theory of senescence Theory that hypothesizes that senescence is due to wearing out of the body.

Withdrawal A psychological retreat from other people, occurs frequently following childhood depression.

Yolk sac The structure that feeds the embryo until the umbilical cord is fully developed.

Young–old stage Stage of life defined by Neugarten to include adults in their sixties to about age seventy-five who are relatively affluent, healthy, and vigorous.

Youth In Keniston's hypothesis, a period of life in which the maturing individual tries out new life-styles but is not yet ready to accept the responsibilities of young adulthood.

Zygote A fertilized egg cell.

Bibliography

Aaronfreed, J. *Conduct and Conscience: The Social-ization of Internalized Control Over Behavior.* New York: Academic Press, 1968.

Adelson, J. The development of ideology in adolescence. In S. Dragastin, and G. Elder (eds.), *Adolescence in the Life Cycle.* New York: John Wiley and Sons, 1975.

Ainsworth, M. Infant–mother attachment. *American Psychologist,* October 1979, 34(10), 932–937.

Ainsworth, M. *Infancy in Uganda: Infant Care and the Growth of Love.* Baltimore, Maryland: Johns Hopkins, 1967.

Ainsworth, M., M. Blehar, E. Walters, and S. Wall. *Patterns of Attachment: A Psychological Study of the Strange Situation.* Hillsdale, New Jersey: Erlbaum, 1978.

Almquist, E., J. Chafitz, B. Chance, and J. Corder-Bolz. *Sociology: Women, Men, and Society.* New York: West Publishing, 1978, 328–372.

Alpaugh, P. *Variables Affecting Creativity in Adulthood: A Descriptive Study.* M.A. Thesis, University of Southern California, 1975.

Alston, F. Early childhood rearing practices in the People's Republic of China. Paper delivered at the annual meeting of the American Educational Research Association, San Francisco, April 1976.

Altman, J. Nutritional deprivation and neural development. In M. Sterman, D. McGinty, and A. Adinolf, *Brain Development and Behavior.* New York: Academic Press, 1971.

American Federation of Teachers. Hearings explore role of family life. *American Educator, The Professional Journal of the American Federation of Teachers,* Summer 1980, 4 (2), 2.

American Personnel and Guidance Association. Battered women, subject of concern. *Guidepost,* March 20, 1980, 22 (14), 12.

American Psychological Association. *Division of Developmental Psychology Newsletter,* 1968, 1–3.

American Psychological Association. Child abuse called national epidemic. *Monitor,* 1976.

Ames, C., R. Ames, and D. Felker. Effects of competitive reward structure and valence of outcome on children's achievement attributions. *Journal of Educational Psychology,* 1977, 69(1), 1–8.

Anastasi, A. Heredity, environment, and the question, "how?" *Psychological Review,* 1958, 65, 197–208.

Anthony, E., and T. Benedek. *Parenthood: Its Psychology and Psychopathology.* Boston: Little, Brown, 1970.

Apgar, V. Proposal for a new method of evaluating the newborn infant. *Current Research in Anesthesia and Analgesia,* 1953, 32, 260–267.

Apgar, V., and L. James. Further observations on the newborn scoring system. *American Journal of Diseases of Children,* 1962, 104, 419–428.

Apple, R. Britain's notable nonagenarians. *New York Times Magazine,* November 11, 1979, 50–53.

Appleton, T., R. Clifton, and S. Goldberg. The development of behavioral competence in infancy. In F. Horowitz (ed.), *Review of Child Development*

Research. Chicago: University of Chicago Press, 1975, 4.

Arenberg, D., and E. Robertson-Tschabo. Learning and aging. In J. Birren and K. Schaie (eds.), *The Handbook of the Psychology of Aging.* New York: Van Nostrand Reinhold, 1977.

Aries, P. *The Hour of Our Death.* New York: Alfred A. Knopf, 1981.

Aries, P. *Centuries of Childhood.* New York: Alfred A. Knopf, 1962.

Arlin, M., and G. Roth. Pupils' use of time while reading comics and books. *American Educational Research Journal,* Spring 1978, 15(2), 201–216.

Armentrout, J., and G. Burger. Children's reports of parental childrearing behavior at five grade levels. *Developmental Psychology,* 1972, 7, 44–48.

Arms, S. *Immaculate Deception.* New York: Houghton Mifflin, 1975.

Asmussen, I. Smoking moms imperil babies. *Pittsburgh Press,* October 20, 1978, A4.

Atchley, R. Dimensions of widowhood in later life. *The Gerontologist,* 1975a, 15(2), 176–178.

Atchley, R. Adjustment to loss of job at retirement. *International Journal of Aging and Human Development,* 1975b, 6(1), 17–27.

Atchley, R. Retirement and leisure participation: Continuity or crisis? *Gerontologist II,* 1971, 13–17.

Athanasiou, R., P. Shaver, and C. Tavris. Sex. *Psychology Today,* 1970, 4, 37–52.

Ault, R., D. Crawford, and W. Jeffrey. Visual scanning strategies of reflective, impulsive, post-accurate, and slow-inaccurate children in the Matching Familiar Figures Test. *Child Development,* 1972, 43, 1412–1417.

Ausubel, D., J. Novak, and H. Hanesian. *Educational Psychology: A Cognitive View* (2nd ed.). New York: Holt, Rinehart and Winston, 1978.

Babson, S., and R. Benson. *Management of High Risk Pregnancy and Intensive Care of the Neonate.* St. Louis: C. V. Mosby, 1971.

Bachman, J. *Youth in Transition.* Ann Arbor, Michigan: Braun-Brumfield, 1970.

Bailey J., and K. Pierce. The friendship rating scale: A sociometric instrument. *Elementary School Guidance and Counseling.* March 1975, 9, 218–224.

Bandura, A. *Social Learning Theory.* Englewood Cliffs, New Jersey: Prentice-Hall, 1977.

Bandura, A., and M. Harris. Modification of syntactic style. *Journal of Experimental Child Psychology,* 1966, 4, 341–352.

Bandura A., and R. Walters. Reinforcement patterns and social behavior. In A. Bandura and R. Walters, *Social Learning and Personality Development.* New York: Holt, Rinehart and Winston, 1963.

Bardwick, J. Middle age and a sense of future. *Merrill-Palmer Quarterly,* 1978, 24(2), 129–138.

Barfield, R., and J. Morgan. Trends in satisfaction with retirement. *Gerontologist,* 1978, 18, 13–19.

Barnett, J. *Development of Children's Fears: The Relationship Between the Systems of Fear Management,* M. A. Thesis, University of Wisconsin, 1969.

Bart, P. Depression in middle-aged women. In V. Gornick and B. Moran (eds.), *Women in Sexist Society.* New York: Basic Books, 1971.

Bartoshevsky, L. Fetal alcohol syndrome. Paper presented at the National Foundation March of Dimes Birth Defects Conference, Chicago, Illinois, July 1979.

Barry, R., and A. Barry. Stereotyping of sex roles in preschool kindergarten children. *Psychological Reports,* 1976, 38, 948–950.

Baumrind, D. Socialization and instrumental competence in young children. In W. Hartup (ed.), *The Young Child: Reviews of Research,* Vol. 2, Washington, D.C., National Association for the Education of Young Children, 1972, 202–224.

Bayley, N. Comparisons of mental and motor test scores for ages 1–15 months by sex, birth order, race, geographical location, and education of parents. *Child Development,* 1965, 36, 379–412.

Beal, D., and P. Duckro. Family counseling as an alternative to legal action for the juvenile status offender. *Journal of Marriage and Family Counseling,* January 1977, 77–80.

Beatty, F. Model me. *American Education,* January–February 1977, 23–25.

Beck, M., and M. Lord. A family meeting turns into a feud. *Newsweek,* June 16, 1980, 31.

Becker, W. Consequences of different kinds of parental discipline. In M. Hoffman and L. Hoffman (eds.), *Review of Child Development Research.* New York: Russell Sage Foundation, 1964.

Behrman, R. Birthweight, gestation age, and neonatal risk. In R. Behrman (ed.), *Neonatology.* St. Louis: C. V. Mosby, 1973, 45–50.

Bell, R. Parent, child, and reciprocal influences. *American Psychologist,* October 1979, 34(10) 821–826.

Bell, R., and N. Lobsenz. Marital sex. In J. Gagnon (ed.), *Human Sexuality in Today's World.* Boston: Little, Brown, 1977.

Bell, A., and M. Weinberg. *Homosexualities: A Study of Diversity among Men and Women.* New York: Simon & Schuster, 1978.

Bellack, L., and M. Antell. An intercultural study of aggressive behavior on children's playgrounds. *American Journal of Orthopsychiatry,* July 1974, 44(4), 503–508.

Belsky, J., and L. Sternberg. The effects of daycare: A critical review. *Child Development,* 1978, 49, 929–949.

Benedict, R. Continuities and discontinuities in cultural conditioning. *Psychiatry,* 1938, 1, 161–167.

Benson, R., and D. Brodie. Suicide by overdose of medicines among the aged. *Journal of the American Geriatrics Society,* 1975, 23, 304–308.

Bentson, V., P. Kasschau, and P. Ragan. The impact of social structure on aging individuals. In J. Birren and K. Schaie (eds.) *The Handbook of the Psychology of Aging.* New York: Van Nostrand Reinhold, 1977.

Ben-Zeev, S. The influence of bilingualism on cognitive strategy and cognitive development. *Child Development,* 1977, 48, 1009–1018.

Berado, F. Survivorship and social isolation: The care of the aged widower. *The Family Coordinator,* 1970, 19, 11–25.

Berenda, R. *The Influence of the Group on the Judgements of Children.* New York: King's Crown Press, 1950.

Berman, E., W. Miller, N. Vines, and H. Lief. The age 30 crisis and the seven-year itch. *Journal of Sex and Marital Therapy,* 1977, 3(3), 197–204.

Bernard, H. *Child Development and Learning.* Boston: Allyn and Bacon, 1973.

Bernard, J. Divorce and young children: Relationship in transition. *Elementary School Guidance and Counseling,* February 1977, 193–197.

Berndt, R., and E. Berndt. Children's use of motives and intentionality in person perception and moral judgement. *Child Development,* 1975, 46, 904–912.

Bernstein, B. Language and social class. *British Journal of Sociology II,* 1960, 271–276.

Bernstein, B. Some sociological determinants of perception: An inquiry into subcultural differences. *British Journal of Sociology,* 1958, 9, 159–174.

Bettelheim, B. The roots of radicalism. *Playboy Magazine,* March 1971.

Biaggio, M. *Sex Role Preference, Sibling Status, and Bonding Behavior in Children.* Ph.D. Dissertation, Utah State University, 1976.

Bigelow B., and J. LaGaipa. Children's written descriptions of friendship: A multidimensional analysis. *Developmental Psychology,* 1975, II(6), 857–858.

Biller, H. Father absence, maternal encouragement, and sex-role development in kindergarten-age boys. *Child Development,* 1969, 40, 539–546.

Bischof, L. *Adult Psychology.* New York: Harper and Row, 1976.

Blackham, G. *The Deviant Child in the Classroom.* Belmont, California: Wadsworth, 1967.

Blum, J., and L. Jarvik. Intellectual performance of octogenarians as a function of education and initial ability. *Human Development,* 1974, 17, 364–375.

Boarding house concept proposed to provide homes for elderly. *New York Times,* April 17, 1980, C14.

Bock, E., and I. Webber. Suicide among the elderly. *Journal of Marriage and the Family,* 1972, 34, 24–31.

Bodmer, W., and L. Cavalli-Sforza. Intelligence and race. *Scientific American,* 1970, 223, 19–30.

Bohannon, J., and A. Marquis. Children's control of adult speech. *Child Development,* 1977, 48, 1002–1008.

Booth, A. Wife's employment and husband's stress: A replication and refutation. *Journal of Marriage and the Family,* November 1977, 39, 645–650.

Borrow, H. Career development in adolescence. In J. Adams (ed.), *Understanding Adolescence.* Boston: Allyn and Bacon, 1973, 421–452.

Boston Women's Health Book Collective. *Our Bodies, Ourselves* (2nd ed.), New York: Simon & Schuster, 1976.

Botwinick, J. Intellectual abilities. In J. Birren and K. Schaie (eds.), *Handbook of the Psychology of Aging.* New York: Van Nostrand Reinhold, 1977, 580–605.

Botwinick, J. *Aging and Behavior: A Comprehensive Integration of Research Findings.* New York: Springer, 1973.

Botwinick, J. Geropsychology. *Annual Review of Psychology,* 1970, 239–272.

Botwinick, J. *Cognitive Processes in Maturity and Old Age.* New York: Springer, 1967.

Bower, T. G. R. *A Primer of Infant Development.* San Francisco: Freeman, 1977*a.*

Bower, T. G. R. *The Perceptual World of the Child.* Cambridge, Massachusetts: Harvard University Press, 1977*b.*

Bower, T. G. R., J. Broughton, and M. Moore. Infant responses to approaching objects: An indication of response to distal variables. *Perception and Psychophysics,* 1970, 9, 193–196.

Bowes, W., Jr. The effects of obstetrical medication on fetus and infants. *Monographs of the Society for Research in Child Development,* 1970, 137(4), 35.

Bowlby, J. Psychiatric implications in bereavement. In A. Kutscher (ed.), *Death and Bereavement.* Chicago, Illinois: Charles Thomas, 1974.

Bowlby, J. Attachment and loss. In J. Bowlby, *Attachment,* Vol. 6. New York: Basic Books, 1969.

Bowlby, J. *Child Care and the Growth of Love.* Harmondsville, Middlesex, England: Penguin Books, 1965.

Bowlby, J. The nature of the child's tie to his mother. *International Journal of Psychoanalysis,* 1958, 39, 1–34.

Bowlby, J. Maternal care and mental health. *Bulletin of the World Health Organization,* 1951, 3, 355–534.

Brackbill, Y., Notes on the FDA's anesthetic and life support drug advisory committee. *Science,* August, 3 1979, 205, 447–448.

Brackbill, Y. The use of social reinforcement in conditioning smiling. In Y. Brackbill and G. Thompson (eds.), *Behavior in Infancy and Early Childhood.* New York: Free Press, 1967, 616–625.

Brackbill, Y., and S. Broman. Preliminary report on the effects of medicated births to the National Institute of Health. Washington, D.C.: Dept. of Health, Education and Welfare, 1979.

Brackbill, Y., and M. Koltsova. Conditioning and learning. In Y. Brackbill (ed.), *Infancy and Early Childhood.* New York: Free Press, 1967, 207–289.

Bradbury, W. An agony of learning. *Life,* October 6, 1972, 57–58.

Brant, R., and P. Tisda. The sexually misused child. *American Journal of Orthopsychiatry,* January 1977, 80–90.

Braun, C. Teacher expectation: sociopsychological dynamics. *Review of Educational Research,* Spring 1976, 46(2), 185–213.

Brazelton, T. *Neonatal Behavioral Assessment Scale.* London: W. Heinemann, 1973.

Brazelton, T. Effect of maternal medication on the neonate and his behavior. *Journal of Pediatrics,* 1961, 58, 513.

Brecher, E. *Licit and Illicit Drugs.* Boston: Little, Brown, 1972.

Bridges, K. Emotional development in early infancy. *Child Development,* 1932, 3, 324–342.

Brock, C. Menopause. *Human Behavior,* April 1979, 8, 38–46.

Brody, E., W. Poulshock, and C. Masciocchi. The family caring unit: A major consideration in the long-term support system. *Gerontologist,* 1978, 18, 556–561.

Bromley, D. *The Psychology of Human Aging* (2nd ed.). Baltimore: Penguin Books, 1974.

Bronfenbrenner, U. Who cares for America's children? *New York Times Educational Supplement,* December 16, 1977, 15–17.

Bronfenbrenner, U. The roots of alienation. In U. Bronfenbrenner (ed.), *Influences of Human Development.* Hinsdale, Illinois: The Dryden Press, 1972.

Bronfenbrenner, U. *Two Worlds of Childhood.* New York: Russell Sage Foundation, 1970.

Bronfenbrenner, U. The dream of the kibbutz. *Saturday Review,* September 20, 1969, 72–73.

Brook, J., M. Whiteman, E. Piesach, and M. Deutsch. Aspiration levels of and for children: Age, sex, race, and socioeconomic correlates. *Journal of Genetic Psychology,* 1974, 124, 3–16.

Brooks, S. *Fear of success: A motive toward success or a response to violation of sex-role prescriptions.*

Ph.D. Dissertation, Washington University, 1976.

Brossard, M., and T. DeCarie. The effects of three kinds of perceptual–social stimulation on the development of institutionalized infants. In *Early Child Development and Care,* Vol. 1, Great Britain: Gordon and Breach Science Publishers, 1971, 111–130.

Brown, M. Teenage prostitution. *Adolescence,* Winter 1979, XIV(56), 665–680.

Brown, R., C. Cazden, and U. Bellugi-Klima. The child's grammar from one to three. In J. Hill (ed.), *Minnesota Symposia on Child Psychology, Vol. 2,* Minneapolis: University of Minnesota Press, 1969, 28–73.

Bruner, J. Child development: Play is serious business. *Psychology Today,* January 1975, 81–83.

Bruner, J. *Processes of Cognitive Growth: Infancy.* Heinz Werner Lecture Series No. 3. Worcester, Massachusetts: Clark University Press with Barre Publishers, 1968, 35–64.

Bruner, J. *Toward a Theory of Instruction.* Cambridge, Massachusetts: Harvard University Press, 1966.

Bruner, J. The course of cognitive growth. *American Psychologist,* 1964, 19, 1–15.

Bryan, J., and N. Walbek. Preaching and practicing generosity. *Child Development,* 1970, 41, 329–353.

Buhler, C. The course of human life as a psychological problem. *Human Development,* 1968, 11, 184–200.

Buhler, C. The developmental structure of goal setting in group and individual studies. In C. Buhler and F. Massarik (eds.) *The Course of Human Life.* New York: Springer, 1962.

Burnside, I. The later decades of life: Research and reflections. In I. Burnside (ed.), *Psychosocial Caring Throughout the Lifespan.* New York: McGraw-Hill, 1979.

Burnside, I. Depression and suicide in the aged. In I. Burnside (ed.), *Nursing and the Aged.* New York: McGraw-Hill, 1976, 165–181.

Burton, S., J. Calonico, and D. McSeveney. Effects of preschool television watching on first grade children. *Journal of Communication,* 1978, 29, 164–170.

Bushway, A., and W. Nash. School cheating behavior.

Review of Educational Research, Fall 1977, 47(4) 623–632.

Busse, E. Psychopathology. In J. Birren, *Handbook of Aging and the Individual.* Chicago: University of Chicago Press, 1959, 389–391.

Butler, N., and D. Alberman. High risk predictors at booking and in pregnancy. *Second Report of the British Perinatal Mortality Survey, Perinatal Problems.* London: E. and S. Livingstone, 1969.

Butler, R., and M. Lewis. Aging and Mental Health. *Positive Psychosocial Approaches* (2nd. ed.), St. Louis: C. V. Mosby, 1973.

Bynum, J., B. Cooper, and F. Acuff. Retirement reorientation: Senior adult education. *Journal of Gerontology,* 1978, 33(2), 250–253.

Cain, C., and A. Weininger. Economic determinants of fertility: Results from cross-sectional aggregate data. *Demography,* 1973, 10, 205–223.

Caldwell, B., L. Hersher, E. Lipton, J. Richmond, G. Stern, E. Eddy, R. Drachman, and A. Rothman. Mother–infant interaction in monomatric and polymatric families. *American Journal of Orthopsychiatry,* 33 (4), 1973, 653–664.

Call, V., and L. Otto. Age of marriage as a mobility contingency: Estimates for the Nye-Berardo model. *Journal of Marriage and the Family,* 1977, 39, 67–79.

Campbell, P. Adolescent intellectual decline. *Adolescence,* Winter 1976, XI(44), 629–635.

Carey, G. Sex differences in problem-solving performance as a function of attitude differences. *Journal of Abnormal and Social Psychology,* 1958, 56, 156–160.

Carey, R. Weathering widowhood: Problems and adjustment of the widowed during the first year. *Omega,* 1979–1980, 10(2) 163–173.

Carey, R. The widowed: A year later. *Journal of Counseling Psychology,* 1977, 24(2), 125–131.

Carey, W. Maternal anxiety and infantile colic: Is there a relationship? *Clinical Pediatrics,* 1968, 7, 590–595.

Carroll, J., and J. Carroll (eds.). *Language, Thought, and Reality: Selected Writings of Benjamin Lee Whorf.* Cambridge, Massachusetts: MIT Press, 1956.

Carter, H., and P. Glick. *Marriage and Divorce: A So-*

cial and Economic Study. Cambridge, Massachusetts: Harvard University Press, 1976.

Casler, L. Maternal deprivation: A critical review of the literature. *Monographs of the Society for Research in Child Development,* 1961, 26 (2, Whole No. 80).

Cavan, R. *The American Family.* New York: Crowell, 1963.

Center for Disease Control. *Morbidity and Mortality Weekly Report,* Annual Summary, 1979.

Cerra, F. Study finds college women still aim for traditional jobs. *New York Times,* May 11, 1980, A46.

Chen, H., and O. Irwin. Infant speech vowel and consonant types. *Journal of Speech Disorders II,* 1946, 27–29.

Cherry F., and E. Eaton. Physical and cognitive development in children of low income mothers working in the child's early years. *Child Development,* 1977, 48(1), 158–166.

Chesler, J. Twenty-seven strategies for teaching contraception to adolescents. *Journal of School Health,* January 1980, 18.

Chess, S., A. Thomas, and H. Birch. Behavioral problems revisited. In S. Chess and H. Birch (eds.), *Annual Progress in Child Psychiatry and Child Development.* New York: Brunner/Mazel, 1968, 335–344.

Child, I., and J. Whiting. Determinants of level of aspiration. *Journal of Abnormal and Social Psychology,* 1949, 44, 303–314.

Chomsky, N. *Language and Mind.* New York: Harcourt, Brace and World, 1972.

Chomsky, N. *Aspects of the Theory of Syntax.* Cambridge, Massachusetts: MIT Press, 1965.

Chomsky, N. A review of verbal behavior by B. F. Skinner. *Language,* 1959, 35, 26–58.

Chomsky, N. *Syntactic Structures.* The Hague, Netherlands: Mouton, 1957.

Church, J. *Language and the Discovery of Reality.* New York: Vintage, 1966.

Chwast, J. Sociopathic behavior in children. In B. Wolman (ed.), *Manual of Child Psychopathology.* New York: McGraw-Hill, 1972, 436–445.

Citizens' Board of Inquiry into Hunger and Malnutrition in the United States. *Hunger USA (A Report).* Boston: Beacon Press, 1968.

Clark, D. *The Psychology of Education.* New York: Free Press, 1967.

Clark, M., M. Gosnell, and M. Reese. The sex-therapy revolution. *Newsweek,* November 17, 1980, 97–99.

Clarke-Stewart, K. Interactions between mothers and their young children: Characteristics and consequences. *Monographs of the Society for Research in Child Development,* 1973, 38(1), 153.

Clausen, J. Glimpses into the social world of middle age. *International Journal of Aging and Human Development,* 1976, 7(2), 99–106.

Clayton, R., and H. Voss. Shacking up: Cohabitation in the 1970's. *Journal of Marriage and the Family,* May 1977, 39, 273–283.

Cohen, D. Donald Hebb: An inside look at aging. *American Psychological Association Monitor,* February 1980, 4–5.

Cohen, J. High school subcultures and the adult world. *Adolescence,* Fall 1979, XIV (55), 491–502.

Cohen, L., and J. Campos. Father, mother and stranger as elicitors of attachment behavior in infancy. *Developmental Psychology,* 1974, 10, 155–162.

Cohen, S. Maternal employment and mother–child interaction. *Merrill-Palmer Quarterly,* 1978, 24(3) 189–197.

Cohen, S., and A. Sussman. The incidence of child abuse in the United States. *Child Welfare,* 1975, 54, 432–443.

Cohen, Y. The disappearance of the incest taboo. *Human Nature,* 1978, 1, 72–78.

Cole, M., and J. Bruner. Cultural differences and inferences about psychological processes. *National Society for the Study of Education Yearbook on Early Childhood Education,* 1972.

Cole, N. Studies of recent declines in test scores. Symposium presented at the Northeastern Educational Research Association, Ellenville, New York, October 1977.

Cole, S. Hyperkinetic children: The use of stimulant drugs evaluated. *American Journal of Orthopsychiatry,* January 1975, 45 (1), 28–35.

Coleman, J., and W. Broen, Jr. *Abnormal Psychology and Modern Life.* Glenview, Illinois: Scott, Foresman, 1972.

Coles, R., *et al.* Hearing before the U.S. Senate Subcommittee, July 1967. In *Hunger and Malnutri-*

tion in America. Washington, D.C.: U.S. Printing Office, 1967.

Collard, R. Exploratory and play behaviors of infants reared in an institution and in lower- and middle-class homes. *Child Development,* 1971, 42, 1003–1015.

Collins, G. Father. *New York Times Magazine,* June 17, 1979, 31–66.

Collins, J., and J. Harper. Problems of adolescents in Sydney, Australia. *The Journal of Genetic Psychology,* 1974, 125, 187–194.

Comfort, A. *Aging: The Biology of Senescence.* New York: Holt, Rinehart and Winston, 1964.

Condry, J., and S. Dyer. Fear of success: Attribution of cause to the victim. *Journal of Social Issues,* 1976, 32(3) 63–80.

Connell, D. *Individual Differences in Attachment: An Investigation into Stability, Implications, and Relationships to the Structure of Early Language Development.* Syracuse University, Unpublished Doctoral Dissertation, 1976.

Constantine, L., and J. Constantine. *Group Marriage.* New York: Collier Books, 1974.

Cooper, J. Application of the consultant role to parent–teacher management of school avoidance behavior. *Psychology in the Schools,* 1973, 10, 259–262.

Coopersmith, S. *The Antecedents of Self-Esteem.* San Francisco: Freeman, 1967.

Cornelius, S., and N. Denney. Dependency in daycare and homecare children. *Developmental Psychology,* 1975, 11(5), 575–582.

Costanzo, P., and M. Shaw. Conformity as a function of age level. *Child Development,* 1966, 37, 967–975.

Costello, C. Childhood depression. *Psychological Bulletin,* 1980, 87, 185–190.

Cox, R. *Youth into Maturity: A Study of Men and Women in the First Ten Years After College.* New York: Mental Health Materials Center, 1970.

Cragg, B. Plasticity of synapses. *British Medical Bulletin,* May 1974, 30(2), 141–144.

Craik, F. Age differences in human memory. In J. Birren and K. Schaie (eds.), *The Handbook of the Psychology of Aging.* New York: Van Nostrand Reinhold, 1977.

Cramer, J. Employment trends of young mothers and the opportunity cost of babies in the United States. *Demography,* 1979, 16(2), 177–197.

Crandall, R. *Gerontology: A Behavioral Science Approach.* Reading, Massachusetts: Addison-Wesley, 1980.

Cratty, B. *Perceptual and Motor Development in Infants and Children.* Engelwood-Cliffs, New Jersey: Prentice-Hall, 1979.

Cravioto, J. Symposium presented at the Meeting of the American Association for the Advancement of Science. Boston, December 1969.

Crawford, J. Career development and career choice in pioneer and traditional women. *Journal of Vocational Behavior,* 1978, 12, 129–139.

Cross, M. *The Effects of Normal and Atypical Infants on Maternal Attitudes and Expectations.* Unpublished Ph.D. Dissertation, University of South Florida, 1978.

Crow, J. Genetic theories and influences: Comments on the value of diversity. *Harvard Educational Review,* 1969, 39, 301–309.

Culbertson, F. An effective low-cost approach to the treatment of descriptive school children. *Psychology in the Schools,* 1974, 11, 183–187.

Cumming, E. New thoughts on the theory of disengagement. In R. Kastenbaum (ed.), *New Thoughts on Old Age.* New York: Springer 1964.

Cumming, E., and W. Henry. *Growing Old: The Process of Disengagement.* New York: Basic Books, 1961.

Curran, B. *Getting by With a Little Help From My Friends: Informal Networks Among Older Black and White Urban Women Below the Poverty Line.* Ph.D. Dissertation, University of Arizona, 1978.

Dale, D. *Language Development.* Hinsdale, Illinois: Dryden Press, 1972.

Darwin, C. A biographical sketch of an infant. *MIND* 1887, 2, 285–294.

Dasen, P. (ed.). *Piagetian Psychology: Cross-cultural Contributions.* New York: Garden Press, 1977.

David, H., and W. Baldwin. Childbearing and child development. *American Psychologist,* October 1979, 34(10), 866–871.

DeGuimps, R. *Pestalozzi, His Life and Work.* New York: Appleton-Century-Crofts, 1906.

DeLamater, J., and P. MacCorquodale. *Premarital Sexuality: Attitudes, Relationships, Behavior.* Madison, Wisconsin: University of Wisconsin Press, 1979.

deLissovoy, V. High school marriages: A longitudinal study. *Journal of Marriage and the Family,* 1973, 35, 245–285.

Demming, J., and S. Pressey. Tests indigenous to the adult and older years. *Journal of Counseling Psychology,* 1957, 4, 144–148.

DeMott, B. Culture watch. *Atlantic Monthly,* September 1977, 86–88.

Dennis, W. Creative productivity between the ages of 20 and 80 years. *Journal of Gerontology,* 1966, 21, 1–8.

Dennis, W., and P. Najarian. Infant development under environmental handicap. *Psychological Monographs,* 1957, 71(7), 1–13.

DePaulo, B., and J. Bonvillian. The effect on language development of the special characteristics of speech addressed to children. *Journal of Psycholinguistic Research,* 1978, 7(3), 189–210.

Deutscher, I. The quality of post parental life: Definitions of the situation. *Journal of Marriage and the Family,* 1964, 26, 52–59.

Devereux, E. Authority and moral development among German and American children: A cross-national pilot experiment. *Journal of Comparative Family Studies,* 1972, 3, 99–124.

Diamond, M., and A. Karlen. *Sexual Decisions.* Boston: Little, Brown 1980.

Dick-Read, G. *Childbirth Without Fear.* New York: Harper and Row, 1953.

Diepold, J., and R. Young. Empirical studies of adolescent sexual behavior: A critical review. *Adolescence,* Spring 1979, XIV(53) 45–65.

Digges, J. *Psychosocial Stress as a Factor in the Assessment of Risk in Pregnancy.* University of Oklahoma Health Sciences Center, 1978.

Dimitrovsky, L., and M. Almy. Linkages among concrete operations. *Genetic Psychology Monographs,* 1975, 92, 213–229.

Dion, K., and S. Stein. Physical attractiveness and interpersonal influence. *Journal of Experimental Social Psychology,* 1978, 14, 97–108.

Dishotsky, N., R. Loughman, R. Mogar, and W. Lipscomb. LSD and genetic damage. *Science,* April 30, 1971, 431–440.

Divoky, D. Can diet cure the LD child? *Learning,* March 1978, 6(7), 56–57.

Dobbing, J., and J. Smart. Vulnerability of the developing brain and behavior. *British Medical Bulletin,* May 1974, 30(2), 164–168.

Doberstyn, J. *The Effects of Education, Social Background and Job Satisfaction Factors on Attitudes Toward Job Change and Career Change.* Ph.D. Dissertation, University of Michigan, 1978.

Doggett, L. Hospice vs. hospital. *The Plain Dealer,* May 25, 1980, 25.

Dohrenwend, B., and B. Dohrenwend (eds.). *Stressful Life Events, Their Nature and Effects.* New York: John Wiley and Sons, 1974.

Douvan, E., and J. Adelson. *The Adolescent Experience.* New York: John Wiley and Sons, 1960.

Downing, J. Bilingualism and learning to read. *The Irish Journal of Education,* 1974, 8(2) 77–88.

Doyle, G., and R. Freedman. Anxiety in children: Some observations for the school psychologist. *Psychology in the Schools,* 1974, 11, 161–164.

Driscoll, J., Jr. Infants of addicted mothers. In R. Behrman (ed.), *Neonatology.* St. Louis: C.V. Mosby, 1973, 450–452.

Duberman, L. *Marriage and its Alternatives.* New York: Praeger, 1974.

Dubos, R. Introduction. In N. Cousins, *Anatomy of an Illness,* New York: Bantam Books, 1981, 11–23.

Duke, D., and C. Perry. Can alternative schools succeed where Benjamin Spock, Spiro Agnew and B. F. Skinner have failed? *Adolescence,* Fall 1978, XIII(51), 375–391.

Durran, W., J. Smhyg, and H. Beecher. Experimentation in children: A re-examination of legal ethical principles. *Journal of the American Medical Association,* 1969, 10(1), 77–83.

Dyer, E. *The American Family, Variety and Change.* New York: McGraw-Hill, 1979.

Dyer, E. Parenthood as a crisis: A re-study. *Marriage and Family Living,* 1963, 25,196–201.

Dykeman, B. Teenage alcoholism—detecting those early warning signals. *Adolescence,* 1979, XIV(54), 251–253.

Ebersole, P. The vital vehicle: The body. In I. Burnside, P. Ebersole, and H. Monea (eds.), *Psychosocial Caring Throughout the Life Span.* New York: McGraw-Hill, 1979.

Edwards, C. Users' guide to USDA estimates of the cost of raising a child. *Family Economics Review,* Summer 1979, 3–15.

Eichenwald, H., and P. Fry. Nutrition and learning. *Science,* 1969, 163, 644–648.

Eiduson, B. Looking at children in emergent family styles. *Children Today,* 1974, 4, 2–6.

Eiduson, B., and J. Alexander. The role of children in the alternative family. *Journal of Social Issues,* 1978, 34(2), 149–167.

Eiduson, B., J. Cohen, and J. Alexander. Alternatives in childrearing in the 1970's. *American Journal of Orthopsychiatry,* 1973, 43, 720–731.

Eisdorfer, C., and E. Wilkie. Stress, disease, aging and behavior. In J. Birren and K. Schaie (eds.), *Handbook of the Psychology of Aging.* New York: Van Nostrand Reinhold, 1976.

Eisenberg, L. The intervention of biological and experiential factors in schizophrenia. In D. Rosenthal and S. Kety (eds.), *The Transmission of Schizophrenia.* London: Pergamon, 1968, 403–412.

Eisenberg-Berg, N., and P. Mussen. Empathy and moral development in adolescence. *Developmental Psychology,* 1978, 14(2), 185–186.

Eisenstadt, S. Archetypal patterns of youth. *Daedalus,* 1962, 91, 28–46.

Elder, G. *Adolescent Socialization and Personality Development.* Chicago: Rand McNally, 1968.

Elkind, D. *A Sympathetic Understanding of the Child Six to Sixteen.* Boston: Allyn and Bacon, 1971.

Elkind, D. Erik Erikson's eight stages of man. *New York Times Magazine,* April 5, 1970.

Elkind, D. Piaget and Montessori. *Harvard Educational Review,* 1968, 38, 335–545.

Elkind, D. Egocentrism in adolescence. *Child Development,* 1967, 38, 1025–1034.

Elkind, D. Children's discovery of the conservation of mass, weight, and volume. Piaget replication study II. *Journal of Genetic Psychology* 1961a, 98, 219–227.

Elkind, D. The development of the additive composition of classes in the child. Piaget replication study III. *Journal of Genetic Psychology* 1961b, 99, 51–57.

Elkind, D. The child's conception of right and left. Piagetian replication study V. *Journal of Genetic Psychology* 1961c, 99, 269–276.

Ellison, D. Alienation and the will to live. *Journal of Gerontology,* 1969, 24, 361–367.

Eme, R. Sex differences in childhood psychopathology. *Psychological Bulletin,* 1979, 86(3) 573–595.

Eme, R., R. Maisiak, and W. Goodale. Seriousness of adolescent problems. *Adolescence,* Spring 1979, XIV(53), 93–99.

Ende, R., and R. Harmon. Endogenous and exogenous smiling systems in early infancy. *Journal of the American Academy of Child Psychiatry,* 1972, 11, 177–200.

Endsley, R., and S. Clarey. Answering young children's questions as a determinant of their subsequent question-asking behavior. *Developmental Psychology,* 1975, 6, 863.

Englehardt, H. Treating aging: Restructuring the human condition. Seminar on Social Policy, Social Ethics and an Aging Society. Washington, D.C.: U. S. Printing Office, 1976, 33–39.

Englund, S. Birth without violence. *New York Times Magazine,* December 8, 1974.

Erikson, E. *Identity: Youth and Crisis.* New York: Norton, 1968.

Erikson, E. *Childhood and Society* (2nd ed.) New York: Norton, 1963.

Erikson, E. Identity and the life cycle. *Psychological Issues,* 1959, 1, 18–172.

Erlanger, H. Social class and corporal punishment in childrearing: A reassessment. *American Sociological Review,* 1974, 39, 68–85.

Ernst, P., B. Biran, F. Safford, and M. Kleinhauz. Isolation and the symptoms of chronic brain syndrome. *Gerontologist,* 1978, 18, 468–474.

Eron, L., L. Huesmann, M. Lefkowitz, and L. Walder. How learning conditions in early childhood—including mass media—relate to aggression in late adolescence. *American Journal of Orthopsychiatry,* April 1974, 44(3).

Eron, L., L. Huesmann, M. Lefkowitz, and L. Walder.

Does television violence cause aggression? *American Psychologist,* 1972, 27, 253–263.

Espenshade, T. J. Raising A Child Can Now Cost $85,000. *Intercom,* September 1980, 8(9), Washington, D.C.: Population Reference Bureau, 1, 10–12.

Etaugh, C. Effects of maternal employment on children: A review of recent research. *Merrill-Palmer Quarterly,* 1974, 20, 71–98.

Evans, W. The behavior problem checklist: Data from an inner city population. *Psychology in the Schools,* 1975, 12, 300–303.

Exton-Smith, A., and J. Evans (eds.). *Care of the Elderly: Meeting the Challenge of Dependency.* New York: Academic Press, 1977.

Eysenck, H. *The IQ Argument: Race, Intelligence and Education.* New York: Library Press, 1971.

Fabe, M., and N. Winkler. *Up Against the Clock: Career Women Speak on the Choice to Have Children.* New York: Random House, 1979.

Fact-file: College degrees awarded in 1979. *Chronicle of Higher Education,* November 17, 1980, 14.

Faigin, H. Social behavior of young children in the kibbutz. *Journal of Abnormal and Social Psychology,* 1958, 56, 117–129.

Fantz, R. A method for studying depth perception in infants under six months of age. *Psychological Record,* 1961a, 11, 27–32.

Fantz, R. The origin of form perception. *Scientific American,* 1961, 204, 10.

Fantz, R., and S. Nevis. The predictive value of changes in visual preferences in early infancy. In J. Hellmuth (ed.), *Exceptional Infant Vol. 1: The Normal Infant.* New York: Brunner/Mazel, 1967, 351–414.

Farmer, W. No paddle bawl in Sweden. *Parade,* March 16, 1980, 24–26.

Fein, G., and K. Clarke-Stewart. *Day Care in Context.* New York: Interscience, 1973.

Feingold, B. *Why Your Child Is Hyperactive.* New York: Random House, 1975a.

Feingold, B. Hyperkinesis and learning disabilities linked to artificial food flavors and colors. *American Journal of Nursing,* May 1975b, 75(5), 797–803.

Feld, S., D. Ruhland, and M. Gold. Developmental changes in achievement motivation. *Merrill-Palmer Quarterly,* 1979, 25(1), 43–60.

Felner, R. *An Investigation of Crisis in Childhood: Effects and Outcomes in Children Experiencing Parental Death or Divorce.* Unpublished Ph.D. Dissertation. The University of Rochester, 1977.

Felner, R., and R. Francis. Relationships between family background problems and school problems and competencies of young normal children. *Psychology in the Schools,* April 1978, 15(2) 283–290.

Fengel, A. Attitudinal orientations of wives toward their husbands' retirement. *International Journal of Aging and Human Development,* 1975, 6(2), 139–148.

Fenichel, O. *The Psychoanalytic Theory of Neurosis.* New York: Norton, 1965.

Feshbach, S. Aggression. In P. Mussen (ed.), *Carmichael's Manual of Child Psychology* (3d ed.). New York: John Wiley and Sons, 1970.

Fillenbaum, G. Retirement planning programs: At what age and for whom? *Gerontologist,* 1971, 11(1) 33–36.

Finch, C. Biological theories of aging. In I. Burnside (ed.), *Nursing and the Aged.* New York: McGraw-Hill, 1976, 92–98.

Finkelhor, D. *Sexually Victimized Children.* New York: Free Press, 1980.

Fisbe, E. Colleges are finding their honor systems short on honor. *New York Times,* October 11, 1975.

Flanagan, G. *The First Nine Months of Life.* New York: Simon & Schuster, 1962.

Flaste, R. Survey finds that most children are happy at home but fear world. *New York Times,* March 2, 1977, A12.

Flavell, J. Cognitive changes in adulthood. In L. Goulet and P. Baltes (eds.), *Lifespan Developmental Psychology: Research and Theory.* New York: Academic Press, 1970.

Flavell, J. *The Developmental Psychology of Jean Piaget.* Princeton, New Jersey: Van Nostrand Reinhold, 1963.

Flavell, S., and J. Wohwill. Formal and functional aspects of cognitive development. In D. Elkind and J. Flavell (eds.), *Studies in Cognitive Development.* New York: Oxford University Press, 1969.

Fletcher, A. The infant of the diabetic mother. In G. Avery (ed.), *Neonatology.* Philadelphia: Lippincott, 1975.

Flint, J. The old folks. *Forbes,* February 18, 1980, 51–56.

Florida State Department of Education, Division of Elementary and Secondary Education. *District Procedures for Providing Special Education for Exceptional Students: 1974 Guidelines,* 1974, 2 (ERIC Document Reproduction Service No. ED 087 164).

Fouts, G., and P. Liikanen. The effects of age and developmental level on imitation in children. *Child Development,* 1975, 46, 555–558.

Fouts, R. Use of guidance in teaching sign language to a chimpanzee. (Pan Troglodytes.) *Journal of Comparative and Physiological Psychology,* 1972, 80, 515–522.

Fraiberg, S. *The Magic Years.* New York: Scribner's, 1959.

Francoeur, R., and A. Francoeur. Hot and cool sex: Fidelity in marriage. In R. Libby and R. Whitehurst, *Renovating Marriage.* Danville, California: Consensus Pubishers, 1973.

Frankenburg, W., and J. Dodds. *Denver Developmental Screening Test.* Boulder, Colorado: University of Colorado Medical Center, 1969.

Freedman, D. Ethnic differences in babies. *Human Nature,* January 1979, 36–43.

Freedman, R., and B. Berelson. The human population. *Scientific American,* 1974, 231(3), 31–39.

Freedman, R., and G. Doyle. Depression in children. *Psychology in the Schools* 1974, 11, 19–23.

Freud, A., and D. T. Burlingame. *Infants without Families.* New York: International Universities Press, 1944.

Freud, A., and D. T. Burlingame. *War and Children* New York: International Universities Press, 1943.

Freud, S. Three essays on the theory of sexuality. In *The Complete Psychological Works of Sigmund Freud* (Standard Edition), 1905, Vol. 5, Reprint, London: Hogarth Press, 1953.

Freyberg, J. Hold high the cardboard sword. *Psychology Today,* February, 1975, 63–64.

Friday, N. *My Mother My Self.* New York: Delacorte Press, 1977.

Friedan, B. Feminism takes a new turn. *New York Times Magazine,* November 18, 1979, 40–106.

Friedman, W. The development of children's understanding of cyclic aspects of time. *Child Development,* 1977, 48, 1593–1599.

Friedrich, L., and A. Stein. Aggressive and prosocial television programs and the natural behavior of preschool children. *Monographs of the Society for Research in Child Development,* 1973, 38 (4, Serial No. 151).

Frieze, I. Women's expectations for and causal attributions of success and failure. In M. Mednick, S. Tangri, and L. Hoffman, *Women and Achievement: Social Psychological Perspectives.* New York: Holt, Rinehart and Winston, 1974.

Furstenberg, F. *Unplanned parenthood: The social consequences of teenage childbearing.* New York: Free Press, 1976.

Furstenberg, F. Reflections on remarriage. *Journal of Family Issues,* 1980, 1(4), 443–453.

Gagne, R. Contributions of learning to human development. *Psychological Review,* 1968, 75, 17–191.

Gagnon, J. *Human Sexuality.* Glenview, Illinois: Scott, Foresman, 1977.

Garbarino, J., and A. Crouter. Defining the community context for parent-child relations: The correlates of child maltreatment. *Child Development,* 1978, 49, 604–616.

Gardner, D., G. Hawkes, and L. Burchinal. Noncontinuous mothering in infancy and development in later childhood. *Child Development,* 1961, 32, 225–234.

Gass, G. Equitable marriage. *The Family Coordinator,* 23, October 1974, 369–372.

Geber, M. The psycho-motor development of African children in the first year, and the influence of maternal behavior. *Journal of Social Psychology,* 1958, 47, 185–195.

Gecas, V., and F. Nye. Sex and class differences in parent–child interactions: A test of Kohn's hypothesis. *Journal of Marriage and the Family,* November 1974, 36, 742–749.

Gelles, R., and M. Straus. Violence in the American family. *Journal of Social Issues,* 1979, 35(2), 15–39.

Gelman, R. Preschool thought. *American Psychologist,* 1979, 34(10), 900–905.

Genetics Research Group of the Hastings Center, Institute of Society, Ethics, and Life Sciences. *Guidelines for Ethical, Social, and Legal Issues in Prenatal Diagnosis.* Hastings-on-Hudson, New York, 1979.

Gentile, A. A working model of skill acquisition with application for teaching. *Quest,* 1972, 17, 1–23.

Georgiady, N., and L. Romano. Ulcerville, USA. *Educational Leadership,* December 1971, 29(3), 269–272.

Giacoia, G., and S. Yaffee. Drugs and the perinatal patient. In G. Avery (ed.), *Neonatology.* Philadelphia: Lippincott, 1975.

Gibson, E. The development of perception as an adaptive process. *American Scientist,* 1970, 58, 98–107.

Gibson, E. *Principles of Perceptual Learning and Development.* New York: Appleton-Century-Crofts, 1969.

Gibson, E. Learning to read. *Science,* 1965, 148, 1066–1072.

Gibson, E. Perceptual learning in educational situations. In R. Gagne and W. Gephart (eds.), *Learning, Research, and School Subjects,* Itasca, Illinois: Peacock, 1968.

Gibson, E., and R. Walk. The visual cliff. *Scientific American,* April 1960, 202(4), 80–92.

Gibson, J. *Psychology for the Classroom* (2nd. ed.). Englewood Cliffs, New Jersey: Prentice-Hall, 1981.

Gibson, J. The special child: A cross-cultural view of special education in the US and USSR. *Phi Delta Kappan,* December 1980, 264–267.

Gibson, J. *Growing Up: A Study of Children.* Reading, Massachusetts: Addison-Wesley, 1978.

Gibson, J. *Educational Psychology* (2nd. ed.). New York: Appleton-Century-Crofts, 1972.

Gibson, J., K. Wurst, and M. Cannonito. Observations on contact stimulation provided young children in selected areas of Greece, U.S.A., and USSR. In press, accepted by *International Journal of Psychology,* 1982.

Gibson, J., and E. Vinogradoff. *Growing Up in Moscow,* Unpublished manuscript, 1981.

Giele, J. Changes in the modern family: Their impact on sex role. *American Journal of Orthopsychiatry,* 1971, 41, 757–765.

Gilligan, J. Beyond morality: Psychoanalytic reflections on shame, guilt, and love. In T. Lickona (ed.), *Moral Development and Behavior.* New York: Holt, Rinehart, and Winston, 1976.

Gilmartin, B. Swinging: Who gets involved and how. In R. Libby and R. Whitehurst (eds.), *Marriage and Alternatives.* North Scituate, Massachusetts: Duxbury Press, 1977.

Giovannoni, J., and R. Becerra. *Defining Child Abuse.* New York: Free Press, 1980.

Glamser, F. Determinants of a positive attitude toward retirement. *Journal of Gerontology,* 1976, 31(1), 104–107.

Glaser, B. The social loss of aged dying patients. *The Gerontologist,* 1966, 6, 77–80.

Glaser, R., and L. Resnick. Instructional psychology. In P. Mussen and M. Rosenzweig (eds.), *Annual Review of Psychology,* 1972, 23, 207–276

Glass, S., and T. Wright. The relationship of extramarital sex, length of marriage, and sex differences on marital satisfaction and romanticism. *Journal of Marriage and the Family,* 1977, 39, 691–704.

Glenn, N. The contribution of marriage to the pychological well-being of males and females. *Journal of Marriage and the Family,* August 1975, 37, 594–600.

Glenn, N., and C. Weaver. The marital happiness of remarried divorced persons. *Journal of Marriage and the Family,* May 1977, 39, 331–337.

Glick, I., R. Weiss, and C. Parkes. *The First Year of Bereavement.* New York: John Wiley and Sons, 1974.

Glick, P. A demographic look at American families. *Journal of Marriage and the Family,* 1975, 37, 15–26.

Glick, P. The life cycle of the family. *Marriage and Family Living,* February 1955, XVII, 3–9.

Glick, P., and A. Norton. Marrying, divorcing, and living together in the U.S. today. *Population Bulletin.* Washington, D.C.: Population Reference Bureau, Inc., 1977, 32(5).

Goetting, A. The normative integration of the former spouse relationship. *Journal of Divorce,* 1979, 2, 395–414.

Goggin, J. Dependency, imitation learning, and the

process of identification. *Journal of Genetic Psychology,* 1974, 124, 207–217.

Gold, D., and D. Andres. Developmental comparisons between ten-year-old children with employed and non-employed mothers. *Child Development,* 1978, 49, 75–84.

Goldenson, R. *The Encyclopedia of Human Behavior.* Garden City, New York: Doubleday, 1970.

Goldings, H. Development from ten to thirteen years. In J. Noshpitz (ed.), *Basic Handbook of Child Psychiatry.* New York: Basic Books, 1979, 199–205.

Golick, M. *A Parent's Guide to Learning Problems.* Montreal: Quebec Association for Children with Learning Disabilities, 1970.

Good, E. Marijuana and the politics of reality. *Journal of Health and Social Behavior,* 1969, 10, 83–94.

Goodman, B., and N. Goodman. Effects of parent orientation meetings on parent-child communication about sexuality and family life. *The Family Coordinator,* July 1976, 25, 285–290.

Gordon, C. Social characteristics of early adolescence. *Daedalus,* 1971, 100, 931–960.

Gordon, I. Early Child Stimulation Through Parent Education. Final Report to the Children's Bureau for Development of Human Resources. Gainesville, Florida: College of Education, University of Florida, 1969.

Gordon, S. Why sex education belongs in the home. *PTA Magazine,* February 1974.

Gorsuch, R., and M. Key. Abnormalities of pregnancy as a function of anxiety and life stress. *Psychosomatic Medicine,* July–August 1974, 36.

Goslin, P. Accuracy of self-perception and social acceptance. *Sociometry,* 1962, 25, 283–296.

Gottfredson, L. Aspiration–job match: Age trends in a large, nationally representative sample of young white men. *Journal of Counseling Psychology,* 1979, 26(4), 319–328.

Gottman, J., J. Gonso, and B. Rasmussen. Social interaction, social competence, and friendship in children. *Child Development,* 1975, 46, 709–718.

Gotz, I. On children and television. *Elementary School Journal,* 1975, 75(7), 415–418.

Gould, R. *Transformations, Growth, and Change in Adult Life.* New York: Simon & Schuster, 1978.

Gould, R. The phases of adult life: A study in developmental psychology. *American Journal of Psychiatry,* 1972, 129, 521–531.

Graham, F., R. Matarazzo, and B. Caldwell. Behavioral differences between normal and traumatized newborns. *Psychological Monographs,* 1956, 70(5).

Granick, S. Psychological test functioning. In S. Granick and R. Patterson (eds.), *Human Aging II: An 11 year Follow-Up.* Washington, D.C.: U.S. Department of Health, Education and Welfare, 1971.

Graves, P. Infant behavior and maternal attitudes: Early sex differences in West Bengal, India. *Journal of Cross-Cultural Psychology,* 1976, 7, 223–234.

Green, A. Child abuse. In G. Wolman, J. Egan, and A. Ross (eds.), *Handbook of Treatment of Mental Disorders in Childhood and Adolescence.* Englewood-Cliffs, New Jersey: Prentice-Hall, 1978, 430–455.

Gregory, J. Fitness in diapers called healthy idea. *Pittsburgh Press,* March 26, 1979, A14.

Grof, S., and J. Halifax. *The Human Encounter with Death.* New York: E. P. Dutton, 1977.

Grossberg, S., and L. Crandall. Father loss and father absence in preschool children. *Clinical Social Work Journal,* 1978, 6, 123–134.

Gruendel, J. Referential extension in early language development. *Child Development,* 1977, 48, 1567–1576.

Gubrium, J. Marital desolation and the evaluation of everyday life in old age. *Journal of Marriage and the Family,* February 1974, 36, 107–113.

Guidepost, House subcommittee hears Carter's youth initiative. *Newsletter of the American Personnel and Guidance Association,* March 20, 1980.

Guilford, J. Maturation of values in young children. *The Journal of Genetic Psychology,* 1974, 124, 241–248.

Guilford, J. Factors that aid and hinder creativity. *Teachers' College Record,* 1962, 63, 380–392.

Guilford, J. Creativity. *American Psychologist,* 1950, 9, 444–454.

Gullotta, T. Runaway: Reality or myth? *Adolescence,* Winter 1978, XIV(52), 543–549.

Gurdon, J. Transplanted nuclei and cell differentiation. *Scientific American,* 1968, 219(6) 24–36.

Gurin, G., J. Veroff, and S. Feld. *Americans View Their Mental Health*. New York: Basic Books, 1960.

Guthrie, G., Z. Masangkay, and H. Guthrie. Behavior, malnutrition and mental development. *Journal of Cross-Cultural Psychology,* June 1976, 7(2), 169–180.

Guyatt, D. *The One-Parent Family in Canada*. Ottowa: Vanier Institute, 1971.

Gwynne, P., S. Begley, and M. Hager. The secrets of DNA. *Newsweek Science Review,* August 20, 1979, 48–54.

Hacker, A. E.R.A.–R.I.P. *Harper's,* September 1980, 10–14.

Hacker, S. It isn't sex education unless. *Journal of School Health,* April 1981, 209.

Hafez, E. Reproductive life cycle. In E. Hafez and T. F⁓ans (eds.), *Human Reproduction: Conception and Contraception*. New York: Harper and Row, 1973.

Hall, C. *A Primer of Freudian Psychology*. New York: Mentor Books, 1954.

Hall, F., and D. Hall. *The Two-Career Couple*. Reading, Massachusetts: Addison-Wesley, 1979.

Hall, G. The contents of children's minds on entering school. *Pedogogical Seminary,* 1891, 1, 139–173.

Hall, V., and D. Kaye. Patterns of early cognitive development among boys in four subcultural groups. *Journal of Educational Psychology,* 1977, 69(1), 66–87.

Hallock, N., G. Ting, J. Dempsey, C. Daberi, and H. Shuman. A first year follow-up of high-risk infants: Formulating a cumulative risk index. *Child Development,* 1978, 49, 119–131.

Hardt, D. An investigation of the stages of bereavement. *Omega,* 1978–1979, 9(3), 279–285.

Hardy, C., and D. Nias. An investigation of physical personality factors involved in learning to swim. *Personality,* 1971, 2(1).

Haring, N. The new curriculum design in special education. In R. Burns and A. Brooks (eds.), *Curriculum Design in a Changing Society*. Englewood Cliffs, New Jersey: Educational Technology Publications, 1970, 159–184.

Haring, N., and D. Krug. Placement in regular programs: Procedures and results. *Exceptional Children,* 1975, 41, 413–417.

Harlow, H. The heterosexual affectional system in monkeys. *American Psychologist,* 1962, 17, 1–9.

Harlow, H. The nature of love. *American Psychologist,* 1958, 13, 673–685.

Harper, R. *Psychoanalysis and Psychotherapy*. New York: Jason Aronson, 1974.

Harrington, C., and J. Whiting. Socialization process and personality. In F. Hsu (ed.), *Psychological Anthropology* (2nd ed.). Cambridge, Massachusetts: Schenkman, 1972.

Harris, C. *Fact Book on Aging: A Profile of America's Older Population*. Washington, D.C.: National Council on Aging, 1978.

Harris, L., and Associates. *The Myth and Reality of Aging*. Washington, D.C.: National Council on the Aging, 1975.

Harter, S. Developmental differences in the manifestation of mastery motivation on problem-solving tasks. *Child Development,* 1975, 46, 370–378.

Hartshorne, H., *et al.* Testing the knowledge of right and wrong. *Religious Education Monographs,* 1927, 1, 72.

Hartup, W. Peer relations: Developmental implications and interaction in same and mixed-age situations. *Young Children,* 1977, 4–13.

Hartup, W., and E. Zook. Sex role preference in three- and four-year old children. *Journal of Consulting Psychology,* 1960, 24, 420–426.

Harvey, C., and C. Bahr. Widowhood, morale, and affiliation. *Journal of Marriage and the Family,* 1974, 36, 97–106.

Havighurst, P. *Developmental Tasks and Education* (2nd ed.). New York: Longman-Green, 1952.

Havighurst, R. Minority subcultures and the law of effect. *American Psychologist,* 1970, 25, 313–322.

Havighurst, R. Successful aging. *The Gerontologist,* 1961, 1, 8–13.

Havighurst, R., and B. Neugarten. *Society and Education* (3rd. ed.). Boston: Allyn and Bacon, 1967, 19.

Havighurst, R., and G. Sacher. Prospects of lengthening life and vigor. *Social Policy, Social Ethics, and an Aging Society*. Washington, D.C.. U.S. Printing Office, 1976, 13–18.

Hebb, D. A return to Jensen and his social science critics. *American Psychologist,* 1970, 25, 568.

Heckman, N., R. Bryson, and J. Bryson. Problems of

professional couples: A content analysis. *Journal of Marriage and the Family,* 1977, 39, 323–330.

Hedrick, T., and J. Chance. Sex differences in assertive achievement patterns. *Sex Roles,* 1977, 3(2), 129–139.

Heilbrun, A. An exploration of antecedents and attributes of androgynous and undifferentiated sex roles. *The Journal of Genetic Psychology,* 1978, 132, 97–107.

Henry, C., and M. Hiller. *Of Pure Blood.* A film documentary. Paris, France: Ageoco Franchaise d'Images. Presented on TV by Public Broadcasting Service, Washington, D.C., 1975.

Herrmann, R. Expectations and attitudes as a source of financial problems in teenage marriages. *Journal of Marriage and the Family,* 1965, 27, 89–91.

Herrnstein, R. IQ. In *The Atlantic,* September 1971, 228(3), 44–64.

Hess, R., and V. Shipman. Cognitive elements in maternal behavior. *Minnesota Symposium on Child Psychology,* Vol. 1. Minneapolis: University of Minnesota Press, 1967.

Hetherington, E., and B. Martin. Family interaction and psychopathology in children. In H. Quay and J. Werry (eds.), *Psychopathological Disorders of Childhood.* New York: John Wiley and Sons, 1972.

Hetherington, E., and R. Parke. *Child Psychology: A Contemporary Viewpoint.* New York: McGraw-Hill, 1975.

Hewitt, L. Age and sex differences in the vocational aspirations of elementary school children. *Journal of Social Psychology,* 1975, 97, 173–177.

Hilgard, E. The effects of early and delayed practice on memory and motor performances studied by the method of co-twin control. *Journal of Genetic Psychological Monographs,* 1933, 4, 493–497.

Hilgard, E., and G. Bower. *Theories of Learning* (4th ed.). New York: Appleton-Century-Crofts, 1975.

Hill, M. *The decision by young adults to split off from their parental households.* Ph.D. Dissertation, University of Michigan, 1977.

Hillenbrand, E. Father absence in military families. *The Family Coordinator,* October 1976, 451–457.

Hirschhorn, L. Social policy and the life cycle: A developmental perspective. *Social Service Review,* 1977, 51, 434–450.

Hofferth, S. Day care in the next decade: 1980–1990. *Journal of Marriage and the Family,* August 1979, 649–657.

Hoffman, L. Maternal employment: 1979. *American Psychologist,* October 1970, 34(10) 859–865.

Hoffman, L. The value of children to parents and the decrease in family size. *Proceedings of the American Philosophical Society,* 1975, 119(6), 430–438.

Hoffman, L., and J. Manis. The value of children in the United States: A new approach to the study of fertility. *Journal of Marriage and the Family,* August 1979, 39, 583–596.

Hoffman, L., A. Thornton, and J. Manis. The value of children to parents in the United States. *Population: Behavioral, Social and Environmental Issues,* 1978, 1(2), 91–131.

Hoffman, L., and M. Hoffman. The value of children to parents. In J. Fawcett (ed.), *Psychological Perspective on Population.* New York: Basic Books, 1973.

Hoffman, M., and H. Saltzstein. Parent discipline and the child's moral development. *Journal of Personality and Social Psychology,* 1967, 5(1), 45–57.

Holland, J. *Making Vocational Choices: A Theory of Careers.* Englewood-Cliffs, New Jersey: Prentice-Hall, 1973.

Holly, W., A. Rosenbaum, and J. Churchill. Effects of rapid succession of pregnancy. In Pan American Health Organization, *Perinatal Factors Affecting Human Development.* Washington, D.C.: World Health Organization, 1969.

Holmes, T., and R. Rahe. The social readjustment rating scale. *Journal of Psychosomatic Research,* 1967, 11, 213–218.

Holstein, C. The relation of children's moral judgment level to that of their parents and to communication level in the family. Paper presented at the Biennial Meeting of the Society for Research in Child Development, Santa Monica, California, March 28, 1969.

Holz, W., N. Azrin, and T. Ayllon. Elimination of behavior of mental patients by a response produced extinction. *Journal of Experimental Analysis of Behavior,* 1963, 6, 407–412.

Hooper, F., J. Fitzgerald, and D. Papalia. Piagetian theory and aging process. Extensions and speculations. *Aging and Human Development,* 1971, 2, 3–20.

Hopkins, J. Sexual behavior in adolescence. *Journal of Social Issues,* 1977, 33(2), 67–85.

Horance, S. *Awareness of Sex-Role Stereotypes in Young Boys.* Ph.D. Dissertation, Rutgers University, 1977.

Horn, J. Human abilities. A review of research and theories in the early 1970's. *Annual Reviews of Psychology,* 1976, 27, 437–485.

Horner, M. Toward an understanding of achievement related conflicts in women. *Journal of Social Issues,* 1972, 28, 157–176.

Houseknecht, S. Childlessness and marital adjustment. *Journal of Marriage and the Family,* May 1979, 41(2), 259–265.

Howe, L. *The Future of the Family.* New York: Simon & Schuster, 1972.

Hsu, F. American core value and national character. In F. Hsu (ed.), *Psychological Anthropology.* Cambridge, Massachusetts: Schenkman, 1972, 241–266.

Hulka, J., and J. Schaaf. Obstetrics in adolescents: A controlled study of deliveries by mothers 15 years of age and under. *Obstetrics and Gynecology,* 1964, 23, 678–685.

Hull, D., and J. Reuter. The development of charitable behavior in elementary school children. *The Journal of Genetic Psychology,* 1977, 131, 147–153.

Hunt, B., and M. Hunt. *Prime Time.* New York: Stein and Day, 1974.

Hunt, J., and L. Hunt. Race: daughters and father loss: Does absence make the girl grow stronger? *Social Problems,* 1977, 25, 80–102.

Hunt, J. McV. Development and the educational enterprise. Paper delivered at the College of Education at Hofstra University, November 15, 1973.

Hunt, J. McV. Black genes—white environment. *Transaction,* June 1969, 6.

Hunt, M. *Sexual Behavior in the 1970's.* New York: Dell, 1974.

Hunter, M. The role of physical education in child development and learning. In H. Behrens and J. Maynard (eds.), *The Changing Child.* Glenview, Illinois: Scott, Foresman, 1972.

Hurlock, E. *Child Development.* New York: McGraw-Hill, 1972.

Imedadze, N. On the psychological nature of child speech formation under conditions of exposure to two languages. *International Journal of Psychology,* 1967, 2(2), 129–132.

Inflation and a demographic shift pose huge problems for U.S. pension system. *New York Times,* May 18, 1980, 48.

Inflation is wrecking the private pension system. *Business Week,* May 12, 1980, 92–99.

Ingle, D. *Who Should Have Children?* Indianapolis: Bobbs-Merrill, 1973.

Inhelder, B. Criteria of the stages of mental development. In J. Tanner and B. Inhelder (eds.), *Discussions on Child Development: A Consideration of the Biological, Psychological and Cultural Approaches to the Understanding of Human Development and Behavior.* Vol. 1 of the Proceedings of the First Meeting of the World Health Organization Study Group on the Psychological Development of the Child. Geneva, Switzerland: International Universities Press, 1953, 75–96.

Iorio, J. *Childbirth.* St. Louis: Mosby, 1975.

Iorio, J. *Principles of Obstetrics and Gynecology for Nurses.* St. Louis: Mosby, 1967.

Isaacs, S. *The Nursery Years.* New York: Schocken Books, 1968.

Jacobs, C., and C. Eaton. Sexism in the elementary school. *Today's Education,* 1972, 61, 20–22.

Jaffee, B., and D. Fanshel. *How They Fared in Adoption: A Follow-Up Study.* New York: Columbia University Press, 1970.

Jalkanen, A. Drug use and the adolescent. In F. Adams (ed.), *Understanding Adolescence* (2nd ed.). Boston: Allyn and Bacon, 1973.

Jaslow, P. Employment, retirement and morale among older women. *Journal of Gerontology,* 1976, 31(2) 212–218.

Jay, S. Effects of Prolonged I.C.U. Hospitalization on a Young Child. Paper presented at University of

Pittsburgh Maternal Child Nursing Conference, Pittsburgh, Pennsylvania, June 1978.

Jay, S. Pediatric intensive care: Involving parents in the care of their child. *Maternal Child Nursing Journal,* Fall 1977, 6(3), 195–213.

Jeffers, F., and A. Verwoerdt. How the old face death. In E. Busse and E. Pfeiffer (eds.), *Behavior and Adaptation in Late Life.* Boston: Little, Brown, 1969.

Jelliffe, D., E. Jelliffe, L. Garcia, and G. deBarrios. The children of the San Blas Indians of Panama. *Journal of Pediatrics,* 1961, 59, 271–285.

Jensen, A. *Bias in Mental Testing.* New York: Free Press, 1980.

Jensen, A. On "Jensenism": A Reply to Critics. Address for the AERA Annual, Chicago, April 7, 1972.

Jensen, A. How much can we boost IQ and scholastic achievement? *Harvard Educational Review,* 1969, 49, 1–123.

Jensen, C. The reluctant fathers. *Pittsburgh Press Parade,* February 24, 1980, 21–31.

Jerome, I. Catching them before suicide. *New York Times Magazine,* January 1979, 30–33.

Jersild, A., and F. Holmes. *Children's Fears.* New York: Teachers' College Press, 1935.

Jewson, R. *After Retirement: An Exploratory Study of the Professional Woman.* Ph.D. Dissertation, University of Minnesota, 1978.

Johnson, C., and M. Maratsos. Early comprehension of mental verbs: Think and know. *Child Development,* 1977, 48, 1743–1747.

Johnson, E. S., and B. I. Bursk. Relationships between the elderly and their adult children. *The Gerontologist,* 1977, 17(February), 90–96.

Johnston, L. D., J. G. Bachman, and P. M. O'Malley. *Drug Use among American High School Students 1975–1977,* U. S. Dept. of Health, Education and Welfare, National Institute on Drug Abuse, 1977.

Jones, H., E. Cohen, and R. Wilson. Clinical aspects of the menopause. In K. Ryan and D. Gibson (eds.), *Menopause and Aging, Summary Report and Selected Papers from a Research Conference on Menopause and Aging.* Bethesda, Maryland: National Institute of Child Health and Human Development, 1972, 2–4.

Jones, M., and N. Bayley. Physical maturing of boys as

related to behavior. *Journal of Educational Psychology,* 1950, 41, 129–148.

Jung, C. The stages of life. In C. Campbell (ed.), *The Portable Jung.* New York: Viking, 1971.

Jung, C. *Modern Man in Search of a Soul.* New York: Harcourt, Brace and World, 1933.

Kagan, J. Family experience and the child's development. *American Psychologist,* October 1979, 34(10), 886–891.

Kagan, J. Parent anxiety. *Newsweek,* September 22, 1975, 48.

Kagan, J. *Change and Continuity in Infancy.* New York: John Wiley and Sons, 1971.

Kagan, J. A conception of early adolescence. *Daedalus,* 1971a, 100, 997–1012.

Kagan, J. *Understanding Children: Behavior, Motives and Thought.* New York: Harcourt Brace Jovanovich, 1971b.

Kagan, J. The child: His struggle for identity. *Saturday Review,* December 7, 1968.

Kagan, J. Acquisition and significance of sex typing and sex role identify. In M. Hoffman and L. Hoffman (eds.), *Review of Child Development Research.* Vol. 1, New York: Russell Sage Foundation, 1964.

Kagan, J. The concept of identification. *Psychological Review,* 1958, 65, 296–305.

Kagan, J., R. Kearsley, and R. Zelazo. *Infancy. Its Place in Human Development.* Cambridge, Massachusetts: Harvard University Press, 1978.

Kagan, J., H. Moss, and I. Sigel. Psychological significance of styles of conceptualization. In *Cognitive Development in Children.* Chicago: University of Chicago Press, 1970, 203–242.

Kagan, J., and H. Moss. *Birth to Maturity: The Fels Study of Psychological Development.* New York: John Wiley and Sons, 1962.

Kagan, J., B. Hosken, and S. Watson. The child's symbolic conceptualization of the parents. *Child Development,* 1961, 32, 625–636.

Kalish, R. Of social values and the dying. A defense of disengagement. *The Family Coordinator,* 1972, 21(1), 81–94.

Kalish R., and D. Reynolds. *Death and Ethnicity: A Psychological Study.* Los Angeles: University of Southern California Press, 1976.

Kamerman, S., and A. Kahn. *Child Care, Family Benefits and Working Mothers.* New York: Columbia University Press, 1981.

Kamerman, S., and A. J. Kahn. The day-care debate: A wider view. *The Public Interest,* Winter 1979, 81.

Kamii, R., and L. Radin. Class differences in the socialization practices of Negro mothers. *Journal of Marriage and the Family,* 1967, 29, 302–310.

Kandel, D., and G. Lesser. Parent–adolescent relationships and adolescent independence in the United States and Denmark. *Journal of Marriage and the Family,* 1969, 31, 348–358.

Kanter, R. Communes. *Psychology Today,* July 1970, 4(2), 53–57, 58.

Kantner, J., and M. Zelnik. Sexuality, contraception, and pregnancy among pre-adult females in the United States, *Demographic and Social Aspects of Population Growth.* Washington, D.C.: The Commission on Population Growth and the American Future, 1972a.

Kantner, J., and M. Zelnik. Sexual experience of young unmarried women in the United States. *Family Planning Perspectives,* 1972b, 4, 9–18.

Kapp, L., B. Taylor, and L. Edwards. Teaching human sexuality in junior high school. *Journal of School Health,* February 1980, 80.

Karagianis, L., and D. Merricks (eds.). *Where the Action Is: Teaching Exceptional Children.* St. John, Newfoundland: Memorial University, 1973 (ERIC Document Reproduction Service No. ED 984 764).

Karnes, M., R. Zehrback, and G. Jones. *The Culturally Disadvantaged Student and Guidance.* Boston: Houghton Mifflin, 1971.

Kastenbaum, R. On death and dying: Should we have mixed feelings about our ambivalence toward the aged? *Journal of Geriatric Psychiatry,* 1974, 7, 94–107.

Kastenbaum, R., and S. Candy. The five percent fallacy: A methodological and empirical critique of extended care facility population statistics. *International Journal of Aging and Human Development,* 1973, 4(1), 15–21.

Kastenbaum, R., and A. Weisman. The psychological autopsy as a research procedure in gerontology. In D. Dent, R. Kastenbaum, and S. Sherwood (eds.), *Research Planning and Action for the Elderly.* New York: Behavioral Publications, 1972.

Keasey, C. Young children's attribution of intentionality to themselves and others. *Child Development,* March 1977, 48, 261–264.

Keay, A., and D. Morgan. *Craig's Care of the Newly Born Infant.* London: Churchill-Livingstone, 1974.

Kellaghen, T. Relationships between home environment and scholastic behavior in a disadvantaged population. *Journal of Educational Psychology,* 1977, 69(6), 754–760.

Kellogg, M., and A. Jaffee. Old folks commune. In S. Zarit (ed.), *Readings in Aging and Death: Contemporary Perspectives.* New York: Harper and Row, 1977, 247.

Kellogg, R., and S. O'Dell. *Analyzing Children's Art.* Palo Alto, California: National Press Books, 1969.

Kelly, J. Work and leisure: A simplified paradigm. *Journal of Leisure Research,* 1972, 4(1), 50–62.

Kelly, J., and J. Wallerstein. The effects of parental divorce: Experiences of the child in early latency. *American Journal of Orthopsychiatry,* January 1976, 46(1).

Keniston, K. In abdicating American parents. *Newsweek,* September 22, 1975, 55.

Keniston, K. Youth: A "new" stage of life. *American Scholar,* 1972, 109–127.

Keshet, H., and K. Rosenthal. Fathering after marital separation. *Social Work,* 1978, 23, 11–18.

Keyserling, M. *Windows on Daycare.* New York: American Council of Jewish Women, 1972.

Kimmel, D. *Adulthood and Aging.* New York: John Wiley and Sons, 1980.

King, K., J. Balswick, and I. Robinson. The continuing premarital sexual revolution among college females. *Journal of Marriage and the Family,* August 1977, 455–459.

Kinsey, A., *et al. Sexual Behavior in the Human Female.* Philadelphia: Saunders, 1953.

Kinsey, A., *et al. Sexual Behavior in the Human Male.* Philadelphia: Saunders, 1948.

Kistiakovskaia, M. Cited by I. London. A Russian report on the post-operative newly seeing. *American Journal of Psychology,* 1960, 73, 478–482.

Kleiman, D. Anguished search to cure infertility. *New*

York Times Magazine, December 16, 1979, 38–151.

Klemesrud, J. A wife's role in big decisions. *New York Times,* November 23, 1980, 68.

Knapp, J. An exploratory study of sexually open marriages. *Journal of Sex Research,* 1976, 12, 206–219.

Knepler, A. Adolescence: An anthropological approach. In G. Winter and E. Nuss (eds.), *The Young Adult: Identity and Awareness.* Glenview, Illinois: Scott, Foresman, 1969.

Koff, E., J. Rierdan, and E. Silverstone. Changes in representation of body image as a function of menarcheal status. *Developmental Psychology,* 1978, 14(6), 635–642.

Kohlberg, L. Stages of moral development as a basis for moral education. In C. Beck, B. Crittenden, and E. Sullivan (eds.), *Moral Education.* Toronto: University of Toronto Press, 1971.

Kohlberg, L. Stage and sequence: The cognitive–developmental approach to socialization. In D. Goslen (ed.), *Handbook of Socialization Theory and Research.* Chicago: Rand McNally, 1969, 376.

Kohlberg, L. *The development of modes of moral thinking and choice in the years 10–16.* Ph.D. Dissertation, University of Chicago, 1958.

Kohlberg, L., and C. Gilligan. The adolescent as a philosopher: The discovery of the self in a post conventional world. *Daedalus,* Fall 1971, 12–16.

Kohli, L., and A. Sobrero. Vasectomy: A study of psychosexual and general reaction. *Social Biology,* 1973, 20, 298–302.

Kohn, R. Heart and cardiovascular system. In C. Finch and L. Hayflick (eds.), *Handbook of the Biology of Aging.* New York: Van Nostrand Reinhold, 1977, 281–317.

Kompara, D. Difficulties in the socialization process of stepparenting. *Family Relations,* 1980, 29, 69–73.

Konner, M. Infancy among the Kalahari Desert San. In P. Leiderman, S. Tulkin, and A. Rosenfeld (eds.), *Culture and Infancy.* New York: Academic Press, 1977, 287–328.

Koocher, G. Why isn't the gerbil moving anymore? *Children Today,* 1975, 4(1), 18–21.

Korner, A. *Some Aspects of Hostility in Young Children.* New York: Grune and Stratton, 1949.

Korner, A., and E. Thoman. Visual alertness in neonates as evoked by maternal care. *Journal of Experimental Child Psychology,* 1970, 10, 67–78.

Kornetsky, C. Psychoactive drugs in the immature organism. *Psychopharmacologia,* 1970, 105–136.

Kramer, M., C. Taube, and R. Redick. Patterns of use of psychiatric facilities by the aged: Past, present, and future. In C. Eisdorfer and M. Lawton (eds.), *The Psychology of Adult Development and Aging.* Washington, D.C.: American Psychological Association, 1973, 428–528.

Kreps, J. Economics of aging. *American Behavioral Scientist,* 1970, 81–90.

Krogman, W. *Child Growth.* Ann Arbor, Michigan: University of Michigan Press, 1972.

Kron, R., M. Stein, and K. Goddard. Newborn sucking behavior affected by obstetric sedation. *Pediatrics,* 1966, 37, 1012–1016.

Kübler-Ross, E. *Death: The Final Stage of Growth.* Englewood-Cliffs, New Jersey: Prentice-Hall. 1975.

Kübler-Ross, E. *On Death and Dying.* New York: Macmillan, 1969.

Kucharski, L., R. White, and M. Schratz. Age bias, referral for psychological assistance, and the private physician. *Journal of Gerontology,* 1979, 34(3), 423–428.

Labov, W. Contraction, deletion, and inherent variability of the English cupola. *Language,* 1969, 45, 715–762.

Ladimer, I. New dimensions in legal and ethical concepts for human research. *Annals of the New York Academy of Science,* 1969–1970, 230–590.

Lamaze, F. *Painless Childbirth: The Lamaze Method.* Chicago: Markham, 1970.

Lamb, M. The sociability of two-year-olds with their mothers and fathers. *Child Psychiatry and Human Development,* Spring 1975, 182–188.

Landreth, C. *Early Childhood Behavior and Learning.* New York: Alfred A. Knopf, 1967.

Langley, G. Functional psychoses. In J. Howells (ed.), *Modern Perspectives in the Psychiatry of Old Age.* New York: Brunner/Mazel, 1975, 326–355.

Langner, T., J. Gersten, E. Greene, J. Eisenberg, H.

Herson, and E. McCarthy. Treatment of psychological disorders among urban children. *Journal of Consulting and Clinical Psychology,* 1974, 42(2), 170–179.

Langway, L. The binge-purge syndrome. *Newsweek,* November 2, 1981, 60–69.

LaSagna, L. Physicians' behavior toward the dying patient. In 0. Brim *et al.* (eds.), *The Dying Patient.* New York: Russell Sage Foundation, 1970, 83–101.

Later weddings, fewer children, more singles change U.S. family. *Family Planning Perspectives,* 1979, 11, 310.

Lawton, M., and L. Gottesman. Psychological services to the elderly. *American Psychologist,* 1974, 29(4), 689–693.

Leboyer, F. *Birth Without Violence.* New York: Alfred A. Knopf, 1975.

Lee, G. Marriage and morale in later life. *Journal of Marriage and the Family,* 1978, 40, 131–139.

Lee, G. Age at marriage and marital satisfaction: A multivariate analysis with implication for marital stability. *Journal of Marriage and the Family,* August 1977, 39, 493–504.

Lefkowitz, M., L. Eron, L. Walder, and L. Huesmann. Preference for televised contact sports as related to sex differences in aggression. *Developmental Psychology,* 1973, 9(3), 417–420.

Leifer, M. Psychological changes accompanying pregnancy and motherhood. *Genetic Psychological Monographs,* 1977, 95, 55–96.

Leizer, J., and R. Rogers. Effects of method of discipline, timing of punishment, and timing of test on resistance to extinction. *Child Development,* 1974, 45, 790–793.

Lenneberg, E. *Biological Foundations of Language.* New York: John Wiley and Sons, 1967.

Leonard, M., J. Rhymes, and A. Solnit. Failure to thrive in infants: A family problem. *American Journal of Diseases of Children,* 1966, III, 600–612.

Lerner, M. When, why, and where people die. In E. Shneidman (ed.), *Death: Current Perspectives.* Palo Alto, California: Mayfield, 1976, 138–162.

Lerner, R., and J. Lerner. Effects of age, sex, and physical attractiveness on child–peer relations, academic performance, and elementary school ad-

justment. *Developmental Psychology,* 1977, 13(6), 585–590.

Lesnoff-Caravaglia, G. The five percent fallacy. *International Journal of Aging and Human Development,* 1978-1979, 9(2), 187–192.

Lester, B. Psychological and central nervous system consequences of protein–calorie malnutrition: A review of research findings and some implications. *Interamerican Journal of Psychology,* 1976, 10, 17–31.

Lester, B. Cardiac habituation of the orienting response to an auditory signal in infants of varying nutritional status. *Developmental Psychology,* 1975, 11, 432–442.

Levin, R., and A. Levin. Sexual pleasure: The surprising preferences of 100,000 women. *Redbook,* September 1975, 51–58.

Levinger, G. A social psychological perspective on marital dissolution. In G. Levinger and O. Moles (eds.), *Divorce and Separation: Context, Causes and Consequences.* New York: Basic Books, 1979, 37–60.

Levinson, D., C. Darrow, E. Klein, M. Levinson, and B. McKee. *The Seasons of a Man's Life.* New York: Alfred A. Knopf, 1978.

Levinson, D., C. Darrow, E. Klein *et al.* The psychosocial development of men in early adulthood and the mid-life transition. In D. Ricks *et al.* (eds.), *Life History Research in Psychopathology,* Vol. 3. Minneapolis: University of Minnesota Press, 1974, 243–258.

Levy, M. *The Family Revolution in Modern China.* Cambridge, Massachusetts: Harvard University Press, 1949.

Lewin, H., and R. Sears. Identification with parents as a determinant of doll play aggression. *Child Development,* 1956, 27(2), 135–153.

Lewis, M., A. Martels, H. Campbell, and S. Goldberg. Individual differences in attention. *American Journal of Diseases of Children,* 1967, 113, 461–465.

Lewis, R. A longitudinal test of a developmental framework for premarital dyadic formation. *Journal of Marriage and the Family,* February 1973, 35, 16–25.

Lewis, R., G. Spanier, V. Storm, and C. Lehacka. Commitment in married and unmarried cohabitation. Paper presented at meeting of the American Sociological Association, San Francisco, California, August 1975.

Libby, R. Creative singlehood as a sexual lifestyle. In R. Libby and R. Whitehurst (eds.), *Marriage and Alternatives.* Glenview, Illinois: Scott, Foresman, 1977.

Liebermann, G. Children of the elderly as natural helpers: Some demographic considerations. *American Journal of Community Psychology,* 1978, 6, 489–498.

Lieberman, M. Adaptive processes in late life. In N. Datan and L. Ginsburg (eds.), *Life-Span Developmental Psychology.* New York: Academic Press, 1975.

Limber, J. Language in child and chimp. *American Psychologist,* April 1977, 32(4), 280–294.

Lind, M. *Motherhood as Option or Destiny: Pregnancy Decision-Making among Childless Women.* Ph.D. Dissertation, University of Hawaii, 1977.

Lindemann, E. Symptomatology and management of acute grief. *American Journal of Psychiatry,* 1944, 101, 141–148.

Lindsley, R. American way of death. *The New York Times,* March 2, 1980, 51.

Lipsitt, L. Conditioning the rage to live. *Psychology Today,* February 1980, 124.

Lipsitt, L. Critical conditions in infancy: A psychological perspective. *American Psychologist,* October 1979, 34(10), 973–980.

Lipsitt, L. Perinatal indicators and psychophysiological precursors of crib death. In F. Horowitz (ed.), *Early Developmental Hazards: Predictions and Precautions.* Boulder, Colorado: Westview Press, 1978, 11–26.

Lipsitt, L., W. Sturner, and P. Burke. Perinatal indicators and subsequent crib death. *Infant Behavior and Development,* 1979, 2, 325–328.

Lipsitt, L., and H. Kaye. Conditioned sucking in the human newborn. *Psychonomic Science* 1, 1964, 29–30.

Lipton, D., R. Stephens, D. Babst, R. Dembo, S. Diamond, C. Spielman, J. Schmeidler, P. Bergman, and G. Uppal. A survey of sustance use among junior and senior high school students in New York State. *American Journal of Drug Abuse,* 1977, 4(2), 153–164.

Little, A. Eyelid conditioning in the human infant as a function of the ISI. Paper presented at meeting of the Society for Research in Child Development, Minneapolis, Minnesota, 1971.

Little, V. Open care for the aged: Swedish model. *Social Work,* 1978, 23, 282–287.

Livson, F. Patterns of personality development in middle-aged women: A longitudinal study. *International Journal of Aging and Human Development,* 1976, 7(2), 107–118.

Long, J. The death that ends death in Hinduism and Buddhism. In E. Kübler-Ross (ed.), *Death: The Final Stage of Growth.* Englewood-Cliffs, New Jersey: Prentice-Hall, 1975.

Long, K. Johnny's Such a Bright Boy, What a Shame He's Retarded. Boston: Houghton Mifflin, 1977.

Lopata, H. *Widowed in an American City.* Cambridge, Massachusetts: Schenkman, 1973.

Lorenz, K. *King Solomon's Ring.* London: Methuen, 1952.

Lovaas, O. I., J. W. Varni, R. L. Koegel, and N. Lorsch. Some observations on the nonextinguishability of children's speech. *Child Development,* 1977, 48, 1121–1127.

Low, S., and P. Spindler. *Child Care Arrangements of Working Mothers in the United States.* Washington, D.C.: Children's Bureau Publication No. 161, 1968.

Lowe, G. *The Growth of Personalty: From Infancy to Old Age.* Middlesex, England: Penguin Books, 1972.

Lowenthal, M., and C. Haven. Interaction and adaptation: Intimacy as a critical variable. In B. Neugarten (ed.), *Middle Age and Aging: A Reader in Social Psychology.* Chicago: University of Chicago Press, 1968, 390–400.

Luria, A. A child's speech responses and the social environment. *Soviet Psychology,* 1974, 13, 7–39.

Lusk, D., and M. Lewis. Mother–infant interaction and infant development among the Wolof of Senegal. *Human Development,* 1972, 15, 58–69.

Lynn, D. Fathers and sex-role development. *The Family Coordinator,* October 1976, 403–409.

Lytton, H., and W. Zwirner. Compliance and its controlling stimuli observed in a natural setting. *Developmental Psychology*, 1975, 11(6), 769–779.

Maccoby, E. Sex differences revisited: Myth and reality. Paper given at annual meeting of the American Educational Research Association, Chicago, Illinois, 1974.

Maccoby, E. Sex differences in intellectual functioning. In E. Maccoby (ed.), *The Development of Sex Differences*. Stanford, California: Stanford University Press, 1966.

Macklin, E. Heterosexual cohabitation among unmarried college students. *The Family Coordinator*, October 1972, 21, 463–472.

Maddox, G. Themes and issues in sociological theories of human aging. *Human Development*, 1970, 13, 17–27.

Maddox, G. Activity and morale: A longitudinal study of selected elderly subjects. *Social Forces*, 1963, 42(2), 195–204.

Magalhaes, R. Oparto embaixo dagua. In *Manchete* (Rio de Janiero), December 8, 1979, 70–75.

Making millions by baby-sitting. *Time*, July 3, 1978, 65.

Malina, R. Secular changes in age and maturity: Causes and effects. *Monographs of the Society for Research in Child Development*, 1979, 44, 59–120.

Malmquist, C. Development from thirteen to sixteen years. In J. Noshpitz (ed.), *Basic Handbook of Child Psychiatry*, Vol. I. New York: Basic Books, 1978.

Mancini, J., and D. Orthner. Recreational sexual preferences among middle-class husbands and wives. *Journal of Sex Research*, 1978, 14, 96–106.

Manes, A., and K. Melnyck. Televised models of female achievement. *Journal of Applied Social Psychology*, 1974, 4, 365–373.

Marcus, J. Early child development in kibbutz group care. *Early Child Development and Care*. Vol. 1. Great Britain: Gordon and Breach Science Publisher, 1971, 67–98.

Margolin, E. *Sociocultural Elements in Early Childhood Education*. New York: Macmillan, 1974.

Marini, M. The transition to adulthood: Sex differences in educational attainment and age at marriage. *American Sociological Review*, August 1978, 43, 183–507.

Marino, C., and R. McCowan. The effects of parent absence on children. *Child Study Journal*, 1976, 6(3), 165–180.

Marjoriebanks, K. Birth order, age spacing between siblings, and cognitive performance. *Psychological Reports*, 1978, 42, 115–123.

Markides, K., and H. Martin. A causal model of life satisfaction among the elderly. *Journal of Gerontology*, 1979, 34(1), 86–93.

Marmor, J. *Psychiatrists and Their Patients: A National Study of Private Office Practices*. Washington, D.C.: American Psychiatric Association, National Association for Mental Health, 1975.

Marshall, E., and S. Hample (eds.). *Children's Letters to God*. New York: Simon and Schuster, 1966.

Marver, J., and M. Larson. Public policy toward child care in America: A historical perspective. In P. Robins and S. Weiner, (eds.)., *Child Care and Public Policy*, Lexington, Massachusetts: D. C. Heath, 1978, 17–42.

Marx, J. Drugs during pregnancy: Do they affect the unborn child? *Science*, April 13, 1973, 180, 174–175.

Marx, M., and T. Tombaugh. *Motivation*. San Francisco: Chandler, 1967.

Masland, R., S. Sarason, and R. Galdwin. *Mental Subnormality: Biological, Psychological, and Cultural Factors*. New York: Basic Books, 1959.

Maslow, A. Creativity in self-actualizing people. In H. Anderson (ed.), *Creativity and Its Cultivation*. New York: Harper and Row, 1959.

Maslow, A. *Motivation and Personality*. New York: Harper and Row, 1954.

Maslow, A. A theory of human motivation. *Psychological Review*, 1943, 50, 370–396.

Masters, W., and V. Johnson. Human sexual response: The aging female and the aging male. In B. Neugarten (ed.), *Middle Age and Aging*. Chicago: University of Chicago Press, 1978, 269–279.

Masters, W., and V. Johnson. *Human Sexual Inadequacy*. Boston: Little, Brown, 1970.

Masters, W., and V. Johnson. *Human Sexual Response*. Boston: Little, Brown, 1966.

Maurer, A. What children fear. *Journal of Genetic Psychology*, 1965, 106, 265–277.

McCary, J. *Human Sexuality* (2nd. ed.). New York: Van Nostrand Reinhold, 1973.

McClelland, D. What is the effect of achievement motivation training in the schools? *Teachers' College Record,* 1972, 74, 129–145.

McClelland, D. Toward a theory of motive acquisition. *American Psychologist,* 1965, 20, 321–333.

McClelland, D. The importance of early learning in the formation of motives. In J. Atkinson (ed.), *Motives in Fantasy, Action, and Society.* Princeton, New Jersey: Van Nostrand Reinhold, 1958.

McClelland, D., J. Atkinson, R. Clark, and E. Lowell. *The Achievement Motive.* New York: Appleton-Century-Crofts, 1953.

McConville, B., L. Boag, and A. Purohitt. Three types of childhood depression. *Canadian Psychiatric Association Journal,* 1973, 18, 133–138.

McCormack. P. Torment in twilight years. *Pittsburgh Press,* November 13, 1980, B1.

McCullers, C. *The Member of the Wedding.* Boston: Houghton Mifflin, 1946.

McFeatters, A. Debate on child-care rises anew in Congress. *Pittsburgh Press,* March 19, 1979, H6.

McGhee, P. *Humor: Its Origin and Development.* San Francisco: Freeman, 1979.

McGhee, P. Children's appreciation of humor: A test of the cognitive congruency principle. *Child Development,* 1976, 47, 420–426.

McGrath, N., and C. McGrath. Why have a baby? *New York Times Magazine,* May 25, 1975.

McKee, J., and F. Leader. The relation of socioeconomic status and aggression to the competitive behavior of preschool children. *Child Development,* June 1955, 26(2), 135–143.

McKeown, T. *The Modern Rise of Population:* New York: Academic Press, 1977.

McKinney, J. Teacher perceptions of the classroom behavior of reflective and impulsive children. *Psychology in the Schools,* 1975, 12, 348–352.

McNeese, F. Helping hand for "Black English." *Pittsburgh Press,* October 3, 1976.

McTavish, P. Perceptions of old people: A review of research methodologies and findings, Third Report. *The Gerontologist,* 1971, 90–101.

Mead, M. *An Anthropologist at Work.* Boston: Houghton Mifflin, 1959.

Mead, M. *Coming of Age in Samoa.* New York: New American Library of World Literature, 1949, Morrow, 1928.

Mead, M. *Male and Female.* New York: Morrow, 1949.

Mead, M. *Sex and Temperament in Three Primitive Societies.* New York: Morrow, 1935.

Mead, M., and K. Heyman. *Family.* New York: Ridge Press, 1965.

Mech, E. Adoption: A policy perspective. In B. Caldwell and H. Ricciuti (eds.), *Review of Child Development Research.* Chicago, Illinois: University of Chicago Press, 1973.

Meichenbaum, D. Self-instructional strategy training. A cognitive prosthesis for the aged. *Human Development,* 1974, 17, 273–280.

Meltzer, J. *The Child's Socialization to the Culture of Poverty.* Unpublished manuscript, University of Pittsburgh, 1980.

Mendes, H. Single fathers. *The Family Coordinator,* October 1976, 25, 439–444.

Messick, S. The criterion problem in the evaluation of instruction. In M. Wittrock and D. Wiley (eds.), *The Evaluations of Instruction: Issues and Problems.* New York: Holt, Rinehart and Winston, 1970.

Mickelson, K. *The Effects of Father–Daughter Relationships on the Development of Achievement Orientation and Psychological Androgyny in Females.* Ph.D. Dissertation, California School of Professional Psychology, 1976.

Miller, J., J. Piaget, L. Kohlberg, and E. Erikson. Developmental implications for secondary education. *Adolescence,* Summer 1978, XIII(50), 237–250.

Miller, M. Toward a profile of the older white male suicide. *The Gerontologist,* 1978, 18(1), 80–82.

Miller, N. Studies of fear as an acquired drive. I. Fear as motivation and fear-reduction as reinforcement in the learning of new responses. *Journal of Experimental Psychology,* 1948, 38, 89–101.

Miller, N., and D. Dollard. *Social Learning and Imitation.* New Haven, Connecticut: Yale University Press, 1941.

Miller, S. The social dilemma of the aging leisure participant. In A. Rose and W. Patterson (eds.), *Older People and Their Social World.* Philadelphia: F. A. Davis, 1965.

Miller, T. Effects of maternal age, education, and employment status on the self-esteem of the child.

The Journal of Social Psychology, 1975, 95, 141–142.

Milton, G. The effects of sex-role identity upon problem-solving skills. *Journal of Abnormal and Social Psychology,* 1957, 55, 208–212.

Milunsky, A., and L. Atkins. Prenatal prevention of genetic disease and mental retardation. In A. Milunsky (ed.), *National Symposium on Genetics and the Law.* Philadelphia, Pennsylvania: Saunders, 1975.

Mitchell, J. Moral dilemmas of early adolescence. *School Counselor,* 22, 1974, 16–22.

Moenckeberg, F. E. Nutrition and behavior: Practical problems in field studies in an urban community. In D.J. Kallen (ed.), *Nutrition, Development, and Social Behavior.* U.S. Dept. of Health, Education and Welfare: Publication No. 73-242, 1973.

Molinquist, C. Development from thirteen to sixteen years. In J. Noshpitz (ed.), *Basic Handbook of Child Psychiatry,* Vol. I. New York: Basic Books, 1979, 205–213.

Moltz, H., and L. Stettner. The influence of the patterned-light deprivation on the critical period of imprinting. *Journal of Comparative and Physiological Psychology,* 1961, 54, 279–283.

Montemayor, R., and M. Eisen. The development of self-conceptions from childhood to adolescence. *Developmental Psychology,* 1977, 13, 314–319.

Montessori, M. *Dr. Montessori's Own Handbook.* New York: Schocken, 1914.

Morgan, L. A re-examination of widowhood and morale. *Journal of Gerontology,* 1976, 31(6), 687–695.

Morrell, G., and D. Atkinson. Effects of breakfast programs on school performance and attendance of elementary school children. *Education,* Winter 1977, 98(2), 111–116.

Morrow, L. Time essay: Wondering if children are necessary. *Time,* March 5, 1979, 42–47.

Mouly, G. *Psychology for Effective Teaching* (3rd. ed.). New York: Holt, Rinehart and Winston, 1970.

Murphy, L. Later outcomes of early infant and mother relations. Paper read at the annual meeting of the American Orthopsychiatric Association, Washington, D.C., March 1971.

Mussen, P. *The Psychological Development of the Child.* Englewood Cliffs, New Jersey: Prentice-Hall, 1973.

Muuss, R. Kohlberg's cognitive–developmental approach to adolescent morality. *Adolescence,* Spring 1976, XI (41), 39–57.

Naeye, R. Relationship of cigarette smoking to congenital anomalies and perinatal death: A prospective study. *American Journal of Pathology,* 1978, 90, 289–293.

Naeye, R., B. Ladis, and J. Drage. SIDS: A prospective study. *American Journal of Diseases of Children,* 1976, 130, 1207–1210a.

Naeye, R., J. Messmer, III, T. Specht, and F. Merritt. Sudden infant death syndrome temperament before death. *Journal of Pediatrics,* 1976, 88, 511–515.

Nagy, M. The child's view of death. *Journal of Genetic Psychology,* 1948, 73, 3–27.

National Center for Health Statistics. *Teenage Childbearing, United States, 1966–1975.* Monthly Vital Statistics Report, Vol. 26, No. 5, Supplement, Dept. of Health, Education and Welfare Publication No. (HRA) 77-1120, Washington, D.C.: U.S. Printing Office, September 8, 1977.

National Institute on Drug Abuse. *Report of Interviews of 2510 U.S. Men Collected from October 1974 to May 1975.* Washington, D.C.: National Institute on Drug Abuse, February 1976.

Nations, J. *Caring for individual differences in reading through non-grading.* Lecture at the Seattle Public Schools, May 13, 1967.

Neugarten, B. Time, age, and the life cycle. *The American Journal of Psychiatry,* July 1977, 136(7), 887–894.

Neugarten, B. *The Psychology of Aging: An Overview.* APA Masters Lecture. Washington, D.C.: American Psychological Association, 1976.

Neugarten, B. Age groups in American society and the rise of the young–old. *Annals of the American Academy of Political and Social Sciences,* 1974, 415, 187–198.

Neugarten, B. Continuities and discontinuities of psychological issues into adult life. *Human Development,* 1969, 12, 121–130.

Neugarten, B. Adult personality: Toward a psychology of the life cycle. In B. Neugarten (ed.), *Middle Age and Aging.* Chicago: University of Chicago Press, 1968.

Neugarten, B., and K. Weinstein. The changing American grandparent. *Journal of Marriage and the Family,* 1964, 26, 199–204.

Neugarten, B., *et al. Personality in Middle and Late Life.* New York: Atherton Press, 1964.

Neugarten, B., R. Havighurst, and S. Tobin. The measurement of life satisfaction. *Journal of Gerontology,* 1961, 16, 134–143.

Neulinger, J., and C. Raps. Leisure attitudes of an intellectual elite. *Journal of Leisure Research,* 1972, 4(3), 196–207.

Nevaldine, A. *Divorce: The Leaver and the Left.* Ph.D. Dissertation, University of Minnesota, 1978.

Newcomb, P. Cohabitation in America: An assessment of consequences. *Journal of Marriage and the Family,* August 1979, 39, 597–603.

Newman, P. School settings and their significance for adolescent development. *Adolescence,* Fall 1976, XI(43), 403–416.

Newman, P., and B. Newman. Early adolescence and its conflict: Group identity vs. alienation. *Adolescence,* Summer 1976, XI(42), 263–274.

Niles, F. The adolescent girls' perception of parents and peers. *Adolescence,* Fall 1979, XIV(55), 591–597.

Nortman, D. Parental age as a factor in pregnancy outcome and child development. *Reports on Population/Family Planning,* No. 16, August 1974.

Novak, E., *et al. Novak's Textbook of Gynecology* (8th. ed.). Baltimore: Williams and Wilkins, 1970.

Novy, M. Evaluation and treatment of the fetus at risk. In R. Behrman (ed.), *Neonatology.* St. Louis: C.V. Mosby, 1973, 1–45.

Nugent, F. School counselors, psychologists, and social workers: A definition. *Psychology in the Schools,* 1973, 10, 327–333.

Office of Nursing Home Affairs. Long term care facility improvement study. Washington, D.C.: U.S. Printing Office, 1975.

Olday, D. *Some Consequences for Heterosexual Cohabitation.* Ph.D. Dissertation, Washington State University, 1977.

Omenn, G. Behavior genetics. In J. Birren and K. Schaie (eds.), *Handbook of the Psychology of Aging.* New York: Van Nostrand Reinhold, 1977.

O'Neill, N., and G. O'Neill. *Open Marriage.* New York: Avon, 1972.

Orthner, D., T. Brown, and D. Ferguson. Single parent

fatherhood: An emerging family life style. *The Family Coordinator,* October 1976, 25, 429–437.

Osborne, F., and C. Bajema. The eugenic hypothesis. *Social Biology,* 1972, 19, 337–345.

Ounsted, M. Familial factors affecting fetal growth. In Pan American Health Organization, *Perinatal Factors Affecting Human Development.* Washington, D.C.: World Health Organization, 1969.

Owens, W. Age and mental abilities: A second adult follow-up. *Journal of Educational Psychology,* 1966, 57, 311–325.

Oyama, S. The concept of the sensitive period in developmental studies. *Merrill-Palmer Quarterly,* 1979, 25(2), 83–103.

Palmore, E., and V. Stone. Predictors of longevity: A follow-up study of the aged in Chapel Hill. *Gerontologist,* 1973, 13, 88–90.

Papalia, D., and D. Bielby. Cognitive functioning in middle- and old-age adults: A review of research based on Piaget's theory. *Human Development,* 1974, 17, 424–443.

Papousek, H. Experimental studies of appetitional behavior in human newborns and infants. In H. Stevenson, E. Hess, and H. Rheingold (eds.), *Early Behavior: Comparative and Developmental Approaches.* New York: John Wiley and Sons, 1967.

Parke, R. Perspectives on father–infant interaction. In J. Osofsky (ed.), *Handbook of Infant Development.* New York: John Wiley and Sons, 1979.

Parke, R. Children's home environments. In I. Altman and J. Wohlwill (eds.), *Children and the Environment.* New York: Plenum, 1978.

Parkes, C. *Bereavement: Studies of Grief in Adult Life.* New York: International Universities Press, 1972.

Parsons, J., and D. Ruble. The development of achievement-related expectancies. *Child Development,* 1977, 48, 1075–1079.

Passantino, R. Swedish preschools: Environments of sensitivity. *Childhood Education,* May 1971, 406–411.

Patterson, R., R. Abrahams, and F. Baker. Preventing self-destructive behavior. *Geriatrics,* November 1974, 115–121.

Pavlov, I. *Conditioned Reflexes.* Translated by G. Anrep, London: Oxford University Press, 1927.

Pearlin, L., M. Yarrow, and H. Scarr. Unintended effects of parental aspirations: The case of children's cheating. *American Journal of Sociology,* 1967, 73, 73–83.

Peck, E., and J. Senderowitz. *Prenatalism: The Myth of Mom and Apple Pie.* New York: Crowell, 1974.

Peck, R. Psychological development in the second half of life. In B. Neugarten (ed.), *Middle Age and Aging.* Chicago: University of Chicago Press, 1968.

Peretti, P., and C. Wilson. Voluntary and involuntary retirement of aged males and their effect on emotional satisfaction, usefulness, self-image, emotional stability, and interpersonal relationships. *International Journal of Aging and Human Development,* 1975, 6(2), 131–139.

Perkins, S. Malnutrition and mental development. *Exceptional Children,* January 1977, 43, 214–219.

Perlmutter, M. What is memory aging the aging of? *Developmental Psychology,* 1978, 14(4), 330–345.

Peterman, D., C. Ridley, and S. Anderson. A comparison of cohabiting and non-cohabiting college students. *Journal of Marriage and the Family,* May 1974, 36, 344–354.

Peterson, D. Financial adequacy in retirement: Perceptions of older Americans. *The Gerontologist,* 1972, 12(4), 379–383.

Pettigrew, T. *A Profile of the American Negro.* Princeton, New Jersey: Van Nostrand Reinhold, 1964.

Pfeiffer, E. Psychopathology and social pathology, In J. Birren and K. Schaie (eds.), *Handbook of the Psychology of Aging.* New York: Van Nostrand Reinhold, 1977, 650–671.

Pfeiffer, E. Sexuality in the aging individual. *Journal of the American Geriatrics Society,* 1974, 22, 481–484.

Pfeiffer, E., A. Verwoerdt, and G. Davis. Sexual activity in middle life. *American Journal of Psychiatry,* 1972, 128, 1262–1267.

Piaget, J. Intellectual evolution from adolescence to adulthood. *Human Development,* 1972, 15, 1–12.

Piaget, J. *Six Psychological Studies.* New York: Random House, 1967, 100–115.

Piaget, J. *Psychology of Intelligence.* Paterson, New Jersey: Littlefield and Adams, 1960.

Piaget, J. Les stades du developpement intellectual de l'enfant et de l'adolescent. In P. Osterrieth (ed.), *Le Probleme des Stades en Psychologie de l'Enfant.* Paris, France: Presses Universitie de France, 1956, 33–42.

Piaget, J. *The Child's Conception of Number.* New York: Humanities Press, 1952a.

Piaget, J. *The Origins of Intelligence in Children.* New York: Norton, 1952b.

Piaget, J. *Dreams and Imitation.* New York: Norton, 1951.

Piaget, J. *The Moral Judgment of the Child.* New York: Macmillan, 1932.

Piaget, J., and B. Inhelder. *The Psychology of the Child.* New York: Basic Books, 1969.

Piaget, J., and B. Inhelder. *The Early Growth of Logic in the Child.* New York: Harper and Row, 1964.

Pineda, V. Organizacion social en la guajira. *Rev. Institute Etnology Nacional* (Bogota, Colombia), 1948.

Pineo, P. Disenchantment in the later years of marriage. In B. Neugarten (ed.), *Middle Age and Aging.* Chicago: University of Chicago Press, 1978, 258–262.

Platzer, W. Perceptual motor training on gross-motor skill and self-concept of young children. *American Journal of Occupational Therapy,* 1976, 30(7), 423–428.

Pohlman, E. Childlessness, intentional and unintentional. *Journal of Nervous and Mental Disease,* 1970, 151, 2–12.

Pohlman, E. *Motivations in Wanting Conceptions in Psychology of Birth Planning.* Cambridge, Massachusetts: Schenkman, 1969a.

Pohlman, E. *The Psychology of Birth Planning.* Cambridge, Massachusetts: Schenkman, 1969b.

Pollard, L. *The Stephen Smith Home for the Aged: A Gerontological History of a Pioneer Venture in Caring for the Black Aged.* Ph.D. Dissertation, Syracuse University, 1977.

Pollitt, E., and A. Eichler. Behavioral disturbances among failure-to-thrive children. *American Journal of Diseases of Children,* 1976, 130, 24–29.

Pollitt, E., A. Eichler, and C. Chan. Psychosocial development and behavior of mothers of failure-to-thrive children. *American Journal of Orthopsychiatry,* 1975, 45, 525–537.

Pope, H. *Voices from the Drug Culture.* Boston: Beacon Press, 1971.

Portnoy, F., and C. Simmons. Daycare and attachment. *Child Development,* 1978, 49, 239–242.

Powell, G. Psychosocial development: Eight to ten years. In J. Noshpitz (ed.), *Basic Handbook of Child Psychiatry,* Vol. 1. New York: Basic Books, 1979, 190–199.

Poznanski, E. Childhood depression: A psychodynamic approach to the etiology of depression in children. In A. French and I. Berlin (eds.), *Depression in Children and Adolescents.* New York: Human Science Press, 1979.

Poznanski, E., V. Krahenbuhl, and J. Zrull. Childhood depression. *Journal of the American Academy of Child Psychiatry,* 1976, 15, 491–501.

Prehoda, R. *Extended Youth.* New York: Putnam's, 1968.

Price, C., R. Price, and B. Toomey. The pre-delinquent girl: Does a volunteer friend program help? *Adolescence,* Spring 1980, XV, 55–64.

Prinz, P. Sleep patterns in the healthy aged: Relationship with intellectual function. *Journal of Gerontology,* 1977, 32(2), 179–186.

Quinn, J. Divorce economic style. *Newsweek,* June 9, 1980, 82.

Rabkin, L. The institution of the family is alive and well. *Psychology Today,* 1976, 9, 66–67.

Rainwater, L. *Family Design: Marital Sexuality, Family Size, and Family Planning.* Chicago: Aldine, 1965.

Rallings, E. The special role of stepfather. *The Family Coordinator,* October 1976, 25, 445–457.

Ramey, C., L. Hieger, and D. Klisz. Synchronous reinforcement of vocal responses in failure-to-thrive infants. *Child Development,* 1972, 43, 1449–1455.

Ramos, M., and L. Gould. Where have all the flower children gone? A five-year follow-up of a natural group of drug users. *Journal of Drug Issues,* 1978, 8(1), 75–84.

Ramsey, P. Shall we "reproduce?" The medical ethics of in-vitro fertilization. *Child and Family,* 1976, 15(1), 43–53.

Rapoport, R., and R. Rapoport. The dual career family: A variant family and social change. *Human Relations,* 1969, 22, 3–30.

Rawlings, E. A general practitioner short-stay delivery unit. *The Practitioner,* 1973, 211, 329–334.

Rebelsky, F. Father's verbal interactions with infants in the first three months. In F. Rebelsky and L. Dormon (eds.), *Child Development and Behavior* (2nd. ed.). New York: Alfred A. Knopf, 1973.

Redl, F. The concept of punishment. Paper presented at the meeting of the American Orthopsychiatric Association, 1959.

Reese, H. The development of memory: Life-span perspectives. In H. Reese (ed.), *Advances in Child Development and Behavior,* Vol. 11. New York: Academic Press, 1976.

Reese, H., and L. Lipsitt. *Experimental Child Psychology.* New York: Academic Press, 1970.

Research News. Behavioral Teratology: Birth defects of the mind. *Science,* November 17, 1978, 202, 732–733.

Rest, J., M. Davison, and S. Robbins. Age trends in judging moral issues: A review of cross-sectional, longitudinal and sequential studies of the Defining Issues Test. *Child Development,* 1978, 49, 263–279.

Restak, R. Birth defects and behavior: A new study suggests a link in ideas and trends in medicine. *New York Times,* January 21, 1979a.

Restak, R. Psychosocial dwarfism: The evidence grows, the kids don't. *New York Times,* November 18, 1979b, E20.

Rheingold, H. The modification of social responsiveness in institutional babies. *Monographs of the Society for Research in Child Development,* 1956, 22 (2, Serial No. 63).

Rheingold, H., and K. Cook. The content of boys' and girls' rooms as an index of parents' behavior. *Child Development,* 1975, 46, 459–463.

Rheingold, H, and N. Bayley. The later effects of an experimental modification of mothering. *Child Development,* 1959, 30, 363–372.

Rheingold, H., J. Gewirtz, and H. Ross. Social conditioning of vocalizations in the infant. *Journal of Comparative and Physiological Psychology,* 1959, 52, 68–73.

Richards, P. Middle-class vandalism and age-status conflict. *Social Problems,* April 1979, 26(4), 482–497.

Richardson, J. Wife occupational superiority and marital troubles: An examination of the hypotheses. *Journal of Marriage and the Family,* February 1979, 41(1), 63–72.

Richmond, J. Disadvantaged children: What have they compelled us to learn? *Yale Journal of Biology and Medicine,* 1970, 43, 127–144.

Rienzo, B. The status of an education. *Phi Delta Kappan,* November 1981, 192–193.

Riess, A. The mother's eye—for better or for worse. *Psychoanalytic Study of the Child,* 1978, 33, 381–409.

Riessman, F. Styles of learning. *National Education Association Journal,* March 1966, 55, 15–17.

Riessman, F. The "helper" therapy principle. *National Association of Social Workers Journal,* April 1965, 27–32.

Riley, J. What people think about death. In O. Brim, H. Freeman, S. Levine, and N. Scotch (eds.), *The Dying Patient.* New York: Russell Sage Foundation, 1970, 30–41.

Riley, M., *et al. Aging and Society. Vol. 1: An Inventory of Research Findings.* New York: Russell Sage Foundation, 1968.

Ringler, N., M. Trause, M. Klaus, and J. Kennell. The effects of extra post-partum contact and maternal speech patterns on children's IQ, speech and language comprehension at five. *Child Development,* 1978, 49, 862–865.

Rist, R. On understanding the process of schooling: The contributions of labeling theory. In A. Holsey and J. Karabel (eds.), *Power and Ideology in Education.* Oxford, England: Oxford University Press, 1976.

Roberts, S. Cardiopulmonary abnormalities in aging. In I. Burnside (ed.), *Nursing and the Aged.* New York: McGraw-Hill, 1976, 286–316.

Robertson, J. Grandmotherhood: A study of role conceptions. *Journal of Marriage and the Family,* February 1977, 39, 165–174.

Robinson, H., N. Robinson, M. Wolins, V. Bronfenbrenner, and T. Richmond. Early child care in the United States of America. *Early Child Development and Care,* Monograph Issue 2, 1973.

Robinson, J., and P. Converse. Social change reflected in the use of time. In A. Campbell and P. Converse (eds.), *The Human Meaning of Social Change.* New York: Russell Sage Foundation, 1972.

Robinson, P. Parents of "beyond control" adolescents. *Adolescence,* Spring 1978, XIII(49), 109–119.

Rock, M. Gorilla mothers need some help from their friends. *Smithsonian,* July 1978, 9(4), 58–62.

Rogeness, G., R. Bednar, and H. Diesenhaus. The social system and children's behavior problems. *American Journal of Orthopsychiatry,* July 1974, 44(4), 497–502.

Rogers, C., M. Smith, and J. Coleman. Social comparison in the classroom: The relationship between academic achievement and self-concept. *Journal of Educational Psychology,* 1978, 70, 50–57.

Romer, N. The motive to avoid success and its effects on performance in school-age males and females. *Developmental Psychology,* 1975, 2(6), 689–699.

Root, J. The importance of peer groups. *Educational Research,* 1977, 20, 22–25.

Rosen, J., and G. Bibring. Psychological reactions of hospitalized male patients to a heart attack: Age and social-class differences. In B. Neugarten (ed.), *Middle Age and Aging.* Chicago: University of Chicago Press, 1968.

Rosenblatt, P. and M. Cunningham. Television watching and family tensions. *Journal of Marriage and the Family,* 1976, 38, 105–110.

Rosenham, D. The kindnesses of children. *Young Children,* 1969, 25.

Rosenham, R. The role of behavioral patterns and neurogenic factors in the pathogenesis of coronary heart disease. In R. Elliot (ed.), *Stress and the Heart.* New York: Futura, 1974.

Rosenkrantz, A. A note on adolescent suicide. *Adolescence,* Summer 1978, XIII(50), 209–215.

Rousseau, J. *Emile, or Concerning Education, Book 2.* (First published 1762). New York: E. P. Dutton, 1938.

Rossman, I. Human aging changes. In I. Burnside (ed.), *Nursing and the Aged.* New York: McGraw-Hill, 1976, 92–98.

Rowland, K. Environmental events predicting death in the elderly. *Psychological Bulletin,* 1979, 84, 349–372.

Rubenstein, J., and C. Howes. Caregiving and infant

behavior in daycare and in homes. *Developmental Psychology,* 1979, 15, 1–24.

Ruch, L. A multidimensional analysis of the concept of life change. *Journal of Health and Social Behavior,* 1977, 18, 71–83.

Ruebsaat, H. J., and R. Hull. *The Male Climacteric.* New York: Hawthorn Books, 1975.

Russell, C. Transition to parenthood: Problems and gratifications. *Journal of Marriage and the Family,* 1974, 36, 294–302.

Rutter, M. *The Qualities of Mothering.* New York: Jason Aronson, 1974.

Ryan, I., and P. Dunn. Sex education from prospective teachers' view poses a dilemma. *Journal of School Health,* December 1979, 573.

Ryder, R. Longitudinal data relating marriage satisfaction and having a child. *Journal of Marriage and the Family,* 1973, 35, 604–606.

Ryor, J. Declining SAT scores. *Today's Education,* 1977, 66,4.

Sabatino, D., J. Heald, S. Rothman, and T. Miller. Destructive norm-violating school behavior among adolescents: A review of protective and preventive efforts. *Adolescence,* Winter 1978, XIII(52), 675–686.

Sachs, S. Baby growing even more precious. *The Pittsburgh Press,* May 28, 1978, E1.

Sage, W. Classrooms for the autistic child. *Human Behavior,* March, 1975.

Salley, K. *The Development of Competitiveness in Women.* Ph.D. Dissertation, University of Arkansas, 1977.

Saltzstein, H., R. Diamond, and M. Belenky. Moral judgment level and conformity behavior. *Developmental Psychology,* 1972, 7, 327–336.

Sams, A. Conformity and peer groups in remedial nine-year-old children. *The Journal of Genetic Psychology,* 1974, 124, 145–150.

Sanborn, S. Means and ends: Moral development and moral education. In *Harvard Graduate School of Education Bulletin.* Cambridge, Massachusetts: Fall 1971.

Sanders, C. A comparison of adult bereavement in the death of a spouse, child, and parent. *Omega,* 1979–1980, 10(4), 303–321.

Santrock, J. Father absence, perceived maternal behavior, and moral development of boys. *Child Development,* 1975, 46, 753–757.

Sarason, I. *Abnormal Psychology: The Problem of Maladaptive Behavior.* New York: Appleton-Century-Crofts, 1972.

Sarrel, P., and L. Sarrel. The Redbook report on sexual relationships. *Redbook,* October 1980, 73–80.

Savitsky, J., and J. Babl. Cheating, intention and punishment from an equity theory perspective. *Journal of Research in Personality,* 1976, 10, 128–136.

Schacter, F., K. Kirschner, B. Klips, M. Friedricks, and K. Sanders. Everyday preschool interpersonal speech usage: Methodical, developmental, and sociolinguistic studies. *Monographs of the Society for Research in Child Development,* 1974, 39(3 Serial No. 156).

Schaffer, H. Cognitive components of the infant's response to strangers. In H. Lewis and L. Rosenblum (eds.), *The Origins of Fear.* New York: John Wiley and Sons, 1974.

Schaffer, H., and P. Emerson. The development of social attachments in infancy. *Monographs of the Society for Research in Child Development, 1964 (3 Serial No. 94).*

Schaie, K. Toward a stage theory of adult cognitive development. *Journal of Aging and Human Development,* 1977–1978, 8(2), 129–138.

Schaie, K., and W. Gribben. Adult development and aging. In M. Rosenzweig and L. Porter (eds.), *Annual Review of Psychology,* Vol. 26. Palo Alto, California: Annual Review, 1975.

Schaie, K., and J. Schaie. Clinical assessment and aging. In J. Birren and K. Schaie (eds.), *Handbook of the Psychology of Aging.* New York: Van Nostrand Reinhold, 1977, 629–723.

Schmuck, R., and P. Schmuck. *Group Processes in the Classroom* (2nd. ed.). Dubuque, Iowa: Wm. C. Brown, 1975.

Scholtz, G., and M. Ellis. Repeated exposure to objects and peers in a play setting. *Journal of Experimental Child Psychology,* 1975, 19, 448–455.

Schomer, J. Family therapy. In B. Wolman, J. Egan, and A. Ross (eds.), *Handbook of Treatment of Mental Disorders in Childhood and Adolescence.*

Englewood Cliffs, New Jersey: Prentice-Hall, 1978.

Schultz, T. Development of the appreciation of riddles. *Child Development,* 1974, 45, 100–105.

Schultz, T. A preliminary survery of economic analysis of fertility. *American Economic Review,* 1973, 63, 71–78.

Schultz, T., and F. Horibe. Development of the appreciation of verbal jokes. *Developmental Psychology,* 1974, 10, 13–20.

Schulz, R. *The Psychology of Death, Dying and Bereavement.* Reading, Massachusetts: Addison-Wesley, 1978.

Schulz, R., and G. Brenner. Relocation of the aged: A review and theoretical analysis. *Journal of Gerontology,* 1977, 32(3), 323–333.

Schwartz, J. Childhood origins of psychopathology. *American Psychologist,* October 1979, 34(10), 879–885.

Schwartz, T., and S. Sullivan. Special report: How men are changing. *Newsweek,* January 1978, 52–59.

Sears, R., L. Rav, and R. Alpert. *Identification and Child Rearing.* Stanford, California: Stanford University Press, 1965, 1–8.

Sears, R., E. Maccoby, and H. Lewin. *Patterns of Child Rearing.* Evanston, Illinois: Row, Peterson, 1957.

Seelbach, W., and C. Hansen. Satisfaction with family relations among the elderly. *Family Relations,* 1980, 29, 191–196.

Segal, J., and J. Cooper. Television, the mass media, and child development. In J. Noshpitz (ed.), *Basic Handbook of Psychiatry,* Vol. 4. New York: Basic Books, 1979, 426–431.

Selye, H. Stress and Aging. *Journal of the American Geriatrics Society,* 1970, 18(9), 669–680.

Selye, H. *The Stress of Life.* New York: McGraw-Hill, 1956.

Selye, H. *The Physiology and Pathology of Exposure to Stress.* Montreal: Acta Medical Publisher, 1950.

Senility: Myth or madness. *Age Page.* Washington, D.C.: National Institute on Aging, October 1980.

Sex-typing. *Pittsburgh Press,* February, 22 1976.

Sgroi, S. Kids with clap: Gonorrhea as an indicator of child sexual assault. *Victimology,* 1977, 2(2), 251–267.

Shanas, E., and P. Hauser. Zero population growth and the family life of old people. *Journal of Social Issues,* November 4, 1974, 30, 79–92.

Shane, H., and W. Wirtz. The academic score decline: Are facts the enemy of truth? *Phi Delta Kappan,* October 1977, 59(2), 83–86.

Sheils, M., and S. Agrest. Nurseries in the jailhouse. *Newsweek,* January 12, 1976.

Shirley, M. *The First Two Years: A Study of Twenty-five Babies.* Institute of Child Welfare Monographs, No. 7. Minneapolis: University of Minnesota Press, 1933.

Shock, N. The physiology of aging. *Scientific American,* 1962, 206, 100–110.

Shouval, R., K. Venaki, U. Bronfenbrenner, E. Devereux, and E. Kiely. Anomalous reactions to social pressure of Israeli and Soviet children raised in family vs. collective settings. *Journal of Personality and Social Psychology,* 1975, 32(3), 477–489.

Shu, C. Husband-father in delivery room? *Hospitals,* 1973, 41, 90–94.

Shulman, N. Life-cycle variations in patterns of close relationships. *Journal of Marriage and the Family,* 1975, 37, 4, 813–821.

Shumsky, A. *In Search of Teaching Style.* New York: Appleton-Century-Crofts, 1968.

Silberman, A. If they say your child can't learn. *McCalls,* January 1976, 10.

Simpson, D., and A. Nelson. Attention training through breathing control to modify hyperactivity. *Journal of Learning Disabilities,* 1974, 7, 274–283.

Siqueland, R., and L. Lipsitt. Conditioned head turning in human newborns. *Journal of Experimental Child Psychology,* 1966, 3, 356–376.

Skeels, H. Adult status of children with contrasting life experiences: A follow-up study. *Monographs of the Society for Research in Child Development,* 1966, 31 (3, Serial No. 105).

Skinner, B. F. *The Technology of Teaching.* New York: Appleton-Century-Crofts, 1968.

Skinner, B. F. *Science and Human Behavior.* New York: Macmillan, 1953.

Slobin, D. Seven questions about language development. In P. Dodwell (ed.), *New Horizons in Psychology,* No. 2. Baltimore: Penguin, 1972, 197–215.

Smart, M., and R. Smart. *Children* (3d. ed.). New York: Macmillan, 1977.

Smith, J., and L. Smith. *Consenting Adults.* Baltimore: Johns Hopkins University Press, 1975.

Smith, M., S. Zingale, and J. Coleman. The influence of adult expectancy/child performance discrepancies upon children's self-concepts. *American Educational Research Journal,* Spring 1978, 15(2), 259–265.

Snoek, D., and E. Rothblum. Self-disclosure among adolescents in relation to parental affection and control patterns. *Adolescence,* Summer 1979, XIV(54), 333–340.

Social Security Administration Office of Research and Statistics. *Income and Resources for the Aged,* 1980.

Solomon, R. Punishment. *American Psychologist,* 1964, 19, 239–253.

Sones, B. As you are so once you were. *The Plain Dealer,* May 25, 1980, 15–16.

Sontag, S. The double standard of aging. *Saturday Review,* September 23, 1972, 29–38.

Sours, J. Enuresis. In B. Wolman, J. Egan, and A. Ross (eds.), *Handbook of Treatment of Mental Disorders in Childhood and Adolescence.* Englewood Cliffs, New Jersey: Prentice-Hall, 1978, 153–160.

Spar, B. *College students' plans for coping with future family-career conflicts.* Ph. D. Dissertation, University of Wisconsin, Madison, 1977.

Spasoff, R., A. Kraus, E. Beattie, D. Holden, J. Lawson, M. Rodenburg, and G. Woodcock. A longitudinal study of elderly residents of long-stay institutions. *Gerontologist,* 1978, 18(3), 281–292.

Spearman, C. General intelligence objectively determined and measured. *American Journal of Psychology,* 1904, 15, 201–293.

Spilton, D., and L. Lee. Some determinants of effective communication in four-year-olds. *Child Development,* 1977, 48, 968–977.

Spinetta, J., D. Rigler, and M. Karon. Anxiety in the dying child. *Pediatrics,* 1973, 52, 841–845.

Spitz, R. A. Hospitalism: A follow-up report. *Psychoanalytic Study of the Child,* 1946, 2, 113–117.

Spitz, R. Hospitalism: An inquiry into the genesis of psychiatric conditions in early childhood. In A. Freed (ed.), *The Psychoanalytic Study of the*

Child. Vol. 1. New York: International Universities Press, 1945, 53–74.

Spivack, G., and M. Swift. "High risk" classroom behaviors in kindergarten and first grade. *American Journal of Community Psychology,* 1977, 5(4), 385–397.

Sprafkin, J., R. Liebert, and R. Poulos. Effects of a prosocial televised example of children's helping. *Journal of Experimental Child Psychology,* 1975, 20, 119–126.

Stafford, R., E. Backman, and P. DiBona. The division of labor among cohabiting and married couples. *Journal of Marriage and the Family,* 1977, 39, 43–57.

Statchell, M. How to enjoy life up until the last minute. *Parade,* October 16, 1977, 16–18.

Steinberg, L., and J. Hill. Patterns of family interaction as a function of age, the onset of puberty and formal thinking. *Developmental Psychology,* 1978, 14(6), 683–684.

Steininger, M., R. Johnson, and D. Kirts. Cheating on college examinations as a function of situationally aroused anxiety and hostility. *Journal of Educational Psychology,* 1964, 55, 317–324.

Sterman, M., D. McGinty, and A. Adinolf. *Brain Development and Behavior.* New York: Academic Press, 1971.

Stewart, M. Hyperactive children. *Scientific American,* April 1970, 94–99.

Stiver, S. *Fear of Success: A Motive to Avoid Success or a Response to Violation of Sex Role Prescriptions?* Ph.D. Dissertation, Washington University, 1976.

Stockard, J., and M. Johnson. *Sex Roles: Sex Inequality and Sex Role Development.* Englewood Cliffs, New Jersey: Prentice-Hall, 1980.

Stoddard, S. *The Hospice Movement: A Better Way of Caring for the Dying.* Briarcliff Manor, England: Stein and Day, 1978.

Stone, L., H. Smith, and L. Murphy. *The Competent Infant.* New York: Basic Books, 1973.

Stott, D. Children in the womb: The effects of stress. *New Society,* May 19, 1977, 329–331.

Straus, M., R. Gelles, and S. Steinmetz. *Behind Closed Doors: A Survey of Family Violence in America.* New York: Doubleday, 1979.

Streib, G. An alternative family form for older persons: Need and social context. *The Family Coordinator,* 1978, 27(4), 413–420.

Streissguth, A. Maternal drinking and the outcome of pregnancy: Implications for child mental health. *American Journal of Orthopsychiatry,* 1977, 47(3), 422–431.

Suls, J., and R. Kalle. Children's moral judgments as a function of intention, damage, and an actor's physical harm. *Developmental Psychology,* 1979, 15(1), 93–94.

Super, C. Differences in the care of male and female infants: Data from non-American samples. Unpublished manuscript, 1977.

Sutton-Smith, B. A developmental structural account of riddles. In B. Kirschenblatt-Gimblett (eds.), *Speech, Play, and Display.* The Hague, Netherlands: Mouton, 1975.

Sviland, M. Helping elderly couples become sexually liberated: Psycho-social issues. *Counseling Psychologist,* 1975, 5(1), 67–72.

Swan, R., and H. Stavros. Child-rearing practices associated with the development of cognitive skills of children in low socioeconomic areas. *Early Child Development and Care,* 1973, 2, 23–38.

Tallmer, M., and B. Kutner. Disengagement and the stresses of aging. *Journal of Gerontology,* 1969, 24, 70–75.

Tanner, J. Growing up. *Scientific American,* September 1973, 229, 36–37.

Tanner, M. Sequence, tempo, and individual variation in the growth and development of boys and girls aged twelve to sixteen. *Daedalus,* 1971, 100, 907–930.

Taylor, R. Psychosocial development among black children and youth: A re-examination. *American Journal of Orthopsychiatry,* January 1976, 46 (1).

Taylor, W., and K. Hoedt. Classroom-related problems: Counsel parents, teachers, or children. *Journal of Counseling Psychology,* 1974, 21(1), 3–8.

Terman, L. *Genetic Studies of Genius.* Vols. 1–4. Stanford, California: Stanford University Press, 1925–1959.

Terman, L., and M. Merrill. *Stanford-Binet Intelligence Scale (Manual for 3rd Revision, Form L-M).* Boston: Houghton Mifflin, 1960.

Terman, L., and M. Merrill. *Measuring Intelligence.* Boston: Houghton Mifflin, 1937.

The toll of the pension clock. *The New York Times,* June 1, 1980, E20.

Thomas A., S. Chess, and H. Birch. The origin of personality. *Scientific American,* August 1970, 223(2), 102–109.

Thomas, M., and R. Drabman. Toleration of real life aggression as a function of exposure to televised violence and age of subject. *Merrill-Palmer Quarterly,* 1975, 21(3), 227–232.

Thompson, N., and B. McCandless. IT score variations by instructional style. *Child Development,* 1970, 41, 425–436.

Thompson, W., and J. Grusec. Studies of early experience. In P. Mussen (ed.), *Carmichael's Manual of Child Psychology* (3rd. ed.). New York: John Wiley and Sons, 1970.

Thornburg, H. Peers: Three distinct groups. *Adolescence,* 1971, 6, 59–76.

Thurstone, L. Primary mental abilities. *Psychometric Monographs,* 1938.

Tierney, M., and K. Rubin. Egocentrism and conformity in childhood. *The Journal of Genetic Psychology,* 1975, 126, 23–38.

Timiras, P. *Developmental Physiology and Aging.* New York: Macmillan, 1972.

Tobin, S., and M. Lieberman. *Last Home for the Aged: Critical Implications of Institutionalization.* San Francisco: Jossey-Bass Publishers, 1976.

Tome, H. *Myself and Others in Adolescent Consciousness.* Paris: Delachaux and Niestle, 1972.

Toolan, J. M. Therapy of depressed and suicidal children. *American Journal of Psychotherapy,* 1978, 32, 243–251.

Torrance, E. Can we teach children to think creatively? *Journal of Creative Behavior,* 1972, 6, 114–143.

Toseland, P., and J. Sykes. Senior citizens center participation and other correlates of life satisfaction. *The Gerontologist,* 1977, 17(3) 235–241.

Treas, J. Family support systems for the aged: Some social and demographic considerations. *Gerontologist,* 1977, 17, 486–491.

Troll, L. The family of later life: A decade review. *Journal of Marriage and the Family,* 1971, 33, 263–290.

Trotman, F. Race, IQ and the middle class. *Journal of Educational Psychology,* 1977, 69(3), 266–273.

Turchi, B. *The Demand for Children: The Economics of Fertility in the United States.* Cambridge, Massachusetts: Ballinger, 1975.

Ungar, G. Biochemistry of intelligence. *Research Communications in Psychology, Psychiatry and Behavior,* 1976, 1(5, 6), 597–606.

U.S. Bureau of the Census. Current Population Reports, Special Studies. *American Families and Living Arrangements.* Washington, D.C.: U.S. Printing Office, 1980, 23–104.

U.S. Bureau of the Census. *Report on Living Practices of Americans.* Washington, D.C.: U.S. Printing Office, July 1979.

U.S. Bureau of the Census. *Statistical Abstracts of the United States* (99th edition). Washington, D.C.: U.S. Printing Office, 1978.

U.S. Bureau of the Census. Educational attainment in the United States. *Current Population Reports* (Series P-20, No. 295). Washington, D.C.: U.S. Printing Office, 1976.

U.S. Bureau of the Census. Some demographic aspects of aging in the United States. *Current Population Reports* (Series P-23). Washington, D.C.: U.S. Printing Office, 1973.

U.S. Dept. of Commerce, Bureau of the Census. Population profile of the United States, 1978, population characteristics. *Current Population Reports* (Series P-20, 336). Washington, D.C.: U.S. Printing Office, April 1978.

U.S. Dept. of Commerce, Bureau of the Census. *Population profile of the United States* (Series P-20, No. 239). Washington, D.C.: U.S. Printing Office, September 1972.

U.S. Dept. of Health, Education and Welfare. *The Health of Children.* Washington, D.C.: U.S. Printing Office, 1970.

U.S. Dept. of Health, Education and Welfare. *One parent families. Case history #1* (Publication No. OHD-74-44), Office of Human Development, Children's Bureau, 1974.

U.S. Dept. of Health, Education and Welfare. *A consumer's guide to mental health services* (Publication No. ADM 75–214). Rockville, Maryland: Public Health Service, Alcohol, Drug Abuse, and Mental Health Administration, 1975.

U.S. Dept. of Health and Human Services. High blood pressure: A common but controllable disorder. *Age Page.* Bethesda, Maryland: National Institute on Aging, September 1980.

U.S. Dept. of Labor. *Marital and Family Characteristics of the Labor Force.* U.S. Dept. of Labor: Bureau of Labor Statistics, 1980.

U.S. Dept. of Labor, Women's Bureau. *Working Mothers and their Children.* Washington, D.C.: U.S. Printing Office, 1977.

U.S. National Center on Child Abuse and Neglect. *Child Sexual Abuse: Incest, Assault, and Sexual Exploitation.* Washington, D.C.: U.S. Printing Office, 1978.

Vail, E. What will it be? Reading or machismo and soul? *Clearing House,* October 1970, 45, 92–96.

Vaillant, G. *Natural History of Male Psychologic Health, II, Empirical Dimensions of Positive Mental Health.* Presented at the Annual Meeting of the American Psychiatric Association, Dallas, May 1–5, 1972.

Vaillant, G., and C. McArthur. Natural history of male psychologic health. The adult life cycle from 18–50. *Seminars in Psychiatry,* 1972, 4(4), 415–427.

Vaitenas, R. *The interest and personality correlates of voluntary career change in young adulthood and mid-life.* Ph.D. Dissertation, Case Western Reserve, 1976.

Vaitenas, R., and Y. Wiener. Developmental, emotional and interest factors in voluntary mid-career change. *Journal of Vocational Behavior,* 1977, 11, 291–304.

Vandell, D. A microanalysis of toddlers' social interaction with mothers and fathers. *The Journal of Genetic Psychology,* 1979, 134, 299–312.

Vander Zanden, J. *Human Development.* New York: Alfred A. Knopf, 1978.

Vasudev, J. An exercise testing a Piagetian-type task. Unpublished manuscript, University of Pittsburgh, 1976.

Vener, A., and C. Stewart. Adolescent sexual behavior in middle America revisited: 1970–1973. *Journal of Marriage and the Family,* 1974, 36, 728–741.

Vickers, R. The therapeutic milieu and the older depressed patient. *Journal of Gerontology,* 1976, 31(3), 314–317.

Vidal, D. Quaker project gives instructions by games. *New York Times,* May 23, 1976.

Villet, B. Opiates of the mind. *The Atlantic Monthly,* June 1978, 82–89.

Vincze, M. The social contacts of infants and young children reared together. *Early Child Development and Care.* London: Gordon Breach Science Publishers, 1971, 99–109.

Vinogradoff, E. Childbirth in Moscow. In *Growing Up: A Book of Readings,* Reading, Massachusetts: Addison-Wesley, 1978, 4–8.

Vulliamy, D. *The Newborn Child.* Baltimore: Williams and Wilkins, 1972.

Vygotsky, L. *Thought and Language.* Translated by E. Hanfmann and G. Vakar. Cambridge, Massachusetts: MIT Press, 1962.

Waechter, E. Children's awareness of fatal illness. *American Journal of Nursing,* 1971, 71, 1168–1172.

Wallach, L., M. Wallach, M. Dozier, and N. Kaplan. Poor children learning to read do not have trouble with auditory discrimination but do have trouble with phoneme recognition. *Journal of Educational Psychology,* 1977, 69(1), 36–39.

Wallerstein, J., and J. Kelly. *Surviving the Break-up: How Children Actually Cope with Divorce.* New York: Basic Books, 1980.

Wallerstein, J., and J. Kelly. Divorce and children. In J. Noshpitz (ed.), *Basic Handbook of Child Psychiatry,* Vol. 4, 1979, 339–346.

Walster, E., J. Traupman, and G. Walster. Equity and extramarital sexuality. *Archives of Sexual Behavior,* 1978, 7, 127–142.

Wasow, M., and M. Loeb. Sexuality in nursing homes. In R. Solnick (ed.), *Sexuality and Aging* (revised ed.). Los Angeles: University of Southern California Press, 1978, 159.

Watson, E., and G. Lowrey. *Growth and Development of Children.* Chicago: Year Book Medical Publishers, 1967.

Watson, J. *Psychology from the Standpoint of a Behaviorist.* Philadelphia: Lippincott, 1919.

Watson, J., and R. Raynor. Conditioned emotional reactions. *Journal of Experimental Psychology,* 1920, 3, 1–4.

Wechsler, D. *Wechsler Intelligence Scale for Children Manual.* New York: Psychological Corp., 1949.

Weg, R. Normal aging changes in the reproductive system. In I. Burnside (ed.), *Nursing and the Aged.* New York: McGraw-Hill, 1976, 99–112.

Weg, R. Physiology and sexuality in aging. In I. Burnside (ed.), *Sexuality and Aging.* Los Angeles: University of Southern California Press, 1975, 7–17.

Weisman, A., and R. Kastenbaum. The psychological autopsy: A study of the terminal phase of life. *Community Mental Health Journal,* 1968, Monograph No. 4.

Weithorn, C., and R. Ross. Stimulant drugs for hyperactivity: Some additional disturbing questions. *American Journal of Orthopsychiatry,* January 1976, 46 (1), 168–172.

Werner, E. *Cross-Cultural Child Development.* Montery, California: Wadsworth, 1979.

Westlake, H. *Children: A Study in Individual Behavior.* Lexington, Massachusetts: Ginn, 1973.

Westoff, C., and J. McCarthy. Population attitudes and fertility. *Family Planning Perspectives,* March/April 1979, 11(2), 93–97.

White, R. Motivation reconsidered. *Psychological Review,* 1959, 66, 297–333.

Whiting, B., and J.W.M. Whiting. *Children of Six Cultures: A Psycho-Cultural Analysis.* Cambridge, Massachusetts: Harvard University Press, 1975.

Whiting, J.W.M. Socialization process and personality. In F.L.K. Hsu (ed.), *Psychological Anthropology.* Homewood, Illinois: Dorsey Press, 1961.

White, B. Mothering! A vastly underrated occupation. *Interchange: A Journal of Educational Studies,* 1971, 2(2).

Whiting, J.W.M., and B. Whiting. Contributions of anthropology to the methods of studying childrearing. In P. Mussen (ed.), *Handbook of Research Methods in Child Development.* New York: John Wiley and Sons, 1960.

Williams, J., S. Bennett, and D. Best. Awareness and expression of sex stereotype in young children. *Developmental Psychology,* 1975, 11(5) 635–642.

Williams, L. *Analysis of Social and Community Needs of Black Senior Citizens in Inner City Detroit.* Ph.D. Dissertation, University of Michigan, 1977.

Willis, R. A new approach to the economic theory of

fertility behavior. *Journal of Political Economy,* 1973, S14–S64.

Wilson, K., L. Zurcher, D. McAdams, and R. Curtis. Stepfathers and stepchildren: An exploratory analysis from two national surveys. *Journal of Marriage and the Family,* 1975, 37, 526–535.

Winick, M., K. Meyer, and R. Harris. Malnutrition and environmental enrichment by early adoption. *Science,* 1975, 190, 1173–1175.

Winter, J., C. Faiman, and F. Reyer. Norms and abnormal pubertal development. *Clinical Obstetrics and Gynecology,* March 1978, 21(1), 67–86.

Witkin, H., C. Moore, D. Goodenough, and P. Cox. Field-dependent and field-independent cognitive styles and their educational implications. *Review of Educational Research,* 1977, 47(1), 1–64.

Wittrock, M. *Education and the Brain.* Chicago, Illinois: University of Chicago Press, 1978.

Woestehoff, E. Students with reading disabilities and guidance. *Guidance Monograph Series.* Boston: Houghton Mifflin, 1970.

Wohlwill, J. *The Study of Behavioral Development.* New York: Academic Press, 1973.

Wolff, P. Observations on the early development of smiling. In B. Foss (ed.), *Determinants of Infant Behavior* II. New York: John Wiley and Sons, 1966, 113–138.

Wolk, S., and J. Brandon. Runaway adolescents' perceptions of parents and self. *Adolescence,* 1977, XII(46) 175–187.

Wolk, S., and S. Telleen. Psychological and social correlates of life satisfaction as a function of resident constraint. *Journal of Gerontology,* 1976, 36(1), 89–98.

Women and retirement income programs: Current issues of equity and adequacy. *A Report of the Select Committee on Aging, House of Representatives, Ninety-Sixth Congress.* Washington, D.C.: U.S. Printing Office, 1979.

Wood, L. *An analysis of motivational reading task reinforcers used in selected grade four classes.* Ph.D. Dissertation, The University of Akron, 1977.

Wooden, H., S. Lisowski, and F. Early. Volunteers, Head Start children and development. *Academic Therapy,* 1976, 11(4), 449–453.

Woods, M. The unsupervised child of the working mother. *Developmental Psychology,* 1972, 6, 14–25.

Wright, H. *Eighty Unmarried Mothers Who Kept Their Babies.* Sacramento: State of California Department of Social Welfare, Los Angeles, Children's Home Society of California and Los Angeles County Bureau of Adoptions, 1965.

Wurst, K. Caretaker–child Interactions in Greek and American Cultures. Paper presented at the annual meeting of the Northeastern Educational Research Association meetings. Ellenville, New York, October 25–27, 1978.

Wyden, B. Growth: 45 crucial months. *Life,* December 17, 1971, 93.

Wynne, E. Behind the discipline problem: Youth suicide as a measure of alienation. *Phi Delta Kappan,* January 1978, 307–315.

Yarber, W., and G. McCabe. Teacher characteristics and the inclusion of sex education topics in grades 6–8 and 9–11. *Journal of School Health,* April 1981, 288–291.

Yarrow, M., P. Blank, O. Quinn, E. Yomans, and J. Stein. Social psychological characteristics of old age. In *Human Aging,* Publication No. 71–9051. Washington, D.C.: U.S. Printing Office, 1975.

Zajonc, R. Family configuration and intelligence. *Science,* 1976, 192, 227–292.

Zelnick, M., and J. Kanter. Sexuality, contraception, and pregnancy among unwed females in the United States. In C. Westoff and R. Parke (eds.), *Demographic and Social Aspects of Population Growth.* Washington, D.C.: U.S. Printing Office, 1972, 355–374.

Zentall S. Optimal stimulation as theoretical basis of hyperactivity. *American Journal of Orthopsychiatry,* July 1975, 45(4), 549–560.

Zeskind, P., and C. Ramey. Fetal malnutrition: An experimental study of its consequences on infant development in two caregiving environments. *Child Development,* 1978, 49, 1155–1162.

Zimbardo, P., P. Pilkonis, and R. Norwood. The social disease called shyness. *Psychology Today,* May 1975, 69–72.

Zimmerman, D., and D. Wieder. You can't help but get stoned: Notes on the social organization of marijuana smoking. *Social Problems,* 1977, 25, 198–207.

Photo Credits

Author Index

Subject Index

theory of development; *see also* personality development

ERA, *see* Equal Rights Amendment

Ethical considerations in research, in *in vitro* fertilization, 77–78; *see also* research

Eugenics, 58–59

Euthanasia, 582–583, 597

Executive responsibility, stage of, 421–422, 460, 462; *see also* personality development

Extramarital sexual intercourse, *see* sexual behavior

Failure-to-thrive-syndrome (FTTS), 127, 140

Family counseling, *see* counseling

Family Educational Rights and Privacy Act of 1974, 442

Family planning, 406

Family relationships: in adolescence, 344–348; in middle age with parents, 477–478; *see also* family violence

Family violence, 434

Fantasy play, *see* play

Father-absent homes, *see* deprivation

Fear: in childhood, 265–266; development of, 118–119; in preschool, 191

Fertilization, *in vitro,* 41, 76–78

Fetal alcohol syndrome, 73

Fetal monitoring, 88

Fetal period, 63–68, *see also* prenatal development

"Fitness in Diapers", 146

Fixation, 23

Flextime, 429

Fluid intelligence, *see* intelligence

Fontanels, 98

Formal operations stage of development, 330–333; *see also* cognition, stages of development

Freudian theory, *see* personality development; psychoanalytic theory

Friendship groups, *see* peer relationships

Functional disorders of later adulthood, *see* mental health problems in later adulthood

General factor theory of intelligence, *see* intelligence

Generativity versus self-absorption, stage of, 418, 463–469; *see also* personality development

Generosity, development of, 222–223

Genetics, *see* hereditary bases of development

Genital stage, 324; *see also* psychoanalytic theory

Good-boy/good-girl orientation stage of moral development, *see* moral development

Gonorrhea, *see* sexually transmitted diseases

Grammar, kernel, 182

Grandmothering, *see* grandparenting

Grandparenting, 478–482, 517

Group marriage, *see* life-styles

Group playpens, *see* communal childrearing

Group tests of intelligence, *see* intelligence

Growth, 9

Habituation, 114

Handicapped children: later childhood, 292–299; learning disabilities, 250–252; middle childhood, 246–248; preschool, 209; *see also* mental retardation

Health care of the elderly, 550–551

Hedonistic orientation with an instrumental view of human relations, *see* moral development

Hereditary bases of development, 53–58

Hereditary versus environment controversy, 52–54

Herpes, *see* sexually transmitted diseases

High blood pressure, *see* hypertension

High-risk infants, 127, 138

Holophrastic speech, *see* speech

Homosexuality, in adolescence, 329–330; *see also* life-styles

Hospice movement, 575–576; *see also* dying, support systems

Hostile aggression, *see* aggression

Humor, development of: in adolescence, 314–315; in later adulthood, 261–263

Hyperactivity, *see* handicapped children, learning disabilities

Hypertension, 535–536

Hypochondriasis, *see* functional disorders of later adulthood

Iconic mode of responding, *see* cognitive modes of responding in the preschool years

Identification, 149–151

Identity development, 369; in young adulthood, 389–390; *see also* personality development

Image-based thinking, *see* symbolic representation

Imitation, *see* learning, types of

Imprinting, 12–13

Impulsivity-reflectivity, *see* cognitive styles

Incest, *see* abuse of children

Incipient cooperation stage, *see* moral development

Independence: in adolescence, 347–348; as a developmental task, 390; in middle age, 472; in middle childhood, 232; in preschool years, 189–191; in young adulthood, 390

Individual differences in development: in infancy, 127; in preschool years, 207–209

Individual tests of intelligence, *see* intelligence

Industry versus inferiority, *see* personality development, stages of

Infancy and toddlerhood, stages of, 7, 98–133; perceptual development during, 101–107; physical development during, 101–102

Infant amaurotic family idiocy, 56

Infant learning, 116–118

Infertility after age 30, 418–420

Initiative versus guilt stage, *see* personality development, stages of

Innate mechanism theory of language development, *see* language development, stages and theories of

Inner speech, *see* speech

Institutionalization, effects on development, 151–154

Instrumental aggression, *see* aggression, types of

Instrumental dependence, *see* dependence, types of

Integrity versus despair, stage of, 464; *see also* personality development, stages of

Intelligence, 239; in adolescence, 333; classifications, 242; crystallized, 471; fluid, 462, declines in adolescent IQs, 333; IQs in young adulthood, 420; in later adulthood, 500–503; in middle age, 461–462; testing, 239–243; theories of, 240–241

Intelligence Quotient (IQ), *see* intelligence

Intelligence tests, *see* intelligence, testing

The Desire of All Nations

This book is a part of a curriculum that is built upon the life of Christ entitled, "The Desire of All Nations," for grades 2-8. Any of the books in this curriculum can be used by themselves or as an entire program.

INFORMATION ABOUT THE 2-8 GRADE PROGRAM

Multi-level

This program is written on a multi-level. That means that each booklet has material for grades 2-8. This is so the whole family in these grades may work from the same books. It is difficult for a busy mother to have 2 or more children and each have a different set of books. Remember, the Bible is written for all ages.

The Bible—the Primary Textbook

The books in this program are designed to teach the parent and the student how to learn academic subjects by using the Bible as a primary textbook.

The Desire of Ages

The Desire of Ages by Ellen G. White is used as a textbook to go with the Bible. This focuses on the early life of Christ, when He was a child. Children relate best to Christ as a child and youth.

Lesson Numbers

The big number in the top right corner on the cover of this book is the Lesson Number and corresponds with the chapter number in the book *The Desire of Ages*. For example, Lesson 1 in the school program will go along with chapter 1 in *The Desire of Ages*. Usually each family starts at the beginning with Lesson 1. Most children have not had a true Bible program, therefore they need the foundation built. If there is academic material that they have already covered, they do the Bible part and review then pass quickly on.

Seven Academic Subjects

There are seven academic subjects in this program—Health, Mathematics, Music, Science–Nature, History/Geography/Prophecy, Language, Voice–Speech.

Language Program

A good, solid language program is recommended to be used along with the SonLight materials.

The Riggs Institute has a multi-sensory teaching method that accommodates every child's unique learning style. Their program is called *Writing and Spelling Road to Reading and Thinking*. Order by calling (800) 200-4840 or visit www.riggsinst.org. (Disclaimer: SonLight does not endorse the reading books recommended in the Riggs' program.)

Another option which you might find more user friendly and is similar to the Riggs program but from a Christian perspective is *Spell to Write and Read* by Wanda Sanseri. To order, call Wanda Sanseri at (503) 654-2300 or visit https://www.bhibooks.net/swr.html

"The Fullness of Time"
Lesson 3 – Alertness

The following books are those you will need for this lesson.
All of these can be obtained from www.sonlighteducation.com

The Rainbow Covenant – Study the spiritual meaning of colors and make your own rainbow book.

Health
The Heart

Math
Addition I

Music
Musical and Non Musical Sounds

Science/Nature
Stars and Constellations

A Casket – Coloring book and story. Learn how to treat the gems of the Bible.

H/G/P
Continents

Language
History of the Word

Speech/Voice
Voice Culture

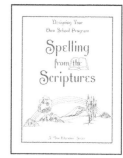

Spelling from the Scriptures

Bible Study – Learn how to study the Bible and helpful use tools.

Bible
*The Desire of all Nations I
Teacher Study Guide*

Student Study Guide

Bible Lesson Study Guide

Memory Verses
*The Desire of all Nations I
Scripture Songs Book*

and MP3 files

Our Nature Study Book – Your personal nature journal.

Table of Contents

God's Kind Eyes

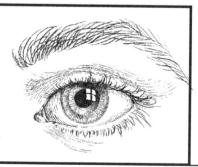

Pretty stars overhead,
Looking down on my bed,
Can you be God's kind eyes
Watching me from the skies?

Teacher Section

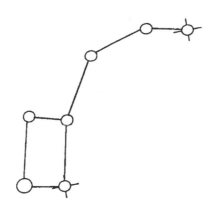

"The heavens declare the glory of God; and the firmament sheweth his handiwork."

Job 37:14

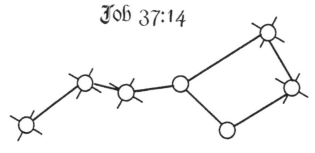

INSTRUCTIONS
For the Teacher

Step 1

Study the Bible Lesson and begin to memorize the Memory Verses. Familiarize Yourself With the Character Quality.

The student can answer the Bible Review Questions. See page 6. Use the Steps in Bible Study.

Bible Lesson

"The Fullness of Time" – Ecclesiastes 3:1-15; Luke 1:26-35; Galatians 4:4-5

Memory Verses

Galatians 4:4-5; *The Desire of Ages* 32; Acts 3:22; Isaiah 61:1-3; 60:1-3; Genesis 49:10; John 3:16-17

Character Quality

Alertness – quick to understand and watching very carefully: vigilance; watchfulness; moving with celerity or briskness; nimbleness; sprightliness

Antonyms – carelessness; indifference; unawareness; levity

Character Quality Verse

Mark 14:38 – *"Watch ye and pray, lest ye enter into temptation. The spirit truly is ready, but the flesh is weak."*

Step 2

Understand How To/And

A. Do the spelling cards so the student can begin to build his own spiritual dictionary.

B. Mark the Bible.

C. Evaluate your student's character in relation to the character quality of **alertness**.

D. Familiarize yourself with the "Stars and Constellations." Notice the Projects.

E. Review the Scripture References for the "Stars and Constellations."

F. Notice the Answer Key.

A. Spelling Cards

Spelling Lists

Star Words

Place I - II	Place II - III
angels	Arcturus
Big Dipper	astrology
clocks	astronomy
brightness	atmosphere
clusters	Betelgeuse
color	Big Dipper
creation	Bootes
distance	brightness
duty	Castor and Pollux
gas	classifying
gem	clusters
giants	companions
guardian	constellations
guides	counterfeits
host	dependable
jewel	dwarfs
Little Dipper	emission
motion	gamma
Morning Star	helium
northern	hemisphere
Orion	hieroglyphics
Pleiades	Horsehead Nebula
polestar	hydrogen
regular	inclination
seasonal	influences
sequence	irregularly
size	Little Dipper
stars	magnitude
twinkling,	Mazzaroth
twinkle	Morning Star

Place II - III continued	Bible Words continued
multiple	faileth
navigational	favour (favor)
nebula	favoured
neutron	forever
nebulae	fullness
northern	Galilee
Orion	Israel
Pleiades	Jesus
Polaris	Joseph
polestar	kingdom
prophetic	law
Proxima Centauri	made
radiation	Mary
Rigel	Nazareth
sextant	prolonged
Southern Cross	proverb
super-giants	redeem
Swan (Cygnus)	reign
sword	sent
twinkling, twinkle	sons (Son)
unique	stand
variations	throne
	time
Bible Words	troubled
adoption	under
alertness	virgin
blessed	vision
conceive	
David	
end	
espoused	

See the book,
Spelling From the Scriptures
for instructions about
the spelling cards.

B. How to Mark the Bible

1. Copy the list of Bible texts in the back of the Bible on an empty page as a guide.

2. Go to the first text in the Bible and copy the next text beside it. Go to the next one and repeat the process until they are all chain referenced.

3. Have the student present the study to family and/or friends.

4. In each student lesson there is one or more sections that have a Mark Your Bible about the subject studied. (See the student's section, pages 16 and 149.)

C. Evaluate Your Student's Character

This section is for the purpose of helping the teacher know how to encourage the students in becoming more **alert**.

See page 7.

Place I = Grades 2-3-4
Place II = Grades 4-5-6
Place III = Grades 6-7-8

D. Familiarize Yourself With the "Star and Constellations" – Notice the Projects

Projects

1. Sleep outside under the stars. Use your binoculars to enjoy the beauty of the heavens. Find Orion and discuss Jesus' Second Coming.

2. For a family building project, build a tree house or elevated deck. The child can do much of the work with proper supervision. The family can sleep outside in the tree house, or on the deck, and observe the stars.

3. Purchase a space puzzle and put it together as a family, while discussing God's stars and constellations.

4. Neatly copy Bible verses about the stars. Then place them in different places in the home.

5. Make cookies in the shape of stars to serve at a special space meal.

E. Review the Scripture References for "Stars and Constellations"

Teacher, read through this section before working on the lesson with the student, also see the student section pages 16 and 149 .

See page 8.

F. Notice the Answer Key

The Answer Key for the student book is found on page 15.

Step 3

Read the Lesson Aim.

Lesson Aim

"But like the stars in the vast circuit of their appointed path, God's purposes know no haste and no delay." When the time came, God sent forth His Son. Some people were ready to receive Him, but most were not **alert** to how late the hour was.

"Outside of the Jewish nation there were men who foretold the appearance of a divine instructor. These men were seeking for truth, and to them the Spirit of Inspiration was imparted. One after another, like **stars** in the darkened heavens, such teachers had arisen. Their words of prophecy had kindled hope in the hearts of thousands of the Gentile world." (*The Desire of Ages* 32-33)

As we study the gems from the treasure box of heaven, we need to be **alert** to two parallels:

(1) Stars remind us that God will fulfill His purposes in this world and "these purposes know no haste and no delay." He will come again. I Peter 4:7 says, *"But the end of all things is at hand: be ye therefore sober, and watch unto prayer."* Read the lesson about Orion in the student section.

(2) There are many, like the stars in the sky, **alert** and shining, showing others that Jesus is coming again. I Corinthians 16:13 says, *"Watch ye, stand fast in the faith, quit you like men, be strong."* Read the lesson about magnitude in the student section.

Step 4

Prepare to begin the Stars and Constellations lesson.

To Begin the Stars and Constellations Lesson

Discuss the difference between God's stars and Satan's stars. Use a picture of a Hollywood star or picture of a rock star. Compare these to Jesus (the Star of all stars) and use pictures of John the Baptist, Joseph, Mary, and other Bible stars.

Step 5

Begin the Stars and Constellations lesson. Cover only what can be understood by your student. Make the lesson a family project by all being involved in part or all of the lesson. These lessons are designed for the whole family.

Steps in Bible Study

1. Prayer.

2. Read the verses/meditate/memorize.

3. Look up key words in *Strong's Concordance* and find their meanings in the Hebrew or Greek dictionary in the back of that book.

4. Cross-reference (marginal reference) with other Bible texts. An excellent study tool is *The Treasury of Scripture Knowledge.*

5. Use Bible custom books for more information on the times.

6. Write a summary of what you have learned from those verses.

7. Mark key thoughts in the margin of your Bible.

8. Share your study with others to reinforce the lessons you have learned.

Bible Review Questions

1. Does God have a time table? (Ecclesiastes 3:1-15)

2. To whom was the angel Gabriel sent? (Luke 1:26-27)

3. In what town did Mary live? (Luke 1:26)

4. Who was to be Mary's husband? (Luke 1:27)

5. How did the angel greet Mary? (Luke 1:28)

6. What did the angel say to remove her fear? (Luke 1:29-30)

7. Who did the angel say should be born to her? (Luke 1:31-33)

8. What would He be called? (Luke 1:31)

9. What does "Jesus" mean? (See a concordance.)

10. What did the angel say of Jesus' throne and kingdom? (Luke 1:32-33)

11. When did God send His Son to this earth? (Galatians 4:4)

12. What does it mean *"the fullness of time had come?"* In God's reckoning or man's?

Thought Question: Why was it necessary for Christ to come to earth as a man to save man? (He came to fulfill what Adam failed to do in the flesh, and He lived a perfect example of righteousness.)

Notes

Evaluating Your Child's Character

Check the appropriate box for your student's level of development,
or your own, as the case may be.

Maturing Nicely (MN), Needs Improvement (NI), Poorly Developed (PD), Absent (A)

Alertness

1. Does the child show **alertness** and recognize opportunities and dangers on his own?

MN NI PD A
❏ ❏ ❏ ❏

2. Is the child able to visualize the consequences of subtle dangers and act according to the wisdom of Scripture? *"A prudent man forseeth the evil, and hideth himself"* (Proverbs 22:3).

MN NI PD A
❏ ❏ ❏ ❏

3. Does the child act quickly upon command?

MN NI PD A
❏ ❏ ❏ ❏

4. Is the child sluggish in the morning?

Yes No
❏ ❏

5. Is the child **alert** to the special needs of others about him?

MN NI PD A
❏ ❏ ❏ ❏

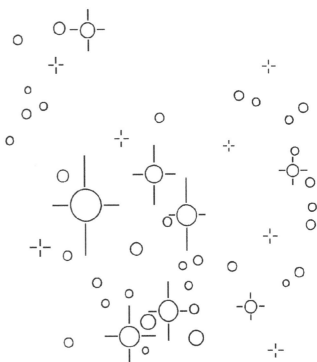

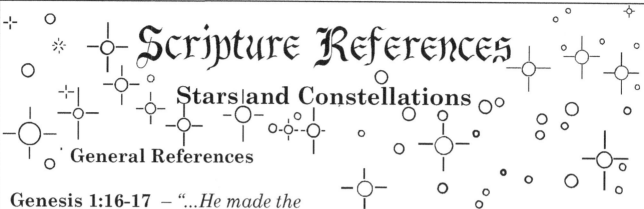

Scripture References
Stars and Constellations

General References

Genesis 1:16-17 – *"...He made the stars also. And God set them in the firmament of heaven to give light upon the earth."*

Psalm 8:3-4 – *"When I consider thy heavens, the work of thy fingers, the moon and the stars, which thou has ordained; What is man that thou art mindful of him? and the son of man, that thou visitest him?"*

Psalm 33:6 – *"By the word of the Lord were the heavens made; and all the host of them by the breath of his mouth."*

Psalm 19:1 – *"The heavens declare the glory of God; and the firmament sheweth his handywork."*

Psalm 148:3 – *"Praise ye him, sun and moon: praise him, all ye stars of light."*

Nehemiah 9:6 – *"Thou, even thou, art Lord alone; thou hast made heaven, the heaven of heavens, with all their host, the earth, and all things that are therein, the seas, and all that is therein, and thou preservest them all; and the host of heaven worshippeth thee."*

Isaiah 45:12 – *"I have made the earth, and created man upon it: I, even my hands, have stretched out the heavens, and all their host have I commanded."*

Job 22:12 – *"...Behold the height of the stars, how high they are!"*

Job 25:5 – *"...The stars are not pure in his sight."*

Stars Have Names

Isaiah 40:26 – *"Lift up your eyes on high, and behold who hath created these things, that bringeth out their host by number: he calleth them all by names by the greatness of his might, for that he is strong in power; not one faileth."*

Job 38:32 – *"Canst thou bring forth Mazzaroth in his season? or canst thou guide Arcturus with his sons?"*

Acts 28:11 – *"And after three months we departed in a ship of Alexandria, which had wintered in the isle, whose sign was Castor and Pollux."*

Psalm 147:4 – *"He telleth the number of the stars; he calleth them all by their names."*

See also Amos 5:8, Job 38:31, and Job 9:9.

Constellations

Isaiah 13:10 – *"For the stars of heaven and the constellations thereof shall not give their light: the sun shall be darkened in his going forth, and the moon shall not cause her light to shine."*

Job 9:9 – *"Which maketh Arcturus, Orion, and Pleiades, and the chambers of the south."*

Amos 5:8 – *"Seek him that maketh the seven stars and Orion, and turneth the shadow of death into the morning...."*

Job 38:31-32 – *"Canst thou bind the sweet influences of the Pleiades, or loose the bands of Orion? Canst thou bring forth Mazzaroth in his season? or canst thou guide Arcturus with his sons?"*

Job 26:13 – *"By his spirit he hath garnished the heavens; his hand hath formed the crooked serpent."*

The Number of Stars

Jeremiah 33:22 – *"As the host of heaven cannot be numbered, neither the sand of the sea measured..."*

Genesis 15:5 – *"...Tell the stars, if thou be able to number them...."*

Genesis 22:17 – *"...Thy seed as the stars of the heavens, and as the sand which is upon the sea shore...."*

Psalm 147:4 – *"He telleth the number of the stars; he calleth them all by their names."*

Magnitude of the Stars

I Corinthians 15:41 – *"There is one glory of the sun, and another glory of the moon, and another glory of the stars: for one star differeth from another star in glory."*

Gravitational Attraction of Stars

Job 38:31 – *"Canst thou bind the sweet influences of the Pleiades, or loose the bands of Orion?"*

Stars as Guides

Matthew 2:1-2, 7, 9-10 – *"Now when Jesus was born in Bethlehem of Judaea in the days of Herod the king, behold there came wise men from the east to Jerusalem, Saying, Where is he that is born King of the Jews? for we have seen his star in the east, and are come to worship him....Then Herod when he had privily called the wise men, enquired of them diligently what time the star appeared....When they had heard the king, they departed; and, lo, the star, which they saw in the east, went before them, till it came and stood over where the young child was. When they saw the star, they rejoiced with exceeding great joy."*

Acts 27:19-20 – *"And the third day we cast out with our own hands the tackling of the ship. And when neither sun nor stars in many days appeared, and no small tempest lay on us, all hope that we should be saved was then taken away."*

Figurative Guides

Daniel 12:3 – *"And they that be wise [teachers] shall shine as the brightness of the firmament; and they that turn many to righteousness as the stars for ever and ever."*

Jude 11, 13 – (Bad Guides) *"Woe unto them! for they have gone in the way of Cain, and ran greedily after the error of Balaam for reward... wandering stars, to whom is reserved the blackness of darkness for ever."*

Symbolic of Christ

Revelation 22:16 – *"I Jesus have sent mine angel to testify unto you these things in the churches. I am the root and the offspring of David, and the bright and morning star."*

Revelation 2:28 – *"And I will give him the morning star."*

Numbers 24:17 – *"I shall see him, but not now: I shall behold him, but not nigh: there shall come a Star out of Jacob, and a Sceptre shall rise out of Israel, and shall smite the corners of Moab, and destroy all the children of Sheth."*

II Peter 1:19 – *"We have also a more sure word of prophecy; whereunto ye do well that ye take heed, as unto a light that shineth in a dark place, until the day dawn, and the day star arise in your hearts."*

Other Symbolic Meanings

Revelation 1:16, 20 – *"And he had in his right hand seven stars: and out of his mouth went a sharp two-edged sword: and his countenance was as the sun shineth in his strength....The mystery of the seven stars which thou sawest in my right hand, and the seven golden candlesticks. The seven stars are the angels of seven churches."*

Revelation 12:1 – *"And there appeared a great wonder in heaven; a woman clothed with the sun, and the moon under her feet, and upon her head a crown of twelve stars."*

Genesis 37:9 – *"And he dreamed yet another dream, and told it his brethren, and said, Behold, I have dreamed a dream more; and, behold, the sun and the moon and the eleven stars made obeisance to me."*

Isaiah 14:12-13 – *"How art thou fallen from heaven, O Lucifer, son of the morning! how art thou cut down to the ground, which didst weaken the nations! For thou hast said in thine heart, I will ascend into heaven, I will exalt my throne above the stars of God: I will sit also upon the mount of the congregation, in the sides of the north."*

II Peter 1:19 – *"We have also a more sure word of prophecy; whereunto ye do well that ye take heed, as unto a light that shineth in a dark place, until the day star arise in your hearts."*

Revelation 12:4 – *"And his tail drew the third part of the stars of heaven, and did cast them to the earth."*

Genesis 22:17 – *"That in blessing I will bless thee, and in multiplying I will multiply thy seed as the stars of the heaven, and as sand which is upon the sea shore; and thy seed shall possess the gate of his enemies."*

Judges 5:20 – *"They fought from heaven; the stars in their courses fought against Sisera."*

Job 38:7 – *"When the morning stars sang together, and all the sons of God shouted for joy?"*

Daniel 8:10 – *"And it waxed great, even to the host of heaven; and it cast down some of the host and of the stars to the ground, and stamped upon them."*

See also Exodus 32:13; Genesis 15:5; Genesis 26:4; Deuteronomy 1:10; 10:22; 28:62; Daniel 12:3; Hebrews 11:12; Revelation 2:1; 3:1; 9:1.

Stars Worshiped

Deuteronomy 4:19 – *"And lest thou lift up thine eyes unto heaven, and when thou seest the sun, and the moon, and the stars, even all the host of heaven, shouldest be driven to worship them, and serve them, which the Lord thy God hath divided unto all nations under the whole heaven."*

II Kings 17:16 – *"And they left all the commandments of the Lord their God, and made them molten images, even two calves, and made a grove, and worshipped all the host of heaven, and served Baal."*

Amos 5:26 – *"But ye have borne the tabernacle of your Moloch and Chiun your images, the star of your god, which ye made to yourselves."*

Jeremiah 10:2-3 – **"Thus saith the Lord, Learn not the way of the heathen, and be not dismayed at the signs of heaven; for the heathen are dismayed at them. For the customs of the people are vain."**

See also Zepheniah 1:5; Acts 7:42-43; II Kings 21:3; 23:5, Jeremiah 8:2; 19:13; Isaiah 47:13; II Chronicles 33:3-5; Daniel 2:27-28; 4:7; 5:15.

As Signs

Genesis 1:14-18 – *"And God said, Let there be lights in the firmament of the heaven to divide the day from the night; and let them be for signs, and for seasons, and for days and years: And let them be for lights in the firmament of the heaven to give light upon the earth: and it was so. And God made two great lights; the greater light to rule the day, and the lesser light to rule the night: he made the stars also. And God set them in the firmament of the heaven to give light upon the earth, And to rule over the day and over the night, and to divide the light from the darkness."*

Luke 21:25-26 – *"And there shall be signs in the sun, and in the moon, and in the stars; and upon the earth distress of nations, with perplexity; the sea and the waves roaring; Men's hearts failing them for fear, and for looking after those things which are coming on the earth: for the powers of heaven shall be shaken."*

Jeremiah 10:2-3 – *"Thus saith the Lord, Learn not the way of the heathen, and be not dismayed at the signs of heaven; for the heathen are dismayed at them. For the customs of the people are vain."*

Darkening of the Stars

Job 9:7 – *"Which commandeth the sun, and it riseth not; and sealeth up the stars."*

Ecclesiastes 12:2 – *"While the sun, or the light, or the moon, or the stars, be not darkened, nor the clouds return after the rain."*

Isaiah 13:10 – *"For the stars of heaven and the constellations thereof shall not give their light."*

Isaiah 34:4 – *"And all the host of heaven shall be dissolved, and the heavens shall be rolled together as a scroll: and all their host shall fall down, as the leaf falleth off the vine, and as a falling fig from the fig tree."*

Joel 2:10 – *"The earth shall quake before them; the heavens shall tremble: the sun and the moon shall be dark, and the stars shall withdraw their shining."*

Joel 3:15 – *"The sun and the moon shall be darkened and the stars shall withdraw their shining."*

Revelation 8:11-12 – *"And the name of the star is called Wormwood: and the third part of the waters became wormwood; and many men died of the waters, because they were made bitter. And the fourth angel sounded, and the third part of the sun was smitten, and the third part of the moon, and the third part of the stars; so as the third part of them was darkened, and the day shone not for a third part of it, and the night likewise."*

See also Ezekiel 32:7.

Falling of the Stars, Symbolic and Literal

Daniel 8:10 – *"And it waxed great, even to the host of heaven; and it cast down some of the host and of the stars to the ground, and stamped upon them."*

Matthew 24:29 – *"Immediately after the tribulation of those days shall the sun be darkened, and the moon shall not give her light, and the stars shall fall from heaven, and the powers of heaven shall be shaken."*

Mark 13:25 – *"And the stars of heaven shall fall, and the powers that are in heaven shall be shaken."*

Revelation 8:10 – *"And the third angel sounded, and there fell a great star from heaven, burning as it were a lamp, and it fell upon the third part of the rivers, and upon the fountains of waters."*

Revelation 9:1 – *"And the fifth angel sounded, and I saw a star fall from heaven unto the earth: and to him was given the key of the bottomless pit."*

Revelation 12:4 – *"And his tail drew the third part of the stars of heaven, and did cast them to the earth."*

Isaiah 34:4 – *"And all the host of heaven shall be dissolved, and the heavens shall be rolled together as a scroll: and all their host shall fall down, as the leaf falleth off from the vine, and as a falling fig from the fig tree."*

Notes

Answer Key

Page 2

Be teachers of spiritual light from earth to heaven

Page 6

God's people will glitter as the precious stones of a crown.

Page 10

1. gems or jewels

2. God invites us to gaze heavenward to see the message traced in the night sky.

3. Each teacher of righteousness will be encircled by those souls that have been saved through their efforts.

4. It taught the glory of their Creator. It led to the Hebrew Scriptures.

5. Each star is a unique creation of God, with its own brightness and its own particular divinely designed structure for its role in God's creation.

God's children are like the stars that shine in a dark place. Each soul

has a distinct mission to fulfill in showing God's glory.

6. one host

7. lines, order, harmonious, individual Christians and churches

8. the sun

9. hydrogen and helium

10. light, heat, and radio waves
We should shine with God's glory, give the warmth of His love, and sing His praises.

11. For answers see page 16 below.

Page 11

1. heavens, glory, firmament

2. Teacher, check.

3. sun

4. hydrogen, helium

Page 16

1. Genesis 1:16

2. Genesis 15:5, Abraham

Page 16 continued

3. Judges 5:20 (See page 13.)

4. Nehemiah 4:21, Nehemiah and the Jews who had returned to Jerusalem

5. Daniel 12:3, *"they that be wise"* or teachers

6. Acts 27:20, Paul

7. Revelation 1:16, angels of the seven churches, the Son of man

8. Revelation 22:16, the *"Bright and Morning Star"*

Page 17

Teacher, check.

Page 18

1.   **L** laboring, loving, large-hearted, liberal, long-suffering

I impartial, industrious

G generous, genial, gentle, good, genuine, giving, gladsome

H happy, healthy, heedful, helpful, honest, honorable, hospitable, humble

Page 18 continued

T tactful, temperate, tender, thankful, thoughtful, tolerant, trusting, truthful

2.   **L** lazy, lawless, lying, loafing, lush, loud-mouthed, littering

I idolatrous, idle, ill-natured, immodest, immoral, impatient, impenitent, imposing, impulsive, impure, indulgent

G giddy, glaring, gloomy, gossiping, greedy, guileful

H hard-headed, hard-nosed, hasty, heedless, hypocritical

T tactless, talebearing, teasing, temperamental, thankless, treacherous

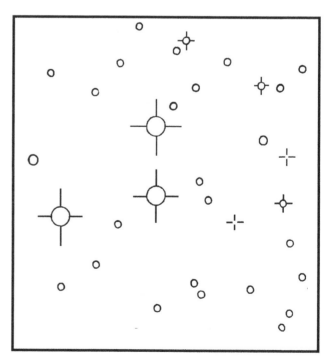

Page 28

1. Some stars are so large that they would more than fill the space between the earth and the sun (93 million miles or 150 million kilometers). Some stars are smaller than the earth.

2. See page 24 and the Covenant Notebook.

3. flares of gamma radiation

4. the larger and hotter stars

5. astronomers' arrangement of stars from cool, faint stars about one-tenth as big as our sun to bright stars ten times the size of the sun

6. a star that doesn't fit in the main sequence
100 times as big as our sun

7. even larger stars
Antares is 6,300 times more luminous than the sun.

8. small, but dense, stars with very hot temperatures

We should be content to be unnoticed and unknown and yet be on fire with the love of God and full of His drawing power.

Page 28 continued

9. See page 27.

(1) red; (2) white;
(3) yellow; (4) blue-white;
(5) orange

Page 29

1. Red, White

2.
   63
+ 32
   95   white

   28
+45
   73   blue-white

   57
+22
   79   orange

   18
+26
   44   yellow

   16
+22
   38

Page 36

1. yes
See page 31.

Page 36 continued

2. Student, answer.

3. super-giant cepheid

4. We should refrain from comparing ourselves with others.

5. 5,000

6. See pages 34-35.

7. stars we can see unaided, limited to the first six visual magnitudes

8. Magnitude is related to distance See page 35.

9. Teacher, check.

Page 37

1. Sirius, −1.46
2. Arcturus, −0.04
3. Alpha Centauri, −0.03
4. Rigel, 0.12
5. Betelgeuse, 0.50
6. Aldebaran, 0.85
7. Antares, 0.96
8. Pollux, 1.14
9. Castor, 1.60
10. Polaris, 2.00

Page 38

1. Yes. Teacher, check.

2. Student, answer.

Page 38 continued

3. height, high, numbered

Page 40

magnitude

Page 56

1. a pair of stars

2. Sirius

3. Sirius B or the "Pup"

4. guardian angel

5. several stars moving around a common center of gravity
the North Star (or Polestar)
Our family should have a common center, Christ

6. Teacher, check.

7. flock of stars
"little flock"

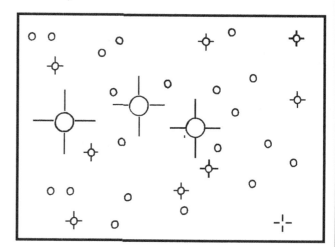

Page 56 continued

P perfection, ploughing time

L light years—250

E eye test

I influences, or icy-blue

A axle (hinge or pivot)

D dipper

E example of spiritual lessons

S sweet, seven stars seen
    by naked eye

Page 57

1. Teacher, check.

2. Sirius, Sirius B (the "Pup")

3. guardian angel

4. Teacher, check.

5. Teacher, check.

6. little flock

Page 58

great multitude

Page 62

Teacher, check.

Page 63

1. Proxima Centauri

2. 25,275,400,000,000 miles
40,440,640,000,000 kilometers

3. Teacher, check. See pages 60-61.

4. Teacher, check. See pages 61-62.

5. The sun lights up the earth's atmosphere giving the sky a blue appearance that is brighter than the stars.

Jesus, the *"Sun of Righteousness,"* will eclipse all the glory of man when He returns.

Page 90

1. the earth spinning

2. The stars can be used for navigation.

3. A star helped guide the wise men to Christ.

4. polestar (or North Star)
See pages 68-70.

5. Student, do.

Page 90 continued

6. The two stars on the cup part opposite the handle of the Big Dipper point to the polestar, the last star in the handle of the Little Dipper.

7. by the sky

8. no
the stars; Heaven's standard
Student answer.

9. Teacher, check.

1. The earth rotates.

2. compass

3. star (like a cloud of angels)

4. Teacher, check.

5. Student, do.

6. Student, do.

7. the sky

8. Teacher, check.

Page 95

By denying self and faithfully doing your duty each day.

Page 96

1. cross

2. cross

3. S

4. I

5. I

6. cross

7. I

8. I

9. I

10. I

11. cross

12. cross

Page 102

1. We do not know.
Southern Cross

2. group of stars that form a pattern in the sky

3. None but Christ can fashion anew the character that has been ruined by sin.

Page 102 continued

4. westward

5. the time when a constellation reaches its highest point in the sky

6. constellations that can be seen at any time of the year

Page 109

1. Arabic

2. ancient learning

3. Flamsteed numbers, which are numbers given to the stars by an English astronomer John Flamsteed

(across)
21, 23, 25, 26, 28, 31, 36, 38
99, 87, 82, 78, 69, 53, 41, 39

Telescope

Page 119

1. Jesus Christ

2. Venus
The Day Star

3. Venus is covered with clouds. As Venus is covered with clouds, so Christ is enshrouded with glory.

Page 119 continued

4. Castor is a second magnitude white star. Pollux is a first magnitude yellow star, the brightest star in the northern winter sky.

Page 132

1. Orion
"Strong One"

2. Teacher, check.

3. that our Lord will come back to earth the second time to execute judgment

4. The main outline is formed by seven stars. The whole constellation contains 17 stars (78 with a telescope).

5. around the central star in the sword

6. a magnificent red super-giant star named Betelgeuse

7. The divine perfection of His offices are shown in His being:
(1) Prophet, (2) Priest, and (3) King.

8. Rigel
It is a long, faint, winding snake-like constellation traditionally known as the River and it looks like that *old serpent.*

Page 132 continued

9. December through March

10. seven
spiritual perfection

11. east
because it moves constantly over the equator

Page 133

1. Bootes
Arcturus

2. Orion
Betelgeuse

Page 142

1. Proxima Centauri, Canopus

2. the Southern Cross and the Swan (or Northern Cross)

3. Teacher, check.

4. Teacher, check.

5. Teacher, check.

Page 147

Orion

Page 156

BinocularS
     STar chart
  AlmAnac
CountRy

Page 172

1. Bootes
2. Southern Cross
3. Leo
4. Perseus

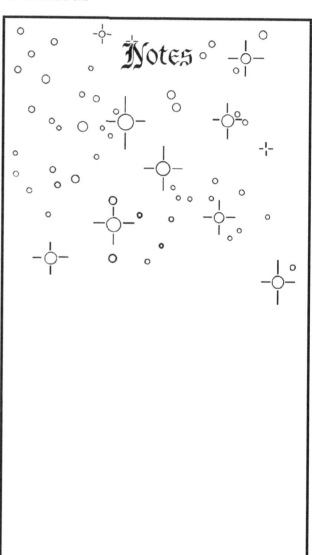

Notes

Music Schedule

Song Titles	Teacher Section	Student Section
1. "The Hand That Made Us"	Page 24	Page 2, 12
2. " 'Tis Shining Still"	Page 26	Page 3
3. "Jewels"	Page 28	Page 30
4. "Who Are These"	Page 29	Page 53
5. "Give Me the Bible"	Page 30	Pages 90, 136
6. "Near the Cross"	Page 32	Pages 116, 120
7. "Lord of All Being"	Page 33	Page 120
8. "Redemption Nigh"	Page 34	Page 121
9. "The Beautiful Beyond"	Page 35	Page 137

THE HAND THAT MADE US

(Creation. L. M. D.)

Addison

Haydn

1. The spa - cious firm - a - ment on high, With all the blue, e - the - real sky, And spang - led heav'ns, a shin - ing frame, Their great O - rig - i - nal pro - claim: Th'un - wear - ied sun from day to

2. Soon as the eve - 'ning shades pre - vail, The moon takes up the won - drous tale; And night - ly, to the list - 'ning earth Re - peats the sto - ry of her birth; While all the stars that round her

3. What tho' in so - lemn si - lence, all Move round the dark ter - res - trial ball? What tho' no real voice nor sound A - mid their ra - diant orbs be found? In rea - son's ear they all re -

'TIS SHINING STILL

"...There shall come a Star out of Jacob, and a Sceptre shall rise out of Israel" (Numbers 24:17).

F. E. B.

F. E. Belden

Children's Duet if preferred.

1. A beau - ti - ful star a - rose one night, Di - vine - ly it shone with
2. They knew by the word of truth di - vine, 'Twas time that the guid - ing
3. We'll fol - low its light, like those of old, The "Light of the World," by

pur - est light; Its won - der - ful rays the wise men led To
star should shine; They fol - low'd its light which shone a - far.— 'Twas
seers fore - told; We'll fol - low His light till we shall come To

find the Sav - iour's low - ly bed.
Christ, "the bright and morn - ing star."
per - fect rest in heav'n, my home.

Chorus

'Tis shin - ing still, 'tis

shin - ing still, That beau - ti - ful star, o'er plain and hill; 'Tis

shin - ing still, 'tis shin - ing still, Sal - va - tion's star of God's good will.

"For God,
who commanded the light to shine out of darkness,
hath shined in our hearts,
to give the light of the knowledge of the glory of God
in the face of Jesus Christ."

II Corinthians 4:6

WHO ARE THESE?
(Neander. 8, 7, 8, 7, 7, 7.)

H. T. Schenck

J. Neander

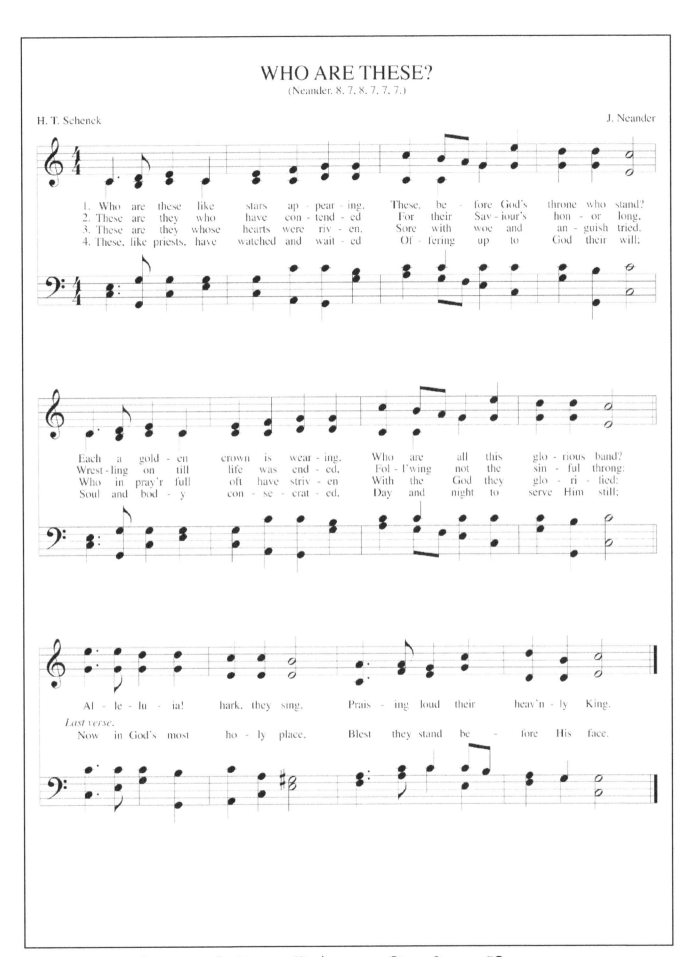

1. Who are these like stars ap - pear - ing. These, be - fore God's throne who stand?
2. These are they who have con - tend - ed For their Sav - iour's hon - or long.
3. These are they whose hearts were riv - en, Sore with woe and an - guish tried.
4. These, like priests, have watched and wait - ed Of - fering up to God their will;

Each a gold - en crown is wear - ing. Who are all this glo - rious band?
Wrest - ling on till life was end - ed, Fol - l'wing not the sin - ful throng;
Who in pray'r full oft have striv - en With the God they glo - ri - fied;
Soul and bod - y con - se - crat - ed. Day and night to serve Him still;

Al - le - lu - ia! hark, they sing. Prais - ing loud their heav'n - ly King.

Last verse.
Now in God's most ho - ly place, Blest they stand be - fore His face.

GIVE ME THE BIBLE

"Thy word is a lamp unto my feet, and a light unto my path" (Psalm 119:105).

Priscilla J. Owens

E. S. Lorenz

1. Give me the Bi - ble, star of glad - ness gleam - ing, To cheer the wan - d'rer
2. Give me the Bi - ble when my heart is bro - ken, When sin and grief have
3. Give me the Bi - ble, all my steps en - light - en, Teach me the dan - ger
4. Give me the Bi - ble, lamp of life im - mor - tal, Hold up that splen - dor

lone and tem - pest tossed; No storm can hide that peace - ful ra - diance beam - ing,
filled my soul with fear; Give me the pre - cious words by Je - sus spok - en,
of these realms be - low; That lamp of safe - ty, o'er the gloom shall bright - en,
by the o - pen grave; Show me the light from hea - ven's shin - ing por - tal,

Chorus

Since Je - sus came to seek and save the lost.
Hold up faith's lamp to show my Sav - iour near.
That light a - lone the path of peace can show.   Give me the Bi - ble,—
Show me the glo - ry gild - ing Jor - dan's wave.

GIVE ME THE BIBLE (2)

Ho - ly mes-sage shin - ing. Thy light shall guide me in the nar - row way.

Pre-cept and pro-mise, law and love com-bin-ing, Till night shall van-ish in e - ter - nal day.

"It is our part to give the word to the people;
we are to sow the seed.
We know not which shall prosper, whether this or that;
but God will give the increase."

Pamphlets 004- 15.3

NEAR THE CROSS

LORD OF ALL BEING

(Park Street. L. M.)

O. W. Holmes

1. Lord of all be - ing, throned a - far, Thy glo
2. Sun of our life, Thy quick'n - ing ray Sheds on
3. Our mid - night is Thy smile with - drawn, Our noo
4. Lord of all life, be - low, a - bove, Whose ligh
5. Grant us Thy truth to make us free, And kin

flames from sun and star, Cen - ter and soul
path the glow of day; Star of our hope,
is Thy gra - cious dawn, Our rain - bow arch
truth, whose warmth is love, Be - fore Thy ev
hearts that burn for Thee, Till all Thy liv

ev - 'ry sphere, Yet to each lov - ing heart
soft - ened light, Cheers the long watch - es of
mer - cy's sign, All, save the clouds of sin,
blaz - ing throne We ask no lus - ter of
al - tars claim One ho - ly light, one heav'n

near! Yet to each lov - ing heart how near!
night. Cheers the long watch - es of the night.
Thine. All, save the clouds of sin, are Thine.
own. We ask no lus - ter of our own.

REDEMPTION NIGH
(Pleyel. 7s.)

Reginald Heber

Ignace Pleyel

1. In the sun, and moon, and stars, Signs and won-ders have ap-peared;
2. Soon shall o-cean's hoar-y deep, Tossed with stron-ger temp-ests, rise;
3. Dread a-larms shall shake the proud, Pale a-maze-ment, rest-less fear;
4. But, tho' from His aw-ful face, Heav'n shall fade, and earth shall fly,

Earth has groan'd with blood-y wars, And the hearts of men have fear'd.
Dark-er storms the moun-tains sweep, Fierc-er light-ning rend the skies.
And a-mid the thun-der cloud Shall the Judge of men ap-pear.
Fear not ye, His cho-sen race, Your re-demp-tion draw-eth nigh.

"When the signs predicted begin to come to pass,
the waiting, watching ones are bidden to look up
and lift up their heads
and rejoice because their redemption draweth nigh."

5 Testimonies 9

THE BEAUTIFUL BEYOND

"Beautiful for situation, the joy of the whole earth, is mount Zion,
on the sides of the north, the city of the great King" (Psalm 48:2).

F. E. B.

F. E. Belden

1. A - bove the clouds that veil the blue, Be - yond the
2. The stream of life with cease - less flow, The ho - ly
3. The flow'rs that sleep neath win - ter's snow, The loved ones

A - bove the clouds that veil the blue,

stars that glim - mer through, There is a home
joy that an - gels know, The gold - en harp,
lost to us be - low. The voic - es hush'd

Be - yond the stars that glim - mer thro', There is a home

un - known to care.— Its gates a - jar in - vite me
the song di - vine, The spot - less robe— Faith calls them
that used to sing.— We'll find them all where Christ is

un - known to care.— Its gates a - jar

THE BEAUTIFUL BEYOND (2)

Gardening Sheet

Lesson **Three** Subject **Nature**

Title **Stars and Constellations"**

In Season	Out of Season
Plant roots are amazing as they work their way through the soil. One scientist measured the roots of a young rye plant and found 387 miles (619.2 kilometers) of them!	Learn more about how roots help the soil. Draw illustrations and find pictures. Dig away a bank so you can look at roots growing.
For proper root growth, soil should be well drained, well aerated, well supplied with organic matter of the right kind, and well fertilized. If water and air cannot get through the soil, neither can the roots.	Deep, wide-spreading roots help when it is very dry. Your plants get water by the roots from deep underground. Roots take up water through minute root hairs. They take in water and dissolve mineral salts from the soil. They take up the minerals required for plant growth. Wilting occurs when these root hairs are destroyed or injured by reckless cultivation.
Deep-penetrating roots are soil builders since their decomposition provides humus deep in the soil and leaves countless channels through which water and food can seep underground. If the subsoil is not too hard, the root is the next best thing to a well digger for burrowing after deep moisture.	In the same way, mankind was dying spiritually and God sent forth His Son to redeem them, to nourish, and save all who would be **alert**.
This underground world is moving, living, and can be paral-	Deep, wide-spreading roots gather plant food from a large volume of soil. When you feed your plants, spread the plant food over

Gardening Sheet

"Stars and Constellations," continued

with the vast world out in space of the stars and constellations. Space is like soil with each constellation a unique garden and the individual stars as plants.

As you check your soil bring to mind the universe God is planning for you to explore.

the whole area occupied by the feeder roots, down both sides of row crops. The influence of Christ is wide-spread.

Student Section

"There is one glory of the sun,
and another glory of the moon,
and another glory of the stars:
for one star differeth
from another star in glory."
I Corinthians 15:41

"...The stars of heaven
and the constellations thereof..."
Isaiah 13:10

"Seek him that maketh
the seven stars and Orion."
Amos 5:8

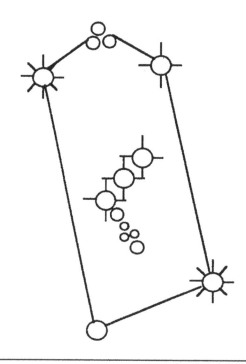

Stars and Constellations

"The heavens declare the glory of God; and the firmament sheweth his handywork."
Psalm 19:1

Research
God's Great Jewel Chest

"There is gold, and a multitude of rubies: but the lips of knowledge are a precious jewel."
Proverbs 20:15

In the creation of the heavens God poured out His jewel case in the sky and from a distance they look like so many diamonds sparkling as if the light catches them first from one angle then another. But upon closer inspection we see they shine with the many colors of gems—one like an emerald, another like a ruby, a third like a sapphire, and a fourth like a topaz—the whole nocturnal heavens appearing to sparkle with a blaze of jewels. It reminds us of the breastplate of precious stones carried on the chest of the high priest in Old Testament times. (See Exodus 28:15-30.)

Hieroglyphics of the Sky

The stars are the hieroglyphics of the sky. They speak of the power and faithfulness of God to all who are <u>alert</u>. But they also enable him to see, as in a glass darkly, a glimmer of the design of the heavens.

These gems were to be teachers so that the study of the stars should have been a science, and it should have reared a pathway of spiritual light from earth to heaven. It should have built shining steps, on which mortals might reverently climb in the ever-ascending way to the throne of the infinite Creator. But ignorance and superstition made the study of the stars a religion (astrology). They changed the myriad host into deities, whose mysterious power was supposed to rule over men with an all-pitiless destiny. They made malignant demons of the burning orbs of the sky, whose fickle favor must be secured, and whose fiery wrath must be averted by strange offerings and forbidden sacrifices. *And they forsook the Lord, and served Baal and Ashtaroth* (Judges 2:13).

God had designed these gems in the sky to be beautiful pictures, called constellations, of the plan of salvation written there by God's foreknowledge in past times. Then to make it real on planet Earth, He placed *one pearl of great price* (Matthew 13:46) among the sinful humanity—in the midst of the Hebrew people in the Babe of Bethlehem. However, as a people, Israel were not **alert** to the great value or knowledge to be gained from the Gem of all gems.

"...One pearl of great price...."
Matthew 13:46

**Sing the hymn,
"The Hand That Made Us."**

Reinforce
Jewel Case

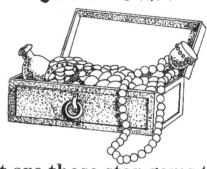

What are these star gems to do? To answer the question arrange the words below in the blanks.

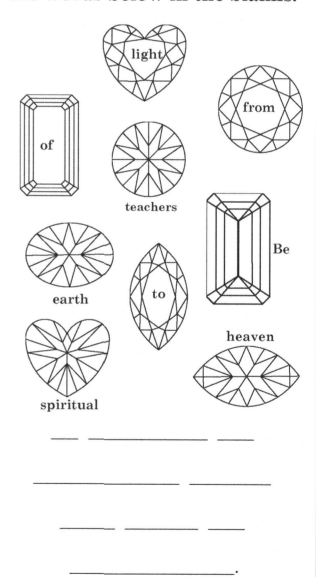

light

from

of

teachers

earth

to

Be

heaven

spiritual

___ ___ ___ ___

___ ___ ___

___ ___ ___

___ .

The Glorious Gems

From the creation of this world, the perfect order and arrangement of the beautiful gems studding the night sky have revealed the plan of redemption; but men, not having the Spirit of truth to guide them, could not understand the alphabet of the celestial dome. Even though God has mercifully and patiently repeated the story night after night, mankind for the most part has not perceived the law of God in the star-spangled firmament.

Our heavenly Father graciously invites us to gaze heavenward even as He called Abraham to his tent door to see the message traced in the night sky. *"And he brought him forth abroad and said, Look now toward heaven, and tell the stars, if thou be able to number them: and he said unto him, So shall thy seed be"* (Genesis 15:5).

Just as each sun is encircled by the planets of its system, so in the kingdom of God each teacher of righteousness will be encircled by those souls that have been saved through their efforts. And as each galaxy revolves around one spot in the heavens, in like manner, the redeemed of all ages will be gathered around Christ the center Jewel, the Saviour of mankind.

The Magi were **alert** to the messages of the sky and sought to fathom the mystery hidden in their bright paths. In it they beheld the glory of their Creator. Then, seeking clearer knowledge, they turned to the Hebrew Scriptures for more gems. Let us humbly follow their example as we also *"seek him"* through a study of the stars (Amos 5:8).

**Sing the hymn,
" 'Tis Shining Still."**

Instruction From Heaven

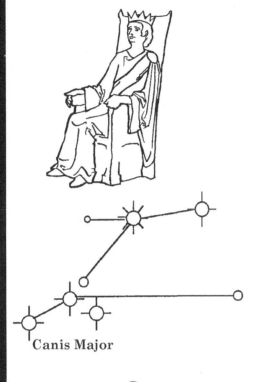

Canis Major

Canis Minor

Stars that on your wondrous way,
Travel through the evening sky,
Is there nothing you can say
To such a little child as I?
Tell me, for I long to know,
Who has made you sparkle so?

Yes, me thinks I hear you say,
"Child of mortal race, attend,
While we run our wondrous way;
Listen; we would be your friend;
Teaching you that Name Divine,
By whose mighty word we shine.

"Yes, and God, who bade us roll,
God who hung us in the sky,
Stoops to watch an infant's soul
With a condescending eye;
And esteems it dearer far
More in value, than a star!

"Oh then, while your breath is given,
Pour it out in fervent prayer,
And beseech the God of heaven
To receive your spirit there;
Like a living star, to blaze
Ever to your Saviour's praise."

—*Isaac Watts*

Stars as Unique Creations

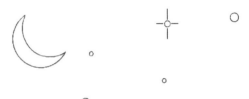

"There is one glory of the sun, and another glory of the moon,
and another glory of the stars:
for one star differeth from another star in glory."

I Corinthians 15:41

In this study of the stars we will explore some of the many ways stars differ from one another just as diamonds and rubies are different from each other. Each one is a unique creation of God just the same as each person is. The phrase in the previous text, *"differeth…in glory"* may also be translated, "differeth in dignity," or "honor," "praise," or "worship." Not only do the stars differ in their brightness, but as this text indicates, each one has its own particular divinely designed structure for its own particular role in God's creation. *"Praise ye him, sun and moon; praise him, all ye stars of light"* (Psalm 148:3).

God's children are like the stars that shine in a dark place. Each soul has a distinct mission to fulfill in showing God's glory.

"Every shining star which God has placed in the heavens obeys His mandate, and gives its distinctive measure of light to make beautiful the heavens at night; so let every converted soul show the measure of light committed to him; and as it shines forth the light will increase and grow brighter. Give out your light, pour forth your beams mirrored from heaven. Oh daughter of Zion, *'Arise, shine; for thy light is come, and the glory of the Lord is risen upon thee* (Isaiah 60:1)." (4 *Bible Commentary* 1153)

> **Do the Reinforce on the next page.**

Reinforce
Explain this verse.

"And the Lord their God shall save
them in that day as the flock of his people:
for they shall be as the stones of a crown,
lifted up as an ensign [glitter or twinkle]
upon his land."
Zechariah 9:16

_____

_____

_____

_____

_____

_____

_____

_____

_____

The Jewish nation was given the special role of preparing the world to receive the Saviour when He came to earth the first time. God had shed upon them the special light of the Old Testament prophecies which they, in turn, were to reflect to the heathen about them. But because they were not **alert** to the influence of the Holy Spirit, they failed to shine as they should have. "As the Jews had departed from God, faith had grown dim, and hope had well-nigh ceased to illuminate the future" (*The Desire of Ages* 32). They had become like fallen stars whose light went out in obscurity.

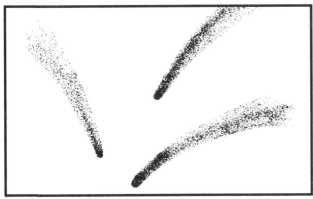

Like the Jews, Christians have been given the divinely ordained role of preparing a people to receive Christ when He returns the second time. May God help each to be **alert** to the influence of the Holy Spirit that all may faithfully shine in this present darkness. Let Christians determine to be like the stars who praise their Creator by shining with a radiant glory like His giving light to all within their sphere of influence.

"But You Will Leave Us the Stars"

During the French Revolution an atheist said to a Christian peasant, "We are going to destroy Christianity. We will pull down your churches, burn your Bibles, and demolish everything that speaks to you of God." The peasant replied, "But you will leave us the stars!" *"And God set them in the firmament of the heaven to give light upon the earth, and to rule over the day and over the night, and to divide the light from the darkness: and God saw that it was good. And the evening and the morning were the fourth day"* (Genesis 1:17-19). The stars are an everlasting witness to God which man cannot remove or destroy!

One Host

"Thou, even thou, art Lord alone; thou hast made heaven, the heaven of heavens, with all their host, the earth, and all things that are therein, and thou preservest them all; and the host of heaven worshippeth thee."
Nehemiah 9:6

It is a fact with which we are familiar from infancy, that all the heavenly bodies, sun, moon, and stars, seem to be set in an azure* vault, which, rising high over our heads, curves down to the horizon on every side. This celestial vault above us, with a corresponding one below us, forms a complete sphere, which has been known in all ages as the celestial sphere. True, it is imaginary, but that does not diminish its value as enabling us to form definite ideas of the directions of heavenly bodies from us. Think of it! Those bright gems, well-nigh innumerable, are scattered everywhere throughout the stellar space, and yet as the eye looks heavenward they seem smoothed out upon the plane of the celestial arch, and move in groups and constellations of individual stars and suns as **one host**—the mighty host of the heavens of God. Their lines are never broken, their order is never disturbed; but they march on forever in harmonious line, and unity so perfect that

*blue

the expression, "the music of the spheres," is rather a fact of science than a figure of poetry.

Thus it is, as it seems to me, individual Christians, with those groups and constellations known as churches, when they are **alert** to the infinite and eternal world, they are all projected upon the celestial sphere as **one harmonious host**. When we lift our eyes from earth's narrow fields, when our vision rises above it, where we take the wider range and clearer view which come from those who have eternity in sight; one after another the differences that had seemed to us great are overbridged, and men in Christ can dwell together as **one host** in unity.

One Harmonious Host

What Is a Star?

Do you know the name of the brightest star we can see from earth? Take a little time to form your answer. Here is a hint: This star is so bright, it can be seen during the daytime! The answer will, perhaps be a surprise to some of you because it is the sun. Yes, our sun is actually a star because, by definition, a star is basically a huge ball of glowing hydrogen gases. Reactions in the heart of stars, like those in nuclear bombs, generate heat and light. It is held together by its own gravity. The middle of a star is so hot, it may reach temperatures of 29 million degrees Fahrenheit (16 million degrees Celsius). The sun seems so bright because it is so much closer to us than all the other stars in the sky.

Israel was not **alert** and did not see the "Son" in their midst shining upon them.

By analyzing starlight, astronomers have found that the stars are made up of elements like those found in the sun. Hydrogen is the most abundant element with helium being the second. Stars shine as they undergo powerful atomic reactions which produce the energy that streams through space in the form of light. Hydrogen gas is changed into helium gas by a process known as nuclear fusion. This creates so much energy that the temperature inside a star is thought to reach millions of degrees. This energy passes from the star's surface in such forms as:

1. light,
2. heat, and
3. radio waves.

These powerful internal reactions in the stars can encourage us to believe that the power of God can fill us too. Then we can

1. shine with God's glory (light),
2. give forth the warmth of His love (heat), and
3. sing His praises (radio waves).

An Unusual Name

One star is called Shurnarkabtishashutu. It is Arabic, meaning "under the southern horn of the bull."

"The morning stars sang together, and all the sons of God shouted for joy"
Job 38:7

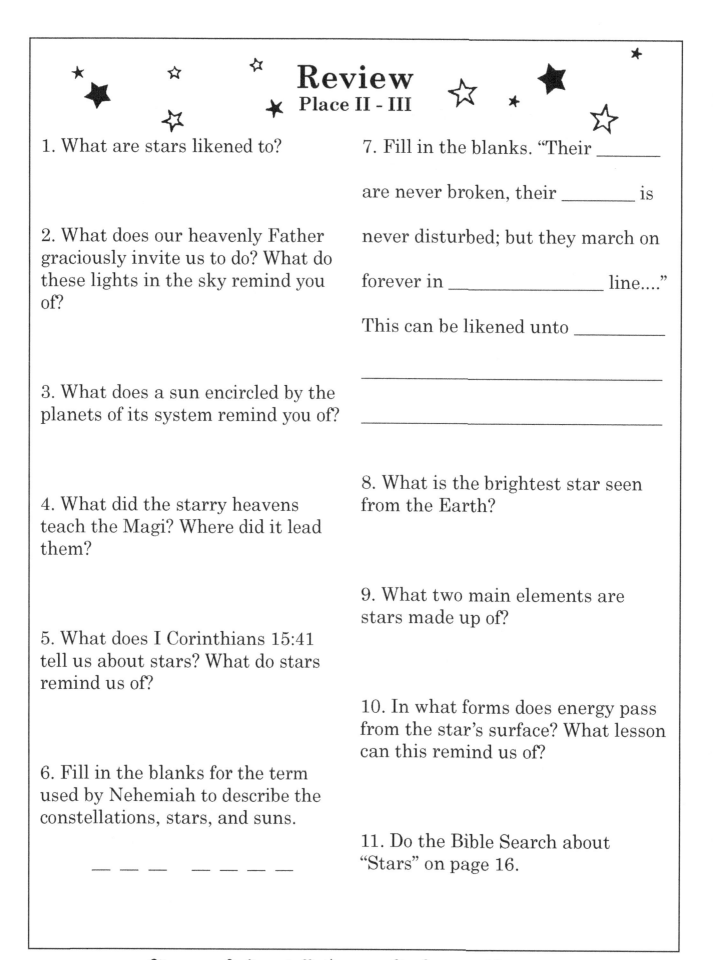

Review
Place II - III

1. What are stars likened to?

2. What does our heavenly Father graciously invite us to do? What do these lights in the sky remind you of?

3. What does a sun encircled by the planets of its system remind you of?

4. What did the starry heavens teach the Magi? Where did it lead them?

5. What does I Corinthians 15:41 tell us about stars? What do stars remind us of?

6. Fill in the blanks for the term used by Nehemiah to describe the constellations, stars, and suns.

__ __ __   __ __ __ __

7. Fill in the blanks. "Their _____ are never broken, their _____ is never disturbed; but they march on forever in _____ line...."

This can be likened unto _____

_____

_____

8. What is the brightest star seen from the Earth?

9. What two main elements are stars made up of?

10. In what forms does energy pass from the star's surface? What lesson can this remind us of?

11. Do the Bible Search about "Stars" on page 16.

Place I - II

1. Fill in these blanks.

"The _____ declare the _____ of God;

and the _____ sheweth his handywork."

Psalm 19:1

2. Draw the spiritual lessons below that you learned in this section.

3. This star is closest to us and its name is the _____.

4. Stars are made up of two main elements which are:

        1. _____

        2. _____

★ Reinforce ☆

1. Visit a jewelry shop to observe the beautiful gems and how they reflect the light.

2. There once was a book entitled Stars of the Reformation. It told of the men who fought for the religious liberties we now enjoy. They were called stars because they were full of the light of God, and they let it shine out boldly and beautifully. Read a book or story about one of these stars. (Examples: Wycliffe, Huss, Jerome, or Luther.)

3. Read the article, "Stars."

4. Sing the hymn, "The Hand That Made Us."

5. Look for star shapes in nature, kitchen, or woodshop.

6. Sleep out under the stars and learn to identify the most common constellations, such as Orion, Pleiades, and Dipper.

7. Look at grains of sand under a microscope (if you do not have that equipment, use a magnifying glass). Each grain is uniquely different.

8. Become familiar with a star guide and star charts.

9. Learn how to draw stars. See the page 17, "How to Draw Stars."

10. Do the "Light Synonym Puzzle" on page 18.

★ Remind ★

1. As you look at the starry night sky, think of Abraham, Job, and the Magi who looked at some of these same stars.

2. When you see the light over the kitchen table, consider how you have a measure of light to shine to those around you.

3. Daily we can observe the sun, our closest star. It can remind us of how Israel's lack of **alertness** caused them to look beyond the "Son." They did not recognize Him in their midst. Do you by faith see Him each day in your life?

Stars
"...He made the stars also."
Genesis 1:16

And what a lot of real pleasure God gave to the world when He did that. When I was a child I looked at the star maps my father used to show me; I thought that the stars were not only beautiful, but very interesting. Many a time, sitting at my room window, I used to try and puzzle out the two Bears, Hercules, the Harp, and many others away up there in the sky. Often on cold, clear nights I thought of the sailors of the past, steering their ships by these stars. I tried to imagine how great God must be to create so many bright suns. And now I know that the number of these stars, these suns, is more than I can count, my wonder and reverence for my Creator is even greater. Truly, ours is a great God.

Astronomy is the oldest of all sciences. Adam and Eve began the study of the stars in their garden home. And they had the Creator who came in the *"cool of the day"* to answer their questions. Abraham and others looked heavenward for lessons from the stars. The Egyptians and Chaldeans in very early times were close observers of the face of the sky. The interiors of some of the Pyramids are scored with astronomic symbols, and contain records of the more remarkable early phenomenon which attracted their attention. The writer of the Book of Judges knew something about the science of astronomy. He tells us that the stars *"in their courses"* fought against Sisera. This was not a miracle. The autumn shower of falling stars and meteors was just due. It is thought the path of the meteor shower lay across the battlefield, and perhaps many of Sisera's host was smitten by them.

Our Place

The whirlpool attracts
more notice than
the quiet fountain;
a comet draws more attention
than the steady star;
but it is better to be the fountain
than the whirlpool,
the star than the comet,
following the sphere and orbit
of quiet usefulness
in which God places us.

There are many other interesting astronomical references in the Bible. The sky always has been, and always will be, full of wonders to men. It seems marvelous, but it is true, that one might look at stars through a mighty telescope every night throughout a long life, never looking at the same spot twice; and even then the whole would not be seen.

One has said—

"The stars are but the shining dust
    Of my divine abode—
The pavement of those heavenly courts
    Where I shall see my God."

And our God, our Father, "made the stars!" How great our God must be! How safe we are in trusting in His power and His love.

"The Voice that rolls the stars along
    Speaks all the promises."

Think of that—all the promises, and all the power behind them. Cannot God help you? He made you as well as the stars, and His promises are yours if you are His.

Our God,
"made the stars!"
How great He is!

Think of the immense distances of the stars. The nearest fixed star is 19 billion miles away. A billion as you, I daresay, know is a thousand millions. Most of the stars are so far away that their distance cannot be accurately measured.

A German astronomer had a dream. He wished to find God's throne. In his dream an angel came to conduct him thither. He was taken to the nearest star, and as he looked back the moon and the earth were both lost to sight. On they went, the various constellations opened out—well-known star after star disappeared behind them. With constellations ever changing their appearances, they dived deep into that countless multitude of stars, the Milky Way, till, almost tired, he asked how much further. The angel replied, "We are only in the vestibule of heaven as yet." Oh how little we are, and yet how precious and how grand we are! How God cares for us! How He takes those stars and their vast distances to tell how completely He forgives us! He says: *As the heaven is high above the earth, so great is his mercy toward them that fear him. As far as the east is from the west, so far hath he removed our transgressions from us.*

The night sky is full of wonders for fallen man.

It is as useless seeking for God's throne now, as that astronomer sought to find it in his dream; the best way is to fix your heart and your eye on Jesus—the Bright and Morning Star; and one day, by the law of the gravity of souls, your Saviour and you will be drawn together.

There is a peculiar star in the sky called Algol, an eclipsing binary. Owing to its habit of shining brightly for 2.87 days, and then growing faint for a short space of time, presently to renew its former brightness, just for all the world as though it were winking. The explanation of Algol's winking is that it revolves round another star; and in crossing the path of this star it has the appearance of winking, being temporarily obscured for ten hours. One day, if we are God's, we shall shine like the stars in our Father's kingdom. Take care that you do not become a fallen star. Rather let your lives be like a great star that blazes the heavens for His glory.

Paul was such a flaming star, always shining, always pointing one way—to Christ. May God raise up many such bright, burning stars from the ranks of Christians today!

We shall shine like the stars in our Father's kingdom.

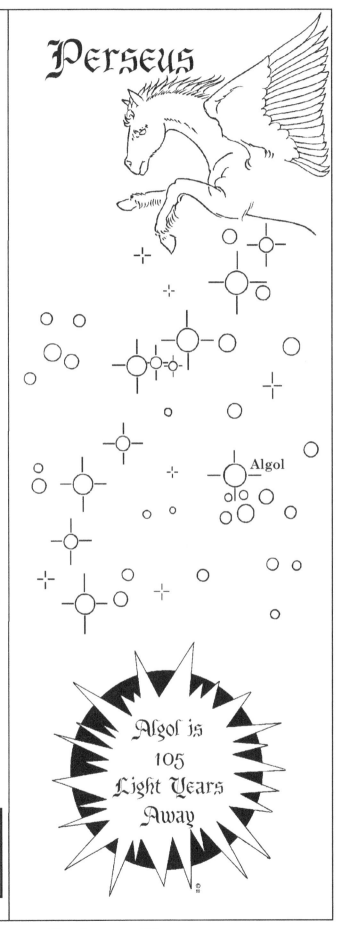

Perseus

Algol

Algol is 105 Light Years Away

 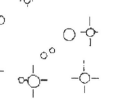

Bible Search
Stars

1. What is the first verse in the Bible that mentions the creation of stars?

2. Who was challenged to number the stars? (Genesis 15:5)

3. Explain the verse *"stars in their courses fought against Sisera."* (Judges 5:20)

4. Who labored to rebuild the ancient walls of Jerusalem *"from the rising of the morning till the stars appeared?"* (Nehemiah 4:21)

5. Who shall *"shine as the brightness of the firmament"* and *"as the stars for ever and ever?"* (Daniel 12:3)

6. Who was in a fierce storm on his last voyage to Rome so that *"neither sun nor stars in many days appeared?"* (Acts 27:20)

7. What were the seven stars held in the right hand and who held them? (Revelation 1:16)

8. What kind of star is Christ called? (Revelation 22:16)

"Arise, shine; for thy light is come, and the glory of the Lord is risen upon thee."
Isaiah 60:1

How to Draw Stars

Draw stars in the picture below, filling the sky with stars.
Then color the picture.

Light Synonym Puzzle

1. Use the letters below to list ways we can let our light shine in our daily life.

L   laboring, _____

_____

_____

I   impartial, _____

_____

_____

G   generous, _____

_____

_____

H   happy, _____

_____

_____

T   tactful, _____

_____

_____

2. What are ways that keep your light from shining?

L   lazy, _____

_____

_____

I   idolatrous, _____

_____

_____

G   giddy, _____

_____

_____

H   hard-headed, _____

_____

_____

T   tactless, _____

_____

_____

You Will Learn

Put this page before page 1 of Student Section.

The night sky is God's great jewel chest.

• God invites us to study His star studded sky.

• Stars differ from one another as do people.

• Stars shine as they undergo powerful atomic reactions which produce the energy that streams through space in the form of light. The Christian like the star can shine for God.

• The heavenly bodies are one harmonious host marching through the sky. This was God's plan for Israel of the past and His desire for His church today.

• Stars or suns are made up of elements some are of the main elements which are hydrogen and helium.

• Energy passes from the star's surface in three forms as the glory of God radiates in three ways from the Christian's life.

Research
Colors, Brightness, and Sizes

"And they that be wise shall shine as the brightness of the firmament; and they that turn many to righteousness as the stars for ever and ever."

Daniel 12:3

"Let there be light..."

On the first day of creation, God spoke, *"Let there be light: and there was light"* (Genesis 1:3). The creation of light meant the creation of color, for in simple white light are all the colors found in the rainbow. When light passes through a prism, it is refracted into the many colors called the spectrum. An object that reflects one color will look that color; while an object that reflects all colors appears white, and one that does not reflect any color is black. Therefore, a yellow flower is not really yellow, it simply absorbs all other colors and reflects yellow. A white lily reflects all the colors, while a black tulip absorbs all colors.

God especially enjoys painting the heavens with varied tints. He gives us a picture of His heavenly city and the beautiful colors there. See Revelation 21:9-21.

Some stars appear brighter than others because they are closer to us, but this is not always the case. Although the stars look like tiny pinpoints of light in the night sky, they are really enormous objects of various colors. Amazingly enough, some stars are so large that they would more than fill the space between the earth and the sun, a distance of 93 million miles (150 million kilometers). The diameter of these stars is about 1,000 times as large as our sun. Then again, on the other end of the scale, there are stars that are smaller than the earth.

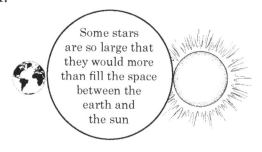

Some stars are so large that they would more than fill the space between the earth and the sun

Colors

As jewels are colorful, so stars also come in a delightful variety of colors. They sparkle in all the colors of the rainbow. It is interesting to note how much astronomers have been able to discover from starlight. They have learned that the color of a star is a good indication of its temperature. Notice the chart on page 24 to see which stars are the hottest and which are the coldest. The different colors of the stars are silent reminders of how each of God's children reflect different "colors" or aspects of His character. The color of a star depends upon its temperature. Spiritually speaking, you might say the "color" of our lives is influenced by our predominating (usual) temper.

Cooler stars are red; intermediate stars, like our sun, are yellow; and the very hottest stars are blue or white. Red can symbolize the blood of sacrifice, such as the martyrs of the past portrayed. The red stars can remind us of their shining witness for God. The yellow stars could bring to mind the gold tried in the fire, that which Christ promises to give to the Laodicean "stars" (Revelation 3:18). The blue stars speak of faithfulness to God and His commandments. The plate of gold with the inscription *"Holiness to the Lord"* on Aaron's mitre was hung by a blue lace (Exodus 28:36-37). The Israelites also wore a ribbon of blue to indicate their fidelity or obedience to Jehovah. Those faithful ones would be like the lovely blue stars. Lastly, we come to the white stars which speak to us of the righteousness of saints (Revelation 19:8), especially of the 144,000 who reflect the image of Jesus fully even as the color white is composed of all the colors combined (Revelation 14:1-5).

Reflect

Observe the Colorful Heavens

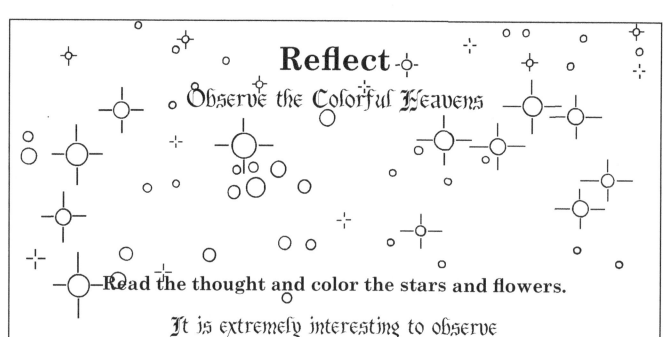

Read the thought and color the stars and flowers.

It is extremely interesting to observe
the same variety and harmony of color
prevailing on a stupendous scale among the orbs of heaven,
as among the colored petals of the lowliest wayside flower.
Both, though separated so widely from each other
by size, distance, and importance, belong to one grand system,
all whose parts are perfect. The rainbow flowers of the footstool,
as well as the starry flowers of the throne,
proclaim them to be the work of one all-wise
and all-powerful Artist.

☆ Brightness of Stars Differ

The differences of the brightness of stars are enormous. The variation is shown in the forms of radiation that they emit.

We observe only visible light with our unaided eye. But stars also transmit invisible rays, like x rays and gamma rays. This is noted on star maps, which show the intensity of x-ray and gamma ray magnitude.

"Good deeds will shine as the stars in heaven."
— J. Chalmers

What do you suppose are the most powerful rays produced by stars? The gamma rays! It is recorded that the strongest gamma ray emission ever measured was from a galaxy called Markarian 421. It is only a mere 400 million light years away from planet earth! The gamma rays from this galaxy give out trillions of electron volts of energy, while visible light gives out only two electron volts!

One puzzling type of gamma ray emission, picked up by sensors, is a powerful burst. These bursts may last from less than a thousandth of a second up to two minutes. There is no particular pattern to them and they appear from any point at any time in the heavens. Therefore, astronomers have a difficult time studying them since they do not know when or where the next one will appear. These powerful super rays momentarily burst causing them to be the brightest spot in the sky.

These flares of gamma radiation are called "gamma ray busters" by astronomers. They can remind us of fireflies which are there and then gone and seem never to appear in the same place more than once. There is also no pattern to the location of the gamma flashes. Their brief glory is studied by **alert** scientists as entomologists study the fireflies.

Reinforce
Place I - II

Color the picture of the firefly on the next page.

"Gamma Ray Busters" and Fireflies

"Gamma ray busters" can remind us
of fireflies which are there and then gone
and seem never to appear in the same place more than once.
Their brief glory is studied by <u>alert</u> scientists
as entomologists study the fireflies.

Illustration

Color each circle the color it is marked.

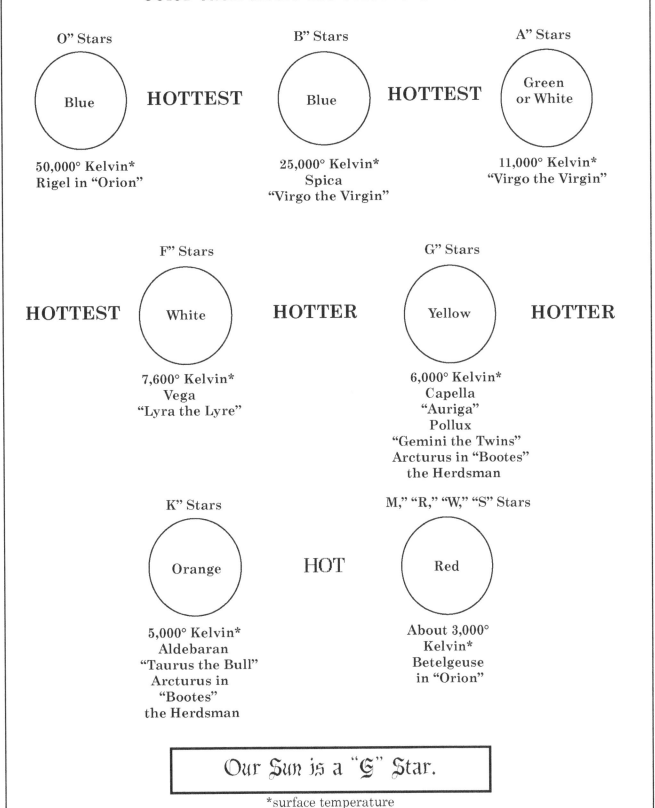

O" Stars

Blue

HOTTEST

50,000° Kelvin*
Rigel in "Orion"

B" Stars

Blue

HOTTEST

25,000° Kelvin*
Spica
"Virgo the Virgin"

A" Stars

Green
or White

11,000° Kelvin*
"Virgo the Virgin"

HOTTEST

F" Stars

White

7,600° Kelvin*
Vega
"Lyra the Lyre"

HOTTER

G" Stars

Yellow

HOTTER

6,000° Kelvin*
Capella
"Auriga"
Pollux
"Gemini the Twins"
Arcturus in "Bootes"
the Herdsman

K" Stars

Orange

5,000° Kelvin*
Aldebaran
"Taurus the Bull"
Arcturus in
"Bootes"
the Herdsman

HOT

M," "R," "W," "S" Stars

Red

About 3,000°
Kelvin*
Betelgeuse
in "Orion"

Our Sun is a "G" Star.

*surface temperature

Main Sequence

Generally speaking, the brightest stars that grace the heavens are the larger and hotter ones. Astronomers have arranged most of the stars in a sequence from cool, faint stars about one-tenth as big as our sun, to bright stars ten times the size of the sun. This group of stars is called the "main sequence."

Reinforce
Place III

Do more research about the main sequence stars.

Giants

God made some stars that do not fit in with the main sequence group. One example would be giant stars. Are you wondering how big a giant star would be? Well, a typical giant star is about 100 times as big as our sun and about 100 to 300 times as bright! If you would like to locate one of these king-sized stars, look for the star called Aldebaran located in the "nose" of the "Taurus, the Bull" constellation. In many parts of the world, this shimmering ruby-colored star is known as a Royal Star. Aldebaran, not being part of the main sequence of stars, can teach us that not everyone can qualify as a king. Jesus, of the royal line of King David is our *"King of kings"* (Revelation 19:16), who shed His crimson blood that we might share His kingdom.

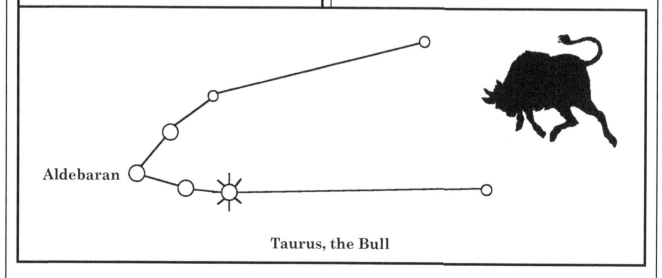

Aldebaran

Taurus, the Bull

Super-Giants

Some other examples of stars that do not fit into the main sequence would be the super-giants such as Antares, a reddish star at the heart of the constellation known as Scorpio. This lantern of the summer night is about 10,000 times more luminous than the sun. Antares is estimated to be 500 light-years away from our earth. With its being that bright we can be glad God keeps it in its place.

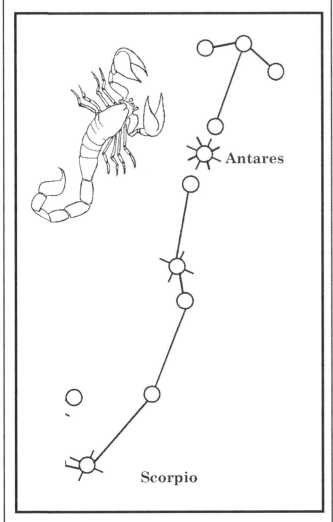

Scorpio

White Dwarfs

The Pup (white dwarf) is a companion to Sirius which orbits it every 48.9 years.

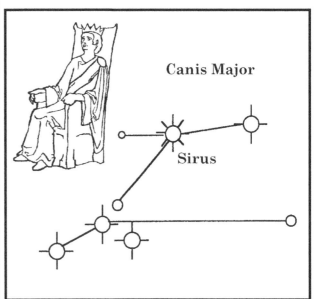

Canis Major

Sirus

The little white dwarf stars are very hot with temperatures several thousand degrees hotter than our sun. These stars are thought to be extremely dense. For example, a little white dwarf known as Sirius B is estimated to contain the mass of our sun packed into a sphere only 2% of the sun's diameter. That makes it over 100,000 times denser than water. There seems to be some kind of gravity (think of the drawing power of God) that squeezes the electrons of white dwarfs as closely together as is physically possible. It would be wonderful if we could be like the little white dwarf stars—content to be unnoticed and unknown—and yet be on fire with the love of God and full of His drawing power.

Neutron Stars

Some neutron stars are also called pulsars. **Can you guess why?** Because of the pulsating radio waves that they emit. A pulsar is a rapidly spinning neutron star. Its fierce magnetic field squirts light and radio waves into beams of energy that sweep around as the star turns. If the beam crosses Earth the star is detected by the pulse of its radiation. The first radio waves were detected in 1967 when radio telescopes picked up the pulsating radio waves.

It was first thought that the radio waves might be messages from outer space and they were called LGM ("Little Green Men"). It was determined that pulsars are not space messages.

Why are they called neutron stars? One theory is that the astronomical bodies consist completely of subatomic particles called neutrons. In atoms protons repel as electrons repel other electrons.

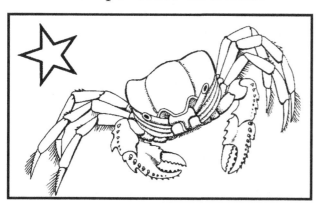

But neutrons do not have an electrical charge, so they pack together very tightly. Therefore, a neutron star can be much denser than our larger gaseous sun. One teaspoonful of matter from a neutron star would weigh billions of tons on earth.

Another theory is that there are protons and electrons, but that they are forced together because of the enormous pressure that occurs when a star runs out of nuclear fuel and collapses.

Besides the radio waves, some pulsars emit x-rays as well as visible light. A familiar pulsar is the bright star at the center of the Crab Nebula.

Some neutron stars spin around very fast, as much as 622 times a second.

A 9-pound (4-kilogram) baby could weigh 90,000 million pounds (40,000 million kilograms) on the surface of a neutron star because of the strong force of gravity.

★ Review ★
Place II - III

1. How big are some stars? How small are some stars?

2. Use a colored pencil or crayon to represent the main colors of stars, then tell the spiritual meaning of that color.

3. Explain what a "gamma ray buster" is.

4. Which stars do we generally see in the heavens?

5. What is the "main sequence"?

6. What and how big is a giant star?

7. What are super-giants? Give an example of a super-giant.

8. What are white dwarfs? of what do white dwarfs remind us spiritually?

9. Explain what a neutron star is.

★ Reinforce
Place I - II

What colors are the stars?

To answer the question fill in the puzzle below.

Review
Place I - II

1. Fill in the blanks and color these stars the correct color.

___ ___ ___ Giants and ___ ___ ___ ___ ___ Dwarfs

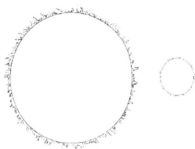

2. Solve these addition problems in the stars below. Put the sum in the box by the star. Use the key to color the stars.

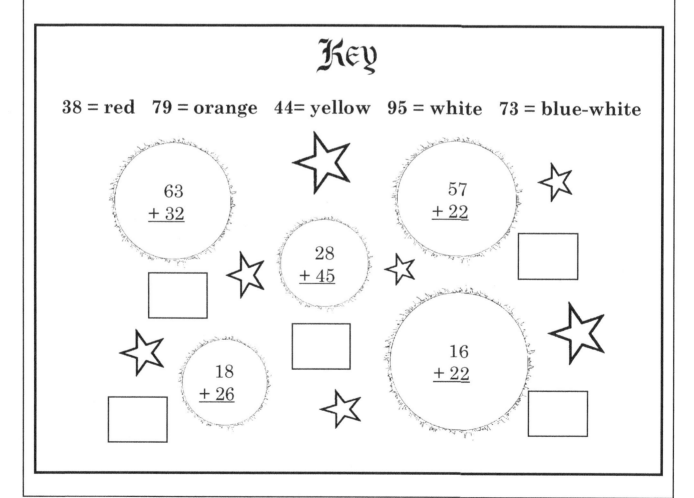

Key

38 = red   79 = orange   44= yellow   95 = white   73 = blue-white

63
+ 32

57
+ 22

28
+ 45

18
+ 26

16
+ 22

Remind

1. Have you ever looked from a hill down upon a town with its many lights—some colored? Let it turn your eyes upward to the brightly colored lights of the heavens.

2. When looking at a gas flame, notice its color. Then think of the star that color and what it means.

3. Notice the size of balls in the toy department of the store next time you are there. Let it remind you of the different sizes of stars.

4. Fireworks on the Fourth of July are just man copying the beautiful lights of heaven.

Reinforce

1. Form a circle and use the following colors of balls—red, orange, yellow, blue, and white. One person throw one ball to another. The one who catches it calls out what the colors mean in star language. (Example—catches a red ball—calls out "cooler star.")

Or, use balls of varying sizes to represent the sizes of the stars. (Example—when a child catches the largest ball, he could call out "supergiant!")

2. Colored jewels represent character, as found on the breastplate of the high priest. The many tinted star-gems in the heavens remind us of this. Some day the faithful saved people of God will be represented by jewels in His crown.

3. Sing the hymn, "Jewels."

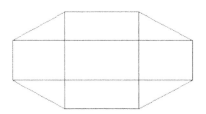

Research
Other Variations

Scientists are finding that stars, like people, have so many variables in their makeup that the probability of two identical stars existing is practically zero. Each one displays God's creative glory. Do you think that Someone as imaginative and powerful as God can figure out the solutions to all your problems?

Many stars have thick, turbulent atmospheres around them while some even appear to smoke and fume. Some stars tick almost like a clock. Even more puzzling, some stars flash a kind of code like dots and dashes. Besides these, there are also stars that change their color and brightness slowly and irregularly. These stars are called variable stars. They sometimes change in size as if they were breathing—expanding and contracting, growing hotter then cooler, brighter then fainter.

Variety is nice, but I think I would rather be more like the Cepheid stars, at least as far as my Christian experience is concerned. Cepheids are stars quite regular and dependable in their changes. They have a regular schedule of things they do and you can count on them to do them on time. The North Star, the famous Polestar, is a supergiant Cepheid. Because a Cepheid is so dependable in its schedule, astronomers "take their pulse" to help them estimate distances to stars far off in space.

A Cepheid variable is a class of stars with exceptionally regular periods of light pulsation.

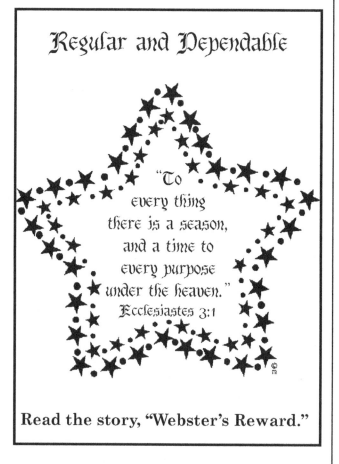

Regular and Dependable

"To every thing there is a season, and a time to every purpose under the heaven."
Ecclesiastes 3:1

Read the story, "Webster's Reward."

Webster's Reward

Regular and **dependable** movements as the stars can make a **light**.

An insurance case was brought to Daniel Webster when he was a young lawyer in Portsmouth, New Hampshire. Only a small amount was involved, and a $20 fee was all that was promised. He saw that to do his client full justice, a journey to Boston would be desirable, in order to consult the law library. He would be out of pocket by the expedition, and for the time he would receive no adequate compensation. But he determined to do his best, cost what it might. He would always be regular and dependable in his work. He accordingly went to Boston and looked up the authorities, and gained the case.

Years after, Webster, who had meanwhile become famous, was passing through New York. An important insurance case was to be tried that day, and one of the counsel had suddenly been taken ill. Money was no object, and Webster was begged to name his terms and conduct the case.

"I told them," said Mr. Webster, "that it was preposterous to expect me to prepare a legal argument at a few hours' notice. They insisted, however, that I should look at the papers; and this I finally consented to do. It was my old $20 case over again; and as I never forget anything, I had all the authorities at my fingers' ends. The court knew that I had no time to prepare, and were astonished at the range of my acquirements. So you see, I was handsomely repaid in both fame and money for that journey to Boston; and the moral is that good work regular and dependable is rewarded in the end."

> It was my old
> $20 case over again;
> and as I never forget anything,
> I had all the authorities
> at my fingers' ends.

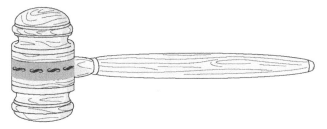

A Lesson

*"For we dare not make ourselves of the number,
or compare ourselves with some that commend themselves:
but they measuring themselves by themselves,
and comparing themselves among themselves,
are not wise."*
II Corinthians 10:12

There is a wonderful lesson in the vast differences that exist among the stars. We should refrain from comparing ourselves with others. *"For we dare not make ourselves of the number, or compare ourselves with some that commend themselves: but they measuring themselves by themselves, and comparing themselves among themselves, are not wise"* (II Corinthians 10:12). God has made you different from anyone else that ever existed with special talents. And "the Giver expects returns corresponding to the gifts. The humblest gift is not to be despised or left inactive....The lamp does not refuse to give its light because it is not a star. The moon and stars do not refuse to shine because they have not the brilliant light of the sun. Every person has his own peculiar sphere and vocation. Those who make the most of their God-given opportunities will return to the Giver, in their improvement, an interest proportionate to the entrusted capital" (*Fundamentals of Christian Education* 48).

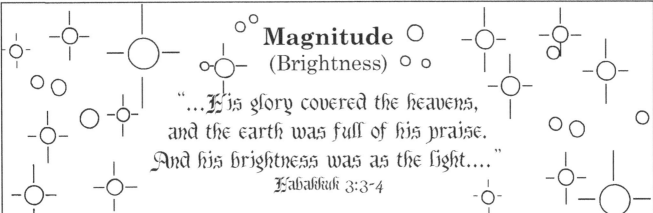

Magnitude
(Brightness)

"...His glory covered the heavens,
and the earth was full of his praise.
And his brightness was as the light...."
Habakkuk 3:3-4

There are at least 5,000 stars that the sharpest human eye can see unaided. And, as you know, this celestial dome of stars is not uniform in its distance from us. Many of the nearest stars are too dim to see without a telescope, while others that look near are really very far away. In this realm, as in so many others, we must not judge according to appearance. "Judge not according to the appearance, but judge righteous judgment" (John 7:24).

Astronomers have a way of classifying stars according to how bright they are. A certain degree of brightness is called first magnitude. A brightness that is 2-1/2 times less than second magnitude is called third magnitude and so on. The dimmer the star, the higher the magnitude; and the brighter the star, the lower the magnitude. The very brightest stars have magnitudes so low that they are less than zero, being expressed as negative numbers. For example, a star with a magnitude of −1.00 is brighter than one with a magnitude of 1.00, but not as bright as a star with a magnitude of −2.00. This seemed a little backward to my mind at first, but an easy way to remember it is to think of the spiritual principal that he that is greatest (brightest) is lowest in his own estimation (magnitude). "And he sat down, and called the twelve, and saith unto them, If any man desire to be first, the same shall be last of all, and servant of all" (Mark 9:35).

There are at least 5,000 stars that the sharpest human eye can see unaided.

"...Servant of all..."

The glittering orbs that we can see unaided in the night sky are limited to the first six visual magnitudes. These stars are commonly referred to as "fixed" stars, but actually they are moving all the time, some of them hundreds of miles per second. We just do not notice their movement because they are so far away.

Beyond this first layer of stars lies layer after layer of stars of the seventh magnitude and fainter. This continues on to the 20th magnitude, which is just beyond the limit of visibility. Through the 100-inch reflector on Mt. Wilson, the stars have been counted at about 5,000,000,000. But now, with the famous 200-inch telescope on Mt. Palomar in southern California, several billion more stars have been individually seen! With Eliphaz we can exclaim, "...*behold the height of the stars, how high they are!*" (Job 22:12). Even beyond what can be seen through the Mt. Palomar observatory or Hubble and other telescopes, the light from even more distant stars can be caught by long time exposures on sensitive photographic plates, each star of the last layer being no brighter than would be the beam of a pocket flashlight aimed at us from the moon. Yet we know by faith that even this vast number, extending to the 24th magnitude, is only a small fraction of the stars in our galaxy and its outlying clusters, many of which overlap each other so densely that they are buried in light, while others are shrouded in mysterious space clouds of utter darkness. "*I would seek unto God, and unto God would I commit my cause: which doeth great things... without number*" (Job 5:8-9). "*...The hosts of heaven cannot be numbered, neither the sand of the sea measured...*" (Jeremiah 33:22).

> "*...Righteousness thereof go forth as brightness....*"

The world is as dark now as it was before Christ's first advent with a misunderstanding of God's love. It is time for the gospel to be proclaimed with such power that the whole earth will be brightened with its glory (Revelation 18:1). The Lord says, "*For Zion's sake will I not hold my peace, and for Jerusalem's sake I will not rest, until the righteousness thereof go forth as **brightness**, and the salvation thereof as a lamp that burneth. And the Gentiles shall see thy righteousness, and all kings thy glory; and thou shalt be called by a new name, which the mouth of the Lord shall name. Thou shalt also be a crown of glory [stars] in the hand of the Lord, and a royal diadem in the hand of thy God*" (Isaiah 62:1-3).

> Beyond this first layer of stars lies layer after layer of stars.

Because the Jews at the first advent of Christ were not alert to their responsibilities, God passed them by. "Outside of the Jewish nation there were men who foretold the appearance of a divine Instructor. These men were seeking for truth, and to them the Spirit of Inspiration was imparted. One after another, like stars in the darkened heavens, such teachers had arisen. Their words of prophecy had kindled hope in the hearts of thousands of the Gentile world."*

Men Like Stars

"Outside of the Jewish nation there were men....like stars in the darkened heavens...."

The Desire of Ages 33

☆ Review
Place I - II - III ☆

1. Are stars different from each other? Describe.

2. Are you a Cepheid star, or a variable star?

3. What is the Polestar (North Star) classified as?

4. What is the lesson for us in the differences that exist among the stars?

5. How many stars can the human eye see unaided by any mechanical device?

6. What is magnitude? Describe.

7. What are fixed stars?

8. What does Job 22:12 tell us about magnitude?

9. Reread Jeremiah 33:22.

Place II - III
Apparent Magnitudes

Arrange the following star names covered in this lesson from brightest to the dimmest.

Stars	Apparent Magnitude
Pollux (Gemini)	1.14
Rigel (Orion)	0.12
Alpha Centauri	− 0.03
Antares (Scorpio)	0.96
Polaris (North Star)	2.00
Castor (Gemini)	1.60
Aldebaran (Taurus)	0.85
Sirius (Canis Major)	− 1.46
Arcturus (Bootes)	− 0.04
Betelgeuse (Orion)	0.50

1. _____   _____

2. _____   _____

3. _____   _____

4. _____   _____

5. _____   _____

6. _____   _____

7. _____   _____

8. _____   _____

9. _____   _____

10. _____   _____

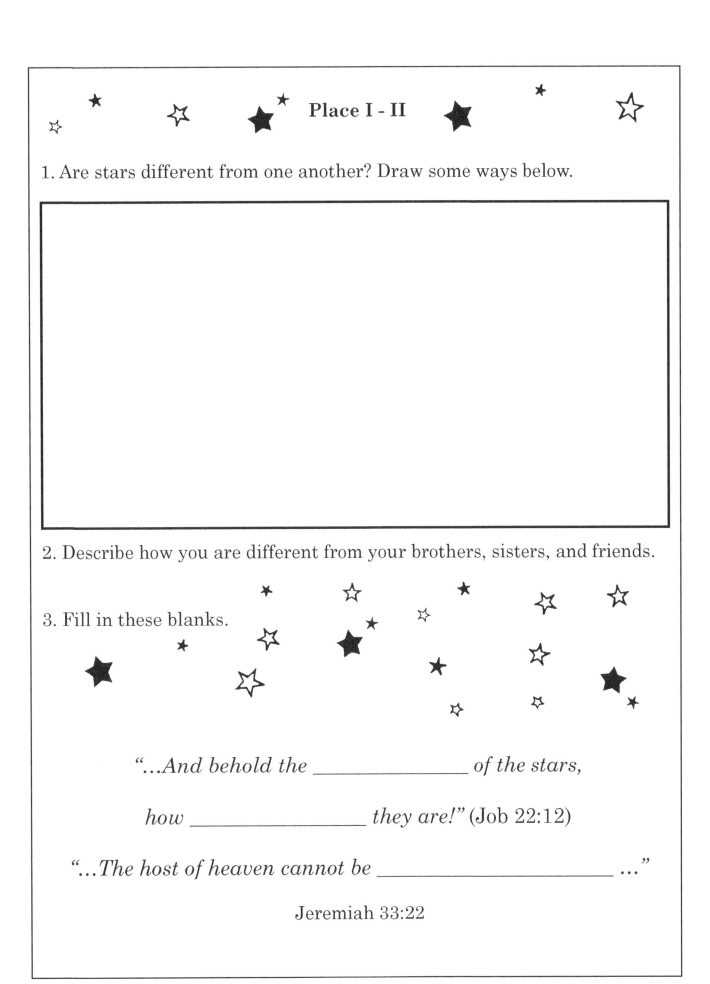

Place I - II

1. Are stars different from one another? Draw some ways below.

2. Describe how you are different from your brothers, sisters, and friends.

3. Fill in these blanks.

"...And behold the _____ of the stars,

how _____ they are!" (Job 22:12)

"...The host of heaven cannot be _____ ..."

Jeremiah 33:22

Remind

1. As you notice how different each person in your family is, think about the multitude of differences in the host of stars!

2. Practice only thinking the best about everyone you come in contact with and memorize John 7:24.

3. Darkness that the clouds may bring to our day is similar to the space clouds of utter darkness, except the space clouds are mysterious.

4. Are you **alert** to someone teaching about Christ's second coming as a few were before His first coming?

Reinforce

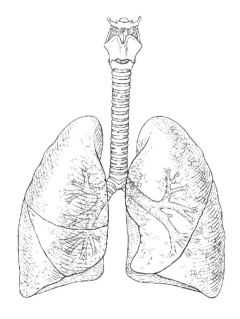

1. Breathe in, then out and notice how your body seems to change sizes. That is what some variable stars seem to do.

2. Take several dry beans of the same variety. Use a magnifying glass and make a list of their differences. Memorize and repeat II Corinthians 10:12.

3. Do the puzzle, "An Astronomical Term."

4. Memorize the poem, "Stars."

An Astronomical Term

**What astronomical term means
the brightness of a star to earthly view?**

Cross out any letter that appears in this graph more than two times.
The letters that are left will give the answer to the question above.

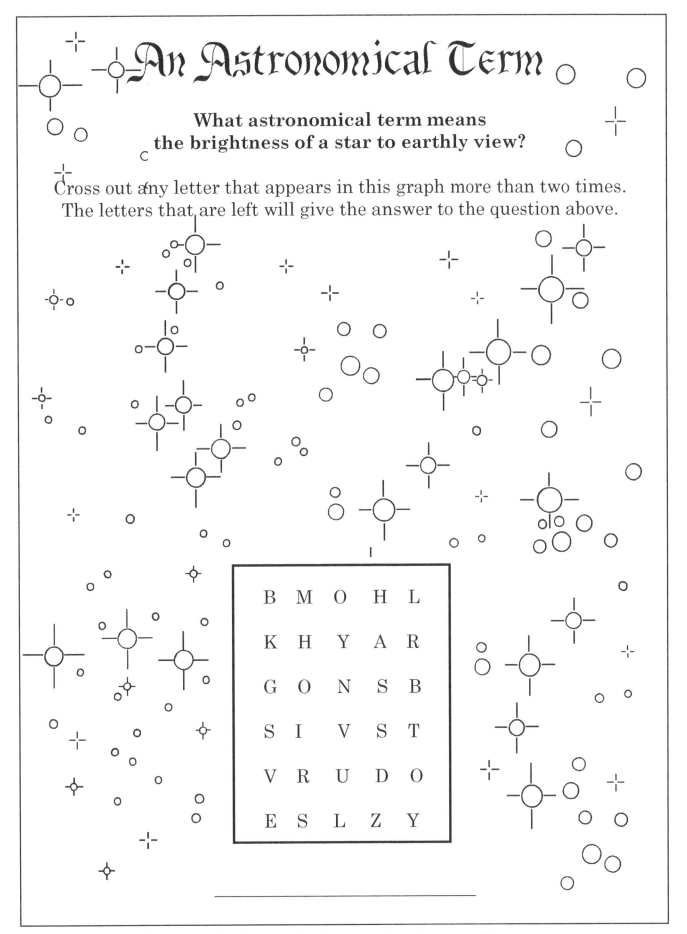

B	M	O	H	L
K	H	Y	A	R
G	O	N	S	B
S	I	V	S	T
V	R	U	D	O
E	S	L	Z	Y

_____

Stars

Memorize this poem.

Ye stars of light in heaven,
How brilliantly ye shine!
And, Oh, what wondrous glory.
What heights on heights, are thine!

—Unknown

Reinforce
Place III

Make a Magnitude Measuring Tool

Materials Needed:
glue, scissors, ruler, pencil, a small coin, one piece of cardboard 2 x 10 inches (5 x 25 cm.), and 5 strips of cellophane 1 1/4 inches wide (3 cm.)

Directions:

1. Divide the cardboard into five 2 inch (5 cm.) sections, drawing a line from the top to the bottom edge.

2. Trace around your coin which should be put in the center of each section.

3. Cut out the circles in each of the five sections.

4. Glue one strip of cellophane onto the strip of cardboard so that it covers all five of the holes. Be care-ful not to get glue on the cellophane inside the hole area.

5. Glue the 2nd cellophane strip onto the first strip so that it covers only four of the cardboard holes.

6. Glue the 3rd cellophane strip onto the second strip so that it covers just the last three holes in the cardboard and so forth, until the last strip covers only one hole in the cardboard.

7. Print the number 1 in the section on the cardboard below the hole with the five layers of cellophane; then label the next space with the four layers over the hole number 2, etc., until the last hole which should be number 5 has only one strip of cellophane.

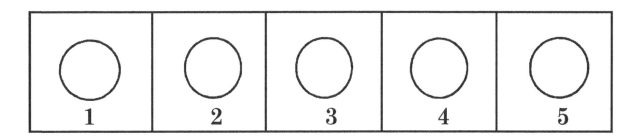

To Use Your Magnitude Measuring Tool

Look at a constellation through your magnitude tool. If a star can be seen through hole number 1, that star is a first magnitude star. If you can see a star through the hole number 2, that star is a second magnitude star, etc. (down through the fifth magnitude).

People in the northern hemisphere can use the four stars in the head of the constellation Draco (the Dragon) to check their tool. The brightest star in Draco is a first magnitude star. The second brightest is a second magnitude; the next brightest is a third magnitude; and the next brightest is a fourth magnitude. There are also four stars in the Great Bear constellation that can be used in the same way. Southern sky watchers can use Centaurus with stars ranging in magnitude from 0.27 to 5.

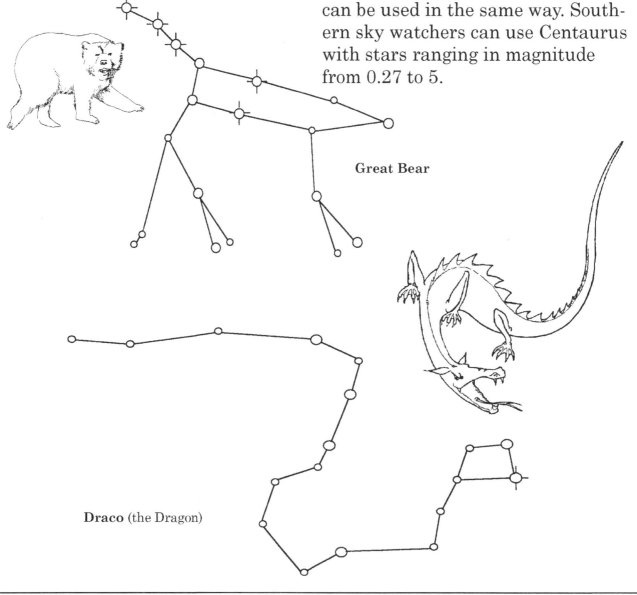

Great Bear

Draco (the Dragon)

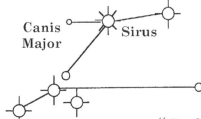

Canis Major   Sirus

Research
Star Companions

Canis Minor

Double Stars

*"And he called unto him the twelve,
and began to send them forth by two and two...."*
Mark 6:7

Like people, stars tend to be involved in relationships. Nearly half of the known stars do not travel alone but have at least one companion to go around with them. When stars are found in pairs they are called double stars. These can call to mind how Jesus sent His disciples *"forth by two and two."*

The brightest gem in the sky is a double star by the name of Sirius. The magnitude of this blue-white main sequence star is –1.46. Its brilliance is due to the fact that it is only 8.6 light years away from earth. The belt of Orion points toward Sirius which is in the Big Dog (Canis Major) constellation. Sirius is called the Dog Star; and if you live in the south, perhaps you have heard the term, "dog days," which refers to the peak weeks of summer's heat beginning about July 23 when Sirius and the sun are closest to each other in the sky.

The name Sirius comes from a Greek word *seirios*, meaning "scorcher," a term coming from an ancient Egyptian word. The star played an important role in the lives of the ancient inhabitants of the Nile River valley. The Nile annually overflowed its banks at that time of year when Sirius rose at daybreak—during the summer months. During this time Sirius is mostly invisible at night because it is in the sky during the day. The ancients thought that the heat of Sirius, "the scorcher," was added to that of the sun during this period, and to this day we call the hottest portion of summer the "dog days."

Sirius is about twice as large as our sun. It has a little white dwarf companion it travels with. This little star, nicknamed the "Pup," was seen for the first time in 1862 when an optician was testing a new, big object glass. The official name for the Pup is Sirius B. You pronounce it like "be serious." This little star is so dense that scientists calculate that the material it is made out of weighs 18 tons (16.2 metric tons) a pint (0.47 liter). It orbits Sirius once every 50 years.

One great mystery about this brightest of stars continues to puzzle modern astronomers: about 2,000 years ago Sirius was described in such terms as "red," "fiery," and "coppery," whereas today and even in A.D. 1000 it is very white, with a tinge of blue.

Often stars having unexplainable variations in their brilliancy or paths have later been found to have an unseen traveling companion. Once these are discovered, astronomers are able to explain the variations in the star since all its movements had been regulated by this unsuspected and unseen center. God has given children an unseen companion—their guardian angel. Like the companion white dwarf star, our **alert** guardian angel has an unseen drawing influence for good on our lives. Guardian angels are robed in white light like the white dwarf star gives off beams of pure white light. Our guardian angels are so humble that they are content to remain unnoticed like the little white dwarf stars. How much we owe to their companionship, eternity alone will reveal.

God has given children
an unseen companion—
their guardian angel.

Angels

How much
we owe
to angel companionship,
eternity alone
will reveal.

**Read the story,
"Guardian Angels,"
and the poem,
"A Little Star."**

Guardian Angels

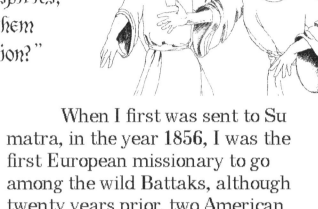

"Are they not all ministering spirits, sent forth to minister for them who shall be heirs of salvation?"
Hebrews 1:14

Through all Scripture we catch frequent glimpses of angels, tireless in their ministry for God to man. At times they appeared in form visible to the natural eye; but more often they were seen in vision or dream. Sometimes they came in the guise of men, so that, as the apostle says, men entertaining strangers *"have entertained angels unawares"* (Hebrews 13:2).

Angels on Guard

The following story of deliverance is preserved in the records of a missionary pioneering in the Dutch East Indies now known as Indonesia, the populous islands which once gave Holland a dominion in the Orient. The incident occurred in the life of Von Asselt, a Rhenis missionary in Sumatra from 1856-76, and was related to him when on a visit to Lubeck.

When I first was sent to Sumatra, in the year 1856, I was the first European missionary to go among the wild Battaks, although twenty years prior, two American missionaries had come to them with the gospel; but they had been killed and eaten. Since then no effort had been made to bring the gospel to these people, and naturally they had remained the same cruel savages.

What it means for one to stand alone among a savage people, unable to make himself understood, not understanding a single sound of their language, but whose suspicious, hostile looks and gestures

> Men entertaining strangers *"have entertained angels unawares."*
> Hebrews 13:2

> Nothing gives us a greater idea of our soul than that God has given us, at the moment of our birth, an angel to take care of it.
> —Jerome

speak only a too-well-understood language—yes, it is hard for one to realize that. The first two years which I spent among the Battaks, at first all alone and afterward with my wife, were so hard that it makes me shudder even now when I think of them. Often it seemed as if we were not only encompassed by hostile men, but also by hostile powers of darkness; for often an inexplicable, unutterable fear would come over us, so that we had to get up at night, and go on our knees to pray or read the Word of God, in order to find relief.

"After we had lived in this place for two years, we moved several hours' journey inland among a tribe somewhat civilized, who received us more kindly. There we built a small house with three rooms—a living room, a bedroom, and a small reception room—and life for us became a little more easy and cheerful.

"When I had been in this new place for some months, a man came to me from the district where we had been, and whom I had known there. I was sitting on the bench in front of our house, and he sat down beside me, and for a while talked of this, that, and the other. Finally he began: 'Now, *tuan* [teacher], I have yet one request.'

" 'And what is that?'

" 'I would like to have a look at your watchmen close at hand.'

" 'What watchmen do you mean? I do not have any.'

" 'I mean the watchmen whom you station around your house at night, to protect you.'

" 'But I have no watchmen,' I said again; 'I have only a little herd-boy and a little cook, and they would make poor watchmen.'

"Then the man looked at me incredulously, as if he wished to say: 'Oh, do not try to make me believe otherwise, for I know better.'

"Then he asked: 'May I look through your house, to see if they are hid there?'

" 'Yes, certainly,' I said laughing; 'look through it; you will not find anybody.' So he went in and searched in every corner, even through the beds, but came to me very much disappointed.

"Then I began a little probing myself, and requested him to tell me the circumstances about those watchmen of whom he spoke, and this is what he related to me:

" 'When you first came to us, *tuan*, we were very angry at you. We did not want you to live among us; we did not trust you, and believed you had some design against us. Therefore we came together, and resolved to kill you and your wife. Accordingly, we went to your house night after night; but when we came near, there stood always, close around the house, a double row of watchmen with glittering weapons, and we did not venture to attack them to get into your house. But we were not willing to abandon our plan, so we went to a professional assassin [there still was among the savage Battaks at that time a special guild of assassins, who killed for hire any one whom it was desired to get out of the way], and asked him if he would undertake to kill you and your wife. He laughed at us because of our cowardice, and said, 'I fear no God and no devil. I will get through those watchmen easily.' So we came all together in the evening, and the assassin, swinging his weapon about his head, went courageously on before us. As we neared your house, we remained behind and let him go on alone. But in a short time he came running back hastily, and said, 'No, I dare not risk it to go through alone; two rows of big, strong men stand there, very close together, shoulder to shoulder, and their weapons shine like fire.' Then we gave it up to kill you. But, now, tell me, *tuan*, who are those watchmen? Have you never seen them?'

" 'No, I have never seen them.'

" 'And your wife did not see them?'

" 'No, my wife did not see them.'

" 'But yet we have all seen them; how is that?'

"Then I went in and brought a Bible from our house, and holding it open before him, said:

" 'See here; this book is the Word of our great God, in which He promises to guard and defend us, and we firmly believe that Word; therefore we need not to see the watchmen; but you do not believe, therefore the great God has to show you the watchmen, in order that you may learn to believe.' "

May none of us lose the blessedness and the comfort of the doctrine of the ministry of angels in this unbelieving age.

"I dare not risk it to go through alone; two rows of big, strong men stand there, very close together, shoulder to shoulder...."

A Little Star

In the blue expanse of heaven,
Undiscerned by human vision,
    Shines a little star:
Hidden 'mong its brighter neighbors.
Like an atom in a brilliant,
    It's unseen from afar.

Just as the retiring crescent
Melted in the glare of noonday
    Still delights to smile.
So this star unknown, unheard of,
Joyfully is twinkling, twinkling,
    Twinkling all the while.

He who hath created these things,
Who doth bring their host by number,
    Calleth each by name:
For that He is strong in power
Not one of them ever faileth,
    He upholdeth them.

Fear not in this world of sorrows,
Little soul unknown, unheard of,
    Just act well thy part:
He who laid the starry heaven
Will sustain, protect, and guide thee.
    Trust Him and take heart.

—*C. C. Roberts*

Multiple Stars

"And I, if I be lifted up from the earth, will draw all men unto me."

John 12:32

Multiple stars are families consisting of several stars quite close together all moving around a common center of gravity. The North Star, also known as the Polestar, is a multiple star. The multiple stars can remind us of how all our family members should have a common center, Christ Jesus, that they are drawn to. If someone in your family is not making Jesus the center of their lives, do what you can by prayer and love to uplift Jesus to them because the Saviour has promised, *"And I, if I be lifted up from the earth, will draw all men unto me."*

Illustration
Spectroscope

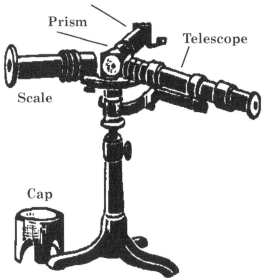

The spectroscope is used to tell whether stars are coming towards the earth or traveling away from it. When a star is approaching earth, the bands in the spectrum are moving toward the blue end of the spectrum; while it is going away from earth they are shown toward the red.

Star Clusters

"Canst thou bind the sweet influences of the Pleiades?"
Job 38:31

The Pleiades

*"And he had in his right hand seven stars:
and out of his mouth went a sharp two edged sword:
and his countenance was as the sun shineth in his strength."*
Revelation 1:16

The Pleiades, also known as the Seven Sisters, is a lovely cluster of icy-blue stars that are all moving through space together in the same direction and at about the same speed. The Pleiades, which is translated from the Hebrew word, "kimah," means "herd" or "cluster." This word, "kimah," is translated in two different ways in relation to the Pleiades. In some cases it is translated as the Pleiades and in other places it may be translated as the Seven Stars. An example of the word being translated in the last mentioned way is: *"Seek him that maketh the seven stars and Orion"* (Amos 5:8). Later on in this study you will see how this variation in the way "kimah" is translated is an important clue as to God's meaning for the Pleiades.

The Pleiades appear in the November skies of the Northern Hemisphere above Orion's left shoulder toward which they are moving. This star cluster looks somewhat like a small, short-handled dipper. Traditionally used as a test of vision, the Pleiades appear as five stars to some persons, while most others see six, and only a few people with the sharpest eyes can see seven stars.

If you have a pair of binoculars, you can see dozens of stars. With a small telescope, you can see one of the most beautiful sights in the heavens because over a hundred stars will be visible, clothed in nebulous clouds of glory.

*"Seek him that maketh
the seven stars and Orion."*
Amos 5:8

The Seven Stars

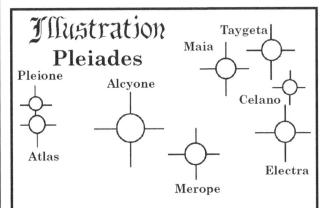

Illustration

Pleiades

Pleione
Maia
Taygeta
Alcyone
Celano
Atlas
Merope
Electra

- The Seven Sisters were called the "Sailing Stars."
- They are about 541 light-years away.
- 250 stars in this cluster can be seen with a telescope.
- The brighter of the group appear to us as just six or seven stars.

From the Greeks it was called Pleiades, from the word "plecin," to sail, because it indicated the time when the sailor might hope to undertake a voyage with safety. It was also called Vergilliae, from "ver," the spring, because it ushered in the mild vernal weather favorable to farming and pastoral employments.

In ancient times, the date of the Pleiades' setting was the signal that it was time for the spring sowing of grain. The season of navigation began with their rising again in the sky. The following quotation from the eighth century before Christ refers to the importance of this star cluster: "When the Pleiades... first arise, begin your harvest: when they leave the skies, plough" (Hesiod).

An intriguing parallel with the Seven Stars (Pleiades) is found in the text, Revelation 2:1. Be alert to the fact that the prophet uses the same words in Revelation 2:1 that the Bible uses in describing the *"sweet influences"* of the Pleiades (Job 38:31). Before we quote from Revelation 2:1 you should understand that the term *"sweet influences"* is from the Hebrew *ma'adannoth* for "bonds," "chains," or "fastenings." Here is the text from Revelation: *"These things saith he that holdeth the **seven stars** in his right hand...."* These words are spoken to the teachers in the church—those entrusted by God with weighty responsibilities. The *"sweet influences"* that are to be abundant in the church are bound up with God's ministers, who are to reveal the love of Christ. The stars of heaven are under His control. He fills them with light. He guides and directs their movements. If He did not do this, they would become fallen stars. So with His ministers. They are but instruments in His hands, and all the good they can accomplish is done through His power. Through them His light is to shine forth. He will give them His brightness to reflect to the world.

"Sweet Influences"

Whenever you look up at the Pleiades, please send a prayer to heaven for God's teachers of righteousness that they, like the Seven Stars, may also be clothed with clouds of glory, while traveling their parallel paths towards Orion (which we will see later in our study is symbolic of Christ). May God's teachers reach the state of spiritual perfection which is implied in the number seven. Even the dipper shape of this cluster can remind us that God's teachers offer the *"water of life"* to thirsty souls (Revelation 21:6). *"And they that be wise* [margin, "teachers"] *shall shine as the brightness of the firmament; and they that turn many to righteousness as the stars for ever and ever"* (Daniel 12:3).

**Sing the song,
"Who Are These," first verse.**

The influences of the Pleiades may be called "sweet," as indicating the harmonious operation of those great laws by which our system revolves. In this vast and complex arrangement, not one wheel jars or creaks—not a single discordant sound disturbs the deep, solemn quietude of the midnight sky. Smoothly and silently each star performs its sublime revolutions. Although our system is composed of so many bodies—differing in size, form, and consistence—they are

Another Pleiades Meaning

It also has another meaning in the Chaldaic which is a hinge, pivot, or axle, which turns round and moves other bodies along with it. And with a telescope we can view the more than 250 stars traveling with the Seven Sisters.

As the pastor ministers to his flock, he influences others to travel with him towards Christ.

all exquisitely poised in space in relation to one another, and to their common center. Each is in its destined path to preserve the safety and harmony of the whole. Moons revolve around planets; comets and planets around the sun; the sun around the center of the galaxy; and grand beyond conception, this cluster of systems around the center of ten thousand centers—the great white throne of the Eternal and the Infinite, and all with a rhythm so perfect that it is called in poetry "music of the spheres." In this vision of orbits and revolutions, more awful and stupendous than Ezekiel's vision of wheels within wheels, we see seated on the throne above the firmament, not a blind chance or a passionless fate, but one like unto the Son of Man—He whom John saw in Patmos, holding the mystery of the seven stars in His right hand—possessed of infinite love as well as infinite power—binding the sweet influences of Pleiades solely for the order and good of His creation.

> Each is in
> its destined path
> to preserve
> the safety
> and harmony
> of the whole.

Reflect
Other Clusters

There are hundreds of other star clusters in our system. Most of these have over 100 star members loosely organized in what we might think of as a flock of stars. As you know, God speaks of His people as a *"little flock"* (Luke 12:32). As the family of God we are like a cluster of stars that influence each other in powerful though often unseen ways. We are bound together by the cords of love. "The stars of heaven are all under law, influencing each other to do the will of God, yielding their common obedience to the law that controls their action. And, in order that the Lord's work may advance healthfully and solidly, His people must draw together" (*My Life Today* 39).

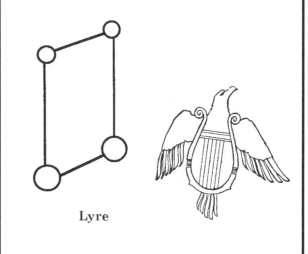

Lyre

Remarkable Facts – About the Pleiades

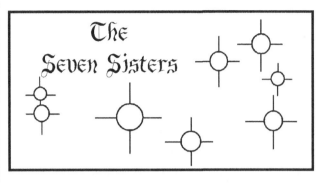

The
Seven Sisters

• The Japanese word for Pleiades is Subaru. This star cluster is the trademark on the Japanese car of that name. The company chose the design because the beginning six companies merged to begin the super company that produces the Subaru automobile. Contracts and corporate relationships now bind the six companies, so they move as one unit. And that is the same relationship the stars of the Pleiades have with one another. They are a moving unit.

• The Pleiades is 541 light-years from earth. They move like a flock of birds.

• The six visible stars in the cluster are six very large suns, each being about 800 times larger than our own sun.

• There are more than 250 stars in the Pleiades cluster, all traveling in the same direction and at the same speed.

• When you look at the Pleiades, you will see light that left it 500 years ago. For fun, look on a time chart to see what was happening in the world 500 years ago when light left the Pleiades!

God designed Israel to be a "cluster," to draw together.
Like stars in the darkened heavens
they were to shine out to the world
of the Hope that soon was to be born.
But Israel as a people were not <u>alert</u> to their great destiny.

Review
Place II - III

1. What is a double star?

2. What is the brightest star in the night sky?

3. Name the companion that travels with Sirius.

4. Who is your constant companion who is unseen?

5. What are multiple stars? Give an example. Of what does it remind us?

6. Write several paragraphs describing the Pleiades and the lessons learned from them.

7. What might we call clusters of stars? What does God call His people?

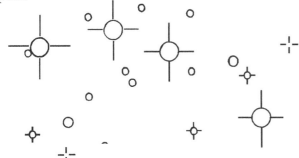

Reinforce

Fill in the blanks with a word or words that describe the Pleiades which start with the following letters.

P_____

L_____

E_____

I_____

A_____

D_____

E_____

S_____

Place I - II

1. Draw a double star.

2. What does the picture remind you about two certain stars in the sky?

   Write their names in the blanks below.
   Pronounce their names for teacher.

   _____

   _____

3. Who is your constant companion who travels with you?

4. Draw your family on a separate piece of paper.
   They are like multiple stars that stay together.

5. Draw the Pleiades.

6. This picture can remind you of the Pleiades and other families of stars.
   It can also remind you what God calls His church family.

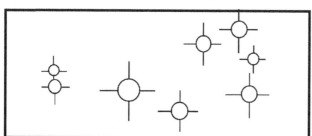
   "__ __ __ __ __ __ __

   __ __ __ __ __ __ __"

★✦Word Find★
Beautiful Cluster

One beautiful cluster of stars has about 100,000 stars in it!
It is called the Great Cluster in Hercules. It is sometimes called
M13. This is because the Frenchman Charles Messier made a list
of stars in the 18th century. This cluster was number 13 on the
list. Another beautiful cluster of stars are mentioned in Revelation
7:9. What are they called?

— — — — — — — — — — — — — — — — — — — —

Another name for them is Spiritual Israel.

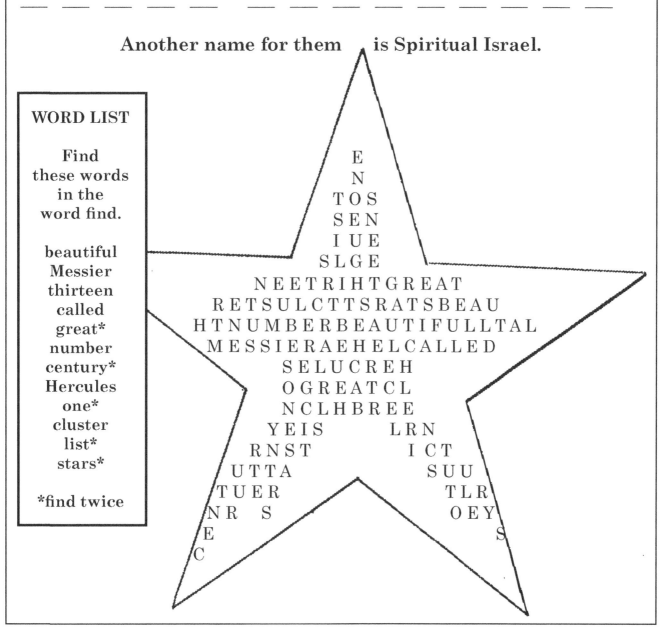

WORD LIST

**Find
these words
in the
word find.**

beautiful
Messier
thirteen
called
great*
number
century*
Hercules
one*
cluster
list*
stars*

*find twice

```
                    E
                    N
                  T O S
                  S E N
                  I U E
                  S L G E
          N E E T R I H T G R E A T
        R E T S U L C T T S R A T S B E A U
      H T N U M B E R B E A U T I F U L L T A L
      M E S S I E R A E H E L C A L L E D
            S E L U C R E H
            O G R E A T C L
            N C L H B R E E
          Y E I S         L R N
        R N S T             I C T
        U T T A             S U U
        T U E R             T L R
      N R   S               O E Y
      E                           S
      C
```

Remind

1. When seeing twins, think about the double stars. Often, like double stars, twins are not identical.

2. When seeing a group of friends walking along together, think how multiple stars move together through space.

3. When seeing a flock of birds flying through the sky, it is similar to the more than 250 stars of the Pleiades "flying" through space.

4. Have you ever attended a church meeting with your parents? That group could be like the "little flock" or star clusters out in space. Then each church is like another star cluster.

Reinforce

1. There are many "unseen" people in our lives that have traveled a long or short distance with us. They have contributed to our happiness. Think of one or more persons in your life and write them a letter of gratefulness or, tell them in person. Be **alert** from now on to give these people special thanks. (Example: box boy at store, parents, pastor, or elderly.)

2. Look at the middle star in the handle of the Big Dipper. It appears as one star, but use binoculars and you will see two points of light.

3. To demonstrate the movements of a double star, take your brother's or sister's hands and skip in circles. As you do this, move across the yard. Now you are like a double star journeying through space. Dad and mom can now take hands and do the same and move with you. Now you are a double-double star traveling across the sky. *"Thou, even thou, art Lord alone; thou hast made heaven, the heaven of heavens, with all their host, the earth, and all things that are therein, the seas, and all that is therein, and thou preservest them all; and the host of heaven worshippeth thee"* (Nehemiah 9:6).

4. Look at Pleiades with binoculars.

Research
The Distance of the Stars
"...Behold the height of the stars, how high they are!"
Job 22:12

Stars are not spread out evenly in the universe but appear in groups called galaxies. The distance between the stars in our galaxy, the Milky Way, averages four to five light years although they are closer together in the central part of the galaxy.

The closest star to us is Proxima Centauri which is 4.3 light years from our sun.

Light-year

A light-year equals 186,282 miles (299,792 kilometers) per second or 5,878,800,000,000 miles (9,460,700,000,000 kilometers) per year.

See the lesson "Universe and Galaxies" for more information about light-years.

Twinkling Stars

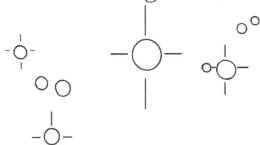

Have you ever noticed how the light coming from some stars seems to flicker or twinkle? Layers of air moving around the earth are part of the reason they appear that way. The tiny stream of light coming to us from a star can be distorted or even cut off by the slightest atmospheric disturbance such as strands of relatively warmer air called striae that rise wavelike on the wind. These differences in air density bend light by refraction; that is what causes a star to twinkle. This is especially true for those low in the sky whose light must pass through more of these lens-like striae. For an illustration of how this works, look at distant railroad tracks in the sun; the lively striae just above the hot surface makes the tracks seem to twist and shimmer and sometimes actually wink like stars.

Just as the atmosphere of the earth affects the light coming to us from the stars, so the atmosphere around our souls affects the clearness of the light coming to us from the *"Star out of Jacob,"* Jesus Christ. *"I shall see him, but not now: I shall behold him, but not nigh: there shall come a Star out of Jacob, and a Sceptre shall rise out of Israel, and shall smite the corners of Moab, and destroy all the children of Sheth"* (Numbers 24:17). There are impressions that are going forth all the time. There is an atmosphere that surrounds the human soul and that atmosphere is a heavenly atmosphere or a hellish atmosphere. There are but two distinct lines. Either we are on Christ's side of the question or on the enemy's side. And if we are continually drawing rays of divine light from glory, angels of God are around about us and there is an atmosphere that surrounds the human soul.

Daytime Stars

Even though we cannot see the stars in the daytime, they are there just the same. It is the sun that lights up the earth's atmosphere, giving the sky a blue atmosphere that is brighter than the stars. The sun's surpassing brightness that eclipses (hides) the lesser glory of the stars, reminds us of Jesus, *"the Sun of righteousness,"* (Malachi 4:2), whose dazzling brightness will eclipse all the glory of man when He returns. His glory was concealed as a test when He came to earth the first time and only those who were **alert** to the Holy Spirit were aware of the time of His coming. His glory will be revealed as a test the second time He comes, and only those who have purified their souls through obedience to the truth will be able to endure His brightness without being destroyed.

The Sun of Righteousness Shall Arise.

> The Lord
> has faithful servants,
> who in the day of trial
> will be disclosed to view.

The invisibility of the stars during the daytime, has another parallel. The Lord has faithful servants, who in the day of trial will be disclosed to view. There are precious ones now hidden who have not bowed the knee to Baal (I Kings 19:18). They have not had the light which has been shining in a concentrated blaze upon some. But it may be that under a rough and uninviting exterior the pure brightness of a genuine Christian character will be revealed. In the daytime we look toward heaven but do not see the stars. They are there fixed in the firmament, but the eye cannot distinguish them. In the night we behold their genuine luster.

The time is not far distant when the test will come to every soul. In this time the gold will be separated from the dross in the church. True godliness will be clearly distinguished from mere appearance and tinsel. Many a star that we have admired for its brilliancy will then go out in darkness.

★ Reinforce ☆

Read the following poem. Write a second verse remembering there are seven syllables in each line.

Twinkle, twinkle little star;
How I wonder what you are.
Up above the world so high,
Like a diamond in the sky.

_____

_____

_____

_____

_____

_____

_____

_____

_____

_____

_____

Remind

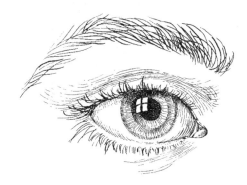

1. Watching people's eyes blink can remind us of twinkling stars. The eyelid hides the eye for a moment just as the layers of air in atmospheric disturbances distort or cut off the light from the stars for a fraction of a second.

2. What is the spiritual atmosphere around your soul?

3. Have you ever seen the moon in the daytime? That shows the difference between the greater light and the lesser light.

4. Maybe you and your family have felt like you were the only ones following Bible principles. If so, remember, *"Yet I have left me seven thousand in Israel, all the knees which have not bowed unto Baal, and every mouth which hath not kissed him"* (I Kings 19:18).

5. Blinking Christmas tree lights calls to mind twinkling stars.

 Review
Place II - III

1. What is the closest star to planet Earth?

2. How far is the closest star in miles (kilometers) from our sun?

3. Write a paragraph telling why stars twinkle.

4. Use a dictionary and define atmosphere. Give a spiritual parallel to atmosphere.

5. Why cannot we see stars in the daytime? Give a spiritual parallel.

Read the stories of people who shone like little stars in the sky, "Queen Alexandra's Favorite Needlewoman," and "I Did Not Do the Job for Money."

Reinforce
Why Stars Twinkle

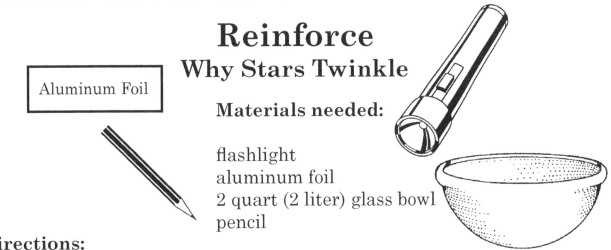

Aluminum Foil

Materials needed:

flashlight
aluminum foil
2 quart (2 liter) glass bowl
pencil

Directions:

1. Tear off a sheet of aluminum foil big enough to fit under the bowl. (See diagram.)

2. Wrinkle the aluminum foil with your hands, then spread it out gently.

3. Fill the bowl half full of water and put it on top of the wrinkled aluminum foil sheet. This needs to be done in a room you can darken.

4. Darken the room and hold the flashlight about 12 inches (30 centimeters) from the top of the bowl.

5. Observe the foil and notice how it appears when viewed through undisturbed water.

6. Keep shining the light through the water, but this time gently tap the surface of the water with a pencil.

7. Notice the difference in the way the foil looks when viewed through moving water.

Results: Moving water causes the light that is reflected from the aluminum foil to be blurred.

Reason: Light travels in a straight line, but the little waves caused by tapping the water's surface cause the light rays to leave in different directions. This is called refraction. Starlight behaves in a similar manner as it passes through layers of moving air before reaching your eyes. This twinkling effect is called scintillation in scientific terminology.

Queen Alexandra's Favorite Needlewoman

The favorite needlewoman of Queen Mother Alexandra was said to be Miss Lottie Flegg, an invalid who worked for Her Majesty many years. The queen mother generally paid a visit to her cottage at Christmas.

"Her own words to me," said Miss Flegg, "were, 'As long as we are both alive, Lottie, you will always see me at least once a year.'"

Miss Flegg is proud of the beautiful workbasket and the silk quilt which were Her Majesty's latest gifts. "See," she said, "that is my royal corner. Everything you see—the china, the pictures, and the knickknacks—were all given me by the queen."

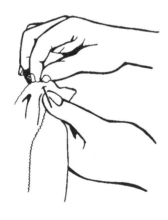

This invalid woman, who could not leave her room in Dersingham village, was reputed to be the finest needlewoman in the world. The queen, twenty-three years ago, discovered Lottie Flegg patiently at work in her room, saw how beautiful was the work done by her fragile white fingers, and immediately asked her to make some things. After that Her Majesty's influence had worked miracles. American millionaires sent to Miss Flegg for her marvelously fine baby clothes; and long ago at the World's Fair in Chicago, the judges gave her the first prize for the best sewing exhibited. She shone like a little star in her small spot.

The queen mother visited the needlewoman with little ceremony. Her Majesty would walk to the door, open it without knocking, and cheerily say, "I'm coming to see you, Lottie," and so walk up to the trim little bedroom. There her own chair waited for her, and she would sit chatting while the invalid worked. The queen recognized what a special person Lottie was.

"I Did Not Do the Job for Money"

One day, early in the reign of the Merry Monarch, the shades of a stormy autumn afternoon closed over the North Sea. The howling wind and rising waves foretold a coming storm; but the English fleet, under as much sail as the ships could safely carry, steered seaward.

The admiral of the fleet, Sir John Narborough, was not a man to fear danger or shun difficulties. Many years before he had been a cabin boy, but by his cleverness, courage, and good conduct, he had raised himself to the highest rank in his profession. From the very bottom of the ladder he had climbed to the highest rung.

On that gloomy afternoon the admiral slowly paced the quarter-deck and gazed eastward. England was then at war with Holland, and at any moment, the Dutch men-of-war might come in sight.

All of a sudden there was joy on board, as, far away, the tall masts of the enemy's ships appeared on the horizon. The English blood was up, and the sailors eagerly awaited the approach of the Dutch fleet. The enemy on his part was equally ready for action, and as soon as the opposing ships were within musket range, they entered into a deadly combat.

During the fierce struggle that ensued, the English flagship was surrounded by the enemy, several of her guns were disabled, her masts were shot away, and her decks strewn with dead and dying. Those on board could tell that on the whole the English were getting the best of the fight, but they feared that help would come too late to save them. The admiral wished to draw assistance from another quarter, but he could hold no communication beyond the circle of ships which enclosed him, as no signal would be visible on account of the blinding smoke.

Not knowing what else to do, Sir John Narborough wrote a note, and offered fifty guineas to the man who would deliver the message. The sailors knew that death was probably in store for him who attempted such a task, but at once many offered to perform the daring feat, and among the number was the cabin boy whose childish voice was heard above the rest. "Let me go, your honor," said he, "let me go." And as he spoke he stepped forward and saluted the admiral and pleaded so hard that at last he was permitted to undertake the task. "Off with you," said Sir John, "and may God keep you safe."

The boy placed the message in his mouth: then there was a plunge, and he was gone. The billows ranged and the shot fell thick around the boy while those on board strained their eyes to catch the first sign that he had passed the enemy's line and accomplished his mission. Soon the mighty English ships bore down upon the Dutch vessels, and the flag of England once more ruled the waves.

It was a proud moment for the youthful hero when he stood on deck surrounded by the crew, who had been called together to do him honor. The admiral advanced and handed him a purse of gold: but to the surprise of all, the poor lad indignantly refused the reward. "I did not do the job for money," he said. "I did it for the sake of the flag; and if you are satisfied, that is all I want."

"I did not do the job for money," he said. "I did it for the sake of the flag; and if you are satisfied, that is all I want."

Sailors can bravely face death, and remain quite cool in the hour of danger, but even the presence of the admiral of the fleet was insufficient to maintain order, and a deafening cheer arose from the assembled crew. "God bless you, my boy," said Sir John. And the sailors knew by the admiral's cheery tone and smiling face that their little breach of discipline had met with his approval.

The brave cabin boy rose step by step to the highest rank in the navy, and thirty years after, when, as Admiral Sir Cloudesley Shovel, he returned to England in triumph, one of the first to welcome him was Sir John Narborough.

Research
Motion

"That bringeth out their host by number...."
Isaiah 40:26

The stars appear to parade across the night sky from east toward the west, but this appearance is due to the earth spinning rather than from the motion of the stars themselves. Stars do move, but their movement only makes a slight change in their position among the other stars. Our sun, which is a star, moves at a speed of 12 miles (19 kilometers) per second through the Milky Way.

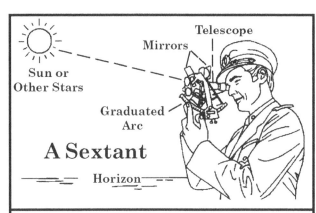

A Sextant

Illustration

The stars are like gems spilled out upon their black velvet container.

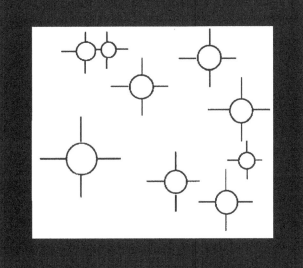

A sea captain of old, using the stars to help him sail his ship in the right direction.

The Most Necessary Star

If you were asked which is the most important star to be seen in the sky at night, what should you answer?

Come, let us step outside and name only a few that we may have learned to recognize. Most conspicuous of all, because it is the brightest, away out in the southwest, shines Sirius. More nearly south is Procyon; while almost directly east of it and almost as high in the heaven, lies Regulus. West from Sirius lie the bluish-white Rigel and the ruddy Betelgeuse; and still nearer the western horizon is Aldebaran, always following the twinkling Pleiades. Higher up is the beautiful Capella. Castor and Pollux are also in view.

But while some of these shine clearer than do others, and there are differences in color, yet who would venture to say that a red star is more important than a yellow one, or a dull orange better than a brilliant white?

Yet there is one star which, to us, next to the sun and moon, is of more importance than any other object in the heavens. Its name is Polaris. **Where is it?**

Let us step around to the other side of the house and view the sky toward the north. Ah, there is the Big Dipper, with its handle. Of course, you all recognize it. This beautiful group of stars is without doubt the best-known constellation in our northern heavens. See, it is pretty well turned over tonight. Notice the two stars—fairly bright ones—which mark the corners of the outside edge of the bowl. They are called the "pointers."

If you could draw a line through these two stars, beginning at the one nearest the bottom, and extend it about the length of the dipper, handle and all, this line would pass very near a solitary star of about equal brightness with these two pointers. This is Polaris, called also the North Star and the polestar.

Were we to look out at midnight, we should see this star in the same place that it now occupies. The Big Dipper would have moved farther to the west overhead, but the two pointers would still direct to the North Star. A few hours later the Dipper would lie underneath the polestar, but still the pointers would sustain the same relation to Polaris.

The great value and importance to us of the polestar lies in this very fact—that it is always found in the same place, or so nearly so that in looking at it in the usual way we cannot see any change. Also, its position is almost directly north. That is why it is called the North Star. It is the hub around which the rest of the stars seem to revolve. The focus of all heaven *is mount Zion, on the sides of the north, the city of the great King"* (Psalm 48:2).

**Read the story,
"A Boy Who Was Wanted."**

Guide

Half the wrecks that strew life's ocean,
 If some star had been their guide,
Might have now been riding safely,
 But they drifted with the tide.

Stars as Navigational Guides

"When he prepared the heavens... he set a compass upon the face of the depth."

Proverbs 8:27

Pilots, sailors, and map makers are some of the people that have relied upon the stars to find exact directions and locations. You can imagine that before the invention of electric lights, the nights were darker and almost more mysterious. The diamond-studded heavens helped people find their way across unknown seas and deserts even as Jesus, our "Star of Light," guides His children on their pilgrimage through this dark night of sin.

It is believed God used a cloud of angels like a star to guide the wise men to Christ (Matthew 2:7, 9-10). They were among the few who were **alert** to and welcomed light from heaven. Because of their appreciation for heaven-sent truth, it was shed upon them in brighter ways. We must be as **alert** to heaven as they were if we would also be guided to the personal presence of Christ.

A Boy Who Was Wanted

**The polestar is dependable and steady.
This story is about a boy who could always be found
in the right place. He was <u>alert</u> to his duty.**

"Well, I've found out one thing," said Jack, hot, tired, and dusty, as he came to his mother.

"What is that?" she asked.

"That there are a great many boys in the world."

"Didn't you know that before?"

"Partly; but I didn't know there were so many more boys than are wanted."

"Why do you think there are more than wanted?"

"Because I've been round and round till I am worn out, trying to find a place to work. Wherever I go, there are more boys than places. Doesn't that show there are too many boys?"

"Not exactly," said his mother with a smile. "It depends entirely on the kind of boy. A good boy is always wanted somewhere."

"Well, if I am a good boy, I wish I knew where I was wanted."

"Patience, patience, my boy. In such a great world as this is, with so many places and so many boys, it is no wonder some of them do not find their places at once. But be sure, dear," as she laid a caressing hand on his arm, "that every boy who wants a chance to do fair, honest work will find it."

"That's the kind of work I want to do," said Jack. "I don't want anybody's money for nothing. Let me see—what have I to offer?—All the schooling and all the wits I've been able to get up in thirteen years; good, stout hands; and a civil tongue."

"And an **alert** mind and heart set on doing faithful duty," suggested his mother.

"I hope so," said Jack. "I remember father used to say: 'Just as soon as you undertake to work for anyone, you must bear in mind that you have sold yourself for the given time. Your time, your strength, your energy are his, and your best efforts to seek his interests in every way are his due.'"

The earnest tone in which the boy spoke seemed to give assurance that he would pay good heed to the words of the father whose counsel could no more reach him.

For two or three days longer Jack had reason to hold his opinion that there were more boys than the world wanted, at the end of which time he met a businessman who, questioning him closely, said, "There are a great many applications for the place, but a large number of the boys come and stay a short time, and then leave if they think they can do a little better. When a boy gets used to our routes and customers, we want him to stay. If you will agree to stay at least three years, we will agree to pay you three dollars a week as errand boy."

"That is just what I wanted to do, sir," said Jack, eagerly. So he was installed and proud to bring his wages home every week, realizing that, small as they were, the regular help was of great value to his mother.

It is not to be wondered at that the faithful carrying out of his father's admonition after a while attracted the attention not only of his employers, but of others with whom he was brought in contact in the pursuit of his duties. One day he was asked into the office of Mr. Lang, a gentleman to whom he frequently carried parcels of value.

"Have you ever thought of changing your situation?" asked Mr. Lang.

"No, sir," said Jack.

"Perhaps you could do better," said the other. "I want a boy who is quick and intelligent, and who can be relied on, and, from what I see of you, I think you are that sort of boy. I want you to drive a delivery wagon, and will pay you five dollars a week."

Jack's eyes opened wide.

"It is wonderfully good pay for a boy like me, I'm sure. But I promised to keep on with Mr. Hill for three years, and the second year is only just begun."

"Well, have you signed a regular agreement with Mr. Hill?"

"No, sir; I told him I would stay."

"You have a mother to assist, you told me. Couldn't you tell Mr. Hill that you feel obliged to do better when you have a chance?"

"I don't believe I could," said Jack, looking with his straight, frank gaze into the gentleman's face. "You see, sir, if I broke my word with him, I shouldn't be the kind of boy to be relied on that you want."

"I guess you are about right," said Mr. Lang with a sigh. "Come and see me when your time is up. I dare say I shall want you then."

Jack went home very much stirred by what had been said to him.

After all, could it be wrong to go where he would do so much better? Was it not really his duty to accept the position? He could then drive a wagon instead of trudging wearily along the streets. They had never felt so hot and dusty as they did just now, when he might escape from the tiresome routine. Might, but how?—By the sacrifice of his pledged word; by selling his truth and his honor. So strongly did the reflection force itself upon him that when he told his mother of the offer he had received, he merely added, "It would be a grand good thing if I could take it, wouldn't it, mother?"

"Yes, it would."

"Some boys would change without thinking of letting a promise stand in their way."

"Yes, but that is the kind of boy who, sooner or later, is not wanted. It is because you have not been that sort of boy that you are wanted now."

Jack worked away, doing such good work, as he became more and more accustomed to the situation, that his mother sometimes wondered that Mr. Hill, who seemed always kindly interested in him, never appeared to think of raising his pay. This, however, was not Mr. Hill's way of doing things, even though he showed an increasing disposition to trust Jack with important business.

So the boy trudged through the three years, at the end of them having been trusted far more than is usually the case with errand boys. He had never forgotten the offer made by Mr. Lang, and one day, meeting that gentleman on the street, ventured to remind him that his present engagement was nearly out, adding, "You spoke to me about driving the wagon, sir."

"Ah, so I did; but you are older now, and worth more. Call around and see me."

One evening, soon after, Jack lingered in Mr. Hill's office after the other errand boys had been paid and had gone away.

"My three years are up to-night, sir," he said.

"Yes, they are," said Mr. Hill, looking at him as if he had remembered it.

"Will you give me a recommendation to someone else, sir?"

"Well, I will, if you are sure that you want to leave me."

"I did not know that you wanted me to stay, but"—he hesitated, and then went on—"my mother is a widow, and I feel as if I ought to do the best I can for her, and Mr. Lang told me to call on him."

"Has Mr. Lang ever made you an offer?"

Jack told him what Mr. Lang had said nearly two years before.

"Why didn't you go then?" asked Mr. Hill.

"Because I had promised to stay with you. But you wouldn't blame me for trying to better myself now?"

"Not a bit of it. Are you tired of running errands?"

"I'd rather ride than walk," said Jack with a smile.

"I think it about time you were doing better than either. Perhaps you think you have been doing this faithful work for me through these years for next to nothing; but if so, you are mistaken. You have been doing better work than merely running errands. You have been serving an apprenticeship to trust and honesty. I know you now to be a straightforward, reliable boy, and it takes time to learn that. It is your capital, and you ought to begin to realize it. You may talk to Mr. Lang if you wish, but I will give you a place in the office, with a salary of six hundred for the first year, with the prospect of a raise after that."

Jack did not go to see Mr. Lang, but straight to his mother with a shout and a bound.

"You're right, you're right, mother!" he cried. "No more hard work for you, mother. I'm wanted, you see! Wanted enough to get good pay. All the hardest part is over."

> "I know you now to be a straightforward, reliable boy."

The Polestar or Polaris

"He stretcheth out the north over the empty place, and hangeth the earth upon nothing."

Job 26:7

The most important navigational guide in the Northern Hemisphere is the North Star or polestar. It is located very near the imaginary point called the Celestial North Pole, or in other words, the North Pole of the sky. The polestar appears to move very little. This star can help a person find out how far north they are on the earth. If the polestar is right overhead, a person would be up in the Arctic Circle right at the North Pole. If the polestar is on the horizon, then a person looking at it would be at the equator. If the polestar is halfway up in the sky, that would mean that a person is located halfway between the North Pole and the equator. When you are looking at the polestar, you are facing north, and to your right is east, and to your left is west, and the south is at your back.

With the polestar to help you know your directions, you will not need a compass if you get lost on a cloudless night because, as our previous text stated, *"when he prepared the heavens...he set a compass upon the face of the depth"* (Proverbs 8:27). Our loving God designed the heavens in such a way as to help those who were lost to find their way. This can picture to us of how God has also planned a way for lost sinners to find their way to *"Zion, on the sides of the north"* (Psalm 48:2). Jesus said, *"I am the way"* (John 14:6), and we learn how to follow Him from the Bible.

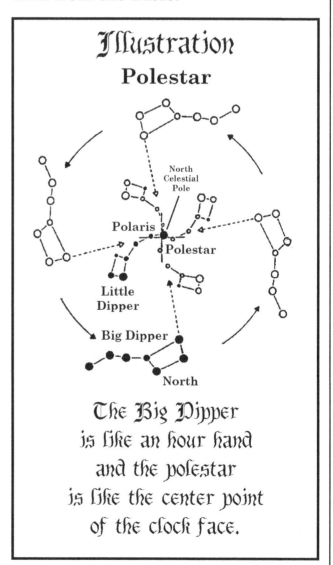

Illustration
Polestar

The Big Dipper is like an hour hand and the polestar is like the center point of the clock face.

Stars and Light

A star is beautiful, but it pours no light into the midnight of a sinful soul. The flower is sweet, but it exudes no balm for the heart's wound. All the odors that ever floated from royal conservatory or princely hanging gardens, give not so much sweetness as is found in one waft from this Scripture mountain of myrrh and frankincense. All the waters that ever leaped in torrent, or foamed in cascade, or fell in summer shower, or hung in morning dew, give no such coolness to the fevered soul as the smallest drop that ever flashed out from the showering fountains of God's Divine Book. Ah! beautiful stars: it is not in guiding us over the seas of our little planet, but out of the dark waters of our own minds, that word is of much more significance.

Color the ship.

Give me the Bible, star of gladness gleaming,
    To cheer the wanderer lone and tempest tossed,
No storm can hide that peaceful radiance beaming,
    Since Jesus came to seek and save the lost.

Give me the Bible—holy message shining,
    Thy light shall guide me in the narrow way.
Precept and promise, law and love combining,
    'Till night shall vanish in eternal day.

               —Priscilla Owens

 # Big Dipper

There are two constellations in the northern hemisphere that will help you to find the North Star. These are the Big Dipper and the Little Dipper. The seven stars in the Big Dipper form a cup with a long handle on it which looks something like a ladle. People used to use dippers (long-handled cups) to drink their freshly-drawn well water with right from the bucket.

It is easy to see the Big Dipper on a clear night if you face north. The two stars on the cup or bowl part opposite the handle point directly to the polestar. If you connect these pointers with an imaginary line and run it out from the top of the bowl as far as about five times the distance between the pointers you will find the polestar. The polestar is an object lesson of Jesus, our Heavenly Guiding Star. Five times the distance between the pointers to the polestar can remind you that five is the number of grace, and it is only through grace that we can find Jesus.

The polestar just happens to be the last star in the handle of the Little Dipper. The Little Dipper revolves around the Polestar and the Big Dipper also circles around the same spot, making a complete circle in 24 hours. During the night the Big Dipper swings halfway around the sky and then it completes the circle during the daytime. This perfect timing reminds us that like the stars in the vast circuit of their appointed path, God's purposes know no haste and no delay. You can actually learn to tell what time it is at night if you get acquainted with the position of the Big Dipper because it is like an hour hand on the clock with the Polestar being the center point of the clock face. This reminds me how others should look at us and tell what time it is in this earth's history. Are you **alert** to how late the hour is?

North Star (Polestar)

Little Dipper

Illustration

The Dippers

Big Dipper

Little Dipper

Did you know that the Little Dipper is positioned in such a way that it is always "pouring" into the Big Dipper? This can remind us of how Jesus (like the Little Dipper) is always pouring the *"water of life"* into thirsty souls (who are like the Big Dipper). *"Whosoever drinketh of the water that I shall give him shall never thirst"* (John 4:14); He is so generous we can say, *"my cup runneth over"* (Psalm 23:5).

For the people of the Lord who pass through the time of trial, there is also another parallel we can draw from this arrangement of the Little Dipper pouring into the Big Dipper. In Mark 10:36-39 we read: *"And he said unto them, What would ye that I should do for you? They said unto him, Grant unto us that we may sit, one on thy right hand, and the other on thy left hand, in thy glory. But Jesus said unto them, Ye know not what ye ask: can ye drink of the cup that I drink of? and be baptized with the baptism that I am baptized with? And they said unto him, We can. And Jesus said unto them, Ye shall indeed drink of the cup that I drink of; and with the baptism that I am baptized withal shall ye be baptized."* We may pass through a Gethsemane-like experience and must be willing to say like Jesus did, "the cup which my Father hath given me, shall I not drink it?" (John 18:11). In our parallel the Father would be represented by the polestar in whose hand is the Little Dipper pouring into Christ's (or His people's) Big Dipper.

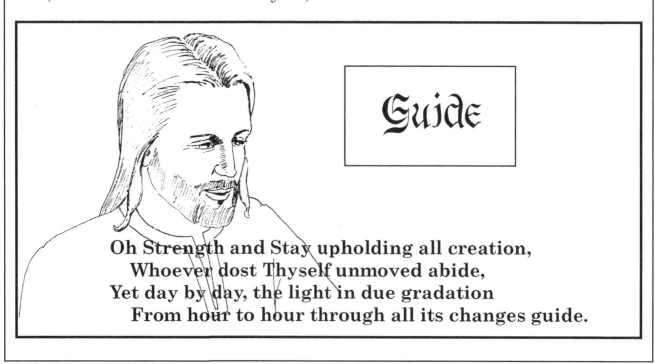

Guide

Oh Strength and Stay upholding all creation,
Whoever dost Thyself unmoved abide,
Yet day by day, the light in due gradation
From hour to hour through all its changes guide.

Long ago, before the invention of the wristwatch, people told time by the sky. They used the sun and certain stars to tell them the correct time of the day or month. The moon gave them the time of the month and the stars measured out the seasons and years. The Hebrew children had a calendar based on the moon and the sun which they used to plan their farming as well as religious events. God has marshaled some of the most majestic objects in His creation to help mankind with their daily needs.

The stars move so regularly in their courses that astronomers use them as an exact measurement of time. Stars make the standard by which all our clocks are set. If people always had to set their clocks according to each other's, what would happen if some of the clocks they were depending upon did not keep the exact time? Soon everyone would be confused. Just as we need to look to the stars for an exact standard as far as correct time is concerned, so we need to look heavenward for the other standards in our lives and not be confused by the world around us.

To be **alert** to our time and use it wisely is illustrated by the story, "Doing and Being." Read it.

Read the poem,
"What the Minutes Say," page 84.

Stars as Prophetic Clocks

"And there shall be signs in the sun, and in the moon, and in the stars."
Luke 21:25

God has used the stars to witness to this world that Christ's coming is nigh at hand. The prophecy regarding the stars being darkened in Joel 3:15 was fulfilled on May 19, 1780. You can read about this great Dark Day in the encyclopedia. *"The sun and the moon shall be darkened and the stars shall withdraw their shining."* Then the stars fell in great numbers as prophesied in the great star shower on November 13, 1833, which was a fulfillment of Mark 13:25, *"And the stars of heaven shall fall, and the powers that are in heaven shall be shaken."* The manner of their falling was predicted in Revelation 6:13, *"And the stars of heaven fell unto the earth, even as a fig tree casteth her untimely figs, when she is shaken of a mighty wind."* Are we **alert** to the hour in which we are living? Just as God gave a star as a witness before Jesus' first coming, so He has given a star witness to us to confirm the nearness of His second coming. Will we be "wise men" and order our lives accordingly?

Doing and Being

"There!" exclaimed Marion, fretfully, as she turned from the window, "the day is all gone, and I haven't done anything. I haven't done *anything*," she repeated discontentedly; "and I meant to do so much."

"What have you done?" inquired Elizabeth, closing her work basket. "Sit down and tell me."

"Well," answered Marion, seating herself, "you know my day as well as I do. This morning I read three chapters in the Bible, as usual. I do want to get through it this year. Then I was gone an hour on that errand for father; then I wrote three letters, mended Tom's mittens and corrected Nellie's composition; then mother called me to set the dinner table. After dinner I directed a magazine and two papers to your missionary; then—oh! Nellie's arithmetic—that took me an hour, she was so stupid; then father asked me to copy a deed for him, and then that tiresome Mrs. Green called, and I entertained her for an hour; and then—how little it all seems!—I went out to get sewing silk for mother, and buy that ball I've been promising Georgie for a month and now the man is lighting the gas over the way, and my day is gone! I can't help feeling dissatisfied; I haven't done anything good today."

Elizabeth was rocking lazily to and fro in her chair. "You think a great deal about doing—don't you?"

"Yes, and so do you! You are always at work doing something."

"It's a good thing to be so. God gives us many things to do; but don't you think He gives us something to be, just as well?"

"Oh, yes!" very quickly answered Marion. "Of course."

"May I speak plainly, Marion? May I tell you all about your unsatisfying day?"

Marion sprang up, and threw both arms about Elizabeth's neck, and said, "Yes, you may tell me; for *'faithful are the wounds of a friend.'* Shoot me through and through, I will not even groan." Nevertheless Marion's lip trembled as she dropped down on the carpet at her friend's feet and laid her head on her lap.

Before speaking, Elizabeth bent over to kiss her; "I've been thinking all day as I watched you, that I would like to say this to you. I see that in trying to **do** what He commands, you forget to **be** what He commands. I know all about it. First, about reading the three chapters every day. How did you read them?"

"Hurried through the last," confessed Marion; "and I did look to see if it was short. I feel condemned if I don't read it through when I set myself to do it."

"You poor child! We will talk about that some other time. Then came the errand for your father; you fretted about that, because you said you were wasting your time. You answered your mother saucily when she inquired whom your letters were written to; you scolded Tom for burning his mittens; you made fun of Nellie's spelling, and set her lips quivering. You spoke impatiently to your mother about setting the dinner table. You slapped Georgie for hiding the paper you were looking for."

"I am sorry for that," said a voice from under Marion's curls.

"You scolded Nellie for being stupid, until she cried; you frowned over the paper you copied for your father, and did you not make fun of Mrs. Green before she had reached the corner?"

"Oh, dear! tell me about **being**." Marion looked up with penitent eyes. "I will think about **being** if you will help me."

"God says, *'Be kindly affectioned one to another'* (Romans 12:10)."

" *'Be ye also patient'* in James 5:8. *'Be ye thankful'* in Colossians 3:15. *'Be not conformed to this world'* in Romans 12:2. *'Be ye therefore perfect'* in Matthew 5:48. *'Be courteous'* in I Peter 3:8. *'Be not wise in your own conceits'* in Romans 12:16. *'Be not overcome of evil'* in Romans 12:21."

Marion listened, making no reply.

Twilight grew into darkness. The tea-bell sounded, bringing Marion to her feet. In the firelight, Elizabeth could see that her cheeks were wet.

"I'll have a better day tomorrow, God helping me. I see that doing grows out of being."

"We cannot be what God loves, without doing all that He commands. It is easier to do with rashness than to be patient, or kind, or forgiving, or gentle, or regularly unselfish, or humble, or just, or watchful."

"Yes, I think it is," returned Marion emphatically.

Color this picture.

What the Minutes Say

We are but minutes: little things,
Each one furnished with sixty wings,
With which we fly on our unseen track,
And not a minute ever comes back.

We are but minutes: each one bears
A little burden of joys and cares.
Take patiently the minutes of pain,
The worst of minutes cannot remain.

We are but minutes: when we bring
A few of the drops from pleasure's spring.
Taste their sweetness while yet you may,
It takes but a minute to fly away.

We are but minutes: use us well,
For how we are used we must one day tell.
Who uses minutes has hours to use;
Who loses minutes whole years must lose.

Stars as Seasonal Clocks

"Let them be for...seasons...."
Genesis 1:14

In Job 38:32 we read, *"Canst thou bring forth Mazzaroth in his season?"* The word Mazzaroth means constellations. Different constellations or star patterns appear during different seasons of the year so that those seen during the spring and summer differ from those seen in the autumn and winter.

We have already mentioned how the Pleiades served as an important seasonal indication for ancient farmers. In Egypt, the star Sirius was worshipped as the Nile star because its appearance in the pre-dawn sky in late June heralded the beginning of the annual Nile flood which rejuvenated the soil of that great river valley. Sirius is a variation of the name Sirus which was one of the names of the Nile River.

**Read the poem,
"Where Are the Sun and Stars?"**

Illustration
Big Dipper

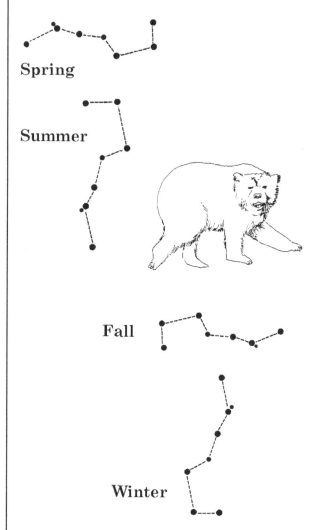

Spring

Summer

Fall

Winter

Nature gives
to every time and season
some beauties of its own;
and from morning to night,
as from the cradle to the grave,
is but a succession of changes
so gentle and easy that we can
scarcely mark their progress.

Where Are the Sun and Stars?

Julia

Where is the sun when his robe of light
Behind the hills has fled from sight;
When the birds are still in their leafy nest,
And the world lies hushed in calm, sweet rest;
Where is the sun then, Mother?

Mother

When his glowing beams from us are gone,
A far-off land he shines upon;
Whose people rouse when his car is near,
With the same blithe hum that greets him here.

Julia

Where are the stars when their silvery beam
Quivers no more in the gliding stream;
When thick, dark clouds hang in the sky,
Like a curtain of sable drapery;
Where are the stars then, Mother?

Mother

When no more they shine on the trembling rill,
Beyond the clouds they are gleaming still;
And mountains that rise to cleave the sky,
Above the gloom in the starlight lie.

The Runaway Sun

The brilliant Arcturus, is so much brighter than our sun, that, could we remove our sun to an equal distance, it would require a fairly powerful telescope to show it as a faintly glimmering star of about the tenth magnitude. Could we be removed 140,000 times farther from our sun than we are now, then would our sun appear to us about as bright as Arcturus. But if we increased our distance the same amount from this stellar giant Arcturus, the difference in his brightness would probably not be appreciable, for Arcturus is 16.2 times farther away than 140,000 times 93,000,000. His brightness has been computed (assuming that a given area of his surface gives out the same amount of light as an equal area of our own sun) to be about 558,000 times as bright, and that in size he is more than a million times as large as our own sun. His heat is about proportionate to his light, and, if we were placed as near Arcturus as we are to our own sun, the very rocks and metals would melt and turn to vapor like a drop of water in a sea of fire.

Arcturus is 36 light-years from earth and looks like an amber stone.

The star Arcturus is located in the constellation known as Bootes, the Herdsman. According to legend, the Herdsman was the keeper of the bear, helping the Great Bear constellation (Ursa Major) follow its assigned track around the northern sky.

Arcturus is mentioned in Job 9:9. *"Which maketh Arcturus, Orion, and Pleiades, and the chambers of the south."* Arcturus is taken from two Greek words which mean "bear guard."

Arcturus can also mean "guardian of the north."

Illustration
Bootes

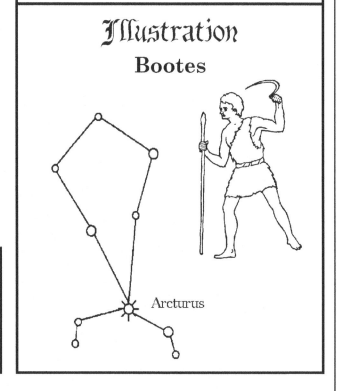

Arcturus

Sometimes the word Arcturus refers only to the brightest star in the constellation Bootes, but it formerly also meant that whole constellation and sometimes the Great Bear constellation itself. For our purposes we will consider Arcturus as a star which is the brightest star in the Northern Hemisphere and which can be located by following where the curving handle of the Big Dipper points. Arcturus is a giant orange star about 22 times the diameter of our sun and about 100 times as luminous. Its orange color is noticeable to the naked eye, but is more striking with optical aid (binoculars or a telescope).

In addition to all this, Arcturus is a runaway. That is, his velocity is so great that the combined attraction of all the stars we know cannot stop him nor swerve him from his course: no, not even if the universe is many times older than the wildest conceptions of astronomers. Our sun is journeying through space at "only" 12.5 miles a second. Long ago Sir Isaac Newton calculated that, in general, the stars move at controlled speeds that do not exceed 25 miles a second. Arcturus is one of a very few stars that break this rule.

> *"Canst thou guide Arcturus with his sons?"*
> Job 38:32

Arcturus is a runaway.

The unaided eyes of ancient astronomers could not have detected that Arcturus is actually a "runaway" sun. Since the star is 36 light-years away from us, even the great speed at which it moves would have gone unnoticed to them. In 100 years the star shifts across our sky only one-eighth of the apparent diameter of the moon. And this magnificent globe, with its attendant worlds, is sweeping majestically on, passing through the universe. How grand the words we find in Holy Writ: *"Canst thou guide Arcturus with his sons?"* (Job 38:32).

The arrival of Arcturus in the eastern evening sky is a sure sign of the spring season. In late spring and early summer, it is the first star seen after sunset, shining high up in the sky. Arcturus is known as a high-velocity star which simply means it is traveling about 85 miles (136 kilometers) per second. That is more than 300,000 miles (480,000 kilometers) an hour! In His sight who guides alike the star and the atom, there is nothing unimportant. Order and perfection are seen in all His work.

Remarkable Facts
Arcturus

• Arcturus is a yellow-orange star, the fourth brightest in the sky.

• Arcturus is 20 times larger than the sun.

• It is called Job's star, because it is mentioned in Job 9:9 and 38:32.

• As publicity, light from Arcturus was used to trigger the 1933 opening of the "Century of Progress" Exposition. A telescope was placed so that when the star moved in front of it, it triggered a light-sensitive switch. The reason Arcturus was chosen was because it was believed Arcturus was 40 light-years away, therefore, the light had left the star the time of a previous fair in Chicago in 1893. The distance to Arcturus is really 36 light-years by more recent measurements.

• Arcturus moves at over 300,000 miles (480,000 kilometers) per hour.

• In March Arcturus can be found by following the handle of the Big Dipper to Arcturus in the constellation Bootes, which comes up in the east.

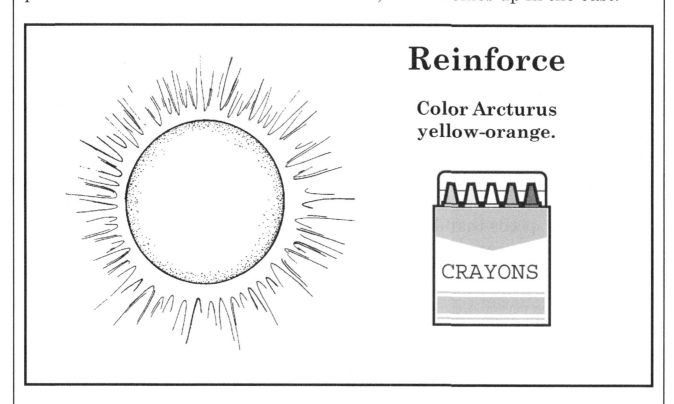

Reinforce

Color Arcturus yellow-orange.

CRAYONS

★ Review ★

Place II - III

1. What makes the stars in the sky seem to move?

2. What does Proverbs 8:27 tell us?

3. Can you think of a Bible story where stars helped guide people?

4. What is the most important navigational guide in the Northern Hemisphere? Explain how it works.

5. Sing the hymn, "Give Me the Bible."

6. Explain how to find the North Star in the sky. Find the North Star in the sky.

7. How did people tell time before there were watches and clocks?

8. Can we depend on other people's clocks to set ours? What standard are all our clocks set by? What standard do we use for our spiritual life?

9. Write a paragraph about stars as prophetic clocks, and stars as seasonal clocks.

Place I - II

1. Why do the stars in the sky seem to move? _____

2. The stars have many purposes. One purpose is to serve as a _____ _____.

3. What guided the wise men to boy Jesus? _____

4. Draw the Big Dipper, Little Dipper, and Polestar (North Star) in the square below.

5. Sing the hymn, "Give Me the Bible."

6. Find the polestar or North Star in the sky.

7. What served man as watches and clocks before they were invented?

8. Find pictures of the night sky for each season (use a star guide book). Notice how the sky changes.

★ Remind ☆

1. When looking at a map, consider the stars as destinations on the sky map.

2. Notice street signs next time you are in town. Some may say north on them—think of the North Star!

3. Maybe you have used a cup or dipper to drink from at one time. What does it remind you about in our lesson?

4. When using your watch to tell time, thank God for the North Star.

5. Watch for falling stars in the sky—think about the falling stars on November 13, 1833.

★ Reinforce★

1. Find pictures or look at a real sextant.

2. Learn to use a compass.

3. Use a ladle or dipper to drink out of for a day to remind you of the spiritual lessons of the Big Dipper.

4. Find the following in the sky if it is the season:

Polestar or North Star,

Little Dipper,

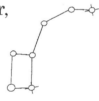

Big Dipper, and

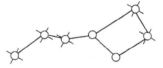

Bootes.

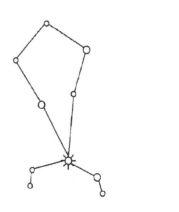

Research
More Sky Clocks

*"And let there be lights in the firmament of heaven
to divide the day from the night;
and let them be for...seasons, and for days, and years."*
Genesis 1:14

When explorers from Europe sailed into the seas of the Southern Hemisphere a few centuries ago, they did not find a guiding star at the pole. But God had not forgotten the people that live "down under" for He gave them the Southern Cross, a beautiful constellation which is useful because its longer arm points south. This illuminated cross in the heavens circling around the South Celestial Pole can remind us that only those who realize that the cross is the **center of hope** for the human family can understand the gospel that Christ taught. Obedience requires a sacrifice and involves a cross; and this is why so many of the professed followers of Christ refused to receive the light from heaven, and, like the Jews of old, knew not the time of their visitation.

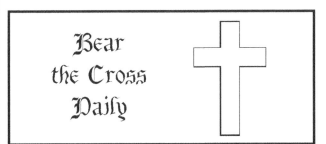

Bear
the Cross
Daily

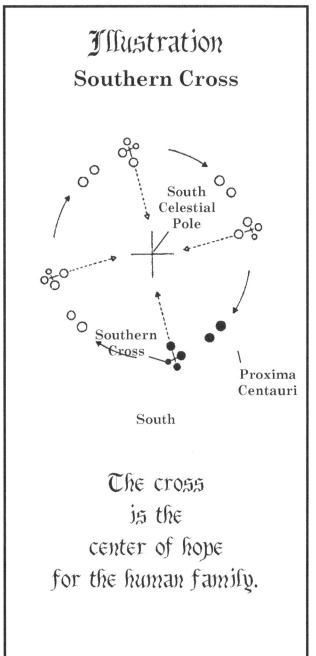

Illustration
Southern Cross

The cross
is the
center of hope
for the human family.

Are we **alert** to the real meaning of the cross? Let us think prayerfully about the following words which deal with this most important subject. Still there is urged against it one objection which our ablest ministers cannot remove. Christ Himself could not remove it. It has effectually barred the way of life to thousands. This hindrance is the **cross**. The cross, covered with shame and reproach, which Jesus bore for us, stands directly in the Christian's path. To evade that cross, the selfish, the world-loving, and the pleasure-seeking turn from the light that would guide their feet to Heaven. They choose doubt, unbelief, and infidelity,* that they may have the pleasure of following inclination,** and giving loose rein to the promptings of the carnal heart. Those who accept and obey the truth, must deny self, bear the cross daily, and follow in the footsteps of Jesus.

> ✝ The cross,
> covered with shame
> and reproach,
> which Jesus bore for us,
> stands directly
> in the Christian's path.

*lack of belief in religion, unfaithfulness
**the act of bending or inclining, natural disposition or tendency

The Cross

We need as Christians to understand the true meaning of the cross. Satan does not want us to understand this. He would rather us focus our attention on symbols rather than the real things they represent. He has made some people attach a lot of reverence to the symbol of the cross. They put crosses on top of their churches, inside their sanctuaries, and some even wear crosses hanging from chains around their neck. This last example would be like what the Jews did when they copied the Ten Commandments and put them on their foreheads when God really meant them to be in their minds as a part of their character. These are all examples of reverencing the symbols rather than experiencing the real meaning of things. People who reverence the outward symbol of the cross often do not understand that the cross is a real experience. To bear the cross of Christ is to control our sinful passions and daily practice self-denial, cheerfully. The real cross Jesus was talking about is the place in our experience where duty crosses (goes against) inclination. Inclination is doing what comes naturally to our sinful nature.

Reflect
Duty and Inclination

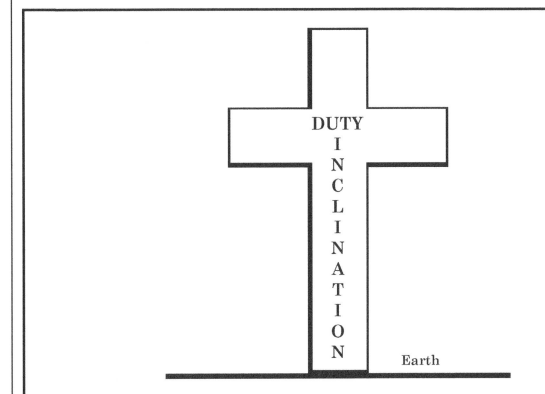

Southern Cross

Inclination starts with the letter **I** and that is the problem with following inclination; **I** always comes first, instead of *"not my will, but thine be done"* (Luke 22:42).

Duty lifts us above our earthly natures; it goes in the opposite **d**irection of inclination.

Following inclination attaches us more to the things of this earth.

Reinforce

Place I - II

Color the words and picture, then read the verse for your teacher.

"...If any man will come after me, let him deny himself, and take up his cross, and follow me."
Matthew 16:24

How can you take up your cross and follow Jesus?

Reinforce
Place I - II - III

Read the following passages and figure out which ones are examples of bearing a cross. Put a little cross after them. If they are only a symbol of the cross and not the real experience, put an S after them. If they are inclination, put an I after them.

1. There is only time for one more sled ride before lunch, and a girl decides to let her younger sister take the last turn. _____

2. A boy is invited to eat at a table where there are many delicious-looking dishes upon the table, but he decides to try only three of them. ____

3. A person decides to hang a crucifix (a figure of Christ dying on the cross) on his wall. _____

4. Mother has called her daughter to come into the house, and as she is on her way she stops to play a little with her dog. _____

5. A boy is visiting at a relative's house for dinner and just after he has eaten a good meal, they surprise him by bringing out a big plate of his favorite kind of cookies. He decides to eat some because they smell so delicious, even though he is full. _____

6. Baby sister is crying and big sister asks Mother if there is something she can do to soothe the little one instead of going outside where she will not be bothered by the noise. _____

7. It is time for prayer before bed and a little boy has played very hard and is tired so he decides to skip kneeling by his bed to pray that night. _____

8. Sabbath has come. But even though a boy outwardly obeys, his mind is on what he is going to do after the Sabbath school is over instead of on his lesson. _____

9. A little girl is taking a walk on someone else's property and finds an old apple tree and decides to eat one. _____

10. Mother comes in to wake her son up on a cold winter morning, but he is so cozy and warm underneath the covers that he waits for her to call him again before rising. _____

11. A friend makes fun of what a young girl is wearing, but she refuses to cherish hurt feelings about the matter, and continues on as though nothing was said. _____

12. There are not enough pieces of pie left at dinner for everyone to have one, so sister volunteers not to have a piece, even though she would enjoy one very much. _____

The Countersign of Service
Acrostic

Red ruin—wreck of impious war—
Effaces beauty years have gained.
Denies ideals so long maintained.

Charged with the Master's higher law—
Rescript* for service and noblesse.**
Oh Sisterhood of Helpfulness,
Still strive to ease the sufferer's loss,
Stretch farther thy protecting Cross.

*officiate, order, decree or announcement **nobility, or of noble birth

Crosses

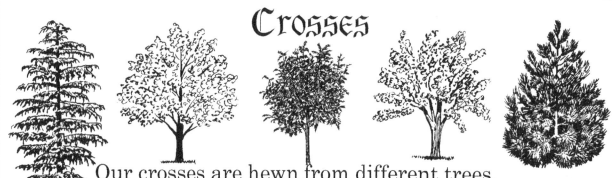

Our crosses are hewn from different trees,
But we all must have our Calvaries.

We may climb the height from a different side,
But we each go up to be crucified.

As we scale the steep, another may share
The dreadful load that our shoulders bear:

But the costliest sorrow is all our own,
For on the summit we bleed alone.

Constellations

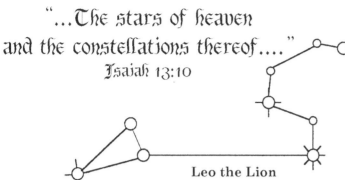

"...The stars of heaven
and the constellations thereof...."
Isaiah 13:10

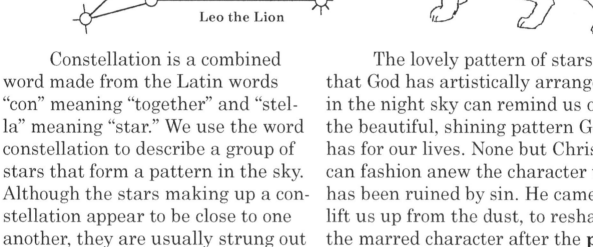

Leo the Lion

Constellation is a combined word made from the Latin words "con" meaning "together" and "stella" meaning "star." We use the word constellation to describe a group of stars that form a pattern in the sky. Although the stars making up a constellation appear to be close to one another, they are usually strung out in space at different distances.

Today astronomers recognize 88 constellations, however, the ancient astronomers described only 48. The more modern constellations are small and obscure because they seem to fill the space between the older and better known constellations.

Concerning constellation names, before the International Astronomical Union's ruling in 1930, there were no officially defined constellation boundaries. They fixed the number at 88 officially recognized constellations.

The lovely pattern of stars that God has artistically arranged in the night sky can remind us of the beautiful, shining pattern God has for our lives. None but Christ can fashion anew the character that has been ruined by sin. He came to lift us up from the dust, to reshape the marred character after the **pattern** of His divine character, and to make it beautiful with His own glory.

Each constellation has a certain time of the year when it reaches its highest point in the sky. This is called its culmination. At latitudes very far north or south of the equator, many constellations do not culminate high enough in the sky to be seen. The constellations appear to move westward as the earth moves around the sun and this is the reason why some constellations can be seen during only one season of the year.

In most of the United States (except Florida and Hawaii) the six constellations near the Polestar can be seen at any time of the year. These are called the circumpolar constellations.

The constellations with their seasonal appearance are silent reminders that "To every thing there is a season, and a time to every purpose under heaven" (Ecclesiastes 3:1). "But of the times and the sea-sons, brethren, ye have no need that I write unto you, for yourselves know perfectly that the day of the Lord so cometh..." (I Thessalonians 5:1-2). These people that Paul was talking to were alert to the times and the seasons but Jesus addressed people in a different spiritual condition in Luke 12:56. "Ye hypocrites, ye can discern the face of the sky and of the earth; but how is it that ye do not discern this time?"

Read the story, "A Remarkable Incident."

A Remarkable Incident

Many years ago, a visitor among the poor was one day climbing the broken staircase which led to a garret in one of the worst parts of London, when his attention was arrested by a man of peculiarly ferocious and repulsive countenance, who stood upon the landing, with folded arms against the wall.

There was something about the man's appearance that made the visitor shudder, and his first impulse was to go back. He made an effort, however, to get into conversation with the man, and told him that he came there with the desire to see him happy, and that the book he had in his hand contained the secret of happiness.

The man shook him off as if he had been a viper and bade him begone with his nonsense, or he would kick him downstairs. While the visitor was endeavoring with gentleness and patience to argue the point with him, he was startled by hearing a feeble voice, which appeared to come from behind one of the broken doors opening upon the landing, saying, "Does your book tell of the blood which cleanses from all sin?"

For a moment the visitor was too much absorbed in the case of the hardened sinner before him to answer the inquiry, and it was repeated in earnest and thrilling tones:

"Tell me, oh tell me, does your book tell of the blood which cleanses from all sin?"

The visitor pushed open the door and entered the room. It was a wretched place, wholly destitute of furniture, except a three-legged stool, and a bundle of straw in a corner, on which was stretched the wasted form of an aged woman. When the visitor entered, she raised herself upon one elbow, fixed her eyes eagerly upon him, and repeated her question:

"Does your book tell of the blood which cleanses from all sin?"

He sat down upon the stool beside her, and inquired, "My poor friend, what do you want to know of the blood which cleanses from all sin?"

> "Does your book tell of the blood which cleanses from all sin?"

There was something fearful in the energy of her voice and manner as she replied, "What do I want to know of it? Man, I am dying! I have been a wicked woman all my life. I shall have to answer for everything I have done," and she groaned bitterly as the thought of a lifetime of iniquity seemed to crush her soul. "But once," she continued, "once, years ago, I came to the door of a church and I went in: I don't know what for. I was soon out again, but one word I heard I could never forget. It was something about blood which cleanses from all sin. Oh, and if I could but hear it now! Tell me, tell me, if there is anything about that blood in your book!"

The visitor answered by reading the first chapter of the first epistle of John. The poor creature seemed to devour the words, and when he paused, she exclaimed, "Read more, read more!"

He read the second chapter—a slight noise made him look around: the savage man had followed him into his mother's room, and though his face was partly turned away, the visitor could perceive tears rolling down his cheeks. The visitor read the third, fourth, and fifth chapters before he could get the poor listener to consent that he should stop, and then she would not let him go till he promised to come the next day.

He never from that time missed a day reading to her until she died, six weeks afterward: and very blessed was it to see how, almost from the first, she seemed to find peace by believing in Jesus. Every day the son followed the visitor into his mother's room, and listened with silent interest: and blessing came not alone to the mother, for the remarkable change wrought in the son also testified to the saving power of God's grace.

On the day of her funeral he beckoned the visitor to one side as they were filling up her grave, and said: "Sir, I have been thinking there is nothing I would so much like as to tell others of the blood which cleanses from all sin."

> Every day
> the son followed the visitor
> into his mother's room,
> and listened with silent interest:
> and blessing came not alone
> to the mother,
> for the remarkable change
> wrought in the son
> also testified
> to the saving power
> of God's grace.

★ Review ★

Place I - II - III

1. How big is the universe? What beautiful constellation is found in the Southern Hemisphere that points south? Draw it below in the square.

2. What is a constellation?

3. The patterns constellations make in the sky remind us of what in our lives?

4. In what direction do constellations move?

Place III

5. What does culmination mean?

6. What are circumpolar constellations?

Remind

1. When exploring a new area where you live, think about the explorers of the past who explored the Southern Hemisphere. They used the Southern Cross as a navigational guide.

2. Whenever seeing a cross on a church, consider the cross God placed in the sky.

3. Notice the patterns on people's clothing or a quilt—God has a pattern in the sky and for our lives.

Reinforce

1. Have a treasure hunt and look for crosses in nature.

2. Those living in the Southern Hemisphere, identify the following constellations if they are in the sky at this time:

Leo the Lion

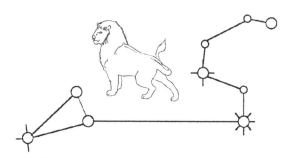

Southern Cross

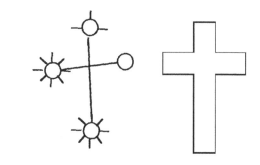

Scorpio

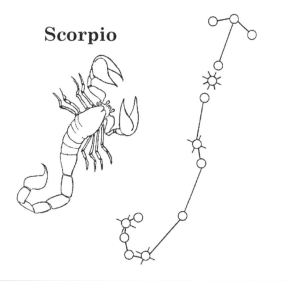

★ Research ★
Names of Constellations and Stars

"...He calleth them all by their names."
Psalm 147:4

In the Bible we can find a few names of constellations and stars, some of which we have already mentioned. However, many of the star names we use today are Arabic since these people have been great admirers of the night sky for many centuries. When much of the ancient learning was lost in Europe during the Dark Ages, Arab scholars carefully preserved what they learned and added much more to the science of astronomy.

In later times the main stars of each constellation have been labeled with a letter of the Greek alphabet, the brightest star usually, though not always, being termed alpha. In some constellations Roman letters have been assigned to fainter stars such as L Puppis and P Cygni. Another way of identifying stars is that of Flamsteed numbers which are numbers given to the stars by John Flamsteed, England's first Astronomer Royal. An example would be 70 Ophiuchi.

It will be wonderful to learn from God someday what He calls each star. We know He names things according to their character and so in learning the stars' real names we will learn something about their unique qualities.

There are many books that can aid you in becoming acquainted with the stars in your area of the sky. Some of these books give the old, traditional names of the constellations while other books rename them and give simpler, easier to identify line drawings. Be prayerfully **alert**, perhaps God will impress your mind as you study the patterns in the heavens with a new, spiritual meaning. After all, He is the "True Interpreter."

Many of the names of the traditional constellations that are referred to in astronomy books reflect pagan mythology. The twelve signs (constellations) of the zodiac have their origin in Chaldean astrology. The Hebrews learned the signs of the zodiac during their exile in

> Much of the ancient learning was lost in Europe during the Dark Ages.

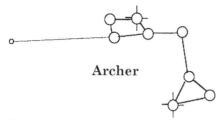

Archer

Babylon and then translated the names of the signs into Hebrew. This mixing of the Hebrew culture with the Babylonian has caused confusion, making some people think when they see Hebrew names attached to these signs or their stars that God was the author of the zodiac. Some of the pictures associated with the zodiac constellations are quite strange. There are amalgamated* animals and people in the zodiac which have long been known to be an earmark of Babylonian confusion. It is true that some of the pictures associated with the zodiac

*mixed

hint at Biblical themes, but the Babylonians corrupted their knowledge of the plan of redemption and the zodiac reflects this perversion. The zodiac reminds us how Satan's errors are always a twisted or perverted truth. He perverted the light of truth at Jesus' first advent so that most of Israel were not **alert** to who Christ really was.

The idea of seeing the Gospel in the stars was popularized in the 1800's. While the stars are pictures of the Plan of Salvation, they are probably not the same pictures taught by the zodiac.

Read the poem, "God Keeps the Stars."

The Zodiac

Constellation	Picture	Christian's Interpretation
Virgo	Virgin	Virgin Mary
Libra	Scales	Sin must be paid for
Scorpius	Scorpion	Sin brings death
Sagittarius	Archer	Demonism
Capricorn	Goat-fish	Earth corruption
Aquarius	Water pourer	Living water or Noah's flood
Pisces	Fish	God's remnant
Aries	Ram	Sacrifice
Taurus	Bull	Resurrection
Gemini	Twins	Christ's dual nature
Cancer	Crab	Gathering of redeemed
Leo	Lion	The King

God Keeps the Stars

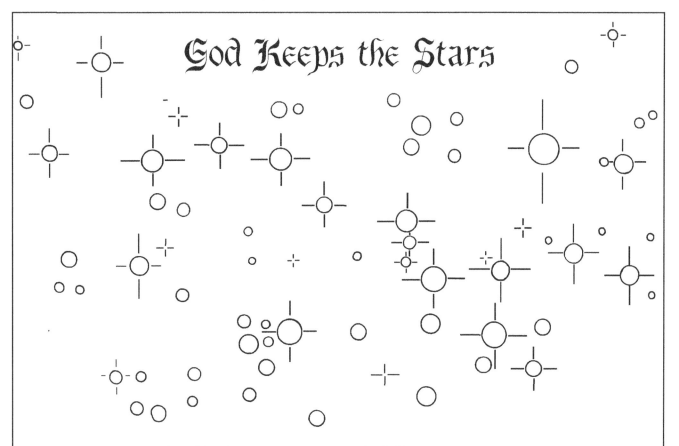

The little stars are twinkling now,
    Above us in the sky;
Earth's fading light makes them more bright,
    As sunset glories die.
Thou callest each by name, Oh Lord,
    All countless though they be;
In boundless space they have a place,
    Obedient unto Thee.

Our little lives are passing now,
    Soon each of us may die;
But earth's dark night shall change to light,
    If "Jesus passeth by."
Thou callest us by name, dear Lord,
    All sinful though we be;
In death's long sleep the Lord shall keep
    And through eternity.

Astrology

"Daniel answered in the presence of the king, and said,
The secret which the king hath demanded cannot the wise men,
the astrologers, the magicians, the soothsayers, shew unto the king."
Daniel 2:27

Satan's Counterfeits

The practice of astrology is Satan's substitute for the true science of astronomy. The Scriptures sharply condemn astrology. People who believe in astrology think that the stars have a controlling influence on people's lives. Deuteronomy 4:19 warns against this type of idolatry: *"And lest thou lift up thine eyes unto heaven, and when thou seest the sun, and the moon, and the stars, even all the host of heaven, shouldest be driven to worship them, and serve them, which the Lord thy God hath divided unto all nations under the whole heaven."*

Instead of looking to God and His word for direction and guidance, people who believe in astrology look to their horoscope which is a prediction of what will happen to a person that day depending upon the position of the stars when he was born.

Whenever you hear the word **hor**oscope, let it remind you of the *"great **whore**,"* Babylon, because she is the mother of this form of idolatry (Revelation 17:1, 5).

Place III

Concerning horoscopes and astrology, the precession of the equinoxes has not been taken into consideration in this pseudo-science of astrology and the resulting discrepancy now amounts to an entire sign. This means that people who think they were born under a certain sign are wrong even on this most basic assumption, as they are at least one sign off now. Also the so-called Age of Aquarius, much heralded by astrologers, is a long way off—600 years in fact because of the effect of precession. If you do not understand what is involved in precession, a good astronomy book will have an explanation.

The practice of astrology is Satan's substitute
for the true science of astronomy.

More About the Zodiac

In the ancient Babylonian astrological system, the sun god was the main god of the constellations, especially of the twelve constellations known as the zodiac. The stars were also worshiped because they were considered offspring of the sun, being thought of as manifestations of heat, fire, and light flowing from the sun. The Babylonians also believed that nature had its origin in the sun god. In worshiping the sun god, they were actually worshiping Satan whose original name, Lucifer, meant the "Shining One." Satan, *"the prince of the power of the air,"* (Ephesians 2:2) used man's curiosity about the heavenly host to cause mankind to worship them rather than their Creator. *"The ordinances of heaven"* (Job 38:33), which God Himself had appointed were made the means of blinding the mind and hardening the heart.

> "Thus saith the Lord,
> Learn not
> the way of the heathen,
> and be not dismayed
> at the signs of heaven;
> for the heathen
> are dismayed at them."
> Jeremiah 10:2

Israelite Apostasy

The Golden Calf (Bull)

Remember when the Israelites made a golden calf and offered sacrifice to it (Acts 7:41)? Well, the next verses reveals that at that time God *"gave them up to worship the host of heaven...Yea, ye took up the tabernacle of Moloch, and the star of your god Remphan, figures which ye made to worship them: and I will carry you away beyond Babylon"* (Acts 7:42-43). In fashioning the golden calf, the Israelites were imitating the worship of the Egyptian bull god, Apis. The golden calf was just a physical idol of the supposed constellation deity, Taurus the Bull. They *"changed the glory of the uncorruptible God into an image made like to corruptible man, and to birds, and four-footed beasts, and creeping things"* (Romans 1:23).

By leading Israel to this daring insult and blasphemy to Jehovah, Satan had planned to cause their ruin. Thus would be secured the extinction of the seed of Abraham, that seed (like stars too numerous to count) of promise, that was to preserve the knowledge of the living God, and through whom Christ was to come—the True Seed, that was to conquer Satan. But again, Satan was defeated. Sinful as they were, the people of Israel were not destroyed.

By causing men to violate the second commandment, Satan has used the constellations (zodiac) to degrade their conceptions of God. **Alertness** to study the word and understand the heavens is very important.

Review
Place II - III

1. In what language are many of the star names called today?

2. What was lost during the Dark Ages?

3. What other ways are stars identified?

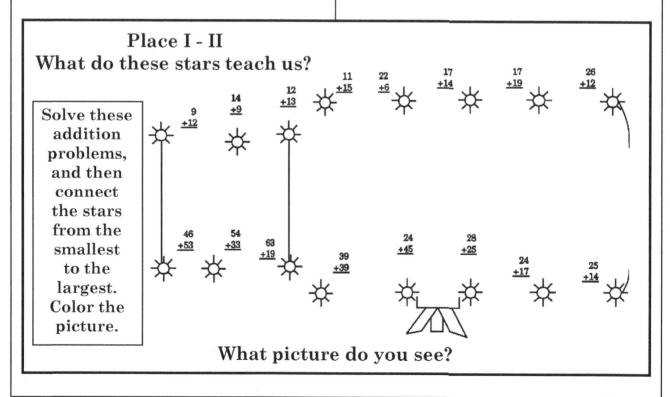

Place I - II
What do these stars teach us?

Solve these addition problems, and then connect the stars from the smallest to the largest. Color the picture.

What picture do you see?

Remind

1. When hearing your name called, be reminded how the stars each have a name. Amazing! God knows each and He knows all about you.

2. When hearing the pagan names of stars, be **alert** and decide in your heart never to be involved in reading horoscopes and sinning as Israel once did.

Reinforce

1. Learn the names and identify the stars in the sky. Find the constellations of the zodiac (which will depend on the time of the year) and give them new names and different objects to represent them that have a spiritual basis.

2. Read the whole story about Israel's apostasy in Exodus chapter 32.

Place I

Color the words below.

Place I

Read the words below.

"Thou shalt not make unto thee any graven image,
or any likeness of any thing
that is in heaven above,
or that is in the earth beneath,
or that is in the water
under the earth:

"Thou shalt not bow down thyself
to them, nor serve them..."
Exodus 20:4-5

Research
More Bible Stars

"Morning Star"

"I Jesus have sent mine angel to testify unto you these things in the churches. I am the root and offspring of David, and the bright and morning star."
Revelation 22:16

The brightest object in the heavens outside of the sun and moon is the planet Venus which is also known as both the *"morning star"* and the "evening star." And because it is the only "star" bright enough to be seen in the daylight, it is also called the "day star." The Scriptures refer to this "star" as a symbol of Christ several times. In II Peter 1:19 Christ is called the *"Day Star." "We have also a more sure word of prophecy; whereunto ye do well that ye take heed, as unto a light that shineth in a dark place, until the day dawn, and the day star arise in your hearts."* Christ is referred to again in Revelation 2:28 as the *"morning star."* He is the *"bright and morning Star,"* shining amid the moral darkness of this sinful, corrupt world.

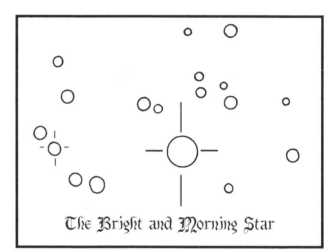

The Bright and Morning Star

The brilliance of Venus in the sky is not due only to its size and closeness to the earth, but because it is cloaked in unbroken clouds that reflect 76% of the light hitting them. The presence of these clouds has prevented astronomers from being able to look directly at the planet's surface. What a fitting object lesson to represent the glory that enshrouds Christ. *"Thick clouds are a covering to him...and he walketh in the circuit of heaven"* (Job 22:14).

Christ is called the "Day Star."

Mercury is sometimes called the morning star.

That Star of Light stooped low to take on humanity. His glory was veiled by human flesh that the majesty of His outward form might not become an object of attraction. Jesus purposed that no outward attraction should call men to His side. Only the beauty of heavenly truth must draw those who would follow Him. A few in Israel were **alert** to His beauty of character.

The clouds of Venus are not made of water vapor but of sulfuric acid and from these clouds descend showers of corrosive, sulfuric acid rain. This calls to mind the solemn fact: *"Upon the wicked he shall rain snares, fire and brimstone, and an horrible tempest: this shall be the portion of their cup"* (Psalm 11:6).

Did you know that **brimstone** is another name for **sulphur**?

Venus is an extremely hot planet, registering a temperature of 475 degrees (890 degrees Fahrenheit) Centigrade according to Venus 7, a probe that landed there intact in 1970. Venus 4, a previous probe, was destroyed by the intense heat and crushing pressure when it parachuted into the Morning Star's atmosphere in October 1967. These facts can remind us of the fate of the two different classes of people when Christ returns the second time. *"The sinners in Zion are afraid; fearfulness hath surprised the hypocrites. Who among us shall dwell with the devouring fire? who among us shall dwell with everlasting burnings?"* (Isaiah 33:14).

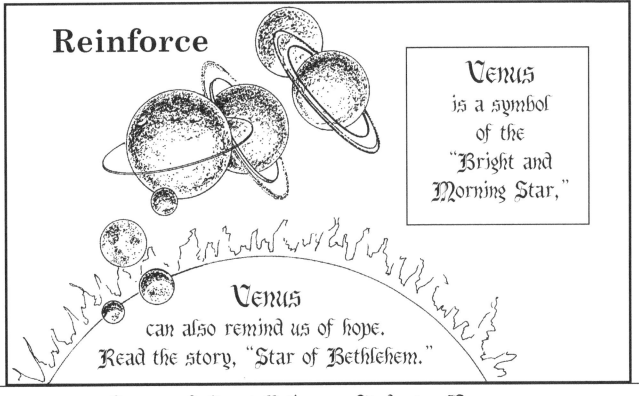

Reinforce

Venus is a symbol of the "Bright and Morning Star,"

Venus can also remind us of hope. Read the story, "Star of Bethlehem."

Remarkable Facts
Venus

• Venus is earth's twin because the two planets are so similar in size. Jesus lived a perfect life and we are to be like Him.

• At certain times of the year Venus is the first planet or star that can be seen in the western sky in the evening. At other times, it is the last planet or star that can be seen in the eastern sky in the morning. *"I am… the first and the last"* (Revelation 1:11).

• When Venus is near its brightest point, it can be seen in daylight.

• Venus is named for the Roman goddess of love and beauty. While we do not believe in mythology, Jesus is truly love and beauty.

• Venus is closer to the sun than any other planet except Mercury. Jesus is the closest to the Father.

• Venus travels around the sun in a nearly circular orbit, taking about 7 1/2 months to go around the sun once.

• When viewed through a telescope, Venus can be seen going through "changes" in shape and size or phases. Jesus went through changes when He came from heaven to earth.

• When Venus is moving toward the earth, the planet can be seen in the early evening sky. When moving away from the earth, Venus is visible in the early morning sky. *"I love them that love me; and those that seek me early shall find me"* (Proverbs 8:17).

• Venus is the only planet that does not rotate in the same direction it travels around the sun. Venus rotates in the opposite direction. Jesus is always in opposition to sin.

• Although Venus is called the earth's twin, its surface condition appears to be very different from those of the earth. The planet is surrounded by thick clouds of sulfuric acid and sulfur. Jesus was very different from those on earth as He never sinned and was covered with a cloud of purity.

• The temperature of the planet's surface is higher than that of any other planet. Jesus is the brightest star.

• Being a planet Venus reflects the light of the sun. Jesus showed man how to live on earth by reflecting the Father's glory to man. *"…The Son can do nothing of himself, but what he seeth the Father do…"* (John 5:19).

Venus • Venus • Venus • Venus • Venus • Venus • Venus

Illustration

Morning Star and Evening Star
Venus

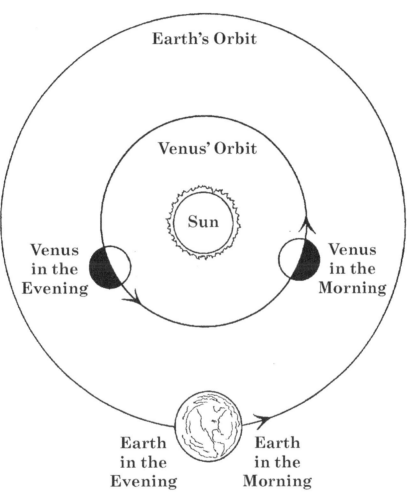

Earth's Orbit

Venus' Orbit

Sun

Venus in the Evening

Venus in the Morning

Earth in the Evening

Earth in the Morning

Long ago
the Sumerians discovered
that the morning star and the evening star
were really the planet Venus.
At some points in its orbit,
the planet can be seen in the early evening,
and at other points, in the early morning.

Sumerian Man

-◯- Star of Bethlehem

When I was at Constantinople, I went to see the English burial-ground at Scutari, on the opposite or Asiatic side of the narrow strait. There is no lovelier cemetery in the world than that, and it commands a glorious view. It is surrounded by high walls, and is admirably kept— the ground being covered with the smoothest and greenest turf, and shaded with cypresses and pine trees. In the center is a tall granite monument, erected by the queen of England. Around it are many graves of those who fell in battle or died afterwards of their wounds during the Crimean War. The dead were mostly young men, who were cut off in the bloom and vigor of life; and here and there you see the record on the marble tombstone of the devoted life and the earnest Christian faith of the sleeper below. No one could read these inscriptions, and know from them of the great sorrow caused to some fond wife or mother by the loss of the beloved dead, without being deeply moved.

There was one thing that touched me greatly, and that was the appearance on the graves of a little lily-like flower, called the Star of Bethlehem. It grows in the southern parts of our own country, and is thus a link of connection between this faraway burying-ground and the green fields of England where the sleepers used to play as boys. It grew in myriads over the green mounds, and opened its pure white starry rays to the sunbeams of April, that shone brightly upon them. The flowers almost hid the grass, they were so numerous; and they looked as if they had newly fallen from the sky, instead of growing up through the dark soil—they were so pure and bright. With the utmost impartiality they covered the grave of officer and private soldier, and seemed especially to distinguish the last resting-places of the unknown and unnamed dead, over whom there was no monument.

This starry flower spoke to me, in a most impressive way, of the morning star of the resurrection, which is promised to him that overcometh. This little earth-star bloomed over the graves of the English soldiers, in token that for them there was a star of hope in the heavenly sky that would usher in the eternal day, when the sleepers would awake to newness of life. That earth-star itself rose from the death of Nature in Winter, under the quickening influences of Spring; and so those who were planted in that God's acre in the likeness of

Christ's death, would be planted together in the likeness of His resurrection. Over the whole burial-place was the holy light of self-sacrifice; for each one that slept in it overcame the selfishness of human nature, and counted not his life dear to him for the sake of his country.

Each of you is a soldier. You have to fight the good fight of faith. You have to struggle with your own besetting sins, and with the evils of the world. And, if you overcome, the promise of the Morning Star is given to you. That promise is not meant to mock you with a false hope. The morning star is not so high above you that you cannot attain to it.

Now, what is meant by this morning star? In the first place it is the emblem of royalty. It is linked with the scepter. When a general returns as a conqueror from some great war, he gets from his sovereign a decoration made in the shape of a golden and jewelled star connected with it, and everyone who receives it feels proud of it in the highest degree. It exalts him above his fellows. And so God gives to each conqueror in the spiritual warfare the jewelled star of honor. If you overcome in the strife with temptation and evil, you will be decorated with a star that shines brighter than any jewel, and you will have

the scepter of dominion over self and the world. The star that arose out of Jacob will crown you with glory and honor. That fair white orb whose "dewdrop of light trembles on the front of dawn," will sparkle on your brow; and all who see you will know that by God's grace you have conquered the world, the flesh, and the devil.

**Sing the hymn,
"Near the Cross,"
the second verse.**

The morning star
is the emblem of royalty.
It is linked
with the scepter.

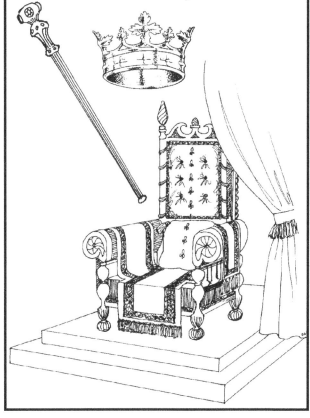

"Castor and Pollux"

"And after three months we departed in a ship of Alexandria, which had wintered in the isle, whose sign was Castor and Pollux."
Acts 28:11

Castor and Pollux, according to *Strong's Exhaustive Concordance* is translated "the Twins." These are twin stars located in the constellation known as the Twins (Gemini), and they form such a striking pair that they have been associated with each other for thousands of years. Castor is a second magnitude white star and Pollux is a first magnitude yellow star, being the 12th brightest star in the northern winter sky. Pollux is also the closest giant star to the earth. These two stars are five degrees apart which makes them good measuring points. On Paul's final journey to Rome, the boat he was on displayed a representation of these twin stars (Acts 28:11).

The bottom stars in the Big Dipper's bowl (cup) point toward Castor, and a line drawn through the stars Rigel and Betelgeuse in Orion points to Pollux. Castor is a triple star and each of its three components is a double star which makes six in all. Castor and Pollux picture to us the twin nature of our Lord Jesus Christ. In Him, divinity was joined to humanity. Since six is the number of man, Castor can re-mind us of Jesus' human nature. Yellow is the color of divinity and Pollux being yellow and also being the brighter of the two stars can represent our Lord's divine nature. Since Pollux is also a first magnitude star it speaks of Christ as God who is first in priority of time, first in superiority, and first in absolute supremacy. *"Hear, O Israel: the Lord our God is one Lord."* Five is the number of grace and there are five degrees between Castor and Pollux. Four is the number of the world and represents man's weakness. Castor and Pollux are a star promise God has placed in the sky to help us remember *"My grace is sufficient for thee: for my strength is made perfect in weakness"* (II Corinthians 12:9). Humanity must be partakers of the divine nature in order to reflect the image of Jesus fully.

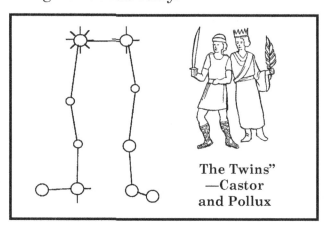

The Twins"
—Castor
and Pollux

Both Greek and Roman sailors regarded Castor and Pollux as patrons of navigation, which means that they thought the stars were looking out for their safety. As Christians, we know Who is really responsible for our safety and so we sing, "Jesus, Saviour, pilot me over life's tempestuous sea. Unknown waves before me roll, hiding rock and treacherous shoal. Chart and compass come from Thee. Jesus, Saviour pilot me." Let us have faith that God is going to carry the noble ship which bears the people of God safely into the heavenly port.

Reinforce
Place I - II

Color the picture
of Paul on the ship
on his last
missionary journey.

Review
Place I - II - III

1. Who is called the Morning Star in Scriptures?

2. What is the name of the "morning star" that is also known as the "evening star"? What is still another name for it?

Place II - III

3. Why does Venus remind us of Job 22:14? Of what can the clouds of Venus remind us?

4. Describe Castor and Pollux.

Twins in Nature

Pampas Cat from South America

Remind

1. When noticing the morning or evening star, think about Jesus the Star of light and hope in this dark world.

2. Do you have any twins in your family? Castor and Pollux are the twins of the sky.

Twins

3. When you see a boat on the water, remember the boat Paul traveled on with the signs of Castor and Pollux on it.

4. Read the story, "Matabele Astronomy."

Matabele Astronomy

I cannot speak of astronomical ideas among the Matabeles,* but only of astronomical names. In their Sintabele tongue they have given names to some of the stars that show how truly the heavens are for "times and seasons" among every tribe and people. The evening skies are bright on the high tablelands of the African interior, brighter than with us in America. The atmosphere is clear, and the stars fairly seem to overflow and drip with light.

"What kind of names do the Matabeles give to the stars?" I ask Brother George Hutchinson at the Somabela Mission, as we talked of some of the picturesque phrases of the Sintabele tongue.

"Well," he said, "the evening star they call *iCelankobe*."

"And what does it mean?"

"Well, *inkobe* means boiled mealies [maize], and *iCelankobe* means to ask for boiled mealies." Thus, when the evening star begins to rise, it is time for supper.

"Then there is the morning star," said Brother Hutchinson. "It is called *iKwazi*. The meaning of this is 'to make to get up.'"

Very expressive names the Matabeles give to the stars, surely. They make all the starry heavens talk of the little round of their circumscribed daily lives.

"Then there are the Pleiades," said Brother Hutchinson, "the seven stars. They are called *isiLimela* which means 'the digging time' or 'the digging season.' When the seven stars are visible just after sunset, as they are about the last of September, it is time to get the ground ready for planting."

When the Matabeles see the full moon, they cry *Ikolive*—it is satisfied. The same verbal root is used to express satisfaction over a full meal.

The rainbow is *umcilo wenkosikazi*, or "whip of the moon."

Reinforce

Sing the hymn, "Near the Cross," the second verse, and "Lord of All Being," verses 1 and 2.

*A Zulu tribe

Research
Orion

"Seek him that maketh the seven stars and Orion."
Amos 5:8

Orion is the most brilliant constellation in all the heavens and has appropriately been termed "the lord of the sky" even by those who do not realize that this constellation represents the Lord of glory Himself. Orion is visible from every inhabited part of the globe and as an object of celestial beauty, it has no peer. Regions of the sky to the east as well as to the west of Orion have comparatively dim stars thus enhancing the surpassing splendor of Orion, which in the Hebrew, means "Strong One." This brings to mind the text: *"Who is this King of glory? The Lord* **strong** *and mighty, the Lord mighty in battle"* (Psalm 24:8).

The fullness of time had come at the very crisis. When Satan seemed about to triumph, the Son of God had come to this world as a babe in Bethlehem. So in the closing scenes of this earth's history He will appear the second time at the appropriate moment as the Strong One. Be **alert!**

The "Strong One"

As we study this constellation further, you will see how Orion especially represents our Lord coming back to earth the second time to execute judgment. At that time Babylon *"shall be utterly burned with fire: for* **strong** *is the Lord God who judgeth her"* (Revelation 18:8).

**Sing the hymn,
"Redemption Nigh."**

The Body

The main outline of this magnificent constellation is formed by seven stars. Seven symbolizes the spiritual perfection of our Lord.

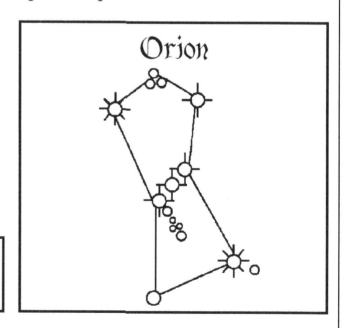

Orion

As you look at the constellation, the arm seems to be holding a mighty sickle speaking to our hearts prophetically of Revelation 14:15-16. *"And another angel came out of the temple, crying with a loud voice to him that sat on the cloud, Thrust in thy sickle, and reap: For the time is come for thee to reap; for the harvest of the earth is ripe. And he that sat on the cloud thrust in his sickle on the earth; and the earth was reaped."* The whole constellation, containing 17 (perfection of spiritual order) stars to the unaided eye, but exhibiting 78 in an ordinary telescope.

The Hands

In the constellation Orion, the left hand appears to be holding a trumpet which Christ will blow at His second coming. *"And then shall appear the sign of the Son of man in heaven: and then shall all the tribes of the earth mourn, and they shall see the Son of man coming in the clouds of heaven with power and great glory. And he shall send his angels with a great sound of a trumpet, and they shall gather together his elect from the four winds, from one end of heaven to the other"* (Matthew 24:30-31).

The Belt

The Strong One is also girded with a three-jeweled belt of very bright white stars each of them being of the second magnitude. *"The Lord reigneth, he is clothed with majesty; the Lord is clothed with **strength**, wherewith he hath girded himself"* (Psalm 93:1). These three brilliant stars being of equal magnitude and white are a symbol of the Heavenly Trio that Christ is a member of. The Three Kings were what they used to be called.

White represents righteousness and it is a character quality shared equally by the Father, Son, and the Holy Spirit. Astronomers use these three stars in Orion's belt as a **ruler** in the heavens because they form a glorious line three degrees long. We know that three is the number of divine perfection. The perfection that it is possible for us to reach through Christ should be the **Ruler** we measure all our actions by.

> The glittering stars of its belt are strung like diamonds on its invisible line.

Each of these three stars, which together are part of a pattern, are traveling at three different speeds in three different directions. *"Canst thou...loose the bands of Orion?"* (Job 38:31). Actually each star that forms the constellation of Orion is moving on a course different from all the rest. This can represent the three unique responsibilities that each member of the Godhead assumes. The "Everlasting Father" who is the supreme ruler, the "Prince of Peace" who is the Son who represents God, and the "Mighty Wind" who is the Holy Spirit who moves on the hearts of men bringing them to repentance.

The Godhead

The **"Everlasting Father"** who is the supreme ruler.

The **"Prince of Peace"** who is the Son who represents God.

The **"Mighty Wind"** who is the Holy Spirit which moves on the hearts of men bringing them to repentance.

The Sword

A short row of stars hanging from Orion's belt make up the full flaming sword of the Lord. *"For my sword shall be bathed in heaven: behold, it shall come down upon Idumea, and upon the people of my curse, to judgment"* (Isaiah 34:5). *"For I lift up my hand to heaven, and say, I live for ever. If I whet my glittering sword, and mine hand take hold on judgment; I will render vengeance to mine enemies, and will reward them that hate me...Rejoice, O ye nations, with his people, for he will avenge the blood of his servants, and will render vengeance to his adversaries, and will be merciful unto his land, and to his people"* (Deuteronomy 32:40-41, 43).

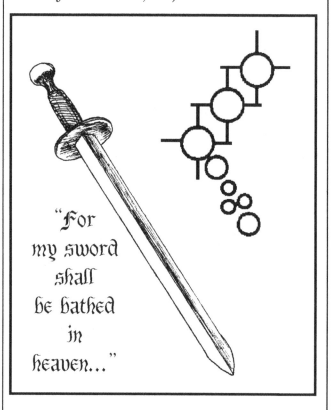

"For my sword shall be bathed in heaven..."

Nebula

The stars in the heavens look close together, but they are really separated by large stretches of space. This space has very small gas and dust particles in it called interstellar matter.

Some of the interstellar matter in space has collected together to form clouds called nebulae. The term nebula comes from the Latin word for cloud. There are two types of nebulae.

1. The diffuse nebulae are the larger of the two types. It may occur near an extremely hot, bright star. The intense ultraviolet light from the star energizes the gas atoms of the nebula and enables the cloud to emit light. It is also called an emission nebula.

If a diffuse nebula occurs near a cool star, the ultraviolet light from the star is too weak to make the nebula's gas atoms give off light. But the dust particles in the nebula reflect the starlight. This kind of diffuse nebula is called a **reflection nebula**.

Sometimes diffuse nebulae occur in areas that have no nearby stars, so it neither emits nor reflects enough light to be seen. Therefore, its dust particles block out the light from the stars behind them. These diffuse nebulae are called dark nebulae.

2. Planetary nebulae are ball like clouds of dust and gases that surround certain stars. When seen through a small telescope, these nebulae appear to have flat, rounded surfaces like that of planets. Early astronomers called these nebulae planetary nebulae.

Nebulae abound along the Milky Way. Some appear as little more than faint wisps. But time exposure photographs reveal beautiful clouds. The Veil Nebula is about 2,500 light years from earth and is one you might like to explore with binoculars or a telescope.

A very large cloud of gas called the Cygnus Superbubble is located about 6,500 light-years from our solar system.

Ring nebulae are formed from the puffs of gases given off by giant red stars. The expanding, glowing gases form rings around the stars. They remind us of smoke signals made at an Indian fire.

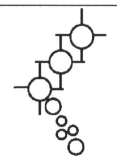

The Great Orion Nebula
(M-42)

"Canst thou...loose the bands of Orion?"
Job 38:31

The Great Orion Nebula is located around the central star in the sword. It is barely perceptible to the naked eye. It is the main attraction in the sky for astronomers today as they are led by an intense fascination to this majestic cloud which is gloriously lit up by four stars arranged in a diamond shape called the Trapezium. In addition to the Trapezium, astronomers have detected hundreds less bright stars within the Orion Nebula, moving in different directions and at different speeds. *"Canst thou...loose the bands of Orion?"*

In the nebula there is what appears to be a gigantic cavern in space, which is 19 trillion miles across and 51 trillion miles deep. It appears to be an entrance to an unseen section of space. The changing colors and the delicately swirling gases in this nebula are breathtaking. All agree that there is no sight equal to it in the heavens. It is, as it were, a visible representation of the fact that the temple of God is opened in heaven, and the threshold is flushed with glory. Perhaps this is the gateway to heaven.

The changing colors and the delicately, swirling gases in this nebula are breathtaking.

Modern IRAS* satellite photographs confirm a mysterious "hole" in "the open space of Orion." Thus we see that the glittering sword of Orion is somewhat like the *"flaming sword which turned every way, to keep the way of the tree of life"* (Genesis 3:24). What is this sword symbolic of? Ephesians 6:17 tells us, *"The sword of the Spirit...is the word of God." "Repent; or else I will come unto thee quickly, and will fight against them with the sword of my mouth"* (Revelation 2:16). *"And out of his mouth goeth a sharp sword, that with it he should smite the nations"* (Revelation 19:15).

"And out of his mouth goeth a sharp sword, that with it he should smite the nations."
Revelation 19:15

*Infra-Red Astronomy Satellite

The Sword

For the warfare gird it on,
Nor until the fight be won,
And the day's sharp work is done,
      Lay it by!

Sharp its edge; oh, use it well;
Strong against the strongest spell
Ever framed in earth or hell,
      It will prove!

Bright its blade; oh, keep it bright,
For the battle, day and night;
Stainless as the flashing light
      Let it shine!

With it hew thy onward way,
Through hell's thickest war-array:
Nothing let thy soul dismay;
      To the last!

Weapon of the true and just,
Trust it strongly, warrior, trust,
Keep it free from earthly rust;
      Win it must!

Strike for God, and let each blow
Tell on Satan's overthrow,
Be the ruin of a foe;
      Strike for God!

Not for angels was it made,
Man alone can wield that blade,
Soldiers of the great crusade—
      Host of God!

Sword of God, thy power we hail;
He who has thee cannot fail,
He who trusts thee must prevail,
      Mighty sword!

Rich in victories untold,
Still the precious sword of old,
Steel and gems and glorious gold,
      To the last!

Till the warfare shall be done,
Till the victory be won,
Till the triumph be begun,
      Grasp we thee!

— H. Bonar

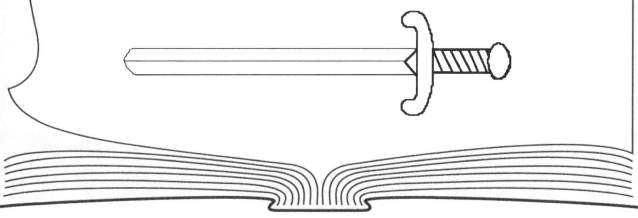

The Shoulders

The shoulders of the Strong One are decked each with a bright star even as Christ our High Priest wears a precious stone on each shoulder inscribed with the names of the children of Israel. *"Thou shalt take two onyx stones, and grave on them the names of the children of Israel.... And thou shalt put the two stones upon the shoulders of the ephod for stones of memorial unto the children of Israel"* (Exodus 28:9, 12). These stars on Orion's shoulders can remind us that Christ never forgets His children for a moment and soon He is coming to take them home with Him.

The Foot

Orion stands with his left foot poised in a position higher than his right foot. The bright, blue-white star marking the left upraised foot of Orion is called Rigel, which is Arabic for "foot." Rigel is a true celestial searchlight, being the seventh brightest star in the sky. It is 60,000 times more luminous than the sun; but since it is so far away we cannot appreciate its true brightness. Rigel has three faint companion stars which give Rigel a bluish cast from one which has a deep blue color. This lovely white-bluish star can signify Christ's faithfulness in obeying the law of God. *"I have refrained my feet from every evil way, that I might keep thy word"* (Psalm 119:101). Rigel's companion stars tell us about those saved from the earth. *"I am a companion of all them that fear thee, and of them that keep thy precepts"* (Psalm 119:63).

Just to the left of this foot is a long, faint, winding snakelike constellation traditionally known as the River (Eridanus). Its snake-like

Illustration

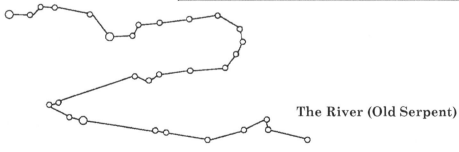

Orion

The River (Old Serpent)

appearance pictures to our minds that *"old serpent called the devil and Satan"* (Revelation 12:9). I like to think of this dull-looking constellation as the constellation mentioned in Job 26:13 as the *"crooked serpent."* In Genesis 3:15 we are told about the conflict between Christ and the serpent, *"And I will put enmity between thee and the woman, and between thy seed and her seed; it shall bruise thy head, and thou shalt bruise his heel."* Think of Orion with his uplifted foot as about to bruise the serpent's head which Christ did at the cross and will finish at His second coming.

Remember earlier in our study where we learned that the Pleiades are moving towards Orion's left shoulder? Well, now that you know the spiritual meaning of both the Pleiades and Orion you will understand how God's teachers of

righteousness are drawn toward Him. *"I drew them with cords of a man, with **bands** of love"* (Hosea 11:4). (Cross-reference with *"**bands** of Orion"* in Job 38:31 to find a very provocative concept that warrants scientific study.) The fact that the Pleiades and Orion are mentioned together in the same verse constitutes one of the most important and profound scientific statements in the Bible.

The Pleiades being drawn toward the Strong One's shoulder brings to remembrance these touching verses: *"And he spake this parable unto them, saying, What man of you, having an hundred sheep, if he*

> *"Blessed are they that do his commandments, that they may have right to the tree of life, and may enter in through the gates into the city."*
> Revelation 22:14

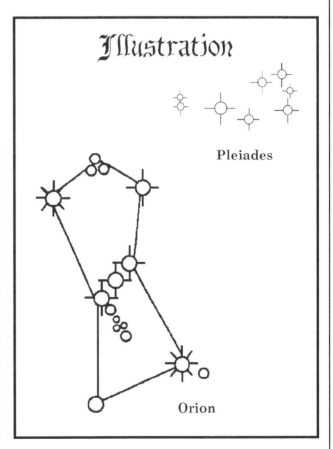

Illustration

Pleiades

Orion

lose one of them, doth not leave the ninety and nine in the wilderness, and go after that which is lost, until he find it? And when he hath found it, he layeth it on his shoulders, rejoicing" (Luke 15:3-5). *"The beloved of the Lord shall dwell in safety by him...and he shall dwell between his shoulders"* (Deuteronomy 33:12). Incidentally, the right shoulder star of Orion is a magnificent red super-giant star named Betelgeuse. You can easily see the red color of this star with the naked eye. May its crimson color speak to your heart of the blood Christ shed on Calvary for you.

Viewed
December Through March

December through March are the most favorable months for viewing The Strong One from the northern skies. The whole constellation is surrounded by a halo of light. There are seven first magnitude stars in this constellation that mark it with incomparable splendor. These seven stars, speaking of spiritual perfection, can remind us that *"It is God that girdeth me with **strength**, and maketh my way **perfect**"* (Psalm 18:32).

The Head

At the head of the Strong One there are three stars that represent the divine perfection of Christ. The perfection of His offices are shown in His being: (1) Prophet, (2) Priest, and (3) King. It could be a reminder of the Headship of the Father, Son, and Holy Spirit—one, yet three.

> Betelgeuse's crimson color
> can remind you
> of the blood Christ shed
> on Calvary for you.

Rising

Orion is seen rising in the east by all observers on earth, due to the fact that it moves constantly over the equator. Straddling the equator as it does, it is shared almost equally by the northern and southern hemispheres. It is a visible object lesson of the fact that no matter where we live on the earth, Jesus will appear to return from the east. *"For as the lightning cometh out of the east, and shineth even unto the west; so shall also the coming of the Son of man be"* (Matthew 24:27). *"Behold, he cometh with clouds; and every eye shall see him..."* (Revelation 1:7).

It is also an interesting parallel to note that the constellation Orion can be seen rising in the east around midnight during the months of September and October when Yom Kippur, the typical Day of Atonement can occur. On the typical Day of Atonement the sanctuary and the people were cleansed from their sins by a special service involving the High Priest, Christ's representative, going into the Most Holy Place of the sanctuary. When the High Priest came out of the sanctuary on that day he had *"made an end of reconciling"* (Leviticus 16:20) and had changed his priestly garments. So Christ lays aside His priestly robes and comes to earth clothed in His royal apparel as King of kings and Lord of lords.

What is the Day of Atonement? At-one-ment or being one with God. We are living in the antitypical Day of Atonement right now. God is waiting with longing desire to come for His people. It will be the darkest period of this earth's history when Jesus returns. Orion's midnight rising during the Day of Atonement season is a promise to us of that deliverance.

Horsehead Nebula

Orion has another famous nebula. It is known as the Horsehead Nebula. It is located near the left-most star of Orion's belt. Seen on photographs as a jet of unilluminated (dark) dust, this silhouette (outline) of a noble steed's head can remind us of the horse Christ will ride when He comes *"forth conquering, and to conquer"* (Revelation 6:2). *"And the remnant were slain with the sword of him that sat upon the horse, which sword proceeded out of his mouth: and all the fowls were filled with their flesh"* (Revelation 19:21).

The Horsehead Nebula is a dark nebula because there are no stars to light up the unusual-shaped horsehead cloud in it. The light from stars behind the cloud outlines the nebula and allows us to see it. This small dark cloud is a silent reminder of the small dark cloud that we will see in the distance when Christ returns. The Scriptures refer to this cloud as the *"sign of the Son of man in heaven"* (Matthew 24:30).

Orion is seen rising in the east by all observers on earth, due to the fact that it moves constantly over the equator.

I am sure Orion is one constellation you will want to look into more deeply. And just think, one day, if faithful, you literally will!

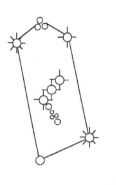

The Horsehead Nebula is a dark nebula because there are no stars to light the unusual-shaped horsehead cloud in it.

I Know He Will Come

I have a Friend so kind and true,
But the miles are far and the time seems long;
He has said to watch and He'd come again;
I sit in the gloaming—'tis even-song.

Said the Friend, "If I go, I will come again,
So watch til my chariot you shall hear.
It may be at cockcrow; it may be at even.
It will not be long—even now I'm near."

The glorious day has waned to its close,
And the sunset gleams across the sky
Have faded into the tender gray;
And the morning watch is a far cry.

But I know He'll come; it will not be long;
So I calmly wait as the moments fly.
Over the hills the morning breaks;
I see His sign in the pearly sky.

And when He comes, I shall no more think
Of the long dark hours I waited here;
I shall run and clasp His garment's hem,
Who has promised no more a pain or tear.
—*Mary M. Morse*

Review
Place II - III

1. What constellation is called "the Lord of the Sky"? What is the Hebrew meaning of this constellation?

2. Draw a picture of Orion. Find Orion in the sky.

3. What does the constellation Orion especially remind us of in these last days?

4. Describe Orion.

5. Where is the great nebula in Orion located?

6. Tell about the right shoulder star of Orion.

7. What can the three stars in the head of Orion signify about Christ?

8. What is the bright, blue-white star called on Orion's upraised foot? What is to the left of this foot?

9. When can the Strong One best be observed in the northern sky?

10. How many first magnitude stars are in Orion? What do they symbolize?

11. Where is Orion seen rising in the sky? Why?

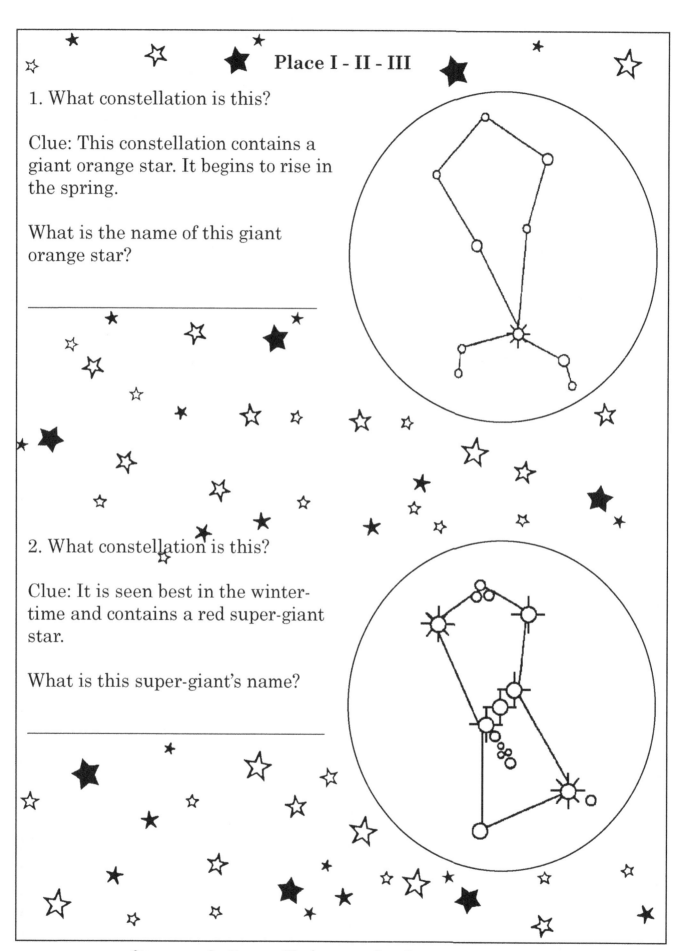

1. What constellation is this?

Clue: This constellation contains a giant orange star. It begins to rise in the spring.

What is the name of this giant orange star?

_____

2. What constellation is this?

Clue: It is seen best in the winter-time and contains a red super-giant star.

What is this super-giant's name?

_____

Research
Southern Hemisphere Stars

"He is wise in heart, and mighty in strength...which maketh Arcturus, Orion, and Pleiades, and the chambers of the south."
Job 9:4, 9

Because of the tilt of the earth, people in the Northern Hemisphere never see the stars in the far southern skies. Important stars in the Southern Hemisphere include Proxima Centauri, the earth's closest star after the sun, and Canopus, the second brightest star after Sirius. Of course, there is also the famous Southern Cross constellation which several Southern Hemisphere countries display on their flags.

There are cross constellations in both the southern and northern skies. In the north the cross constellation is known as the Swan (Cygnus). We have already mentioned some facts about the Southern Cross in the section, "More Sky Clocks," but in passing, it is interesting to note that the Southern Cross was just visible in the latitude of Jerusalem at the time of the first coming of our Lord. Since then, because of the gradual recession of the pole star, it has not been seen in the northern latitudes. It gradually disappeared and was not visible in Jerusalem when Christ was crucified. It seems like it was a "sign" God gave to those who were **alert** foreshadowing the cross of Calvary. I wonder how many people noticed?

Illustration

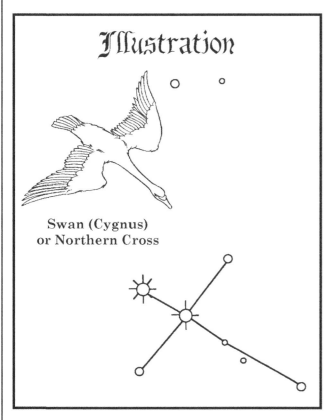

Swan (Cygnus)
or Northern Cross

Read the poem, "The Cross."

The Cross

God laid upon my back a grievous load,
A heavy cross to bear along the road.

I staggered on, and lo! one weary day
An angry lion sprang across my way.

I prayed to God and swift at His command
The cross became a weapon in my hand.

It slew my raging enemy, and then
Became a cross upon my back again.

I reached a desert. O'er the burning track
I persevered, the cross upon my back.

No shade was there, and in the cruel sun
I sank at last, and thought my days were done.

But lo! the Lord works many a blest surprise—
The cross became a tree before my eyes!

I slept: I woke, to feel the strength of ten,
I found the cross upon my back again.

And thus through all my days, from that to this,
The cross, my burden, has become my bliss:

Nor ever shall I lay the burden down,
For God some day will make the cross a crown.

— Amos R. Wells

Jewel Box

The Jewel Box, also known as NGC 4755 and Kappa Crucis, is a glittering star cluster in the Southern Cross constellation. It is a group of more than a hundred variously colored red, green, blue, and bluish-green suns so closely throned together as to appear in a telescope like a superb bouquet or a piece of fancy jewelry. The cross was a bouquet of love to man.

The fact that these beautiful gems in the night sky are not seen in their true beauty by the naked eye can remind us that the jewels of truth in the Bible do not lie upon the surface as many suppose. Let us be like those who have been seeking the hidden treasure and have been opening up the jewel box and letting the jewels of truth shine forth.

The Magellanic Clouds, two fuzzy patches of light, are galaxies of stars which can be viewed in the Southern Hemisphere. There is a remote (distant) star named S Doradus in the Larger Magellanic Cloud that is 400,000,000,000 times as bright as the dimmest star known. As you gaze upon the Magellanic Clouds, think of the other worlds God has created and His own heavenly home. The heavenly universe is watching with intense interest the conflict between good and evil. They rejoice as Satan's subtleties one after another, are discerned and met with *"It is written,"* as Christ met them in His conflict with the wily foe. Every victory gained is a gem in the crown of life.

Sing again the song, "Give Me the Bible."

The Jewel Box, also known as NGC 4755 and Kappa Crucis is a glittering star cluster in the Southern Cross constellation.

Remind

1. When seeing the Orion constellation meditate on the second coming and Bible texts that relate to it.

2. As you look at your hands, think what Jesus will hold in His when He returns to the earth the second time.

3. Sometimes we wear a belt—it is a reminder of Orion and the lessons about it.

4. A color wheel in a store display shows a small glimmer of the changing colors in the Orion Nebula.

5. Every time we read the Bible it is a reminder of the sword in Orion.

6. Playing with magnets is an object lesson of how the Pleiades are being drawn toward the Strong One.

7. Stepping on a destructive, pesky insect is symbolic of Christ crushing the serpent.

8. The rising sun from the east calls to mind the second coming of Christ.

Reinforce

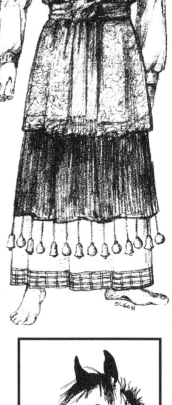

1. Sing the hymn, "The Beautiful Beyond," verse one.

2. Look at a picture of the High Priest in Old Testament times. Especially observe his shoulders.

3. Use binoculars to observe Orion in the sky.

4. Look at a picture of the Horse- head Nebula. Then observe a horse's head. Do you now see why it is called by that name?

5. Read the poem, "It Doth Not Yet Appear What We Shall Be."

"Behold, he cometh with clouds; and every eye shall see him...."
Revelation 1:7

It Doth Not Yet Appear
What We Shall Be

The gems of earth are still within
    Her silent unwrought mines;
There hide they, all unknown, unseen:
    No sparkle upward shines.

The stars of heaven how few and wan
    Are all we see below,
Compared with what remain unseen
    Beyond all vision now.

Who knows the untold brilliance there,
    The wealth, the beauty hid?
Like sparkle of a lustrous eye
    Beneath the eyelid hid.

So with the heaven of better stars
    Of which these are but signs;
So with the stores of wisdom hid
    In everlasting mines

For what we shall in that day be
    It doth not yet appear;
But when we see Him as He is
    We shall His likeness wear.

— *H. Bonar*

Stammerjohan

Research
Star Watching Tips

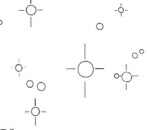

"When I consider thy heavens...."
Psalm 8:3

If you lived back in Bible times you probably would not have needed any tips for star watching. Back then, parents taught their children about stars like parents today teach their young ones about street signs because the information could be necessary for survival. If someone was lost at night back then, the stars might have been their only method of finding their way. Such people could rely upon the stars because they are kept in their appointed places by the power of God. God can use us as guides to help others just as He uses the stars when we, like they, are willing to always be at the right place at the right time.

The best place to view these precious gems of light studding the heavens is the country because there is less interference by pollution and electric lights. Flashing neon lights and glaring headlights and even street lights blind the eyes to the beauty of the natural lights God has created; just as the glare and glitter of the things of this world can make it hard to discern the beauty of spiritual things. We must separate ourselves from all this interference. If you cannot avoid bright lights altogether, try to place yourself so that buildings or a tree can screen them out somewhat. A simple sighting tube can also help screen out light.

Do not strain your eyes trying to see a constellation when it is very low on the horizon because the atmosphere near the horizon is denser and may make the stars look dimmer or even blot them out. Try to choose a moonless or near moonless night to watch stars. Winter nights are a wonderful time for sky watching because it is often dry and clear then while air pollution is usually less then than in the summer. Also, darkness comes earlier in the winter giving you extra time for star study before bedtime. Just as the stars arise and shine in darkness while many people sleep, so the spiritual darkness in Israel was great when the Star of Bethlehem arose. Most of God's people were asleep in their sins and not **alert** and missed the glorious occasion. Let us, *"Arise, shine; for thy light is come, and the glory of the Lord is risen upon thee"* (Isaiah 60:1).

It is best to wait until an hour after sunset when the sky has completely darkened if you want to see the most stars. But if you are just starting to learn the constellations, you may want to come out earlier because then only the planets, sometimes also referred to as the wandering stars (the word planet means wanderer), and brighter stars will be showing, and you will be less confused by the many fainter stars. The five visible planets—Mercury, Venus, Mars, Jupiter, and Saturn—wander among the "stationary" stars. The planets teach us about keeping our appointments because that is exactly what they do. The almanac, like an appointment book, can **alert** you when and where to look for each one. Then you can keep your part of the appointment by being there to look for each planet as it appears. The precision of the heavenly bodies reflects God's punctuality. At just the precise moment, *"when the fulness of the time was come,"* Christ came to this earth (Galatians 4:4). He was exactly on time according to the prophetic clock.

Reflect
God's Punctuality

The precision of the heavenly bodies reflects God's punctuality.
At just the precise moment, "when the fulness
of the time was come," Christ came to this earth.
He was exactly on time according to the prophetic clock.

Depending upon their relative positions, you can usually find Mercury and Venus just before sunrise or just after sunset. But Mars, Jupiter, and Saturn travel in their own way and might be visible at any time during the night. It is helpful to know that the planets and the sun all move through the heavens following a common line called the ecliptic. You can find the ecliptic marked in your star guide books to help you know where to look for the planets, but basically it is the region of the sky the sun passes through.

Jude 13 refers to *"wandering stars"* as being symbolic of professed ministers who wander around from place to place preaching truth mixed with error. These false teachers, though they may appear brilliant for a time, give neither constant light nor guidance. We must beware of making such people our guides. Just before Jesus came the first time, the bigotry of the Jewish leaders hindered the spread of the light. Intent on maintaining the separation between themselves and other nations, they were unwilling to impart the knowledge they still possessed concerning the symbolic service. The True Guide would arise to teach the people.

As you are looking at the night sky remember that the constellations you will see will depend upon the season of the year as well as the time of the evening. If you are looking for a particular constellation, that means you may have to wait until an hour later to see it or even a later month in the year.

Binoculars are helpful for looking closely at planets and star clusters but they narrow your field of vision too much for looking at constellations.

A flashlight is helpful to see the star charts in your astronomy field guide, but it will keep your eyes from adjusting to the dark unless you cover the end with red cellophane or tissue paper. Red fingernail polish accomplishes the same purpose and can be removed later with nail polish remover. Just as your physical sight is more discerning in the darkness when you use a red shield, so penetrating spiritual vision is only possible through the crimson blood of Jesus.

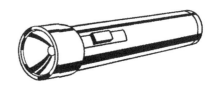

Jude 13 refers to *"wandering stars"* **as being symbolic of professed ministers who wander around from place to place preaching truth mixed with error.**

When enjoying the night sky, it is best to lie on the ground or in a lawn chair so that your neck will not get stiff from looking up constantly. If you will also close your eyes and count slowly to 200 before looking up at the stars, your eyes will have time to adjust making it possible for you to see many more of the fainter stars.

As you look at the wonderful things God's hand has made, let your proud, foolish heart feel its dependence and inferiority. As you consider these things, you will have a sense of God's condescension.

The heavenly treasure chart is worthy of our contemplation. God has made them for the benefit of man, and as we study His works, angels of God will be by our side to enlighten our minds, and guard them from satanic deception.

May God richly bless you as you *"lift up your eyes on high, and behold who hath created these things"* (Isaiah 40:26).

"Lift up your eyes on high,
and behold
who hath
created these things."
Isaiah 40:26

Review
Place II - III

1. What are some important stars in the southern skies?

2. Name two cross constellations?

3. Choose a constellation. Research more about it, and write several paragraphs describing it. Draw a picture of that constellation and make spiritual parallels.

4. Describe for your teacher how to star watch.

Place I - II

5. Choose a constellation. Study more about it and do the following:

    A. Draw a picture of it.

    B. Write out the important information about it.

    C. Make spiritual parallels with the Bible lesson.

    D. Find it in the sky.

**For Place I - II - III
have your teacher dictate
your spelling words.**

Illustration
Why Does the Sky Change?

Why does our view of space change during the year?

**This movement is really caused
by Earth revolving around the sun.**

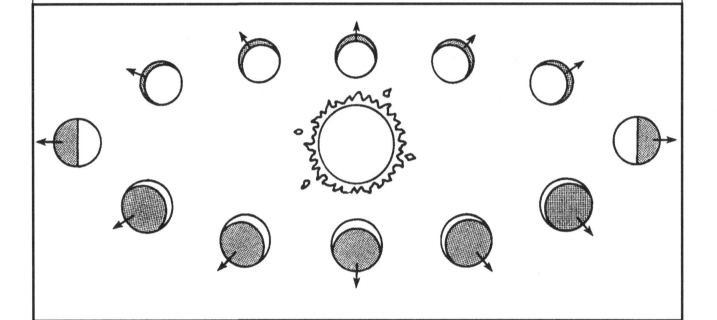

If you would stargaze
every night for one year,
you would see more than
6,000 different stars in the sky.

Find a star map that shows
the constellations
that may be seen
at different times of the year.
Choose one time of the year
and draw three constellations
that can be seen at that time.

Instruction From the Heavens

Stars that on your wondrous way
  Travel through the evening sky,
Is there nothing you can say
  To such a little child as I?
Tell me, for I long to know,
  Who has made you sparkle so?

Yes, me thinks I hear you say,
  "Child of mortal race, attend,
While we run our wondrous way;
  Listen: we would be your friend;
Teaching you that Name Divine,
  By whose mighty word we shine.

"Child, as truly as we roll
  Through the dark and distant sky,
You have a precious soul,
  Born to live when we shall die:
Suns and planets pass away;
  Spirits never can decay.

"When some thousand years, at most,
  All their little time has spent,
One by one our sparkling host
  Shall forsake the firmament;
We shall from our glory fall;
  You must live beyond us all.

"Yes—and God who bade us roll,
  God, who hung us in the sky,
Stoops to watch an infant's soul
  With a condescending eye;
And esteems it dearer far,
  More in value than a star!"

O then while your breath is given,
  Pour it out in fervent prayer,
And beseech the God of heaven
  To receive your spirit there:
Like a living star to blaze
  Ever to your Saviour's praise.

— *Ann Taylor*

The Soothing Colors of Evening

While you are waiting for darkness to fall, take some time to enjoy the soft colors of different areas of the sky beginning at sunset. As your eyes adjust to the darkness, you will see different layers of color in the atmosphere.

Color this chart showing the different layers of the evening sky colors. Notice how these colors change over a period of time.

The softness of the colors can remind you of the gentleness of God. He gradually prepares us for nightfall by covering His children with beautiful blankets of lovely colors. Then as the day fades away, He lights the stars to let His children know that the light of His presence is always with them. *"When I sit in darkness, the Lord shall be a light unto me"* (Micah 7:8).

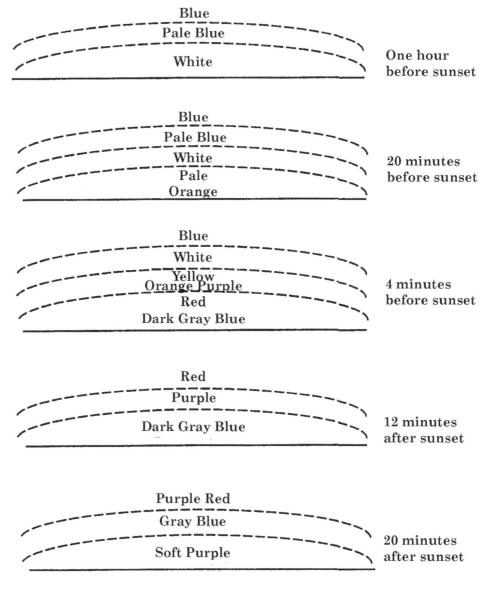

One hour before sunset

20 minutes before sunset

4 minutes before sunset

12 minutes after sunset

20 minutes after sunset

Day Is Dying in the West

Day is dying in the west;
Heaven is touching earth with rest;
Wait and worship while the night
Sets her evening lamps alight
Through all the sky.

Lord of life, beneath the dome
Of the universe, Thy home,
Gather us who see Thy face
To the fold of Thy embrace,
For Thou art nigh.

While the deepening shadows fall,
Heart of love, enfolding all,
Thro' the glory and the grace
Of the stars that veil Thy face,
Our hearts ascend.

When forever from our sight
Pass the stars, the day, the night,
Lord of angels on our eyes
Let eternal morning rise,
And shadows end.

# Christ's Second Coming

The morning is a beautiful figure of the opening glory of the day of God. The "Day Star" first appears, then the dawn of the day. And, as the light of day increases, our eyes are enabled to endure it, and view the sun shining in his strength. But should the light of the sun burst upon the world suddenly at midnight, no human eye could endure it. So will the people of God be prepared to meet their coming King. They must first break away from the love and cares of this world and consecrate all to the Lord. Then they will in due time, share the outpouring of the Holy Spirit *"as the rain, as the latter and the former rain unto the earth"* (Hosea 6:3). The *"Day Star"* will arise in their hearts. (See II Peter 1:19.) Those who have taken heed to the sure word of prophecy through the dark watching night will then raise their heads in triumph. They are filled with faith, and with the Holy Spirit. Glory is poured upon them till they can gaze on Christ and the angels.

Reinforce

Place I - II

Connect the large stars as a dot-to-dot to help you fill in the blank below.

This constellation is called _____ .

Finally

Everywhere God shines through matter. His voice is in the rolling air; His robe is in the sunset sky and the green earth; His path is in the deep waters. The method and order of His purposes are seen in the laws of Nature. Like Moses, with unshod feet, let us be **alert** and draw near to learn the mysteries of Nature.

Beneath the midnight gem-studded skies the naked eye discerns several thousand stars; a telescope reveals many millions, and out of range there are millions more in infinite space—like gold dust upon the great highways of heaven, rising and falling before God's throne.

Remember God has designed these gems in the sky to be beautiful pictures of the plan of salvation written there by God's foreknowledge in past times. These jewels can give spiritual light as you travel the path heavenward.

These jewels
can give
spiritual light
as you travel
the path heavenward.

𝕸𝖆𝖗𝖐 𝖄𝖔𝖚𝖗 𝕭𝖎𝖇𝖑𝖊

The Stars

Place I

Underline the answers in each verse before marking your Bible.

1. Who made the stars?

Genesis 1:16 – *"And God made two great lights; the greater light to rule the day, and the lesser light to rule the night: he made the stars also."*

2. How were the stars made?

Psalm 33:6 – *"By the word of the Lord were the heavens made; and all the host of them by the breath of his mouth."*

3. Do the stars have names? And what keeps each star in its proper place?

Isaiah 40:26 – *"Lift up your eyes on high, and behold who hath created these things, that bringeth out their host by number: he calleth them all by names by the greatness of his might, for that he is strong in power; not one faileth."*

4. Can we learn the names of any of the constellations from the Bible?

Job 9:9 – *"Which maketh Arcturus, Orion, and Pleiades, and the chambers of the south."* (Others are also mentioned.)

5. How many stars are there?

Jeremiah 33:22 – *"As the host of heaven [stars] cannot be numbered, neither the sand of the sea measured...."*

6. How will stars show that Christ's coming is near?

In two ways:

A. By being darkened

Joel 3:15 – *"The sun and the moon shall be darkened, and the stars shall withdraw their shining."*

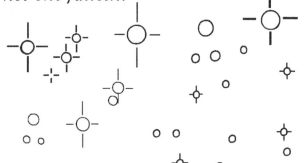

B. And by falling from heaven

Mark 13:25 – *"And the stars of heaven shall fall, and the powers that are in heaven shall be shaken."*

7. When were these things predicted to happen?

Matthew 24:29 – *"Immediately after the tribulation of those days shall the sun be darkened, and the moon shall not give her light, and the stars shall fall from heaven, and the powers of heaven shall be shaken."*

(Immediately after the tribulation which ended in 1798 A.D. the Dark Day occurred on May 19, 1780.[1] The great star shower occurred on November 13, 1833, and their manner of falling was predicted graphically in Revelation 6:13.)

[1] Mark 13:24 says the sun would be darkened *"in those days after that tribulation."* Persecution ceased before the tribulation period itself ended.

Place II

1. Who made the stars?

Genesis 1:16 – *"And God made two great lights; the greater light to rule the day, and the lesser light to rule the night: he made the stars also."*

2. How were the stars made?

Psalm 33:6 – *"By the word of the Lord were the heavens made; and all the host of them by the breath of his mouth."*

3. Do the stars have names? And what keeps each star in its proper place.

Isaiah 40:26 – *"Lift up your eyes on high, and behold who hath created these things, that bringeth out their host by number: he calleth them all by names by the greatness of his might, for that he is strong in power; not one faileth."*

4. How many stars are there?

Jeremiah 33:22 – *"As the host of heaven [stars] cannot be numbered, neither the sand of the sea measured...."*

5. What does the Bible mean when it says in Genesis 1:14 that the stars are "for signs, and for seasons, and for days, and years?"

A. Signs of prophetic events – Matthew 24:29

B. Seasons – Job 38:32 (Different stars and constellations indicate different seasons of the year.)

C. Days – Genesis 1:14

D. Years – Psalm 19:6 (The sun, a star, marks off the year in his *"circuit."*)

6. Do any of the prophetic star "signs" have special significance for God's people today?

Luke 21:25-28 – *"And there shall be signs in the sun, and in the moon, and in the stars; and upon the earth distress of nations, with perplexity; the sea and the waves roaring; Men's hearts failing them for fear, and for looking after those things which are coming on the earth: for the powers of heaven shall be shaken. And then shall they see the Son of man coming in a cloud with power and great glory. And when these things begin to come to pass, then look up, and lift up your heads; for your redemption draweth nigh."*

7. How will stars show that Christ's coming is near?

In two ways:

A. By being darkened

Joel 3:15 – *"The sun and the moon shall be darkened and the stars shall withdraw their shining."*

B. And by falling from heaven

Mark 13:25 – *"And the stars of heaven shall fall, and the powers that are in heaven shall be shaken."*

8. When were these things predicted to happen?

Matthew 24:29 – *"Immediately after the tribulation of those days shall the sun be darkened, and the moon shall not give her light, and the stars shall fall from heaven, and the powers of heaven shall be shaken."*

(Immediately after the tribulation which ended in 1798 A.D. the Dark Day occurred on May 19, 1780.[1] The great star shower occurred on November 13, 1833, and their manner of falling was predicted graphically in Revelation 6:13.)

---

[1]Mark 13:24 says the sun would be darkened *"in those days after that tribulation."* Persecution ceased before the tribulation period itself ended.

Place III

1. Who made the stars?

Genesis 1:16 – *"And God made two great lights; the greater light to rule the day, and the lesser light to rule the night: he made the stars also."*

2. How were the stars made?

Psalm 33:6 – *"By the word of the Lord were the heavens made; and all the host of them by the breath of his mouth."*

3. What is one of the reasons God made the stars?

Genesis 1:17 – *"…God set them in the firmament of the heaven to give light upon the earth."*

(Remember, the sun is a star also.)

4. Do the stars have names? And what keeps them in their proper place?

Isaiah 40:26 – *"Lift up your eyes on high, and behold who hath created these things, that bringeth out their host by number: he calleth them all by names by the greatness of his might, for that he is strong in power; not one faileth."*

5. Does the Bible mention constellations?

Isaiah 13:10 – *"For the stars of heaven and the constellations…."*

6. Can we learn the names of any of the constellations from the Bible?

Job 9:9 – *"Which maketh Arcturus, Orion, and Pleiades, and the chambers of the south."*

7. How many stars are there?

Jeremiah 33:22 – *"As the host of heaven* [stars] *cannot be numbered, neither the sand of the sea measured…."*

8. Are the stars different from each other?

I Corinthians 15:41 – *"There is one glory of the sun, and another glory of the moon, and another glory of the stars: for one star differeth from another star in glory."*

9. Do the stars influence each other?

Job 38:31 – *"Canst thou bind* [to tie] *the sweet influences* [bond] *of Pleiades, or loose* [open] *the bands of Orion?"*

10. Are the stars useful as navigational guides?

Acts 27:19-20 – *"And the third day we cast out with our own hands the tackling of the ship. And when neither sun nor stars in many days appeared, and no small tempest lay on us, all hope that we should be saved was then taken away."*

(See also Matthew 2:1-2. The Bible also speaks of stars as figurative guides in Daniel 12:3 and Jude 10-13.)

11. Does the Bible have anything to say about astrology which claims that the fate of everything is dependent on the stars?

Daniel 2:27-28 – *"Daniel answered in the presence of the king, and said, The secret which the king hath demanded cannot the wise men, the astrologers, the magicians, the soothsayers, shew unto the king; But there is a God in heaven that revealeth secrets, and maketh known to the king Nebuchadnezzar what shall be in the latter days."*

Deuteronomy 4:19 – *"And lest thou lift up thine eyes unto heaven, and when thou seest the sun, and moon, and the stars, even all the host of heaven, shouldest be driven to worship them, and serve them...."*

12. Was the idolatrous practice of worshiping the stars ever practiced by God's people?

II Kings 17:16 – *"And they left all the commandments of the Lord their God, and made them molten images, even two calves, and made a grove, and worshipped all the host of heaven, and served Baal."*

(See also Amos 5:26, II Kings 23:5, Jeremiah 19:13.)

13. What does the Bible mean when it says in Genesis 1:14 that the stars are "for signs, and for seasons, and for days, and years?"

A. Signs of prophetic events – Matthew 24:29

B. Seasons – Job 38:32 (Different stars and constellations indicate different seasons of the year.)

C. Days – Genesis 1:14

D. Years – Psalm 19:6 (The sun, a star, marks off the year in his "circuit.")

14. Do any of the prophetic star "signs" have special significance for God's people today?

Luke 21:25-28 – *"And there shall be signs in the sun, and in the moon, and in the stars; and upon the earth distress of nations, with perplexity; the sea and the waves roaring; Men's hearts failing them for fear, and for looking after those things which are coming on the earth; for the powers of heaven shall be shaken. And then shall they see the Son of man coming in a cloud with power and great glory. And when these things begin to come to pass, then look up, and lift up your heads; for your redemption draweth nigh."*

15. How will stars show that Christ's coming is near?

In two ways:

A. By being darkened

Joel 3:15 – *"The sun and the moon shall be darkened, and the stars shall withdraw their shining."*

B. And by falling from heaven

Mark 13:25 – *"And the stars of heaven shall fall, and the powers that are in heaven shall be shaken."*

16. When were these things predicted to happen?

Matthew 24:29 – *"Immediately after the tribulation of those days shall the sun be darkened, and the moon shall not give her light, and the stars shall fall from heaven, and the powers of the heavens shall be shaken."*

(Immediately after the tribulation which ended in 1798 A.D. the Dark Day occurred on May 19, 1780.[1] The great star shower occurred on November 13, 1833, and their manner of falling was predicted graphically in Revelation 6:13.)

17. What did Jesus mean in Mark 13:25 when He said, "...And the powers that are in heaven shall be shaken?"

(Genesis 1:16-18 explains that the sun, moon, and stars rule or have power in the heavens.)

Genesis 1:16-18 – *"And God made two great lights; the greater light to rule the day, and the lesser light to rule the night: he made the stars also. And God set them in the firmament of the heaven to give light upon the earth, And to rule over the day and over the night...."*

[1]Mark 13:24 says the sun would be darkened *"in those days after that tribulation."* Persecution ceased before the tribulation period itself ended.

The powers of heaven are the sun, moon, and stars. They rule in the heavens. The powers of heaven will be shaken at the voice of God.

18. How is this event of the powers of heaven being shaken described in the Bible?

Isaiah 34:4 – *"And all the host of heaven shall be dissolved, and the heavens shall be rolled together as a scroll."*

We might say, dark heavy clouds came up and clashed against each other. The atmosphere parted and rolled back.

19. What causes these powers to be shaken?

Joel 3:16 – *"The Lord also shall roar out of Zion, and utter his voice from Jerusalem; and the heavens and the earth shall shake."*

(See Job 38:31 concerning the bands of Orion being loosed.)

20. How close are we to the Second Coming of Christ?

Matthew 24:32-33 – *"Now learn a parable of the fig tree; When his branch is yet tender, and putteth forth leaves, ye know that summer is nigh: So likewise ye, when ye shall see all these things, know that it is near, even at the doors."*

21. What assurance do we have that we shall be able to "live in his sight"?

Hosea 6:2-3 – *"...We shall live in his sight. Then shall we know, if we follow on to know the Lord: his going forth is prepared as the morning; and he shall come unto us as the rain, as the latter and former rain unto the earth."*

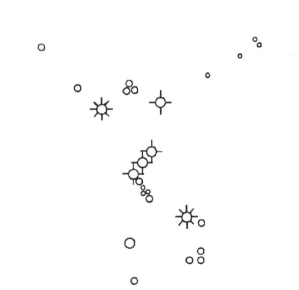

"The atmosphere parted and rolled back; then we could look up through the open space in Orion, whence came the voice of God."
Early Writings 41

Remind

1. You might have a box you keep special treasures in. Think of the Bible as such a box or even the sky as a huge treasure chest.

2. When driving in the country with your family, remember how the country is the best place to star watch.

3. A watch or clock is a reminder of heavenly punctuality.

4. Have you ever seen a dog wandering about? It can remind you of a wandering star. Read Isaiah 56:10-11.

5. Lawn chairs that lay down call to mind the position we can best study the stars.

Reinforce

1. Sleep out some night under the starry heavens. As a test, see how many stars and constellations you can identify.

2. Identify all or at least some of the five visible planets in the sky.

3. Read the story, "What the Boy Thought of the Falling Stars."

4. Read the information about Johann Kepler and Tycho Brahe.

Tools

**Fill in the blanks
to remember some of the things
that help in star watching.**

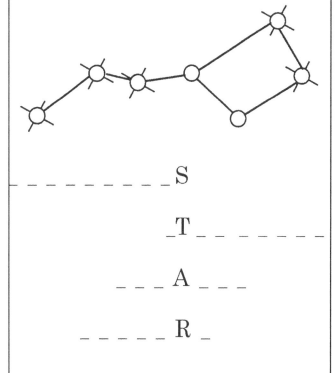

_ _ _ _ _ _ _ S

_ T _ _ _ _ _ _ _

_ _ _ _ A _ _ _

_ _ _ _ _ R _

What the Boy Thought of the Falling Stars

A very extraordinary exhibition of "falling stars," meteorites, took place in America, November 13th, 1833. It is thus described by an eyewitness:

We were about five miles southwest of Boston, and a little before five in the morning, on looking out of the window saw several stars shooting downward, leaving behind a shining train. This excited our attention, and calling up a learned friend who was sleeping in an adjacent room, we set forth.

The scene was indeed beautiful, and almost fearful. On all sides of us nearly without cessation, the meteors were streaming through the heavens: sometimes one alone, sometimes two or three or more together. Some of them were small and soon disappeared; others were more brilliant, and had a longer and more glorious career. We were standing among some trees, the strong shadows of which were often thrown upon the ground, as the meteors hurried by.

There was a boy with us, whose exclamations were amusing and descriptive. "See, there, see, see!" said he, "there goes a whole handful! there's one, cracked all to pieces! Look up there; that one's made a mark on the sky like a piece of chalk!"

It may well be believed that our feelings became deeply interested, and that an exhibition so wonderful, produced emotions amounting to awe. It seemed as if the very stars were leaping from their places, and after a rapid flight, vanishing into air. If philosophy taught us better, still the imagination could not be restrained, and the mind pressed forward to that predicted hour when the heavenly bodies shall vanish like a scroll, and the glittering vault above, like a vesture, be finally rolled up.

This phenomenon was seen nearly over the whole of North America, and far out to sea.

"Some of them were small and soon disappeared;
others were more brilliant,
and had a longer and more glorious career."

Great Astronomers of the Past

Johann Kepler
(1571-1630)

Tycho Brahe
(1546-1601)

Some materials were adapted from the following sources:

The Desire of Ages
The Acts of the Apostles
The Corn of Heaven
Patriarchs and Prophets
A Cyclopedia of Nature Teachings
Misc. Addresses
Saunder's Readers
Our Father's House
Addresses to Young Folks
The Wonderful River
Heroes of the Scientific World

Johann Kepler
(1571-1630)

**From a boy who served drinks in a tavern
to imperial mathematician and astronomer**

Although Johann Kepler served drinks in a tavern, his parents were both of noble families. But Johann got a very bad start in life. His parents had degraded themselves; they had come down in the world. The last straw seems to have been that Johann's father had become security for a friend, and this friend had absconded, leaving Johann's father to pay the piper. It was then that he sold off everything of value that he possessed and became a tavern-keeper, and it was in this tavern the son worked for several years.

There was no happy home life for the boy. His mother was a woman with a terrible temper, so much so that her husband was glad to go abroad as a soldier. Just when Johann should have been sent to school he became a victim to smallpox. On his recovery he went to school, but after two years of irregular attendance he was withdrawn so that he might serve drinks in his father's tavern. He seems to have been kept at this menial work for five years, by which time he was fourteen years of age. He then returned to school, but only for a very short time, as he developed a severe illness, while his parents at the same time, were both suffering from smallpox.

We see that Kepler had passed the ordinary school age without any proper schooling. How different from Tycho Brahe who entered the university at thirteen years of age. But at the age of fifteen years Kepler was admitted to a monastery which prepared students for the University at Tubingen.

We have been picturing this unfortunate boy without placing him in any particular part of the world, except for the preceding paragraph. The name Johann will probably have placed him in his native land of Germany. It is usual to speak of Kepler as John Kepler, but this has always seemed to me unfortunate; indeed, I have found some young friends thinking of Kepler as an Englishman. Probably this error has arisen through these young people only hearing of Kepler in connection with Sir Isaac Newton's work. However, the birthplace of Johann Kepler was a small town about ten miles from Stuttgart, and he was born prematurely a few days before the Christmas of 1571. He remained delicate throughout life.

His time at the university was interrupted not only by repeated illnesses, but by family troubles. It was at this time that the mother's violent temper drove the father to a foreign land, where he died. It is reported that the mother quarrelled with every one of her relations. It is to Johann Kepler's credit that, despite all these troubles, he succeeded in gaining his degree of Bachelor, coming out second in the examination.

It is interesting to note that when Kepler was about twenty years of age he became a convert to the Copernican theory, which brought the sun to a standstill and set the earth in motion. His conversion was due to a lecture on the subject delivered in the university. Galileo's conversion to this theory is supposed to have taken place about this time also, but we must remember that the surroundings of the two men were very different. Kepler was allowed perfect freedom of thought in Germany, whereas Galileo had no such liberty in Italy. It is interesting to note that when Galileo first heard of the Copernican theory, he thought it was "a piece of solemn folly."

At the age of 23 years Kepler became Professor of Astronomy at Gratz, but this science was not accounted of much importance in these days, except so far as it was of value to astrology. Kepler was not physically fit to become an astronomer such as old Tycho was in Denmark at that time. Kepler suffered from weak eyes, and his delicate constitution prohibited him from exposing himself to the night air. Neither was it as a mathematician that Kepler excelled, but he had a wonderfully vivid imagination, and so his strength lay in devising theories concerning the motions of the heavenly bodies. Some people think that theories are mere guesses at the truth, but unless a "guess" or hypothesis can be supported by established facts it is not allowed to remain. Kepler made many very wild guesses, he has left us a record of some of these, but he did not stop there. He put all his theories to the test. Sometimes he thought he had established them, but when he found out some error later, he never failed to make it known, and to demolish his own theory.

> **Kepler was allowed perfect freedom of thought in Germany, whereas Galileo had no such liberty in Italy.**

But when considering the theories of others Kepler sometimes became very sarcastic. For instance, when a new or temporary star appeared, similar to that seen by Tycho Brahe some 30 years previously, those philosophers who were known as Epicureans put forward a theory that the new star was due to a fortuitous concourse of atoms. Kepler wrote a good deal of sarcastic nonsense about this, finishing up in the following fashion: "I will tell those disputants, not my own opinion, but my wife's. Yesterday, when weary with writing, and my mind quite dusty with considering these atoms, I was called to supper, and a salad I had asked for was set before me. 'It seems then,' said I, aloud, 'that if pewter dishes, leaves of lettuce, grains of salt, drops of water, vinegar and oil, and slices of egg had been flying about in the air from all eternity, it might at last happen by chance that there would come a salad.' 'Yes,' says my wife, 'but not so nice and well dressed as this of mine.'"

As Kepler was not capable of being an active observer of the heavens, it was necessary that he should reply upon the observations of others in constructing his theories. For this reason Kepler paid a visit to Tycho Brahe at Prague. At that time Tycho was about 54 years of age, while Kepler would be 29. After returning home from that visit, Kepler received a pressing invitation from Tycho to become his assistant, and so Kepler and his wife set out for Prague. Again misfortune overtook our hero. He fell ill on the journey and was delayed for seven months. During that time all his savings disappeared, and he had to ask Tycho for financial assistance.

Tycho and Kepler became the best of friends. They undertook to compute a new set of astronomical tables, which would entail an enormous amount of labor, but Tycho died in that same year.

Kepler was appointed to Tycho's post of Imperial Mathematician, and he was promised a liberal salary by the Emperor, but unfortunately the treasury was already overtaxed by heavy war expenses, and Kepler's salary was always in arrears. Indeed, Kepler did not receive enough to keep him and his family, and he had to set up as an astrologer, while he continued his real astronomical work in earnest. He was not in earnest about astrology. Tycho Brahe was a real astrologer, believing in his own predictions. Kepler was only an astrologer in the sense as we have fortune-tellers at country fairs today; merely as a means of livelihood. There was this difference, that the modern astrologer often knows nothing of astronomy.

Kepler did not like to resort to this means of making money. A few years later, when he had to raise funds in a similar manner, he wrote: "I have been obliged to compose a vile prophesying Almanac, which is scarcely more respectable than begging." Kepler was scarcely ever free from money difficulties, and it is all the more creditable to him that he did such excellent work.

The most outstanding of Kepler's discoveries are those truths known to the student as Kepler's Laws. The first of these laws states that the planets move in ellipses, with the sun in one focus. This was a truly great discovery. The famous philosopher Aristotle had said that the heavenly bodies moved in circles, and we have seen that there was no doubt in Aristotle's mind, for the circle was the only perfect and natural motion. And because Aristotle had declared this long ago, generation after generation accepted the statement as an established fact. Astronomers however, could not get the motions of the planets to agree with a simple circular motion. They made an elaborate system of one circle carrying another circle. Then, believing the earth to be the center around which the planets moved, they placed the earth at some distance from the true center in order to try and account for the different positions of the planets at different times. All this arrangement developed by Ptolemy, and known as the Ptolemaic System, was very much complicated.

How, then, did Kepler discover that the path of a planet is an oval or elliptic form? Simply by guessing one thing, and when he found that would not do, guessing another possible solution. But it required a strong mind to break away from the universally accepted doctrine of Aristotle.

As we are considering only the life of Kepler, we need not detail the other two laws which he discovered. We are more concerned about the welfare of our hero, whose scientific ardor could not be extinguished by all the worries of this life.

About this time his wife became very seriously ill, and before she had recovered, their three children were attacked by smallpox, which caused the death of his favorite son.

The most outstanding
of Kepler's discoveries
are those truths known
to the student as Kepler's Laws.

There seemed little use in Kepler remaining at Prague, as mere promises of payment of salary would not meet his household bills. And so he set out for Austria, where he believed he might obtain a Chair of Mathematics. On his return home, he found his wife in a very despondent condition, and not long afterwards she was attacked by an infectious fever which proved fatal.

Kepler felt that his son and daughter required the care of a mother, so he decided to marry again. He asked his friends to select a suitable wife for him. Why he adopted this plan is not quite clear. To suppose that it was because he was too engrossed with his studies to trouble about the details of such an affair does not explain matters, for he had to consider no less than eleven different candidates.

The first candidate was a widow, who had been a family friend. But when Kepler, who had not seen the lady for some years, heard that she had decided in the end not to accept his offer, his description of her was that "there is no single pleasing part about her." This lady had two marriageable daughters, and later on these young ladies were added to Kepler's list. His reason for refusing one of the other candidates was that she had learned nothing but showy accomplishments. Another was too old, while another was "too proud of her birth and quarterings." In one case the courtship lasted several months, but in the end the lady jilted him.

Kepler's description of another selected candidate makes amusing reading: "She has, undoubtedly a good fortune, is of a good family, and of economical habits; but her physiognomy is most horribly ugly; she would be stared at in the streets, not to mention the striking disproportion of our figures. I am lank, lean, and spare; she is short and thick: in a family notorious for fullness, she is superfluously fat."

Kepler was at this time a little over 40 years of age, but he refused the 11th selection of his friends because of her excessive youth. The final result was that he went back to number five on his list, and declared that she was the one he had really been in love with all the time. Kepler says of her: "Her person and manners are suitable to mine, no pride, no extravagance. She can bear to work; she has a tolerable knowledge how to manage a family; middle-aged, and of a disposition and capability to acquire what she still wants."

Kepler had settled down with his new wife, when he received the offer of a professorship in Italy. This offer was respectfully declined; his reason was that he would not have the freedom of speech to which he was accustomed.

Kepler's financial troubles were not at an end yet, the government was always far in arrears with his salary.

It is interesting to note that he dedicated one of his books to King James I of England. But why he did so is not quite clear. Possibly because King James had shown interest in the work of Tycho Brahe. Of this book Kepler wrote: "The die is cast; the book is written, to be read either now or by posterity, I care not which. It may well wait a century for a reader, as God has waited six thousand years for an observer." However, not long after the publication of his Harmonies of the World Kepler received a visit from the English Ambassador at Vienna, and we may presume that this visit was owing to the dedication of the book to King James. The Ambassador urged Kepler to take up his residence in England, but Kepler declined this invitation. It is amusing to read that one of Kepler's reasons was that he "dreaded the confinement of an island." One wonders if Kepler's geography were at fault.

Kepler received a very handsome offer from the Duke of Friedland, one of the most distinguished men of that day, to take up his residence in Silesia. At last Kepler's misfortunes seemed to be at an end. The Duke treated him liberally. He provided him with an assistant for his calculations, and he presented him with a printing press. He also obtained for Kepler a professorship.

Later we find Kepler making one more attempt to get his arrears of pension paid by the Imperial Assembly. Probably Kepler thought to provide for his wife and family; he was now 58 years of age. However, his mission was useless, and this seems to have worried him. His health, never good, was weakened by over-study, and he died at the close of his 59th year, leaving his wife and seven children. They were left very poorly off, but they would have been comparatively rich had the long arrears of their father's pension been paid.

Kepler led a very busy life. He published no less than 33 separate works, and left 22 volumes of manuscript. In addition to his astronomical work, he was a pioneer in the region of optics. He was a devout Christian, and a serious student of the Holy Scriptures.

Tycho Brahe
(1546-1601)

Astrologer, alchemist, and medical quack, but a most distinguished astronomer

The name of Tycho Brahe, though foreign to us, would not seem strange to his fellow countrymen in Denmark. Indeed, the name Tycho is still used among the Danes.

In the ordinary course of events Tycho would have become a soldier. He was born at a time (1546) when learning was left very much to the monks. He came of a noble family who lived on the estate of their ancestors, but the present owners were not wealthy. It was usual that the sons of gentlemen should devote their lives to the protection of their country, or spend their time in hunting. For such avocations it was considered that no book-learning was necessary; and had the intentions of Tycho's father been fulfilled, it is probable that we should never have heard his name. But it so happened that an uncle, who had no family, desired to adopt one of his nephews. The uncle and aunt were desirous of having the entire upbringing of the boy, but so long as Tycho was the only son, his parents could not part with him. However, there seems to have been a definite understanding that ulti-mately the boy would go to the uncle, for we find Tycho getting special instruction in reading and writing, and later on in Latin and literature. All this was in opposition to his father's ideas, but the uncle, on the other hand, was a well-educated man.

After the death of Tycho's father, who left five sons and five daughters, the uncle sent Tycho to the University of Copenhagen. The boy was then only 13 years of age, so he must have been a very apt pupil, though it is interesting to note that Lord Kelvin entered Glasgow University at an earlier age even than this. Tycho's uncle's ambition seems to have been to give his nephew a good education in philosophy and law, so that he might be able to fill some of the great political offices.

While Tycho was a law student at Copenhagen, there was a great deal of talk about an eclipse of the sun which had been prophesied to occur on a certain day. The interest of the people was not a scientific one; science was a thing of the past so far as these people were concerned. But, according to their notions, this eclipse of the sun might carry with it the destiny of a whole nation, and no doubt the astrologers would have been busy in framing predictions.

Of course, all this about astrology seems strange to us, but if we picture a people totally devoid of all knowledge of astronomy, we can understand that when they found that astrologers were able to predict definite happenings in the heavens, it seemed natural that they should be able to predict also what should happen on this earth.

When the 21st day of August, 1560, dawned, there would be considerable excitement, for that was the very day upon which the astrologers had said the sun would be darkened. Tycho, now a boy of 14 years, was one of the anxious watchers, and when things happened in the heavens just as they had been predicted, he was carried away with enthusiasm. He, too, would learn to predict not only what should take place in the heavens, but among the nations also. In other words, Tycho decided there and then that he would become an astrologer; a profession far removed from that of an astronomer. He purchased books dealing with the planetary motions, which books would, of course, state

that the earth was the center of the universe.

We may presume that Tycho's uncle was not party to this idea of the youth becoming an astrologer, for we find Tycho, at the age of 16 years, being sent with a tutor to Leipzig to extend his knowledge of law. But his hobby had a far greater fascination for him than the study of law. All his spare time was devoted to a study of the heavens, and all his spare pocket money went to the purchase of books on astronomy. Tycho would sit up at night, presumably without his tutor's knowledge, and study the stars. He could soon distinguish the different planets and trace their apparent motions. With the aid of a pair of rude compasses and a celestial globe no larger than an orange, this youthful astronomer found that some of the accepted calculations of the planetary motions did not agree with his own calculations, and so Tycho resolved to devote his life to obtaining accurate information concerning the motions of the heavenly bodies.

To the average youth such a task would have seemed impossible, for the whole of Tycho's training had been in philosophy and law; he had never studied mathematics. But he had reached that stage at which he could learn on his own account, and so, without the aid of any master, he gained the necessary knowledge of arithmetic and geometry. Tycho found some of the predicted motions of the planets so very far out, in some cases whole months, that he determined to make more accurate instruments for observing. Telescopes were not invented until the succeeding generation.

Tycho had practically completed his study of law, when news came that his uncle had died, leaving his fortune to Tycho.

Now he was free to settle in Denmark to pursue his astronomical studies with freedom. But we are told that his relatives and friends were not pleased that he should have abandoned law for what seemed to them a ridiculous and useless occupation; that, indeed, they made things so uncomfortable for Tycho that he left Denmark and settled in Germany.

We must remember that Tycho's study of astronomy was closely connected with astrology. The great plague which devastated Europe later was believed by him to be due to the conjunction of two of the planets having taken place in a certain part of the heavens which had a special connection with pestilence.

While pursuing his astronomical observations in Germany Tycho attended a wedding feast. He may have attended many more, but we know of this one because while at this feast he had a quarrel with a fellow countryman. The occasion of the dispute had reference to their mathematical acquirements. Matters were evidently smoothed over for the time, but about a fortnight later Tycho and this quarrelsome guest happened to meet again at some festive games. Instead of letting bygones be bygones, they revived the former quarrel. So serious did the matter appear to them that they decided to fight a duel with swords, but how this should decide which was the better mathematician is difficult to see. However, the fight did not take place in the heat of the moment, but two days later. It was a dark December evening and one biographer states that they fought in total darkness. But surely there must have been sufficient light to enable the combatants to see the position of each other, or the seconds might have fared badly. However, the result was that Tycho had his nose cut off by his opponent. To lose one's nose would not improve one's personal appearance. And if we try to picture Tycho as described by some of his biographers, we can well imagine that the loss of his nose would not add to his good looks. He was of middle size, and had "reddish yellow hair" and a ruddy complexion.

Tycho did the best he could under the circumstances. He had an imitation nose made. The artificial nose has been described by some as a nose of gold and silver; by others it is spoken of as a construction of putty and brass. His nose would be a decided novelty in these days, and would be of general interest. He seems to have had some difficulty in getting the nose to remain in its proper place, for he is said to have carried with him a box of cement with which he could replace the nose when it fell off.

While Tycho was still a young man of 22 years, he had a very large quadrant instrument made by which he could make more perfect observations. The best workmen were employed for a month making this huge instrument, which required 20 men to carry it to its place of fixture.

At the age of 25 Tycho had become famous as an astronomer, and when he returned to Denmark he was received as a great man. The king invited him to court, an uncle provided him with an observatory and a laboratory, and for a time Tycho became a very keen alchemist. There have been many honest alche-mists who earnestly sought to produce gold from silver, and to discover not only a panacea for all ills, but a tonic which should prolong life indefinitely.

Tycho worked hard in his laboratory; he was an enthusiast in everything he took up of his own accord. Upon leaving his laboratory one night, the sky happened to be very clear, and Tycho observed overhead a bright star which he had never seen before. Of course, Tycho was so familiar with the heavens by this time that he would very quickly spot a stranger. But this seemed so impossible a thing that he called his servants out to assure him that the star was really there. He hurried off to his observatory and noted down the exact position of this new star, so that he might find out if it moved or if it were a fixed star. Tycho's friends teased him about this new star, but he was able to point it out to them, for it was as bright as Venus at her best. Strange to say, the new star began to diminish; it remained visible for a little more than a year, then faded out altogether. Tycho was able to say definitely that this temporary star was very far distant, away among the fixed stars. Other temporary stars have appeared and disappeared in similar fashion, and we believe these to be great masses of incandescent gas produced by some collision or disruption far off in space.

Tycho, who was now 27 years of age, fell in love with a peasant girl. He shocked the dignity of his friends by marrying this girl who had been brought up in so humble a position. Some two years later Tycho decided to remove from Denmark, so he set off by himself on a tour of inspection on the Continent, ultimately fixing upon Basle as a permanent residence "not only from its centrical position, but from the salubrity of the air, and the cheapness of living."

Tycho returned home and made all preparations for the departure of himself and family to Basel, Switzerland. Just then a messenger arrived with a letter from the King of Denmark asking Tycho to meet him at Copenhagen. To Tycho's great surprise the king entreated him to remain in Denmark. He offered Tycho a certain island where he could have peace to make celestial observations. His Majesty presented Tycho with the sum of 20,000 pounds wherewith to build a large observatory on the island. He also gave to him an estate in Norway, which would yield him an income, and in addition to all this he undertook to give him a pension for life of 400 pounds a year. Needless to say, Tycho gladly accepted this very handsome offer, and he expressed the hope that by such means he might make discoveries that would be a credit to his native land.

Tycho's observatory was a veritable castle, but it was no plaything. Tycho put in 20 years' earnest work, and work that counted much for future generations of men. He did the first really accurate work in astronomy, and all without the aid of any telescope, the discovery of which we shall consider when we inquire into the life of Galileo, who was born in Italy when Tycho was a lad of 18. These two great men never met. A mutual friend recommended Tycho to write to Galileo. This he did, but the acquaintance went no further.

We must not picture Tycho as a recluse away in his island home. He had always a number of students resident at the observatory, and he had constant visitors from many different countries. Among the royal visitors we find James I of England, who spent eight days at Tycho's observatory. Of course, it was King James' marriage with Anne of Denmark that took him to these quarters.

The description of Tycho's house in the observatory reminds one of the country mansion of the great French conjurer, Robert Houdin. Tycho had invisible bells which communicated with every part of his establishment, and with the gentlest touch he could summon any of his pupils before him. When some stranger was present Tycho would mutter in a mysterious manner, "Come hither, Peter!" whereupon one of his pupils would suddenly appear before them. In this and similar ways Tycho would mystify his visitors. Then he had a great collection of automatic devices of his own invention, which interested all visitors.

But there was one of Tycho's "curiosities" which must have been very unpleasant to his guests. He kept an feebleminded boy named Lep, who lay at Tycho's feet during meals, and whom he fed with his own hand. Tycho imagined this feebleminded to be something wonderful, and no matter what guests were present, everyone had to keep quiet when this boy spoke, so that Tycho might note down what the boy said. Tycho believed that the boy's mind could foretell the future. Such scenes must have been most distressing.

Tycho was so superstitious that if, on leaving his house, he happened to meet an old woman or a hare, he would not proceed farther, but returned immediately to his home.

In the sub-title Tycho was described as a medical quack. This is quite justified, for although Tycho was not a trained physician, he doctored many invalids who flocked to his island. One must suppose that his cures were, like those of present-day quacks, performed on persons who were hypochondriacal, or highly imaginative and nervous persons. However, he had invented what we might call a patent medicine, which was in great demand and is said to have been on sale in every apothecary's shop in Germany.

Such things aroused the jealousy of the medical profession, and when Tycho's great benefactor, the king, died, leaving his young son to fill the throne, the physicians helped to stir up a feeling against Tycho. So many adverse things were said about Tycho and his work that a committee, what we should call now a royal commission, was appointed to inquire into the value of Tycho's work, for he was still drawing his income from the state. This committee had the audacity to report that Tycho's work was absolutely worthless and that it would be ridiculous to allow him to draw any income from the treasury.

> **In the sub-title Tycho was described as a medical quack.**

Deprived of his estate in Norway, and of his pension, Tycho was compelled to give up his great observatory, in which he had worked and lived for 20 years. It will be remembered that Tycho had been left his uncle's fortune, amounting to about 20,000 pounds, and he had doubtless accumulated money from his famous medicine. But all his fortune had been spent upon his great observatory, which in all must have cost not less than 40,000 pounds. We can understand what a heartbreak it must have been for Tycho to be forced to abandon all this. He had to retire to a house in Copenhagen, to which he carried all his smaller instruments.

Not long after this Tycho determined to leave Denmark altogether. He returned to his island and collected all the other instruments that were movable, along with his books and crucibles. He hired a ship and set sail, accompanied by his wife, his family of nine, many pupils and assistants, and a number of servants. The plague, which was then spreading in Europe, prevented Tycho taking up a permanent residence.

He was introduced to the Emperor of Bohemia, who was "addicted to alchemy and astrology." The Emperor gave Tycho the choice of several castles for an observatory.

In addition to this he settled a very substantial annual pension upon him. And so Tycho established a school at Prague, where he employed many good calculators as assistants. Among these assistants was Johann Kepler.

Tycho's health gave way, and he lived only four years after leaving his happy island home in Denmark. His life of 55 years was a crowded one. He was a devout man, a great student of the Holy Scriptures, and there is no doubt that it was on religious grounds that he did not accept the theory of Copernicus that the earth was not the center of the universe.

One is pleased to know that Tycho's widow and family were not left in want, for the emperor purchased Tycho's instruments for a very large sum of money.

The great value of Tycho's work was his making astronomy an accurate science, and something more than a mere aid to astrology. Considering the instruments with which he had to work, Tycho's observations are a marvel of accuracy; he never made one careless mistake. Tycho Brahe laid the foundations upon which modern astronomy was built.

Reinforce

Identify these constellations.

_____

_____

_____

_____

Outline of School Program

Age	Grade	Program
Birth through Age 7	Babies Kindergarten and Pre-school	*Family Bible Lessons* (This includes: Bible, Science–Nature, and Character)
Age 8	First Grade	*Family Bible Lessons* (This includes: Bible, Science–Nature, and Character) + Language Program (*Writing and Spelling Road to Reading and Thinking* [WSRRT])
Age 9-14 or 15	Second through Eighth Grade	*The Desire of all Nations* (This includes: Health, Mathematics, Music, Science–Nature, History/Geography/Prophecy, Language, and Voice–Speech) + Continue using WSRRT
Ages 15 or 16-19	Ninth through Twelfth Grade	9 – *Cross and Its Shadow I* + Appropriate Academic Books 10 – *Cross and Its Shadow II* + Appropriate Academic Books 11 – *Daniel the Prophet* + Appropriate Academic Books 12 – *The Seer of Patmos* (Revelation) + Appropriate Academic Books *or you could continue using *The Desire of Ages*
Ages 20-25	College	Apprenticeship

Made in the USA
Monee, IL
21 August 2022

11941352R00125